P9-ARC-548

THE
PRAIRIE
PEOPLE

THE PRAIRIE PEOPLE

Continuity
and
Change
in
Potawatomi
Indian
Culture
1665 ~ 1965

JAMES A. CLIFTON

THE REGENTS PRESS OF KANSAS
Lawrence

© Copyright 1977 by The Regents Press of Kansas
Printed in the United States of America
Designed by Fritz Reiber

Library of Congress Cataloging in Publication Data

Clifton, James A
The prairie people.

Bibliography: p.
Includes index.
1. Potawatomi Indians—History. I. Title.
E99.P8C55   970'.004'97   76-51774
ISBN 0-7006-0155-4

to
the
memory
of
my
good
friends

JAMES WABNOSAH
MINNIE EVANS
CURTIS PEQUANO
SCOTT NANOGAH
JOHN WAHWASSUCK

May their tribe increase

CONTENTS

ILLUSTRATIONS

PREFACE

This book is for a general audience as well as serious students of history and anthropology interested in understanding the sense and meaning of the experience of one North American Indian tribe over the course of three centuries of interaction with Euro-Americans. These readers should understand that a work of this nature is a reconstruction, based—particularly in the early years—upon fragmentary materials and not always unambiguous facts. Rather than clutter up the narrative with scholarly hedgings and qualifications, I have reserved commentary on alternative interpretations for the notes located in the back of the book.

I have tried to present a view of the Potawatomi tribal experience through the centuries as a whole. However, the narrative is pointed down the years toward a description of the evolution of the so-called Prairie Band of Potawatomi, today located in Kansas. The distinction between Prairie and other varieties of Potawatomi is one which arose only in the early nineteenth century; and then it was a conception of American Indian agents and traders, one which was never well defined but always used with a mainly geographic reference. The contemporary Prairie Band of Kansas is in fact a composite, made up of descendants of Potawatomi from different localities in the Great Lakes area. Indeed, the Kansas Potawatomi were not always known as the Prairie Band. Before moving to Iowa Territory in 1838 their ancestors had been identified as the United Band of Ottawa, Chippewa, and Potawatomi of the Chicago region. In Iowa they were shortly joined by some Potawatomi from other parts and there became known as the Bluffs or Council Bluffs Band of Potawatomi. For a short while in 1842 they wanted to be called the Billy Caldwell Band of Potawatomi, in commemoration of that recently deceased and most interesting frontier personality who was by birth Irish-Mohawk and by later disposition a defender of the Chicago area Potawatomi. Only after moving to Kansas Territory in 1847 did these Potawatomi come to be called the Prairie Band, and again the distinction was largely American-made, for administrative convenience.

I will use the words "Prairie Band" merely to refer to the Kansas Potawatomi, since this is the phrasing they use—when speaking English—to refer to themselves. Lest I cause certain Indian Claims attorneys shudders of anticipation, let me emphasize that I use the word "band" not in the technical anthropological sense of an autonomous economic, geographic unit, but in the common English meaning that has been standard usage since the late eighteenth century. In this sense "band" means group and no more; and in the early nineteenth century one can readily show that observers identified anywhere from fifty to sixty different bands (i.e., groups) of Potawatomi, ranging in size from a few dozen or less to a thousand or more individuals.

This book is specially focused on the Prairie Band because they are the most culturally conservative of all modern Potawatomi. They are, in fact, the major repository of the modern versions of ancient Potawatomi ethos, value system, language, and cultural and social patterns. The only other Potawatomi group which approaches the Kansas population in the amount of retention of older culture forms are the Potawatomi of Forest County, Wisconsin. But these are the descendants of refugees who fled into the northern forests from Milwaukee, Manitowoc, and Lake Geneva, and from other Potawatomi villages in Illinois and Indiana, to avoid removal west of the Mississippi in the 1830s. Their history is very different from that of the Kansas group, and they are heavily intermixed with nearby larger Ojibwa and, to a lesser extent, Odawa populations, which blurs their cultural and linguistic outlines.

There are a great many people legally defined or culturally recognizable as Potawatomi in other locations as well. In the Upper and Lower peninsulas of Michigan there are three scattered Potawatomi groups. In southwestern Canada a large number of people of Potawatomi ancestry since 1840 have blended into more than a dozen widely separated reserves with members of other tribes, principally Odawa and Ojibwa. In Oklahoma there is a very large population of legally defined Potawatomi, while in the Kickapoo Reservation in Kansas, on the Menomini Reservation in Wisconsin, and adjacent to the line of Winnebago homesteads in western Wisconsin are other enclaves of Potawatomi who have moved in with different tribes.

Until the 1830s all these Potawatomi constituted a single tribal society with villages distributed in the four-state area around Lake Michigan. After that point it was no longer feasible for the tribe to function or sustain itself in that area, and the constituent villages scattered to seek out new habitats and to find different adaptations. Until that point they are part of the Potawatomi *tribal* experience, and long afterwards—even until today—the scattered local groups kept in contact and frequently exchanged population. Consequently, to appreciate the sense of the Prairie Band's experience will require comparing it with the fate and situation of other Potawatomi communities in more recent decades.

The approach used in this book is called ethnohistorical. This involves intertwining facets of Potawatomi culture and social structure with discussions of historical events and processes. In the three centuries covered—as well as before and after—the Potawatomi were ceaselessly adapting to an always changing physical and social environment. Their social milieu was particularly fluid, being composed of numerous other societies, each trying to come to grips with its place in the destiny of a continent. The ethnohistorical approach recognizes that cultural strategies and social institutions are not static and frozen in time, hence it stresses the fact of change and adaptation over the decades and centuries. Yet it also recognizes that the nature of a tribal culture such as the Potawatomi has to be understood partly in its own terms, world view, and beliefs. In this way we will have to read the past through an understanding of some of the current features of Potawatomi culture. Put simply, neither Potawatomi culture nor history can be understood separately from one another.

In important ways Potawatomi history is part of the history of three colonial empires and two emergent nation states: New France, the British North American Colonies, and Spanish Louisiana; and Canada and the United States. In the midnineteenth century some Potawatomi even got themselves involved in the history of the Republics of Texas and Mexico, but this fortunately was a minor and tangential episode. In the three centuries covered here the Potawatomi were also endlessly and variously entangled with a large number of other tribal societies, from the Seneca in the northeast to the Dakota in the northwest, and the Chickasaw and Comanche in the southeast and southwest. In 1653, when the Potawatomi first met the Eastern Iroquois, who had come pillaging into northeast Wisconsin, they met them with bows and arrows, spears and clubs, all tipped with stone and bone points. Just two centuries later the Potawatomi in turn were intruders in the tall-grass buffalo country of the High Plains, and a combined force of Dakota, Comanche, and Kiowa came to evict them. These Potawatomi met the attack by dismounting from their ponies, forming ranks, and firing their long rifles by volleys. Changes of such magnitude are only part of this tribe's experience.

I first encountered the Potawatomi in Kansas in 1962. The meeting was an accidental one, and I had no intention of spending much time in the study of this community. At the time, I was interested in something I called "resistance to cultural change" and had the conviction that groups like the Potawatomi were largely deculturated and assimilated. The Kansas Potawatomi welcomed me with grave and great hospitality, and they soon disabused me of this notion. I came quickly to the understanding that they were one of the most stubborn people I had ever met—firmly, bitterly, and successfully resistant to enforced cultural change, outside domination, and assimilation. So far as they were concerned—they made perfectly clear to me—the great melting pot was a place to cook fried bread, not to lose one's identity in.

My own research among the Kansas Potawatomi ended in 1965, although I have visited them occasionally in the years since. Beginning in 1970, I have been able to work among the Potawatomi of Wisconsin and Michigan, and in 1973 and 1974 I conducted a survey and a historical study of the several thousand Potawatomi who migrated into Upper Canada after 1835.

This book expresses an attitude as well as a theme. My personal sentiments do not allow me to express pity for the Potawatomi, and I certainly feel no personal guilt at the "fate of the Indian." In this respect this book strikes an attitude that differs from much recent historical and anthropological writing about Indians, which tends to be shallowly moralistic, carping at the behavior of Americans caught up in the swirl of historic events in the past, and excessively maudlin, patronizing, and condescending toward Indians of the present. I personally believe that pity is a scarcely disguised form of contempt, while the Potawatomi I know never asked for the former and certainly do not deserve the latter. Moreover, I remember that when the Potawatomi first came on the historic stage in 1667 in northeast Wisconsin they numbered few more than 2,400 and used and occupied a territory hardly more than 3,000 square miles in extent—much of this shared with several other tribes. Over the years they had trebled in population to more than 9,000, and they had increased their territorial range to more than 28,000 square miles (including large portions of Wisconsin, Michigan, Indiana, and Illinois), land which by 1837 they had sold to the United States in their numerous treaties. These two facts of population growth and territorial expansion well argue the case that this tribe's adaptive strategy was for many decades a highly successful one. Indeed, one might well summarize the history of the Potawatomi since 1800 by asserting that this highly successful, predatory raiding tribe met with a society who bested them in the struggle for territory. Such an interpretation, however, calls for analysis and understanding, not sentimental moralizing.

For similar reasons I will not use the noxious racist tag "white man" in referring to persons of European ancestry, their descendants, or their culture and communities. Contemporary Potawatomi use the word "Chimokman" to designate Americans, and some of them will translate it as "White Man," but this is not what it means. It is instead an abbreviation of "Kitchimokman," which properly translates as "Great Knives," and this phrase their ancestors used to designate only Virginians and, especially, Kentuckians. It was a respectful term rightfully applied by one group of warriors to another in praise of their prowess in battle. The point is that the traditional Potawatomi recognized numerous categories of persons of European ancestry, including Postonnene—Boston Men, i.e., New Englanders; Sakonosh—Anglo-Canadians; and others. Their relations with all these groups varied considerably from time to time, and they appropriately distinguished between them. They were not then prone to racial labels; this they have learned since. Thus I use "Euro-American" to indicate groups of European descent in North America, or the appropriate national name. Similarly, I use "Indian" with no racial overtones or suggestions of shared characteristics—merely to indicate collectively several or more tribal societies when a full listing becomes tiresome.

The research on which this book is based was supported by a number of foundations and institutions whose generous aid is gratefully acknowledged. The Kansas Potawatomi research was funded by grants from the University of Kansas General Research Fund, the National Science Foundation, the Wenner-Gren Foundation, the Society of Sigma Xi, and the Kansas City Association of Trusts and Foundations. My work in Canada during 1974 was aided by a grant from the National Museum of Man, Ottawa. I was able to spend time among the Wisconsin and Michigan Potawatomi while serving as director of the Action Program at the University of Wisconsin–Green Bay; and that institution provided clerical help in preparing the final manuscript.

Properly speaking, a research program of this nature is a group effort with a single name attached in the end. I must bear with any blame that is due, but much of the credit belongs to a number of other able people. First are the Potawatomi themselves, whose fine and numerous contributions I will have to acknowledge jointly and collectively. The time has passed when an anthropologist can gratuitously name names and tell all. These are a literate folk, and they read extensively. Most of our Potawatomi associates in Kansas asked that they not be identified; some were deeply injured that earlier anthropologists had done so. In the traditional Potawatomi community, revealing the identities of those who had assisted researchers might expose them to risk from rivals and enemies. In the current highly militant, violence-prone atmosphere of Indian-American relations this risk is even greater. I will say that there are twenty-odd people in Kansas to whom I will always be grateful for the weeks and days of their time that they willingly gave, as well as several hundred others who allowed themselves to be interviewed, recorded, photographed, visited, and observed for shorter periods.

Because it is sometimes necessary to personalize this narrative by using the words and ideas of a particular individual or by describing the doings of several in a case presentation, I have honored the Potawatomi's request for privacy by using pseudonyms and fabricating dates, ages, and circumstances to prevent identification of the true source. Thereby, except for historic figures long dead, all Potawatomi names used in this study are fictitious.

My associates in the Kansas Potawatomi research in 1962–1965 were Faye Clifton, Robert L. Bee, Ann McElroy, Gary Gossen, and Barry Isaacs. I have drawn freely on their field notes and publications concerning the Potawatomi, as cited in the text. In Wisconsin, Lynn Johnson and Mary Schauer worked with the Forest County Potawatomi in 1973–1974 and shared numerous insights about this group. I am particularly grateful to Professor George Waggoner, then dean of the College of Liberal Arts and Sciences, Vice-Chancellor William Argersinger, and Professor Charles Warriner, all at the University of Kansas, who encouraged my early work there and aided in funding the research program. They are good friends, indeed.

Long ago, my friend and teacher Theodore S. Stern provided a model for this kind of study, while Ruth Landes was kind enough to send me her manuscripts on Potawatomi medicine and culture well before they were published. For some years Nancy O. Lurie of the Milwaukee Public Museum has provided a continuing stream of useful suggestions and commentary. At one time or another Helen Hornbeck Tanner, Charles Callender, Bruce Trigger, Ives Goddard, Gordon Day, Barry Reynolds, Ted Brasser, David Baerreis, Ghisiline LeCour, Leonard Plotnikov, A. F. C. Wallace, David French, John Nichols, Deward Walker, Alan Beals, Ernestine Friedl, Murray and Rosalie Wax, Erminie Wheeler-Voegelin, Louis A. Zurcher, and the late Harold Hickerson have provided insights, corrected misconceptions, offered fresh facts, or have otherwise helped—wittingly or not—to set me straight.

In the United States, Robert Bell, Robert Johnson, Sam Crow, H. E. Bruce, James H. Hyde, Buford Morrison, and Jack Carson have shared their personal experience with the Potawatomi. I have, moreover, profited from numerous interchanges with the excellent historian R. David Edmunds. In Canada, Constance Chisholm, Dean Jacobs, Clarence Rogers, Carol Nahmabin, the Band Council at the Saugeen Reserve, Donald Isaacs, Carl Johnson, Flora and Goldyn Tobobondung, and Father James E. O'Flaherty have aided me in various essential ways. E. G. Rogers kindly made available the manuscript of the book on Parry Island farmers he has written with Flora Tobobondung.

The staffs of various libraries, archives, and depositories gave absolutely essential help, including that at the University of Wisconsin–Green Bay, particularly Mary Nauman at the Inter-Library Loan desk; the Milwaukee Public Museum; the Green Bay, Manitowoc, Sheboygan, and Milwaukee public libraries; the staffs of the Public Archives of Canada, the National Map Collections, and the Parliamentary Library, Ottawa, Ontario; the Library of the Department of Indian Affairs, Ottawa; the archivists at the Ft. Malden National Historic Park, Amherstburg; the National Museum of Man, Ottawa; the Royal Ontario Museum, Toronto; the Drummond Island Historical Museum; the Chicago Historical Society; the Newberry Library; the Field Museum of Natural History; the Chicago Public Library; the Kansas State Historical Society; the *Topeka Daily Capital*; the Council Bluffs Free Library; the Council Bluffs Historical Society; the Missouri Historical Society; the Wisconsin Historical Society, particularly the curator of the Draper Collections; the Detroit Public Library, particularly the curator of the Burton Historical Collections; the Kenneth Spencer Research Library at the University of Kansas; the reference section of the Bureau of Indian Affairs, Washington; the National Archives, Washington; and the Federal Archives and Records Center in both Chicago and Kansas City. Obviously, records concerning the Potawatomi are somewhat scattered; and if the good people at these institutions did not care for and make them available, this book would have been impossible.

Earlier versions of some of the thoughts, interpretations, and conclusions presented in this book were published in *Transactions of the Kansas Historical Society*; *Search*; *Plains Anthropologist*; *Chicago History*; the Mercury Series of the Ethnology Division, National Museum of Man; *Midcontinent American Studies Journal*; and volume 12 of the second edition of the *Handbook of North American Indians*. However, these pieces have in each case been substantially reworked and/or revised to fit them into this larger whole.

Field notes and supporting documentation for the Canadian research are on deposit in the Archives of the Ethnology Division, National Museum of Man, Ottawa. Similar materials on the Potawatomi in the United States are deposited with the Wisconsin Historical Society.

Unless otherwise noted, all photographs, maps, and figures are my own work. I am grateful to Bernie Hoffman Labs., New York, for converting my sensitized film into sparkling negatives and fine photographs. I pointed the camera; Bernie's people were the artists.

The orthography used in spelling Potawatomi names and phrases in this book is discussed fully in Appendix A. My efforts to convert the spoken Potawatomi word into writing involve what the professional linguists call an "ethnographer's impressions." However, I did employ alphabets which were developed by linguists for this language. One difficulty is that in the 1960s I used Charles Hockett's phonemic alphabet for recording Potawatomi speech, while recently I have begun using the more useful alphabet developed for teaching purposes at the University of Wisconsin–Milwaukee. This latter alphabet is a morphophonemic one, different from Hockett's, and there are certainly unavoidable errors of cross-transcription in this text.

Converting older, historical renditions of Potawatomi speech into this new morphophonemic alphabet is hazardous at best. Wherever possible, I have had a Potawatomi speaker try to pronounce the name or phrase drawn from some old document, and then have retranscribed it. Frequently, however, they cannot even recognize it as Potawatomi in origin. To illustrate, the tribal name is pronounced "Bodēwadnene" by some contemporary Wisconsin Potawatomi—but there are on record more than 140 extremely creative misspellings of this one name alone. Wherever possible, I cite the form in the original spelling used in the historic source, provide a retranscription in the contemporary alphabet, and then try to translate the phrase. Readers should remember that such translations, indicated by quotation marks, are glosses—rough approximations only. For example, the personal name "Onangizes" in various old documents is spelled "Onougesa," "Unangisa," "Dounnanghisse," and numerous other ways. This may be roughly translated as "Shimmering Light of the Sun," but it has other connotations, for the Potawatomi were and are most imaginative and poetic in their use of this complex, sophisticated language.

Citations in the text proper are enclosed within parentheses. These, together with citations in the notes, follow the style of the *American Anthropologist,* and consist of the author's surname, year of publication, and page. References to multivolume series are abbreviated (e.g., WHC) and such abbreviations will be found in alphabetical order in the bibliography, cross-referenced to the full source.

I am very grateful to Elizabeth Tiedemann and Patricia Raether for typing the final manuscript. Joel B. LeGrande is the artist responsible for transforming my maps and sketches into finished form.

THE
PRAIRIE
PEOPLE

1

Introduction

In the early seventeenth century the first contacts of Europeans with the Indian tribes of the Upper Great Lakes—one of whom later was to be identified as the Potawatomi—came in consequence of the need to place the colony of New France on a sound economic footing. The means for this development had to be trade, between the agents of New France and those of the interior tribes. French-made products—steel knives and axes, awls, firearms, and other goods—were to flow into the interior, and a harvest of Indian-produced furs were to pass east and north of the French posts along the lower St. Lawrence River, ultimately to France itself.

Until 1613 trade with the interior tribes had been an occasional, limited, and unsatisfactory affair. In the view of the tribes of the far and—to the French—unknown interior, there were few visible advantages to making the long journey to and down the St. Lawrence to Lachine and other market places. The distances, time, and labor involved were great, the hazards of combat with rivals and enemies many, and the rewards unclear.[1] New France needed a new and mutually profitable relationship with these tribes, few of whom were known firsthand.

The prime mover in the development of this new policy was Samuel de Champlain—soldier, seaman, author, geographer, and woodsman-explorer extraordinary. In 1603 Champlain had undertaken his first voyage to New France, up the St. Lawrence to the site of the later Montreal. There, at a trade fair, the Indians told him of a southern route to the west from the St. Lawrence—via a great lake (Ontario) and a strait (Niagara), another large lake (Erie), through another strait (the Detroit–St. Clair rivers), into even a third vast body of water (Lake Huron). As one journeyed farther west, he was told, the waters of these lakes got increasingly brackish until—past the head of Lake Erie—it was as salty as the sea.

Champlain's informants could tell him no more; they had no firsthand knowledge of what lay beyond the second strait. But these suggestions could only have whetted the appetite of an accomplished seaman and explorer, a man who lived in an era clouded with dreams of a short water-route west to the Orient. Champlain returned to France that year, coming back to the New World in 1609 to explore the Richelieu south to Lake Champlain. In 1611 he learned more of the interior country west of the St. Lawrence from his able aide, Étienne Brulé, whom he had sent to live among the Algonquin tribes of the upper St. Lawrence waterway (Grant 1907: 207–20; 302–3).[2] But he lost his patron and then spent the next four years in France or in fruitless exploration of the northern tributaries of the Ottawa River.

In 1615 Champlain again set forth for New France, this time with firm plans to advance to the shores of the great upper lakes. He contacted a group of Huron and Algonquins trading at the Lachine Rapids on the St. Lawrence. They had come also to prepare for a raid on their enemies, the Iroquois of New York. It was plain to Champlain that a trading alliance with these interior tribes could be created only on the foundation of a display of military support, and so he promised to visit the Huron country to help with a large attack on the Iroquois (Heidenreich 1971: 237).

Champlain sent ahead of him the first missionary to the upper country, a French Récollet priest, who traveled west with a dozen French *voyageurs* in the Huron trading fleet. Three weeks later—accompanied by a servant, ten Indians, and his interpreter Brulé—came Champlain. In their birch-bark canoes this party followed an unfamiliar route which was soon to become a great avenue of trade between the upper lakes and New France. They paddled up the St. Lawrence to the Ottawa, thence westward and up the Mattawan, then portaged to Lake Nippising, and down the French River to the sheltered inlets of the Georgian Bay and the waters of La Mer Douce (the Sweet Water Sea), later known as Lake Huron after Champlain's hosts and allies (Kellogg 1925: 55–58).

Champlain joined the Huron in a half-successful raid against the Onondaga, one of the five Iroquois tribes of New York. Wounded in this encounter, he had to stay the winter with his new allies, who had now seen the strength of Champlain's friendship amply demonstrated. During that winter and the spring of 1616 he explored the southern reaches of Lake Huron, portaging and canoeing across the Ontario Peninsula to discover Lake Ontario. Traveling outward from the Huron villages, he became familiar with closely related peoples to the west, the Petun or Tobacco Huron and the Neutral. In the Huron country Champlain again met with representatives of a different society, whom he at first called Cheveux Relevés (Standing Hair People), after their fashion of doing their hair in a tall roach. These were an Algonquian people, with home villages on Manitoulin Island. They were trading partners of the Huron and were known to travel 1200 to 1500 miles each summer in a grand circuit which reached from the Huron country past Lake Nippising west and northwest to the Upper Great Lakes (Heidenreich 1971: 239).

It was from the Cheveux Relevés—soon to be known as the Odawa—that Champlain first learned of yet another people farther to the west. The Odawa told Champlain that they were continuously "at war with another nation of savages, called Asistagueroüon, which means *Gens de Feu* (the Fire People), who are distant from them ten days' journey" (Grant 1907: 303).[3] Champlain also learned of the Gens de Feu from the Neutral, who informed him that they regularly aided their allies the Odawa in their wars against that people. Champlain placed this newly identified people somewhere west of La Mer Douce in a region whose geography was only dimly and imperfectly understood.

Those who came after Champlain kept on the outlook for the Fire People, or Fire Nation, fully expecting someday to come across them directly. As knowledge of the land forms in the Upper Great Lakes improved, cartographers located the Gens or Nation de Feu first one place, then another (see Figures 1 & 3). Many years later the identity of the Gens de Feu continued to

Figure 1. Section from Nicolas Sanson's map "North America in 1650" (from copy in the Library of Congress). Note the N. du Feu located south of the Lac des Puans, which confuses Green Bay and Lake Michigan.

cause confusion and controversy. They were finally equated with first one known tribe, then another. Finally, some agreement was reached—quite in error as it turned out—that the Asistagueroüon (the Fire Nation) were specifically the Mascouten or the Potawatomi (Hodge 1910 I: 810–11; II: 289).

The Odawa and the Neutral might have informed Champlain that they used the phrase "Asistagueroüon" in a very general sense, as a cover term for all of those tribes immediately to their west and southwest who were enemies of the Huron, the Petun, the Neutral, and the Odawa (Goddard 1972). In its seventeenth-century usage, then, this phrase apparently referred to most of the tribes that anthropologists today classify together as the Central Algonquians, including possibly the Shawnee, the Miami, and the Illinois, and certainly the Sauk, the Fox, the Kickapoo, the Mascouten—and the Potawatomi. As soon as the French traders, missionaries, and agents came in firsthand contact with these separate tribes, the use of the general term "Nation de Feu" disappeared.

TRIBAL NAMES AND IDENTITIES

It is possible that the Huron-Odawa reference to the Fire People alluded to the regular, extensive use of fire by the Central Algonquians both for clearing new garden lands and for communal hunting of large game animals. Be that as it may, in this fashion the Potawatomi almost entered the historical scene as a named, identified people in 1616. They were instead classed together with a number of other tribes quite similar in language, culture, and social organization. This was not to be the last confusion of the Potawatomi with one or more tribes.

Identifying a particular society in the historical development of the Upper Great Lakes has always been a problem complicated by the variety of names used to label one or another of them, as well as by the variant pronunciations and creative efforts at spelling each name in different languages—Indian and European. Of the tribal societies geographically closest to the Potawatomi in 1616 (see Figure 5), the word "Sauk" derives from that tribe's own expression "Osagiwug" (People of the Inlet, i.e., Saginaw Bay). But the Sauk were also known to the Huron and the early French as Hvattoehronon (the Sunset People, i.e., the Westerners). The Fox, close neighbors of the Sauk and later allied with them, acquired from their early contacts with the French a name which derives from their word "Wagosh" (Red Fox); but this was the name of only one of their clans. This tribe actually called itself Muskwakiwuk (the Red Earth People). However, they were also known for many years to the

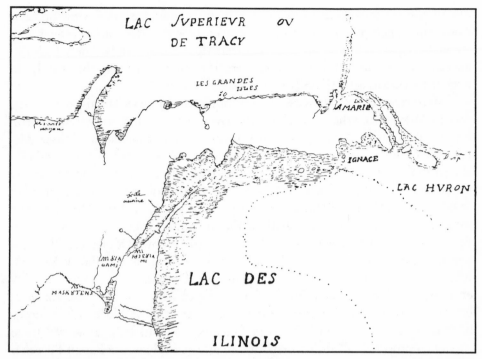

Figure 2. Section from Father Marquette's manuscript map of 1674 (copy in the UW-Green Bay library). Note the "P8t8iami" (i.e., Poutouimai) located at the head of Green Bay and the "Mask8tens" (i.e., Maskoutens) farther south. At this date the French knew firsthand only the north and west shores of Lake Michigan.

French as the Outagami, derived from the Ojibwa-Odawa word "Utugamig" (People of the Other Shore).

Farther south of the Sauk and Fox were the Kickapoo and their close relations the Mascoutens. The Kickapoo were first known to the French as the Lake People, from the Huron expression "Ontarahronon"; but their own name for themselves derives from the word "Kwigapaw" (He Moves About Here and There). The Mascoutens in turn were also known to the Huron as Oherokouaehronon (People of the Grassy Place), whereas the tribal name proper comes from the Ojibwa-Odawa expression "Mashkode" and the related Sauk-Fox form "Muskuta" (both meaning Prairie), to which is added a diminutive ending, making People of the Small Prairie. It is the Mascoutens who create additional confusion. For awhile they seemed prime candidates for identification as the true Fire People, first mentioned to Champlain. However, this apparently stems from mistaking the word "Mashkode" (Prairie) for "Ishkote" (Fire). Moreover, for many years beginning in the late seventeenth century, "Mashkode" (Prairie People) was used as a general label to describe *any* of the tribes who lived in the savannahs below, east, and west of Lake Michigan. There is now no doubt, however, that the Mascoutens proper constituted a separate tribe within the Central Algonquian family, one which disappeared as an autonomous group before 1812 by assimilating into the Kickapoo tribe (Goddard 1971; Silverberg 1957).

More remote from the Central Algonquians of Lower Michigan were the related Menomini, who lived along the river of that name in extreme northeastern Wisconsin. Menomini comes from the Ojibwa-Odawa phrase "Menominiwok inniwok"—literally, the People of the Good Seed, that is, the Wild Rice People, after this important natural food on which they were heavily dependent. But the French and, later, the English also used the expression "Folles Avoines"—literally, the Crazy Oaters or the Wild Oats (Rice) People —for the Menomini. Farther south of the Menomini, along and below Green Bay, was a very large, powerful tribe whom the Ojibwa-Odawa called Winipeg and the Sauk-Fox called Winipyagohah (People of the Filthy Water), from whence comes the modern Winnebago. Thinking filthy water a reference to a salt sea, the early French for awhile called them the Gens de Mer; but later—after determining that Green Bay was truly an algae rich, odorous body of water—they created the usage "Puants," or Stinkards. However, these tribesmen properly called themselves Hochagra (People of the Parent Speech). They were not an Algonquian society; instead, they were a tribe of the Chiwere subfamily of Siouans, most closely related to the Iowa, Ota, and Missouri west and south of them.

Although each of these five Central Algonquian tribes and the Siouan Winnebago had numerous other less common names, none of them poses a truly serious problem of identification.[4] They were all semisedentary societies, each a single, unitary, tribal-level organization. The organization of the societies to the east, north, and south of these Central Algonquians was quite different. To the east on the Ontario Peninsula were several societies of the Iroquoian family. The largest of these were the Huron, which is a word of French derivation. Some of the first French in the New World apparently believed the Indians looked like wild boars—from the men's hair styling—and called them Hure (JR 16: 231–33).[5] This name was later applied to a people who actually called themselves Wendat (The One Island), after the insular topography of their territory (Heidenreich 1971: 22). The Wendat, or Huron, were not a single tribal society but a closely cooperating coalition of four or more Iroquoian tribes in what is now Simcoe County, Ontario. Eastward of them were the so-called Petun or Tobacco Huron and the Neutral, each also a coalition of several tribal societies of Iroquoian language and culture.

Immediately to the south and west of the Sauk, Fox, Kickapoo, and Mascouten of the Lower Peninsula of Michigan were other closely related

Algonquian societies. These became known later as the Miami and the Illinois. The name "Miami" is Ojibwa-Odawa in origin, from "Omaumeg" (People Living on the Peninsula); but Illinois derives from this people's own self-name, "Ilini" (which simply means the Men or the People). These together constituted some ten or more separate, named societies grouped in two loose coalitions, all speaking dialects of one mutually intelligible language. There is good evidence to indicate that at least some of these societies had advanced to a more complex level of social organization than that of their relatives immediately to the north. The Miami, for example, were probably organized as a centralized chiefdom when the French first came in contact with them in 1668 (Clifton 1975a).

On the north shore of Lake Huron, in the vicinity of Sault Ste. Marie, and along the Lake Superior shore the situation was very different from the prairielands of Indiana and Illinois. In 1616 all of the groups living in this cold northern woodlands were Algonquians, but they lived in smaller communities, not organized into tribal-level societies. These communities were

Figure 3. Section of the map "Carte de la Louisiane et du cours du Mississippi," 1718, by Guillaume Delisle (from a copy in the Newberry Library). In this map the Potawatomi are shown in three locations: on the islands at the mouth of Green Bay, on the St. Joseph River, and at Detroit. The Mascoutens are now shown as near Chicago.

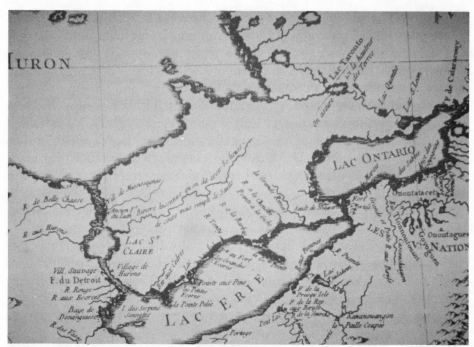

Figure 4. Section from M. Bellin's map "Partie Occidentale de la Nouvelle France," 1755 (from a copy in the UW-Green Bay library). Note that the name "Onankissus" in corrupted form—"Donanguasse"—is here given to the bay at the head of Lake Erie.

localized clans, each autonomous of the other, all subsisting by fishing and hunting (Hickerson 1963: 67). It was certain of these communities which first became involved with the French in the early fur trade. The Nippising —trading partners of the Huron—were one. Another was the group called by Champlain the Cheveux Relevés, later identified as the Odawa. The name "Odawa" comes from a generic Northern Algonquian verb stem meaning "to trade." Eventually the French used this word on two levels of meaning, (1) to refer to all the Algonquian communities who were involved with the French in the fur trade, and (2) in a narrow sense to designate the Odawa proper.[6] At the time Champlain first met them in 1615 picking blueberries near the mouth of the French River, the Odawa were not a single tribe, but four or more autonomous clan communities. The largest and most influential of these were the Kiskakon (Cut Tails, i.e., Bear Clan), and the Sinago (Squirrel Clan). Two other Odawa communities are known by geographical references: the Sable, likely, the People of the Sandy Country, and the Nassau-aketon, or People of the Fork (in a river).

To the east of the Odawa communities, which were centered on Mani-toulin Island, were the small scattered communities of master hunters and fishermen who later became known collectively as the Ojibwa. "Ojibwa," however, was the name of only one of the communities which made up this group. Others included the Amikwa—Beaver, the Nokwet—Bear, the Mara-meg—Catfish, and the Saulteurs. "Saulteur" was a French name for the several groups of Ojibwa clansmen clustered around Sault Ste. Marie. This prime location on the strait separating Lakes Superior and Huron was the focal point for Ojibwa economic, subsistence, and ritual activities. By 1680, as fur trade activities in this area reached their zenith, a number of these small Algonquian communities consolidated at Sault Ste. Marie to take advantage of these new opportunities. The French first called this new tribal aggregate the Saulteurs, and only later did they become known as the Ojibwa (Hickerson 1962, 1963, & 1970).

Of the Central Algonquians located on the Lower Peninsula of Michigan, the Potawatomi were probably the ones least well known to the Hurons. All available evidence points to the Potawatomi occupying the far western edge of Michigan, a strip of land stretching from the St. Joseph River north to Big Sable Point, and perhaps as far as Traverse Bay. In this location they were oriented to Lake Michigan fisheries and transportation routes, and were isolated from direct contact with the Huron and their allies by the Sauk, Fox, Kickapoo, and Mascoutens to the east of them.

POTAWATOMI IDENTITY

The first unmistakable evidence of the existence of the Potawatomi dates to 1634 but was not recorded until six years later. The contact was made because of difficulty in trading relations between several of the interior tribes. The Odawa had sent a trade delegation to Green Bay, where the Winnebago demonstrated a certain inhospitality by eating them, and the Odawa retaliated by sending war parties against the Winnebago. Since these Odawa were acting as advance agents for the French, some action for peace was called for. Samuel de Champlain, managing affairs from his Quebec post, wanted to establish friendly relations with these identified but unvisited Winnebago, the People of the Filthy Water or, perhaps, the Salt Water. He still hoped to find a short route to the Orient; but the business of trade was uppermost in his thoughts. To accomplish the dual aims of reestablishing trade relations and exploration of unknown territory, he selected another of his able aides, the accomplished *voyageur*, interpreter, and forest diplomat Jean Nicolet (Smith 1973: 7–10; Kellogg 1925: 75–83).

Nicolet left the St. Lawrence posts of New France with the Huron-Odawa trading fleet in the summer of 1634. Traveling via the familiar Ottawa and

French river route to the Hurons and then to Manitoulin Island, in late August he struck out westward in one large canoe with seven Indian companions. First visiting Sault Ste. Marie, he observed the productive fishing there and heard of the lake beyond the Sault. From there the eight men paddled along the shore of the Upper Peninsula of Michigan southwestward, finally entering Green Bay. Beyond Manitoulin Island this had all been uncharted territory.

The exact nature of Nicolet's discoveries and the specifics of the business he conducted are unknown. He left no journal of this voyage, and what is recorded of it is contained in a few brief paragraphs in the *Jesuit Relations* in words set down secondhand by other men. The later of these two brief accounts was written at the time of Nicolet's death in 1642. It describes in glorious phrases how Nicolet—arriving in Winnebago country on Green Bay —dressed in Chinese damask robes and a mandarin's cap, stepped ashore and fired a pistol from each hand. This astonishing sight frightened the women and children; but the Winnebago reception party recovered and feted him, and so a peace was concluded and he soon returned to the St. Lawrence (JR 18: 237; 23: 275–79).

It was in the earlier report of Nicolet's voyage that the Potawatomi are first specifically mentioned in a historical document. The context was a de-

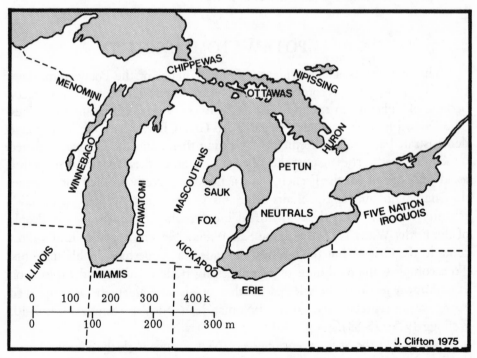

Figure 5. Distribution of Upper Great Lakes tribes about 1634.

scription of the western country, the upper lakes, and the tribes thereof. It was written in 1640 by Father Le Jeune—a French priest—from information supplied him by others. Because this brief recitation of secondhand facts has been often used to make the Potawatomi prehistoric residents of Wisconsin, it needs to be examined carefully and in detail.[7] After accurately describing the location of the Winnebago on the shores of Green Bay, Father Le Jeune had only this to say about other tribes in these western waters (JR 18: 231–33).

> In the neighborhood of this nation [the Winnebago] are the Naduesiu, the Assinipour, the Eriniouai, the Rasaouakoueton, and the Pouutouatami. These are the names of a part of the nations which are beyond the shores of the great river Saint Lawrence and of the great lakes of the Hurons on the North. . . . I will say, by the way, that sieur Nicolet, interpreter of the Algonquin and Huron languages for the Gentlemen of New France, has given me the names of these nations, which he himself has visited, for the most part in their own country.

Aside from the Pouutouatami (this is only one of more than 140 known spellings of the name), we need to identify and locate the other four tribes which in 1634 were "in the neighborhood" of the Winnebago.

The Naduesiu are clearly the Nadowesiw, which was the common Ojibwa-Odawa name for the Dakota, who in fact got their popular name, Sioux, from "-siw," the diminutive ending of this word. It means Little Timber Rattlesnakes, which is what the northern Algonquians called their western Dakota enemies (they reserved Nadowe proper—the Big Rattlesnakes—for the New York Iroquois, also long-term enemies). This was long before the Dakota tribes had moved out of the woodlands of Minnesota onto the plains. In 1634 the nearest Dakota were probably the Santee, living near Milles Lacs, Minnesota, as many as twenty-five days' journey distant from Green Bay.

Similarly, the Assinipour are unmistakably the society later known as the Assiniboine—He Cooks with Stones, from the Ojibwa-Odawa name for them. Until about 1630 the Assiniboine were one tribe with the Yankton Dakota, and lived in the boundary-waters area between Minnesota and Ontario as well as in southern Manitoba; and when they split away from the Yankton they moved farther north and west of there (Ray 1974: 4). The Assinipour, in short, were many days' travel farther away than the Naduesiu.

The Eriniouai are the Illinois, whose northernmost villages above Chicago were much closer than were the Santee or Assiniboine villages to the Winnebago country around Green Bay. But still, by canoe—taking the shortest route along the west shore of Lake Michigan—the Illinois were a good 360 miles round-trip away. Assuming the best weather and the freshest, most eager paddlers, this is at a bare minimum ten days' travel distant from the Green Bay site of Nicolet's visit.

The Rasaouakoueton make a slight puzzle. For some years it was thought that this was a corruption or a misspelling of Mascoutens, which might have placed that tribe in Wisconsin in 1634. However, it is known that the Mascouten in this period were still li. .ng in Michigan, south of Saginaw Bay, adjacent to the Fox, Sauk, and Kickapoo. This information comes from later pages of Le Jeune's 1640 relation, where he lists tribes known to him from the so-called Lost Huron Map, which apparently was the base from which Nicolas Sanson d'Abbeville drew his 1650 and later maps (see my Figure 1; and Goddard 1972: 123–24). In a careful philological and historical analysis of "Rasaoua-koueton" and other names, Goddard concluded that there was indeed a misprint or a confusion of the first letter of this name, substituting an R for an N. This would make them Nasaouakoueton, which is one alternate spelling version of Nassauaketon, People of the Fork, the Odawa group just mentioned, who were known to have traded in the Green Bay area (1972: 130). The People of the Fork may well have maintained a temporary trading settlement on the south shore of the Upper Peninsula of Michigan in this era, directly along Nicolet's route from Sault Ste. Marie to Green Bay. They were known to have done so later in the seventeenth century.

This leaves the Pouutouatami identified but not firmly located in space. As will be seen, in 1634 the Potawatomi were still based in their villages on the *eastern* shores of Lake Michigan. The northernmost of these known prehistoric village—on Dumaw Creek—was less than one hundred miles distant in a straight line from the head of Green Bay—fifty-five miles west across the open waters of Lake Michigan and another forty by portage and streams to the bay. However, it is doubtful if any Potawatomi attempted such a long open-water journey across this great lake. In the historic period they were known to be cautious coast-wise sailors, with an anxious, healthy respect for open-water travel in their fragile birch-bark canoes. If Nicolet had visited them in their "own country," or, as is more likely the case, if some Potawatomi had visited the Green Bay area, the likely route would have been across the northern route of Lake Michigan. This round-trip journey—dead reckoning from points of land to islands along the way—is about six hundred miles from the center of Green Bay to Big Sable Point on the Michigan shore. Thereby, the Potawatomi homeland was considerably farther away than that of the northernmost Ilini villages.

Jean Nicolet is known to have arrived in Green Bay in mid- or late summer, 1634. And he returned to the St. Lawrence River that fall, before the November freeze-up. Therefore, he could not have visited many, certainly not all, of the tribes Le Jeune mentioned "in their own country" in the short few weeks available to him. Judging from the experience of later travels in the area, the trip from the St. Lawrence to both the foot of Lake Michigan and the head of Lake Superior, then back to New France, would have required at least two full summer seasons and a winter spent in the upper lakes—more than sixteen months. The "neighborhood" mentioned by Le Jeune was indeed a very considerable one. We must appreciate the range of geographic knowledge of the French in this period. They knew for example that there was a lake beyond the rapids of Sault Ste. Marie, but they believed it to be a small one. Moreover, the actual shape and orientation of Lake Michigan was unknown. It was confused with the much smaller Green Bay and was believed to lie slanted in a nearly east-west direction (see Figure 1).

Except for the People of the Fork (Odawa), who may have had a trading station somewhere along the Upper Michigan shore or on an adjacent offshore island, it is far more likely that *some* of the Illinois and the Potawatomi visited the Winnebago and Nicolet in Green Bay. Like Sault Ste. Marie, the Green Bay area had long been a prehistoric focal point for Lake Michigan area Indian trade, and news of the impending arrival of this mysterious Waybaymishetome (Long Beard, i.e., Frenchman) would have attracted any visiting tribesmen to the meeting place. The Assiniboine and the Santee Dakota, in contrast, Nicolet more likely may have visited at Sault Ste. Marie, which was a similar focus for trade in Lakes Superior and Huron.

As the root of this problem of the Potawatomi location in 1634 lies an interesting fact. Unlike the Ojibwa and the Odawa, for example, the French always identified and called the Potawatomi by a single name, as did most of the other tribes of the Great Lakes area. To be sure, there were many variant pronunciations and spellings of this name, but these represent either an effort to pronounce or write down "Bodēwadmi" in some other language, or to translate its supposed meaning into the terms of that language. Examples are "Oupouteouatamik" (a Frenchman's effort to say the word with an Algonquian plural "-k" tagged on), "Atowateteany" (an eastern Iroquois version), and "Putewata" (a Dakota version). Invariably, such efforts to pronounce "Bodēwadmi" were further corrupted when, say, a French official tried to write down a Seneca's effort to pronounce the Algonquian word in an Iroquoian language.

Examples of the latter—efforts to translate the supposed meaning of "Bodēwadmi" into some other language—are "Wahonahah" (Fire-Makers, in Miami-Illinois) and the Europeans' own efforts, "Gens de Feu" and "Fire People." Much later in their history, among different tribes, the Potawatomi were known by several other words with different meanings, such as "the Aliens" and "the Watermelon People," but these are not relevant to the key point. This is that from the time of first contact all Potawatomi, regardless of clan or village affiliation or area of residence, were known by a single tribal name. On the one hand, the use of just one name leads to a possible confusion.

Le Jeune's mention of *the* Potawatomi in 1634 is a case in point. It leaves open the possibility that all Potawatomi were in the Green Bay area in that year, although different evidence suggests otherwise. Similarly, in later years there are occasional, fragmentary references to *the* Potawatomi, which may or may not imply that all of the villages or clans making up this tribe were in one or another locale.

On the other hand, the use of a single name to identify the whole society does clearly suggest that at the time of first contact the Potawatomi constituted a single, unitary, cohesive tribal society. In this respect the Potawatomi were entirely like the other Central Algonquian societies of Michigan—the Sauk, Fox, Kickapoo, and Mascoutens. These too were invariably called by one or another name which always designated the tribal whole. And in this respect the Potawatomi were very much unlike their northern kinsmen, the peoples who later became known as the Ojibwa and the Odawa. At the time of first contact these were never known by a single, overall tribal name. Instead, they were identified as separate, smaller, autonomous groups—bands, clans, or villages. In the instance of the Ojibwa clans, for example, it is clear that only about 1670 did they coalesce into a larger aggregate with a tribal structure (Hickerson 1970: 37–50), and that this Ojibwa—or Saulteur—tribal system was an emergent, an outgrowth of their participation in the fur trade. Therefore, like the Mascoutens or the Sauk, the Potawatomi had evolved a single tribal structure prior to contact with Europeans. When the first useful descriptions of Potawatomi social life start being reported, about 1667, it is clear that the Potawatomi tribe was made up of a number of segments—clans or clan-villages—but also that these were well organized into a larger functioning whole, the tribe.

Efforts to trace the meaning of "Potawatomi" back to its roots in the Potawatomi or any Algonquian language are not very fruitful. As Henry R. Schoolcraft noted a good many years ago, "To search for analogies of etymology amid such mere incidental forms [tribal names], which were sometimes imposed in irony or jest, is a mere waste of philological labor" (1851–57 V: 40). In this strict, etymological sense, it is clear that "Potawatomi" in the 1640s did not and could not have a meaning anything like "Fire People" in any Algonquian language. Modern efforts to trace this tribal name to its roots have rested on the definitions given by one or another speaker of some Algonquian language (see Hodge 1910 II: 289). The primary form of the name was assumed to be "Potawatamink" or "Potawaganink," supposedly translating out directly as "People of the Place of the Fire." However, the Algonquian pronunciations used were apparently distorted inventions, pieced together to make an approximation of the English expression "Fire People." They are based upon a popular, or folk, etymology, not one that is justified by the nature of Algonquian grammars. The informants seemingly assumed the derivation had to be from the Ojibwa-Odawa "po:tawe," which is made up of "-awe," "to make a fire," plus "po:t-," "by blowing." This does not and cannot be made to mean "Fire People" or "People of the Place of the Fire" (Goddard 1972: 131).

What apparently happened historically is that an Algonquian language speaker told some Frenchmen with an inadequate understanding of an Ojibwa or Odawa dialect something about blowing on a fire—perhaps, in irony or jest, pointing to a visiting Algonquian from the Lake Michigan shore. Then the French, assuming this to be a tribal name, used it in speaking about or to the people who thus became identified as Potawatomi. Thereafter, these people themselves picked up the new name and used it, knowing that the French— and later the English and Americans—were comfortable with it. In this fashion the word "Potawatomi" could have gotten assimilated into the lexicons of several languages as a useful neologism.

There is no evidence that the people called Potawatomi used this word when speaking in their own language. Even today, it is rarely if ever heard when Potawatomi are joined together in ritual or other business conversing in their own language. Then they use the singular "Neshnabē," Man, or the plural "Neshnabek," People. This once had the connotation of the True or Real People—themselves in contrast to others, strangers. Today it has the sense of *Indian* people in contrast to Euro-Americans. In the 1640s, when the French first made lasting contacts with them, the ancestors of the people who later were to be called the Potawatomi had no problem with identifying themselves, nor of contrasting themselves linguistically or culturally with other societies. This was a problem for Europeans new on the scene, who wished to draw maps, fix tribal districts, and otherwise communicate their new understanding of unknown societies.

Contemporary Potawatomi will not agree with these observations. This is because the tribal name has been well established as a *modus communicandi* for more than three centuries, well known and undoubted as an authentic word in several languages, including their own. As such, it should properly have an equally authentic, ancient meaning. No one, myself included, has ever followed Schoolcraft's advice. The number of efforts to search out the true meaning of the word are many. Indeed, the pronunciation used earlier, "Bodēwadnene," is the result of one such effort. This is a kind of back-formation type of linguistic invention. Starting with the assumption that the tribal name means "People Who Make a Fire by Blowing" (one old translation), it is then pieced together like this: "bod- + ewa + "-(n/d)ini," which, via clumsy grammar, makes "by blowing" + "to make a fire" + "people." Requesting a Potawatomi speaker to translate the tribal name, or even to give one the slightest opportunity to do so, is to ask him to scratch where he itches.

It is an old puzzle about which there are many individual opinions; and all use it as an opportunity to indulge in group-glorification. Thus some examples of other inventive translations are: Those Who Are Capable of a Separate Sovereignty (by building their own council fire); Those Who Are Economically Independent; The Chosen People or Leading Tribe (by virtue of the right to kindle a ceremonial intertribal council fire); and Those Who Have a Special and Unique Way of Building a Fire (by blowing). We can have no objections to these Potawatomi efforts to characterize their own distinctiveness. Therefore, with no further effort at definition, the most common standard form, "Potawatomi," will hereafter be used in discussing this society of Neshnabek.

POTAWATOMI
OR MASCOUTENS?

We have seen that the Huron used the word "Atsistaehronon" (Fire People) as a general cover name for the Central Algonquians to their west. The French picked up this expression temporarily, but then—as they became acquainted with the separate tribes firsthand—they dropped it, substituting particular names for each individual group. Since the Fire People thereby in effect disappeared from the historical scene, the imaginations of various scholars have been greatly stimulated. One result of this has been a series of efforts to identify the Fire People with other specific, known tribes. The Shawnee and the Sauk were briefly candidates for this honor, as were the Mascoutens, since they had—seemingly—conveniently disappeared.

However, because "Potawatomi" was supposed to mean "People of the Place of the Fire," it was easy to conclude that the Atsistaehronon, the Gens de Feu, and the Potawatomi were one and the same society. This is precisely the conclusion James Mooney and J. N. B. Hewitt drew in describing the Potawatomi in the first edition of the *Handbook of American Indians North of Mexico*, while also rejecting the Mascoutens–Fire People identification (Hodge 1910 II: 289).

A few years later, Alanson Skinner developed a different opinion in writing up his study of Kansas Potawatomi culture. He became convinced that the Potawatomi had long been partitioned into two grand divisions, the Forest Potawatomi—whom the Kansas people called Nanosi—and the Muskodanenek, which means, literally, "People of the Prairie." The Forest Potawatomi, Skinner believed, were a group who had always lived in the forests of northern Wisconsin, who spoke a different dialect and evidenced a different, simpler, more archaic culture than the Prairie Potawatomi. Moreover, the Prairie Potawatomi represented, Skinner thought, a prehistoric migration from the eastern seaboard of the United States into the Great Lakes region (1924–27: 9–17). Apparently, some of the Kansas or Oklahoma Potawatomi had told Skinner of a vaguely remembered migration from the east, although he did not record the details of this legend.

In this fashion, since the Potawatomi were supposedly two separate groups with different cultures and histories, Skinner was able to accept and mesh two apparently contradictory interpretations: the Potawatomi (of the Forest division) were truly the Huron's Fire People, while the Potawatomi (of the Prairie division) were the long lost Mascoutens.

The difficulty with this conclusion is that it is contradicted by linguistic, historical, and cultural facts. "Potawatomi" does not properly mean "Fire People." "Fire People" was no more than a convenient cover label for a number of separate Algonquian tribes. The Mascoutons were quite definitely a separate tribe which eventually merged with the Kickapoo: in eighty known historical references to the Mascoutens, they and the Kickapoo are described sixty-two times as coparticipant tribes engaged in joint activities (Silverberg 1957: 134). And, as we shall see in later chapters, all of the Potawatomi once lived in far northeastern Wisconsin—temporarily—as refugees, before moving out from there in the 1670s to expand their tribal estate, while the Potawatomi now found in northern Wisconsin are yet another group of refugees, but these fled north from various parts of the tribal estate to evade removal to Kansas and Iowa hardly eighty years before Skinner studied their relatives in the western prairielands.

What of the Nanosi? Skinner's Kansas and Oklahoma informants told him that this meant "the Between People," applied to the Forest Potawatomi in Wisconsin. These of course are to the east of Kansas. But in Wisconsin the Potawatomi there also recognize the Nanosi, which word they use to refer to Eastern Algonquians such as the Mahican or the Wabunaki. In its usage this is apparently a directional term used to refer to kindred peoples living to the east of the speaker.

And what of the legend of a prehistoric migration of a group from the east into the Great Lakes area across the southern shores of Lakes Erie and Ontario? Here is where a small amount of history rather than conjecture would have helped Skinner immeasurably, for there was indeed such a migration of people, some of whom joined the Potawatomi in the Lake Michigan region, but it was historically documented, not a prehistoric movement.

This migration occurred in 1681. It consisted of an odd-lot group of Eastern Algonquians (Nanosi!) who accompanied René Robert Cavelier, Sieur de La Salle on his 1680–1681 expedition to the Lake Michigan area. These were said to come from near Boston or Bristol—that is, they were New England Algonquians. Driven from the New England homelands by the pressures of

English colonists and Mohawk invasions, they had affiliated themselves with the French and had joined La Salle's party as his special aides for the expedition into the upper lake country. They represented refugee fragments of several different Eastern Algonquian tribes, identified as the Minissens (the Minisink division of the Munsee), the Mahingans (Mahicans), the Abenaki (Wabunaki), and the Sokoki (the Sakukiak, a tribe closely related to and part of the Wabunaki confederacy). Bitterly anti-English and anti-Iroquois, they were deeply loyal to and dependent on the Sieur de La Salle.

These Eastern Algonquians were at a loss as to where they should settle. Returning east to give themselves up for adoption into the Mohawk tribe was one possibility tentatively raised. But another was to remain in the Lake Michigan area serving the French and particularly La Salle's interests. The leader of the Minisink group put it to La Salle that he would remain and attract others from the east if La Salle would appoint him a chief. A second, a man named Ouioulamet or Ouilamette, the son of a chief of a village "near Boston," was a particular favorite of La Salle's, who did appoint him a chief of the Indians of the area. La Salle made Ouilamette his chief go-between in negotiating with the tribes in the Lake Michigan region (Margary 1878 I: 551–72, 575–85, 629–35).

The appointment of Ouilamette as chief by La Salle is of very special interest to the history of the Potawatomi. For, only a few years later, Ouilamette, or Catfish, emerges identified as a so-called chief of that tribe. Later the Eastern Algonquian version of the name "Catfish"—Wilamet—is converted into Potawatomi sounds with the same meaning, Winamek. It remains very prominent throughout Potawatomi history, on the one hand as a very powerful Fish Clan name distinguished by its use by a long series of warriors and leaders, and on the other as a European-style surname of a French-Potawatomi family line which was still influential in Oklahoma and Kansas when Skinner did his work.

THE TRIBAL
SOCIETY

The arrival of a group of Eastern Algonquians in the Great Lakes region, some of whom merged with the Potawatomi (and other societies already there), illustrates a kind of experience which was common throughout the latter half of the seventeenth and eighteenth centuries. This event will also serve to raise a question, what type of society were the Potawatomi at that time?

The arrival of the Mahican, the Wabunaki, and their colleagues is, first, an example of a common process—they carried in with them novel ideas about social and political life. These intruders represented societies organized as chiefdoms, further arranged into political confederacies. Moreover, they had already committed themselves to an alliance with the French and worked—in part—as the servants of French interests. Further, the relationship between La Salle and the several appointed "chiefs" was a relationship between patron and client. Then too, this assimilation of groups of people of somewhat different language and culture illustrates the fact that a society like the Potawatomi can be heterogeneous in its composition. But the important issue is the exact nature of a "tribal society," of which we have so far assumed the Potawatomi were one example.

Three key words have to be understood: "band," "tribe," and "chiefdom." The first two of these have been in common English usage for several centuries; the last is a recently coined technical term. All three are used in this book, each in a very special sense.[8] They represent, in order of their appearance in cultural evolution, three different kinds of primitive social organizations.

Of the three words, both "band" and "tribe" have long been in common (if not everyday) usage with different, nontechnical meanings. Of the two, over several centuries "band" has retained a single, hardly changing connotation of some kind of human group organized for some purpose or another. The situation with "tribe" is otherwise. Although its roots in European languages are ancient, it reappeared by the early nineteenth century as an educated person's word, refurbished and put back to work in an effort to understand the kinds of societies that Europeans had been discovering all over the world. By analogy with the ancient *tribus* of Rome and Israel, the meaning was a group of persons forming a community and claiming descent from a common ancestor. This meaning today—with some special addenda—is generally attached to the technical word "clan," and is so used in this book.[9] Thus, in consulting old documents concerning the Potawatomi, one is on safe ground assuming that when the word "band" is encountered, the word "group" can be substituted with no loss in meaning, if with no gain in understanding either. However, when we read lines written in 1812 describing how the Potawatomi were divided into tribes, the modern, ordinary meaning of this word is not intended, much less the technical meaning, which will be given shortly. In this case, one is on fairly safe ground in supposing that the author meant something like clan, and this information is at least potentially illuminating.

The connection between the special definitions of "band," "tribe," and "chiefdom" is that the first is—in terms of the evolution of types of societies— the more ancient, while the latter are similarly the more recent. Bands, in human history, were the kind of society characteristic of paleolithic hunters and gatherers. These were very small-scale societies, each an intimate face-to-face community which shared a life in a limited geographic area. Whole band communities in some seasons camped together, depending on the locally available richness or scarcity of foods, but in other periods they dispersed in smaller family groups over a larger territory. In 1634 the northern kinsmen of the Potawatomi—the forerunners of the later Odawa, Ojibwa, and Cree—were clearly band-level societies. Indeed, sometime before 1634 the ancestors of the Potawatomi themselves had constituted several separate, autonomous hunting and gathering bands. This is a very safe statement to make: in truth, sometime before 4000 B.C. *all* of our ancestors lived in foraging band-level societies. In the Potawatomi instance the important matter is not *that*, but *when* they became organized as a tribe. This is an issue we will reserve for a subsequent chapter.

The transition from band-level to tribal-level societies was an outgrowth of the misnamed neolithic revolution. This important series of technological-economic developments had nothing to do with improved techniques for fabricating—or more loving care given to the creation of—stone tools and weapons. The critical invention was the domestication of plants and animals, which offered a more secure and substantial food supply. Tribal peoples, worldwide, are generally people who husband the soil or animals or both.[10] In this respect the Potawatomi were no exception. Moving southward prehistorically from a more northern area, they entered a region where the climate allowed the planting of crops and there mastered those skills necessary to improve their conditions of subsistence.

Husbanding the soil means placing a greater value on territory and the possibility of subsisting a larger population in one area. These features also characterize tribal societies, and they bring in train other developments. Larger, semisedentary populations require different kinds of social organization from those exclusive to band societies. However, there are no very sharp breaks. Tribes, like bands, remain societies emphasizing and based upon a network of kinship ties; and tribes, like bands, remain profoundly equalitarian both in ethic and practice. Hierarchies of power, authority, wealth, or personal value are little known to tribes such as the Potawatomi. Moreover, tribal societies are acephalous societies. They get on quite adequately without prime ministers or chiefs. There are no formal offices occupied by full-time, political officials.

Instead, the management of social life, the business of social control, is a responsibility distributed throughout the tribe. It is the business of almost anyone who can gossip about someone else's deviance, although it may be more the special interest of grandfathers, elder brothers, magicians, sorcerers, the leaders of ritual congregations, clan elders, or other persons occupying special kinds of status positions.

We observed that bands in the aggregate developed into tribes. But a tribe is not simply an assemblage of formerly autonomous bands. It is an organized kind of a larger whole. Part of the connective tissue tying a tribe together consists of specialized secondary associations, such as secret societies, ritual congregations, ceremonial organizations, and military sodalities with limited police functions. All of these were characteristic of the Potawatomi tribe. But the most important binding element remained extended kinship ties, consanguineous and affinal, real and fictional. In the Potawatomi case a strong emphasis on patrilineage and a system of linked clans (within each of which men and women were like brothers and sisters to one another) had great force in unifying scattered tribal segments with sometimes widely different interests. The constituent elements of a tribal society like the Potawatomi, the knots in the social fabric, were clan villages.

These economically self-sufficient local communities were bonded together for certain common purposes. Together they constituted—borrowing Morton Fried's phrase—a society of nonbelligerents (1968). Within the tribal whole, peace was the idealized rule, although scarcely controlled conflict and concealed hostility were often the reality. Thereby, a tribe was capable of channelizing its angers into external wars in defense of the tribal estate. Further, as we have seen earlier in the case of the Potawatomi, tribes generally had two sorts of names: those given them by other societies—such as the name "Potawatomi" itself—and those they used in discussing themselves, which generally meant simply "human being or person"—such as the Potawatomi word "Neshnabē."

In studying tribal societies a number of historians and anthropologists have been disturbed and struck by the lack of linguistic and cultural homogeneity characteristic of some. They seem to believe that tribes by definition must be pure in language and ethnic composition. Tribes not so characterized, they assume, represent a fall from grace, societies blemished by variant and discordant human elements.[11] The truth is that tribal societies normally are societies adulterated by the process of incorporating aliens into their ranks. In Fried's words most "tribes seem at close range to be curious melanges rather than homogeneous units." Assimilation of culturally and linguistically different groups was a recognized tribal policy, an effective means for recruiting new members. The Potawatomi, for instance, had traditional and often-employed rituals for just this purpose. As we will see, these were rituals of identity transformation which made kinsmen out of strangers. A tribe, in brief, was an organization, a distinctive social system, not a particular population or a piece of real estate.

Several different kinds of tribes are recognized. In the Potawatomi instance we are dealing with the segmentary variety. The segments—building blocks of the tribal edifice—were the just-mentioned clan villages. In each such village was accomplished most of the work of the society. Each had its own internal organization, largely duplicative of that of the others. There marriages were arranged, children born, food produced, and the sick attended to. Each had its sphere of influence and interests, and each was—within limits, and most of the time—autonomous. But individuals, families, clans, and congregations were also autonomous, within limits and much of the time. The qualifications to individual or village autonomy are the subject and substance of the larger, inclusive tribal organization.

Chiefdoms contrast with tribal-level societies of the segmentary variety first and foremost by the presence of chiefs. That is to say, they are societies characterized by a formal office with established, legitimate powers of political leadership over the whole society. Such chiefly offices, as might be expected, require the support of an administrative branch which mediates between the chief and the ordinary people. Some limited amount of hierarchy, a ranking of the whole population into those more or less unequal, is the rule. Similarly, the authority of a chief backed by his administrative branch tends to weaken the power and to reduce the autonomy of the local communities. A leader in a segmentary tribe is first among equals (and they are mostly close kinsmen); the chief, on the other hand, may have no peer.

Coming from excessively hierarchical societies, the early European visitors had grave difficulties understanding how any society could manage without a king and a nobility. In the case of societies like the Potawatomi, they were forever confusing clan elders, speakers, ceremonial hosts, religious leaders, and other traditional Potawatomi functionaries with chiefs. There is no evidence to indicate that the Potawatomi had chiefs (in this technical sense) when the French first visited them; but there is ample evidence to indicate that they acquired some soon afterwards. Not finding chiefs already on the scene, the French began making them. The example of La Salle's appointment of Ouilamette, as discussed earlier, is only one case in point. This does not say that this segmentary tribe was thereby quickly and easily converted into a chiefdom. It does indicate how this tribe acquired a new kind of social role, and it does suggest one direction of social change. To the details of these developments we will now turn.

2

Before History

Locating the Potawatomi homeland and describing their cultural adaptation prior to 1640 is a mildly hazardous enterprise. We will see that following Nicolet's ambiguous reference to them in 1634, 1641 is the next occasion that they are even mentioned; and it is not until the late 1660s that there are Frenchmen on the scene amongst these tribesmen to leave behind full descriptions of their locations and activities. By then the Potawatomi had long since fled the country they occupied in 1634.

The evidence available consists of information about their language; conclusions drawn from archeological studies; the traditional oral histories of the Potawatomi, Odawa, and Ojibwa; analysis of cultural materials described soon after the French first arrived on the scene in northeast Wisconsin (whence the Potawatomi had by then moved); and recorded fragments of descriptions of their activities between 1641 and 1660. Taken together, this evidence encourages a firm conclusion: the protohistoric territory of this tribe consisted of a long belt of Lake Michigan shoreline on the western edge of the Lower Peninsula of the area which now bears that same name.[1] Dating the period of Potawatomi occupancy of that coastal zone is somewhat more difficult. The latter end of the period is easiest to fix. They were clearly in this area between 1605 and 1640, but by 1641 they were on the move out of and away from it. The beginning of the period of the occupancy of the Lower Peninsula has to be conjectured. An educated speculation would be A.D. 1500, plus or minus fifty years. Altogether about 140 years: not particularly a long period of occupation—true. But the archeological evidence suggests a recent arrival there and a kind of transitional adaptation to a new type of environment.

THE PROTOHISTORIC ESTATE

The southwestern Michigan homeland may be called the protohistoric estate since it was occupied when the Potawatomi were on the edge of history.

Of course, it was occupied for more than a century before 1634, and consequently prehistory overlaps with protohistory. The exact limits of this area cannot be specified precisely since there was no one on the scene to map it, and unfortunately the Potawatomi picked locations for their villages which were the same as those Americans later selected for their most intensive urban, industrial, and agricultural development. Most prehistoric Potawatomi sites are thereby obliterated by the cities of Niles, Benton Harbor, South Haven, Muskegon, and Ludington. Others have been despoiled by amateur pot-hunters who treat a prehistoric village site as if it were private property and buried treasure. The few remaining sites available for careful archeological study are not necessarily the largest nor the most typical. However, the Moccasin Bluff site just north of the town of Buchanan in extreme southeastern Michigan and the Dumaw Creek site on the drainage of the Pentwater River west of Big Sable Point roughly fix the southern and northern limits of Potawatomi territory before 1640.

If population estimates made by the French of the Potawatomi in the 1650s are approximately correct, and if there had not been earlier too sharp a decline in population occasioned by the hardships of the period of migration north and west into Wisconsin, then we may estimate some twenty-five hundred Potawatomi in the Michigan protohistoric estate about 1634. Calculating an average summer village size of about two hundred persons, this would make some dozen or more semipermanent major villages. Of course, there would have been many more smaller winter-hunting camps, fishing-station camps, maple sugar–making sites, and smaller satellite villages scattered about some distance from the major villages.

Reading from the kinds of locations indicated in the known archeological example, and from the types of village sites favored by the Potawatomi on the opposite shore of Lake Michigan in the years soon after, we can identify the probable locations where these Michigan villages might have been found, say, in 1634. These were in open lands—small prairies, near a forest edge, adjacent to a substantial stream, where there were loose sandy or sandy-loam soils to be easily worked, in an area picked for good hunting and fishing. It is doubtful that all or even many of these dozen villages were clustered close together. They were more likely separated from one another by ten or more miles of unoccupied country.

THE PROTOHISTORIC
HABITAT

This territory in western Michigan was rich, fertile, Indian country. It was especially suitable for a tribe such as the Potawatomi whose subsistence economy combined maize horticulture with pedestrian hunting in nearby areas, long-distance hunting using birch-bark canoes for transport, extensive fishing from dugout and birch-bark canoes or using traps and weirs in local streams or along the lakeshore, and the gathering of vegetal foods. It was adjacent to the upland savannahs of Indiana and Illinois, which were made easily accessible via canoe down the lakeshore to the Calumet region at the foot of the lake, or to and up the St. Joseph River and thence by a comfortable portage and the Kankakee River to the blue-stem prairies of Illinois.

This southeastern Michigan habitat is part of the Carolinian biotic prov-

Plate 1. Drawing reconstructing the appearance of a Potawatomi man of Dumaw Creek, Michigan, about 1600 A.D. (Courtesy of the Chicago Natural History Museum.)

ince, marked by an average growing season allowing between 140 and 180 frost-free days, a mean annual temperature of 46° to 50° Fahrenheit, and a well-distributed annual precipitation averaging 28–36 inches per year. The winters provided snow cover for many months, easing the Potawatomi hunter's burden in tracking deer and elk. The long growing season combined with rich soils allowed the practice of agriculture, which was difficult if not impossible north of Michigan. In the northern part of the region were hardwood forests mixed with Great Lakes pines; and in the south oak and hickory forests were mixed with beech and maple stands (Cleland 1966: 2–10; Fitting and Cleland 1969).

This habitat provided a rich flora and fauna for exploitation by the Potawatomi. Game animals in abundance ranged in size from muskrat to buffalo, and also included oppossum, raccoon, cottontail rabbit, whitetail deer, turkey, passenger pigeon, various turtles, black bear, beaver, and elk. The streams and lakes provided whitefish, lake herring, lake trout, pike, perch, lake sturgeon, suckers, burbot, catfish, white bass, and other species. The Potawatomi were specialized in river and inshore lake fishing, but they did not exploit all species of fish or game animals equally. The security of the food supply created by corn farming in time made hunting and fishing more of an auxiliary subsistence activity. Meat was still quite important as a source of protein, or was valued for reasons of ritual, hospitality, or taste, but hunting to an increasing extent became supplementary to domesticated crops (Cleland 1966: 84).

At the Moccasin Bluff site, for example, the Potawatomi and other tribesmen who occupied that area had evidently specialized in taking three main species. Together, these accounted for 82 percent of the meat consumed. Deer accounted for 39 percent of this consumption, elk 33 percent, and sturgeon 9 percent, while beaver was only 6 percent, bear 5 percent, dog 2 percent, and other species much less (Bettarel & Smith 1973: 130).[2] A wide variety of vegetal foods were also collected and consumed: acorns, walnuts, plums, butternuts, wild rice, various berries, and the white water lily (*Nymphaea tuberosa*), which the Potawatomi call mkopin, bear potato. Berries were much used as condiments, as was maple sugar, especially in early spring when it gave a welcome lift from the hard times and food shortages of late winter. Nuts were a sometime, starvation period, emergency food supply, not relied on regularly for a substantial part of the diet.

LINGUISTIC EVIDENCE

Potawatomi is one member of the Central Algonquian subfamily of languages which were spoken from the northern part of Canada west to the Great Plains, and in the Upper Great Lakes area. Taken together, these languages do not constitute a single genetic group—they apparently are not descended from a single common ancestral language of the larger Algonquian family. Instead, they constitute only a convenient geographic grouping (Goddard 1976). Although it was once believed that Potawatomi was no more than a mutually intelligible dialect of Ojibwa-Odawa, as are Mississauga, Nipissing, and Algonkin, for some years now it has been recognized that Potawatomi constitutes a separate language in its own right (Hockett 1942: 541). However, in sound and structure Potawatomi is very close to Ojibwa, Odawa, and their congeners; but it also shares much vocabulary with other Central Algonquian languages such as Sauk and Kickapoo (Hockett 1942 & 1975). For example, some 90 percent of Potawatomi morphemes have cognates in languages such as Ojibwa, Menomini, Cree, and Fox, although these are altered by regular sound shifts between these languages (Hockett 1942: 541).

Unfortunately, no linguist has expended the time and labor necessary to do a systematic quantitative study of the Central Algonquian languages which might help fix a more exact date for the point of separation of Potawatomi from Ojibwa-Odawa. However, the facts available indicate that the ancestral Potawatomi speakers were separated from their Ojibwa-speaking kinsmen some several hundred years ago, which rough time frame is consistent with other estimates of the point of Potawatomi entry into the Lower Peninsula of Michigan. More importantly, the markers of close linguistic relationship are in sound patterns and the fundamental structure of the languages involved, and here the evidence points to the derivation of Potawatomi from Ojibwa. The acquisition of new vocabulary items like those used by Sauk or Kickapoo speakers indicates later contact between speakers of these languages. Both conclusions point to one interpretation: sometime before 1550 the Potawatomi spoke a dialect of Ojibwa but broke away and migrated into the Michigan habitat, there to come into extensive contact with speakers of other Central Algonquian languages already there.

This interpretation has to be clarified and somewhat qualified. The statements made are about the nature of the Potawatomi *language*, not about the linguistic skills of those many individuals who spoke this—and often other —languages. Saying that Potawatomi was mutually unintelligible with Ojibwa does not say that numerous Potawatomi speakers were not versed in the use of that second language. Indeed, soon after the arrival of the French in the upper lake country, Ojibwa became the preferred language of trade and other intertribal dealings. It was sometimes, in fact, called the court language of the upper lakes. French missionaries, traders, and agents came into the lake country already speaking dialects of Ojibwa, which they had learned from the Algonkin and Nipissing farther east. Later on in Potawatomi history, a considerable number of Ojibwa and Odawa were assimilated into several major

Potawatomi villages, which undoubtedly made some such communities poly-
glottal. As we will soon note, in the 1660s the Potawatomi also assimilated a
group of Sauk, which may be the origin of some vocabularly similarities in
these languages. In point of fact, after 1667 the Potawatomi were in very
frequent contact with most other Central Algonquian tribes. All of these
mixed experiences tend to confuse efforts to track exactly the time of separation
of Potawatomi from its nearest linguistic relatives.

TRADITIONAL HISTORY

The traditional histories of the Ojibwa, Odawa, and Potawatomi are in
agreement that these three once constituted a single people with a common
culture and language. Such orally transmitted accounts depict a migration
from the east and a splitting into three divisions at some unspecified date. This
division, traditionally, occurred at the Straits of Mackinac, and the narratives
remark that those who became known as Potawatomi moved southward into
Lower Michigan.[3]

Such traditional accounts of distant prehistoric happenings have to be
approached with some caution and used with care. They cannot be accepted
directly without questioning them as valid, specific accounts of developments
in the remote past (Vansina 1965: 8–18). But they cannot be entirely discounted either. From what has been said of the Ojibwa, Odawa, and Potawatomi peoples earlier, it should be evident that such a recital has to involve considerable simplification. This is so because neither the Ojibwa nor the Odawa
had a tribal organization or a group identity much before 1670. Before that
date they constituted a number of scattered local communities. Moreover, the
examination of the story given by Skinner, already discussed in chapter one,
indicates that at least one of the "migrations from the east" was a dated, historic event, and it did not involve any of the three Great Lakes tribes. One key
to understanding oral traditions of this sort is to understand that the Potawatomi and kindred peoples place very great stock on relative age. The greater
the supposed antiquity, the more valued the thing, ritual, person, or process.
Today's tradition often enough is last year's novelty.

Several examples will help in understanding what is involved in creative
fabrications of this sort. One involves a relatively recent event, dated in the
1830s. A good many historians and anthropologists believe that in those years
a group of Potawatomi from Drummond Island (off the eastern tip of the
Upper Peninsula of Michigan) migrated into Ontario. This is of some interest
because Drummond Island is far to the north of other known Potawatomi
villages at that time.

The conviction stems from the acceptance of the words of George Copway, self-styled as Kah-Ge-Ga-Gah-Bowh, Chief of the Ojibwa Nation, who in 1850 published this information in a book called *The Traditional History and Characteristic Sketches of the Ojibwa Nation*. Copway may have been a chief; he was certainly a Wesleyan missionary, which fact might serve to explain a certain predilection to pretentiousness and copying. Surely an event happening only fifteen years prior to its telling should be validly transmitted via traditional oral accounts. But this is not a traditional account at all. Copway actually copied the description of the supposed Potawatomi migration word for word directly from the pages of an official British government document published in 1844.[4] The report happened to contain a printer's error, substituting "Potawatomie" for the word "Potaganasus"—the name of an Ojibwa village—in the original, handwritten copy, which had been prepared by an experienced British Indian agent (Clifton 1975b: 105–9).

A second traditional account of the division into three parts of an older Ojibwa-Odawa-Potawatomi grouping was given to Henry R. Schoolcraft about 1838 by a man whose name he wrote down as "Ossigunac." Phonetically this is "Assikinak" (Blackbird), the name of a prominent Odawa chief (British appointed) of that time.[5] Since a later author, Andrew J. Blackbird, may have gotten his 1897 version of the tripartite division secondhand from the elder Assikinak, it will bear some examination. These are the words of Assikinak, which follow a description of the separation at Michilimackinac: "The Ottawas went at first to live among the men called the Potawatomies, about the southern shores or head of Lake Michigan; but the latter used bad medicine, and when complained of for their necromancy, they told the Ottawas they might go back towards the north if they did not like them. They had made a fire for themselves." Now this Blackbird throughout his life had been loyal to the interests of Great Britain, and during the War of 1812 he had watched and attempted to delay the loss of Michigan-area Potawatomi support to the British cause.

Blackbird's account may refer to any one of several time periods when the Potawatomi and Odawa separated. It is doubtful that the reference is directly to a time well before 1600 when the original division of Northern Algonquian peoples occurred. It may refer to a period sometime between 1700 and 1720. By then some Potawatomi had moved back from Wisconsin into the St. Joseph River area in Michigan, and Potawatomi-Odawa relationships were very definitely strained at the time. However, it is more likely that the reference to a division was even more recent, to a time post-1743. About that date the three tribes had forged a coalition at Michilimackinac for the purpose of territorial expansion and war against other tribes. However, by 1780 the St. Joseph area Potawatomi had drifted away from that alliance and were going their own way with little regard for the northern Odawa interests. The symbolism of "building a fire for themselves" thus likely refers not to the original split but to a later dissolution of a sometime political coalition.

The value of traditional accounts such as these—when they are in fact traditional and not cribbed—is that they reflect a continuing sense of belonging together that has rather consistently characterized Odawa, Ojibwa, and Potawatomi relationships. These convictions, in part, reflect many similarities in language and culture, which in turn are the residue of a more ancient togetherness. In this sense the oral histories support the sketch of Potawatomi movement away from a northern homeland shared by other societies like themselves.

ARCHEOLOGICAL
AND POST-CONTACT
CULTURAL EVIDENCE

Archeologists are understandably reluctant to identify prehistoric sites with known historic tribes; and as noted above, the well-studied, undisturbed prehistoric sites on the western shore of Michigan are few. Two of these are of special interest, as they have been tentatively identified as involving Potawatomi occupation, the Dumaw Creek and the Moccasin Bluff sites (Quimby 1966; Fitting & Cleland 1969; Bettarel & Smith 1973). The Dumaw Creek site is of special interest because it dates to the period 1605–1625, immediately prior to the arrival of the French. The Moccasin Bluff site, on the other hand, is somewhat earlier.

In both of these instances we find evidence of large, semipermanent summer villages. The Potawatomi living therein practiced a dual economy, involving digging stick and hoe farming, hunting, fishing, and the gathering of wild plant foods. In summer they grew maize, pumpkins, squash, beans, and tobacco, and hunted deer, elk, and beaver nearby. In the Moccasin Bluff site there is evidence of year-round occupancy, with at least part of the population remaining in the main village in the winter months. However, as a general rule much of the population likely scattered to winter hunting sites in the late fall. The deer were hunted by driving and surrounds in late fall, with the heaviest kill occurring then. Sturgeon were probably speared in the spring spawning runs, while other fish were taken with nets, weirs and traps, or spears as they spawned. The Moccasin Bluff site is particularly important since it suggests that the Potawatomi were in transition from less to more dependency on farming (Bettarel & Smith 1973: 134–36).

The Dumaw Creek and Moccasin Bluff peoples made triangular arrow and spear points and blades of stone which had been imported from other places. Similarly, the grit used to temper the pottery identified with the Potawatomi was nonlocal in origin. They lived in dome-shaped wigwams constructed of bent saplings covered with woven mats or sheets of bark. The mats are especially distinctive and are characteristic of the Odawa and Ojibwa as well. When Champlain first saw them among the Cheveux Relevés he commented how industrious these people were in plaiting these mats, which he called "their Turkish carpets" (Grant 1907: 304). This is an apt analogy. The Potawatomi—and other tribes—used them both as coverings for the floors of their wigwams and as roofing and siding as well. They could be rolled up and transported to other locations, where only a framework was then needed to provide shelter.

The Potawatomi made their clothing of sewn skins and of simple fabrics constructed by plaiting, not true weaving. Their hair, bodies, clothing, and goods they decorated extensively with paints and ornaments. Native copper they got from the shores of Lake Superior; their shell beads, gorgets, and pendants were made from materials obtained from the Atlantic coast. Tobacco —or powdered red sumac bark—was smoked in carved stone or fired-clay pipes. Some of these were elbow shaped, others molded or carved as animal effigies. All of them used long wooden or reed stems. Burials were elaborate. Those at the Dumaw Creek site were oriented in an east-west direction. Many years later, an early American settler in the area noticed this customary orientation and used his surveying instruments to determine that the body was aligned precisely with the rising sun (Turner 1911). However, we cannot conclude from the Dumaw Creek site that all Potawatomi burials were alike. Later evidence indicates that the Rabbit Clan cremated their dead (JR 51: 33), while the Eagle Clan used trees or scaffolds for disposing of theirs (Skinner 1924/27: 49–50). Generally, the corpse was interred with an array of grave goods, in full finery, with personal weapons or tools, food, and other necessaries for the four-day journey to the spirit world.

By this time the Potawatomi had likely developed a special kind of patrilineal kinship system which anthropologists classify as the Omaha type (Callender 1962). This kind of patrilineal system does not exclude women from consideration in calculating descent and affiliation. Indeed, it emphasizes the vital functions of women in the economy—farming work was largely their responsibility—by aligning each individual secondarily with the descent line of his mother's father. This kind of kinship system was based on corporate clan organizations. Each village proper was at root a clan group, that is, a corporate, patrilineal, exogamous, totemic descent group. The term "totem" here is used in the technical English sense, while the word in fact derives in a corrupted form from a Potawatomi expression, "ototeman," which means "those who are related (to him) as brothers and sisters," i.e., those who are actually or putatively descended from the same (male) parent. The Potawatomi use "totem" both as the name of the clan group and the name of the clan eponym, e.g., Bear or Eagle. The word for village, "otan," derives from the same root used to make "totem." "Otan" literally means "dwelling place of the brother-sister kin group." That is, Potawatomi clans were villages.

Support for these conclusions concerning protohistoric Potawatomi culture is contained in the first useful description of this tribe (JR 51: 26–41). The author of this report was Claude Allouez, a Jesuit missionary newly arrived in the upper lakes. The place was Chequamegon Bay, then a flourishing trade center and assembly point for the Ojibwa bands on the southern shore of Lake Superior. The time was winter, spring, and summer, 1667–1668. By then the Potawatomi had migrated from the protohistoric estate to the western shores of Lake Michigan, being situated from near Manitowoc north to the tip of the Door Peninsula.

Allouez reported that the Potawatomi spoke an Algonquian "dialect much harder to understand than that of the Outaouacs."[6] They then lived along the west shore of Lake Michigan, were warlike, hunted and fished, and had large fields covered with corn. They practiced polygamy, worshiped the Sun, and were very civil and deferential to strangers like the Jesuit father. The Potawatomi, hearing of the arrival of the Jesuits at Chequamegon, had come visiting, "to the number of three hundred men bearing arms." Since the Potawatomi habitually traveled as village groups, and because they promptly put in a corn crop (which was women's work) upon arriving at Chequamegon, this indicates that at minimum some fifteen hundred Potawatomi had made the long journey from eastern Wisconsin to Chequamegon. It is very doubtful that the entire tribe had come to Chequamegon in 1667, for this would have meant abandoning their hard won territory along the Lake Michigan shore. Hence, the Potawatomi population at this point must have been well in excess of fifteen hundred persons.

Allouez's relation allows us some of the first close glimpses at the inner workings of Potawatomi culture and society. He had converted (he believed) a very old man, whom Allouez said was "about a hundred years old, who was regarded by the Savages as a sort of divinity. He was wont to fast twenty days at a time, and had visions of God—that is, according to these people, of the Maker of the Earth." Here Allouez records the special spiritual importance of the very aged, the importance of fasting as a means of seeking supernatural, visionary experiences, and the name of a principal superhuman figure. We should emphasize that the French word "*sauvage*" as used by Allouez did not have the later English connotation of vicious and undisciplined; it meant undomesticated, uncorrupted by the influence of civil society, and—particularly —non-Christian.

Allouez went on to write how surprised he was when, upon the death of this elder, "his relatives, contrary to all the usages of this country, burned his body and reduced it to ashes." Allouez was accustomed to witnessing burials, and he inquired why this variation. The relatives replied that the old man was a member of the Hare (Rabbit) Clan and explained that the rabbit was "an animal which runs over the snow in winter,—and that thus the snow, the Hare, and the old man are of the same village,—that is they are relatives." The elder's niktotem (clan-mates) further explained that the Rabbit Clan prohibited burial of its members in the depths of the earth, for if they did so the Great Hare would prevent the arrival of spring.

The kinsmen went on to explain that this old observance had weakened and that several years earlier, forgetfully, they had buried the old man's brother in the earth when he died. In consequence of this violation of Rabbit Clan custom the winter had been very prolonged, bringing great hardship and starvation, and the Potawatomi had despaired of ever seeing spring. After many councils were held to discuss this near disaster, someone recalled the clan prohibition and the terrible error committed, whereupon the body was exhumed and cremated; warm weather followed. In this account Allouez provides us with the Potawatomi's own identification of the clan with a village, the supernatural identification of the clan village with the totemic animal, and a good look at their style of explaining natural events. This recitation also correlates with the experiences of the Potawatomi in the twenty-six years previous to 1667. For by migrating north out of western Michigan, they had entered a much colder zone, with longer winters and a shorter growing season. During this period of migration it is likely that some of the niceties of traditional ritual observance had been neglected, for the Potawatomi in those years were refugees. Once reassembled in their new Wisconsin territory, they were in process of both reasserting their old culture and adapting to the new habitat.

DIASPORA
AND RESETTLEMENT:
1641–1667

Following Nicolet's 1634 visit to Green Bay, there are only five specific but critical historical references to the Potawatomi until Allouez reported their visit to Chequamegon in 1668. These were years of great changes and trials for the tribe, as they were for all the populations of the upper lakes. A series of events outside the Potawatomi territory in Lower Michigan soon forced them to migrate, while other factors drew them towards a new territory in Wisconsin. Soon after Nicolet's visit, the tribes of the Upper Great Lakes had been drawn into the fringes of the fur trade. This was before many French traders and missionaries had penetrated much past Lake Huron. The trade in the fur country was carried on by Indian middlemen—the Algonquian Odawa and Nipissing, and the Iroquoian Huron. This trade was initially in small goods—steel knives, awls, and axes and cloth; but these were so valued that they brought about rearrangements of tribal territories and the development of new alliances (Hickerson 1960: 81). The trade also brought about devastating wars.

Previous to 1634 the Huron and their Petun allies had been regularly embroiled in mutual back-and-forth raiding with the Five Nations Iroquois of New York—the Seneca, Onondaga, Cayuga, Oneida, and Mohawk. The New York Iroquois were allied with Dutch and English interests on the Atlantic coast, while the Huron—through Champlain's intervention in 1615—had tied themselves firmly to a military and trading relationship with the French. The Neutral—westernmost of the Iroquoian peoples on the Ontario Peninsula— were so called because they maintained relations with both the Huron and the Five Nations. They had need to, for their primary economic interests and the attentions of their war leaders were directed to the west, to the country of the Atsistaehronon, the Fire Nation—the Algonquians of Lower Michigan.

Earlier the intertribal raiding had had slight effect on the populations involved. But in the 1640s these wars took on a new and devastating aspect. The war parties were larger; they stayed out on the war roads longer; and they came to conquer and destroy. In 1644 Father Jerome Lalemont (JR 27: 25–27) from the Huron mission reported a visit from the Neutral, who told him of their raid on the Michigan Algonquians during the previous summer, where they went

> to the number of two thousand, and attacked a village well protected by a palisade, and strongly defended by nine hundred warriors who withstood the assault. Finally, they carried it, after a siege of ten days; they killed many on the spot, and took eight hundred captives,—men, women, and children. After having burned seventy of the best warriors, they put out the eyes and girdled the mouths of all the old men, whom they afterward abandoned to their own guidance, in order that they might thus drag out a miserable life. Such is the scourge that depopulates all these countries; for their wars are but wars of extermination.

Which of the Central Algonquian tribes had been the target of this ruinous assault is unknown, although from the size of the village destroyed it was more likely Sauk or Fox. However, this kind of invasion of Algonquian territory had been going on for several years. Even before 1643, some of the Sauk and the Potawatomi had been driven out of Michigan by Neutral raids.[7]

In 1642 Father Lalemont reported on the knowledge that had been obtained the previous year while visiting the Nipissing near the northern shores of Lake Huron. The occasion had been the annual Feast of the Dead, a great intertribal ritual which was Huron in origin, but which now attracted many of that tribe's trading partners and their allies, as it was a mechanism for creating and solidifying alliances (Hickerson 1960). At the feast were a group of Algonquians from Sault Ste. Marie, whom the French now called Saulteurs (the later Ojibwa). These Ojibwa of the Sault invited the Jesuits to visit them in their own country (JR 23: 225), and Father Lalemont reported that the fathers were eager to do so, particularly because they also learned that "a more remote Nation whom they call Pouteatami had abandoned their own Country and taken refuge with the Inhabitants of the Sault, in order to remove from some other hostile Nation who persecuted them with endless wars." Here—in 1641—the Potawatomi have fled their Michigan estate for the north country in the face of Neutral assaults in their homeland.

Some if not all of the Sauk had similarly left Michigan and soon arrived in northeastern Wisconsin. There they were attacked by the Winnebago, who lost more than five hundred men in the subsequent battle. Soon afterwards, the Winnebago were prey to an unidentified epidemic which further reduced their population. And they then became embroiled in a war with the Illinois tribes who had sent them provisions and other assistance (La Potherie in Blair 1911 I: 293–301). These three disasters reduced the Winnebago tribe to a small fragment of its earlier size, eliminating this tribe as a serious power in Wisconsin (Kellog 1925: 88).

Meanwhile, in the Ontaria Peninsula the Five Nations Iroquois had stepped up their attacks on the Huron and Petun. Their aim was to eliminate these tribes as rivals in the fur trade and to gain control of their lands. They too switched their tactics from hit-and-run raids to organized, sustained assaults on the main Huron villages. While the Mohawk supported by Oneida operated along the Ottawa and St. Lawrence rivers, interdicting the trading flotillas from the upper lakes, the Seneca, Onondaga, and Cayuga carried out the principal invasion of Huron and Petun country. In the three years between 1647 and 1650 the Five Nations Iroquois totally destroyed the Huron and Petun confederacies. The remnants of the Huron fled to join the French on the St. Lawrence, and the surviving Petun joined the Odawa on Manitoulin Island. But there was no safety even in that remote area from Iroquois attacks, so that soon the Odawa and Petun again were forced to migrate west to Lake Michigan and Lake Superior, while the Nipissing fled north to the boreal forests (Heidenreich 1971: 260–76). In the spring of 1650 the Five Nations turned their attack on the Neutral and then the Erie, killing all the men and older women. In consequence of these invasions the Ontario Peninsula, the Lower Peninsula of Michigan, and most of Ohio and Indiana were abandoned by the tribes that had lived there in 1640. These areas remained unpopulated

—Five Nations Iroquois controlled hunting territory—until a peace was made in 1701 (Voegelein 1974a: 65; ICC 1974 III: 175–80).

In consequence of these wars came massive population dislocations. In general, the surviving groups fled westwards into and beyond Wisconsin. Those of the Michigan Algonquians who were skilled in the use of birch-bark canoes and accustomed to long-distance travel in them migrated first to Sault Ste. Marie, which had become a rally point as well as a focus for the remains of the fur trade.[8] The Potawatomi and the Sauk made up most of those to make this northwestward voyage. The other Michigan tribes were pedestrians: their route took them by land south of Lake Michigan to a western prairie refuge. Moving from Sault Ste. Marie, the Potawatomi and some of the Petun and Ottawa soon began congregating near the mouth of Green Bay.

Since the 1660s the islands at the entrance of Green Bay have been known as either the Huron or the Potawatomi islands (see Figure 3). Generally, it has been assumed that the larger of these, Washington Island (35 square miles), was the principal place of occupancy and trade for the Potawatomi, Odawa, and Petun after about 1645. However, in the past several years a combination of archeological and ethnohistorical studies have demonstrated that the smaller Rock Island (1.5 square miles), adjacent to and north of Washington Island, was the actual village and trading location for these tribes. Here on Rock Island, then, is where Radisson and Groseilliers, La Salle, Hennepin, Tonty, and other French travelers met and dealt with the Potawatomi in subsequent years (Mason 1974 & 1975).

The archeological evidence from the Rock Island I site points to a very brief period of Potawatomi occupancy about 1648–1649, followed by a longer period of Petun-Odawa occupation which, according to historical documentation, ran to about 1667 (Perrot 1911 I: 148–49). Thereafter, the Potawatomi were dominant on Rock Island and—as will be seen—on the mainland to the south as well. Apparently, Rock Island was used principally as a village and trading center, as well as for a fishery. It is much too small to support many game animals or even to provide adequate space for corn fields. Apparently, Washington Island to the south was used for the latter purpose, while the Potawatomi hunted on the mainland to the west and south of their village and trading center.

There is a documented report of Potawatomi activities in 1653 in northeast Wisconsin which demonstrates their relative strength in that area. The Five Nations Iroquois had not abandoned their pursuit of the scattered Algonquians, but instead they sent large parties of warriors into Wisconsin after them. The Journal of the Jesuit Fathers reported that on July 29, 1653, news had arrived from the upper lakes at Quebec that all of the Algonquians, together with the remains of the Petun and Neutral, were assembling at Green

Bay to meet the Iroquois invasion (JR 38: 181). The journal lists the number of warriors contributed by each tribe as :

    400 Ondatonateni [the Huron pronunciation of Potawatomi];

    200 Outawek, or cheveux releve;

    100 Awe,atsiwaen'ronnons, and people from the Nation of A'chawi [Win-nebago];

    200 Enskia,e'ronnons [Saulteur-Ojibwa];

    100 Awechisae'ronnons and Achirwachronnon [Missisaugi & French River Algonquians].

Thus the Potawatomi constituted 40 percent of this fighting force, while all the Algonquians together made up 90 percent of the total. How effective the Iroquois had been in interdicting the fur trade to New France and how important this Wisconsin alliance was can be seen in the fact that in this year only two canoes of furs arrived in Montreal. Ten years earlier a hundred Huron canoes had made the journey safely (Smith 1973: 14).

The name the Potawatomi gave to the place where this force was assembled was Mechingan (Mitchigami—Great Lake).[9] It was a large, intertribal, and very strongly fortified village located on the Lake Michigan shoreline, somewhere north of the present Manitowoc, Wisconsin (Perrot 1911 I: 151–54). Here in the summer of 1653 the Potawatomi and their allies met the invading Iroquois tribesmen. Scouting parties had been sent out which located the Iroquois, whereupon all the scattered villagers moved into the safety of the fort. The Iroquois found the fort impregnable; and they were unable to sustain a protracted siege, for they were far distant from their own homeland and lacked adequate supplies. The allies in the fort agreed to a truce with the Iroquois, then attempted trickery by sending the invaders poisoned corn. When the Iroquois discovered this, they divided into two parties and retreated, pursued by the Algonquians. Few of this group of invaders made it safely back to their homes in New York.[10] In consequence of this great defeat Wisconsin thereafter remained secure to invasion from the east, and the Five Nations made a temporary peace with the French and their allies, which allowed the fur trade to the upper lakes to reopen.

In this fashion the Potawatomi took the lead and provided the largest contingent of fighting men for a force which successfully blocked an invasion from the dreaded Nadowe—the Iroquois. The cultural and historical consequences of this Potawatomi tribal victory were considerable. A success of this magnitude intensifies tribal morale and solidarity, and it generates a high order of prestige among other neighboring tribes. Shortly, the Potawatomi were to make it plain to others that they had a very high opinion of themselves and set a lesser value on their neighbors. At this point they began attempting to establish themselves as arbiters for all the tribes in the Green Bay area (La Potherie 1911 I: 302).

The tentative peace with the Iroquois which developed after this successful defense allowed a reopening of trade between the upper lakes and the St. Lawrence. Taking advantage of this opportunity, the Odawa reasserted their position as the key middlemen in the trade between the French and the interior Indians. In 1654 they sent a trade flotilla to New France that arrived safely, bringing great joy to the colony, which had barely survived the depression caused by the rupture in trade (Kellogg 1925: 103). In the fall, when the trading fleet returned westward, it was accompanied by two young Frenchmen sent by the governor to establish alliances with the tribes in the upper lake country. These were the famed Pierre-Esprit Radisson and his brother-in-law, Médart Chouart, Sieur de Groseilliers.[11]

In a second voyage to the upper lakes, Radisson and Groseilliers accompanied their Odawa partners (whom Radisson wrote of in English as "our Wild-Men") to the northern end of Lake Michigan. They arrived at an island where they found the Odawa and Petun well established in trade but in conflict with another tribe just to the south of them who had emerged as rivals (Adams 1961: 89; Scull 1967: 148–149). The Odawa wished the two Frenchmen to do for them what Champlain had done earlier for the Huron—aid them in military action against their trade rivals. But the Frenchmen counseled diplomacy and negotiation and arranged a council between the contending tribes. The year was likely 1658, and the location, the Odawa-Petun trade station on Rock Island, with the Potawatomi on Door Peninsula just to the south.[12]

Radisson and Groseilliers persuaded both parties to come together peaceably to discuss their grievances. The brothers-in-law advised the Odawa that if the Potawatomi did not cooperate, then they would make use of their "thunders" (muskets). But Radisson reported that the efforts at diplomacy were successful (Scull 1967: 148), for—responding to the Frenchmen's advances—the Potawatomi "without more adoe comes and meets us wth the rest & peace was concluded. Feasts were made & dames wth guifts came of each side, wth a great deal of mirth." Forest diplomacy in the mid-seventeenth century apparently had its satisfactions. The exchange of women (who were highly valued commodities) and other "guifts" guaranteed that the negotiations were serious and successful. This device put hostages (and informants) in the other party's camp and linked the two tribes together as affinal kinsmen as well as (supposedly) cooperating allies.

Here we have the Potawatomi well established on Green Bay, in a position to challenge Odawa supremacy for their position as the key middlemen in the fur trade. By this time, then, the Potawatomi were journeying down Green Bay and the Fox River to the headwaters of the Wisconsin, thence to the

Mississippi. In terms of trade the Potawatomi on Green Bay had situated themselves at a very strategic place, at the entrance of the main waterway leading from the Upper Lakes to the Mississippi River valley. There they proceeded to establish themselves as hosts for peaceful visitors, welcoming them to their villages on Rock Island and the Door Peninsula. Profit and ascendancy over neighboring tribes were their chief goals. The instrument to these ends was to be a strong alliance with the French.

3

The Quebec Connection

Their experience in 1658 with Radisson and Grosielliers—who had acted as powerful supporters of the Odawa—was firm testimony of the value of an alliance with the distant French, one which the Potawatomi were not likely soon to forget. Yet the Odawa and their allies—the remnants of the Huron and the Petun—maintained their dominant position as middlemen in the trade into the upper lakes for some years. In this the Odawa followed prehistoric practice—the right of a tribe to control a trade route and a trading relationship they had pioneered. Seen from the perspective of Quebec, the French moving towards the interior had constantly met with new tribes, each with vested interests in a territory straddling the route, wanting a say in the management of and a share of the profits in the exchange. Prehistorically, Indian trading relationships between the Great Lakes and the Atlantic coast had constituted a long chain, each tribe being one link, each controlling one or more points on the route, each traveling a relatively short distance to a trading point controlled by another tribe, there to engage in ritualized barter and exchange before returning to base. In this respect the Odawa were truly remarkable: they had opened a route that sliced through the territories of several other tribes between Chequamegon Bay on Lake Superior and the St. Lawrence.

It was a dangerous water route, limited by distance, climate, and mode of transportation to one round-trip each year. The trade flotillas had to leave Lake Superior in June or July to return by early September (Hickerson 1960: 96). It was a path easily and frequently cut at numerous points by Iroquois ambushes, lying in wait to gather in the furs harvested by other tribes. The Iroquois in turn were supplied and encouraged mainly by the Dutch in the New Netherlands, their major trading partners. The Odawa were few in number to supply the growing wants of the people of the upper lakes across this long route. The more distant tribesmen at the western end of Lake Superior and on Lake Michigan got only the leavings—a few trinkets and small wares, worn-out knives, dulled axes, and broken brass kettles. It was, however, more than enough to whet appetites and drive up expectations for the new tools, weapons, and goods. The Potawatomi and other tribes looked with envy on the wealth, power, and prestige of the Odawa.

In the east New France had a large name but a small population. There were in fact as many Potawatomi in northeast Wisconsin as there were Frenchmen on the banks of the St. Lawrence in 1658. New France was a struggling infant of a colony, tiny, weak, hardly capable of defending and unable even to feed itself, nearly strangled by strictures in the flow of furs on which the economic wealth of the settlements depended.

The loose end to this tangle lay in the distant court of the French king. Once it was pulled, the Potawatomi far to the west were shortly presented with an opportunity they quickly seized on. In 1661 Cardinal Mazarin died, allowing Louis XIV to assume personal control of the French government. One of the king's first acts was to appoint Jean Baptise Colbert as minister of the colonies. Colbert in turn took personal charge of the development of New France, where agriculture would now be stressed as well as commerce. In 1663 he persuaded Louis XIV to make New France a royal province, to be governed by an appointed council whose agent would be a governor, but with an intendant to act as the king's own representative, carrying out his policies. In 1663 a detachment of agricultural colonists and a contingent of regular troops were sent to New France (Kellogg 1925: 118–23; Billington 1960: 106–7). Then in 1664 the New Netherlands colony was ceded to Charles II of England, an ally and dependent of Louis XIV, opening the possibility of an end to the Iroquois wars. The next year the marquis de Tracy was appointed governor and Jean Talon intendant of New France, starting a decade of unparalleled colonial development and expansion.

By 1665 the population of New France had grown to three thousand civilians and thirteen hundred officers and men of the Carignan regiment. In August of that year detachments of this regiment—moving up the St. Lawrence—met the Odawa trading flotilla. The Odawa were flushed with success: they were bringing in many packs of prime furs from Lake Superior, and they had driven off two Iroquois attacks along the way. On their return voyage the Odawa carried with them more French traders and Claude Allouez, who journeyed west to open a mission at Chequamegon. But Allouez was also carrying a message from the intendant, Talon. He was to announce to all the tribes that the French king had sent his personal troops to destroy the Iroquois. In 1666 Talon dispatched a thousand men of the Carignan regiment and colonial auxiliaries into the Iroquois country. The blows they struck were so hard that the next year the Iroquois arrived in Quebec to sue for peace. It was news of these developments that in 1667 had brought the Potawatomi from Green Bay to Chequamegon, along with thousands from other tribes.

At Chequamegon in 1667 the Potawatomi met Allouez, as described in chapter two. They also met another young Frenchman who arrived that year, a man they would name Mtamins, Little Corn. This was Nicholas Perrot, formerly employed by the Jesuit fathers in Quebec, soon to become the most influential of all Frenchmen among the tribes of the Upper Great Lakes. Perrot had gone west to trade in company with a partner, Toussaint Baudry. He stayed to act as principal agent for the governor of New France in the Upper Great Lakes. In the year of Perrot's arrival at Chequamegon the interests of New France began to shift from Lake Superior to Lake Michigan. On visiting with the Potawatomi at Chequamegon, Perrot undoubtedly showed an interest in the Green Bay area. The Potawatomi offered him their warmest invitations, imploring him to come and stay with them in their own villages so that they might have the advantages of the trade heretofore enjoyed by the Odawa. Perrot agreed, arriving at Green Bay in the early summer of 1668 (La Potherie, in Blair 1911 I: 308).

In the 1650s the Potawatomi had not selected the Green Bay area because they anticipated its later value to New France. But from the point of view of a tribe interested in increasing its own wealth and power, no more strategic location could have been found. The region had ample, fertile soils for Potawatomi cornfields; the waters of the bay and lake were rich in fish; the area was a major fly-way for migratory waterfowl; and the surrounding forests and openings had an adequate supply of game animals (Wilson 1956; JR 55: 184–95). It had been prehistorically a natural trading center for exchange relationships with distant tribes. With the depopulation of the Winnebago and Menomini, these lands were open to new settlement. This was enough to attract the harried Potawatomi, refugees from Iroquois incursions, even without the French presence in the upper lakes.

In addition to their strategic location and possession of a rich subsistence base, the Potawatomi possessed several other notable advantages in 1667. They were yet the numerically dominant tribe in northeast Wisconsin, while the only other powerful society there was the Sauk, who were also Central Algonquian refugees from Michigan and close allies of the Potawatomi. But the Potawatomi were also highly skilled in handling birch-bark canoes, which gave them a technological advantage even over the Sauk, who were less disposed to long-distance, open-water travel, more so over the soon-to-arrive Fox, Mascouten, Kickapoo, Miami, and Illinois, all of whom lacked birch-bark canoes and were known as "excellent pedestrians" (La Potherie, in Blair 1911 I: 322).[1] The Potawatomi also had an ambition, clearly stated to Perrot at Chequamegon: they desired to rival the Odawa as middlemen in the fur trade.

Perrot—followed shortly by Allouez—had hardly arrived at Green Bay when the area achieved even greater worth to both the French and the Potawatomi. By 1670 the intendant of New France conceived a larger design—to penetrate the far interior and to discover another great waterway, one vaguely described thirdhand by traders, one which might finally prove to be the illusive short route to the Orient. As the French soon discovered, there were just three ways to the Mississippi via the Great Lakes. In 1668 the Potawatomi were already astride two of these. Indeed, their trading station at Rock Island was at the natural fork in canoe traffic coming down from Lake Huron. One track from Rock Island led down Green Bay to the Fox River, then to the Wisconsin and Mississippi. The other went down the west shore of Lake Michigan to the Chicago River, then to the Illinois and the Mississippi. There was a third major route on the eastern shore of Lake Michigan, via the St. Joseph and Kankakee rivers to the Illinois. The Potawatomi, under French auspices, reoccupied that third strategic place by 1695 (Kinietz 1940: 309; Charlevoix 1870: 141–42).

French influence in the Green Bay area began with the arrival of Perrot in 1668. Formal French sovereignty in the upper lakes dates to 1671, when François Daumont de St. Lusson—acting under Jean Talon's orders—conducted a grand annexation ceremony at Sault Ste. Marie. Fifteen tribes—including the Potawatomi—sent delegations who fixed their totem marks to the annexation document. In that year a firm alliance was solemnized linking the Potawatomi with the French in Quebec. At that moment the Potawatomi were still mainly confined to the Door Peninsula in Wisconsin, but they had already begun a process of expanding their tribal estate. The French alliance came to a nominal end in 1760, when the British sent Major Robert Rogers and George Croghan to take possession of the French posts at Detroit, St. Joseph, Green Bay, and Michilimackinac. It came to a formal ending three years after with the treaty terminating the French and Indian Wars. In that year, 1763, the Potawatomi still occupied the Green Bay area, but they had their villages also in the St. Joseph River valley, in northern Indiana, near Detroit, Chicago, and Milwaukee, and their winter hunting grounds were even farther into Illinois and Indiana. But the treaty between France and Britain did not, as we shall note, end the connection between the Potawatomi and the French. This relationship was to continue strong for many years thereafter.

POTAWATOMI IDEOLOGY I

There is a tale recorded by Alanson Skinner in 1912, but which a few elderly Potawatomi still related with delight in the 1960s (Skinner 1924–27: 400–2; Clifton 1962–65). The story is based upon a very old folk tale to which are added more recent ingredients. Some of these additions reflect—in a distinctive Potawatomi literary style—certain of their memories of the French alliance and what it meant to them. Other features of the tale have a different and no less valuable interest. These exhibit aspects of Potawatomi ideology, particularly certain fundamental postulates or assumptions concerning human nature. To underscore the latter will help us appreciate how the Potawatomi perceived and responded to such figures as Nichols Perrot and Claude Allouez in the late 1660s.

The hero of the tale is Tisha, an odd name which contemporary Potawatomi informants claimed they did not understand.[2] Tisha is said to be the youngest of four pitifully poor brothers, who lacked even a scrap of hide to cover their nakedness, and who had not even fish to eat. They had to subsist on a few berries and the inner bark of certain bushes.

One night in a dream-vision a stranger came and told Tisha that he would try to help, but his instructions would have to be followed exactly, else his power would not work. The stranger then said he would have to leave but would return in four days and would meet Tisha if he promised to come alone.

Four days later Tisha went to the appointed spot and found the stranger dressed in the finest and most beautiful clothing the young neshnabē had ever seen. The stranger then said if Tisha paced off the length he desired, he would then build him a boat that size, one which would travel over land. Tisha took more than two dozen long strides, and then suddenly there appeared in front of them a huge sailing ship. They boarded it and started traveling over the earth.

As Tisha sailed along over the earth he met with four or five (the several versions differ) unique kinds of individuals.[3] One was a champion hearer, the second a champion seer, the third a champion eater, the fourth a champion runner, and the last a masterfully powerful wind-maker. These were named, respectively, Listens Far, Sharp Shooter, Dirt Eater, Rabbit Catcher, and Great Farter. All of them joined Tisha and became his companions. Their trials soon began.

As they traveled along they came across a strange town. There they were received by a messenger who said he would tell his okama (leader) of their arrival. The messenger told the head man in the village that Tisha was much too poor and ragged to be anybody much, but the young neshnabē was invited in anyhow. The okama wanted to gamble with him for his life. He wagered Tisha that he had a follower who could out-eat anyone in Tisha's small band, but Dirt Eater easily defeated his adversary. So also did Dirt Eater's fellows overwhelm the champions from the enemy camp in each of the trials that followed. Thus did Tisha and his allies overcome all, even when the okama used a beautiful woman to try to bequile them. Thus Tisha won many valuable prizes.

Afterwards Tisha and his companions inspected the enemy camp and found its inhabitants were man-eaters. There were piles of bones all over the place, the remains of others who had come, gambled their lives, and lost. Boat Maker suggested a new game. When Tisha gave the order, Rabbit Catcher threw a big iron ball way up in the air, and Great Farter bent over and blasted it even higher. Then Tisha hollered, "All you people better jump out of there. The ball's going to fall on you." All of a sudden then, the bones popped together, and all those people were alive again. Tisha and his companions, aided by Boat Maker, then destroyed that evil village.

The narrator concludes his story with a commentary: that village was Wiske's village. Wiske was Matjimanito, the Evil Spirit himself. Ever after that, Tisha was a wealthy and a well-respected man. He was a great sailor, traveling around the earth on his ship with his guardian, Boat Maker: Boat Maker was a Frenchman.

Indeed he was. We can even give a name to one of the French prototypes for Boat Maker; it was Robert Cavelier, Seiur de La Salle. The name of his great ship was the *Griffon,* the first sailing vessel on the Great Lakes, constructed by La Salle at Niagara on Lake Ontario in 1679 and sailed from there to the Potawatomi trade station on Rock Island, after which it foundered with all hands at some unknown place in the upper lakes (Mason 1974: 150–51).

As indicated, this is an old tale modified in recent centuries by adjustments and additions. In fact, in this version of the story the ancient culture hero of the Potawatomi, Wiske, who likely first appeared in the guise of Boat Maker, is here made into the devil. This reflects Potawatomi acceptance of the teachings of Tecumsah and his brother Tenskwatawa, the Shawnee prophet, both of whom set out to extirpate Wiske from the Potawatomi pantheon and to convince them he was an evil figure. It used to be Wiske, in various guises, who came to the poor, destitute Potawatomi and gave them help and new things. In this version of the tale Boat Maker is an encapsulation of all Frenchmen who provided valuable aid and property. This is more than just a distorted memory of a particular historical event; it is a distinctive Potawatomi literary expression of a long series of warmly remembered experiences.

The French origin of Tisha's name (from *tissu*—fabric or textile) is less important than the literary fashion in which it is used to denote the hero of this tale as the archetypical neshnabē. The hero figures in Potawatomi myths and tales are just that. As such, they are generally made to be poverty stricken and relatively helpless. This is the nature of a neshnabē; he is dependent on external aid and support. In this story Tisha is just a little worse off than most —as the youngest of four brothers he is at the bottom of the family heap. Neshnabē gets relief—the necessaries to obtain recognition, conquer enemies, gain wealth—from mysterious contacts with strange, generally supernatural figures. Such contacts are made through deliberate vision-seeking behavior, during normal sleep, but occasionally in a day-dream as well. The postulate is clear: neshnabē is relatively helpless to correct his impoverished condition without the intervention of powerful benefactors and skilled allies. It is a Potawatomi-style success story.

The business of the pile of bones coming to life is literally contrivance based upon an ancient belief, namely, that the essential spirit of people and animals is lodged within the skeleton. Here it is used to stress the value of what the Frenchmen brought: new life for old bones. But it also expresses another constant theme in Potawatomi culture, one which is found throughout their oral literature. Once hero figures like Tisha achieve power, they are expected to use it to benefit others; the wealth they obtain in this fashion must be shared around. Associated with this is yet another even more pervasive assumption that underlies much of Potawatomi ideology—there is a fundamental good and evil division built into the nature of man and the universe. Boat Maker and Matjimanito are two sides of the human condition. Evil can be controlled by the neshnabē of good will who secures external power, but not always, and not inevitably. Men who secure much power, in particular, have to be watched. Finally, living is a gamble where the stakes are high; but it helps to play with a little extra on your side.

PERROT AND ALLOUEZ:
1688–1671[4]

By inviting Nicholas Perrot and later Claude Allouez to their Green Bay villages the Potawatomi sought just such an edge over their rivals. Both were clearly powerful figures, how powerful and in just what ways the Potawatomi were not too certain. The former represented new technological riches and economic potential; the latter claimed to have access to a different kind of resources, supernatural ones. The Potawatomi could have interpreted the meaning of both men in just one fashion, by using the terms and assumptions of their own ideology. At first, many thought these two Frenchmen likely were some kind of Manito (Spirit-Power).

Claude Allouez's principal business in the upper lakes was to convert many to Catholicism; however, he practiced a number of sidelines, from occasional diplomacy to minor surgery. While at Chequamegon his conversions were few, just five adults, one of whom was the elder of the Rabbit Clan whose death and cremation was discussed earlier. Before his death the elder asked to be baptized. During a visit to his family, Allouez inquired about the status of the old man's new faith. The elder replied, "Know, my brother, that I am continually throwing tobacco into the fire, and saying, 'Thou maker of

Heaven and Earth, I would honor three.'" The Jesuit was mildly disturbed, and instructed him that it was unnecessary to honor his God in quite that way. Allouez commented also that the old man was particularly given to fervent prayer, saying "My Father who art in Heaven, my Father hallowed by your name" (JR 51: 31).

The Rabbit Clan elder was here in the process of assimilating this new spirit into a distinctively Potawatomi frame of thought and worship. The Christian God was identified with a major Potawatomi Manito, the Maker of the Earth, and he worshiped him by casting tobacco on the fire, as one properly did for the Manitowak. But the old man also thought of this new spirit as a very personal guardian of himself alone—as "My Father." Thus new cultural materials were identified with old, with little change in form or meaning. Allouez did report that after his conversion the elder would not allow a juggler (i.e., a Potawatomi religious practitioner) into his presence to try a cure.[5]

That same winter, Allouez came into competition with the jugglers over the seriously ill body of an important young man who had come down with what Allouez diagnosed as pleurisy. In the jugglers' medical doctrine the cure required extraction by sucking of the foreign body which had poisoned his body, in this case two dog's teeth that some enemy had "shot" into the young man's chest. Allouez, after watching the rites of this sucking doctor as he extracted the dog's teeth, accused him of fakery and explained that, in the best European medical doctrine, the cure for the ailment required an extensive bleeding. He then proceeded (after a cautionary baptism) to draw a bowl of blood from the young man's arm.[6] This he showed the juggler with the admonition that drawing out "corrupt blood" was the proper cure, not the "alleged dog's teeth" (JR 51: 35–39). The young man seemed to improve, whereupon the juggler poured a potion down his throat, and the patient then fell into a deep, lengthy coma. Confounded, the juggler acknowledged that Allouez's medicines were the more powerful, confessing he would have killed the patient. We have here two opposed medical doctrines as well as two associated sets of rival religious beliefs, for Allouez believed the juggler represented the devil. Fortunately, the young man had an unusually strong constitution, as he recovered from his treatment by these two specialists.

Allouez's invitation to the Potawatomi villages came while he was at Sault Ste. Marie in 1669. He reported that the Potawatomi wanted to take him there, but not because they wanted instruction in the Catholic faith. They had no interest in this. Instead, they wanted him to "curb some young Frenchmen, who, being among them for the purpose of trading, were threatening and maltreating them" (JR 54: 197). Allouez left the Sault by canoe on the third of November in the face of a winter storm on Lake Huron. As they passed the Island of Michilimackinac, the Potawatomi told him of some of their gods,

"Michabous" (the Great Hare), or perhaps it was "Ouisaketchak" (the Maker of the Earth)—Allouez's account is a little confused. These are, in later Potawatomi phrasing, Chipiyapos and his elder brother Wiske. The Potawatomi told Allouez that they believed Lake Superior was a pond made by Beaver. One day, long ago, Wiske had been chasing Beaver, who fled before such a mighty enemy. He went first to Lake Nipigon and from there by the rivers to Hudson Bay, with the intention of crossing over to France. But Beaver did not like the salty water. He turned back and spread throughout the rivers and lakes of this country. The Potawatomi narrator concluded this tale with a small moral coda, "And that is the reason why there are no beavers in France, and the French come to get them here" (JR 54: 201–3). This early in their contacts with the French, the Potawatomi had already constructed an explanation of what they were doing in the New World, and had imbedded it in their folklore.

Nicholas Perrot had been operating in the Green Bay area for eighteen months when Allouez first arrived there. His invitation from the Potawatomi expresses how they perceived him: Perrot was to be an instrument serving the tribal aim of establishing themselves in a position like that of the Odawa. The Potawatomi intended to replace the Odawa as middlemen in the fur trade, using their position at Green Bay to profit from the role of brokers between the French and the tribes to the south and west of them. However, Perrot was himself an agent of the governor of New France. He had been directed to Green Bay with the specific mission of breaking the monopoly of the Indian middlemen (Innis 1962: 54–55; Kellogg 1925: 123–25). Perrot and his partner, Baudry, were commissioned to open direct contact with the interior tribes, to encourage them to deal firsthand with French traders at Green Bay, and to transport their furs straight to the St. Lawrence. There was from the start a conflict of policy between the Potawatomi and New France. Much of Perrot's work in the first year thus consisted of efforts to alter the nature of Potawatomi participation in the trade.

When Perrot arrived in Green Bay he found that a large group of Potawatomi had already departed for Montreal with their furs, guided by the Odawa (La Potherie 1911: 309). These were men from the Potawatomi villages who had not gone to Chequamegon the previous year. Perrot's reception by the Potawatomi at Green Bay that early summer of 1668 reveals how this tribe perceived him. Some—never having known a Frenchman—were surprised to see that he was human. They had heard the French were all covered with hair. A major reception was staged in his honor. He was told that the Potawatomi believed "the sky and the spirits had made them [a present] in permitting one of the celestial beings to enter their land." A calumet ceremony —a new ritual for the Potawatomi that year—was performed in his honor. The smoke from the calumet was blown, like incense, over Perrot's body and on his iron tools and weapons. He was told, "Thou art one of the chief spirits, since thou usest iron; it is for thee to rule and protect all men" (La Potherie 1911: 309).

All this was the ritual trappings of Potawatomi diplomacy. Perrot set to work, explaining his position, role, and intentions to the Potawatomi, and developing his own influence. He began visiting the surrounding tribes, opening relations with them, trying to settle intertribal feuds which would disturb the tranquil atmosphere needed for successful trade, encouraging them to benefit from a direct trading relationship with the French.

Perrot's guide in his travels was another juggler, but of a different variety from the medical practitioner Allouez had confronted earlier. The Potawatomi had grown concerned over the fate of the young men who had gone to Montreal, having no understanding of the distance or time required to make the round trip, fearing that the French had mistreated them or that they had been intercepted by the Iroquois (La Potherie 313–14). The juggler, actually the kind of specialist the Potawatomi called chaskyd, a diviner, proceeded in traditional fashion to allay their anxieties, performing his rites and predicting that the trading party was three-days' journey distant, safely on their way home. Perrot called him a liar, and in turn calculated time of departure, rate of travel per day, distance, and estimated time spent in Montreal—forecasting that the party would not return for some two weeks. Perrot's prediction was nearly correct, and his prestige was enhanced thereby.[7]

However, Perrot's renown did not automatically erase the Potawatomi resolve to establish themselves as trading brokers for the distant tribes. The success of their first Montreal trip encouraged them, and they quickly dispatched messengers to notify the Miami, Illinois, Fox, Mascouten, and Kickapoo to the south that they were ready to do business, with an ample stock of trade goods brought back from New France. These tribes, by the standards of those already in the trade, were impoverished. In the fall of 1668 they sent envoys to the Potawatomi, asking them to visit, bringing the Frenchmen with them.

The Potawatomi concealed this invitation from Perrot and his associates, made the visit, and returned laden with gifts of buffalo meat. Some of the newly arrived Algonquians accompanied the Potawatomi back to Green Bay. When they saw the French there they rebuked Perrot for not having accepted their invitation—by Algonquian standards, a gross incivility. As Perrot made plans to visit the tribes south of Green Bay, the Potawatomi intervened, attempting to block the contact. They told the Frenchmen that "there were no beavers among those people—who, moreover, were very boorish—and even that they were in great danger of being plundered." The Frenchmen departed anyway, and were warmly received by the Miami and other tribes. At this point, the Potawatomi sent a slave (i.e., a captive who had not been killed or adopted) to the Miami to spread rumors about the French. The French countered by putting this agent "into a condition where he could say no more outrageous things," much to the pleasure of the Miami (La Potherie 322–34).

The Potawatomi effort at diplomatic maneuver had failed, and when reproached by Perrot they had little choice but to make an accommodation. Whatever else, they had to stay on friendly terms with the French, for they were now dependent on imported goods, and were locked into a relationship they neither desired to lose nor cared to abandon. Thereby, the Potawatomi made their peace with Perrot, sending him gifts of corn so that he might "eat and swallow the suspicion that he felt toward them" and beaver furs to act as an "emetic for the ill-will and vengeance which he might retain in his heart" (La Potherie 333).

Soon Perrot was involved in discussions with the Potawatomi concerning their proper role in the fur trade and as allies of New France. This required a reversal of settled Potawatomi tribal policy, necessitating lengthy councils, achievement of a consensus of the nature of a desirable relationship, and a ritualized demonstration that this position was acceptable to all. Once this policy was approved, the Potawatomi settled into a long and mutually beneficial alliance. We will see that this new tribal policy did not mean subservience to French mandates; although they greeted Perrot, the Potawatomi did not literally intend that they would accept his, or anyone's, rule. Nor did the agreement mean the Potawatomi would accept a position of parity with other neighboring tribes—the Potawatomi set too high a value on themselves to allow this. It did mean a willingness to arbitrate and compromise with the French, but only in an atmosphere of reciprocity and mutual need.

This critical three-year period, 1669–1671, is well documented in the commentaries of Allouez, Perrot, and—to a lesser extent—those of several other Frenchmen involved with the Potawatomi in these years. After agreement on a new tribal policy was achieved and ritually certified, the Potawatomi in 1669 dispatched another trading fleet to the St. Lawrence. This one was accompanied by Perrot. While in Montreal that year the Potawatomi got into some difficulties with the French which reveal important features of their social organization. At Green Bay, too, strained relationships were evident between the Potawatomi and the traders, which also indicate how the Potawatomi were adapting to the new alliance. An intratribal rivalry between Potawatomi clans was developing; and the new alliance affected relationships with other tribes as well. Finally, the Potawatomi began the process of expanding their tribal estate, and in 1671 they journeyed to Sault Ste. Marie to participate in the grand annexation ceremony.

The sources for this period specify some four Potawatomi summer villages on the shores and near the head of Green Bay proper. Later materials indicate that in the same period there were probably at least four more located on the Lake Michigan shoreline, from the large old composite village, Mitchigami, established to thwart the 1653 Iroquois invasion, north to the trading station on Rock Island (see Figure 6). Mitchigami no longer served as a fortress, nor could its population have been very large in this period. It is clear that some of these Potawatomi villages on Green Bay were jointly occupied by members of other tribes, particularly the Sauk, but including a few Winnebago and Menomini.

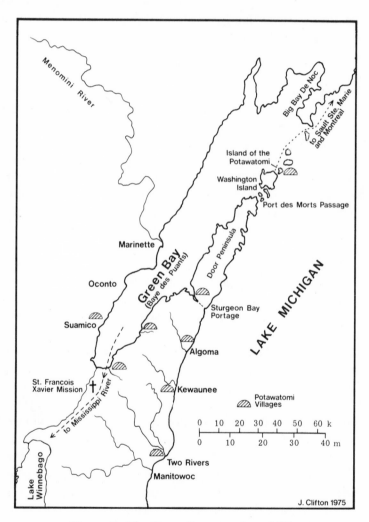

Figure 6. The Green Bay area about 1680.

In 1670 Claude Dablon—the Jesuit superior of the western missions—journeyed to Green Bay to visit Allouez and to inspect the missions there. In describing the tribes that lived around the bay, Dablon confirms our earlier conclusions about the origins of the Potawatomi. After commenting that the native Winnebago had been nearly exterminated by wars with the Illinois, he added that the Potawatomi and Sauk also lived there, "but as foreigners, driven by their fear of the Iroquois from their own Territories, which lie between the Lake of the Hurons and that of the Illinois [Lake Michigan]" (JR 55: 182).

LEADERSHIP
AND GOVERNANCE I

The standard position on Potawatomi leadership is that they were governed by hereditary chiefs capable of issuing authoritative edicts to their tribesmen. If there is little evidence that there were such chiefs in the later years of Potawatomi history or, for example, if supposed chiefs complained that their followers no longer accepted their dictates, then this is explained as one consequence of acculturative contact with Euro-Americans. By intervening in tribal affairs, it is argued, the authority of traditional chiefs was undermined and destroyed by outsiders (Baerreis 1973; Conway 1972). If this were the case, then Allouez, Dablon, Perrot, and other Frenchmen who were in intimate contact with the Potawatomi in the first years of the French alliance should have left some evidence of the presence of chiefs, together with descriptions of their powers and perogatives. They did not do so. Instead they described a quite different pattern of tribal governance, one that neither responded to nor was dependent upon the dictates of the powerful chiefs. We will see that within a few years the Potawatomi did acquire chiefs; but this was a newly emergent role, one that developed out of the relationships between the Potawatomi and the French, a process of social change that came in consequence of the changing adaptation of the tribe.

Three separate kinds of questions have to be asked and answered to avoid confusion in attempting to understand how the Potawatomi governed themselves. The first of these deals with the Potawatomi's own understanding of the nature and limits of leadership and the forms of governance they found agreeable. The second concerns how the French saw and described these matters, while the third involves a comparative, scientific effort to conceptualize, to explain, and to achieve general understanding of the patterns of leadership and governance in societies like the Potawatomi's.

There is no direct access to observation of Potawatomi leaders in action in 1669. Neither historians nor anthropologists possess the time machines to put them on the scene where they might ask the right questions. We are dependent upon the contemporary witnesses, Perrot and Allouez, and the testimony they left. In that instance it is required that we try to see through their prejudices and stereotypes in an effort to visualize what they might have described had they asked our questions for us. We can add a check on such interpretations, one derived from more recent knowledge of other aspects of Potawatomi culture. For example, the behavior of leaders in folk tales, myths, and rituals constitutes a kind of model for proper leadership behavior as practiced in past times. And we can also test our conclusion by asking the question "If the Potawatomi did not have chiefs in 1668, where did they come from later?" Two sources have already been suggested in chapter one—they came from other tribes, or were appointed by influential Frenchmen.[8]

Allouez, Perrot, Dablon, and others in the first years of contact very rarely used the French word "*chef*" in describing Potawatomi leadership roles. When they did, translators automatically converted it to "chief," which is unfortunate since this English word does not necessarily have the appropriate connotations. Generally, when the Frenchmen did use "*chef*," it was in the plural. That is, they mentioned the doings of chiefs or, better, leaders. However, the *chefs* far more frequently were known as elder or elders, council or general council, juggler (both the medical and prophetic varieties), principal man, important man or men, captain, hosts, master of the feast, heralds, singers, waiters, head (of a clan or a clan segment), and speakers. Again when "*chef*" was used, it was in the plural, and the kind of group led was always specified (Clifton 1975a: 37). *Chefs*, as described by Allouez and Perrot, were only leaders of (1) trading fleets, (2) war parties, and (3) villages, clans, or clan segments. There was no hint of a *chef* of the tribe in this period. Lest it be supposed that Perrot, Allouez, or Dablon could not recognize a proper chief when they saw one, we may consult their observations upon first visiting the Miami. There—much to their apparent relief—they spoke of the great chief of the Miami, who was like a prince in his palace, surrounded by retainers and a bodyguard—all showing proper respect and deference to the exalted presence of their chief, who was like a king in his nation (JR 55: 215–17; Perrot 1911: 222–23; La Potherie 330–31).

Unfortunately, neither Perrot nor Allouez nor any other early French observer recorded the Potawatomi's own name for any of the roles they observed and described. But they do describe in some detail what the speakers or the elders did, how they behaved, what they said, and how they conducted themselves with respect to others. That is, they gave these leadership roles descriptive names in French but not in Potawatomi; and they proceeded to describe the roles as they were acted out. These descriptions enable us to co-ordinate knowledge of Potawatomi social organization obtained many years later with these early portraits of the Potawatomi in process of making group decisions, settling conflicts, generating new tribal policies, and contending with other tribes. Sorting out obvious ambiguities and duplicate French names for single roles as identified by the Potawatomi, there is remarkable correspondence. The Potawatomi's own names for some of these roles witnessed by Perrot and Allouez are listed in Table 1.

The one word most used by the Potawatomi to denote leadership roles is "okama."[9] This is an animate, intransitive noun stem. As such, by various grammatical devices, it can be transformed and used in a variety of different kinds of statements. It is sometimes used alone, in which case the exact reference (okama of what?) must be inferred from context. But it is more often combined with various prefixes and suffixes to designate which specific kind of okama is intended, for the Potawatomi's okamek came in various shapes, sexes, and sizes. Consulting Table 1, we see for example that the warriors had their okamawokitchita, the youth their shkenwēyowokama, and the women their wokamakwē. Moreover, rabbits (in a legend) might also have waposowokama; supernatural figures, theirs; and so on. "Okama" is thus a flexible word, much used to name a variety of different leadership roles. It does not simply mean "chief of the tribe"; there is no such word that does. If the Potawatomi want to conceptualize and speak of such a personage, even if no real tribal chief is actually present, they might say "neshnabēwokama," which is only "leader of all the people." Moreover, the table also lists several other

TABLE 1: Traditional Leadership Roles

Potawatomi Word	Translation
neshnabēwokama	leader of (all) the people
(w)okama	leader (of a village, clan, extended family, etc.)
kiktowenene	one who impersonates (i.e., speaker)
okamawokitchita	leader of the warriors
pu'akneyonene (or skepu'akeneyonene)	pipeman (pipe-lighter man)
skabewis	one who runs before (i.e., crier/herald)
wigwameyonene	houseman (i.e., janitor)
shkenwēyowokama	leader of the youth
okamakwē	leader of the women
patopit	stand-in (i.e., alternate or substitute for each of the above)

SOURCE: Clifton 1975a: 43–44.

kinds of leadership roles which have different names not including this noun stem. Kiktowenene (literally, man who impersonates, but generally translated as speaker) is one such. Shkapewis (the herald who also serves as head waiter) is another.

There are numerous other ways, not listed here, in which the Potawatomi spoke about leadership. Like many of the birch-bark canoe–using Algonquians, the Potawatomi often used names drawn from that activity to speak figuratively of a leader—bow man or steersman. And like all peoples, the Potawatomi did not have names for everything. There were men—and women—who from their own ambitions and performance had won positions of personal prominence that were not well conceptualized or named as formal roles. To anticipate later discussion, we can call these kinds of individuals "big men," remembering that this is a technical, not a Potawatomi classification. Finally, we may conclude that to translate "okama" as "chief" would do something of an injustice to both Potawatomi and English semantics. Leader is a less binding and more suggestive gloss for this Potawatomi noun.[10]

With these observations in mind we can fit them into the kinds of descriptions of Potawatomi activities left by Perrot, Allouez, and others. What they were watching were a number of Potawatomi individuals acting out a number of well-formalized traditional roles. Some of these descriptions are easily identified with Potawatomi ideas about and names for these roles. Others less so. For example, clearly the Frenchmen saw elders involved in positions of responsible decision-making. In Potawatomi society age had (and has) its perogatives. Some of these elders were likely okamek, or they acted out other formal roles. Those elders who held positions as okamek were leaders of a clan, a clan segment (i.e., a lineage), or a village composing two or more clan segments. But they met and deliberated jointly.

At least one of the elders, at one time or another, might take the role the French and English called "speaker." The Potawatomi phrasing for this— "man who impersonates"—is better, because it specifically indicates what they had in mind. The kiktowenene was a mature man selected on the basis of two qualities. One of these consisted of a very high order of skill in public oratory, which the French quite clearly appreciated. But the second was equally important to the Potawatomi. The man who was kiktowenene had also to be unusually capable in listening to the joint deliberations of everyone, and skilled enough to state in public a position which represented the consensus of all, inoffensive to the sentiments of anyone. That is, he impersonated others by stating their views for them. The kiktowenene was always very prominent at tribal and intertribal councils, and often enough the French, English, or Americans confused him with a chief. But he was no chief—he was a master spokesman. The pu'akneyonene also filled a role easily confused with that of a chief, because the man in this position was highly visible as he passed around the elaborate calumet for all to smoke in ritualized deliberations. On the other hand the person Perrot sometimes called the master of the feast might have been playing just half a role, that of shkapewis. This functionary had dual responsibilities—outside of and preliminary to the council meeting as herald or crier announcing the affair and inviting the guests; and inside, during the deliberations, as the head waiter (for the Potawatomi, this was an honorable, not a servile position). Or the master of the feast might have been an ambitious big man, trying to gain the limelight so as to increase his prestige and influence.

The evidence from both the perspective of the Potawatomi and the French who described their activities seems to square nicely with general, theoretical ideas concerning the nature of leadership and governance in tribal societies like the Potawatomi. What we are dealing with here is a variety of interlocked leadership roles with none having much ascribed, legitimate power. Leadership was largely expressive of kinship ties: some key okamek drew their support from and were responsive to the needs of their clans. Governance consisted of all varieties of leaders coming together in open council and there deliberating on their opinions and wishes until some consensus position was achieved. They were not isolated from their followers. Indeed, there were no followers. Leaders did not have the power to command, although they might suggest, encourage, or point out possible directions or solutions.

The Potawatomi had no chiefs issuing authoritative edicts to obedient Indians. To assume they did would give a much too simplified portrait of Potawatomi social life in the early years. But waiting in the wings were some ambitious men who saw the possibilities for themselves in the new association with the French, men who were willing to manipulate the traditional tribal system and this opportunity to personal or group advantage. These were the potential big men, people who might achieve great personal influence through their skill at managing a rapidly changing situation. Such individuals also in time would be identified by the French, English, and Americans as chiefs, but they were not born to that status. They were participating in the creation of a new role, that of middleman, an intercultural broker helping to link the interests of two very different societies (Paine 1971: 4–7).

Some examples of Perrot and Allouez's reports on the processes of leading and governing will illustrate how Potawatomi society worked. In a simple example, La Potherie reports that the Potawatomi who first brought Perrot to Green Bay and introduced him was thereafter "treated as a Captain" (1911: 310). Here we have an instance of an ambitious Potawatomi man achieving recognition, prestige, and influence by doing something worthwhile. This is probably the same individual identified later as chief of the feast, for there he is involved in the same activity—promoting an alliance with Perrot and New France. This is an emergent big man.

In the spring of 1669 at Green Bay there was a dispute between two French traders and "an old man who was one of the leaders among the Pouteouatemis." The old man was a leader of the Black Carp Clan segment (i.e., lineage).[11] The Frenchmen had been dunning him for payment for goods advanced the previous fall. Hence the basis for the dispute is clear. This was the Potawatomi's first experience with credit. The French traders habitually advanced supplies in the fall, anticipating repayment in the early spring from the winter's harvest of furs. The Potawatomi had yet to learn this. The Black Carp leader resisted, there was a scuffle, and one of the Frenchmen pulled the earrings off the old man. The Black Carp lineage people ran up to help, and were joined by their clan brothers of the Red Carp lineage. The Frenchmen were attacked, and one was left unconscious on the ground following a hard blow from a war club. So far we have an example of intraclan solidarity; two lineages of the same clan pooling their efforts in defense of a clan-mate.

But the Frenchmen had many Potawatomi friends in the village, particularly so the leader of the Bear Clan, who came up with reinforcements to aid the downed Frenchmen. Moreover, the Bear Clan leader's son-in-law was the chief of the Sauk living nearby, and he rushed up to help his father-in-law. The situation is now more delicate. We now have an intratribal, interclan dispute between the Bear and the Carp people complicated by the loyalty of the Sauk to the Bear Clan through their leader. Note that all the relationships are so far those of kinsmen, consanguineous or affinal. There was no mention of a Potawatomi chief, even with regard to the two clans. If there had been a tribal chief, this is precisely the kind of setting in which he should have appeared—to keep the peace between feuding segments of the society. But none came forward. The Frenchman regained consciousness, and it was he who calmed everyone down (La Potherie 319).

The process of decision-making on very large matters becomes very clear in the narrative of how in 1669 the Potawatomi achieved consensus on the implications and the specifics of their growing alliance with the French. La Potherie rightly states one of the key issues as involving deferred as opposed to immediate gratification (1911: 336–38). "As the savages give everything to their mouths, they preferred to devote themselves to hunting such other wild beasts as could furnish subsistence for their families, rather than seek beavers, of which there were not enough [in the immediate Green Bay area]; they preferred the needs of life to those of the state." The Potawatomi fully appreciated that if they failed to cooperate the French would seek an alliance with other tribes. Their rivals the Odawa, for example, were close by, waiting for just such a development. Moreover, they had had their first taste of the luxuries of Montreal. It was time for the Potawatomi to reach agreement on a new tribal policy.

Perrot's narrative (through his editor, La Potherie) of how the Potawatomi achieved and solidified this new policy is one of the richest of all available descriptions of an early-contact–period Algonquian society at work. It was a tribal affair, one which mobilized the full force of the society in a collective, magical play for control of the elements, solicitation of spiritual aid, and the development of group confidence in the new enterprise, all aimed at achieveing success in a highly hazardous activity. It began with days of deliberations in which a consensus position was finally reached and it ended with a two-day ritual. All of the leadership roles described earlier were enacted, with each adult male then in turn rising and improvising a song expressing his personal commitment to a French alliance, declaring his readiness to make the trip to Montreal, praying to the French manito for his aid and support, expressing hope that the French in Montreal would find him acceptable and that it might be a profitable trip.

The chief of the feast in this affair is an interesting figure. Likely the same man who the previous year brought Perrot to Green Bay, the man who was treated like a captain, he was the organizer, host, and sponsor of the ritual, and was obviously elated by the success of the whole affair. He is given no other title of office. Indeed, he was identified by personal name only a decade later, at which time he is firmly established as the major figure at the Potawatomi trading station on Rock Island and a frequent visitor to Montreal and the council chambers of Governor Frontenac. This was Onangizes, the Shimmering Light of the Sun. At the Potawatomi policy-making session in 1669, however, he was simply an ambitious host, a friend to Perrot, a man who saw new advantages in a French alliance. There was no mention of a tribal chief at this affair at all, only elders, hosts, heralds, singers, waiters, and other involved participants.

The French thought very highly of the Potawatomi system of governance. They characterized these tribesmen as stubborn: once the Potawatomi set their minds on a course of action, it was difficult to turn them in a different direction. The tribal elders were described as "prudent, sensible, and deliberate; it is seldom that they undertake any unseasonable enterprise" (La Potherie 302). But following an incident at the council house in 1670, when Dablon and Allouez tried to reprimand them for the behavior of the warriors (see page 65), the elders replied with an explanation which was to be regularly repeated to Euro-Americans over the next three centuries. They declared that "their young men had no sense, and would not listen to the elders" (JR 55: 189). Potawatomi leaders exercised no authority. They could not command or control, manage or coerce anyone. The absence of authoritative chiefs was a basic feature of Potawatomi society, not a consequence of experiences with Europeans.

EXTERNAL RELATIONS

The initial advantages to the Potawatomi of the French alliance were several. Since the French were then at peace with the Iroquois, the Potawatomi immediately gained increased security both in their home territory and during the long journey to Montreal. In 1669 even the suggestion that there were Iroquois in the upper lakes was enough to create panic. Indeed, the change in Potawatomi policy had been precipitated partly by two such scares. In early 1669 a small trading fleet en route to the St. Lawrence had been frightened into retreating at Michilimackinac by the sight of several Iroquois. Their return had increased rumors of coming Iroquois attacks, and several weeks later the appearance of a large fleet of unidentified canoes at the mouth of Green Bay terrorized the Potawatomi. As it turned out, these were a flotilla of Odawa—chief rivals of the Potawatomi—who had come to trade. They were hardly more welcome than the Iroquois. One other advantage of the French alliance became apparent in 1670. That year the Seneca had attacked the Potawatomi, taking many prisoners (JR 54: 265). This brought quick reaction from Governor Daniel de Courcelles, who insisted that some thirty Potawatomi captives be returned to their villages (Charlevoix 1870 3: 161). It was imperative that the Potawatomi secure themselves from further Iroquois attacks and avoid competition with established trading tribes. Both, it was now apparent, could result from a French alliance.

Thereafter, Potawatomi policy aimed at maintaining a balance of alliances with other tribes advantageous to themselves, particularly with those who shared a relationship with the French and against common enemies, together with periodic hostilities directed against other tribes. The rivalry with the Odawa was eased, for example, when that tribe in 1671 shifted its base east to Michilimackinac and Manitoulin Island; but relations with the Odawa were never entirely serene (Perrot 1911: 188–190). In the Green Bay area the Sauk were closely allied to the Potawatomi, and this relationship proved durable for many years.

The Menomini on the northwest shores of Green Bay were held in mild contempt by the Potawatomi. There were very few of them in this period, and they were less than cautious in their relations with surrounding tribes. Soon after Perrot arrived in Green Bay, a Menomini killed a Potawatomi. The tribe retaliated by tomahawking a Menomini who was in a nearby Winnebago village (La Potherie 310–11). As most of the Potawatomi warriors were absent at that time, the Menomini gave indication of attacking the Potawatomi vil-

lage; but Perrot intervened, informing them that the French and the Pota-
watomi were friends and would fight together, reminding them that the
Potawatomi greatly outnumbered the Menomini and were returning from
Montreal with new muskets. Coming back from the Menomini village in the
same period, Allouez related something of the Potawatomi attitude towards
that tribe. An old Potawatomi wanted intelligence of the situation in the
Menomini camp but would not ask Allouez directly. Instead, he spoke to
Allouez's dog, saying, "Tell me, O Captain's dog, what is the state of affairs
among the Oumacouminetz [Menomini]? Thy Master has told thee; thou
hast followed him everywhere. Do not conceal the matter from me . . ." (JR
54: 237). Allouez reported with dark suspicion that he saw what the Potawatomi's design was.

Potawatomi efforts to block contacts between the French and the Miami
and other Central Algonquians to the south were described earlier. If, because
of the French alliance, the Potawatomi could not carry out their original design of creating a trade monopoly in the Green Bay area, neither were they
willing to accept a position of equality with other tribes. Throughout the
French era the Indian tribes called the French governor, in Montreal, Onotio
and addressed him in the idiom of nuclear family relations.[12] Onotio was
addressed and spoken of as father; the tribes therefore were his sons, hence
brothers to one another. However, the Potawatomi carried an additional distinction into diplomatic fiction, insisting that they were the elder sons of
Onotio, and thereby elder brother to the other allied tribes. This metaphor
carried the implication of a measure of precedence, seniority, and authority.
When they first met, for example, the Miami tried to impose this distinction
on the Potawatomi, who would not have it and managed to have their seniority
recognized (Keating 1824: 93).

There was more to this than merely a metaphor of kinship. The Potawatomi were entirely serious about maintaining a position of dominance with
respect to other tribes. In 1671, for example, the Potawatomi escorted Perrot
to a visit with the Miami in the Chicago area. Perrot went to invite the Miami
to attend the forthcoming annexation ceremony at Sault Ste. Marie. On approaching the large Miami village Perrot and his bodyguard were met with
a mock attack from the Miami side (La Potherie 343–47). The Potawatomi
joined in this ritualized combat, assaulting the Miami with fierce cries, firing
their muskets into the air. With the preliminaries over and the independence and strength of the tribes properly symbolized, the parties joined in discussion of the coming French ceremony to the north. But when it came time
for the Miami to undertake the voyage up the shore of Lake Michigan, the
Miami chief, Tetinchoua, was frightened by the stormy weather. The Potawatomi encouraged Tetinchoua's anxieties about the long lake voyage, suggest-

ing that such a journey might injure his health. At the Miami chief's suggestion, the Potawatomi expressed their willingness to represent that tribe at
the Sault Ste. Marie ceremony, where they spoke for and signed the annexation
documents on behalf of their younger sibling (Parkman 1879: 59–60; Charlevoix 1870 3: 166–68).

Potawatomi alliances with other tribes were often cemented by the exchange of women (La Potherie 301). Indeed, even among a group of tribes
where this practice was common, the Potawatomi were notorious for sending
their daughters and sisters as wives into the villages of other tribes. In the fall
of 1671 this practice got the Potawatomi embroiled in war with the Eastern
Dakota. The Odawa, then newly established on Manitoulin Island, had gone
to Montreal, where they traded furs exclusively for guns and munitions, planning war against the Dakota. The head of the Sinago (Squirrel Clan) Odawa
was brother-in-law of the chief of the Sauk, who was similarly related by
marriage to the head of the Potawatomi Bear Clan. The Odawa sent presents
through this linkage, inviting the Sauk and their allies to join them in their
planned raid. Perrot reported that Potawatomi performance in the ensuing
battle was not commendable and their losses few, for they "took to their heels
at the beginning of the combat" (1911: 188–90), while their retreat had to be
covered by the Sinagos, Huron, and Sauk.

Relationships with the French were not always smooth and painless. The
partnership often increased friction with other tribes. Following the ritual
celebration of the new compact in 1669, the Potawatomi sent off thirty canoes
loaded with furs to Montreal. This would make a party of at least one hundred and fifty men. They were joined by seventy more canoes from other
tribes below the Sault Ste. Marie, and the two groups went on from there
together. As they passed Lake Nipissing, the Algonquians at that location
delayed the fleet, resentful that the flotilla did not intend to pay the traditional
toll. The Nipissing men themselves were just returning from the St. Lawrence,
and, when the two fleets met, the Nipissing tried to persuade the Potawatomi
and their associates that the St. Lawrence was being ravaged by a smallpox
epidemic (La Potherie 339–41). But the travelers from the upper lakes recognized this deception when they saw that all the Nipissing were untouched by
the disease, and proceeded.

Once in Montreal the traders discovered that the new French policy of
opening the upper lakes had combined with the Iroquois peace to bring a flood
of furs into market. Prices were depressed, and the exchanges were unsatisfactory to the western Indians. Some of the Algonquians caused a disturbance
and their leaders were arrested. Those Iroquois present tried to take advantage
of the situation and offered their services to the French in an effort to undermine the French-Algonquian relations. The Potawatomi themselves were not

directly involved in the dispute and were very uncomfortable with the whole affair. They proved to be "the most discreet . . . continually dreading lest some disagreeable consequences would happen to them" (La Potherie 342).

The effects of this kind of experience in Montreal were soon displayed in Green Bay. Many Potawatomi returned badly annoyed with the treatment they had received, and they worked off their spite against the French in their home territory. When Allouez and Dablon arrived at the bay in the fall of 1670, they found affairs in disarray. The Potawatomi were "highly incensed against the French" and were maltreating them "in deed and word, pillaging and robbing them of their goods . . . subjecting them to unbearable insolence and indignity" (JR 55: 185–87). Dablon was greatly amused at the form taken by some of those deeds and words of protest (JR 55: 187–89). The Potawatomi—so as to mock the French—

> had chosen two-score of their young men, appointed a Captain over them, and thus formed a Company of Soldiers, for the purpose of treating our Frenchmen who were in those regions in the same way as the Soldiers at our French settlements had treated them. . . . Those newly-made Soldiers took it upon themselves to honor us with the same ceremonies that they had seen practiced by ours, but . . . absurdly, as they were unaccustomed to such things. . . . two of them came to call us, muskets shouldered and war-hatchets, instead of swords, at the belt; and throughout the sitting of the assembly they continued this species of sentry duty at the Cabin door . . . pacing back and forth . . . with their muskets now on one shoulder and now on the other, striking the most astonishing attitudes, and making themselves the more ridiculous, the more they tried to comport themselves seriously.

The Potawatomi obviously had been greatly impressed by the pomp and ceremony witnessed in Montreal and Quebec. But among the sources of their annoyance was the fact that French sentries there had tried to segregate Potawatomi warrior from Potawatomi chief, allowing only the highest ranking visitors into the council chambers of the governor. Hence their angry mimicry of French manners in their own villages.

The imitative role-reversal in this Potawatomi reaction is understandable. But by itself it was not to lead to any lasting change in the structure of Potawatomi society. Their displeasure came, in part, from being treated like a stratified society divided neatly into ranks of authority and worth. Imitating the French in this manner could provide only passing satisfactions, for to continue this practice would mean leaving some of the lower ranks on sentry duty outside their own council house, where the "soldiers" could not—as they expected to be able to do—fully participate as equals in the deliberations.

This kind of reaction, moreover, deflected Potawatomi energy away from the central interests of tribal policy. A workable alliance with the French was, in the eyes of the Potawatomi of the time, one instrument which could be used for tribal advantage. They had set a large ambition for themselves. As Perrot reported to La Potherie, the Potawatomi had "so good an opinion of themselves that they regard other nations as inferior to them. They have made themselves arbiters for the tribes about the bay, and for all their neighbors; and they strive to preserve for themselves that reputation in every direction" (1911: 302). The proper interests of the Potawatomi lay in their position relative to other tribes. The next century of their history centers on the unfolding of that principle.

TERRITORIAL EXPANSION I

The Potawatomi did not long remain confined to the northeastern Wisconsin refuge area. They soon began expanding into a much larger tribal territory in a pattern of centrifugal migration which often was at the expense of other tribes. Always they maintained alliances with strong tribes but intruded themselves into the lands of weaker ones. The French alliance facilitated the beginning of this expansion. The waning of the Iroquois threat encouraged it. The ambitions of the Potawatomi's own clan leaders gave it impetus. But there was opportunity for many, not simply those elders who saw an opportunity to increase their standing and influence. Population expansion also likely provided a push, and the exhaustion of resources in the Green Bay area added even more pressure. Too many Indians had sought refuge in this area. The fur-bearing animals in the region were depleted, and to secure the most valuable kind of pelts required hunting in other locales. For many years after, the whole Lake Michigan shore south to Sheboygan was understood to be poor in large game animals. Many of the Potawatomi who eventually remained in that area increasingly relied on fishing for basic subsistence.

But there were internal—cultural—pressures as well which added their weight to the press for outward movement. This pattern of centrifugal migration could not have been centrally planned or directed. The fact that the clan elders lacked the means of disciplining their young men in fact fueled the flow of Potawatomi elsewhere. The fundamental structure of Potawatomi society, divided as it was into segments, provided the basis for the migration. Whatever the several pressures towards movement elsewhere, it was the clan structure which provided the mechanism for the expansion into a far greater estate.

Perrot, who was on the scene and intimately familiar with Potawatomi aspirations and activities, carefully assessed the factors involved. As recorded by La Potherie in a passage which is sometimes quoted and as often misunderstood, Perrot observed how the Potawatomi elders labored to win the respect, esteem, friendship, and trade of neighboring tribes. He added that to do so the Potawatomi elders had to "make presents of all their possessions, stripping themselves of even necessary articles, in their eager desire to be accounted liberal." Perrot also carefully explained the consequences of this extreme generosity. "Their ambition to please everybody has of course caused among them jealousy and divorce; for their families are scattered to the right and to the left along the Méchéygan [Lake Michigan]" (La Potherie 302–3).

An understanding of Potawatomi social organization has to be read into these statements. By "families" Perrot referred to clans or, more likely, parts of clans or lineages. The emphasis on generosity is important: this was how an ambitious Potawatomi won prestige and influence, and how a clan leader was expected to maintain his influence among his own kinsmen. Economic exchange was conceived of and conducted as gift-giving. But this was also how a clan leader obtained influence in other tribes. What Perrot here described was a normal set of values which had been pushed too far. The enterprising elders were being overly generous—with the wrong people.

The Potawatomi were still trying to be traders. Regardless of Perrot's persuasions or their acceptance of an alliance with France, they had not abandoned the concept of themselves as middlemen. But they were caught in the position of middlemen at the lower end of a complex exchange network which operated with two sets of often contradictory principles.[13] The French in Montreal operated by the doctrines of a capitalized market economy. The prices they paid for furs fluctuated widely with the supply delivered and the demand for same in the home market. An overabundance of furs delivered to Montreal in 1669 had indeed caused prices to collapse, creating the disturbances among the visiting Indians just noted. But in the Green Bay area the Potawatomi bartered goods in an atmosphere of gift-exchange, with no concept of abstract unit values, debt repayment, or equivalences.

Therefore, to obtain a continuous supply of furs and equally valuable commodities such as prestige and influence, the Potawatomi leaders had to deprive themselves, their immediate families, and their villages and clan-mates of basic necessities. This brought on the great intratribal jealousy Perrot observed. The clan members were not attending to their most fundamental obligation, generosity to kinsmen within the village and clan. What Perrot called "divorce" consisted of schisms within the clans. Parts of the clans—the "families"—were moving elsewhere. Such migration was eased by the fact that each smaller group was economically viable—a producing, processing, and consuming unit—in its own right. It was encouraged by the value placed on autonomy. In this fashion, fueled by other forces, the segmentary clan structure of Potawatomi society provided the social mechanism for territorial expansion.

Patrilineal societies, such as the Potawatomi, which have a strong clan system, are forever generating the social materials for new clans by the mechanism of simple intraclan schisms. The necessary ingredients are only one or perhaps several young men—likely brothers, their wives, and a friend or two, with their basic economic skills, a sense of being denied or thwarted, and a conviction of better opportunity elsewhere. As the elders told Dablon and Allouez, there was none who could say no to the young men. Or—given interclan rivalry and conflict—a larger unit such as a whole clan would readily pack its canoes and paddle away. We will see later that this fundamental process of sloughing-off clans or clan segments remained the basis for territorial expansion and migration through the American treaty period in the 1830s and even well beyond that decade (Clifton 1975b).

4

Chronicles of
the French Regime:
1668 - 1760

The Potawatomi story of how Tisha acquired power and prosperity from Boat Maker reflects a much later, sweetened and simplified perception of their alliance with the French. Like many societies, the Potawatomi glamorize the distant past, convincing themselves that there must have been earlier eras when life was far more satisfactory than presently experienced, with game animals numberless and easily taken, when all men lived to a ripe and respected old age, and where opportunities for glory and wealth came in ample supply. The French alliance did not begin that way.

For some years—until about 1690—there were strains aplenty, while the disadvantages of the compact seemed to outweigh the benefits. Thereafter, until 1760 when the English appeared in force and ousted the French, the partnership was mutually satisfactory if not always easy or totally harmonious. The Potawatomi quickly discovered that the French came in different stripes and inclinations. Not all wished or were able to satisfy Potawatomi wants. But prosperity—indeed wealth—did come, wealth relative to the Potawatomi standards of 1665. So did greater power and influence, and a profuse variety of new experiences and things, which were unanticipated consequences of the Quebec connection.

The Potawatomi in 1671 understood perfectly well that an alliance meant mutual support and service. They did not understand it to mean subordination. Thus one point of stress involved balancing Potawatomi interests and needs for autonomous action against French demands and rewards. But by 1700 the Potawatomi had become technological dependents. They had absorbed new wants which could only be satisfied by French—or other European—suppliers. In this period there was just one other available source for the goods the Potawatomi now had to have—the English of the Atlantic seaboard. However, extensive trade with the English would have meant a rupture of the French relationship, for whom the economic and political dimensions of the alliance were cemented tightly together.

The Potawatomi were not the sole tribe in the Great Lakes region to be in this predicament. They were, though, almost the only one not to seek out and attempt either of the two available alternative strategies. They never abandoned the French for an English alliance. And they did not work systematically at playing off the English against the French, although they were sorely tempted to do so.[1] For this they received high praise for fidelity and warm recognition for services performed. The history of their relationships with Champlain's successors can be briefly summarized: from 1690 to 1760 the Potawatomi loyally served the French as their most reliable allies against—first —those tribes who threatened the preeminence of New France by making accommodations with the English and—eventually—the English themselves.

An intensification of intertribal wars in the Great Lakes was one unexpected consequence of the French alliance. Indeed, although the Potawatomi in 1668 had expected some relief from Iroquois assaults, this did not come immediately. Through 1687 large parties from the Five Nations regularly traveled the war road from upstate New York to northern Illinois, devastating the Miami and Illinois and threatening the Algonquians on the northern shores of Lakes Michigan and Huron. It was not until 1687 that the French assembled their allies and effectively carried the war into the Iroquois homeland, so that by 1689 the Iroquois altered their tactics, abandoning their attacks on the west and turning their warriors against the French settlements on the St. Lawrence River. Peace with the Iroquois came in 1701. Thereafter, the Five Nations hovered on the sidelines, watching for an opportunity in the west, skillfully playing French against British for their own advantage. The prolongation of the Iroquois threat had been a major source of Potawatomi dissatisfaction with the French alliance, but hardly the only one.

Meanwhile, in the west the Potawatomi continued in periodic hostilities with the Dakota tribes of Minnesota, western Wisconsin, and northern Iowa. These were intermittent, back-and-forth, small-scale raids aimed at gaining and controlling access to prime hunting grounds. Generally, they were conducted by small numbers of Potawatomi in support of Odawa or Ojibwa interests, and they continued until the Ojibwa drove the Dakota out of Wisconsin in the 1740s. Because such raids interrupted trade, the French were displeased with them. Such hostilities expressed Ojibwa, Odawa, or Potawatomi interests, not French, and on occasion this provided some additional strain.

Throughout the French period the Potawatomi had as their chief rivals the Odawa, proving that near neighbors who are close kin with similar economic interests do not make the best bedfellows. The Odawa periodically experimented with the English trade, played at working the English as a check against the French, and intrigued with other tribes who were openly willing to go much further into the English camp—the Potawatomi were much less disposed to this strategy. Indeed, throughout the era there is evidence of two parallel, if loose, intertribal alliances, the Odawa striving to manipulate one, the Potawatomi the other. The Odawa's chief allies in this game of ascendancy were mainly the Huron, Fox, Kickapoo, Mascouten, and Miami; the Potawatomi's were most of the Sauk, La Salle's Eastern Algonquians who had settled around the St. Joseph River after 1670 and whom the Potawatomi eventually assimilated, and some Ojibwa. These alliances, if this is not too strong a word, were not hard and fast arrangements but fleeting affairs which shifted with the fortunes of the participating tribes. On occasion, for limited ends, the Odawa themselves were allied with the Potawatomi. Nor did the two coalitions involve whole tribes in perpetual friendship or enmity. By 1714 both the Potawatomi and the Odawa were well dispersed over a large territory, and the interests of the Potawatomi at, say, Detroit did not necessarily coincide with those at Chicago. Nonetheless, there is a clear pattern: the Odawa were the weaker and tended to waver, the Potawatomi were stronger and more steadfast in their relationships with the French. The Odawa similarly tended to support, the Potawatomi more strongly to oppose those tribes who were antagonistic to the French and who sought accommodations with the English.

With the Great Lakes area relatively secure from Iroquois assaults by 1701, peace was still not obtained. Instead, an incendiary tribe—the Fox, notorious as the most independent and combative of all Central Algonquians—lighted fires which inflamed the whole region for thirty-five years. The Fox had settled astride the Fox River south of Green Bay and thus controlled the most convenient route from the upper lakes to the Mississippi and to prized hunting lands in Iowa and Minnesota as well. They constantly angered the French and other tribes by their perpetual demands for tribute and were in turn angered by the French trade with the Dakota tribes, which put firearms into the hands of their closest major enemies. Thereupon, joined by their close allies the Kickapoo and Mascouten, they launched a series of attacks on French traders and allied tribes which persisted until they were in turn nearly exterminated in the early 1730s. The Potawatomi were among the prime movers in putting out the Fox conflagration.

With the Fox wars behind them the Potawatomi soon were employed by the French as mercenary warriors in support of their efforts to defend their teetering position in the Great Lakes and Mississippi valley. In 1733 the immediate threat was from the Chickasaw, a large and powerful Muskhogean tribe of northern Mississippi. The Chickasaw—closely allied with English interests—had been raiding French shipments on the Mississippi River, threatening to sever connections between New Orleans and the Illinois country. The French reacted by loosing war parties of their allies from the lake country into Chickasaw territory, which periodically provided some Potawatomi employment and adventure for the next twenty years.

Following the 1701 peace with the Iroquois, the French had been able to open a major new post at Detroit, which commanded access to the upper lakes from Lakes Erie and Ontario and hence blocked English entry into important French territory. But Detroit also provided access to the Ohio area which, due to Iroquois threats, had not been systematically hunted or exploited for half a century. The tribes which soon relocated and remained in the Detroit area—Potawatomi, Odawa, Huron, and Miami—were naturally drawn to this valuable hunting ground. Of these, most were also attracted by the possibilities of an English connection, for traders from New York and other eastern colonies too were penetrating Ohio. The lure was almost irresistible, for the English offered clearly superior goods at much lower prices than those available from the French in Detroit. Of the Detroit tribes two succumbed, the Huron and the Miami. In 1747–1748 the Huron conspired to raise a coalition against the French, as did the Miami between 1747 and 1752. Neither were successful, as the Potawatomi and other tribes stood fast to the French alliance, resisting overtures to defect.

In 1750 many Potawatomi from the St. Joseph area began moving into southern Wisconsin and northern Illinois; other Potawatomi from the villages along the Door Peninsula of Wisconsin had been there earlier. The occasion for this increased migration was an opportunity presented by a weakening of the Illinois tribes. Once strong and populous, the Algonquian tribes of Illinois had been severely depopulated by Iroquois raids and newly introduced epidemic diseases (Blasingham 1956). Weakened, they had begun shifting their territory southward into central and southern Illinois before 1750. By listening to Miami overtures of an English alliance, some of the remaining fragments of the Illinois tribes raised the ire of the French, which provoked the Potawatomi and their allies into action. Not that they needed an additional excuse: a large and relatively unpopulated territory lay before them. They were encouraged by the French in Illinois to settle the area. Between 1750 and 1760, then, the Potawatomi and other tribes intruded themselves into formerly Illinois lands, driving the remnants of these tribes before them until they abandoned the state altogether or cowered amidst the French settlements at Cahokia and Kaskaskia.

This was the last major act in the drama of intertribal rivalries during the French regime. Hardly had the move into the Illinois territory begun when the Potawatomi warriors were again employed as mercenaries to serve against English forces in the east and as raiders terrorizing the frontier settlements of Virginia, Pennsylvania, and New York. The Potawatomi were now caught up in the throes of a major international convulsion—in Europe called the Seven Years' War, and in North America the French and Indian War. With the fall of Montreal to British forces in September 1760 came the end of the formal

French alliance. British Indian agents and traders shortly appeared in Detroit, Michilimackinac, St. Joseph, Green Bay, and Chicago to pick up the pieces.

With this overview of the long French alliance accomplished, we can proceed to a sampling of a vast thicket of historical trees.

AGENTS
AND AGENCIES

The formal beginning of the French alliance ended on a note of healthy skepticism. On the fourteenth of June, 1671, by the fall of water named St. Marie, the pageant was ended, speeches made and translated, a mass celebrated, feasting done, calumets passed around for all to smoke, a tall cedar pole raised bearing the royal arms of France on an escutcheon and another in the form of a cross symbolizing a different kingdom. As the French were leaving, one folded and slipped a written report of the annexation proceedings behind the iron escutcheon. When they were gone, some of the Indians came up, removed the document, and burned it (La Potherie 347). Perrot explained to La Potherie that the Indians feared the paper was a spell which would cause the death of all those who resided in the district.[2] Certainly the participating Indians were unsure of French plans or intentions; and they had yet to see much in the way of tangible benefits from the association. The French, on the other hand, were positive all had gone successfully; above all else, the Indians had given them piles of rich furs, sufficient to meet all the costs of the expedition.

The Indians present that day had seen all of the kinds of Frenchmen most were ever to see. There was a nobleman, St. Lusson, clothed in silks and satins, representing the government of New France; there was an agent-translator representing the economic interests of the colony; there were *engagés*—indentured servants who supplied the labor for the trip; *coureurs des bois,* the lusty wood-rangers (better, fur bootleggers), with as little respect for constituted authority as the Indians themselves, were numerous; and there were also a few soldiers and the priests. All male, no children, and no elderly, it was an odd sampling of the population of France. These were the kinds of French agents with whom the Potawatomi thereafter conducted their business. They had to travel the long route to the St. Lawrence to see other kinds of French people, women or infants, for example, and only a minority ever did so.

At first the major contact of Potawatomi with Frenchmen involved agents like Father Allouez, Nicholas Perrot, and the often unidentified *coureurs des bois*. All such—with the likely exception of Perrot—caused frequent consternation and anger. Perrot had great presence and power, called, elegantly, charisma (recognized by the Potawatomi as manito). All were in open competition with their Potawatomi counterparts, and each served as a model for these new kinds of learning which are called acculturation. Allouez (and other priests who followed him) made Potawatomi religious functionaries his adversaries. Since the Potawatomi did not have full-time religious practitioners —theirs was a religion where most adults had roles to play—those potentially annoyed were numerous. Perrot was in competition with Potawatomi political leaders, but on occasion he trod on the toes of a diviner or a curer. The *coureurs des bois,* the most numerous and the least disciplined, were the greatest potential threat, for they promised to usurp the Potawatomi male's economic position as primary producer and trader of furs. They also had no French-women with them, and this in quick time posed other problems.

Claude Allouez had built the mission of St. Francis Xavier close to the mouth of the Fox River, and near there in 1672 he planted a large cross. Sometime later a group of young Potawatomi warriors pulled it down and burned it, so Allouez thought, as an offering to their gods (JR 58: 36-43, 267, 287). He himself had earlier destroyed an Indian idol on the Fox River near Kaukana, an idol set by the Potawatomi to placate and appease Nampizha, the Underwater Panther, who threatens unwary neshnabek with drowning. When the Potawatomi were later defeated in the joint expedition against the Dakota, Allouez chastised them and argued that their defeat had been caused by their disrespect to his god. This was the kind of argument that the Potawatomi could understand, for ritual and worship for them was an aspect of technology, a labor-saving device aimed at securing success in risky enterprises. Thereafter, for a short while, the Potawatomi festooned the cross with offerings of tobacco, food, and water. They could understand Allouez's promise of new powers through his variety of worship; but they could not have understood his style. He gave his powers away, asking no compensation. For the Potawatomi, spiritual powers were personal or group property, a valuable intangible which would be used or exchanged only for an adequate fee.

The converts of Allouez and his Jesuit successors among the Potawatomi were few, and these were mainly very small children and the elderly—those about to die. The Jesuit policy of working among the children was a source of annoyance to the Potawatomi. Potawatomi socialization practices did not and do not involve excessive amounts of nurture or attention given to the young (McElroy 1968; F. Clifton 1963–64). Children anywhere are most susceptible to new teachings, being the less well socialized, while Potawatomi children grew up with a net deficit need for recognition. Thus the children and the very old—those most vulnerable—responded to the attentions of the missionaries. But there seems to have been little impact, for few practicing Catholics were the result of these great labors.

The attentions of the Jesuits continued. The mission at Green Bay continued in operation for many years, but as a lonely outpost, for French attention soon shifted elsewhere. Marquette and Joliet passed by Green Bay in 1673 on their way to the Mississippi, and while on the return trip Marquette spent the winter recuperating at the Green Bay mission. On his trip down, Marquette reported that he found some young Potawatomi men preparing to travel south to trade with the Illinois, to the consternation of the elders who wanted them to remain, anticipating raids from the Dakota. The young men were going to the Kaskaskia village near Chicago to hunt beaver and to trade. Marquette also reported that there was little game on the Lake Michigan shore until one had traveled far south of the Potawatomi villages (JR 59: 164–81). In 1676 Allouez left Green Bay mission for the Illinois country.

In 1669 and 1670 François Dollier and René de Galinée of the Sulpician order traveled from Montreal to Sault Ste. Marie via Lakes Ontario and Erie. They had been accompanied part way by the intensely ambitious young Robert de La Salle, who parted company at the head of Lake Ontario to explore the Ohio River. Dollier and Galinée had planned on accompanying La Salle, but on Lake Ontario they accidentally encountered Louis Joliet traveling east from the upper lakes. From him they learned of "a very numerous nation of Ottawas [trading Indians] called the Pottawattamies, amongst whom there had never been any missionaries" (Galinée 192). At Sault Ste. Marie they discovered that their competitors the Jesuits were already on the scene in force, and they returned to Montreal, thus completing the first known journey to the upper country via Lakes Ontario and Erie. Thus was an alternate route to Lake Michigan opened, and a foretaste provided of later interdenominational competition for the bodies and souls of the Potawatomi.

The Sulpician journey had been occasioned by factional strife in Montreal. Governor Frontenac had been planning a great expansion of the fur trade, hoping to achieve personal wealth. Opposed by the intendant, the merchants, and the Jesuits, Frontenac backed many personal supporters, one of whom was Robert La Salle. La Salle's success in securing a monopoly of the Lake Ontario trade sharply threatened the Montreal merchants, for the market was flooded with furs and La Salle planned to deflect trade with the upper country to Fort Frontenac at the head of Lake Ontario (Phillips 204–5). This was the setting for La Salle's later journeys to the Potawatomi country along the Lake Michigan shore.

It was nearly a decade before La Salle embarked on his trip to the upper lakes, the prelude to his expeditions into the Illinois country and the Mississippi valley. In the interim the Potawatomi regularly visited Montreal, expanded their trading partnerships in Wisconsin, and fended off the Dakota and Iroquois. When La Salle returned to the west in 1679 he planned to establish a post in the Illinois country and to improve the transportation of furs and goods between Lake Michigan and Fort Frontenac on Lake Ontario. For this reason he had constructed the first sailing ship on the Great Lakes, the *Griffon*. As he journeyed west with his party on the *Griffon* he discovered the area in an uproar. More than six hundred *coureurs des bois* were trapping and trading in the western country illegally, under sentence of imprisonment or death from the governor of New France. La Salle's own crew and his advance party were mutinous. The Jesuit missionaries were suspicious; and the Indians were increasingly tense.

La Salle went first to Michilimackinac and thence to the Island of the Potawatomi, now identified as Rock Island (Mason 1974). There he anchored the *Griffon* a hundred feet off the protected sandy shore, on the southwest side of this small island. He was warmly welcomed by the Potawatomi, who carried him about on a red blanket and honored him with a calumet ceremony (Tonty 1693; Margary 1: 487–92). He found some of his *engagés* waiting impatiently with a rich hoard of furs obtained from the Illinois country. His host was the first Potawatomi okama identified by name, Onangizes—the Shimmering Light of the Sun, who wore the silver medal presented to him years earlier by Governor Frontenac (Hennepin 1683). The weather was stormy, and the *Griffon* tossed at its open roadstead anchorage. Onangizes paddled out to the vessel in a small canoe and joined the Frenchmen, telling them "he was ready and willing to perish with the children of Onnontio." This was a grand and politic gesture, as much for the benefit of his own tribesmen as for the French, since Onangizes was personally familiar with sailing ships from his earlier visits to Montreal and Quebec. Later, the okama of the Rock Island Potawatomi presented La Salle with a calumet of peace, to serve as his passport for his trip south.

Having only four canoes at his disposal, on September 18 La Salle dispatched the *Griffon*—laden with most of his merchandise and supplies—back to Michilimackinac and Niagara. At this point the *Griffon* disappeared, whether foundered in an autumn storm, abandoned by a mutinous crew, or waylaid by hostile Indians is unknown. The next day La Salle and his party proceeded south. In their trip down the west shore of Lake Michigan they visited and were resupplied at a village of Potawatomi somewhere between the present Jacksonport and Manitowoc, Wisconsin. One night they camped on a river called Mellioki, then the location of a Fox and Mascouten summer village, later to become a major Potawatomi stronghold. But they met no other Indians until arriving at Chicago. There they encountered a hostile group of Fox, who had to be driven off with a show of force. From Chicago, La Salle proceeded to the mouth of the St. Joseph River (then called the River of the Miamis) where he built a log fort as a trading establishment and waited for his lieutenant Henri de Tonty to join him. Tonty arrived in December, and the group proceeded up the St. Joseph until they located hunting parties of Miami and Mascoutens, who showed them the way to the portage leading to the headwaters of the Kankakee River. Down the Kankakee and Illinois they traveled until they reached Lake Peoria on 3 January 1680. It was a hard winter's journey, with angry Indians and hostile Jesuits giving them no welcome.

At Peoria, La Salle built another post, Fort Crêvecour, and departed for the east, leaving Tonty in charge of the operations in Illinois. The situation there soon turned into calamity. The garrison mutinied, burned the fort, and fled, leaving Tonty with two Sulpician chaplains and three *engagés*. Then began what Louise Kellogg (1924) was to call Tonty's Anabasis. Tonty retreated south seeking refuge among the Kaskaskia, but there calamity turned to catastrophe. A large war party of Seneca and Onondaga came up, bent on destroying the Kaskaskia and other Illinois tribes. Tonty intervened, unsuccessfully, arguing that since the Iroquois were at peace with New France and the Illinois tribes were French allies, the invading Iroquois should stay their attack. He received a severe knife wound for his efforts, was captured and nearly killed. He then gathered up his five companions and began a long flight north towards the friendly Potawatomi village on Lake Michigan. There the five surviving Frenchmen arrived on 11 November 1680—Father Gabriel had been killed by the Kickapoo near Chicago (Tonty 1693: 136). But the Potawatomi had left the lakeside village for their winter hunting camps, so Tonty's hungry party headed north for the Sturgeon Bay portage and—they hoped—the Potawatomi camps along the Green Bay shore.

Arriving starved and frozen on Green Bay, they were found by a party of Kiskakon Odawa hunters who guided them to the Potawatomi. There they found five Frenchmen, and again they were welcomed by Onangizes, who fed and warmed them (Margary 1: 629–31). Father Zenobius Membre, Tonty's remaining chaplain, recorded Onangizes's words and behavior on that occasion, writing that "he used to say, that he knew only three great captains, M. de Frontenac, M. de la Salle, and himself." After placing himself in high company, Onangizes then went out among his people and harangued them to donate food for the starving Frenchmen (Shea 1853: 10–11).

It was the summer of 1681 before Tonty and La Salle were again reunited, now at Michilimackinac. In the early spring La Salle had returned to the upper country and had gone to the St. Joseph River fort and Illinois searching for Tonty. It was in the spring of 1681 at the St. Joseph River post that La Salle joined forces with the Eastern Algonquians—the Minisink, Mahicans, Wabunaki, and Sukukiak—who were resettling in that area. As described earlier (see page 20), one of them, Nanagoucy, petitioned La Salle to appoint him a chief. Another, Ouilamette (later Winamek or Catfish), was particularly useful to La Salle in the latter's efforts to create a coalition of tribes near the southern end of Lake Michigan.

La Salle's aim was to achieve such an assembly of united Algonquians as would block Iroquois invasions of the Illinois country. This tactic was essential if he were to obtain a monopoly of the fur trade in that rich area (Margary 1878 1: 551–74). La Salle was partly successful in this, attracting most of the Algonquian tribes from central and southern Wisconsin into Illinois, leaving the Potawatomi in northeastern Wisconsin in relative peace, dominating the trade in that region (Kellogg 1925: 220). The Eastern Algonquians, particularly, continued to serve La Salle's interests. On his next journey south, for example, Henri de Tonty had a guard of eighteen men and ten wives from the Mahican, Wabunaki, and Sukukiak groups (Margary 1: 629–32). These Eastern Algonquians are of particular interest because some of them at least remained attached to the St. Joseph River area, where a few years later a few reappear in the guise of Potawatomi "chiefs." Of these, Ouilamette or Winamek remained the most prominent.

While in the Illinois country, 1680–1681, La Salle reported that the bison were getting scarce there. Too many Indians had been crowding into these prairie lands, hunting and killing this prime game animal continually and indiscriminately, upsetting the delicate ecological balance between the Illinois tribes proper and their environment (Margary 1: 97). By the time the Potawatomi moved into central Illinois—some seventy years later—the bison herds were nearly gone. La Salle also noted that while at Michilimackinac in 1681 he observed a number of Potawatomi flaunting—in the faces of visiting Iroquois—the scalps of several Iroquois they had recently killed. This did not endear the Potawatomi to the Five Nations, and undoubtedly it contributed somewhat to continuing hostilities between these tribes. But the Five Nations were moved by larger issues, matters that went far beyond ordinary revenge seeking.

These issues were well stated by those who governed New France. In 1681 the intendant, Jacques Du Chesneau, summarized the situation in the west. He wrote that the Algonquian tribes in the Great Lakes area for the most part did not hunt beaver, as there were few such in their own territory. Instead, they "went in search of it in the most distant places" and there exchanged French merchandise for furs. His policy for maintaining French control of the fur trade was to keep peace between the tribes, to control the undisciplined *coureurs des bois,* and to keep the Algonquians united against the Iroquois. He pointed out that if the Iroquois were allowed to proceed unchecked they would destroy the Illinois and ruin other Algonquian tribes. But the only long-range, permanent solution he could recommend to his king was the purchase of the English colonies (Du Chesneau 1681).

In 1683 Le Febure de La Barre, the new governor of the colony, commented on the "secret springs that move the Iroquois" in a report urging that he be granted permission to wage war against the Five Nations. The Iroquois, he recognized, sought to stop the flow of furs from the Algonquians to Montreal and to control Michilimackinac. The key issue was simple: "Who will be the Master of the Beaver Trade in the interior?" (La Barre 1683). In the upper lakes things were in an uproar. The Potawatomi resented the growing number of *coureurs des bois* staking out claims in areas the Potawatomi thought of as theirs. They had taken to stealing goods from the French traders. Governor La Barre responded by sending an inadequately small force to Green Bay to impress the Potawatomi and to restore their allegiance to New France.

Father Jean Enjalran, a good Jesuit stirring deeply into already troubled waters, was disdainful of the effect of this weak demonstration. Writing from Michilimackinac to La Barre, he accused the Potawatomi of conspiring against the French. They were going about the country, he wrote, "inspiring the other nations with their own hostile spirit. It is the policy of the wretched Ounanghisse [Onangizes], with the view of shielding himself, to induce others to join him; and, what-ever goodwill he may display, there is no doubt he is urging the Illinois, Miamis and others to do without the French—leading them to hope that he and his adherents will supply them with goods. . . . [he] assuredly will have to be humbled sooner or later" (Enjalran 1683). Enjalran and his fellows were reasonably certain that Onangizes and his like had been tutored by a certain Machiavelli. But Enjalran overstated his case. Onangizes was not anti-French; he was overly friendly to Frontenac and La Salle, which made him the enemy of the Jesuit-prompted faction in New France.

La Barre received permission to wage open war against the Iroquois. In 1684 he sent the Sieur de La Durantaye to raise the Western Algonquians against the Five Nations, but Durantaye was quite inadequate to the task of enlistment and a complete failure as commander of the Indians who were brought together. Nicholas Perrot had to be called back into service to assemble warriors from Green Bay, Michilimackinac, and Lake Superior; however, the expedition proved to be a comedy of errors (Perrot 1911: 232–37). The Odawa were reluctant to participate at the start; and on the trip west, if one Odawa was not wounding another accidentally, a Frenchman—mistaking the Indians for elk —was. Needed weapons and supplies were ostentatiously promised and never delivered. And the Indian allies finally arrived at Niagara to find that Governor La Barre had already made a dishonorable peace with the Iroquois on their terms. Whether or not the Potawatomi participated in this ludicrous effort at impressing the Iroquois is uncertain. Perrot did enlist a hundred warriors—their tribes unidentified—from Green Bay; he was well supported by an unnamed leader there. These likely included some Potawatomi. However, the Algonquians did considerably better on their own. In 1686, when a large Seneca party struck at the Miami near Chicago, the Potawatomi, Mascouten, and Fox came to the rescue, pursued the Seneca eastward, killing many and releasing most of the Miami captives (La Potherie 14–16).

FRIENDS
AND FOES

In 1685 the English finally penetrated the upper lakes, sending eleven canoe loads of merchandise to Michilimackinac safely (Smith 1973: 37). The Indians now in their own country got a taste of English prices, goods, and rum. Already unsettled, the French-Indian alliance was further shaken by this event. Under its fresh governor, Jacques Denonville, New France stirred into action in 1686. That year Sieur Duluth was instructed to establish a post at the "straights of Lake Erie" (Detroit) so as to control access to Lakes Huron and Michigan and to the Illinois country (Denonville 1686). Duluth opened a small post there, although it was fifteen more years before this vital narrows was strongly fortified. A French strategy was emerging. For 1687 Denonville planned a major assault on the Iroquois in their home villages and again required the services of the Indians from the upper lakes. Meanwhile, thirty more Englishmen had arrived laden with goods at Michilimackinac, but they were captured and their goods confiscated.

Early that spring the Potawatomi had been working with Perrot in his efforts to establish new posts on the Mississippi and to expand trade with the Dakota. When the French traders were trapped on the frozen Wisconsin River, the Potawatomi sent two hundred men to their aid (La Potherie 30). In May, when Perrot received Denonville's call to arms, he set out for Michilimackinac with one hundred Potawatomi, Menomini, and Sauk warriors. As Perrot's fleet approached the French post, they were met by the Odawa, who staged a mock battle to welcome them (La Potherie 21). The Odawa and their allies the Huron had been playing a double game. Their warlike reception seemed to signal their readiness for battle with the Iroquois, but earlier they had tried to aid the English trading fleet, while what the Odawa actually planned was to turn back the Potawatomi force from Green Bay. When persuasion and negotiation did not work, the Odawa tried to use British rum to immobilize the Potawatomi war party, for the bumbling Durantaye had grandly presented the captured liquor to the Odawa (La Potherie 21–23; Perrot 1911: 249–50).[3] But the Potawatomi had been forewarned of the Ottawa-Huron conspiracy, and Perrot worked with the former's war leaders to maintain discipline.[4]

Although sorely tempted by repeated offers of "Indian milk," the Potawatomi warriors held fast and refused to succumb to the Odawa stratagem. Perrot and his Potawatomi joined Tonty, Duluth, Durantaye, and their Indian forces, proceeded to Lake Ontario where they united with Governor Denonville and the French regulars, and successfully invaded the Seneca territory, fighting off a massive ambush and driving away the Seneca forces (Margary 2: 46–52).[5] This was short of a decisive victory, for—although urged to do so by the jubilant Algonquians—Denonville failed to pursue and destroy the Seneca forces. However, this success ended major Iroquois assaults on the west. The Iroquois now turned their war parties against the French in their St. Lawrence River settlements, with disastrous consequences for a great many habitants there.

On 28 April 1688 another group of refugees from La Salle's Gulf Coast enterprise barely managed to reach sanctuary in a Potawatomi village north of Milwaukee. This party was led by Henri Joutel, who headed for Michilimackinac following La Salle's assassination in the south lands (Margary 2, Part 2; Joutel 1962). Like Marquette and Tonty before him, Joutel reported how poor the hunting was along the Lake Michigan shore north of Milwaukee. Joutel replenished his supplies among the "tribe called the Poutouatamy. . . . [we] bought corn from them. They sell it very dear, we paid 20–25 livres per bushel and a half . . . [we] paid for it in beaver and otter skins." The Potawatomi were still in the business of exchanging local produce for furs. The high price is not as surprising as the fact that they had any corn left at all to exchange in late spring. It is quite possible that they bartered part of their seed corn for the 1688 planting to Joutel and had to replenish their supply from other villages.

Later in 1688 some Potawatomi joined with other tribesmen to hunt far south of their home territory. That year they were observed by Henri de Tonty's nephew hunting buffalo and deer along the Illinois River (Deliette 1724: 307–08, 312–13). The following year Baron Louis La Hontan visited the Potawatomi on Green Bay, where he verified that a major economic activity was raising corn, which the Potawatomi traded to the *coureurs des bois*. La Hontan commented that he had been welcomed with impressive ceremonies during which he "entreated one of the Grandees to sing for *me* . . . for . . . in all the ceremonies made use of among the Savages, 'tis customary to imploy another to act for 'em" (1905: 168, 170–71, 341, 398).

Among its other problems, New France had been suffering from poor leadership at the top. This was resolved in 1689 when Frontenac returned as governor. Frontenac moved promptly and decisively, dispatching a large body of troops to Michilimackinac to temper the rebelliousness of the Odawa and Huron, and sending Perrot as the manager of the western trade. Shortly, Perrot moved his operations to Green Bay where he had greatest influence.

Near the St. Francis Xavier mission he assembled the Sauk and Potawatomi village and clan leaders, praised them for their fidelity, encouraged them to continue the war against the Iroquois, and supplied them with new muskets and ammunition (La Potherie 60). The Iroquois had been too successful in their raids against the French settlements. Visiting Algonquians, on witnessing some of the most destructive raids, had returned to the upper country with tales of a French debacle. A coalition of anti-French Odawa, Fox, Mascouten, and Kickapoo now emerged in full force, and New France was badly in need of allies in the west. The support offered by Potawatomi and Sauk was thereby the more welcome. Combining with the Menomini, Winnebago, and Illinois, they consistently opposed the Iroquois, raiding so effectively into Seneca territory that by 1694 the Iroquois—seemingly—begged Frontenac for peace (Kellogg 1925: 248-54). The Potawatomi, unknowingly, had been caught up in the fringes of a European conflict, the war of William III of Orange, king of England, who opposed the efforts of Louis XIV to expand the borders of continental France.

Frontenac did not accept the Iroquois peace proposal. Instead he called for a visitation from his western allies. The delegation of Potawatomi, Odawa, Menomini, Sauk, and Miami was escorted by Perrot and Cadillac. Onangizes in the public sessions acted as the speaker for the group, and in private he was Frontenac's trusted confidant (Perrot et al. 1695). Onangizes in open councils complained that many of the western tribes were deranged. How he wished they could be restored to their senses! Oh, that the Miami, Fox, Sioux, and Sauk might listen to their Father! "I am yours," he said; "I always obey your wishes. . . . When those other seemingly faithful Indians are out of your presence they act contrary to what they promised. No matter what injury I suffer from others—I always obey you." Onangizes claimed for the Potawatomi and other tribes at Green Bay the honor of a greater loyalty and most active service against the Iroquois. He later acted as speaker for the Fox, who were—judiciously—sitting quietly in the background.

Here Onangizes casts a wider net of influence than that of an ordinary Potawatomi village leader. His behavior suggests aspirations of leadership in an intertribal coalition, made up of the Indians located on Green Bay. Later —in the privacy of Frontenac's chambers—this Shimmering Light of the Sun explained that, had it been up to him, he would not have invited the Fox. That was Perrot's doing. The hearts of the Fox were false, he said. They despised the French and other peoples as well. But the Mascoutens were even worse (Perrot et al. 1695: 163-65). Perhaps Father Enjalran had been right in his thought that Onangizes had been exposed to the writings of an Italian statesman. In any respect, as events developing later indicated, the intelligence Onangizes provided Frontenac was a sound forecast of things to come.

While Onangizes was in Montreal impressing Frontenac, the Potawatomi around Lake Michigan were stirring. Cadillac reported that in 1694 two hundred Potawatomi warriors—which means a total population of as many as twelve hundred—were once again settled in the St. Joseph River area (Kinietz 309). After an absence of fifty-three years, some Potawatomi were again living in their Lower Michigan lands. How they got there is undocumented, but it is likely that this migration occurred at the request of Cadillac or another French agent, for their strategy called for a build-up of forces in that area to further block Iroquois advances. Later in the year, Cadillac organized an expedition against the Iroquois, who were accustomed to hunting in the lands near Detroit (Margary 2: 95–104). The force he assembled included warriors from two Odawa clans and a group of thirty Michigan Potawatomi under a leader named Ouilamek. The spellings of this name vary, but here again we likely have the Eastern Algonquian Ouilamette who was so loyal to La Salle in 1681. Some of these refugee Algonquians had settled in with local groups of Potawatomi and were achieving some considerable influence. Apparently, they had assembled near Michilimackinac under Cadillac's influence and by 1695 had migrated to the St. Joseph where they settled. Onangizes and his Green Bay Potawatomi now had competition.

In late 1695 serious—indeed, disastrous—news reached New France. Again the markets in France had been flooded with beaver pelts, causing a depression in prices, and simultaneously the Jesuits had won the ear of Louis XIV. The Jesuits wanted to isolate the Great Lakes Algonquians from what they considered the disturbing influences of the *coureurs des bois*. Well persuaded, Louis XIV planned on ordering the closing of the western posts and a prohibition on trade in that area. Frontenac, fully appreciating the dependency of the Western Algonquians on French goods, and as well the barely contained threat of the English to dominate the trade in the upper lakes, held off enforcing the edict for several years (Margary 2: 98–104). But by 1697 trade with the western Indians had slowed to a trickle, with potentially disastrous consequences for the French alliance.

Again the St. Lawrence was threatened with Iroquois raids, and Cadillac brought three hundred western Indian reinforcements down to Montreal in late summer. The Potawatomi, led by Onangizes, used the visit as an occasion to voice their grievances to Frontenac. This was to be the last council between the Potawatomi okama and the ablest governor New France had ever known, for Frontenac died the next year. The Algonquian delegation explained to Frontenac that the west was in total disarray, with all the tribes at one another's throats, all suffering from the shortage of supplies on which they were now dependent, the Odawa and the Fox taking advantage of the situation to promote further disorder. Even Perrot had been plundered by the Miami, who threatened to eat him before he was rescued by the Sauk (Anon. 1697).

At this council, when the Odawa speaker finished, Onangizes rose and indicated that the Odawa had not explained the whole situation sufficiently well. He said that he well understood that men often promised more than they were able or intended to deliver, but the western Indians had not received new supplies of ammunition for more than a year. The comparison he drew was invidious: the English treated the Iroquois far better than the French, their allies (Charlevoix 1870 5: 67–69). The French traders no longer visited the Algonquians in their own country; soon the Indians would no longer visit the French in theirs. "If the French leave us," he said harshly, "this is the last time we shall come and speak to you" (Margary 2: 150–55). Frontenac made feeble excuses and half-hearted promises, the reply of a discouraged, dying man. The secretary keeping the minutes of the council observed of Onangizes, "His speech was so bold it shut everyone's lips."

It was Cadillac who proposed a fresh and, he hoped, a viable alternative: accept Baron La Hontan's old scheme. Close the several expensive posts at St. Joseph and Michilimackinac and develop a less expensive, closer post which would block access to the upper lakes—Detroit. Congregate all the faithful tribes at this one large installation. Stop the trade in beaver for at least three years. Substitute other peltries which were not in oversupply. Give him command at Detroit (Margary 2: 186–92). Cadillac's plan was accepted, the St. Joseph and Michilimackinac posts closed, and for the next three years he worked at developing Detroit as a barrier to the English.

When the French interests shifted to Detroit, so did many of the Algonquian tribes. The eastern shore of Wisconsin was no longer of much concern to the French, and between 1699 and 1795 there were almost no travelers to report on the whereabouts and doings of the Potawatomi in that area. The last to leave a substantial report on the Potawatomi presence in Wisconsin was Jean François Buisson de St. Cosme, one of three priests representing the Société des Missions Étrangers, who in 1699 traveled with Henri Tonty south along the Lake Michigan west shore on their way to the Mississippi River (St. Cosme 1917). Once again in St. Cosme's journal it is reported that the west shores of the lake were poorly stocked in game animals. This party had planned on using the Fox River route to the Mississippi (see Figure 6), but on reaching Green Bay they discovered it blockaded by the Fox tribe. They doubled back north to the "crossing of the bay" (either the Sturgeon Bay portage or the Port des Morts passage, which is unclear) and from there traveled south along the lakeshore. Twenty leagues (about sixty miles) south of the "crossing," they came to what St. Cosme reported once had been a very large Potawatomi village, then in the process of being "abandoned" due to the "death of its Chief."[6]

The information given by St. Cosme leaves his exact locations uncertain. Sixty miles south of the Sturgeon Bay portage would have placed him at Sheboygan, a very likely location for a large Potawatomi village since it is on a point of land which serves as the outlet of a large stream, a prime location for taking the staple whitefish. If this is so, then by 1699 the Potawatomi had already expanded their territory well south of their old refuge area on the Door Peninsula. The migration of a thousand or more Potawatomi to the St. Joseph in the same period adds to the indications of a combined population increase and territorial expansion. But St. Cosme's statement that the large village was being abandoned "because of the death of its Chief" has to be discounted.[7] He arrived at the (Sheboygan) village September 29, which is precisely the time the large villages broke up into smaller, winter hunting camps.

St. Cosme's party proceeded, finding another Potawatomi village farther south, and on October 9 they reached Milouakik (Milwaukee), where they discovered yet another large village inhabited by Mascouten, Fox, and Potawatomi. Thus, in 1699 St. Cosme reported a string of Potawatomi villages down the entire Wisconsin shore. Therefore we know that in that year the Potawatomi were well established at the St. Joseph River, on Green Bay proper, and on the Wisconsin shore from Rock Island to Milwaukee. The phase of territorial expansion was well begun. And in their several locations the Potawatomi practiced a mixed economy—producing corn, fishing, and hunting for both subsistence and barter, and being extensively involved in the fur trade (Margary 2: 306).[8]

The next decade was a period of further expansion and considerable prosperity for the Potawatomi. They were now firmly entrenched as the favored allies of New France, and were caught up in the military, political, economic, religious, and social entanglements of this alliance (Phillips 318–19). In the St. Joseph River valley the population was mixed—composed of Miami, Fox, Huron, Mahican, Wabunaki, and Potawatomi (Charlevoix 1870 5: 141–42). Increasingly, the Potawatomi were in a dominant position there, pressing against their principal competitors, the Miami. In 1701 the St. Joseph Potawatomi received a substantial infusion of new residents from Green Bay, a migration fostered by Ouilamette (Winamek—Catfish). Ouilamette made a grand gesture to Cadillac, offering to send his young men to Detroit often if Cadillac would pledge himself to be generous and to sell goods at low prices. Cadillac replied that Ouilamette would always be welcome at his post, and added disdainfully, "It was I who made him Chief. If he wished to go elsewhere for his goods, he may do so as he thinks fit; it will not disturb my rest" (Margary 2: 395–98). Thus, whatever the original sources of the position and influence of Onangizes, his rival Ouilamette was clearly a French-appointed *chef*.[9]

Ouilamette was attracted by the growing power of the French at Detroit, which was now the major center of French power in the upper lakes. For peace—between the French, their allies, and the Iroquois—had finally been concluded. In the spring of 1701 the western Indians—including the Potawatomi (who were at that moment busily sending off war parties against both the Dakota and the Iroquois)—had been called to Montreal for the July 21 peace conference. Onangizes and Ouilamette (now spelled by the French as Ouilamez or Ouilamek) served as representatives and speakers for the Potawatomi (Charlevoix 1870 5: 142–53). Onangizes showed up at the peace council wearing the head of a young buffalo bull, with the horns dangling down over his ears. He continued to embrace interests larger than those exclusive to the Potawatomi, acting as negotiator for the Sauk and Illinois, and as speaker for all the Wisconsin tribes. He was a man who served the French well, and he stood high in their esteem. Peace was successfully concluded and prisoners exchanged. Fifty years of Iroquois raids into the upper lakes had ended.

With peace achieved, it was possible to fully develop the French position at Detroit, for no longer was this exposed location subject to regular assaults from the east. In late summer of 1701 Cadillac built Fort Pontchartrain, together with many cabins and storehouses near its walls, and he had lands cleared for the planting of wheat. His policy was to relocate as many tribes as possible in the immediate area around Detroit, and in a few years he had attracted more than six thousand Indians to his domain (Kellogg 1925: 271–73). The Potawatomi were among those invited. Beginning in 1703, at least some were settled and there they remained until well into the American treaty era (ICC 2: 133–205). However, except for brief periods, the St. Joseph River valley remained the main settlement area for those Potawatomi in close association with French interests.[10] The St. Joseph Potawatomi obtained their own mission in 1703 (JR 1: 219–21) and continued to expand in population. By 1707 they and the Sauk had replaced the Miami, who earlier had dominated that region (Marest 1706). They were drawn by the rich land and ample game known to be available, and there can be no doubt but that the eldest men in the tribe spoke glowingly of the time before the French when the Potawatomi had occupied Michigan in relative peace.

Cadillac's policy of concentrating the tribes at Detroit soon ran into competition and misfortune. In 1699 Pierre le Moyne d'Iberville founded the Louisiana colony, while Henri de Tonty maintained his post on Lake Peoria in the Illinois country; these were two other major French strongholds with similar goals, competing for the affection and services of the tribes. And some tribes were not disposed to abandon their own established positions to migrate to the

Detroit area. The Odawa, yet dominant at Michilimackinac, were one. They refused to move to Detroit, demanded they be sent a French agent, and threatened uncooperation if not hostilities (WHC 16: 221–23).

Similarly, the Illinois tribes and the displaced Miami south of Detroit in 1701 and afterwards were hostile to the newly settled tribes around Fort Pontchartrain. In 1704 the Wea (a Miami subtribe) raided the area, killing a few Potawatomi, Odawa, and Huron. The Illinois claimed they had been encouraged in their hostile acts by the Odawa at Michilimackinac (Cadillac 1704: 234). However, it was the Fox—still holding sway astride the river that bears their name in Wisconsin—who replaced the Iroquois as the terror of the French posts and allies. As early as 1701 at the Montreal peace council, one Fox leader had declared that although the Iroquois had now become his brothers the Dakota remained his enemies and the Fox would prevent French access to their country.

Through the remainder of the decade the Potawatomi at St. Joseph and Detroit continued to expand and prosper. They remained on the edge of the growing disputes between dissident tribes and the French but were finally drawn into the fray. In 1708 the St. Joseph area received a new infusion of Potawatomi from those who still remained on Green Bay (Marest 1708). This large, expanding population in Lower Michigan established several villages and hunted far afield down the Kankakee and into the Illinois country. The Detroit Potawatomi, in contrast, utilized the territory immediately to their south, along the River Rouge and the Raisin, and likely into the nearly untouched Ohio country on the south shore of Lake Erie. The Detroit Potawatomi were not numerous and had aroused the anger of the Huron and Miami by opposing their plots against the Odawa. When the Odawa moved back to Michilimackinac and Saginaw Bay, these Potawatomi were left isolated and fearful (MHC 33: 382–35; 287–90). The Potawatomi in their villages near the mouth of Green Bay numbered from five hundred to six hundred, and regularly supplied Michilimackinac with corn (Raudot 381).

In 1711 the Potawatomi were once again called on for service by the French in connection with fears of English-Iroquois invasion of the St. Lawrence during the War of the Spanish Succession, or Queen Anne's War as it was known in North America. Above all else, Vaudreuil insisted Wilamek from St. Joseph must come to help (1711b). Still nominally at peace, the Potawatomi had exhibited little affection for the Iroquois: in 1710, for example, they had captured two Seneca hunting in Michigan and, after toying with them, cut off their ears and dispatched them homeward as a token of Potawatomi esteem for the Iroquois (Vaudreuil 1710 & 1771c). Although the Potawatomi did not see service in the east during 1711 (French fears of invasion were not realized), Governor Vaudreuil took the occasion to hold a council in which he warned the Fox against further hostilities in the west (1711a: 503–6). The Fox listened disrespectfully, and not well.

By 1712 there had been far too large an increase of population from different—and contentious—tribes around Detroit and, to a lesser extent, in the St. Joseph River valley. The prime hunting grounds in the region were now overcrowded, while the Fox alliance dickered with the Iroquois and English for their support. In 1711 a large group of Mascoutens—staunch supporters of the Fox—intruded themselves, settling lands in southwest Michigan that the Potawatomi considered properly theirs. Meanwhile, the Fox had established a large fortified camp adjacent to Fort Pontchartrain and there awaited the arrival of their Kickapoo allies.

Like an overheated boiler, the situation exploded in the early spring of 1712. Then the St. Joseph Potawatomi combined with the Odawa and slaughtered fifty Mascouten—men and women, adults and children. Getting wind of this assault, the Fox at Detroit tried to attack some Odawa who were sheltering in the French fort. The badly outnumbered and increasingly nervous commandant, Charles Dubuisson, promptly dispatched messengers to the Potawatomi and Odawa, calling for reinforcements and relief. Within weeks six hundred and more warriors arrived, principally Potawatomi and Odawa, but including some Huron, Menomini, Sauk, Illinois, Osage, and Missouri. This large force surrounded the Fox camp and set a tight siege which lasted nearly a month (Dubuisson 1712). Several times the Fox and Mascouten tried to parley, seeking to talk their way out of a desperate situation. But Dubuisson and Mackisabe (Matjizibe—Bad River), the Potawatomi leader of the relief forces, refused to talk peace: the intertribal force aimed at "extinguishing the Fire of the Fox."

The end came as the Fox and Mascouten sought to escape during a late night storm. Pursued, they set an ambush but were driven off and again surrounded by Bad River and his warriors. After four more days of futile resistance, the badly mauled Fox and Mascouten surrendered. Only some of the women and children were spared by the victorious Indian allies of the French. Aside from a hundred Fox warriors who managed to elude capture, the balance were instantly killed or taken for later torture and consumption. In all, more than one thousand Mascouten and Fox men, women, and children died in this month-long vengeful battle. The French and their allies lost sixty men (Dubuisson 283).

Following this successful siege, the Potawatomi warned the French that the hostilities were not over. There were more Fox and Mascouten elsewhere, and they would seek bloody reprisals (Vaudreuil 1712). After the victory had been celebrated, Dubuisson sent Bad River with his cohorts to encourage the Miami to settle peacefully on the Maumee River, near present Fort Wayne.

Later, Bad River and Catfish visited Montreal to receive their reward and to further warn of the consequences of the Fox defeat. The Odawa and Potawatomi in western Michigan were particularly apprehensive, for theirs was the area most exposed to Fox retaliation. The Odawa abandoned their villages along the Grand River and moved north, while the St. Joseph Potawatomi temporarily left that area—those led by Bad River moving to join the Illinois near Starved Rock where they had allies, others congregating near the shelter of Fort Pontchartrain.

American historians discussing this period have generally followed the misconceptions of the early French and identified Ouilamette and Mackisabe, respectively, as the civil or peace chief and the war chief of the St. Joseph area Potawatomi.[11] There is no doubt that Catfish was one of the more ambitious and prominent men then dealing with the French, nor any that Bad River was the more capable and notable in military affairs. However, they were likely the okamek of the two largest clans known to have been resident in the St. Joseph area at that time, with Catfish representing the Gigos (Fish Clan) and Bad River the Kitchigami (Ocean or Great Sea Clan).

During much of the next twenty-three years the Potawatomi and their allies were preoccupied by the need to cope with the Fox menace. In 1715 the Potawatomi joined other tribes to attack the Kickapoo and Mascouten in southern Wisconsin, capturing more than fifty and killing nearly one hundred. The Fox counterattacked, but the Potawatomi conducted a skillful retreat to Detroit.[12] The French sent an expedition against the Fox stronghold at Butte des Morts in central Wisconsin in 1716, and the Potawatomi participated in this effort to subdue their chief enemies. But after a short siege the commandant, Louis de Louivigny, allowed an armistice; and, much to the consternation of the Potawatomi, the Fox escaped a thorough beating. The year 1718 saw the annexation of the Illinois territory to the Louisiana colony, which placed the Fox in a more secure position—in a bureaucratic morass. For several years no Frenchman was certain who was supposed to deal with them. The French seemed to incline towards peace, and in 1719 Catfish from St. Joseph escorted a group of Fox leaders to Montreal for an abortive effort at conciliation—while other Fox continued their raids against the French and their allies in the west.

Catfish was rewarded for his efforts in 1720 when the Fox attacked a hunting party of Potawatomi near Chicago, capturing two young men, one of whom was the Fish Clan leader's son. However, the Mascouten and Kickapoo intervened, releasing one of the prisoners unharmed and allowing the other to escape. The Mascouten were now so frightened by the destructive intransigence of the Fox that they broke away and sought permission to live among the Potawatomi along the St. Joseph. By 1722 the Fox considered the Potawatomi their most desperate enemies and threatened to "devour them." They were riding high on the crest of great successes, for they had virtually halted French traffic in Wisconsin and Northern Illinois. Still—because of the vacillating French policy—the Potawatomi held off making major assaults on the Fox. But as the Mascouten defection two years earlier intimated, the Fox alliance was dissolving. Casualties had been heavy, and the booty obtained from predatory raiding could not match the steady supply to be obtained from regular trade. Meanwhile, the French restored their alliance with the Dakota; and in 1726 a new governor, Charles de Beauharnois, demanded and organized a final solution to the Fox problem.

By 1729 Beauharnois had organized his forces and coordinated a policy with the French in Illinois and Louisiana. That year a large party of Potawatomi, Ojibwa, Odawa, Sauk, Miami, and Huron set out to meet the Fox in open battle. The Fox—realizing their weakness—tried diplomacy, seeking an accommodation. Finding Beauharnois determined on their destruction, they sought escape eastwards across the prairies of northern Illinois, aiming towards sanctuary among their long-time supporters in the east, the Iroquois. But hunting parties of Illinois, Potawatomi, Mascouten, and Kickapoo cut their trail, warned their allies, and agreed to hold the Fox in place until reinforcements could come up. This holding operation spoiled the Fox's chances of successful flight. The Potawatomi in this fight were led by a man with an interesting name, Madouche. Not Potawatomi, not even Indian in origin, it is an example of a French nickname. It might be translated from *ma douche*, except that the French were not known to take showers in this period. Hence, it is likely a corruption of *ma douce*, sweet one. Sweet and successful this Potawatomi hunter was, for soon large numbers of reinforcements came up to aid his hard-pressed blockaders.

Between August 17 and September 1 more than thirteen hundred fresh fighting men came up—French soldiers and traders, the Potawatomi, Odawa, Ojibwa, Huron, Kickapoo, Miami, Illinois, and other Indians from St. Joseph, Detroit, Illinois, and the Wabash country. This combined force surrounded and besieged the Fox for more than three weeks, until the Fox again selected a stormy night to attempt their escape. They found less success on this occasion than they had at Detroit sixteen years earlier. Betrayed by the wailing of their starving children, they were pursued and nearly exterminated. Few Fox warriors escaped—no more than half a hundred. The surviving remnants of this once fearsome tribe now fled to the Green Bay area where they amalgamated with their Sauk allies, themselves now stigmatized with the bloody reputation of the Fox. The French again tried to assault the Fox in northern Wisconsin, but with the Sauk they fled across the Mississippi into the Iowa country. This was the effective end of the Fox wars, the finish of more than thirty years of death and disorder in the western Great Lakes. The French even pursued the Fox across the Mississippi, but the Potawatomi and Kickapoo had tired of this bloody game and would no longer cooperate. Instead, the Potawatomi intervened, pleading the case of the remaining Fox so effectively in Montreal that Governor Beauharnois relented, recognized the Fox as a threat no longer, and gingerly accepted them back again as the now far less numerous sons of Onotio.

It is clear that in the experience of the Potawatomi the first thirty years of the eighteenth century were dominated by the Fox wars and their implications. Yet the Potawatomi had interests to pursue and work of their own to do. The business of living had to proceed, irrespective of constant alarums and excursions. Their rivalry with the Miami, for example, continued. By 1712 the Potawatomi were displacing that tribe from its hunting grounds south of the St. Joseph River and Lake Michigan. Indeed, Potawatomi pressure was one cause of Miami opposition to French domination (Anson 8–9; La Potherie 123–32). About the same time that the Miami and Huron were sidestepping east into the Ohio country, two other major tribes were moving westward into that same rich and productive area. These were the Shawnee and Delaware, long-time vassals of the Five Nations, who themselves now began promoting trade with the English. The French had wanted to remove the Miami to the Chicago area and to resettle the Shawnee along the Maumee-Wabash rivers, so as to remove these tribes from English influence. But this was not to be, and the English presence was increasingly felt.

French difficulties were exacerbated by the practices of Jacques de Sabrevois, the commandant at Detroit. In 1717 a delegation of Potawatomi and Odawa visited Governor Vaudreuil in Montreal, complaining of conditions at that post. The Potawatomi were led by Otchik (Chichak—the Crane).[13] The Crane faulted Sabrevois on several grounds. His prices were too high; he was ungenerous and never gave feasts for the tribal leaders; nor did he freely distribute tobacco. But his worse failing was that he refused to provide the Indians with brandy. The delegation begged the governor for relief from Sabrevois's regime and for something to drink. Vaudreuil allowed them "to take away a little milk [liquor], to give your children to suck," but warned them to use it sparingly. He then dismissed Sabrevois and replaced him with Henri de Tonty's younger brother Alphonse (Sabrevois 1717a & 1717b). The governor also reported on what another Potawatomi had obtained when he visited the English post at Orange the previous year. This was Ouytaouikigik (Wizawigizhek—Makes the Sky Yellow, Thunder Clan), who had returned with many kegs of rum, English wampum belts, and a message—the Potawatomi were fools to adhere to the French alliance. See how generous the English were!

In these same years it was reported how far the process of "civilizing"

some of the Indians had proceeded. There are few such commentaries referring specifically to the Potawatomi, but it was evident that farther south,
among the Illinois tribes, a composite Métis culture was emerging. There most
of the Kaskaskias had been Catholicized, and they were heavily intermarried
and interbred with the French. Most continued to go on regular summer and
winter hunts, but there was increasing reliance on agriculture, and some men
had been exempted from hunting responsibilities (JR 66: 219–95).

This process had not developed quite so far among many Potawatomi,
but a distinctive historical process was unfolding: there was emerging a frontier proletariat of mixed ethnic origins. During his secret 1721 mission for the
duke of Orleans to investigate conditions in the colonies, the Reverend Pierre
Charlevoix visited three major Potawatomi locations. At Detroit he found a
man named Onangizes holding forth, acting as "chief and orator for the
tribe." If this was the same Onangizes who had worked with Perrot and welcomed La Salle, he was by now a very elderly man. Assuming he was only
twenty when he first promoted the French alliance, by 1721 he was well over
seventy years, and Charlevoix should have noted it as he did when he observed
that Piremon at St. Joseph was an aged man over sixty (1923 2: 11–13; 95–98).
It is likely that the earlier Onangizes had died, and that his powerful name
had been "resuscitated" and bestowed on a successor.[14] In any respect, he was
obviously a favored man in the Detroit area, for Charlevoix spoke very highly
of him, and his name was left on French maps of that era (see Figure 4). At
St. Joseph, Charlevoix observed that the Potawatomi there were mostly Christian, some, like the aged Piremon, professing their belief; others, such as the
younger Wilamek or Catfish, were much more enthusiastic in this new faith.[15]

At St. Joseph, Charlevoix also noted that the soils were unusually fertile
but that intensive maize farming soon exhausted the cleared plots. This was
one cause of the frequent relocation of Potawatomi villages; since the Indians
did not know how to restore nutrients to the soil, every eight to ten years the
men had to burn off fallow areas and establish new fields for the women to
farm. And Charlevoix left one observation which is powerfully suggestive, if
not conclusive. He wrote that the St. Joseph Potawatomi applied "themselves
more than others to the study of medicine," which is a good hint that St.
Joseph was a major center of the Midewewin (Spirit Doings) cult, which was
the organized focus of Potawatomi religious-medical practice by this era (1923
2: 55–57). Four years earlier at Detroit, Sabrevois had made the earliest historic mention of this important Algonquian religious institution when he
wrote, "often the old men dance the medilinne, they look like a band of
sorcerers" (Sabrevois 1718: 367–68). The implication of this is that, whatever
faith Potawatomi leaders professed publicly to Charlevoix and other priests,
traditional Potawatomi religious institutions were still very strong. When he

reached Rock Island at the mouth of Green Bay, Charlevoix commented that the few Potawatomi remaining there in their "sorry village" obliged him and his companions to accept their hospitality.

During the period of the Fox wars several other specific Potawatomi names are recorded. One St. Joseph Potawatomi war leader killed during the 1730 battle which nearly exterminated the Fox was named Okeia (Wakaya— Bay, Ocean Clan) (WHC 17: 111–12). The principal war leader in charge of the Potawatomi force was Mandiché (untranslatable). Finally, at the 1730 battle came the first hint that the Indians of the Great Lakes were becoming familiar with a new form of transportation, for Vincennes and his reinforcements from the Wabash arrived on horseback. This marks the beginning of a new era of tribal mobility in the region. However, a deadly side effect of these wars was an intensification of the spread of contagious diseases. In 1733 smallpox and malignant fever ravaged the Great Lakes tribes, killing many Potawatomi at Detroit and other locations (Beauharnois 1733).

Even before the Potawatomi had successfully negotiated an end to the French policy of exterminating the Fox, they were involved in new battles against a distant foe, the Chickasaw. But in this struggle they largely served the ends of French foreign policy. Those Potawatomi warriors who set ambushes north of the Beautiful River, hoping to waylay Chickasaw war parties, or who crossed the Ohio in company with French regulars to assault that tribe's towns, were not defending the perimeters of their own hunting grounds. Neither were they safeguarding their women and children in their home villages. Nor were they reacting against repeated provocations, insults, and injuries thrust on them, as had been the case in retaliatory raids against the Iroquois and Fox. The forces that now spurred them into battle were different —personal glory and public renown for valorous acts of war, trophies, subsistence, supplies, booty, and pay. This new role had been anticipated in the years when the French called the Potawatomi to the St. Lawrence to help defend the colony against invasion. But now it had matured—the Potawatomi were providing auxiliary forces for French colonial wars. They had become mercenary soldiers.

Chickasaw attacks on the French lines of communication had begun in the 1720s, directed at both French trading and supply fleets along the Mississippi waterway and at the tribes allied to the Louisiana colony.[16] These incursions mounted in intensity, and in 1730, when Governor Perrier of Louisiana demanded that the Chickasaw return the numerous Natchez prisoners they had taken, he was refused. The governor responded by calling on allied tribes in the Illinois territory, turning their war parties against the bastions of Chickasaw in western Tennessee and northern Mississippi. Beginning in 1731, the Potawatomi of St. Joseph and Detroit joined the Wea, Piankeshaw, Miami,

Illinois, Odawa, and Ojibwa regularly to raid into the Chickasaw homeland or to set ambushes for that tribe's war parties along the Ohio and Mississippi rivers. The employment of Potawatomi warriors for this purpose intensified during the 1740s and continued during the 1750s, but then at a diminishing rate. In 1739 the Potawatomi even participated in an ambitious but unsuccessful French invasion of the Chickasaw homeland in western Tennessee. But as far as reducing or eliminating such English-prompted pressure on the French, the results of all such efforts were inconclusive. The French—employing their Indian allies to the utmost—were fighting no more than a delaying action along too many frontiers. In the Upper Great Lakes, this deflection of manpower to the colonial wars and the decline of productive economic activities resulted in a steady inflation of prices. This combined with the French trade policy of maximizing profits and administrative corruption to rot the foundations of their Indian alliances. Most Potawatomi continued strong in their allegiance, but even those *chefs* most acclaimed by the French were unable to control all their young men. Many were slipping away to do business with the English at the Lake Ontario posts. And with the advance of English traders into the Ohio country, there was increasingly less need to travel so far.

Upon completion of their post at Oswego on Lake Ontario in 1726—constructed specifically to capture the trade from the upper lakes—the English were in a position to protect their influence along the south side of Lake Erie with the Odawa, Potawatomi, Miami, and Wyandot suppliers and customers (Phillips 459–69). Completed the next year, the French post at Niagara supposedly served the same ends, but the military stationed there was successful only in a partial interdiction of Indian traders coming to the English post. The French traders could not compete in the quality of goods made available or prices charged. Following the death of Louis XIV, France had fallen into a decline; and during King George's War, when the English blockaded New France, the French were unable even to maintain a minimal supply of goods to the upper country, further weakening an already unsteady alliance. Those tribes in the Detroit area, long ambivalent in their relations with the French, soon took this opportunity to break away.

Even some of the Potawatomi may have rebelled. In 1742 they stood accused of killing thirty Frenchmen in the Illinois country, and they dispatched a delegation of okamek to Montreal to clear themselves of the charges (WHC 17: 393). Among those who counciled with Beauharnois were Pilemou (Piremon), who was a Sauk, Tchichaakane (Chichakose—Little Crane), and Oquiyaouy (Wakaya—Bay). The governor accepted these leaders' protests of innocence and listened to their demands: they desperately needed a blacksmith, and once again they wanted some of the governor's "milk." Beauharnois offered to send some brandy to their villages, but he required them not "to go and get milk from the English, which spoils your Hearts and Minds and Prevents you from paying your debts" (1742: 393). As the Potawatomi okamek departed, Beauharnois presented each with a silver medal symbolic of their connections with New France, and he also sent medals back with them to Wilamek, Memidokay (Manitoke—Idolator), and Ouasado (probably Wizawdep—Yellow Head).

The Huron were first to break away from the French.[17] As early as 1738, they made peace with the Chickasaw and proceeded to betray a combined Ojibwa, Odawa, and Potawatomi war party from Detroit, which was nearly destroyed in a Chickasaw ambush. The few survivors—on reaching Detroit—accused the Huron, most of whom fled to the interior Ohio country south of Sandusky Bay. From that sanctuary they begged to be allowed to resettle along the St. Lawrence, where they would join the Huron of Lorette, who had taken refuge there in 1651 after Iroquois invasions of their Ontario lands, but permission did not come. Some Huron moved back to Detroit, but the majority, led by Chief Nicholas (or Orontony), settled along Sandusky Bay near Lake Erie. English traders then flocked into the new settlement. By 1747 this was a major, strongly anti-French lodgment, a point of concentration for various tribes doing business with the English. In that year Nicholas conceived a conspiracy aimed both at driving other tribes away from the French and the destruction of Detroit. His allies in this enterprise were the Miami and some of the Odawa and Ojibwa at Michilimackinac and Saginaw Bay. But this plot was betrayed and the conspiracy collapsed. In an atmosphere of near paranoid suspicion the French even came to suspect the Detroit Potawatomi of collaborating with the enemy—but the Potawatomi stood firm in their preferred position as the elder sons of Onontio.

Hardly had the upset over the Huron (or Wyandot) affair subsided when the Miami made their play.[18] Long reluctant associates of the French, they willingly joined forces with the Huron, and in the summer of 1747 had attacked Fort Miami, burning and pillaging the property there. With Nicholas and his Wyandot defeated, in 1748 the Miami built a major town at Pickawillany on the upper Great Miami River in what is now northwestern Ohio. Under the leadership of a man known to the French as La Demoiselle (and to the English as Old Briton), the Miami again sought an Iroquois alliance, and they opened the door of the west to the English traders. These quickly led their pack horses to the new Miami post, penetrated into the Wabash River country, and were soon trying for Illinois.[19]

Although they were fast approaching a dangerous end-game, there were still a few more moves available to the French. Recognizing that they could not compete with British prices or merchandise, Michel La Galissoniere—now governor of New France—tried force of arms and legalistic maneuvering. In the spring of 1749 he dispatched Pierre Celoron with inadequate soldiery and a large supply of lead plates to be buried ceremoniously—declaring the Ohio country French territory. As Celoron came near Pickawillany he entered increasingly hostile territory, managing only to frighten away the English temporarily, but not overawing La Demoiselle. The Miami countered by trying for an alliance with other Algonquians to their west and got some support. But the Potawatomi stood firmly with the French, unwilling to violate their political alliances, not unwilling occasionally to send trading parties to Pickawillany and other English centers of commerce. In 1751 the French tried and failed to mobilize a major assault on the Miami heartland. In this the Potawatomi refused to participate on the grounds that the French had sent too few support troops and Indian auxiliaries from the St. Lawrence. It was now apparent that the Potawatomi were enjoying good things from two opposed empires, benefiting both from their favored position as the strongest allies of New France and from the convenience of doing occasional business with the English.

But in 1752 the French silenced the booming trade at Pickawillany. In that year they launched against the Miami the heir to Nicholas Perrot's influence in the upper country, the young Charles de Langlade, son of an Odawa mother and a French father. Langlade gathered up 240 of his Odawa kinsmen at L'Arbre Croche in northern Michigan, drew a few Potawatomi reinforcements from Detroit, and on June 21 burst into the well-fortified Pickawillany post when most of the Miami warriors were away hunting. There Langlade's warriors killed fourteen of the twenty Miami and Shawnee men present and celebrated their victory by broiling and eating La Demoiselle. New France was once again firmly in control of the western country, from which English traders were excluded until the end of the French regime.

In spite of occasional suspicion, by the 1740s the Potawatomi were solidly placed—among the Indian allies—at the pinnacle of French esteem. In 1747 Lieutenant Jacques St. Pierre at Michilimackinac observed that they were "the only nation to be relied on"; and he remarked how their importance to the French lay in the fact that "being sure of the fidelity of that Nation, it will always be a barrier in the way of others, and the means to keep them in check" (WHC 17: 479). A decade later, when New France had fallen on hard days indeed, the marquis de Montcalm noted that in spite of the great "fermentation" which disturbed most tribes, the Potawatomi yet stood firm. They were, he reported, "the sole savage nation which has never been reproached for any murder," which was something of an exaggeration (WHC 18: 205). This reputation had spread. In the 1740s, not only did Quebec rely on and reward their fidelity, but officials in the Louisiana colony were encouraging them to settle the Illinois country, where they might serve as a stalwart obstacle to English penetration down the Ohio River. But the English had also heard of the Potawatomi reputation for loyal service, and they too wooed them with better blankets, more trustworthy muskets, and rum. In 1749, still loyal to the French, 160 Potawatomi in twenty canoes loaded with 140 packs of furs arrived at Oswego. They constituted more than 10 percent of the western Indians visiting the British post that year (Fernow 1971: 83–84).

However, the major focus of Potawatomi tribal interest then lay in a different direction. The invitation from Louisiana coincided with their own expansionist aims. Long familiar with the lush prairie country to the south, and knowing the Illinois tribes to be severely weakened yet increasingly anti-French, in that direction they turned in the mid 1740s to expand their tribal estate.

The Potawatomi had been raiding into the Illinois country by 1741. As commented on earlier, they were accused of murdering thirty Frenchmen that year. In his memoir of the Indian tribes of Illinois, written in 1816, Auguste Chouteau noted that the Potawatomi began their movement into northern Illinois—then little used by the depopulated Illinois tribes—by 1743, when they settled along the drainage of the Kankakee and Illinois rivers (1816: 131–32). The Potawatomi were not alone in moving to this country. It was a favorite place of trespass for the Odawa and Ojibwa, for other Central Algonquian tribes, and for the Dakota as well. By 1751 some Potawatomi had settled on the Chicago River, and in that year they combined with the Odawa and Ojibwa to stage a raid on the Illinois at Starved Rock, which netted only one unsuspecting Frenchman who was killed (La Jonquiére 1751a & 1751b).[20] The Potawatomi had been active, of course, in the Illinois country since Jacques Marquette observed them heading there to trade in 1674, but these were temporary visitations—hunting, trading, or military excursions. In the late 1740s they had come to stay. Thereafter, they kept up the pressure against the original inhabitants, further contributing to the decline and retreat of the Illinois tribes (Blasingham 206).

In late spring, 1752, the Potawatomi joined a combined force of between four and five hundred Fox, Sauk, Dakota, Winnebago, and Menomini to strike a blow against the Illinois, who were wavering in their allegiance to the French. The French fully approved of this, for they considered the Illinois banditti, and similar assaults were launched in 1753 (Duquesne 1754). In 1756 there had been enough fighting: the French sponsored a peace between the invading tribes and the remnants of the Illinois, who by 1761 had totally abandoned northern Illinois (Blasingham 210–12). Both Chicago and Milwaukee now became major centers of Potawatomi population.

THE QUEBEC
CONNECTION SEVERED

The year before the end of King George's War the Potawatomi got their first experience serving the French as "bloody claws" digging at the backs of the English colonies along the Atlantic seaboard.[21] In 1746 they volunteered their services, and in 1747 several substantial parties of Potawatomi from both St. Joseph and Detroit traveled to Montreal, from whence—operating out of Crown Point between Lake Champlain and Lake George—they proceeded to raid English settlements along the Hudson and Connecticut river valleys (see Figure 7). They left behind them the first of numerous scars to be suffered by frontier farm villages and raw militia units from the weapons of that distant Great Lakes tribe.[22]

But it was seven more years before the French truly needed the Potawatomi and other Indians from the lakes to buttress the hard-pressed borders of the Quebec colony. In 1754 an ill-experienced young major of the Virginia Militia blundered into an advance party of Frenchmen led by Joseph Coulon, Sieur de Jumonville, near Fort Duquesne at the forks of the Ohio. Major George Washington proceeded to attack the French party, killing ten—including Jumonville—and capturing the remaining twenty-two (Flexner 1965: 82–92). On that day were fired the first shots of the Seven Years' War (in North America known as the French and Indian War), which in the end took the lives of more than a million soldiers and civilians, cost France her North American colonies, and caused the Potawatomi to make a wary accommodation to Great Britain, the newly sovereign power in Canada, the Great Lakes, and the Ohio valley.

By 1755 the French sought to block English penetration of the Ohio country with a chain of forts, from Presque Isle on Lake Erie to Venango at the mouth of the Allegheny River, with Fort Duquesne—at the forks of the Ohio —serving as the linch-pin in this barricade. The British counter in the spring of 1755 was to send General Edward Braddock with twenty-five hundred regulars and Virginia militiamen against Fort Duquesne. Inexperienced in forest warfare, Braddock was accompanied by George Washington (with little more experience), who was now a militia colonel, and who acted as Braddock's advisor and commander of the 450 Virginians. The advice Washington gave Braddock was to divide his plodding army and to send the fastest moving troops ahead to attack the French position. Meanwhile, with insufficient regular troops to reinforce Fort Duquesne, the French had called in their Indian allies. Some two hundred Potawatomi from both Detroit and St. Joseph then joined the force of six hundred other Indians and three hundred Frenchmen and assembled near the fort the first week in July, awaiting the approach of Braddock's divided army.

June 8 was the critical day.[23] Braddock was well aware he was opposed. He proceeded with all known tactical caution to capture two fords on the Monongahela and to keep his troops ready and well prepared to withstand an assault. On that day the French had urged their Indian allies to join them in an attack on Braddock's forces; but it was the Potawatomi who stalled—perhaps wary of attacking a well-prepared position—and prevented a fight that day. Braddock then concluded the French intended to defend their position at Fort Duquesne. The next morning he crossed the river unopposed and then, with

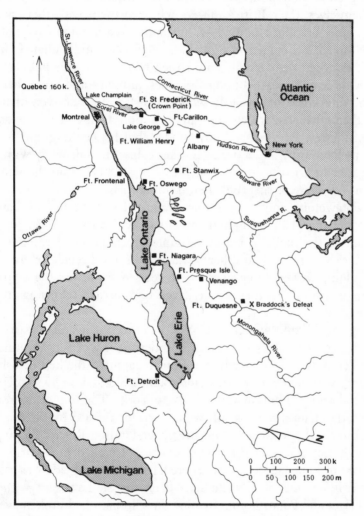

Figure 7. Geography of the French and Indian War, 1754–1760.

too little care, sent his men down the narrow, shrouded, forest pathway that led to the French fort. The English troops and Virginia militiamen were soon strung out in a long, thin column, their flanks unprotected, the high ground on their right untaken, in a position where they could not form ranks and fire volleys at a neatly formed, compactly visible enemy.

The point of the column was attacked first and fell back on the main body. There confusion became pandemonium as the wagons and rearward elements continued marching forward, soon making a disorganized mass out of the disciplined army that had been a few minutes earlier. Meanwhile, the French and Indians swarmed along the flanks half seen and never still, firing and flitting on to new positions. When the Virginia militia sought cover to protect themselves, their British officers whipped them with their swords for cowardice; and Braddock refused—as uncouth—Washington's request that he be allowed to form his men to fight back in French and Indian fashion. Of the twelve hundred regulars and militiamen who started this fight with Braddock, sixty-three officers—including Braddock himself—and more than a thousand men were killed or seriously wounded before the survivors managed to extricate themselves and reach the safety of Fort Cumberland. Washington was one of the few who escaped unwounded, but his clothing and equipment had been punctured by half-a-dozen musket balls. He rode away with a lesson that ever after he tried to impress on his own generals whom he sent against the Indians, "Beware of surprise! Beware of surprise!"

The Potawatomi and other Indians returned to their homes, having suffered no more than half-a-hundred casualties. At Detroit and St. Joseph they rested, counted the spoils of battle, recounted their personal exploits, and received well-earned praise and other rewards from the French before going on the winter hunt. It was to be twenty-five years more before the Upper Great Lakes were anything less than a safe haven for warriors returning from raids on remote frontiers.

During the fall and winter of 1755–1756, other Potawatomi warriors went off in small parties to harry the exposed borders of new York, Virginia, Maryland, and Pennsylvania.[24] Shortly, the French captured the key British post at Oswego and, with access to the interior country blocked, in 1756 prepared an attack on the central Hudson valley in New York. The line of approach was to be down the natural north-south water corridor formed by the Sorel River, Lake Champlain, Lake George, and the upper Hudson River. To prepare for this invasion, they constructed a base of operations named Fort Carillon at the northern end of Lake George. Once more Charles de Langlade was called into service, and in the fall of 1756 he arrived on the St. Lawrence with a large force of Odawa and Potawatomi. By now these Indians had broken away from the traditional pattern of summer raids and winter hunts. This was to be a long campaign, lasting through spring well into the next year, and so they carried their families with them to Montreal. Some Potawatomi had now moved into the role of mercenary soldiers on a full-time basis. They expected their French masters to see to the subsistence of their kin during the long months of the campaign.

In October these Potawatomi were dispatched south of the St. Lawrence to set ambushes and to act as scouts and raiding parties against English troops and settlements south of Lake George. In this work they were most proficient. During the winter and spring of 1756–1757 they attacked the English lines of communication, raided settlements near Albany, and carried intelligence and prisoners back to Fort Carillon. In the spring some returned to the Great Lakes, but other Potawatomi from the west reinforced their kinsmen serving with the French. In July 1757, while waiting for the main French attack on interior New York, the Potawatomi joined with Menomini, Odawa, and Ojibwa to ambush a large force of New Jersey militiamen, who were proceeding north on Lake George in twenty-two clumsy, slow-moving batteaus in a reconnaissance in force.[25] The force—350 untrained New Jerseymen—was insufficient to change the fate that awaited them around a point of land, where there lay waiting for them a group of lakes Indians, some on shore and some in faster and more maneuverable canoes. An advanced party of militia was captured without being able to prime their muskets, and those who came unsuspecting after them were utterly destroyed. Those who were not killed outright were captured, with most subsequently tortured and killed. This was a major victory for the Algonquians and a devastating blow to the English.

The French and Indian forces at Montreal were commanded by the marquis de Montcalm. Those Potawatomi present in July of 1757 were led by five named men: Millouisillyny, Ouakausy, Nanaquiba, Oybischagme, and Ninivois.[26] These are interesting names. The French apparently thought the first worth his weight in precious metal, for his name is mainly French, not Potawatomi—*mille Louis*, with an Eastern Algonquian suffix, "lini" (man), tagged on. That is, the French called this Potawatomi war leader "the Thousand Louis d'Or Man." Ouakausy was Wakwshē, or Fox, of the Wolf Clan; Ninivois was Nenewas, or Little Man; Nanaquiba was Nanokiba, or Water Moccasin (the Snake, Ocean Clan); while Oybischagme was so corrupted in transcription it is difficult to make out, but may have been Wabshchichak, or White Crane (also Ocean Clan). These names suggest that the French had recruited an odd-lots combination of Potawatomi to join them in their military adventures.

With the support of the Thousand Gold Coins Man—and a great many other Indian auxiliaries and French regulars—Montcalm attacked and sacked Fort William Henry in early August. Unknown to the French and their Indian auxiliaries, the English garrison there had been severely weakened by an outbreak of smallpox. Following the surrender of the garrison, Montcalm was unable to control his Indian forces, who broke into the prisoners' camp, killing all of the sick and eating some. The next day they also attacked the unarmed prisoners whom Montcalm was trying unsuccessfully to shepherd away. Before the massacre was ended, the Indians had slaughtered or captured more than five hundred British troopers and militiamen. They had also infected themselves with the smallpox virus. The result—once these warriors dispersed to their homes in the Great Lakes area—was that this deadly disease rapidly spread to the whole region. A massive epidemic resulted, causing the French allies to seethe with discontent. The Algonquians of this era believed that serious illness was the consequence of sorcery, and they soon went looking for those hidden enemies who wanted them sick or dead.

For some while, the Potawatomi continued to support the French, but the tide had turned on the future of the Canadian colonies. In the summer of 1758 the British captured Louisburg and destroyed Fort Frontenac on Lake Ontario, interdicting the French supply line to the western country.[27] Now the French could not support their troops or their allies, either in the Ohio country or on the upper lakes. In the summer of 1759 the French were forced to consolidate their advance positions, drawing back on interior lines. The marquis de Montcalm made a stand at Niagara, where he was aided by a group of Potawatomi, whom some British-allied Iroquois tried unsuccessfully to lure away. The British forces were accompanied by William Johnson at the head of a large party of Iroquois, mainly Mohawk, more than a thousand strong. When the British commander was killed, William Johnson—the most capable Indian diplomat the English colonies had serving them—assumed command and took a stand separating the French fortress from a column of fast-approaching reinforcements. This relieving force included many Potawatomi and other tribesmen, but these French-allied Indians held back, reluctant to attack Johnson's forces. Ambushing half-trained English militia units was one thing, taking on the Mohawk and other Iroquois in a frontal assault quite a different matter. When Johnson's men came over their breastworks and fell on the disorganized French column, the French and their allies beat a hasty retreat. Johnson accepted the capitulation of Fort Niagara that night.

When Quebec fell to the British in September 1759, the French alliance was effectively severed. There was little for the Potawatomi to be connected to. The British blockade had earlier slowed and then nearly stopped the flow of goods into the French colony. And for more than a year the Potawatomi had not received near-adequate supplies of powder, lead, or other goods in the Great Lakes villages. Now it was time for them to think realistically of relating themselves to the British conquerors. They had long had ample experience with the quality and cost of English goods. At issue now was the question of how—after ninety years of faithful service to the French and against British interests—to foster the least painful and disadvantageous relationship. In the Potawatomi tribal experience the losers in a fight sought blood revenge at the earliest moment, while the winners were expected to turn victory into carnage. They had every reason to await the arrival of the British with trepidation. Had they not given the colonists of Virginia, New York, New Jersey, and Pennsylvania more than adequate reason to seek a bloody recompense?[28]

In July of 1759 George Croghan, the principal trade and Indian agent, opened a conference at Pittsburgh with the tribes. No Potawatomi attended. The Wyandot claimed the role of spokesman for the western tribes, capitalizing on their earlier friendly overtures to the British. In August, Croghan held another council. Now a few Detroit Potawatomi appeared, but they remained silent, in the background. In the remaining months of 1759 the Potawatomi of Detroit sent more messengers to the British, cautiously, a few at a time. They declared their willingness to accept peace and friendship and called for the reopening of trade. They wanted to receive the British on their ground.

It is not too much to suppose that the Potawatomi were proceeding with maximum caution, fearing—once they had entered British-controlled terrain in the east—the loss of these small delegations as hostages or worse. These messengers declared themselves a poor people, weak, near defenseless, badly in need of British trade. There were, it is true, other reasons to wait and see. The French had not yet been completely defeated; they still occupied key posts, particularly in the upper country; and there were wishful rumors of massive reinforcements coming from Europe. But in September 1760 Montreal capitulated and the French and Indian War was over. It was another three years before the larger drama of the Seven Years' War ended, but in 1760 the British were visibly victors in North America.

Still the Potawatomi were cautious. Few would reject the British trade goods that now started to move into the upper lake country, but many were yet pro-French and anti-British. These Potawatomi were strong along the St. Joseph River, and the Chicago-Milwaukee area soon became a center of anti-English sentiment. The British—with a small force and a large new territory to command—also proceeded with care, paving the way for the advance of British authority to Detroit and the other posts on the Great Lakes with talk after talk. Another large council was held at Oswego in August 1760, with only a few Potawatomi present, none notable for his previous prominence in political affairs. Then, in the fall of 1760, the British sent their Indian agent George Croghan west under the escort of Major Robert Rogers, with his ranger force, the Royal Americans. Rogers arrived at the mouth of the Detroit River on November 27. He was welcomed by those Odawa, Wyandot (or Huron), and Potawatomi who had their villages in the vicinity. On December 3 these Indians met with Croghan and Rogers at the French fort in Detroit to discuss the terms of their new relationship. The Potawatomi at these councils were initially still backward. They first deferred to the Hurons whom they allowed to speak for them. On December 3, Nenewas—Little Man finally stood and spoke openly for the Detroit Potawatomi. He agreed that the Potawatomi would treat the English as brothers. He reflected that they might jointly arrange a major intertribal council the next spring with the Iroquois present (Where, he was thinking, stood the Iroquois in the British scheme of things?). He asked, What price would the English pay for fresh meat delivered to the garrison? (How, he was reflecting, could the Potawatomi make themselves useful to their new "brothers"?)[29]

At the end of the French regime the Potawatomi were weakened by many years of war. They had suffered a sharp population loss caused by the smallpox epidemic following the Fort William Henry massacre of 1757. And it was years since they had received a really adequate supply of the trade goods on which now they were thoroughly dependent. Yet the names of their clans were found scattered over a far larger territory than they had occupied when the French had first got vague and nonspecific information about their existence in 1615. Large parts of Michigan were their village and hunting grounds, and parts of Indiana, Wisconsin, and Illinois as well. The British alliance would mature and ripen, while the memory of the French would fade slowly, and would affect their behavior in another major war yet to come. In the meantime they would have to learn and react to the fact that the British were not—in consequence of an absolute bungle of a policy decision—to deliver the large quantities of ammunition and supplies they desperately needed. In responding to that piece of British administrative stupidity, they would come to know the name, and many Potawatomi would rally to the cause, of an Odawa named Pontiac.

5

Persistence and Change in the French Era

The Potawatomi gained much from their long relationship with France, but in the process they lost their earlier isolated autonomy. They had become part of an increasingly interdependent world, one in which there was to be little place for small tribal societies. Their progressively frequent contacts with Frenchmen—and later with other Euro-Americans—brought in train an irreversible series of cultural changes in numerous aspects of Potawatomi life. Broadly speaking, in the French era these forces operated on the fringes and details of Potawatomi culture, not upon its central patterns. New things and novel practices that were incorporated into the Potawatomi life-style were drawn from a larger inventory of potential changes that might have been. The tribesmen paid little attention to many aspects of French culture, selecting out what they wanted and needed, and rejecting much. Moreover, what the Potawatomi accepted was made over to fit Potawatomi beliefs and values.

Out of the first meetings of the Potawatomi and the French there developed a new set of relationships, a contact community, consisting of roles and relationships structuring the encounters (Spicer 1961: 4). These relationships were essentially harmonious, with Potawatomi technological dependency balanced by French needs for Potawatomi economic and military support. Potawatomi subordination to French political hegemony, for example, was cast in the traditional idiom of kinship, which—in the view of the tribesmen —required regular generosity from their French "father." Maintenance of the alliance required a regular delivery of valued and needed goods to the Potawatomi in the upper lakes. Without this, as Onangizes warned Frontenac and as the English were shortly to discover, friendship could quickly turn to enmity. There is no suggestion that the Potawatomi ever sought to withdraw from contact with the French, and this is the best measure of the quality of their satisfaction.

The French relationship could be harmonious because it served to further Potawatomi interests and because there was little effort on the part of the French to dominate this tribe. Such was not true of all French. The Jesuits, for example, clung to their dream of somehow converting enough Indians to form the basis of a theocratic state, with themselves as the rulers (Hyde 1962: 111). They wanted to create another Paraguay in the Upper Great Lakes, but they were even less successful among the Potawatomi than they had been among the Huron. However, the major roles assumed by the Potawatomi with respect to the French were those of trapper, trader, warrior, and—increasingly so, as the years progressed—wife. Numerous Frenchmen who settled and stayed in the lake country took Indians wives, which promoted a kind of extensive, durable, and lasting change that eventually made Potawatomi society more heterogeneous. Those Frenchmen who lived among these Indians and took wives raised their sons and daughters with values and beliefs that varied considerably from those of other Potawatomi. But overall, the processes of acculturation growing out of contacts with the French were permissive rather than coercive. Except for the Jesuits (and they were none too successful), few sought to force changes on the Potawatomi. Thus the relationship involved mutually acceptable accommodations, mutual interdependency, and a two-way pattern of beneficial symbiosis.

However, the Potawatomi had relationships with peoples other than the French. Clearly, one of the satisfactions of the French alliance for this tribe was that they were able to achieve through it an important ambition, a position of prestige and ascendancy with respect to other tribes. Beyond this, the arrival of Europeans in the upper lakes added new impetus to earlier migrations and relocations caused by tribal wars. The Potawatomi often came into contact with unfamiliar tribes from unknown regions, and as well they entered into new kinds of relationships in unfamiliar environments. So there was cause for acculturative change in these encounters and experiences as well as those involving Europeans. In sum, during the French era there were increased opportunities for the diffusion of new cultural elements from Indian as well as European societies, and increased pressure stimulating new kinds of adaptations and institutions. But none of these dislocated the dominant patterns of Potawatomi ideology and practice. The tribal society and the tribal culture remained intact; indeed, they flourished throughout the French period.

IDEOLOGY II:
NAMES AND IDENTITY

Naming customs and beliefs of the Potawatomi were much like those of other tribes of the Eastern Woodlands and were among the most persistent of all elements of their culture. Concepts and practices concerning personal names were inextricably tied to ideas about the afterworld and the supernatural, the basic social structure, the typical individual's life-cycle, and the distinctive career path of each particular person. Personal names marked uniquely individual characteristics—flaws and failings as well as extraordinary merit and accomplishment. Moreover, they fixed each individual firmly in social space, identifying each child and adult as a member of one or another important social group.[1] Obviously, a single personal name cannot do all of this important social work. Each Potawatomi individual acquired a number of names during the course of a lifetime. One of these—the most durable and lasting, if the least used—was a clan name. Other kinds included status names, war names, and nicknames. After the arrival of the Europeans, many Potawatomi also acquired French or English names, either baptismal names or nicknames.

Of the different types of names, from the point of view of both Potawatomi society and our efforts to reconstruct their history, the most important is the clan name. Each Potawatomi clan had as a part of its incorporeal property a stock of personal names. Some of these were in active use, having been bestowed on living individuals. Others—the names of deceased members of the clan—were cached, held in reserve. These clan names marked distinctive features of the clan eponym or different animals or aspects of natural phenomena which were thought of as parts of the eponym. Thus the Ocean Clan owned and its members were identified by such names as Trickle, Eddy, Rapids, Waterfall, Cataract, Whirlpool, Bay, Fog, Swan, or Snow Goose. The Potawatomi, no less than other societies, had difficulties forming neatly bounded, mutually exclusive categories; hence, the Ocean Clan included the names of some waterfowl that were also found in one or another of the several Bird clans. The latter also included other names such as Flies Across and White Hair (Eagle Clan), Black Loon, White Turkey, and Duck Hawk. Thunder Clan names expressed a proliferation of different kinds or features of thunder or lightning as well as other aspects of the sky, such as Variable Rain, Brings the Clouds, Yellow Thunder, or Sharp Crackling Sound. Many such clan names are easily recognizable as belonging to a particular clan, but in other instances the connotations are so elusive one has to memorize or be told where they belong. Examples of these are Jumps Backward and Stains the Snow (i.e., urine), both of the Wolf Clan, and Curly Hair or Walks Over the Earth, of the Buffalo Clan.[2]

In Potawatomi thinking, these clan names were more than just words used to identify the living and the deceased. Each in its own right was a repository of the accomplishments, the supernatural power, the social position, and the identities of all the individuals who ever bore the name. There is a fundamental principle of thought involved here, one which recurs in other aspects of Potawatomi life, a principle of unity in multiplicity. Thus, the child who was awarded the name of an ancestor literally became identified as one with that ancestor. The French who observed this practice were much taken by it and called it the resurrection or the resuscitation of the dead.[3] It was associated with the belief that part of the spirit of a person resided in the bones, so that if the bones were properly cared for they could rise and germinate into new flesh housing the spirit of those who had the name in earlier generations. In this fashion the memory of the dead was never lost, and the corporate organization of a clan's membership was carried over the boundary of human mortality.

The clan name was bestowed on a child sometime soon after the infant had survived its first month of life. During that period the child was not presented to the father officially, a custom associated with a high infant mortality rate. Once it was evident that the infant would probably survive, the mother brought it into the father's wigwam and shortly thereafter an elaborate naming ceremony was held. At this point the child was formally incorporated into the patrilineal clan of its father, the most important social group it would ever belong to and the center of the most vital relationships. An alternative to the naming ceremony held for an infant was an adoption ceremony wherein an older child or an adult was renamed—given a new clan name which marked an official change in identity, and sometimes a change in clan membership. Adoption was a fundamental mechanism for replacing deceased kinfolk, whether a son or a mother; and like the naming of a child it signified an official, lasting change in social status. The person who named the child, however, was not obligated to bestow a name drawn from the ancestral dead. Generally a clan elder or a religious specialist, he could create a new name of a kind he believed appropriate for the child, one which was distinctive of the clan eponym.

The continuity of many Potawatomi names across the centuries is remarkable. Onangizes met with Count Frontenac in the mid-1670s; yet Onangizes died in 1930—the last Wisconsin Potawatomi man to bear that name and identity, that is (Brown n. d.). European monarchists would appreciate this principle perfectly: Onangizes is dead, long live Onangizes. In 1681 La Salle demonstrated that he had very keen insight into this custom, which was common to other Central Algonquians. This was the year he was working to promote a coalition of tribes around the St. Joseph River in support of his plans for the development of the Illinois country. One of the devices he employed to persuade the Miami they should support him in this plan was to assume the identity of one of their much respected, deceased chiefs, Wabikolkata. In his speech to the Miami, La Salle told them he had taken on the identity of Wabikolkata, that Wabikolkata was no longer dead, that he lived again in La Salle's person, and that he would assume responsibility for the care of the dead chief's family and people (Margary 1878 1: 575–80). La Salle's grasp of the principle involved was good, but imperfect. Or more likely—since he was an excellent observer of Indian customs—he twisted a native practice to his own ends. The perogative of selecting a replacement for "resuscitation" of the name and identity of the deceased chief was not his, but that of the tribal and clan elders to whom the name belonged.

The French, and later the English, confused Potawatomi naming beliefs and practices with their own patrinominal customs. Hence, they did not understand Potawatomi practice when it came to the problem of selecting a successor for the position of a dead okama. The status of okama was not automatically awarded to a son sired by the deceased, although it might be so. Rather, a successor was selected by the clan elders and, through an adoption and naming ceremony, acquired the identity of the deceased, including his status, powers, position, and responsibilities. Europeans and Americans misperceived and thought of Potawatomi succession to the position of okama in terms of hereditary kingships. But a tribal society such as the Potawatomi had no tolerance for an idiot or even a moderately incapable okama, no such practice as a regency, and hence no custom of automatic, strictly patrilineal succession to the position. On the death of an okama the village and clan needed an adult man of demonstrated talent and ability to fill the position quickly, and their customs were tailored to fit this need.

Nonetheless, the French conceived the issue of succession in terms of their own needs and beliefs. In 1721 when Kouatkougy (Kwakwagesa—Practices Flying, Thunder Clan) died near St. Joseph, the French post commander sought to appoint as his successor as okama the son of the elderly Piremon, who was a French-made chief and a Catholic convert. However, the young man demurred, refusing to accept Kouatkougy's French medal on the grounds that he was not properly qualified to wear it or to assume the position (WHC 17: 365–66). It might well have been that Piremon's son was of a different clan from that of Kouatkougy, but the facts on this are not clear, although Piremon was known to have been an assimilated Sauk. In any respect, here French interests and French ideas were intruding on Potawatomi practices involving the selection of a successor to Kouatkougy. This kind of pressure from both French and English—and later the Americans—eventually led to the acceptance by some Potawatomi of the idea of hereditary succession to office, but it was never a change which became fully popular or generally applied.

Women's clan names were either distinctly female in nature or they consisted of a root name with the suffix "-kwē" added; thus Menisikwē—Swooping-Down Woman (Bald Eagle Clan) and Kitasmo—Spotted Bitch (Wolf Clan). But women and men were also commonly known by other names, for individual clan names were not often used in everyday relationships. Potawatomi clan names do not seem to have been secret and guarded, as was the case for many other Indian tribes, but they were quite formal appellations. More commonly used were nicknames of various kinds, including names acquired for valorous (or less than valorous) behavior in battle. War names tended to be particularly sarcastic or ironic, such as Runs Well (i.e., in the wrong direction). Nicknames and status names were as diverse as the full variable range of Potawatomi shapes, sizes, dispositions, temperaments, habits, defects, or odd experiences could make them. Only a few examples will illustrate this fact: Lop Sided, Fatigued, The Thief, Mr. Solitary, Five Medals, Smallpox, Thousand Gold Coins, He Started It (i.e., a war party), Deaf and Dumb (a war name), Fat Woman, The Hog, Young Chief, The Waiter, and Twisted Hand.

The fact that any one Potawatomi individual had different names poses obvious difficulties for historical analysis. For example, a well-known anti-American okama during the first five decades of the nineteenth century, generally identified as Five Medals, was also sometimes known by one or another of four additional names—including Onangizes! The problem is one of identifying which individual is involved in what activity. It occurs when the same name occurs at times too widely separated to involve a single human career. In such instances, it is generally clear that an ancient name has been "resuscitated" and bestowed on a successor. But the problem also occurs when several different individuals in the same period widely separated in space are identified with the same name. In the instance of nicknames or war names, the reinvention of similar names is responsible for such simultaneous occurrence. But in the instance of clan names, one of two different factors is at work. One example is the situation of the same name—Goose or Gull—which belongs to both the Ocean and the Bird clans. In effect, these are not the same names, as they are property of different clans. The alternative is of more interest, the situation of one name from a single clan being bestowed on several individuals at the same time. This happened frequently later in Potawatomi history, and when it did the cause was the geographic separation of parts of a clan. For this reason the namers—being out of contact with one another—lost track of the names that had been bestowed and unknowingly used them several times.

However, during the French era there is no problem with finding too many names for historical and cultural analysis. The problem was of an opposite nature: only a few dozen Potawatomi individuals had their personal names recorded and preserved. We have mentioned most of these in earlier pages. There are so few of them that the greatest value of the personal name cannot be fully exploited. Most of the names recorded by the French were clan names, and hence we can see that they were involved with the Thunder, Fish, Ocean, and probably the Bald Eagle and the Wolf clans. But what of other Potawatomi clans? In 1667 Allouez identified the Hare Clan at Chequamegon, while in 1668 the Bear Clan was contending with two lineages of the Fish Clan at Green Bay over their relationship with the French, yet through 1760 there is not a single mention in documentary sources of any Bear or Hare clan members identified by clan names. The Bear Clan certainly did not disappear in 1669, and just as certainly other clans went unmarked by the French as well.

One additional type of name used to identify individual Potawatomi are those of French origin, either baptismal given names or nicknames. Examples of the former are Gabiniya—Gabriel, Mani—Mary, Manyan—Marion, and Zozas—Joseph. Such names have long been assimilated into Potawatomi language and cultural patterns and are currently used as regular clan names (Landes 1970: 377). Several French-origin nicknames have been cited earlier —Sweet One and Thousand Gold Coins. Many more were likely in use during the French era and went unrecorded in that period. Another source of personal names was Potawatomi expressions for things of French origin. For example, in 1672 Father Louis André spoke of a Potawatomi man who would pay no attention to Christian teaching and who was indeed the epitome—in André's view—of all that was false and satanic in Potawatomi religion. André said he was named Porceau and that "he was a true hog in his conduct" (JR 57: 293). Only many years later was the Potawatomi version of the name recorded as Kokosh or Coe-Cosh (see Plate 4). The domesticated hog (*Sus scrofa*) was not native to North America but was a European import. In 1672 the Potawatomi could only have seen hogs in French settlements along the St. Lawrence, and hence within a few years of becoming aware of such animals they were using a word of their own invention—"Kokosh" is Potawatomi onomatopoeia for a hog's grunt—as a personal name.[4]

SOCIAL ORGANIZATION I: THE CLAN SYSTEM

Through 1760 the French identified by name only ten totems, which Potawatomi word they borrowed to name clans and clan segments. These were the Bear and Hare totems of the Bear Phratry; the Frog, Crab, Turtle, and Sucker (called Carp by the French)—further discriminated into the Red, Black and Golden Sucker totems of the Water Phratry; and the Crane totem of the Bird Phratry. From the few dozen personal names recorded by the French, we can further identify an additional four clans: the Thunder and Bald Eagle clans of the Bird Phratry, the Ocean Clan of the Water Phratry, and the Wolf Clan of the Wolf Phratry. Two phratries—Buffalo and Man—identified many years later are not mentioned or suggested in the French sources. Similarly, an additional thirty-odd clans and clan segments from all six known phratries go unrecognized in the first century of contact between Potawatomi and Euro-peans. Obviously, French knowledge of Potawatomi social organization was partial and limited. The Potawatomi they seem to have known best were mainly from the clans of the Water Phratry, which apparently were predomi-nant in the St. Joseph River and Detroit areas of southern Michigan. Later observers—inquiring systematically about the nature of Potawatomi social life —added the names of some thirty additional clans and clan segments (see Table 2).

An understanding of the Potawatomi clan system can come only from two separate and different perspectives; the Potawatomi's own view of how the

TABLE 2: KNOWN POTAWATOMI PHRATRIES, CLANS, AND LINEAGES

Phratry	Translation	Phratry	Translation
WATER		MAN	
Kitchigumi	Great Sea/Ocean	Neshabē	Man
Gigos	Fish	Manasano	Warrior
Wasi	(Bullhead)*	BEAR	
Name	Sturgeon	Mko	Bear
Nmapena	(Sucker, Carp)	Kaganwikashi	(Grizzly Bear)
	(Golden Sucker)	Wabozo	Hare—or Rabbit
	(Black Sucker)	Nagig	(Coyote)
	(Red Sucker)	Kētetaj (or, Gmepshkwē)	Otter
Mshike	Turtle	Mek	Beaver
	(Frog)	Ogak (or, Kedēmi)	Porcupine
	(Crab)	Kokagi	(Woodchuck)
BIRD		Wabesheshe	(Martin)
Wamigo	Thunderbird	Sibash	(Wildcat)
Megisi	Bald Eagle	BUFFALO	
Wishkino	(Black Eagle)	Bzheke	Buffalo
Kakak	(Duck Hawk)	Mozo	Moose
Kakashi	(Raven—or Crow)	Mishwawa	Elk
Mkedēwashikakak	(Black Hawk)	Seksi	Deer
Kweyashk	(Sea Gull)	WOLF	
Mak	Loon	Mwa	Wolf
Pina	Turkey	Amo (or, Nemosh)	Dog
Sinkabe	(Mud Hen)	Wakwshe	Fox
Chichak	Crane	Esben	Raccoon

* Totems included in parentheses were probably clan segments, that is, newly formed lineages.

SOURCES: Morgan 1959; Skinner 1924/27; Landes 1970; Rutzenthaler 1951; Kinietz 1940; WHC 17: 251; & JR 51: 33.

system was created and operated, and the technical analysis of an outsider. The former tends to be a timeless, mythic, unquestioning view of the matter, while the latter must include a concern with the history of change and adaptation, as well as an effort to understand how the system functioned at any one time.

In the Potawatomi view the totem was the primary community of kinsmen organized in its fundamental principles as a single, much enlarged family. At the center of a person's life, it was the social place where one was born; then, through the naming ceremony, one was identified with an ancestor and allowed to share in the powers and benefits of the clan eponym.

A person's life, ideally, involved service to the totem group, and in turn each person received support, tangible and spiritual. Without the clan, every man was a helpless creature; but without the individual to add his resources to the fortunes and powers of the group, the clan would not prosper and grow. From his place in a clan, each man faced outward armed with customary rules for relating himself to and interacting with other clans. All of the clans and their powers came originally from the culture hero, Wiske, who created the whole system. All clans were thereby essentially one, an example of the principle of unity in diversity mentioned earlier. As the okama of the Wolf Clan instructed his clan-mates, "always respect the clan you are named in. [But] If a member of any other clan calls you for help, render it to him willingly. We are all one people, only we have been brought up under different [clan] rules" (Skinner 1924–27: 150). Members of the same clan addressed one another as niktotem—clan-mate, or more specifically as elder brother, elder sister, or younger sibling, as father, grandmother, or other extended-family kin terms.

The origin myths of the clans, which form part of the great narrative literature of the Potawatomi, prescribe the ingredients of a strict moral order. Running throughout these myths are a number of thematic constants.[5] One of these expresses the need to recognize and regulate competition within and between the different clans. The Fish and Bear clans, for example, laid claim to such primacy and power as entitled them to ascendancy over the other clans, to be acknowledged by having their okama accepted as the okama of the entire tribe. The other clans never gave much evidence of accepting this arrogance. All clans generally, however, made claims to special powers, perogatives, and dispensations—drawing upon their identification with one or another eponym, whether the special powers and privileges of Water, Wolf, or Hare. Competition within the clan was implicit but dangerous, being controlled through rewards granted the man who sought prestige by obtaining manito powers and using them for the benefit of his niktotem. Those men who did not achieve satisfaction in such intraclan competitions are recognized—in both myth and history—as the founders of new clan segments.

The specific thematic elements are numerous. The condition of Tisha before he met Boat Maker is common to the hero-figures of the clan origin myths. These were poor, insignificant, unsuccessful men. They had no wealth, no children, no wives, no kinsmen—until they had a successful encounter with the supernatural. Again—man is a largely helpless creature dependent for his success on aid from the spirit world. Even then it is not often that man gets that which he wants. He is apt to obtain something important that he did not anticipate, and then he may need the aid of his fellows to recognize its value. These myths teach that a greater wisdom sometimes comes from the spirit world through dreams and visions that can be obtained from parents and elders, yet a man can only uncover the true message in his vision with the aid of others, usually elders. Man is thus doubly dependent—on the spirit world for the original vision, and on the social world to realize its potential. Yet one's niktotem are also dependent on the individual man to make fresh and original, recreative contact with the supernatural, so as to replenish and refurbish the special powers of the clan. The individual and his group are thereby linked in mythic and moral harmony in a fashion expressing both the values of joint, cooperative action with kinsmen and the importance of individual initiative. For, after all, a man's family gave him his main reason for living; without family he is nothing. If his family be poor, there is no worry, for a poor man has as much influence with the spirit world as the richest one. But regardless of wealth and status, a man must honor his clan unto death; whatever special power or wealth he may have must be shared and used for the benefit of all.

The language of Potawatomi myth and morality is not the same as the language of objective analysis, but the former balances and is balanced by the latter. From this external viewpoint, the origin myths and other Potawatomi opinions concerning clans are also partly historical documents and partly evidence of fundamental social structure. In the Potawatomi perspective, each totem is fully the equivalent of every other—each is the same kind of logical social thing. From the outside we have to see their differences: some clans are older, some younger, some larger, some smaller, while all have characteristics which the Potawatomi themselves did not consciously recognize.

There was a time when there were no clans. But this was likely before or early in the period of occupation of the western Michigan protohistoric estate. Little can be said about this prehistoric, preclan condition except that the Potawatomi were then likely organized as small, mobile, hunting and gathering bands, as were their Northern Algonquian kinsmen. With their adaptation to a more sedentary existence came the invention of the clan principle and the expansion of the idea of individual spirit power and identification with a supernatural animal or element to include a whole social group. Early on, the Potawatomi clans were certainly few. There is no way of fully demonstrating this interpretation, but the earliest clans were possibly nearly coextensive with the larger units we call phratries, which are groups of clans linked together in logical, ritual, and social ways. Thus the earliest Potawatomi social clans might likely have been Water, Sky, Horned Mammals, Hornless Mammals, and Man.

If this interpretation is correct, then there must have been some principle at work which encouraged and structured the organization of new social units like the original clans, identified as extensions of them, but duplicating their basic structure and allowing for the growth of new clanlike segments. Potawatomi origin myths, some of which are hardly more than an oral history of fairly recent events, describe precisely this kind of mechanism. The founder of the Kakak—Duck Hawk totem was a famous Kansas Potawatomi war leader of the last half of the nineteenth century, a man known by the same name. His personal spirit-helper—acquired during his puberty fast—became the eponym of the Duck Hawk clan segment. Here one able man, aided by his personal vision power and his spirit-helper, founded a new lineage (Skinner 1924–27: 114–17). The origin story of the Wolf Clan is similar, although the chronology of events is obscured by the antiquity and mythic phrasing of the narrative. This story tells how a man named Wolf claimed to know a lot about leading, governing, and aiding people, and so he gathered together some of his relatives and started a little village of only eight wigwams, a village which prospered. After awhile Wolf invited others in the tribe to a feast and told them that this village was now the Wolf Clan and he described his clan's special characteristics. The mechanism involved in the creation of new totems is thus clear. One individual initiates a move to create a new totemic unit, and after some time the additional clan segment is accepted by others as a valid part of the tribe. Obviously, more efforts to create totemic units were attempted than ever succeeded. Some prospered and grew in size and influence, while others failed. As late as the 1930s, some few Kansas Potawatomi were still creating new clans, the last such being the Angel Clan, which had just one member.

There is no suggestion in Potawatomi thinking of a belief that members of a clan are descended from the totemic animal or phenomena. The relationship was a supernatural one. Each totemic eponym comes to a founder in a vision and promises aid and assistance, specifies rules for dress, face paint, medicines, rituals, feasting, and conduct. As Skinner pointed out in his analysis of clan origin myths, although the Potawatomi say generally that in the beginning Wiske gave man the sacred bundles, which are the most important part of each clan's equipment, the origin myths of the clans suggest a different sequence of events. In each myth the clan organization existed before the sacred bundle, which was acquired as a consequence of the dream experience of a named individual clan member (1924–27: 57). That is, the process of social change was prior and fundamental; the clan system was invented and developed before the sacred bundles were acquired. These bundles, called Pitchkosan—Watches Over Us, consisted of otter or mink skin bags, much decorated with bead and quill work, ribbons, and feathers. Each one contained powerful mementos, heirlooms, talismans, and fetishes appropriate to the clan's eponym. Thus the Pitchkosan housed and embodied the special supernatural powers of each clan. Pitchkosan in turn is one of the alternate names of Wiske, a name used when he was being helpful to poor neshnabē. The bundle was altar and sacrament, the central focus of clan rituals during which it was opened, worshiped, and purified.

In an analytic view, during the French era Potawatomi clans and clan segments were the most important feature of the tribe's social structure. By and large the clans were residential groups, one clan constituting the core membership of the village, or several clan segments that of a larger, composite village. Evidently, during the latter part of the French regime some of the larger Potawatomi clans became dispersed, with segments found among the villages of widely separated locales. This process of dispersion continued and was intensified in the period of British and American sovereignty, but nonetheless the clan principle remained a vital feature of Potawatomi social life well into the twentieth century. The functions of the clans were numerous and critical to the welfare of both the individual and the whole society. They acted as agents of status placement, fixing each child and adult into a particular place in the village and tribe. The most important personal relationships were those involving niktotem—clan-mates, who officiated at life cycle rites from birth to death, and who formed the major cooperating group in between.

The principal collective functions of the clan were the arrangement and conduct of important rituals, feasts, and dances. Each clan had its own unique rules and peculiarities for such ritual work, although all followed a common pattern. Similarly, each clan had specialized rights, obligations, and prohibitions, frequently directly symbolic of the clan eponym. The eponym was the crucial base for much creative elaboration. The sacred bundle of the Warrior Clan, for example, contained magic ties for binding prisoners and a powerful miniature bow and arrow; that of the Buffalo Clan, a buffalo-tail amulet and powerful buffalo medicine. Members of the Wolf Clan were the most savage of all people, and a good present for a member was a mat or blanket, for wolves liked to lie down. The Bear people were easily angered and hard to please, just as are bears. Thunder Clan warriors struck fastest and hardest of all in battle. Members of all clans, in seasonal and special-purpose rituals, mimicked their eponyms in dance and song.

For many purposes each clan was relatively autonomous of others; however, all were ultimately interdependent, and the basic social structure reflected this fact. Since clan-mates were related to one another as close kinsmen, each was an exogamous social group. Bear Clan men, for example, sought their wives from the daughters of other clans, while Bear Clan women, too, married out into other clans, generally changing their residence to live within the village of the husband's people. Thereby, the clans were linked as intermarrying groups, and the Potawatomi tribe in this fashion became a network of affinal kinfolk. However, each clan was also aligned with one or more others with similar eponyms into one of six phratries. These had few specific functions, except to arrange and structure rituals and feasts. Then they had reciprocal relationships, with one phratry obligated to act as host, another to provide the heralds or waiters, and a third to provide the speaker for the ritual. Since much of Potawatomi collective life was oriented around seasonal and special-purpose ritual, the system of providing reciprocal cooperation using the phratries and clans as the basis for organization gave internal cohesion and integrity to the tribal society. In at least these two important ways—the selection of mates and the conduct of group ritual—the clan system operated as an integrative, centripetal force binding together the dispersed parts of the tribe. There were other such centripetal influences as well, since any large-scale activity involving the cooperation of more men and women than there were members of a single clan—warfare or large-scale hunting for example—could be and often was organized in terms of the overall clan system.

In sum, the Potawatomi totem was a patrilineal descent group whose membership formed a corporate organization, which was the core of those residing in the village. A small village, for example, consisted of male members of one or another clan, plus their wives, who were drawn from other clans, and their immature children (see Figure 8). Later in the French era some larger villages were composite units consisting of parts of several clans— of the same phratry or not—and their associated extended family units. These segments, organized by various social and ritual devices, formed the interconnected tribal structure. While for some purposes each clan-village was relatively autonomous, for many others it was dependent upon cooperative relations with others. The corporate functions of these clans ranged from the conduct of ritual, to the socialization of the young, to major economic and political activities. Finally, given the built-in mechanism and propensity for generating new clan-segments, the tribe was well equipped to deal with increased population and with new economic and political stresses and opportunities, and to expand its territory. In this latter sense the Potawatomi clan was self-reproducing, via a process of social mitosis.

In addition to the clan system the Potawatomi tribe had another mechanism for subdividing the entire tribe or village for special purposes. All Potawatomi—regardless of age, sex, clan affiliation, or residence—were assigned to one of two "halves" or "sides." The principle of assignment was simple and

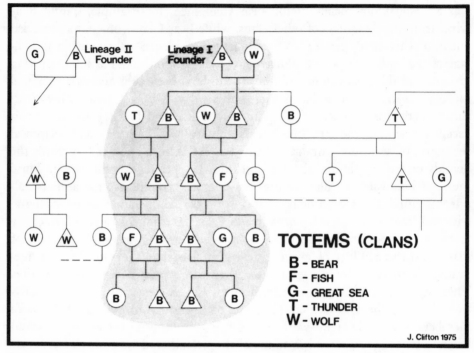

Figure 8. The basic socioeconomic unit, Potawatomi lineage and extended family. Note that all "Bs" are members of Lineage I of the Bear Clan, except the founder of Bear Clan Lineage II. The shaded area includes the members of the coresidential, extended-family group built around the Bear Clan segment. This extended family might constitute one small village or a part of a larger one.

unambiguous. All children whose birth order was first, third, fifth, and so on were assigned to the senior side, called Oshkēsh, while all those whose birth order was an even number were assigned to the junior side—Kishko. This was a dual division or moiety system whose organization had some parallels in Potawatomi beliefs about the spirit world. The dual division thus cuts across lineage, clan, village, and family memberships to create two separate memberships. An important fact about the principle of assignment is that it strictly randomizes the membership of both sides. Each was thereby composed of a random selection of ages, sexes, sizes, talents, skills, and dispositions. This moiety system was called into action only for a few limited purposes, for the organization of La Crosse teams, for the selection of gambling partners, and for similar activities involving the controlled expression of rivalry, competition, and hostility within the larger village or society. Thus the dual division system acted as a tension-relieving mechanism in rule-bound, formalized rivalries. The moiety system has been remarkably persistent: traditional Potawatomi in

Kansas and Wisconsin still use it to organize teams as did their ancestors in the French era.

LEADERSHIP
AND GOVERNANCE II:
THE EMERGENT CHIEF

The historical facts are clear with respect to the creation of a novel political role during the French era. This role, that of the chief, was undoubtedly built upon older Potawatomi ideas and practice concerning the selection and responsibilities of clan leaders. But just as certainly it took on a new form in consequence of French expectations, ideas, and preferences; and it was further structured to fit the new kinds of pressures on tribal leaders that developed as a consequence of European intrusions and the dislocation of many tribal societies. In earlier years much time had to be given to group deliberation on new policies, while the powers of the individual okama were severely limited. The traditional okama was, first and foremost, an agent and a creature of the clan-villages, selected by the clan elders, closely supervised by many, a supremely public if relatively powerless figure. This was not the kind of leadership role compatible with French hierarchical expectations or practice, nor was it one which could be fully effective in an era of frequent migration, grave economic and political stress, and rapid technological and economic change.

The chief's role that emerged was a composite of all these elements and influences. From the French perspective, the chief was their agent, made by their action and kept in power with their support. The practice of awarding "medals" to okamek of demonstrated fidelity symbolized and validated their appointment, while the custom of funneling economic support—the "presents" —through faithful chiefs gave them new status and prestige in the eyes of their own tribesmen. From the point of view of his own niktotem, in contrast, the okama was expected to be generous, true, and faithful to the interests of his own kinfolk. In this fashion the okama became a middleman, an intercultural go-between, a man who had to play an increasingly delicate role in two separate and often opposed social systems. In the longer course of history, what was going on in the Upper Great Lakes between 1668 and 1760 was the invention of a new form of colonial governance. In the later history of European empires, this style of administering native peoples came to be known as indirect rule. It involved, pure and simple, the use of existing, traditional political roles to further the interests of the colonial power.

From the perspective to the individual okama, say Onangizes or Winamek, being a chief was a balancing act. During most of the French era the balance favored the tribal society. The French were never so strong that they did not need Potawatomi loyalty and services. Thus Onangizes could think of himself as an equal to Frontenac and La Salle, and he could travel to Montreal, there to confront the governor in his own chambers with demands, fully expecting that his words would be heeded and respected. However, the seeds of intertribal and interclan conflict were well planted and richly fertilized, although they would not bear their bitter fruits until the time of Tecumsah many years later. The mere fact that the okama of the Potawatomi Thunder Clan could travel to Montreal and there confer in private and make commitments unknown to and unqualified by his niktotem guaranteed later conflict. The fact that one okama might presume to speak for many or all Potawatomi clans simply exacerbated potential dissension. In the French view it was most convenient to have one faithful okama speak for all. Their expectation was that he might command and manage his tribesmen. Nothing was further from Potawatomi thinking. In their view a spokesman was a man who accurately summarized and represented the views of all, not one who took it on himself to make private commitments or to generate new policy. Clearly, men like Onangizes had ambitions which far outreached the grasp of their traditional responsibilities.

Those who pioneer in the acting out of new social roles are always beset by anxieties and conflicts. In the instance of those Potawatomi okamek who began acting and talking like chiefs, we can discern one major different kind of strain. Onangizes himself was apparently Potawatomi by birth and early experience. Hence he matured in an atmosphere where loyalty to the clan was a value most highly stressed. For him to assume responsibilities of leadership which extended beyond the bounds of his clan had to be hazardous. When he did so—it is clear from his words in council—it was by assuming a second traditional role, that of kiktowenene—speaker. But Potawatomi (and other Central Algonquian) speakers were nominated, they were closely observed by those who appointed them, they were disciplined if their words were inappropriate, they could have little opportunity to express personal interest, and their position was temporary. Onangizes, and later others, went beyond these traditional expectations and limitations, added elements of the speaker's role to that of okama, and in the process altered the role of okama in irreversible ways.

There is a fundamental weakness in the structure of political leadership in a segmentary tribe like the Potawatomi. Each okama was first and foremost a representative of one clan group, and he was closely controlled by that clan. When the interests of all constituent clans coincided, there was no serious problem in achieving a durable, shared consensus. But, even then, the process of achieving mutual agreement was vastly time consuming, requiring many days of discussion, deliberation, and ritualized validation. When the interests of the clans did not, however, converge, then it was an entirely different matter. Then the clans would go their separate policy ways. There was none to say no or otherwise to them. The weakness lies on the side of executive management, which is simply another way of expressing the fact that the Potawatomi placed little value on dominance by an individual or group. Both the problems of segmentation and executive control could be partly managed by leaders who were not tied to a particular clan, men perhaps not even Potawatomi in origin. Such men would lack the restrictions placed on traditional okama by clan-mates, and they would be freer to act in their own interests, or in the interests of a new kind of power base or interest group. Some of the earliest Potawatomi chiefs were precisely of this sort. They were Eastern Algonquian (Winamek) or Sauk (Piremon) by birth, and they were appointed by the French to their new roles (Clifton 1975a).

In the latter years of the French regime it is clear that appointed chiefs were starting to proliferate. Not only did the governor of New France have his favored Potawatomi okamek, but on the local scene a Jesuit priest or a commanding officer of a post would have his. Soon thereafter, there were Potawatomi chiefs attached and beholden to very diverse imperial and national interests—French, Spanish, British, and American. By the opening years of the American period, the appointment and management of faithful chiefs was to become a device used by many for subventing special interests within the tribe and for subverting the loyalties of men who came to neglect the needs of their niktotem for the new prestige and power to be obtained for their loyalty to outsiders.

It is clear, therefore, that during the French era the patterns of Potawatomi leadership and governance were changing in adaptation to their altered circumstances. These changes involved actual alterations in the kind of behaviors practiced by some okamek, if not all. What is not clear is that there was little change in the ideals of proper behavior for these clan leaders. Myths, legends, and traditional history materials collected in the twentieth century continue to specify as right and proper an inward-looking, conscientious, generous, powerless leader who thought first and largely of his kinsmen. Thereby, well before 1760, an important source of personal and group conflict had been generated in Potawatomi society. The idealized prescriptions and proscriptions of Potawatomi ideology no longer fitted the actual behavior of many of their leaders.

RELIGION I

The distinction between sacred and secular and the sense of religion being confined to a separate institution are European ideas which had no true counterparts in Potawatomi thought or practice. Much of what we might call religion was intertwined and indistinguishable from routine economic, political, and social activities in the daily life of these tribesmen. The Potawatomi, as is true of most other tribal peoples, were imbued with and expressed a magical world-view that conceived the universe as a society, not a mechanism (Wax 235). The relationship between a Potawatomi and any part of that universe was a social one. Animals, plants, features of the landscape, and events in the heavens had humanlike characteristics which required men to relate to them in a human fashion, with, for example, the emotions of compassion or fear, and in the idiom of kinship or other traditional social relations. But even when the French first made contact with the Potawatomi, their religious beliefs and practices were a complex conglomerate of elements ancient and more recent. Like all the tribes that came from the original Siberian homeland, they had a special, ancient relationship with Bear and worshiped primordial spirits such as Sun and Moon. Soon after their first contacts with the French, new religious practices were added, not by direct diffusion from European sources but through internal change processes, by way of adapting existing tribal ideologies to the stresses caused by these new associations.

Each individual Potawatomi was a religious practitioner in his own right, for his own protection and welfare. All personal power—the possibility of success in hunting or planting for instance—came from visions. All were required through fasting to deliberately seek visionary experiences whereby each person might obtain contact with supernatural figures. The effort made at puberty to achieve such contact was one of the most important experiences of everyone's life. However, Potawatomi practice differed substantially from that of some other Algonquian tribes in this respect, for the youth seeking a vision was closely supervised by elders to insure that his behavior was proper and appropriate, while once the visionary experience was obtained it was publicly discussed to see if it was valid (Landes 1963: 565). Thus the Potawatomi were less individualistic and more subject to external social controls than such societies as the Ojibwa and Odawa. The specific spirit helper obtained in such visionary experiences was believed to represent one aspect of Wiske, one of the numerous disguises assumed by this important supernatural figure, whom the Potawatomi sometimes called the Master of Life. Early French and American observers misperceived Potawatomi ideas about Wiske, believing he was conceived as a single, all-powerful high-god analogous to their own (Keating 119–20). But Wiske was only one of numerous spirits, although one who was recognized as very powerful and who took many forms. The power obtained in vision could be inherently either good or evil, and it could be used for either good or evil, which is why its acquisition was closely supervised by the elders. Spiritual power was a potentially dangerous commodity.

At the time the French arrived the Potawatomi had three different kinds of religious specialists or shamans. One was the Chaskyd—Diviner, who employed a variety of techniques to capture the attention and faith of his audience. He juggled, used ventriloquism, was a master of sleight of hand, and for a price could foretell the future or locate lost objects or loved ones. The second was the Wabino—Dawn Man, a fire-eating, fire-handling, fire-walking specialist who mystified, amused, and provided practical advice. The third practitioner was the medical specialist, the curer, a sucking doctor who was also adept in sleight of hand and similar skills sufficient to capture the faith of the ill and those concerned with their welfare. Beyond these individual shamans and the religious and magical practices of all individual Potawatomi lay the clan rites and observances. These were the prime locus of collective religious observance, practiced mainly on a seasonal basis. Just as individual medicines, fetishes, and charms were lodged in personal medicine bundles, the collective magic of the clan was wrapped in its larger and more powerful bundle. Both the individual and clan bundles were called Pitchkosan (Skinner 1924–27: 55–56; Landes 1963: 576). The clan thus was the largest social unit which could be conveniently and regularly organized as a single religious congregation. In religion the Potawatomi tribe suffered the same weakness characteristic of leadership and governance—too much segmentation.

It must not be supposed that the Potawatomi's faith in any or all of their religious or magical practices was absolute. Their attitudes towards such beliefs were essentially instrumental: these were traditional techniques to be used in achieving desirable ends. And their attitude was also empirical and questioning: if a particular technique or practice did not work well, another might be sought. Father Louis André recorded how this worked in the late winter of 1672 among the Potawatomi near Suamico on the west shore of Green Bay, and also how he sought to exploit their (certainly temporary) loss of faith for his own purposes (JR 57: 297). It had been a cold, hard winter, and by February the Potawatomi were starving. The young men, wrote Father André, were "losing their faith in dreaming" and approached André wishing to try Christian prayer in the hope that it might give them success in sturgeon spearing. André noted, "What served greatly to disabuse them was the Bear-hunt which took place while I was in the village. All the young men were in the field for ten days: they had dreamed of bears; and according to their dreams and their feasts, the Carnage was to be great. They had even invited the neighbors to prepare to visit them and eat bear meat with them; but not one of them was successful, and not a single bear was killed." Under the great physiological stress of starvation, these young Potawatomi warriors were willing to try anything, including the magical practices of the Jesuits. However, Christian prayer is no more effective in soliciting the cooperation of bears than is deliberate vision-seeking, and the hunger-motivated openmindedness towards André's approach did not lead to any known lasting changes in Potawatomi religious practice.

During the French era there were, however, two important changes in Potawatomi religious forms, neither of which had anything to do with European models or teachings. The first represented a borrowing from other tribes of a ritual means for establishing improved, peaceful relations with strange societies. The second was the generation of a nativistic movement among the Algonquian tribes in the Upper Great Lakes which provided them with a new religious institution, one which functioned to improve the solidarity between the separate clans of a tribe, thus contributing to tribal cohesiveness.

The ritual borrowed to provide an improved means of dealing with the problem of increasingly frequent contact with strange, new, and distant tribes was the calumet ceremony. Prior to 1666–1667 this ceremony was not known to the Potawatomi, being confined to the tribes south of them, such as the Illinois (JR 51: 47). The Potawatomi apparently took over this ceremony during their visit to Chequamegon Bay that winter, for the next spring they welcomed Perrot to Green Bay with a calumet ritual. Properly speaking, what the French called the calumet was the stem only of the long, elaborately decorated, highly symbolic pipe. Later usage extended the word to include the separate pipe bowl, which was made of stone or fired clay. Together, stem and bowl were used as an altar in a ritual signifying and validating a compact between different tribes. Tobacco was burned and wafted over visitors, or over things thought to be sacred, "incensing them," as the French described it. The calumet was employed as a passport or safe-conduct pass for travelers into strange parts, and it was also used in ratifying alliances, concluding and sanctifying peace councils, and to attest agreements (Hodge 1911 1: 191–95). The use of the calumet made sacred—at least temporarily—any such agreement. Thereby, in acquiring this ceremony the Potawatomi obtained an improved means of dealing with foreigners, which was needed in those years, especially because of their ambition to achieve greater influence and renown.

The second new institution dealt with the problem of ritual, magical, and religious segmentation within the tribe, a problem common to the Ojibwa and Odawa as well as the Potawatomi. Again, this development occurred at Chequamegon Bay among the Ojibwa clans gathered there, and the period of invention and institutionalization centered around the year 1680 (Hickerson 1963; 1970: 51–163). This was the religious cult later known as the Midewiwin (in Potawatomi, literally Spirit Doings), which also became known as the Grand Medicine Society. Hickerson's careful ethnohistorical analysis indicates that the Midewiwin developed as a nativistic movement among the tribes gathered around the trading posts at Chequamegon. It consisted of a group of religious specialists who sought to obtain a monopoly on supernatural power. This cult group organized itself as a semisecret priesthood who pooled the individual powers of formerly separate and independent religious practitioners. Mide priests were generally men, but in some tribes women were allowed to join. Jointly the Mide priests used their powers for symbolic "killing" and "curing," and a major rite was centered on the death and rebirth of a victim. As an organized priesthood within each tribe, the Mednanenewek—Mide Men (priests) became a special repository for religious lore, tribal history, and tradition. Much of their knowledge was written in pictographs on birch-bark scrolls, which were used as aids to memory for practitioners. Membership in the priesthood was carefully controlled and limited. Candidates were screened, sponsored, and accepted as novitiates only with the unanimous consent of the Mednanenewek, and then only after the payment of large initiation fees.

The Midewiwin was long thought to be a precontact Algonquian and Siouan religious institution common to many of the tribes of the Upper Great Lakes. Hickerson has amply demonstrated that it was not. Instead, it developed out of the contact situation in response to a need for pantribal institutions which could aid in the unification of independent clan groups. Its major functions were such as to have exactly this result: the Mide men kept careful watch on potential deviates and traitors, overseeing any development that might threaten tribal welfare and interests. They casually and mysteriously threatened death to the unwary, the unscrupulous, and the uncertain and hence reinforced traditional norms of conduct in ways that the okamek of the clans could not. There are no clear mentions of the Midewiwin by name among the Potawatomi (or for that matter any other tribe) before 1718 (Sabrevois 1718: 367–68), although there are numerous fragmented descriptions of Mide-like practices well before then. We should not expect casual French visitors or agents to know much of a highly secret society which was in large part anti-alien in its ideology and activities. However, in later years—when Englishmen and Americans were more numerous and the Potawatomi relatively fewer—the descriptions of Mide activities are more frequent, if not particularly perceptive.[6] In 1824, for example, William Keating became convinced that the Mide priests were a specialized society of cannibals who had the privilege and duty of eating the tribe's enemies (1824: 106). This was the kind of thing the Mide men wanted others to believe, but Potawatomi cannibalism was not a practice restricted to the Mednanenewuk.

ECONOMY
AND TECHNOLOGY

It is in the areas of material culture, instrumental skills and techniques, subsistence activities, production, distribution, and exchange that the greatest and most lasting changes in Potawatomi adaptations occurred during the French period. Again we must remember that such rubrics as economics and technology do not neatly fit traditional Potawatomi patterns of thought. Father André's experience with the Potawatomi at Suamico on Green Bay in 1672 illustrates this nicely. The young Potawatomi hunters had become dissatisfied with one of the important "tools" they used to insure success in hunting, namely, their reliance on visionary experience to give directions to the men out seeking bear. To Father André they seemed willing to substitute Christian prayer for dreaming, and thus they saw both as features of their technology, as instruments to be used towards the achievement of subsistence goals. Moreover, the same incident points to another important feature of their life. Success in hunting was not only merely a means to subsistence ends, it was also one way of obtaining prestige in the eyes of the other tribesmen who had been invited to a bear feast. Their growing involvement in the fur trade was substantially motivated by quite this same pattern of prestige and recognition wants. To a very large extent the Potawatomi were concerned with the personal and social benefits that might accrue in their favor from securing European trade goods, at least as much so as the immediate saving in labor, improvement in technique, or increase in volume of game taken that came from accepting a superior technology.

In an important sense, by avidly accepting European-made things, the Potawatomi got more than they bargained for. They could not have foreseen, predicted, or prepared themselves for the new wants and ramifications that came in train with the new tools and materials. By readily accepting copper pots, iron knives and axes, and steel firearms, the Potawatomi had committed themselves to dependency upon distant manufacturers and to a complex web of economic relationships between point of fabrication and point of distribution. They quickly learned to want metal pots and axes, but they could not create these themselves. Once they had firearms, they were dependent upon the necessary supplies for their use—powder, shot, balls, and auxiliary tools. Moreover, having obtained complex machines like muskets, they were also dependent on Europeans for their upkeep and repair, since these were fragile, easily broken tools and weapons, and the Potawatomi had acquired no skills in metal-working.

Beyond this—and more importantly—the availability of these newly valued goods stimulated the need for a means of getting them (Barnett 1953: 150). For the Potawatomi—and many other tribes—this necessarily meant an involvement in the fur trade or in other productive work that could provide them with ample supplies of goods desired by the French and the English. As we have seen earlier, later in their relationship with the French the Potawatomi also moved into service occupations, exchanging their services as warriors in colonial wars for the necessaries of their existence. To anticipate later developments, it must be recognized that the new economic relationships with Europe flourished and were viable only so long as the Potawatomi and other tribes were in a position to supply highly valued commodities. When European tastes changed, or when their markets were flooded, or more critically when the supply of available fur-bearing animals plummeted, the Potawatomi would be left in an extremely disadvantageous position. Long before this happened (in the 1820s), these tribesmen had become involved in the commitment of an intangible—they pledged their political and military loyalties in exchange for the regular delivery of gifts. This involved the establishment by French and English of a custom of annually delivering a basic supply of "Indian presents," in the expectation that this practice would generate faithful loyalty. When the Potawatomi no longer had sufficient furs, and when the value of their services in war declined, they were forced to other expedients so as to assuage their insatiable wants for Euro-American products. At that point (in the 1790s) they started living off their capital, by leasing and selling tracts of land. Thus the generation of new wants for technological novelties conditioned many aspects of Potawatomi relationships to European powers and other tribes.

Some of the European technological novelties were accepted as substitutes for traditional things—steel knives and axes, material for clothing, clay pipes, fish hooks, glass beads. Some were in satisfaction of newly established wants —brandy and rum, horses, mirrors, European-style uniforms and clothing. Some were derivatives of other things—gun flints and gun-worms, cotton and silk thread, medals. By the time the English arrived to replace the French, the Potawatomi shopping list was very long indeed. It included such things as: awls; silver armbands; axes; silver brooches; breastplates; woolen blankets, in a half-dozen weights and sizes and several colors; calico, striped cotton material, and broadcloth; elegant coats for chiefs, ordinary coats for warriors; horn, ivory, and basswood combs; leather; wooden and metal containers in many shapes and sizes for various purposes; silver earbobs; gun flints; flags; feathers; flannel; fish hooks; silver gorgets; fine rifles, excellent muskets for chiefs and other distinguished figures, plain muskets for the common herd; silk and cotton handkerchiefs; gunpowder; brass, tin, and copper kettles; mirrors; large and small medals; butcher knives and clasp knives; bar iron; molten cloth; sewing needles; osnaburg (a rough cotton cloth); clay pipes; ribbons in many widths and colors; scissors; swanskin (a fine cotton material) and cotton shirting; fire steels; stroud (a coarse woolen material); tobacco of various qualities and flavors; thread; iron harpoon heads; vermilion; hats large and small, fancy and common; Irish linen; files, hammers, and tongs; charcoal; rosin; borax; and a large variety of bottled and boxed patent medicines, nostrums, gewgaws, ornaments, and things fancy and frivolous (RG 10 Vol. 37: 21210–12).

One kind of technological change is of very special interest because it has gone almost unmentioned in the records of contact between the Indians of the Great Lakes and the Europeans, and as well because it had a particularly critical impact on the core of subsistence activities of the Potawatomi and similar tribes. In the mid-eighteenth century many Potawatomi were experiencing a revolution in the area of transportation, but of this there is not a single direct reference in the contemporary French sources. By the time of the Revolutionary War, those in the St. Joseph area and certainly Potawatomi in other areas had abandoned the use of birch-bark canoes for long-distance transportation and had substituted for them the use of horses. The early history of the acquisition of the horse by this tribe is unknown, although the basic framework can be ascertained. The substitution of horses for canoes as the favored means of long-distance transportation for Potawatomie of the St. Joseph River villages must have required several decades; hence we conclude these tribesmen acquired horses in substantial numbers in the 1750s, for horses were well established by 1775. The first horse had arrived in New France in 1647 but soon died. In 1667 Louis XIV's colonial minister Colbert sent the first contingent of breeding stock to the colony, where the animals flourished, proliferating and over the years adapting to the rigors of the climate (Kellogg 1925: 121). Thus at the same time the Potawatomi began visiting the settlements on the St. Lawrence River, horses started arriving in sufficient numbers to be useful (Douville & Casanova 100, 185). Here, on the St. Lawrence River, is where the Potawatomi saw their first horses, but it is highly unlikely that they received their first horses directly from New France. The water route taken and the vessels used would have prohibited transportation of horses back to the Lake Michigan area.

But early in the eighteenth century horses from the Spanish Southwest were becoming available in the region immediately south and east of Potawatomi territory. Before 1723 the Illinois and the Missouri tribes were obtaining Spanish horses, and these were being traded east of the Mississippi to the Chickasaw and Creek (Jablow 1974: 161; Swanton 1946: 348–49). The Chickasaw became particularly proficient in horse raising and were famed for their own breed. By the 1750s English traders from the Atlantic colonies too were penetrating the interior country with their pack-horse trains. Thus, by about 1750, the Potawatomi were in a central position with respect to the diffusion and availability of horses. As discussed earlier, the Potawatomi may have gotten their first horses, in any appreciable number, as part of their share of the spoils of General Braddock's defeat in 1755 (Copely 263), although they may have obtained a few earlier. By the time horses became available to them, they had long been familiar with the French use of horses; they already had some knowledge of the care, feeding, and use of these valuable animals. Like other Eastern tribes, the Potawatomi paid little attention to their horses at the end of a day's work, freeing them to forage for themselves but belling them so as to locate them more easily. Their early use of horses was not so spectacular as was the case on the High Plains, for their principal function was as pack animals.

Therein lay the key importance of horses to tribes like the Potawatomi. Before the acquisition of such animals, they were severely limited in the amount of goods they could transport long distances overland. Like other Algonquians, they probably used dogs as pack animals to some degree (Ray 1974: 165), but the principal burden-bearers for the tribe were Potawatomi women. The acquisition of horses and their use as pack animals considerably relieved women from a great deal of drudgery. Moreover, goods carried on horses instead of canoes did not have to be portaged. The new mode of transportation was not limited to watercourses, nor was it entirely closed down in winter. Wherever a man could walk, a pack horse could follow, carrying his goods and supplies. By the mid-seventeenth century the Potawatomi, like other Algonquian tribes of the Upper Great Lakes, could get horses from several different directions. Indeed, the acquisition of horses was a major motivation for raiding the Chickasaw or the Osage or the English settlements on the Pennsylvania and Virginia frontiers (Voegelin & Tanner 1974: 127–28).

The impact of the horse on the cultures of the tribes in the Great Lakes region or in the Eastern Woodlands has not been studied in as great a depth as it has in the case of the tribes of the Great Plains. In the Potawatomi instance, however, some of the consequences of acquiring horses are immediately clear. The use of horses as pack animals (and later for riding purposes) improved the transportation facilities of the tribe, enabling them to travel over more routes during more months of the year. Since horses were self-reproducing and because their numbers could also be augmented through trade or raids, they reduced the amount of labor that formerly had to be given over to the construction and repair of canoes. And they substantially reduced the heavy work that had previously fallen on the women's shoulders. In effect, the horse further opened up the southern and western prairie lands to the Potawatomi. Thus the acquisition of horses certainly facilitated the expansion of the tribal estate as the Potawatomi moved out onto the Illinois prairies in the second half of the eighteenth century and into other areas where birch-bark canoes could not carry them.

6
Contest for Sovereignty: 1761-1795

In the three decades following the British victory in the French and Indian War one paramount issue dominated the affairs of those people who lived and others who had an interest in the Trans-Appalachian West. This was a generation of struggle for supremacy over the vast, rich territory between the Mississippi River and the Appalachians. The parties in contention were many. During most of this period three empires—Great Britain, France, and Spain —and the new United States were embroiled in a diplomatic, economic, and military contest for control and ascendancy in this area. The interests of these Euro-American powers were sometimes compatible but often at odds, resulting in shifting coalitions and alignments either with or against one another. Seldom was any imperial or national policy, founded entirely on interests in the interior country, either long-lasting or consistent with other governmental policies or aims. From the view of the Euro-American officials involved, these were thirty-odd years of temporary ends and makeshift means. It was a period of expediency, with the course of events influenced by forces beyond the control of any government.[1]

Caught on the ground itself were the native tribal societies, the Five Nations Iroquois, Shawnee, Delaware, Wyandot, Miami, Cherokee, Creek, Odawa, Ojibwa, Kickapoo, Mascouten, Menomini, Sauk, Fox—and the Potawatomi. The interests of these societies were also sometimes compatible and sometimes at odds, and so these groups too were thrust into shifting coalitions and alignments for or in opposition to one another, and in concert with or antagonistic to one or another of the Euro-American powers involved. Conventional wisdom has it that these tribes were defending the precious lands they had occupied for untold centuries, but in fact by 1763 none occupied or claimed the same territory they had when Champlain first arrived on the St. Lawrence River. If the French or the newly nationalized Americans had their frontiers to settle and to defend, so too did the native societies on the other side of the always shifting borders.

Historical hindsight suggests that these tribes might have forged a Red

Confederacy and successfully won the battle for sovereignty in the interior of North America, but the facts deny the value of such an interpretation. Each of them was fully as ethnocentric and prideful of its independence as any European principality, while most were in open competition with other tribes for ascendancy in some part of the western country. By 1760 even the Five Nations Iroquois Confederacy had fallen into disrepair and was no longer capable of controlling the actions of the member tribes or its satellites, having to substitute ingenious diplomacy for joint military power. Moreover, none of the tribes was able to develop a consistent, tribal-wide policy of opposition for long. In part this was the result of an old ethos stressing the value of individual, clan, or village autonomy, but equally important were the new developments. Each tribal society harbored within its limits variant opinions and alternative adaptations resulting from their long experience with Euro-American peoples. Further, all of these societies between the Mississippi and the Appalachian Mountains were dependent on both economic and political alliances with some industrialized nation. None was willing or capable of reverting to the level and style of existence they had enjoyed two centuries earlier. Finally, a full understanding of what was coming was not apparent until late in the period, and then the threat did not fall equally upon all to the same degree at the same time. The Potawatomi, in particular, were for a long time well buffered from the more damaging contacts by layers of other tribes between themselves and the westering American frontier. While the tribes of the Ohio valley were losing territory to the new American nation, for example, the Potawatomi were still expanding their tribal estate in the Old Northwest country.

REVOLT
IN THE WEST

The first major episode in this thirty-year contest erupted in the Detroit region. Impoverished and angered by British failure to deliver the expected presents, further antagonized by a flood of unregulated English traders in such extreme competition with one another that profits could be had only by cheating the tribesmen, encouraged by the French inhabitants still living in the upper lakes country and Illinois, excited by the messianic dreams of a Delaware prophet preaching a return to ancient ways and a final victory over Europeans, and nourished by a hope of a return of French power, in May of 1763 the Potawatomi joined forces with the Odawa, Ojibwa, and other tribes in an effort to drive the British from the Trans-Appalachian West (Peckham 1961). Known as Pontiac's rebellion, this pantribal movement aimed at asserting and defending Indian sovereignty over the vast territory as yet unsettled by many Euro-Americans. It met with initial, startling success. By the end of June all British posts west of Niagara had been captured except Detroit and Fort Pitt, and both these positions were under siege. The western tribes had demonstrated that they could effectively engage in massive, concerted action in their own interests, if only in the short term.[2]

Pontiac's efforts to achieve success were dependent upon quick victory over all British positions in the west. His followers soon learned that although they might capture smaller posts by ruse and deception, they lacked the manpower, tactical skills, and artillery needed to reduce the larger, well-defended forts. They were also dependent upon an outside source of supply, for they entered into battle with a limited amount of firearms and ammunition and were resupplied only by what they might capture from the British or requisition from the scanty stocks of French traders and residents in the upper lakes. The rebelling tribes soon discovered that although they might blockade the garrisons at Detroit and Fort Pitt, preventing sorties and maneuvers outside their palisades, they were not strong enough on land or lake to prevent resupply and reinforcement from eastern garrisons. Pontiac's rebellion was undermined by economic realities. His forces were made up of only part-time warriors. By

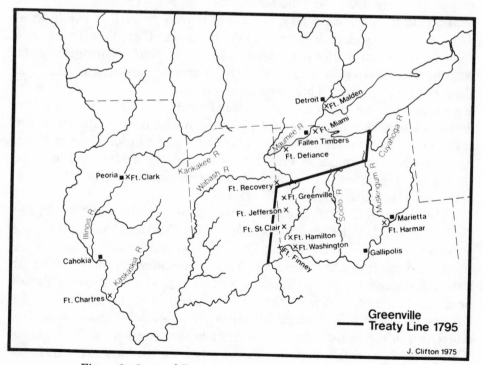

Figure 9. Scene of Battle, the Northwest country, 1761–1795.

fall they had to begin thinking of their winter hunt. But on 3 August 1763, General Henry Bouquet's relief columns defeated the tribes investing Fort Pitt, while in October, Pontiac learned that the British and French had made peace eight months earlier and that he could not anticipate French aid. With his own supporters slipping away, and with increasing dissension among the participating tribes, on November 5 the critical siege at Detroit ended. Pontiac departed for a refuge on the Maumee River, and the rebellion was finished.

BRITISH
ASCENDANCY

The British reconquest of the Great Lakes area did not bring immediate peace to the area. The Potawatomi, in particular, remained at odds with the British; and until the time of the American Revolution some of these tribesmen regularly, each year, plundered English traders or raided incautious troops near the posts in the upper country. The traditions of alliance with France remained strong, although with the Treaty of Paris on 10 February 1763 France lost all of her possessions in North America. Three months prior to that date France had ceded to Spain the Louisiana Territory west of the Mississippi (Kellogg 1925: 439-40; Sosin 1961: 22-24). Yet most Frenchmen remained in the interior country, electing to remain under British rule while they continued to seek their fortunes in the fur trade. There they intermarried with the tribes, eventually developing a Métis subculture—among the Potawatomi, particularly so in the St. Joseph River area, in northwest Indiana, and along the Illinois River. This presence was a constant, seldom entirely mute or neutral reminder of earlier times when French and Potawatomi relations provided satisfactions never obtained under the British regime. Indeed, as late as 1807—long after the United States had emerged as the major power in North America—the mere rumor of French intervention up the Mississippi into the Great Lakes region was enough to cause consternation among British officials in Canada (Horsman 1964: 123-25, 145, 169).

The British did not firmly occupy the Illinois country until 10 October 1765, on which date they took possession of Fort Chartres. Nonetheless, their position was strongest in the Detroit–Ohio valley region, weaker in the country around and south of Lake Michigan. Those Potawatomi in the villages near Detroit and along the Huron River became most closely allied to the British cause and benefited most from the British presence. On the other hand, the Potawatomi villages in western Michigan, Illinois, and Indiana were less closely tied to the British; there trade relations were weaker; and a tradition of anti-English sentiment persisted, particularly so in the Milwaukee area and Illinois.[3]

British imperial policy for the tribes of North America was a product of the practical experience gained during the French and Indian War, the need for economy in administration of the interior country, the goal of maintaining ascendancy in the fur trade and a market for English industries, and the aim of controlling the western expansion of the Atlantic colonies (Sosin 1961: 41–77). The expedient means to these desirable ends were peace and alliance with the interior tribes; however, this required some mechanism for insuring the tribesmen of control over their own lands and protection from an invasion of settlers from the eastern seaboard. The Proclamation of 1763 aimed at achieving these goals by defining a boundary between Indian and Euro-American settlements. It was drawn down the midline of the Appalachian Mountains and was intended to make of the interior country a vast game preserve and Indian reservation. But as soon as 1765 it was evident that this boundary could not be enforced, for by that date there were already widespread violations. This boundary did, however, bring relative peace to the Ohio valley for a period of ten years, until it became evident no imperial or national government could forever control the westward flow of long-hunters, traders, land speculators, surveyors, and settlers who continued to press against and over whatever frontier boundary was defined by the statesmen of London or Philadelphia.

British policy in North America was the product of a dilemma which defied a solution satisfactory to the major contenders. The tribes formerly allied to France had to be pacified while the Atlantic colonies also had to be placated. The wants of both sides, it turned out, were quite incompatible, while British efforts to keep the peace soon exacerbated the existing conflict. Pontiac's rebellion had been caused, in part, by the issue of sovereignty. For the tribes involved, the idea that Britain had acquired control of their lands by a victory over France was a concept both alien and unacceptable. Those tribes just east of the Atlantic colonies were further incensed by unauthorized settlements on their lands (Sosin 1961: 65). But it was the press for economy in imperial management of the Indian country which turned discontent into revolt. Britain ended the Seven Years' War with her treasury impoverished, and when the commander of the forces in North America—Sir Jeffrey Amherst—sought economy by ending the practice of delivering presents to Indians, the tribes erupted (Jacobs 1950: 66–67, 184–85). Then too, Britain wanted to maintain peace at the lowest possible cost by denying the Atlantic colonies jurisdiction over the interior country and by limiting the expansion of their populations westwards. This thwarting of the expansionist aims of the new Americans, when combined with efforts to raise revenues to finance colonial administration, soon precipitated another rebellion of a different order of magnitude.

The boundary line defined by the Proclamation of 1763 had in part been intended to safeguard the lands of those tribes inhabiting western Pennsylvania and the Ohio country. In this period Ohio was occupied by members of a curious conglomeration of societies, none of which were native to the area. During the long period of the Iroquois wars Ohio had been depopulated. The tribes that had lived there earlier—the Erie, Andastes, and Mosopelea—were gone, either exterminated or their remaining population fragments assimilated into other tribes. Unoccupied and unhunted for a half to three-quarters of a century, its large game and fur-bearing animal population increasing in size and its garden lands rejuvenated, Ohio thus became a rich prize for any society which might take possession and protect its treasures (Tanner & Voegelin 1974: 59–88; Clifton 1976c). Following the peace of 1701, several tribes began reoccupying this fallow ground, and by the 1750s they were firmly in possession thereof. These were the Wyandot, dominant in the Sandusky region, the Miami in northwest Ohio, the Shawnee along the Scioto River on the main trail to the rich Kentucky hunting grounds, the Delaware on the Muskingum and Tuscarawas rivers, and the Mingo—a composite aggregation of splinter groups from several Iroquois and Algonquian tribes who were scattered along the Cuyahoga and Scioto rivers. Since the expansionist aims of the northern tier of the Atlantic colonies were centered on the Ohio-Kentucky country, it was these tribes who were directly and immediately threatened. And it was they who for two decades slowed the westward movement of the American frontier, allowing Great Lakes tribes such as the Potawatomi relative peace and buffering them from quick, easy invasion.

Underlying the contest for sovereignty was a major historical process that many contemporary figures recognized, if but dimly and imperfectly. This involved a succession of types of cultural adaptations which structured and sustained whole societies in their relationships to the environment; the struggle itself basically involved conflicts between societies for the perpetuation of one type of adaptation as against the imposition of a new way of dealing with the land (Wax 1971: 16–18, 45–47; Park 1936). In process, tribal societies—their populations limited by their subsistence patterns of hunting, fishing, and gathering supplemented by woman-powered hoe and digging-stick horticulture—were being displaced by large national societies organized as centralized states, nations with rapidly increasing populations in process of industrialization, if yet dependent upon draft-animal–powered, intensive agriculture.

Long before the Atlantic colonies organized themselves as a new nation, the tribal societies of the Eastern Woodlands had already experienced a major shift in their economic adaptation as they became involved in the fur trade. For this reason, and because they were increasingly threatened by invasion of Euro-American agriculturalists, the tribal lands of the Old Northwest took on a new and different value. For the societies most directly and immediately threatened

—those of Ohio—their territories were clearly seen as a critical refuge for a tribal way of life. Other tribes—those more remote from the scene of conflict on the cultural frontiers—on occasion recognized that land had become a commodity, and they sometimes became involved in transactions involving the cession of rights to lands they did not control or utilize. Indeed, the first treaties signed by the Potawatomi with the United States (1787 & 1795) and Great Britain (1790 & 1800) involved the surrender of rights to territories of little immediate value to this tribe.

Those who would interpret this process of ecological succession as involving a basic racial or European-Indian conflict miss an important point. Centuries before the arrival of the first Europeans in the New World, entirely the same kind of processes had developed in Middle and South America. There, similarly, agriculturally based, urbanized societies organized as centralized states and empires had evolved independently of developments in the Old World; and there, too, the powerful new nation-states incorporated and submerged the earlier hunting and gathering tribal societies (Harris 1975: 216–29). The biological ancestors of these Incan, Mayan, and Aztec urbanized states were quite the same as those of the tribal peoples of eastern North America.[4] After 1492 the essential process was one of ecological succession and a conflict of cultural types, not a racial confrontation.

THE NEW
AMERICAN NATION

In the Atlantic colonies and in the early history of the American Republic, land took on a powerful new meaning, one added to its basic value in agricultural development. Land became a medium of exchange, a determiner of wealth and status, a major source of economic and political power, and a means of capital development which supported both public works and administration and private business transactions. By obtaining land from tribal societies and putting it on the market, it became a speculative commodity, which —increasing in value—provided the capital needed for national development (Rogin 1975: 79–80, 179). In the decade between the Seven Years' War and the American Revolution, it was the land speculators who most stridently pressed to have the western country open to settlement. Well before the British victory in the Seven Years' War—in 1747—the Ohio Company had been formed to promote settlement along the Upper Ohio and Kanawha rivers. However, after 1763 dozens of new land companies sprang up. One such aimed at establishing the colony of Charlotina on the Wabash River in the Illinois country, while another—the Mississippi Company—hoped to promote development of the region around the junction of the Ohio and Mississippi rivers, just to the south of the expanding Potawatomi tribal estate. Those English traders who had suffered losses during Pontiac's rebellion sought compensation through a grant of lands in Illinois. The line of colonial and shortly American national expansion thus was down the Ohio River to the Mississippi, and later up the Mississippi and its tributaries (Billington 1960: 132–48). In consequence, it was the southernmost Potawatomi villages which first came into extensive contact with Americans, while those in Michigan remained closer to and more influenced by British posts in the upper country.

American expansion into the Ohio valley was facilitated by the 1768 Treaty of Fort Stanwix at which the Five Nations Iroquois ceded their feeble claims to Kentucky, to the great consternation of their former vassals, the Delaware and Shawnee, who actually hunted these rich lands. This treaty gave recognition to the fact that the 1763 proclamation line could not be held against the land hunger of American colonists. Yet British imperial authorities insisted on their authority over the interior country, until they were bypassed by groups of speculators who formed the Illinois and Wabash Land Companies in 1774, seeking to buy land directly from the tribes, thereby avoiding British regulation and management of such transactions. However, in 1774 the Quebec Act was also passed by the House of Lords, restoring the boundaries of Quebec to the limits that had obtained under the French regime, with the French-speaking settlements of Illinois and Indiana added thereto (Kellogg 1971: 115–29; Sosin 1961: 231–35). Under this act, aimed at placating the interior tribes and the French-speaking inhabitants of English North America, as well as protecting British interests in the fur trade, the area available for the expansion of the American Atlantic colonies was to be limited to the region west of the Allegheny Mountains and east and south of the Ohio River. Here was one more effort to define an effective boundary between the expanding agriculturalists and interior tribesmen. The American colonists saw it as another of the "Intolerable Acts," and hence this effort to keep the peace with the tribal societies was one important factor leading to the declaration of independence. As Louise Kellogg has commented, before the provisions of these new regulations could be put into effect, "the American revolution overwhelmed British rule in the Northwest and annexed that region to the new nation born of the struggle" (1971: 129).

The American settlers on the western frontiers had little sympathy for many of the issues which fomented the revolution and continued to push settlements westwards into Tennessee and Kentucky. For several years their antagonists were British-sponsored tribal raiding parties and British-led units of irregulars—ranger forces. American policy was to keep the western tribes neutral, but in this for years they had little success. The British offered their strong presence, protection, and supplies at the interior posts of Michilimackinac, Detroit, Oswego, and Niagara, a well-established fur trade which flourished and expanded during the war years, an opportunity for many young warriors to continue in their now familiar role of service as mercenaries raiding the weak and difficult-to-defend American frontier settlements, as well as the long-range promise guaranteeing the boundaries of the western tribal lands.

Encouraged by Lieutenant Governor Henry Hamilton and Captain Arent De Peyster—British commanders at Detroit and Michilimackinac—the Detroit-area Potawatomi declared themselves in the British cause and, in company with other tribesmen from the upper lakes, in 1776 began raiding American positions in New York and Kentucky. The raids continued successfully into 1778; however, they remained largely unsupported by the Potawatomi villages and clans in western Michigan, Illinois, and Wisconsin. These western and southern Potawatomi were not so much pro-American as they were anti-British —increasingly these Potawatomi had turned to the Spanish posts in Missouri for their trade. The British policy of centralizing the trade and Indian affairs at a few strong posts had failed. The western tribesmen found it more convenient to trade with the French and Spanish on the Mississippi, while the traditions of the older French relationship remained influential and the antagonisms generated during Pontiac's rebellion were yet unquieted (Sosin 1961: 104). This seeming division of loyalties between Detroit and certain of the western Potawatomi villages never developed into internal conflict within the tribe. A few years later in 1781 Sigenak—Blackbird, who led the opposition to the British in the Lake Michigan area and who was most strongly allied with the Spanish, joined with Spanish troops and sympathetic French traders to raid the British at St. Joseph. The raiders cautioned the St. Joseph villagers to stand aside and, following their victory, shared the captured British trade goods with them.

Precipitating this raid on the British posts was an earlier American show of force in southern Illinois and Indiana. By 1777 the American defensive strategy in the frontier settlements was an obvious failure. The frontier communities could barely manage to survive by congregating in small forts, but they could not safely work to produce sufficient food to sustain themselves. Then, in 1777, George Rogers Clark persuaded the Virginian authorities to back what amounted to a demonstration-in-force in the Illinois and Indiana country. By August 15 of 1778 Clark and his tiny contingent of fast-moving frontiersmen had captured Kaskaskia, Cahokia, and Vincennes. He then controlled the Illinois country and called the surrounding Indian tribes into council, where his forceful words and bold manner blinded them to the weakness of his military posture. Then, in February of 1779, Clark captured Hamilton, who was trying to counterattack and dislodge him, and at this point British influence in the prairielands south of Lake Michigan fell to a low ebb. Increasingly, the Potawatomi and other tribes of that area turned to the Americans and Spanish, talking of peace and neutrality. But Clark lacked the manpower, supplies, and backing necessary to carry through with an attack on Detroit and soon had to retreat from his dangerously advanced position.

Thereafter, until the Revolutionary War came to an end in 1783, the Detroit Potawatomi gave occasional, desultory support to British military efforts. Then, in April 1783, Captain De Peyster at Detroit called the tribes in to inform them that the war was ending and no more raids were to be made. But when the American peace commissioner, Ephraim Douglas, arrived to discuss the terms of the peace settlement later in the summer, De Peyster would not allow him to meet directly with the tribes to discuss the facts of British land cessions. At the peace settlement the British had sought to outmaneuver French and Spanish influence by granting to the new American nation the lands west to the Mississippi and south of the midline of the Great Lakes, but they soon had second thoughts concerning the implications of this hasty settlement with respect to their relations with the western tribes. At the Treaty of Paris the Americans had gained nominal sovereignty but not actual control over the west. The British were determined to maintain their influence with their tribes and their ascendancy in the fur trade. The conflict over the expanding agricultural frontier thus continued for another decade (Horsman 1964: 42–43; Billington 1960: 191–99).

BRITISH-AMERICAN CONFLICT: 1783-1795

The Americans were left with a new, weak, ill-experienced and untried government and the same problems that had plagued the British with respect to western Indians and lands. In addition, they were faced with the British as an adversary for control of tribal loyalties and as competitors in the western trade. Meanwhile, Spain remained influential in the Mississippi posts, concerned with safeguarding the vitals of her southwestern empire—always willing to lure tribesmen or American frontiersmen west of the Mississippi to fight Spanish battles or to reduce frontier tensions, while the specter of French intervention hovered just over the horizon as one more possible complication in the contest for control of the American heartland. The Potawatomi were thereby engrossed in a complex international and diplomatic situation, at the geographic center of the controversy. In 1784 the American Congress took up the problem of dealing with the Indians of the Trans-Appalachian country, settling the conflicting claims of seven states to western territories, and providing for the orderly development and management of federal lands. The Ordinance of 1785 and the Northwest Ordinance—passed in 1787—provided for the development of new western territories and states and for the sale of public lands, well before the tribes occupying these lands were willing to concede that Americans had rights to them.[5]

In the fall of 1783 the United States informed the western tribes that they had lost their claims to the lands west of the Ohio, which brought these societies to an immediate recognition of their mutual threat and joint interests. British Indian agents moved among them encouraging them to believe that the peace had not deprived them of their rights to the lands, while the view of the Potawatomi and other tribes was that, since they had not ceded their territories to France or England, thereby they had not lost them due to the defeat of their European allies. Encouraged by Iroquois diplomats and British agents, the idea of a Western Confederacy was born.

At the second Treaty of Fort Stanwix, in 1784, the United States forced the Five Nations Iroquois into abandoning their claims west of Pennsylvania and New York; but the Iroquois—now almost surrounded by American settlements—did not readily give up their efforts to maintain their position of influence among the western tribes. In 1784, also, at the Treaty of Fort McIntosh, the Ojibwa, Odawa, Delaware, and Wyandot ceded their lands in Ohio except for a reserved tract between the Cuyahoga and Tuscarawas rivers—but the Shawnee refused to participate. Later in 1785 another treaty at Fort Finney was attempted. This time the Potawatomi, Miami, Wea, Piankashaw, and Kickapoo were invited, but only the Shawnee arrived and bowed to the terms dictated to them. Instead of negotiating with the Americans, the increasingly concerned tribes met at Detroit under British auspices, where they rejected the treaties dictated by the United States and agreed to negotiate as a unit, hoping to gain strength in their joint numbers, supported with British advice and supplies. At this point the Shawnee, Potawatomi, and other tribes erupted, following their old tactics of small raids against settlements along and across the Ohio, and the Americans counteracted with raids against the Shawnee villages. Until this moment the Potawatomi had enjoyed the booty and the glory they obtained in substantial quantities from this pattern of hit-and-run surprise attack, while their casualties were few and their villages and cornfields were too remote for American retaliation. They continued to profit from a sheltered geographic position.

By 1787 the Americans were again determined to negotiate, but Arthur St. Clair, governor of the Northwest Territory, was unable to bring the tribes together for councils. The Western Confederacy was in fact seriously divided. The Delaware and Wyandot were wary of armed opposition; the Mohawks,

Kickapoo, Miami, and Shawnee favored war; and the Potawatomi counseled conciliation and compromise. By this time the St. Joseph–area Potawatomi were becoming hostile to the Wea, Kickapoo, and other tribes along the Wabash and even offered to aid the Americans against them, continuing their tribal expansion southwards. The Americans tried negotiation and treaty-making again in midwinter of 1788–1789 at Fort Harmar and managed to bring together small delegations (which were later discredited) of Potawatomi, Seneca, Sauk, Ojibwa, Odawa, Delaware, and Wyandot to reaffirm the terms of earlier treaties at Forts Stanwix, McIntosh, and Harmar. Of those present only the Delaware, Wyandot, and Seneca had any claims to the lands involved, while others who did—the Shawnee and Miami—avoided the treaty proceedings. This was a treaty agreement in name only, accomplished because the United States was still too weak to expand its territory by force of arms, with most of the Indians present unwilling or unaccredited representatives. These departed with their presents, convinced that little could be accomplished by negotiation, encouraged by promises of British support, and unconcerned with abiding by the terms of the document to which they had affixed their names and totem marks.

In 1789 a new Indian war exploded a fresh wave of violence on the northwest frontier. For four hard years the Americans took the worst of the raids, skirmishes, and pitched battles which disrupted life in Kentucky and Ohio. In 1790 an expedition led by General Joseph Harmar lost 183 men when ambushed on the Maumee River in western Ohio. That year also, on May 19, the Potawatomi of the Detroit area joined with their Ojibwa, Odawa, and Huron neighbors to cede a large tract of land in the Ontario Peninsula to Great Britain—this was land the Potawatomi did not use or occupy (Canada 1891 1: 1–4; Clifton 1975b: 58–59). Another American expedition directed at the heartland of the Western Confederacy by General Arthur St. Clair in 1791 suffered 630 killed and 283 wounded out of the three thousand troops involved (Billington 1961: 223–24). Meanwhile, small raiding parties from the tribes of the confederacy—including Potawatomi warriors—regularly assaulted American frontier settlements, and the Kentuckians retaliated with raids against the tribal villages most accessible to them. On the diplomatic front Great Britain tried to obtain the creation of an Indian buffer state, a proposal rejected by the United States government, which pressed forward with a dual strategy of negotiations with the tribes backed by more effective preparations for military action. By 1793 the British were moving overtly and positively in support of the Indian confederacy and were soon informing the tribes that war was expected between the United States and Great Britain, promising active military support of their tribal allies (Horsman 1964: 94–95). The ultimate symbol of active British support—Fort Miami, garrisoned with British regulars—was constructed on the lower Maumee River in the spring of 1794.

In these same years the United States seemed to be having some success with negotiations with the Potawatomi of the Illinois River valley. The tribesmen in the villages of this area were still strongly under the influence of the Spanish from St. Louis, who were trading northward to Lake Michigan (Voegelin & Stout 1974: 154–58; Jablow 1974: 320–21). In 1792 Secretary of War Knox had dispatched General Rufus Putnam west to treat with all of the tribes of the Western Confederacy, but he was able to meet only with representatives of some, those from western Indiana and Illinois. In September, Putnam concluded a treaty of peace with a mélange of supposed representatives from eight of these tribes, a treaty which was never ratified by the Senate (ASP–IA 1: 319; Buell 1903: 118–21). Included among the signatories were three young Potawatomi men who presented themselves and were accepted by the unsuspecting Putnam as "chiefs" of the Illinois Potawatomi, a claim later discredited by other Potawatomi in the region (Voegelin & Jones 1974: 181). While their allies in the Western Confederacy had their attention riveted to the east, trying to meet and counter the threat of American invasion, the Illinois Potawatomi were oriented south and west, raiding and countering the raids of the Osage tribe in Spanish territory (Jablow 1974: 317–19, 323–24).

In the Ohio country during 1793 the double thrust of American policy continued. The major aims were to achieve peaceful relations through negotiation and to reduce tensions on the frontier through control of frontier expansion and effective management of the fur trade (Flexner 1969b: 102–3). But British officials in Upper Canada counseled armed opposition, and the tribes of the Western Confederacy rode high on the glories of their earlier major victories over American forces (Horsman 1964: 95–96). The American peace commissioners met with representatives of the Western Confederacy in the summer of 1793, but the parties remained deadlocked. The easternmost tribes of the confederacy adamantly held out for the Ohio River as a final boundary between the United States and Indian territory, and they were reluctantly supported in this position by the Ojibwa, Odawa, and Potawatomi, who had been agreeable to surrendering the lands east of the Muskingum River. By September it was evident to the American commissioners that all attempts at peaceful negotiation had failed, and the now well-trained troops in western Ohio were released so as to attempt to secure in battle the objectives denied by diplomacy.

The American forces in the west were under the command of General Anthony Wayne, who through 1792 and 1793 had been mobilizing and molding his troops into a well-trained, highly disciplined frontier army. Denied the option of aggressive action until the outcome of treaty negotiations were known, upon receiving permission to attack in September 1793, Wayne held back, unwilling to engage in a hazardous late fall campaign. Wayne had been moving northward slowly, extending the chain of American fortified positions begun two years earlier by General St. Clair. In the spring he built Fort Recovery on the site of St. Clair's overwhelming defeat (Billington 1961: 226). While Wayne was moving north, the Western Confederacy—encouraged and well supplied by the British at Detroit—had been gathering their forces. By late June more than fifteen hundred warriors had been assembled along the Maumee River, including Potawatomi from the St. Joseph River as well as Detroit and northern Indiana villages. On June 30 the Potawatomi—joined by the Ojibwa and Odawa—assaulted a supply train departing Fort Recovery and made an abortive attempt to overwhelm the fort's defenses. The net result of this action was fifty Americans killed and wounded, with some twenty of the attacking Indians killed and an unknown number wounded (Edmunds 1972: 296). The attacking Indians captured more than three hundred American horses and departed the next day, returning to their homes angered because the Shawnee and Delaware had not joined them in the attack.

By midsummer some two thousand warriors had been gathered, seemingly prepared to stand and fight together (Billington 1961: 224). At the point of final battle they were reinforced by fifty-three Detroit militia mustered and led by William Caldwell, together with a number of English traders. But the British Indian agents were having difficulty in holding the confederates together: the tribesmen from the upper lakes particularly were hard to keep in check, and they continued to slip away. When the moment of confrontation came, only thirteen hundred were assembled to meet Wayne's advance—these from the Wyandot, Delaware, Shawnee, Miami, and Odawa tribes, with no more than fifty Potawatomi present, mostly from the St. Joseph area (Edmunds 1972: 302; Horsman 1964: 102–3). Meanwhile, Wayne had received very substantial reinforcements in the welcome form of fifteen hundred mounted Kentucky volunteers. By July 28 his forces totaled thirty-five hundred well-armed and combat-ready men, and he marched north, halting at the mouth of the Auglaize River to build one more of the line of defensive positions, Fort Defiance. General Wayne then issued one last call for negotiations on August 13, which went unanswered. The tribesmen were stalling for time: their scouts (including some Potawatomi) had carefully watched Wayne's advance and were well aware of the size of his force. They had sent out messengers calling for reinforcements from the western tribes, but the Potawatomi, Odawa, and Ojibwa of western Michigan were slow in responding. The fatal weakness of the Western Confederacy was now becoming apparent: they could not maintain a large enough force of warriors in the field for long enough periods to seriously contest Wayne's advance, while intertribal jealousies and frictions weakened their efforts at concerted military action.

One last hasty fortification—Fort Deposit—Wayne built to safeguard his baggage and supplies on August 18, just ten miles south of the British Fort Miami. On that same night the opposing Indian warriors began their pre-battle rituals and started their fast, preparing their spirits and bodies for the coming ordeal. Wayne, adding guile and intelligence of his enemy's customs to his own weight of arms, had feinted, letting it be broadcast that he intended battle on the nineteenth (Billington 1961: 226). On the morning of that day the warriors and the Detroit militia took up defensive positions in a natural breastwork of storm-felled trees on the north bank of the Maumee River. Now Wayne stalled as the tribesmen fasted. On the twentieth, five hundred of the thirteen hundred warriors available left their positions to obtain provisions at Fort Miami—and then Wayne assaulted their weakly held position amidst the fallen timbers. At first Wayne's right flank column was halted and driven back, but the Indians were badly outnumbered. They were weakened by their fast, and they had no reserves. Quickly Wayne's tactics prevailed, combining a frontal infantry assault with a fast-moving double cavalry envelopment of the Indians' flanks. The Indians broke and retreated rapidly towards Fort Miami, anticipating support from the British garrison there. Their retreat was covered by the Detroit militia and the remaining Wyandots—who had taken the full force of the American bayonet attack and suffered the greatest casualties (Horsman 1964: 103–5).

Compared with St. Clair's and Harmar's defeats three years earlier, Fallen Timbers was not much of a battle. It lasted hardly two hours, and the casualties on both sides were very low. The Americans lost 133 killed and wounded —a small fraction of the total engaged when compared with the staggering 32 percent losses of St. Clair in 1791, while the Indians lost no more than fifty dead and an unknown but probably comparable number of wounded. However, by tribal standards these numbers were large, particularly so because the Odawa and Wyandots suffered the majority of the Indian casualties, with the latter losing many of their chiefs (Horsman 1964: 104; MPHC 20: 370–72; Case 1963: 54–68). More seriously, the tribesmen were not accustomed to defeat at the hands of the Americans on ground of their own choosing, and they carried away neither glory nor booty to warm them in later days. The new United States, under General Wayne's leadership, had finally developed a winning combination of military organization and tactics which could successfully meet and defeat the warriors of the Western Confederacy. An American general had at last heeded George Washington's hard-earned lesson of forty years earlier and had avoided surprise, the Indians' most potent tactical maneuver.

But it was not so much the American mastery of the Fallen Timbers battleground which brought victory—in the scale of battles of that time this was little more than a large skirmish. The real victory came when the fleeing warriors reached the gates of Fort Miami. They had been urged into battle by British Indian agents and traders in the Detroit–Maumee River area, backed—they believed—by the full weight of British policy and arms. But British policy had changed since February 1793, when Lord Dorchester had told the tribal representatives that war between Britain and the United States was inevitable. Major William Campbell, the British regular officer commanding Fort Miami, was under orders to do no more than safeguard the integrity of his post. When the stricken Indian allies appeared below the walls of the fort, they found the gates closed and no shelter, much less reinforcement, awaiting them there.

The tribes of the Western Confederacy learned a hard lesson at Fallen Timbers and Fort Miami on 20 August 1794, one which was strongly enough remembered twenty years later that it was to condition the brilliant Tecumsah and his allies to a profound skepticism as regards the amount of British backing the western tribes might safely count upon (Horsman 1963: 74; Clifton 1975b: 37–38). They discovered that standing alone—even backed by local British militia units—they could neither muster nor sustain sufficient force to meet well-disciplined American infantry and cavalry in open battle. And they learned that British policy in North America was a maple leaf blown by the vagaries of distant winds: the Indian need of British support was greater and more consistent than was the British need of their services. The Western Confederacy was a weak and readily sacrificed pawn in a much larger game of empire. Wayne stayed in the vicinity of his victory just two days, impressing Major Campbell with the American presence without forcing a fatal confrontation, but burning and destroying the nearby Indian villages and cornfields as well as the houses and posts of the British traders in the area.

The Indians departed the area demoralized, and the British found them increasingly difficult to control, although badly in need of their supplies and rations. The Western Confederacy had been defeated and divided and soon came to recognize the United States as the major force in the area, a power capable of dictating the terms of relationships between the tribes and the expanding American frontier. By the fall and early winter of 1794 the Potawatomi and other tribes began making their peace with the United States. In January 1795 the Potawatomi accepted an armistice and committed themselves to join in a major council the following summer (ASP-IA 1: 559–60). British efforts at maintaining their allegiance were listened to but rebuffed. Simultaneously, some Indiana Potawatomi began moving their village from the Tippecanoe farther south to the Wabash River so as to be closer to the American trading stations; but this initial peace did not hold long for the Potawatomi. A few, particularly those along the Tippecanoe River and in Illinois, continued their older pattern of raiding isolated homesteads, stealing horses and trade goods, and killing unwary travelers and families. This outbreak of hostilities seemed to threaten the fragile armistice, for the American frontiersmen demanded the protection of federal forts, and some retaliated wherever possible. But these hostile acts were the actions of unruly warriors from a minority of the Potawatomi villages, and they did not in fact impede the participation of representatives from all parts of the tribal estate in the treaty council at Greenville in June 1795.

THE GREENVILLE
TREATY, 1795

The treaty council which was to settle the question of sovereignty in the northwest country opened under the firm direction of Anthony Wayne at Fort Greenville on 16 June 1795. Before the end of the council more than eleven hundred Indians representing eleven groups of tribesmen had assembled, although the majority of the Shawnee delegates did not arrive until very late in the proceedings—July 31. Wayne came to the council armed with the sole power of negotiating on behalf of the United States but under careful and detailed instruction from Secretary of War Timothy Pickering and President Washington. In general, Wayne was instructed to follow the same guidelines as had been carried by the unsuccessful treaty commissioners in 1793 and to obtain a surrender of lands which followed the boundaries of the 1789 Treaty of Fort Harmar. In addition, he was to obtain a cession of ten specified tracts west of the Ohio cession, which would later be developed as American posts. Wayne was specifically cautioned to avoid the spread of infectious disease among the many assembled Indians, to prevent drunkenness, and to be especially on his guard against surprise attack—by this time his military force had dwindled considerably. The treaty was finally signed on August 3, while supplementary councils continued until the tenth of that month.[6]

In important ways Wayne's situation and instructions differed from those of earlier treaty commissioners. He was a victorious general who had demonstrated to the assembled tribes that American troops could successfully meet them in battle, and for this reason had earned the respect of the assembled chiefs and warriors. Similarly, the tribes had recently learned that they could not obtain adequate British support in battle against the United States; and, as the events of the proceedings indicated, most came to the council grounds willing to accept a transfer of their allegiance. The tribesmen arrived much subdued, if not cowed. Indeed, some of the tribes who had long defended the

Ohio country—particularly the Shawnee and soon the Delaware—had already begun migrating westward across the Mississippi into Spanish territory (Kellogg 1971: 224). But a major American policy aim was to reduce tensions; hence Wayne, unlike earlier commissioners, was instructed not to assert that the lands east of the Mississippi were fully and absolutely the property of the United States, theirs in consequence of the 1783 Treaty of Paris with Great Britain. Indeed, Wayne was to admit that the tribes had free and exclusive use of all lands not specifically ceded; but the tribes were to acknowledge that they were under the sole protection of the United States and that the United States alone had exclusive right to preemption of such lands in subsequent treaties. With those words and understandings accepted by the tribes, the contest for sovereignty ended.

The British continued their involvement with the tribes and against the interest of the United States before, during, and after the treaty proceedings. While British ministers in London were commending Wayne for his restraint following the battle at Fallen Timbers and denouncing Lord Dorchester for his inflammatory speech and advice to the tribes, British traders and Indian agents in the Detroit area worked to prevent or to subvert the treaty and to undercut the growing American influence among the tribes that formerly had been dependent upon them (Knopf 1960: 369–70, 386–89; Horsman 1964: 113; ASP-IA 1: 566–68). One agent, the half-Odawa son of a wealthy Detroit trader, attended the Greenville proceedings under instructions to persuade the tribes to insist on their sovereignty, but Wayne soon placed this young man— John Askin, Jr.—under arrest and held him in confinement until after the treaty was signed, certified, and distributed (Quaife 1931 1: 550–52, 561–65).

Wayne conducted the treaty proceedings according to his understanding of tribal customs for such affairs. He approached the meetings slowly and deliberately, allowing ample time for discussion, interpretation, and debate of issues and details. Indeed, some of the tribesmen—especially the Ojibwa— evinced a greater interest in hurrying matters, signing the treaty, and returning home than did Wayne. The ceremonial council fire was kindled and kept alight throughout the weeks of the meeting. Wayne lit and presented the "calumet of peace of the Fifteen Fires of the United States" for all the tribesmen to smoke, and in appropriate ritual fashion he accepted and smoked the calumets of the tribes when they were presented to him. He exchanged strings and belts of wampum, further symbolizing and recording the importance of the affair. But he was also a strict disciplinarian. Although pressed often for lavish distributions of food and especially liquor, he closely controlled such issues. He offered to share with the chiefs whatever simple fare was on his own table, and issued liquor to the tribes and his own troops only on special occasions, then in small, carefully rationed amounts. Following Washington's injunction to beware of a surprise attack, Wayne kept his troops alert and armed at all times, but with their weapons unloaded so as to avoid accidental misfire and disturbances.

During the treaty proceedings a number of key concerns and issues were raised by the Potawatomi and other tribes, and these matters were debated among themselves and with Wayne. One such issue concerned the Fort Harmar treaty. The Ojibwa particularly complained that they had known nothing of this proceeding in 1789, that the Five Nations Iroquois had conspired to thrust this treaty on the Western Confederacy, and that the Three Fires (i.e., the Ojibwa, Odawa, Potawatomi coalition) had never received any of the payments due from the treaty. Massas—the Ojibwa who acted as speaker for the Three Fires—argued that the Ohio lands truly belonged to the Ojibwa, Odawa, and Potawatomi. To this both the Wyandot and Miami objected most strenuously. Here was a critical matter, with the different tribes issuing conflicting claims for the same territory. Underlying such claims was a related development—the competition between some of the tribes for advantage and a position of ascendancy in American eyes. Tarhe—the Wyandot spokesman—finally argued that the disputed lands belonged to all the tribes for their common welfare, a position which was to be taken up a decade later by Tecumsah and his followers in yet another effort to block American expansion into the Old Northwest.

Wayne countered with the argument that the United States had not been responsible for the distribution of the payment made to the tribes after the Harmar treaty, but would now once again make payment for the lands then ceded. With respect to claims that the lands were the sacred property of all the tribes, Wayne was caustic. He pointed out that if this were so he could not understand how it was that much of this territory had earlier been ceded to the French and the British. Wayne's position was strengthened by two facts. Previous to the Greenville proceedings, the United States had recognized that the claims by the Five Nation Iroquois to the western lands were indeed spurious, and had countered Iroquois machinations by excluding them from the Greenville councils, although one Seneca from Sandusky did sign the treaty document. Moreover, Wayne knew that John Jay had already concluded a successful treaty with Great Britain which provided for the abandonment of their posts south and west of the 1783 treaty line along the midline of the Great Lakes, although Jay's Treaty had not yet been approved by the Senate. At this point Wayne read to the assembled chiefs and spokesmen the relevant section of Jay's Treaty so that they would know that Great Britain had agreed to turn over the border forts in American territory from Niagara to Michilimackinac (Knopf 1960: 435–36, 445–46). The tribesmen were now fully brought to understand the extent of their abandonment by Great Britain.

For a brief period the Wyandot, Delaware, and Shawnee wanted to delay acceptance of the proposed treaty, while the Miami and the Three Fires favored immediate acceptance. The Wyandot, expressing concern with a fundamental weakness within the Western Confederacy—their own tendency to fight among themselves for control of territory—wanted the United States to determine and to fix the territorial boundaries of each tribe west of the proposed treaty line. At the same moment, the Miami complained that the lands to be ceded to the United States included some of the most valuable hunting grounds, and there was a general objection to the idea of leaving behind ten chiefs as hostages until the release of American prisoners held by the tribes had been obtained. There was also concern expressed with safeguarding the interests of long-established French traders and settlers in the tribal lands. Wayne refused to intervene in intertribal politics to set their boundaries for them and pointed out that the treaty provided for free access to hunting grounds so long as the tribes remained peaceful (ASP-IA 1: 575–78).

By July 30 Tahre—speaking for the Wyandot, Delaware, and Shawnee—had acknowledged the sovereignty of the United States, as had Massas in his capacity as spokesman for the Ojibwa, Odawa, and Potawatomi. After expressing fear of British retaliation against himself personally, Massas eloquently summarized what by then must have been the consensus position of the delegates, saying:

> Elder Brother—You asked me who were the true owners of the lands now ceded to the United States . . . I tell you, if any nations should call themselves the owners of it, they would be guilty of a falsehood; our claims to it is equal; our elder brother [the United States] has conquered it.
>
> Brothers, have done trifling. Let us conclude this great work; let us sign our names to the treaty now proposed and finish our business.
>
> Elder Brother: if I can escape the snares of McKee [the British agent at Detroit] and his bad birds, I shall ascend as high as the falls of St. Mary's, and proclaim the good tidings to all your distant brothers in that quarter [ASP-IA: 557].

A week later, after the treaty had been signed, Tahre seconded and carried forward the thoughts of Massas when he told the assembled Indians that hereafter they should acknowledge the United States as their father, and that they should "call them brothers no more." Tahre thereupon delivered a wampum belt to Wayne, symbolizing the Wyandots' acceptance of the status of "children" in the new alliance (ASP-IA 1: 579–80).

On August 8 Gizes—the Sun, who was acting as speaker for the Potawatomi villages along the Wabash River, explained to Wayne that those Potawatomi present belonged to "three classes," those from the Huron River, those from the St. Joseph River, and those from the Wabash. As we will shortly note, this classification was neither complete nor was it followed in the way the several groups of Potawatomi actually signed the Greenville treaty document. However, Gizes's main concern was something else; he was disturbed with the possibility of internal bickering within his tribe if Wayne continued with the plan of distributing the treaty payment in a lump sum and the treaty goods in bulk to one or a few representatives of his tribe. Okia (Wakaya—the Bay), another Potawatomi spokesman of the Detroit area, seconded the objection of the Sun and expressed concern that the Eastern Michigan Potawatomi would not obtain a fair share if the treaty payment were to be handed over to one or a few Potawatomi leaders for further redistribution. The Bay also wanted his own copy of the treaty in addition to the one delivered to the Potawatomi tribe "generally." Wakaya further indicated that he would be ashamed if he was not able to carry home with him a copy of the document (ASP-IA 1: 580–81).

Here we find expressed a fundamental problem stemming from divergent systems of administration and management, the Potawatomi's versus that of the United States. Wayne refused himself to divide the goods between the several Potawatomi groups, explaining that they would understand better than he did their relative numbers and should act so as to provide a fair distribution. He told them he would appoint a storekeeper, and he wanted the Potawatomi —and other tribes—also to appoint two "confidential" (trustworthy) representatives from among themselves to receive and receipt for the goods delivered (ASP-IA 1: 581). Wayne thereby indicated that he expected to proceed with the distribution via a standard administrative-bureaucratic system familiar to himself and other Americans, through an appointed official subject to careful audit. He wanted to have the tribes establish a similar, counterpart official to represent each of them. But such a system was in profound conflict with the values of a highly egalitarian, segmentary, much-dispersed tribal society such as the Potawatomi. Wayne, although proceeding basically along sound understanding of accepted etiquette of treaty councils, did not display similar understanding of the nature of the economy and system of governance of the Potawatomi. Men such as Gizes, who acted as speaker for the Potawatomi villages along the Wabash River, Wakaya, speaking for the Detroit–Huron river villages, and Atsimethe (or Etsimethe—both untranslatable), who spoke for the St. Joseph River villages, were not acting in any authoritative chiefly role but each as kiktowenene—one who speaks for (or impersonates). Each may also have been the okama—leader of a clan or village, but that did not give them the authority to act for others than their own clan-mates. The ill-experienced Americans, like the French and British before them, tended to confuse such roles as speaker with their own ideas of administrative and political authority.

The threat the Sun and the Bay perceived in Wayne's proposal was the concentration of wealth and power in the hands of one or a few men. The British, and the French before them, had made a practice of distributing presents to the leaders of clans and extended families, thereby avoiding the possibility of intratribal conflict. Indeed, the practice initiated by Wayne later contributed to the rise of individual Potawatomi okamek who would lay claim to a range of authority other tribesmen disputed. One of these men, Thupenebu (Topnebi—Sits Quietly), of the Bear Clan on the St. Joseph River, was already present at the Greenville proceedings and signed the treaty document. Within a few years Topnebi would claim to be—and be identified by some confused American agents as—the Red Sovereign of the Potawatomi Nation.

The Treaty of Greenville was signed 3 August 1795 and was ratified unanimously by the United States Senate and proclaimed by President Washington on December 22 of the same year (Tanner & Voegelin 1974: 427). The major provisions of the treaty—with a few exceptions—closely followed the sample draft Wayne had received from Secretary of War Pickering. First and foremost, it was a treaty of peace aimed at promoting friendly relations between the United States and the tribesmen. It provided for the immediate release of all Indian prisoners held by the Americans and for the subsequent release of Indian-held American prisoners, with ten chiefs to remain as hostages until this was accomplished. Except for the northwest quarter, all of the Ohio country was ceded to the United States (see Figure 9). In addition—going beyond his original instructions—Wayne also obtained the cession of a long triangle of land in what is now Indiana, from the mouth of the Kentucky River northwards to the main east-west boundary line. North and west of the United States–Indian boundary, the cession of an additional sixteen tracts of land at strategic locations in Ohio, Indiana, Michigan, and Illinois was obtained. Here again Wayne went somewhat beyond his original instructions, which had specified only ten such tracts. The United States was to be provided free access to these sixteen tracts, either by land or by waterway, and hence this territory would no longer be a British hunting preserve guarded by unfriendly tribes. In turn, the United States relinquished its claim of absolute ownership over the Indian lands west of the Greenville line and east of the Mississippi, while reserving the exclusive right of preemptive purchase from the tribes in subsequent treaties. Thus was the key to future developments written into the Greenville treaty, for it provided the powerful mechanism for obtaining further land cessions in the Old Northwest.

There were certain exemptions made to Indian ownership of the lands west of the treaty line that went beyond the sixteen special tracts which were ceded. These included the cession of 150,000 acres on the lower Ohio River in what is now Indiana—to serve as payment to Wayne and his troops, Post Vincennes on the Wabash River, Fort Massac on the Ohio, and all other tracts which the tribes had previously ceded to the French or British governments or to private citizens. Payment for all these cessions consisted of $20,000 in goods to be distributed immediately at the end of the treaty deliberations, with a perpetual annuity of $9,500 to be paid out annually pro rata to the tribes—$1,000 of this annuity going to the Potawatomi. The treaty deliberations and the document proper were quite specific with respect to the one most critical issue: irrespective of tribal use and occupancy of the lands west of the Greenville treaty line, the United States was the sovereign power in the area. The continuing importance of the French in the western country is marked by an interesting fact. Of the twenty-six names of witnesses and interpreters who signed the document certifying its accuracy, thirteen—just half—were French.

Of the 107 Indian names fixed to the Greenville treaty document, more than one-fourth—thirty of them—were Potawatomi. This is good testimony to the strength and size of this tribe as compared to others in the same area. Moreover, in six instances a Potawatomi signatory signed for himself and then for one of his brothers. Such a practice was followed by no other tribe signing this treaty. This is clear evidence of the strength of the Potawatomi patrilineage system, wherein the tie between male siblings was the strongest and most important social relationship. Apparently, the six Potawatomi whose names were given by their brothers were absent, and their siblings acted as proxies certifying the others' acceptance of the treaty proceedings.

The procedure for signing the treaty had the secretary of the council, Henry De Butts, transcribe the names as best he could. Unfortunately, De Butts was inexperienced with Algonquian languages, and thus many of the Potawatomi names he wrote down are so corrupted that they cannot today be translated. However, opposite De Butts's efforts at a phonetic rendition, each Potawatomi drew his totem mark. The names that can be translated, together with those totem marks which can be deciphered, allow us to identify some of the Potawatomi clans that were participants in the Greenville treaty proceedings. These include the Fish, Great Sea, and Sturgeon clans of the Water Phratry, the Bear and possibly the Otter clans of the Bear Phratry, and the Thunderbird and Eagle clans of the Bird Phratry.

The names that can be translated include Thupenebu (Topnebi—Sits Quietly), Nawac (Nawak—Noon), Nenanseka (probably Nanameski—Rumbling Earth), Keesass (Gizes—Sun), Sugganunk (Sigenak—Blackbird), Wapmeme (Wapmimi—White Pigeon), Pedagoshok (probably Padekoshēk—Pile of Lead), La Chasse (French, the Huntsman), Meshegethenogh (Mzhikteno—Thunder Coming Down, also Barren, i.e., Childless), Wawasek (Wawasēk—Distant Flash of Lightning), Missennogomaw (Matchiwokama—Big Chief, a sarcastic nickname),[7] Waweegshe (Wawiyezhi—Something Round), Le Blanc (French, the Whiteman), Shewinse (probably Shebinse—the Shaker, i.e., prone to fits), Okia (Wakaya—the Bay), Segagewan (either a misprint for Ksanadjiwan—Cold River, or Senajiwan—Stream Splashed Rocks), Marchand (French, the Peddler), and, last of all, the old familiar Wenameac (Winamek—Catfish).

Some comparisons are in order to extract the significance of this list of names. For example, of the three upstart, self-appointed "chiefs" who signed the unratified Putnam treaty in 1792, one certainly appeared again at Greenville in 1795, namely, Gomo (Okama—Leader), who in 1795 appears as Big Chief. Moreover, the Waweachsetoh of the Putnam treaty may also be the Wawiyezhi—Something Round, of Greenville. However, although in 1792 and later years both these men were known as living in the Illinois River area, in 1795 they are listed under the St. Joseph River Potawatomi. Similarly, Sigenak—Blackbird is also known as a northern Illinois or southern Wisconsin Potawatomi, although in 1795 he is listed as coming from the St. Joseph River area. Finally, Michimang arrived at the council with the Ojibwa from Lake Michigan, but likely signed the treaty as Chamung—identified as a Potawatomi from the Huron River, while the aged Mtamins—Little Corn (also known as New Corn or Le Petit Bled) was prominent as a speaker but did not sign the document.

For these specific reasons, it is evident that at least some Potawatomi from Wisconsin, Illinois, Michigan, and Indiana were present at the treaty proceedings regardless of the geographic territories under which their names were listed by De Butts. Indeed, in the original treaty document, the Potawatomi names appear in more of a random order than in the final, published version. In the original there are three blocks of names, two titled as the St. Joseph River and one as Huron River area Potawatomi. Regardless, these geographic categories imposed by the treaty commissioners do not seem to correspond to the far more numerous clan-village divisions of the tribal estate, which the treaty commissioners do not seem to have been aware of.

One more comparison is in order. In 1790 and 1800 some Potawatomi participated in signing British treaties numbers 2 and 12 for lands in the western half of the Ontario Peninsula. In Treaty Number 2 of 1790, the six Potawatomi signatories are all identified as being of the Detroit area, and include Sko-neque (Mskwaneke—Red Goose), Pe-Nash (either Pinase—Little Turkey, or Pinesi—Partridge), and Ke-Wey-Te-Nan (Kiwaytin—North Wind), all of the Bird Phratry and clans, as well as She-Bense (Shebinse—the Shaker). The latter name is the only one appearing on the 1790 Canadian treaty which also appears on the 1795 Treaty of Greenville. Moreover, none of the names on the British Treaty Number 12 in 1800 also appear on the 1795 Greenville treaty. Therefore, the Americans and the British were negotiating with nearly mutually exclusive groups of Potawatomi representatives. In the case of the

Greenville treaty, the Americans clearly were dealing with a more legitimately representative group of Potawatomi from all parts of the tribal estate. Those few Potawatomi who signed British treaties 2 and 12, on the other hand, seem to have been mainly Potawatomi who regularly served the interests of their patron, the influential and powerful Indian Agent Alexander McKee, for the Potawatomi did not occupy or use any of the Ontario lands and had no legitimate claim to them (Canada 1891: 1–4, 30–31; Clifton 1975b: 57–64).

The 1790 and 1800 land cessions to the British, together with similar transactions with other tribes, were accomplished so as to provide a place of retreat for British agents, traders, and settlers. The lands acquired in the Ontario Peninsula were to be opened for settlers (particularly, United Empire Loyalist veterans of the Revolutionary War), developed as military posts and trade stations, and used as a refuge for those tribesmen from west of the international boundary who might be encouraged to resettle on British soil. Soon after Fallen Timbers and the Treaty of Greenville, the main British agents, Alexander McKee and Matthew Elliot, worked at encouraging some of the western tribesmen to move east to a twelve-mile-square reserve at the north end of Lake St. Clair on the Chenail Ecarté. But during the next few years few Indians settled there, and these were mainly Ojibwa. No Potawatomi groups are known to have migrated into British territory until long after the War of 1812. In the three decades after the Treaty of Greenville, the history of the Potawatomi tribe was largely written on the prairies and woodlands in Wisconsin, Illinois, Michigan, and Indiana (Clifton 1975b; Horsman 1964: 113–14).

Jay's Treaty had left the boundary question open so far as allowing the free passage of fur traders into American territory, although the British posts on American soil were moved into Upper Canada in the summer of 1796. Surrendering Michilimackinac, the British soon set up shop on nearby St. Joseph Island in the eastern channel approaches to Sault Ste. Marie. The Detroit post was similary moved to Fort Malden, which soon developed as the town of Amherstburg, on the eastern shore of the Detroit River. For many years thereafter, British traders were very active in the fur trade on the American side of the upper lakes. Indeed, they dominated the trade west of Lake Michigan until after the War of 1812 (Kellogg 1971: 224–25, 233–36). For the next forty-five years, many Potawatomi and other tribesmen annually journeyed to Malden to receive British presents and keep alive the continuing possibility of a British affiliation in time of great need. Eventually, when the time came for the United States to press for the removal of all Potawatomi from the Old Northwest Territory, a great many Potawatomi elected to migrate onto British soil. The treaties of Anthony Wayne and John Jay had settled the question of sovereignty in the west: they did not at that time end British influence.

From the perspective of the tribal societies involved, the thirty-six years between 1760, which ended the effective power of France, and 1796, which saw the establishment of the United States as the legitimate power in control in the Old Northwest Territory, can properly be interpreted as an interregnum. During many of these years, first France and Britain, then Spain, Britain, and the United States contended for the loyalty of the tribes and for control of part or all of this great territory. But in the eyes of the Americans, in 1795 it became the future property of frontier agriculturalists and a potential source of wealth for a new generation of land speculators. Until 1795 the Potawatomi had enjoyed numerous advantages derived from their sheltered and strategic geographic position. All too soon the full weight of the American frontier would fall upon them, and they would lose both their isolation and a large measure of their tribal autonomy.

7

Persistence and Change in the Interregnum

The thirty-five years between 1760 and 1795 are particularly frustrating ones for anyone concerned with reconstructing the processes of adaptation and change in Potawatomi society and culture. There is much information available on a few topics, but even this is fragmented and disconnected, and it consists of the products of men who for the most part had little direct familiarity with the Potawatomi, their language, and their culture. The biases in the kinds of information available are profound, and there are too many serious gaps. There is much information on military activities, for example, particularly Potawatomi participation in wars and raids against the British and the Americans; but much less information is available on Potawatomi feuds with other tribes, except those activities that were in the service of or affected the interests of some Euro-American power. Yet there are whole areas of Potawatomi life which were hardly mentioned. It was, for example, exceptionally rare for any Potawatomi woman's name to be written down, much less a good description of women's work, values, interests, involvements, or participation in these three decades of the tribe's history. These were thirty-five years without an Allouez or a Perrot to comment on developments with a knowledge-ableness based on long-term, firsthand involvement and participation. And there was another twenty-five–year delay before anyone would do so (Marston 1820; Keating 1824).

For this reason, the specifics that are available, biased as they are with respect to a near exclusive focus on political, military, and economic issues involving males, have to be fitted into information available before the period started and after it ends to make culture historical sense out of these three decades. When this is done, one major conclusion stands out unmistakably. In spite of a very rapid, stressful turnover of alliances caused by the decline of French power and the rise of British influence, itself too soon complicated by the American Revolution and the rise of a third continental power, up to 1795 the Potawatomi continued their very successful political-economic adaptation. Until 1760 the Potawatomi and other tribes west of the Appalachian Mountains had constituted the balance-of-power in the struggle between the French and the British. With the French gone and with the British for some few years seemingly alone in a near uncontested position of dominance, some Potawatomi began turning towards the Spanish south of the Illinois country, while others of this tribe maintained alliances with the British.

Then, with the rise of the new American nation, once again the tribes of the Old Northwest seemed to be back in the advantageous position they had exploited prior to 1760, able to play one Euro-American power against another in their own interest. But the Battle of Fallen Timbers in 1794 and Jay's Treaty demonstrated unmistakably that this was not the case, that British interest in the Old Northwest was slight and inconsistent. At this point the Potawatomi and other tribes had to face the Americans alone, with only the possibility of British support in back of them. By 1803—when the Louisiana Purchase gave the United States the territory between the Mississippi River and the Rocky Mountains—the Potawatomi and neighboring tribes were almost completely surrounded by lands under American sovereignty. Only the Great Lakes routes provided direct access to their sometime ally, the British in Upper Canada.

TERRITORIAL
EXPANSION II

Until 1795, and even for some years afterwards, the basic structure of the Potawatomi tribe—the segmentary clan and lineage system—had served as what Marshall Sahlins calls "a social means of intrusion and occupation in an already occupied ecological niche" (1961: 322–24). Beginning in the 1670s when they sought a position of ascendancy in northwest Wisconsin, by 1795 the Potawatomi had successfully moved into territory used or occupied by other tribal societies. In succession, they pushed against and displaced the Winnebago, the Fox, the Miami, the Illinois, and—by the end of the eighteenth century—they were pressing against the Osage and other tribes west of the Illinois country. The segmentary organization of the Potawatomi developed and flourished in an intercultural environment made up largely of other tribal societies. They had, thereby, evolved an effective predatory organization, one which served them well in conflicts with other tribes. It had also, demonstrably, worked well in conflicts with communities that were frontier extensions of a larger, more complex society, when and so long as the scene of battle was remote from the center of Potawatomi territory. However, as the American frontier moved up to and around the tribal estate, eventually penetrating it with settlements of agriculturalists, the Potawatomi were to discover that what had been a source of strength in one era was a weakness in the next.

As Anthony F. C. Wallace has pointed out in his discussion of the origins of the Blackhawk War, American frontier communities and tribes such as the Potawatomi were similar in a number of important ways (1970b: 11–12). They shared a common technology, except that the Potawatomi lacked the skills needed to produce and repair metal tools and weapons. Their primary communities were organized on the basis of kinship ties, and kinship was the main focus of their social life. They were heavy users of hard liquor, although again the Potawatomi were consumers and not producers, for they lacked the technology and knowledge necessary to distill alcoholic beverages. They were given to violence and brawling, but in this respect there were also differences. In American frontier settlements much of this violence was expressed within the community. In tribal societies such as the Potawatomi, peace within the community was the norm, with aggression directed outwards. By the opening of the nineteenth century, however, the Potawatomi were to discover that this outlet for the frustrations and hostilities of community life was curtailed by their incorporation into a larger political community; and, with ample supplies of whiskey to act as a solvent for the limited internal controls of men prone to violence, in-group brawling could become extremely disruptive to their patterns of community life.

Like the American frontiersmen, the Potawatomi also had little regard for order and control imposed by institutions beyond the bounds of kinship relations and the primary community. Moreover, both Potawatomi and frontiersmen relied on force as a preferred, ultimate means of adjudicating disputes. In the instance of tribal societies like the Potawatomi there was, in addition, the alternative of settling disputes by the exchange of gifts and wealth. The frontier community had no counterpart custom until legal institutions were established. Both frontiersmen and tribesmen were also similar in that both were dependent upon distant markets for the exchange of their products; however, the frontier communities were quick to develop local markets, particularly as suppliers for new settlers or for other migrants pushing through already established communities. Moreover, in military affairs there were important likenesses between the frontier community and tribal groups such as the Potawatomi. Both were largely dependent on militia-like fighting forces— part-time, short-term warriors who served more or less by whim, who fought distant battles only under the most unusual circumstances. But here the comparison breaks down. The frontiersmen were only the closest representatives of a far larger society with manpower and resources that far outstripped those available to any one tribe or all of them together. At Fallen Timbers, for example, the assembled Indian warriors were defeated by regular army units of the United States that were supported by local militia. The Potawatomi and their allies had no such reservoir of resources to draw upon, in military or other spheres of life.

By 1795 the Potawatomi were approaching the limits of the full range of the tribal estate they were to surrender to the United States in the first three decades of the nineteenth century (see Figure 10). But they still had a way to go, for the new alliance with the United States gave some of their clan villages an opportunity for further expansion, particularly in southern Wisconsin and in Indiana. In the last decade of the eighteenth century there were numerous Potawatomi villages well established in what are now the states of Michigan, Indiana, Wisconsin, and Illinois.[1]

In northwest Ohio, Potawatomi villages were located on the Auglaize River, the Maumee River, the St. Marys River, and the St. Joseph River. In Michigan, they were found at a half dozen sites along the St. Joseph River as well as the Huron, Raisin, and Rouge rivers in the southeast part of the state. Potawatomi villages were along the Lake Michigan shoreline of northern Indiana, as well as along the St. Joseph River, the Elkhart and Little Elkhart rivers, the Tippecanoe River, and the Upper Wabash. In Illinois, these tribesmen had their villages along the Chicago and Calumet rivers, on the Des Plaines and the Kankakee, on the Fox and Rock rivers, and on the Illinois River south to Lake Peoria. In Wisconsin in this period, the Potawatomi were located between Chicago and Milwaukee on the Lake Michigan shoreline, as well as north of Milwaukee. In 1795 and the years following, when the first French, British, and American traders reestablished posts in the Milwaukee area and north thereof, they found Potawatomi villages between Milwaukee and Kewaunee. Apparently, there were no permanent summer villages north of Kewaunee on the Door Peninsula, and there were some Odawa and a few Ojibwa living with the Potawatomi in their villages in this part of Wisconsin.[2] One of the wokamuk at Milwaukee had a familiar name, Onangizes (Vieau 1888: 219; WHC 11: 238–39). Long unmentioned by whatever visitors passed through their country, the Wisconsin Potawatomi were once again noted on the historical record.

Thus, by the opening of the nineteenth century the Potawatomi were established along the entire length of the Lake Michigan shoreline from the Door Peninsula south to Chicago and then east and north to and beyond the mouth of the St. Joseph River. They occupied Michigan south of the headwaters of the Kalamazoo River, the northern third of Indiana, and about half of Illinois, especially west and north of the Illinois and Kankakee rivers. In few parts of this immense territory were they the sole inhabitants. Most often they shared—sometimes uncomfortably—the same area with other tribes, such as the Kickapoo, the Miami, and the Sauk and Fox. However, they were the dominant and near-exclusive inhabitants of northeastern Illinois, eastern Wisconsin, and the St. Joseph River valley. Their hunting parties ranged farther afield than is indicated by the locations of their summer villages, for by this period they operated west of the Mississippi in Missouri and Iowa, as well as into extreme southern Illinois and Indiana.

This considerable territorial range obviously affected how the widely scattered Potawatomi villages subsisted in the different parts of the tribal estate as well as the nature of their social life. By this period, for example, there was a clear division between those who had abandoned the birch-bark canoe (but not necessarily the dugout for local fishing) in favor of horse transportation, and those who continued to construct and use the bark canoes. The Potawatomi in central Illinois and Indiana were well outside the range where large canoe-birch trees were available, and well into the territory where horses were increasingly at hand. Nonetheless, this contrast does not represent a sharp division. The Potawatomi in eastern Wisconsin and in Michigan continued to make and use birch-bark canoes and to employ horses as well. But the importance of horses to the Potawatomi cannot be underestimated. By 1795 the buffalo were nearly gone from Indiana and Illinois, and only horses could provide the Potawatomi access to this important source of food west of the Mississippi, while the adoption of horse nomadism in general greatly expanded the range of their hunting, trapping, trading, diplomatic, and military activities.

Whatever their habitat, the Potawatomi exhibited a preference for a lakeshore or riverside setting for their permanent summer villages. Even the southernmost Potawatomi of Illinois—who were not yet so designated, but who would shortly be called the Potawatomi of the Prairie by Americans—maintained their summer villages in wooded river valleys. This preference for a waterside location of the summer village involved a number of considerations. Fishing remained important as a dependable source of food; the river valleys provided shelter from the weather, as well as convenient food supplies; the soils in lakeshore and riverside locations were more easily tillable, given the inventory of Potawatomi tools and techniques for raising crops; and the waterways were often paralleled or crossed by trails, giving access to several modes of transportation.

LEADERSHIP
AND GOVERNANCE III:
A PLETHORA OF CHIEFS

In the thirty-five years of the interregnum, there was a considerable proliferation of Potawatomi men who were identified as chiefs, village chiefs, principal chiefs, headmen, and the like. However, it is certain that not all of

the men who occupied and acted out leadership roles in the numerous Potawatomi villages were named in the documented history of this period. This is
particularly true of those who organized and led the many raids against the
British or against American settlements, and who often went unidentified.

In the first years of British control, particularly during Pontiac's rebellion,
several Potawatomi leaders achieved considerable prominence. Ninivois
(Ninewas—Little Man) of Detroit was the great admirer and most consistent
supporter of Pontiac, while Washee (Wishē—Yellow Catfish) was identified
as the war chief of the St. Joseph area Potawatomi, the man who arranged to
capture the British fort on that river (Peckham 1961: 145). In early June 1763
the British captured two St. Joseph area men, one known to them only as Big
Ears, and the second as Nokaming (Nokamin—Early Spring) (Peckham 1961:
181). Big Ears was a much respected leader, and the St. Joseph area Potawatomi badly wanted to exchange their own British prisoners to obtain his
release, although they were much less interested in negotiating the freedom of
Early Spring. When Major Henry Gladwin learned of this, he adroitly bargained for the release of his countrymen; but he freed Early Spring rather than
Big Ears, whom he held captive through much of the siege of Detroit.

After the siege of Detroit was lifted, in late 1763, one St. Joseph River
Potawatomi chief—Machoquise (Mishikese—Little Snapping Turtle)—advised
his fellow tribesmen to make peace, but his advances were not particularly
successful (Flick 4: 408–9). Mishikese seems to have moved to Detroit about
1765, where he remained friendly with the British. In 1764, when Colonel
John Bradstreet came to Detroit to arrange a peace council, two Potawatomi
acted as speakers for the tribe, Kiouqua (Kiyēkwa—He Stands Around) on
behalf of the Detroit villagers, and Nanaquiba (either Nanakibek—He Sheds
His Horns, or Nanokiba—Water Moccasin) speaking for the St. Joseph River
villages (Flick 4: 525–32). In November 1794, following a raid on the Detroit
area organized by some St. Joseph warriors, a delegation went to Detroit to
apologize and makes excuses for the incident, blaming it on irresponsible
young men. The delegation was led by Nangisse (Onangizes) and Peshibon
(Peshabon—Peep, i.e., First Light of Day) (Edmunds 1972: 188).

During the American Revolution, another crop of Potawatomi okamek
achieved distinction. In 1776 and 1780, Peannish (either Pinase—Little Turkey,
or Pinesi—Partridge) was one of several Detroit Potawatomi engaged in selling lands along the River Rouge to Alexander and William McComb, Arent
De Peyster, and other British traders and agents. This was the same man who
in 1790 signed British Treaty Number 2 ceding lands in Ontario (ICC 2: 103;
MPHC 19: 553). He seems to have been an early Potawatomi real-estate
dealer. But in 1777, far to the southwest, other Potawatomi were seizing other
opportunities. In that year Unan Guise (once more the familiar Onangizes)

from St. Joseph led a delegation to St. Louis to receive presents and medals from the Spanish there (WHC 18: 367).

This division of interest, which suggests that the Potawatomi took their opportunities where they found them, persisted throughout the American Revolution. In June 1778 a man whose name is untranslatable—Peemembkee-tach—was sponsored by Henry Hamilton at Detroit as leader of a raid against American settlements along the Ohio River (IHC 1: 322; MPHC 9: 475–77). Similarly, after George Rogers Clark had successfully penetrated the Illinois country in 1778, the aging Nanaquiba, now from Detroit, and backed by the influential French trader Louis Chevalier from St. Joseph, joined Henry Hamilton in his unsuccessful attempt to dislodge Clark (WHC 9: 178–81; Barnhart 1951: 116–18). If not actually a double agent, Louis Chevalier was a man who spent a lot of effort going through the motions of advising and assisting the British, with little or no practical consequence. Three years later his half-Potawatomi son Louison was one of the organizers of the raid on the British position at St. Joseph. Meanwhile, when the aging Nanaquiba met Hamilton at Vincennes, he was still proudly wearing his old French medal, awarded for services rendered to the French in the Seven Years' War.

On 25 December 1778, Hamilton sent a small party of Potawatomi to scout the American position at Kaskaskia. These warriors (who did not go very far or accomplish much) were led by Wyndeego (Windigo—Cannibal) and Eskibee (Ashkibi—New River, i.e., River's Source) (IHC 1: 232; Barnhart 1951: 157–58).[3] Early the following year New River organized a raiding party of Detroit Potawatomi to attack Americans along the Ohio River (Barnhart 1951: 112; IHC 1: 393); and a decade later Windigo would be one of the few Potawatomi to sign the Treaty of Fort Harmar.

Following George Rogers Clark's capture of Henry Hamilton in 1779, Arent De Peyster—now commanding at Detroit—tried to stave off the American threat by arranging an attack on their posts in central Illinois. But the pro-British and the pro-American Potawatomi forces met in transit and decided not to fight among themselves but to remain neutral. This unwelcome news was carried to De Peyster by the St. Joseph "war chief," Le Petit Bled (Mtamins—Little Corn, or Young Corn).[4] When the St. Joseph Potawatomi were later pushed to attack the Americans, Le Petit Bled became very insulting to the British officer, Lieutenant Thomas Hutchins, who was trying to force him into action, reminding him that the Potawatomi had an obligation to their alliance with the Odawa and Ojibwa as well as to their fellow tribesmen and the British (MPHC 9: 395–97, 10: 348–49, 392; WHC 18: 394–95). By 1791 De Peyster was thoroughly put out with the Potawatomi, particularly those of Illinois and southern Wisconsin who had actively sided with the Americans. Thus in 1781 he made one of his several attempts to capture the leaders of the "renegade" Potawatomi. That year he insisted that the St. Joseph tribesmen demonstrate their fidelity by capturing the two most actively opposed leaders. The okama he tried to dispatch on this errand was Wawiaghtemou (Wawiyatin—Whirlpool) (MPHC 10: 589).

By this time De Peyster thought that the Potawatomi were a group of impudent scoundrels, constantly demanding rewards for services they never rendered (MPHC 10: 424). But he best expressed his exasperation and his attitude toward the Milwaukee-Chicago area Potawatomi in a rhyming speech he "sang" to an intertribal council several years earlier at L'Arbre Croche, when he was attempting to raise forces to support Hamilton's operations in Illinois. De Peyster had then chanted these words (10: 188):

> Those runagates at Milwakie,
> Must now *per* force with you agree,
> Sly Siggenaak and Naakewoin,
> Must with Langlade their forces join;
> Or, he will send them *tout au diable*,
> As he did Baptist *Point de Saible*[5]
> And now the convert *Miamies*,
> Must join the Pottawatomies;—
> Who're all true Catholics in religion,
> Yet, as Mohamet let his pigeon,
> Let those who call our bad birds here,
> Whisper rebellion in their ear.
> No wonder, then, their list'ner's stray'd
> From what they should have done or said!
> Thus Pettagouschach said he's take
> The French King's part, for conscience sake;
> And that,—because the priest Gebau
> Cajoled him with a petted crow.

Sly Siggenaak (Sigenak—Blackbird) and Naakewoin (Nakiyowin—Wind Striker) were the two largest thorns in De Peyster's side, of which Mr. Blackbird (as George Rogers Clark called him) was the sharpest and most painful.[6] Pettagouschach (Padekoshēk—Pile of Lead), in turn, was the French loyalist, Catholic okama of a St. Joseph River village. These were not the only American-leaning Potawatomi leaders in the northern Illinois area. Two others, who were identified by Clark's aide, Major Joseph Bowman, were To-Mech-Kigic or Mech Kigie (Matchigizhek—Big Sky) and Nanaloibi (untranslatable), okamek of Chicago area villages (IHC 8: 311–13). With names such as Blackbird, Wind Striker, and Big Sky, it is evident that the opposition to the British in the Chicago-Milwaukee area was led by elements if not all of the Thunder Clan.

Sigenak is of particular interest because he rapidly achieved a position of some fame (or ill-fame, from the perspective of Michilimackinac), and then within a few years seems to have disappeared. Or it is quite possible that he assumed a different name—Onangizes is a real possibility—by which he was later known to Americans. He apparently was one of the anti-British Potawatomi from the St. Joseph River region who migrated to northern Illinois and the Milwaukee area after the failure of Pontiac's rebellion. However, he seems to have spent part of his time in later years at St. Joseph as well, which would not have been unusual for the very mobile Potawatomi. Some have concluded that he was actually an Ojibwa or an Odawa of the St. Joseph River, but this inference is based on an ambiguous reference from the reports of George Rogers Clark, or on secondary commentaries based on Clark's original words (Voegelin & Jones 1974: 171–73).

After Clark's 1778 victory in Illinois he reported that he had turned his "attention to Saguina Mr Black Bird & Nakiowin two Chiefs of the Bands of the Sotairs [Saulteur, i.e., Ojibwa] and outaway Nation bordering on Lake Michigan and the River St Joseph Mr Black Bird and party was in St Louis at the time Majr Bowman took possession Koho [Cahokia]." Clark then commented that Mr. Blackbird and party had been convinced it was in their best interest to ally themselves with the Americans. He then "made strict enquiery about Black Bird I found that they ware chiefs of Considerable Bands about St Joseph then at war that Black Bird had great Influance in that Quarter and that it was thought by some Traders lately arrived that he Really wanted a Conference but wished to have an Invitation &c." Clark dispatched the invitation, and shortly Blackbird with eight companions arrived to visit him in Kaskaskia. There, after "they had Rested and got Refreshed he observed some Utial preparations for an Indian counsel" (James 1912: 125). It was on the basis of such reports that Patrick Henry later reported to Virginia's delegates in Congress: "The Great Blackbird, a Chippewa Chief, has also sent a belt of peace to Col. Clark, influenced, he [Clark] supposes, by the dread of Detroit's being reduced by the American arms" (James 1912: 72–73).

What is evident in this passage is some considerable confusion about the geography of Lake Michigan and the location of Detroit (which was of no particular interest to Blackbird, since he did his business at St. Louis), as well as a lack of sharp understanding of the tribal alignments and affiliations in the area. Clark (much less Patrick Henry) had no firsthand familiarity with the area or its populations, and he was dependent upon what the local French traders in southern Illinois could tell him. His vagueness about tribal alignments is clearly indicated by the lumping of the Ojibwa and the Odawa as one "Nation," while his dependence upon secondhand, likely out-of-date information is suggested by his use of the then obsolescent French term "Saulteur" for the villages then collectively known as the Ojibwa or Chippewa.

However, De Peyster—who was the better-experienced agent in the Lake Michigan area—had no reluctance in identifying Blackbird as a renegade Milwaukee Potawatomi, although he was much less concerned with Sigenak's tribal identity than he was with the great trouble Mr. Blackbird was causing him. It was Blackbird and Wind Striker, first and foremost, who had avoided trading with the British at Michilimackinac or Detroit; it was they who had used their influence to turn Potawatomi (and some Odawa and Ojibwa) attention to the Spanish in St. Louis; and it was they who refused to provide aid to the British in the first years of the revolution. As Clark remarked, once the Americans had conquered southern Illinois and Indiana and started operating in northern Illinois, Sigenak's neutral stance changed to open support of the rebel cause.

Clark and Blackbird hit it off very well in their conference at Kaskaskia in the fall of 1778. Clark found Blackbird to be a most cosmopolitan kind of man with, he thought, the manners of a polite gentleman, and a style of doing business that seemed distinctly un-Indian. Blackbird wanted to get directly to the point, was not concerned with calumet smoking or other ritualized niceties, sat up to table with Clark, listened attentively to Clark's presentation of the American case, asked sharp questions, drove a bargain, shook hands, and went about his own business (IHC 8: 252–58). Thus it was that the influence of Blackbird—and other Potawatomi okamek in northern Illinois and southern Wisconsin—turned the wavering British loyalties of the St. Joseph Potawatomi towards a position of neutrality.

For this alone Henry Hamilton at Detroit and Arent De Peyster had ample reason for concern. But the Milwaukee-Chicago area Potawatomi did not hold to a passive neutrality. Instead, they shortly took the field to attack British traders and posts in the Lake Michigan area. In 1779 Sigenak and his associates in the Milwaukee area were reported as aiding the Americans with supplies and horses, and in the construction of boats (WHC 11: 128; IHC 8: 311–12). Knowing that the Spanish wanted to strike at the British, and after an unsuccessful raid on St. Joseph led by the French of southern Illinois in late 1780, Sigenak journeyed to St. Louis that winter to provide intelligence information and to encourage a substantial assault on British positions in southwestern Michigan. Some six weeks later, on 12 February 1781, some sixty Potawatomi, Ojibwa, and Odawa led by Sigenak and Nakiyowin joined with an equal force of Spanish soldiers in a successful attack on the British post on the St. Joseph River. The local Potawatomi were persuaded to stand aside passively and were rewarded with half the spoils of the battle.[7] All this work had little long-range impact, however, for the Spanish quickly retreated to St.

Louis, while the American forces in Illinois and Indiana moved back south of the Ohio, again shifting the balance of power in the Lake Michigan area back to the British.

In the years following the Revolution other Potawatomi leaders came to the fore. In 1788 it was a "chief" named Le Grande Couete who offered an alliance with the Americans in exchange for support in a war against the Weas and Miamis. When rejected at Vincennes by the suspicious Captain John Hamtramck, this group of Potawatomi then tried to raid American settlements in Kentucky; but during their retreat they were pressed hard by the Kentucky militia and Le Grande Couete was killed (Thornbrough 1957: 122, 159, 162; ASP-IA 1: 10). This is a name of some curiosity, since the French "couette" (phonetically, "kwet") means either "seagull" or "featherbed," while in Potawatomi "seagull" is "kwesk." Hence the deceased war-party leader was likely named the Big Sea Gull (Matchikwesk).

Of the few Illinois River Potawatomi who met with Rufus Putnam in 1792 to sign the unratified treaty mentioned in earlier pages, La Gesse (the Quail) acted as spokesman. La Gesse had accompanied Sigenak in the raid on St. Joseph eleven years earlier, and it was he who persuaded the southeastern Michigan Potawatomi to stay out of that skirmish. After putting his mark on the treaty, La Gesse accompanied a second signer, Gomo, to Philadelphia for a visit with President Washington, and there he died. Gomo, or Missenogomaw as his name appears on the Treaty of Greenville, is the most interesting participant in the Putnam negotiations, for he lived to emerge as the model of an American sponsored "chief" of the Illinois River Potawatomi until his death in 1814.[8] The dealings with Putnam in 1792 are of particular interest, for not one of the participants was an accredited representative of the Illinois Potawatomi, none were recognized as okamek by their own people at the time, and their involvement with Putnam at that moment illustrates the ways in which an upstart "chief" emerged—by successful dealings with an outside power (MPHC 24: 108, 167; ASP-IA 1: 241; Buell 1903: 302-03). At the start, Gomo—the Chief or the Big Chief, or whatever his actual name was—was a fraud, if a successful one.

On 9 August 1792, Captain John Hamtramck reported to General Putnam that he had sent Putnam's message calling for a council to the Illinois Potawatomi "by the son of the first King of that Nation who has been with me for some time (I suppose as a Spye) and he assures me that he will bring this Nation to see you—as they Sincerely wish to be at Peace with the U States—I shall have some Difficulty to send to the Illinois Country, owing to the extravagant Price they ask. however it must be done" (Buell 1903: 320-21). The "son of the first King" of the Potawatomi must have traveled swiftly to Illinois with the "extravagant Price" he had extorted from Hamtramck, upon his arrival making some equally extravagant promises; but he did not return to Vincennes with a legitimate body of Illinois Potawatomi representatives.

What actually happened in Illinois was reported after the treaty by Joseph E. Collins, an American spy who toured the Illinois country in the winter of 1792–1793. He reported that the Potawatomi and other tribes in Illinois had ridiculed the supposed "chiefs" who had done business with Putnam. The Potawatomi okamek in Illinois told Collins that some young men had "imposed themselves upon Genl Putnam, at the Treaty of Vincennes as Chiefs when in fact they were nothing but common men or rather blackguards." When Collins inquired why the okamek themselves had not come to Vincennes they told him that the messengers (including Hamtramck's "son of the first King") had not invited them. Instead, they had "stoped at the first encampments they met with—& and carried off some of there common people with them—we shall see what kind of Chiefs they are when they return—they will probably attempt to give away our Lands—as the others of the same sort of self created Chiefs did at the Treaty of Muskingum" (Collins 1793).

Along with the Potawatomi there were supposed representatives of the Kickapoo, Peoria, Mascouten, Kaskaskia, and several Miami groups present in September 1792 for the Vincennes treaty, all of them elbowing for attention and influence, making up their own protocol as they proceeded. The Potawatomi spokesman, La Gesse, was very deferential to Putnam and addressed him as "Father," while managing to shunt the Miami and Peoria aside as "younger brothers" (i.e., subordinates), and acting as spokesman for the Mascouten as well. La Gesse told Putnam that he had been allied with the French and Spanish during the late war and had never struck against the Americans. What he wanted was peace and prosperity. La Gesse also admonished the other tribes to make peace with the United States (Buell 1903: 329–32). It was an accomplished bit of acting on the part of the Potawatomi "blackguards" present in Vincennes, a performance which Putnam swallowed whole. Out of this first contact, however, emerged a man who well served American interests as their "first chief" of the Illinois River Potawatomi. This was the famous Gomo, who was an okama made, not born.

At the time of the Putnam treaty Gomo was about twenty-seven years old. As a child he had been orphaned, and he and his brother (Senajiwan, or Petcha'o) and sister had been raised near Lake Peoria in the home of a French trader, Louis Chattelrou. He was raised a Catholic and mastered French, and as a growing boy watched George Rogers Clark in operation near Kaskaskia in 1778. His participation in the Putnam treaty and his subsequent visit to President Washington made him a success in the Illinois River valley, in the same manner as a much earlier generation of young and ambitious Potawatomi men, such as the first Onangizes, had made their mark by skillful ex-

ploitation of a relationship with an outside power. In the twenty years following the Putnam treaty, Gomo was to serve as the preferred American chief in
the area; but his role was not one without conflicts. In 1811, on the edge of
another war in the Old Northwest, while being heavily pressured to support
the Americans during a council at Peoria, Gomo spoke these words: "Formerly we all lived in one large village. In that village there was only one
chief, and all things went on well; but since our intercourse with the whites,
there are almost as many chiefs as we have young men" (Edwards 1870: 47).
Like the Potawatomi okamek of 1668 and all the years after, Gomo had to
explain to his patron that he did not have at his fingertips all the power that
the Americans might wish he had over the unruly young warriors. By 1811
Gomo was glamorizing the past, forgetting—or ignoring—the route he and
La Gesse had taken to power and influence.[9]

The idea that the Potawatomi had or, rather, that they might obtain a
single okama with authority and responsibilities going beyond the limits of
a single clan-village was not new in the 1790s. This kind of conception dates
back at least to the time of the first Onangizes in the years when he was doing
private business with Governor Frontenac in Montreal. The historical record
and the contemporary ethnographic record are clear on this point: Potawatomi
men and their okamek have never been noted for allowing their reach to be
limited by their grasp.[10] Throughout their history the tribe has been noted
for an intense rivalry between men seeking influence beyond that allowable
by the norms of their culture. The confrontation of men seeking power with
the available means of exercising controls over those who obtained the strength
to influence or coerce their fellows was a dualistic, conflicted theme, one of the
fundamental dynamics in the adaptation of the Potawatomi to their changing
historical circumstances. However, during the interregnum this conflict of
authority versus autonomy reached toward a new peak, for outsiders increasingly began seeking to identify and support their own candidates for the position of chief supreme over all or some subgroup of Potawatomi.

This process is best illustrated in the advice offered in 1779 by Louis
Chevalier—the supposed British agent in the St. Joseph area—to General Frederick Haldimand, governor-general of Canada (MPHC 19: 375). Haldimand
was concerned with the inroads George Rogers Clark had made among the
Potawatomi, and Chevalier wrote him, saying,

> This nation in general is very inconsistent in its friendships but never in its
> hatred, wavering in their good resolutions even to the point of abandoning
> them. Timid in danger, proud & haughty when they believe themselves in
> safety, credulous to the last degree, easily led away by great promises &
> frightened by threats. These are the two means that the Rebels used to cor-
> rupt part of this nation. . . . The evil is almost without a remedy, it is not

without trouble that I have arrested the progress of this corruption. . . . It does not seem to me, however, impossible to keep this nation in dependence, if they were united under the same chief, but divided as it is into six villages distance fifteen to twenty miles from each other it is very difficult to impose this yoke. Each village has its own chief who dispose his young men according to his private ideas. . . .

Chevalier's reference was to the six Potawatomi villages along the St. Joseph River, and the difficulties he envisioned in imposing the yoke of a single chief were even greater if the remoteness of the Potawatomi of Wisconsin, Illinois, and Indiana were to be considered.

However, the idea of a single chief supported by an outside power was well planted, and it flourished in the years following the American Revolution. The man who emerged as claimant to this incipient office in the St. Joseph area was Topnibe—Sits Quietly, of the Bear Clan. It was he who was later thought to be the "red sovereign of *the nation*" by some American Indian agents (DRC 11YY36–36[1] & 37–37[1]). But Topnibe was not without rivals or competitors. In 1792, for instance, La Gesse told Hamtramck at Vincennes that he was and should be recognized and supported as the "first and great chief of the Pattawatamies" (ASP-IA 1: 241). Three years later, in the preliminaries to the Treaty of Greenville, Gizes—speaking with reference to the Potawatomi villages on the Wabash River—told Thomas Pasteur of the United States War Department, "If anyone should come & tell you they [i.e., that] they are over me, they lie, don't believe them, I am Master, I keeps my people in order."[11] Gizes was addressing himself specifically to the pretensions of Topnibe and the problems posed by American concentration on support of that Bear Clan okama. But he made too much of the degree of his own power even over his own villagers, for later—during the treaty proceedings proper—Gizes had to inform General Wayne of his real limitations, saying, "Father, I have not the same authority over my people, that you exercise over yours. They live dispersed, and it is difficult to reach them on all occasions" (ASP-IA 1: 580–81). It is clear from this passage that Gizes was impressed by and was using Wayne's own position as a standard or reference point for his own position, and equally clear that he misperceived the amount and permanency of Wayne's powers.

Following the Treaty of Greenville, the Americans still seemed convinced that Topnibe on the St. Joseph River was the focal point of political power among the Potawatomi. When the Potawatomi on the Wabash River became unruly, they addressed their complaints to Topnibe, and he had to explain the limits of his authority. But he spoke as if he were the okama of all Potawatomi nonetheless, saying, "I have used every measure to prevent our people from settling on the Wabash . . . last Summer I ordered my people from the Wa-

bash, but they were deaf to me . . . Too many of our nation aspire to be chiefs
—and when they find—they cannot be such in their own Country—they fly to
the woods, and impose themselves upon people of other tribes, as Chiefs—intrude upon Lands not belonging to them, and are not only troublesome to us,
but to all who meet them."[12] Here is an eloquent, succinct statement of the
old mechanism of fission and dispersal of clan-segments and their intrusion
into lands occupied by other tribes, which had been the basis for Potawatomi
tribal expansion since the 1670s. It is also quite clear that Topnibe conceived
of himself as having powers and responsibilities extending well beyond the
limits of either the Bear Clan or the villages along the St. Joseph River, although other Potawatomi did not agree with him in these aspirations.

Such differences of opinion concerning the authority of local okamek
were by no means confined to disputes between those living on the St. Joseph
and the Wabash rivers. There were numerous Potawatomi elsewhere in Illinois and Wisconsin. Although there were some few representatives from all
major areas occupied by the tribe present at the Treaty of Greenville, and
despite the fact that the Potawatomi signatories of that document were the
most numerous of all the tribes present, the Potawatomi villages in Illinois
and Wisconsin were underrepresented. Indeed, so far as American officialdom
was concerned, it was not known that there were Potawatomi villages north
of Milwaukee; and the tribesmen in that area would remain almost unrecognized by American agents as Potawatomi for many years after 1795. Although
not specifically addressing himself to the Potawatomi, upon receipt of the
completed treaty on 27 September 1795 Secretary of War Pickering expressed
grave concern to both President Washington and General Wayne that too few
chiefs had been present to negotiate and sign the document (TP-US 2: 537–38;
Knopf 1960: 562–63). Pickering was worried that land cessions made without
the consent of all the chiefs involved would leave open the possibility of further
strife on the northwest frontier. As events soon demonstrated, he had reason
for some anxiety.

Those Potawatomi who signed the Treaty of Greenville had agreed to the
cession of three parcels of land of direct interest to the Illinois-Wisconsin
Potawatomi. These consisted of one parcel six miles square at the mouth of
the Chicago River, one twelve miles square at the mouth of the Illinois River
on the Mississippi, and one six miles square on the Illinois River near present
Peoria (Kappler 1972: 40). In the summer of 1796 several of the Potawatomi
okamek from the west met with an American representative, probably General
Wayne, and expressed their complaints about what happened (Potawatomi
Chiefs 1796). These included an unidentified okama from the Chicago area,
Wabenaneto (Wabimanito—White Spirit) from the Joliet area, and Sho'cto:to
(probably Shawota—Brings the South Wind) of the Milwaukee area.

The unidentified okama told Wayne that they had not been present at the Greenville treaty and that they wanted to know who of their fellow tribesmen had ceded the Illinois lands without their consent. But White Spirit informed Wayne that they were not displeased with the spirit of the treaty, that they wanted peace and friendship. In addition to not being involved in the treaty deliberations, the Illinois-Wisconsin Potawatomi never received any of the annual annuity pledged to the Potawatomies by the Greenville agreement. The Indiana-Michigan Potawatomi collected the thousand dollars annually and made no provision for sharing it with their western kinsmen (TP-US 17: 228). However, relations with the Western Potawatomi did not remain comfortable for long, and it was eight years before the United States could move to occupy and to establish Fort Dearborn on the lands ceded near Chicago.

By 1796 the Potawatomi tribe was on the edge of a major, disruptive crisis in governance. Political institutions that had served them well during 125 years of tribal growth and territorial expansion had begun to break down. The needs of local groups—the clans and villages—as well as of regional coalitions of villages, were taking precedence over tribal-wide interests and processes of decision making. The vast increase in the size of the tribal estate had placed the villages at such distances from one another that communication and coordination were difficult, if not on occasion impossible. And the interests, concerns, values, and adaptations of the different villages began to diverge, particularly so when after 1800 the American frontier began to press in rapidly on their lands. Accidents of geography combined with American efforts to administer affairs economically so as to result in a differential distribution of payments and rewards to different groups of Potawatomi. The Illinois River–Wisconsin Potawatomi, for example, did not share in the Greenville annuity payment because it was distributed at the American post at Fort Wayne or at Detroit.

With the establishment of numerous agricultural settlements, mission stations, trading posts, Indian agencies, forts, and other elements of the growing American presence in the Old Northwest, the stresses and strains within the tribe increased dramatically. There were in 1795 already numerous Frenchified and a few Americanized Potawatomi to add linguistic and cultural variety to the differences within the tribe. Within a few short years, when the pace of change became too fast for satisfactory group adjustment, much less the creation and perfection of a whole new style of adaptation, the divisions within the tribe would generate intense conflict and schism.

It was problem enough when the ambitions of a few Potawatomi okamek were in concert with the interests of the official representative of the United States government, allowing some to play with the idea of being chief-over-all. Within a few years the number of such upstart chiefs would proliferate dangerously. Shortly, each local Indian agency and every company of traders would be advancing their personal Potawatomi clients as the sole, legitimate, recognized chief. When this process reached full growth, clan and village leaders would find themselves in severe conflict, unable to satisfy the demands of both their American or British patrons and the needs and expectations of their own kinsmen and neighbors. There would then be too many okamek, each with too little legitimate authority, most suffering from the skepticism and anger of their followers. Then few would be able to contribute adequately to the orderly process of Potawatomi tribal or village governance, and a new form of leadership would emerge. Within three decades following the Treaty of Greenville, the basic fabric of the Potawatomi tribe would be dissolved and the tribe would be broken into a number of separate and sometimes antagonistic parts.

PATTERNS OF
FEUDING AND WARFARE

The traditional means of settling extra-village blood feuds were the basis for the patterns of Potawatomi warfare that emerged in the eighteenth century. A feud-precipitating crisis developed when some member of a clan suffered death, injury, or insult at the hands of a second party. Such an injury was felt as a blow to the entire clan, one which weakened the magical power and energy of this primary reference group. The injury or insult did not have to be an actual event: if a clan member apprehended such an outrage in a dream or other visionary experience, it was sufficient to provoke and to validate arrangements for retaliation. Thus the Potawatomi rationalized feuding and warfare in two connected ways: these were a primary means for a man to obtain prestige and renown, and they were a powerful restorative which recharged the energies of the warrior and his clan. A successful war-party, as Landes has noted, "exemplified a high point of group well-being" (1970: 266). The difference between feuding among clans—or between a Potawatomi clan and a group from another tribe—and warfare proper involved a difference of scale as well as kind. Warfare consisted of armed combat between members of different political communities, involving several or more Potawatomi clans, if not the whole tribe, arrayed against one or more other societies.[13] However rationalized by the Potawatomi themselves, beginning in the late seventeenth century their war-parties functioned both to defend as well as to expand the tribal hunting grounds, fishing sites, garden lands, and village locations. War was one of the important mechanisms used in their continuous expansion into new territories. But successful war-parties also added other kinds of wealth to the resources of the tribe, such as booty and prisoners.

The patterns of Potawatomi warfare were similar to those Wallace has outlined for other tribal societies in the Eastern Woodlands of North America (1970b: 7–9). But there were important differences between Potawatomi war customs and those of other tribes (Marston 1820: 161–62; Keating 1824: 122). Once the basic injury was actually experienced or dreamed of, a Potawatomi warrior blackened his face, made his intentions publicly known, and prepared a temporary wigwam with a red wampum belt or a strip of red cloth hanging in the center. There he remained contemplating his plans, receiving volunteers who expressed their wish to join him. The initiator of the war-party did not necessarily have to be a fully experienced or recognized okamawokitchita—warrior leader. The visionary experience of outrage and the determination to seek retribution were sufficient to provoke interest and some support, while even the most experienced war-party leader obviously had to start somewhere with his first effort at organized retribution. The prospective war-party leader might be encouraged or discouraged by his clansmen, especially the women, elders, and village leaders. With their support, and with sufficient volunteers coming in, the group of warriors would then join in ritual fasting, abstaining from sexual intercourse and other sources of pollution, dreaming and comparing their dreams, storing up their magical powers, and working up their courage before starting forth to attack their enemy.

Before departing for their approach to the enemy's camp, the effort to arrange a war-party might be aborted in any of several fashions. The initiator might not draw sufficient support from the warriors. Elders, women, and clan leaders could mobilize public opinion against him. The village okama might even go so far as to confiscate the party's pitchkosan, their sacred bundle around which the preparatory rituals had been centered, and which they would have to carry with them to provide the magical power needed for success. The Potawatomi village okama could also draw a magic net around the war-party by walking around the group, symbolizing opposition and counteracting the war-powers of the party. But no okama would take such an extreme step unless community opposition were great, and even then it would not necessarily work. As many Potawatomi okamek repeatedly told French, British, Spanish, and American officials, in the end they had no effective authority over their young men. Their classic phrase was the invariable "the young men have no sense." A Potawatomi war-party thus consisted of a small or large group of men who had formed a kind of magical-supernatural pact with one another, among other things agreeing to eat portions of any enemies they might kill, an action that would both symbolize their rage and aid them in incorporating some of the personal spirit-power of the people they had killed in battle (Landes 1970: 50–54).[14]

Potawatomi military tactics were similar to those of other Eastern Woodlands tribes. These developed from one central principle: the object of war was to cause the enemy to suffer casualties and to capture prisoners and booty, and to avoid if at all possible any losses to the attacking group. These tribes-men firmly believed that the warrior who fired accurately or who struck a deadly blow and flitted away would survive to reap the glory of his exploit, as well as remaining available for combat on another day. For this reason the Potawatomi and related tribes were masters of the surprise ambush, and they favored guile and deceit to place themselves armed and ready in an unsuspect-ing enemy's camp. As Colonel Henry Bouquet analyzed the tactical maneuvers of the Woodlands tribes, they preferred to fight in a loose, scattered formation from the flanks; they attempted to surround their opponents wherever they could; and they would easily yield ground at any point where they were pressed hard, but would return to the attack at points where their opponents were weakest or unsuspecting (Williams 1959).[15]

Potawatomi military tactics were designed to cope with the war-parties of societies much like themselves; but they worked exceedingly well when di-rected against the defenses of Euro-American frontier settlements, as well as against untrained, ill-experienced militia units and those regular army units that had not learned to cope with the problems of forest warfare. One estimate of the casualties suffered by all tribes as against Euro-American battle losses on the Ohio, Virginia, Pennsylvania, and Kentucky frontiers from the time of first contact to 1825 yielded a count of 7,837 Indians and 12,002 Euro-Americans killed or died of wounds suffered in action (Moorehead 1899). These raw numbers yield a ratio of 1 Indian to 1.5 Euro-Americans killed, and this is a useful if crude measure of the effectiveness of the patterns of warfare employed by the Potawatomi and other tribes. However, such raw numbers are mislead-ing since those killed represented a much higher percentage of the avail-able manpower in the tribes than was the case for the French, British, and Americans.

Potawatomi tactics—as is the case with military tactics of other societies generally—were built around their available technology of war, their weap-onry. For initial shock and long-range killing power the Potawatomi relied on the bow—tikwap and arrow—kitakwen or shati, and later the imported flint-lock trade musket—zigwebaske'gan. Fired in volleys from cover on the flanks of an unsuspecting, unprepared enemy unit, such weapons had great shock value and could effectively disrupt Euro-American formations and demoralize the troops. The Potawatomi, if successful in their initial attack, could follow up immediately with a variety of weapons for close combat, including shield —wawiyashan; a ball-headed war club—pēkwapto or pkēmakēn; tomahawk-- p'kēmasag n; a flat war club—showakta; as well as knives, spears, and lances (Skinner 1924–27: 298–99; Clifton 1972/74). When the shock of the Pota-watomi assault and penetration was great enough to destroy the enemy's capacity for effective resistance, precipitating a rout and retreat, the war-party was capable of immediate and effective pursuit of stragglers and fleeing troops. This was one of the major advantages of the decentralization of command in these tribal war-parties, of the reliance on individual initiative, and of the looseness of the tactical formations. Pursuing the remnants of a defeated enemy force provided an additional opportunity for warriors to obtain a kill or trophies and booty.

The victorious Potawatomi war-leader had charge of any prisoners and a say in their disposal after the return to the home villages (Marston 1820: 162). Prisoners might be tortured and killed, further insulting the enemy group, or they could be adopted by bereaved families as replacements for a lost son or daughter. Successful warriors had their exploits memorialized in several ways. Eagle feathers were awarded to those who had killed an enemy; their deeds were recounted in song and legend; and feats involving man-to-man combat were noted by incising symbols on a coup stick or on a special kind of war-club shaped like the stock of an antique French wheel-lock musket (Landes 1963: 586 & 1970: 262–68). The successful warrior—one who had actually killed an enemy and who carried home a trophy commemorating the event—was considered a man weakened and polluted by powerful supernatural forces. He had to acquire a new name which symbolized a transformation in his identity, although the name was not a proper clan eponym.

Potawatomi war-parties were not always composed exclusively of men. Occasionally a woman was temperamentally disposed or situationally encouraged to adopt the role of watasakwē—warrior woman. A nineteenth-century legend tells how one Potawatomi woman rescued her captive husband from the Kiowa, after the warriors had abandoned hope for his life. The tale concludes with the statement that ever after she went to war with the men, and that she was the first Potawatomi woman to be called watasakwē (Skinner 1924/27: 393–95). This is certainly not true, for in January 1779, during the Revolutionary War, when Henry Hamilton at Detroit was organizing war-parties to send against American settlements, Ashkibi—New River brought with him a "Squaa named Cataboe who insisted on having a gun and going to war with them" (Barnhart 1951: 171–73).[16]

Employed against both frontier settlements and British or American military units, the weapons and tactics employed by the Potawatomi and other tribes frequently had a devastating effect. The techniques of small-party raids employing stealth, ruse, and ambush were particularly effective when used against small parties of settlers in the open or at farmsteads. However, when the settlers banded together into larger parties in forts and blockhouses, the tribal techniques of war were less useful, particularly if long sieges were required, for it was difficult for a war leader to maintain the discipline needed to wear the defenders down, and the tribesmen generally lacked the artillery to take a fortified position by force of arms.

The Potawatomi and their allies generally assaulted large regular-army or militia units when they were the most vulnerable—while they were on the march, or before they had maneuvered into the preferred formation from which the troops had been trained to fight. British tactics in the period were dictated by the main weapon, the flintlock, smooth-bore musket, which had an effective range of no more than about eighty yards (Eccles 1966: xvi). The British, and for a long time many American units, emphasized the use of a line formation composed of three ranks which fired in volleys under the strict management of trained officers. Employed against conventional military forces in defensive positions or in lines and columns in the open, standing ready to meet an attack, such conventional tactics were effective enough. However, such tactics required rigid discipline, long training, and an opponent who was willing to fight in the same fashion.

This the tribal war-parties were rarely willing to do. Instead, they generally assaulted the army or militia units during their approach march, before they had time to form and arrange their ranks, while they were on the move, stretched out in a long, unwary, and uncoordinated column on narrow trails and roads. Under such conditions a war-party could fire and assault from cover before the military units could form ranks, impose discipline, employ the preferred volley fire, and even before they could safely reload. Under such conditions, a smaller war-party could defeat a larger regular or militia force piecemeal, beating up parts of a dispersed column before those attacked could organize an effective resistance and maneuver for a counterassault.

The innovations adopted and perfected by General Anthony Wayne departed far from the tactical doctrine of earlier years. He did not move to the attack before his troops had been effectively trained and disciplined. He never maneuvered far from a strong fortified base. He did not allow himself to be surprised. And when he attacked at Fallen Timbers, he employed three fast-moving, well-coordinated columns against Indian opponents who tried to stand firm in a defensive position. During the next three decades, some Potawatomi and parts of other tribes in the Old Northwest would on occasion meet and defeat regular United States Army units or scratch militia forces; but their main successes would continue to be surprise attacks against small, unprepared groups of settlers or isolated garrisons. In moving up to the edge of the Potawatomi tribal estate, the American frontier had provided a base of operations for swift counteraction. As the patterns of tribal governance began to weaken, the capacity of the tribesmen to mount an effective military effort also started to decline rapidly. Both, combined, would contribute to a loss of the capacity for autonomous political and military action on the part of the Potawatomi and other tribes in the northwest country.

8

The Diminishing Estate: 1796~1837

A rapid advance of the line of American settlements into the Old Northwest Territory marked the four decades following the Treaty of Greenville. In these scant forty years successive administrations—Federalist, Jeffersonian Republican, and Jacksonian Democrat—converted the promise and the mechanisms of the Northwest Ordinance into the reality of organized states and territories, while the nominal American sovereignty seized by Anthony Wayne in 1795 was translated into actual control over and occupation of the ground. These were also years when Potawatomi okamek and their kinsmen had to cope with and adjust to the accelerating growth of the American presence, population, and institutions. In 1800 Americans in the territory numbered 51,000, over 45,000 of whom lived in Ohio, with the balance—mainly old settler French-speaking Métis—clustered in the established centers of trade, around Detroit, or in southern Illinois and Indiana. Another 220,000 Americans in 1800 populated Kentucky, which had achieved statehood in 1792.[1] Ohio became a state in 1803, in the same year the Louisiana Purchase circled the Potawatomi tribal estate with lands subject to American sovereignty. By 1816 Indiana had also become a state, followed by Illinois in 1818, Michigan in 1837, and Wisconsin a decade later in 1848. In 1830 the American population of the states and territories carved out of the Old Northwest Territory swelled to nearly 1,500,000 persons, the vast majority of whom lived south of a line drawn between present Chicago and Detroit.

Commensurate with the expansion of American society and territory came a steady decline in the power and landholdings of the tribal societies that had for long centuries persisted and sustained themselves in the prairies and woodlands of the western Great Lakes. Coupled with the advance of the American frontier had come dramatic changes in the habitats that had supported these tribes. The game was no longer adequate to sustain them, while the fur trade had declined to a scarcely marginal enterprise, insufficient to provide the tribal populations with income adequate to purchase the necessaries of subsistence. Why did the Potawatomi and other tribes assent so readily to many treaties?

"The Indians always arrive at our treaty grounds poor and naked," explained Lewis Cass, then governor of Michigan Territory. "They expect to receive some part of the consideration at the moment of signing the treaty. This expectation, in fact, furnishes the only motive for their attendance, and much the most powerful motive for their assent to the measures proposed to them" (ASP-IA 2: 683–84).

On the day Wapmini, Sigenak, Topnebi, Gizes, Mzhikteno, Wakaya, and their fellow Potawatomi signed the Greenville document, the tribe numbered perhaps six to seven thousand persons. Claiming rights to some eighteen million acres of prairies and woods, bottom lands and marshes, streams and lakes

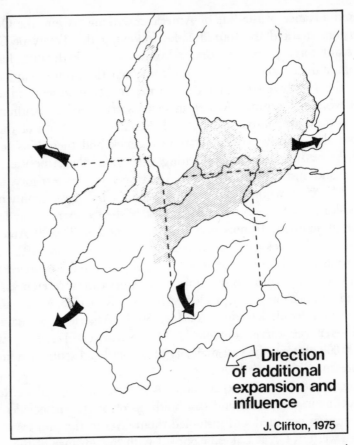

Direction of additional expansion and influence

J. Clifton, 1975

Figure 10. The tribal estate at its peak, 1812. The Potawatomi participated in treaties ceding more territory than they actually occupied or hunted over, while some of the areas used by them longest and most extensively were ceded to the United States by other tribes.

(see Figure 10), it was an intact, autonomous, and flourishing society, one which prospered—in its fashion. Some parts of this huge estate the Potawatomi actively occupied and used intensively. Other portions they dominated and used as hunting grounds, while sharing the fruits of the land with allied tribes. Additional hundreds of square miles they would maintain—if dubiously—were rightly theirs, although such claims were much disputed by other tribes. However, because of the motives suggested by Lewis Cass, as well as for other reasons, between 1795 and 1837 the Potawatomi entered into thirty-eight treaties with the United States. Three of these treaties—in 1814–1815—ended Potawatomi involvement in the War of 1812. These three signified the end of political autonomy for the tribe, for afterward the Potawatomi lacked the capacity to defend themselves by force of arms against American incursions. One other treaty, at Prairie du Chien in 1825, involved little more than an American effort to reach agreement on boundaries between the several tribes of Wisconsin, Illinois, Iowa, and Minnesota—so as to facilitate later land cessions. The remaining thirty-four, six before the War of 1812, twenty-eight after, all involved the surrender of tribal lands to the United States for some consideration (see Figure 11). The payments consisted of cash, rations, and goods-in-hand delivered immediately on the treaty grounds; limited term and perpetual annuities payable in hard money, goods, and services to be delivered annually; and, finally, new reservation lands located west of the Mississippi River.

Swiftly changing conditions of life during the four decades after the Greenville treaty necessitated alterations in the forms and styles of Potawatomi adaptations. Early on, an intensification of the pattern of raiding and warfare, an increased involvement in intertribal alliances, and a renewed reliance on the British in Upper Canada constituted one pattern of adjustment (Temple 1958: 133–34). When war failed them, the Potawatomi turned in other directions, sometimes embracing religious and cultural revitalization movements conceived by prophets from other tribes, sometimes syncretizing new belief systems of their own, sometimes exploring the possibilities of radically different subsistence patterns and new work roles for men, sometimes casting political-military alliances with the United States. Voluntary or encouraged migration was one cultural strategy much employed, at first within the bounds of the old tribal estate, eventually into territory outside the range of American sovereignty and settlement pressure. Throughout, the Potawatomi were rarely entirely without some means—however limited—of influencing the course of events.

American policy, both in conception and execution, was never a monolithic structure dictated in a distant capital and arbitrarily imposed on the tribesmen. The Potawatomi were not helpless, and they had their friends and

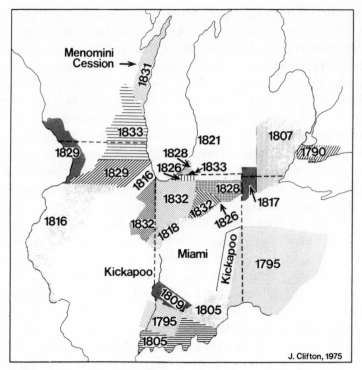

Figure 11. Potawatomi treaties and land cessions, 1795–1837. Some of the minor cessions, especially those of the tiny "band reservations" in Indiana between 1834 and 1837, are not shown.

spokesmen in the other camp, some of whom, too, conceived alternate paths towards the future of the tribe. There were, however, basic themes that underlay the variations in American policy. A choice between diplomacy or force was one such—"there is nothing to be obtained by an Indian War," wrote George Washington in 1783, "but the soil they live on and this can be had by purchase at less expense" (Fitzpatrick 1931/44: 136–37). The preferred tactic, diplomacy, meant dealing with the tribes within the rubric of a legal fiction, as if they were sovereign, independent nations. This required the prescribed format of a treaty council with all its trappings—commissioners appointed by the president, Senate approval, the action of the House of Representatives for any necessary appropriations, and presidential proclamation on the one side; and on the other, the concurrence of tribal representatives with—it was hoped —the acceptance and approval of their kinsmen. If the American preferred policy of diplomacy were to be successful, a minimal amount of cooperation had to be obtained from some Potawatomi. This imperative gave these tribesmen some leverage always, enough that they could often define, sometimes

subvert, or frequently modify the impact of terms dictated by American officialdom. The pattern of relationships between Potawatomi and Americans
throughout these forty years did not simply involve selfish use of the former
by the latter. The basic paradigm was one of reciprocal exploitation, each party
expecting and taking something of value from the other.

The last of the thirty-four treaties surrendering Potawatomi lands in the
Old Northwest was signed in Washington on 11 February 1837 (Kappler
1904: 488–89). On that day seven leaders gave their approval for the extinction of claims to the few remaining fragments of the old tribal estate. This
1837 treaty holds special interest, for in one brief printed page are represented
many important historical and cultural processes. It was the only treaty to
that date the Potawatomi had ever signed outside the boundaries of their own
Great Lakes habitat. But neither at the request of the government nor in consequence of their own promptings had these seven Potawatomi okamek come
to Washington. The prime mover in this treaty was the Reverend Isaac McCoy,
erstwhile self-taught Baptist missionary to the tribe, now self-made authority
on Indian affairs. In 1837, preoccupied still with his personal vision of an all-
Indian state west of the Mississippi, McCoy intended that all Potawatomi
would be assembled in such a Promised Land as where their bodies could be
salvaged, their souls converted, and their customs remade into forms compatible with an American mold.[2] In such ways the 1837 treaty marked the demise of the Potawatomi tribe as a viable political, social, and cultural unit.

Beyond watching the initiative for this treaty come from outside, private
parties, the seven Potawatomi leaders signed the treaty "for themselves and
their respective bands [i.e., villages]"—not on behalf of the tribe proper or any
lesser contained coalition of clans, but severally and individually. A decade
earlier Lewis Cass had tried to secure a final cession of Potawatomi land and
the removal of this people westward, but without success. They had bitterly
resisted such a migration, and Cass predicted that "time, the destruction of the
game, and the approximation of our settlements are necessary before the measure can be successfully proposed to them." Cass believed it of particular importance "that the Indians should be separated into bands [villages], by the
intervention of our settlements." He saw that "as long as they can roam unmolested through the country, we may in vain expect either to reclaim them
from the savage life they lead, or to induce them to seek a residence where
their habits and pursuits will be less injurious to us" (ASP-IA 2: 684).

The successful American tactic of divide and dispossess bore much fruit,
including some unanticipated varieties. By 1837 the Potawatomi tribe was
broken into a number of discordant pieces, each moving in very different cultural and geographic directions.[3] The seven signers of this treaty represented
only one of these segments, which included those most heavily missionized

and least capable of fending off alien influence and pressure. These Potawatomi were destined soon to move west to a reserve in Indian Territory, where they would become part of a community known first as the Mission and later the Citizen Potawatomi (Murphy 1961). In fact, the real business of the 1837 transaction was not land cession; the signers merely gave their assent to cessions specified in earlier treaties, while only an additional thirty-two hundred acres of land (the personal reservation of one participant, Kikito—Sun Goes One Place) were surrendered to the United States. Removal of the remaining Potawatomi from the state of Indiana was the important business transacted; its corollary was acceptance of a new reservation in what is now eastern Kansas on the Osage (Marais des Cygnes) River.

The publicly expressed goals of the treaty covered certain items on a concealed agenda. Senator John Tipton of Indiana (who was Isaac McCoy's accessory) got something for his constituents, the removal of the Indians and additional homestead lands for Indiana. Isaac McCoy's plan of Indian colonization in the West received fresh impetus, which increased his influence on the new reservation and his patronage there. Kikito was paid $4,000 for his personal reservation—$1.25 per acre, about what the land could be had for by Americans in direct purchase from government land offices, but perhaps one-fourth its value on the open market. The seven signatories jointly were designated the beneficiaries of $47,680 due from two treaties for Indiana lands drawn the previous year. They also received an expense-paid tour of the capital city and anticipated future rewards from their patrons, Isaac McCoy and his associates. Although this treaty document identifies these seven as "chiefs and headmen" of the Potawatomi tribe, they are better understood as playing out a special kind of newly emergent intermediary role. They were acting as clients of their American patrons, mediating between them and their own kinsmen, working as brokers persuading other Potawatomi to move westward out of range of the line of established American settlements. Thus the 1837 treaty manifested a sharp decline in the traditional authority and influence of Potawatomi village leaders, who now served others as well as their own people, drawing much of their power and resources from outside the community, more so than from their own kinsmen.

Also expressed in the 1837 treaty was the growing heterogeneity of the Potawatomi population, which was becoming increasingly diversified in linguistic and cultural ways. By that year numerous descendants of the old established French-speaking Métis population had changed their status to "Indian by descent," as had some of the offspring of unions between Scots-Irish or Anglo-Saxon traders and Potawatomi women. Two sons of the latter group—John C. and Abram B. Burnett, both men products of Isaac McCoy's mission school on the St. Joseph River—witnessed the 1837 treaty as official interpreters.

By switching their ethnic identities and aligning themselves with the interests and fortunes of the Potawatomi, such persons of mixed ancestry added further cultural dissimilarities to the population; they acted as skillful middlemen for American authorities; they contributed to the formation of socioeconomic classes; and they formed the nucleus of a new elite which would assist the Potawatomi in dissipating such resources as became available to them. In later years, for instance, Abram B. Burnett—a grotesquely corpulent man—would become identified as a "chief" of the Mission or Citizen Potawatomi in Kansas.[4]

But not all Potawatomi groups were so vulnerable to outside influence and pressure in 1837. Other elements of the tribe in that same year were working out alternative adaptations in different locales. Several thousand Potawatomi —organized in traditional clan and lineage units—were on the move towards a refuge in Upper Canada (Clifton 1975b). Another thousand or more from northern Illinois and southern Wisconsin had already migrated west to a reservation on the Missouri River in what is now western Missouri and Iowa, where they took up a High-Plains, buffalo-hunting style of life. Several hundred more had embraced the new religion of Kenakuk, the Kickapoo prophet, and had moved in with his congregation on the Kickapoo Reservation in northeast Kansas, where they worked at becoming settled agriculturists.[5] Many hundreds more were drifting north on both shores of Lake Michigan, away from the prairies and bottoms where American settlement pressure was heaviest, into the thick forests that were less desirable to the new settlers, or onto lands still reserved for Menomini, Ojibwa, or Odawa use. A few more hundreds held on in southeast Wisconsin and in southern Michigan, the latter especially privileged because of their earlier conversion to Christianity. The history of the tribe in these four decades was not simply one of determinative American action followed automatically by passive Potawatomi response. Throughout these years they sought to fashion—and worked at perfecting—alternative adaptations of their own design and making. Their efforts were not entirely without success.

PRELUDE
TO BATTLE

The decade following 1796 was one of relative peace between Great Britain and the United States along the Great Lakes frontier. In the same period the antagonisms of the tribesmen south of the international border were steadily aggravated by the progressive impact of American expansion (Horsman 1964: 113–14). In the seven years between 1803 and 1809 some Potawatomi entered into six treaties with the United States, treaties which accurately defined the tract near Vincennes that had been ceded at Greenville in 1795, that relinquished claims to large tracts in northern Ohio west of the Cuyahoga River and Michigan, and that transferred ownership of other lands in Indiana and Illinois (see Figure 11).[6] Most striking about these treaties is the fact that all the lands involved were marginal to those actually occupied and used by the Potawatomi. The treaties proper were arranged, on the one side, by the governor of Indiana Territory—William Henry Harrison (who had been General Wayne's aide-de-camp at Fallen Timbers), Charles Jouett (Indian agent at Detroit), and William Hull (governor of Michigan Territory); and by a handful of Potawatomi "Sachems, Chiefs, Headmen, and Warriors" on the other. A total of twenty-one different Potawatomi signed these six treaties, but until 1809 each averaged but three Potawatomi signatories, while in 1809 only ten Potawatomi placed their names and totem marks on the document, which was to be the last treaty ratified by the United States prior to the War of 1812.

The Potawatomi involved in these negotiations and agreements represented villages and clans from two distinct areas, those of southeastern Michigan near Detroit, and those from southwestern Michigan and northern Indiana, particularly the St. Joseph River drainage. From the St. Joseph River–northern Indiana area the participants were Topnebi—Sits Quietly; his brother Shissahecon (possibly Shisamko—Standing Bear);[7] and Mkoge—Bear's Foot, of the Bear Clan; Winamek—Catfish, of the Fish Clan; Gizes—The Sun, of the Thunderbird Clan; Five Medals (or Nyanenseya, also known as Onangizes, as well as by his clan name Onaxa or Onaksa—He Flies Away), his brother Osmet, and Sigenakshēt (possibly Blackbird Flying), all of the Eagle Clan; Nanoseka, the son of Pinamo—Turkey, of the Turkey Clan; Mozo, of the Moose Clan; and several others whose names and clans cannot be translated or identified. The eight Potawatomi signatories from the Detroit area include only three whose names and clans can be recognized: Mogawh (Mko—Bear), of the Bear Clan; Nenewas—Little Man, of the Warrior Clan; and White Pigeon, or Wapmimi, of the Eagle Clan. Skush, another signer, was certainly Oshkēsh, likely the war-leader of the senior moiety, for he was killed while fighting alongside Tecumsah in 1813 (Clifton 1975b: 41); while, in addition to signing the 1807 treaty at Detroit, Tokwish had earlier signed Canadian Treaty Number 12 in 1800. Although the Potawatomi leaders from the villages in these two areas acted more or less independently of one another, it is clear that they were linked in a variety of ways, notably through membership in two of the clans—Bear and Eagle—that can be identified.

Closest to the areas of American expansion, the Potawatomi of southern Michigan and northern Indiana were following a policy of accommodation parallel to that employed by their ancestors when the British displaced the French in 1763. But they were also exploiting for their own purposes opportunities presented by the advent of the Americans. One such aim was to effect an expansion of their influence into areas they had not previously occupied, particularly into northern Ohio, southern Indiana, and the Ontario Peninsula. Similarly, some of these leaders openly and actively aided the American officials in securing the compliance of other tribes at several of the treaties in this period. This was especially true of the 1805 treaty at Grouseland, where the Potawatomi—led by Topnebi and Winamek—strongly supported the now pro-American Miami leader Little Turtle and Governor Harrison against the interests and opposition of the Miami and other tribes involved. It was also true in the 1809 treaty at Fort Wayne, where these Potawatomi again cooperated with Little Turtle and Harrison to force a cession of land in Illinois and Indiana, against the stringent opposition of the Miami. The Potawatomi—led by Winamek and the son of Five Medals—went so far as to threaten the Miami with war if they did not comply with Harrison's demand for a treaty cession. About half of the thousand Indians present at this treaty were Potawatomi; and they anticipated getting, but did not, to their displeasure, receive, the largest share of the treaty goods distributed.[8] They did obtain an advance of $500 against future annuities, which Harrison later converted into a gift, in recognition of services performed.

In the decade after 1795 by such devices did some Potawatomi adapt to the reduced economic circumstances caused by the shortage of game, crop failure, and the decline of the fur trade. By ceding land—preferably land occupied by other tribes—and by supporting American officials in treaty negotiations, leaders such as Topnebi and Winamek were able to extend the range of their influence and to secure access to treaty goods and increases in the annuities paid them. By 1809 they had obtained a total of $5,350 in treaty goods, plus a share of the rations and other payments made available at the treaty grounds, and had added another $2,067 to the annuity payments due them each year. But in so doing they had started to live off sales of pieces of the tribal capital —the lands they occupied; and they were contributing much to the grave tensions that increasingly disturbed the frontier.

American officials were not the only direct sources of additional revenue and rations which could be exploited by the Eastern Potawatomi. In the same years that they were dealing with the Americans at Detroit and Fort Wayne, many Potawatomi, mainly from Michigan and Indiana but also from Milwaukee and Chicago, regularly visited the British post at Amherstburg to declare their fidelity to British interests and to receive their presents.[9] While American officials recognized this duplicity and feared the consequences of an Indian-British alliance, they lacked the means—a constabulary or a customs and revenue service of adequate size—to close this highly permeable border. When Governor Hull complained of these visits on the treaty grounds at Detroit in 1807, a Potawatomi spokesman assured him that their sentiments truly were for the Americans, but that when they visited Amherstburg (Fort Malden) the British bribed them with liquor to keep them there. "At last," he explained coyly, "without his [the British Commander's] knowledge we crossed the River" (Smith 1957: 36). At Fort Malden the British Indian Department—led by such old campaigners as Matthew Elliott, William Caldwell, George Ironsides, and Captain Thomas McKee (the son of Alexander McKee)—were not much concerned with good relations with the United States. They aimed instead at maintaining the allegiance of the Indian tribes, and regularly received, exaggerated, and passed on to their superiors whatever rumors and intelligence information served their personal interests (Horsman 1964: 122–23).

Nor were such exploitable resources limited to British and American officials and governments. In the same period the Potawatomi could count on some aid and assistance from private citizens, particularly Protestant missionary organizations. The involvement of this tribe with such missionary groups began in 1801, when a small group of Potawatomi leaders, including Five Medals and Topnebi, traveled east to visit President Jefferson. On the way the Potawatomi leaders stopped at Baltimore, where they met with a Quaker convention and asked their assistance in the form of a program to develop agricultural enterprises among their kinsmen. Back in Indiana, in 1803 Five Medals again communicated with the Quakers, calling for their help. This request, which coincided with government efforts to develop agricultural programs among the tribes of Indiana and Ohio, brought a quicker response, for the Quakers soon sent a delegation to discuss the matter with the Potawatomi at Fort Wayne.[10] The result of these discussions was the founding of a model farm on the Wabash River, an enterprise which began in the spring of 1804 and failed that same fall. Very few Potawatomi men displayed much interest in farm work, and the discouraged Quaker farmer donated his crop to Five Medals and to Little Turtle (of the Miamis) before departing.

The distinction between public—or government-prompted and -supported programs—and private-sector benevolence in enterprises aimed at "civilizing" Indians was not hard and sharp. Indeed, the government preferred to use missionary organizations as agents and arranged special appropriations to finance their work (Prucha 1962: 219–24). In 1807 the Congress allocated six thousand dollars for a second Quaker effort to teach farming techniques to the Potawatomi and neighboring tribes, but the program was never established. Samuel Kirk, the teacher-farmer sent by the Quakers, fell into a controversy with the Indian agent at Fort Wayne and finally settled elsewhere. The Quakers and the Potawatomi had to discover that, however strong the good intentions of officials in the central government, missionaries and Indian agents were often fractious competitors on the frontier, and without their mutual cooperation development programs could easily fail (Berkhofer 1965: 90–91). Until 1811 Five Medals, Winamek, Topnebi, and other leaders continued to press the United States for help with agricultural development, and the government responded by regularly shipping farm tools and seeds to them, but no Potawatomi men adopted farming as a livelihood. Well before 1811 most Potawatomi males were being caught up in a new wave of excitement which turned their attentions far away from efforts to imitate American economic pursuits. Nonetheless, leaders such as Five Medals and Winamek were not entirely unsuccessful. At the expense of a little talk and persuasion they brought in several missionaries willing to work farms on their behalf and to deliver the proceeds to them, and they obtained quantities of capital equipment and consumables from the government which they could exchange with traders for goods more to their liking.

In the years following the Treaty of Greenville the leaders of the easternmost Potawatomi had also been successful in monopolizing the annual annuity payments that were supposedly destined for the benefit of the entire tribe. Until 1802 these payments had been made at Detroit, but after complaints that year from the Potawatomi along the Tippecanoe River the payments were moved to a more central location at Fort Wayne, while in 1804 the secretary of war determined that part of the payment should be distributed at the new Fort Dearborn, near the mouth of the Chicago River.[11] Up to this moment the American presence had been strongest in the East, in northern Indiana, eastern Michigan, and Ohio, and weakest in the Illinois and Wisconsin area. The Eastern Potawatomi thereby had been forced into making accommodations with Americans while their kinsmen in the west had proceeded along a different path. Even at the time of the Greenville treaty, the Western Potawatomi had been anti-American, and this bent was increasingly expressed in raids against American settlements as well as against tribes, especially the Osage, with whom the Americans desired peace. The unequal distribution of annuities did not cause such grave antipathy in the West, but it certainly fueled an anger which was already present. The American government's response to these raids had been to send a detachment of troops to Kaskaskias in 1802 and to establish Fort Dearborn in 1803; but the display of force was insufficient to the considerable task of pacification that lay ahead.

In the West anti-American sentiments were rooted in the conflicts that preceded and were not resolved by the Treaty of Greenville; but they were exacerbated by Spanish machinations from St. Louis, at least until the Louisiana Purchase removed that source of international irritation. As early as 1795 Anthony Wayne's scouts in southern Indiana and adjacent Illinois had found the Potawatomi in some of the villages there haughty, insolent, and overbearing, prone to extort by threats flour, corn, and tobacco, when their warriors had obviously just returned from successful raids against American settlements in Kentucky or southern Illinois.[12] These Potawatomi were progressively blocked from effective raiding into Kentucky by the intensification of American settlement there and by the propensity of Kentuckians to launch fast-moving, mounted, filibustering raids of their own against Potawatomi and other Indian villages in Illinois and Indiana. One critical source of conflict was the increasing pattern of Kentuckians hunting on lands claimed by the Potawatomi and Kickapoo north of the Ohio River. As each year went by, there was less game for growing numbers of Indians and Americans pursuing pelts and meat. Thus the attentions of the Western Potawatomi were deflected south and west, to the more isolated and vulnerable settlements along the American Bottoms (the fertile river terraces on the east bank of the Mississippi between the mouths of the Illinois and Kaskaskia rivers) and to the newest target for a Potawatomi warrior's efforts to attain glory and plunder, the Osage tribe in present Missouri.

Potawatomi raids against the Osage in Missouri were encouraged initially in 1793 by the Spanish in St. Louis, who were then having difficulties pacifying that tribe. In several ways the Osage were an ideal target for Potawatomi assaults. They were remote from the centers of Potawatomi population, across a major barrier, the Mississippi; and once an attack was completed the Spanish would block Osage efforts to retaliate. The Americans in southwestern Illinois became involved at first simply because their scattered settlements were in the pathway of the Potawatomi approach and retreat, while the best known leaders of their war parties, Pinage—Turkey Foot, of the Tippecanoe River, Main Poche—Puckered Hand, and the younger Sigenak—Blackbird, from northern Illinois, were decidedly anti-American in disposition.[13] These men regularly led war-parties against the Osage between 1793 and 1805, along the way ravaging American settlements in southern Illinois.[14] In 1805, for example, Main Poche's warriors hit an undefended Osage encampment, killing thirty-four women and children and capturing another sixty. This raid came after the Potawatomi—prompted by American authorities—had supposedly made peace with the Osage earlier that same year.[15] The Americans continued to counter with diplomacy, worked to secure the release of the Osage prisoners, and pressed attempts to secure intertribal peace; but the Potawatomi raids into Missouri and against American settlements went on. The small military forces deployed at Kaskaskia and Chicago were totally inadequate to the task of containing, much less pacifying, the aggressively warlike parties under such powerful and effective leaders as Main Poche and Sigenak.

After 1805 the warlike disposition of many Potawatomi began to merge with a general wave of discontent that was sweeping the Northwest Territory. The numerous treaties transferring lands out of the hands of the tribes long established there, squabbles over the distribution of annuities, heightened pressure to adopt a new and radically altered pattern of economic activities as subsistence farmers, further reduction in the supplies of game, continued weakening of the fur trade, increased settlement pressure from Americans, decreased freedom of movement, tribal demoralization exhibited most dramatically by excessive consumption of the ample supply of liquor readily available from numerous whiskey dealers and traders, and an intensifying pattern in ingroup violence—all these combined to generate collective fury out of numberless individual frustrations. The historical and psychological situation was fully ripe for the appearance of someone with a large, appealing, and culturally appropriate solution to the many disturbing problems that plagued the tribes of the region.

The vision of new directions that arose and achieved wide acceptance was the product of a pair of Shawnee brothers, Tenskwatawa and Tecumsah. The former, as much masterful charlatan as powerfully appealing prophet, served as the bearer of fresh supernatural tidings, good news, and pat solutions that were symbolized by the new name—Open Door—he had adopted after a life of dissipation, violence, and alcoholism. Tenskwatawa was not the first prophet carrying visionary solutions to tribal problems whose message appealed to the Potawatomi and other tribes of the area, and he was not to be the last. Nor was he the only prophet who arose in the years following the Greenville treaty. All of the tribes in the area gave fundamental value to dream processes and visionary experiences, which were an important source of innovative solutions to the problems of living, from the most mundane and trivial to the most extraordinary and culture threatening. Full-scale messianic visions of a total new lifeway such as those produced by Tenskwatawa were, basically, only extensions and elaborations of this deep-rooted psychocultural pattern.[16] But Tenskwatawa was the one of numerous prophets who achieved the widest recognition, the largest following, and the greatest influence. That he did so was largely the consequence of his elder brother Tecumsah's pragmatic genius, for it was Tecumsah—a long-experienced, brilliant military leader, astute diplomat, and masterful political organizer—who added rational practicality to the often erratic emotionalism of the ill-experienced Tenskwatawa, whose life previous to his revelatory vision had been one of useless dissipation.

In the fall of 1805 Tenskwatawa underwent a psychotic episode, interpreted by himself and his kinsmen as a religious trance-state during which the Master of Life appeared and presented him with a vision of the new way. Such psychologically devastating and re-creating experiences have since been recognized as the critical defining feature inaugurating major cultural revitalization movements, for while in such a psychological limbo such grossly disturbed individuals as Tenskwatawa experience an overwhelming sense of personal and social death and rebirth.[17] When he emerged as if reborn from his trance, Tenskwatawa began preaching the ingredients of a new and more satisfying cultural adaptation. An outline of the doctrines proposed by Tenskwatawa and refined by Tecumsah reads like a list of major social problems, as they were perceived by those who most suffered from the symptoms of cultural disorganization, together with a set of proposed reforms (see pp. 266–70).[18] The Shawnee brothers promised a variety of new satisfactions, ranging from magical protection against American weapons, to more control over witches and sorcerers, to the benefits of a revitalized intertribal confederacy, which by joint action might stay the advance of the American frontier and reverse the tide of cultural disintegration. Essentially, Tecumsah and Tenskwatawa were the advocates and leaders of a rudimentary intertribal separatist and independence movement, in which the widely respected elder brother acted as the political-diplomatic leader as well as spokesman for the much feared and often preposterously pretentious younger man.

The rise to power of the Shawnee brothers coincided with and was facilitated by an increase in tension between Great Britain and the United States, particularly so along the Great Lakes frontier. By 1807, through numerous treaties with the Potawatomi, Kickapoo, Sauk, Fox, Miami, Delaware, and other tribes, the United States had obtained the cession of eastern Michigan, southern Indiana, and most of Illinois. A new, young generation of Americans in the West saw Great Britain as the cause of all the troubles that plagued them. The West suffered periodic economic depression. American fur traders there were regularly undercut by British intruders. And the Indians continually ravaged the outlying settlements. The aggressive westerners firmly believed that the conquest of Canada would relieve them of all these troubles.

Until this time British Indian agents in Upper Canada had been counseling peace to the tribesmen who regularly visited Fort Malden, advising them that war was a scourge which should be avoided at all costs (MPHC 23: 31–32). But in 1807, when the British frigate Leopard stopped and boarded the American ship-of-war *Chesapeake*, there was an outcry from the American War-Hawks for immediate war against England. The English in Canada fully expected an invasion and once more began girding up their Indian allies in preparation for battle. American policy in the face of the prospect of war was to keep the tribes neutral, the best that could be anticipated, given the assumption that the basic interests of the Indians lay on the British side. But the British aimed specifically at gaining the services of their old allies. In December 1807 the new governor-in-chief of Canada, Sir James Craig, gave specific instructions for the Indian agents in the Sandwich-Amherstburg border region opposite Detroit. They were to prepare the Indians and hold them in check, waiting for the moment when their services would be required. The agents were to avoid specific instructions and incitements; but they were always "to insinuate that as a matter of course we shall look for the assistance of our Brothers. It should be done with delicacy, but still in a way not to be misunderstood" (Brymner 1897: 31). The governor also instructed his agents to look into the possibility of purchasing the loyalty and services of Tenskwatawa. At this point Tecumsah—who was to prove far the more valuable British ally—was still practically unknown to British agents.[19]

Tenskwatawa's early preachings of the new message quickly brought many converts, who carried the new beliefs far and wide, from the Seminole in Florida to the Blackfeet in Saskatchewan. John Tanner (a young Ohioan who had been captured by the Odawa as a boy, in 1807 living as an Ojibwa fur trapper in Manitoba) reported the reception given one such convert-messenger and the great enthusiasm that swept the Ojibwa hunting camps when they were told of the wonders in store for them (James 1830: 144–47). These Ojibwa received Tenskwatawa's messenger "with great humility," Tanner noted in his autobiography, "and they tried to follow the doctrine." The Western Potawatomi were first visited by the prophet's advocates in 1806, and they were invited to a great intertribal conference in western Ohio the next year. Because Tenskwatawa and Tecumsah aimed at eliminating the influence of traditional religious practitioners and political leaders as well, many tribal elders and okamek remained suspicious and distrustful. Tecumsah's ire was directed particularly at such collaborationist okamek as Five Medals, Winamek, and Gizes, who had ample reason for anxious skepticism concerning the new way, for Tenskwatawa soon backed his brother's political maneuvers with a program of witchcraft accusations intended to subdue or assassinate pro-American village leaders. It was the younger tribesmen who were special targets for conversion, who most often responded positively, and who were attracted in large numbers to the support of the Shawnee brothers and their plans for a vast anti-American, intertribal confederacy.[20]

Tenskwatawa's new doctrines and Tecumsah's vision of an effective, intertribal, political-military confederacy were not—in whole or in part—equally appealing to all Potawatomi, much less all Indians. Traditional chaskyd or wabino practitioners, for example, or priests of the Midewiwin religion found the Shawnee prophet's views in open conflict with their own ingrained beliefs and established influence. Village okamek who were accommodating their kinsmen's wants and their own leadership roles to American pressures were openly threatened by Tecumsah's appeals for a revisionist, separatist stance. Moreover, the messages carried by converts were subject to much reinterpretation, for the brothers had no means of insuring doctrinal purity. Tenskwatawa himself had originally insisted, for example, on abandoning European varieties of dogs and domestic cats. By the time this demand reached

Manitoba, it had been broadened to deny Indians the use of all dogs, an idea which John Tanner and his Ojibwa hunter kinsmen thought defied common sense. Giving up flint-and-steel for fire-making was not, similarly, a considerable inconvenience for sedentary Shawnee villages in the temperate climate of the Ohio valley; but for the small bands of Ojibwa hunters in the boreal forests far to the north, it was a great hardship (James 1830: 146–47).

The case of Main Poche is instructive of how the appeal of the new doctrines varied. Puckered Hand had a hard-won personal reputation and a substantial following, obtained through numerous successful raids on other tribes and American settlements. Such triumphs, in Potawatomi belief, manifested the possession of incomparable manito—spirit-powers; and Main Poche was simultaneously known as a major, powerful religious figure, likely as a priest in the Midewiwin religion. Beyond this he was, even in Potawatomi terms, a rogue male, a man with an insatiable desire for killing. And he exhibited an equally strong infatuation for the whiskey jug (Forsyth 1812a: 278, and 1827: 204). Here was a man whose own propensities and career centered on attributes actively opposed by Tenskwatawa and Tecumsah. He was unlikely to surrender his own personal fame, renounce his several powerful addictions, or subordinate himself to the discipline of any new prophet's doctrine or the leadership of a rival political-military leader. He might agree to an alliance of equals that provided fresh opportunities for satisfying old needs, perhaps, but not to an association that required abandoning a firmly established, much-rewarded personal identity. But Main Poche was only an individual who manifested one Potawatomi ideal of proper manliness. There were others who approximated his level of performance, and many more who emulated him, men fashioned from the same sort of cultural cloth, if of weaker warp. Tecumsah would shortly find the Potawatomi to be undependable allies, too prone to acting out their own impulses, contrary to his personal plans for a well-disciplined confederacy.

The unwillingness to accept external discipline, which was characteristic of such Potawatomi warrior-leaders as Main Poche, was demonstrated by a continuing series of hostile actions against the Osage and other tribes between 1806 and 1814. Such raids were generally accompanied or paralleled by similar assaults on American settlements in southern Illinois and eastern Missouri Territory.[21] At a time when they might have heeded Tecumsah's plea to maintain intertribal peace—the obvious necessary precondition for a successful confederation—or at least have concentrated their efforts against American military forces, some Potawatomi, especially those from northern Illinois, continued to raid south into the American Bottoms and across the Mississippi River. One such raid was recorded for 1809 and another larger one in 1810—the latter organized and led by a second and different man bearing the name of Winamek. In 1810, also, Main Poche himself, assisted by one of his brothers-in-law, Neskotnemek—Mad Sturgeon, led another major assault on the Osage; but on this occasion Puckered Hand's spirit-powers failed him, as he was grievously wounded and laid up the entire winter of 1810–1811. Such raids not only disturbed the peace between tribes who might otherwise have sought common ground, they provoked American retaliation and dissipated the limited war-making potential available to the Potawatomi and other tribes.

Main Poche had been relatively inactive in raiding until 1810 because of the large amount of attention he had been receiving from Tenskwatawa and Tecumsah, the Americans, and British agents in Upper Canada, all of whom were vying for his support and allegiance. The contest for the loyalties of such powerful tribal leaders as Main Poche arose out of the growing influence of Tecumsah and the continuing antagonism between the United States and Great Britain. Although British-American relations along the Great Lakes frontier after 1807 had quieted somewhat, British Indian agents continued to make preparations for war, and the tribes south of the boundary were prime targets for their attention. "The British did not create Indian discontent," Reginald Horsman noted, but they "took advantage of it to win the Indians for the defense of Canada in the event of war" (1964: 176). These agents stirred up resentments, held out the promise of British support, made ambiguous, innocuous speeches in public, and saved their true plans and instructions for secret conferences, exacerbating existing antagonisms (Horsman 1964: 167–76.) Until 1810 Tecumsah and his confederacy did not receive much attention from the British, partly because he was too independent and prone to issue caustic reminders of the British failure to support the Western Confederacy at Fallen Timbers (where he had fought) fifteen years earlier, partly because the old veteran Indian agents in Upper Canada preferred dealing with established tribal and village leaders. Tecumsah remained for the British an unknown quantity, an upstart who was in effect organizing a third force of unpredictable disposition.

In 1808 Tecumsah had moved the beginnings of his coalition of forces away from Fort Greenville to a new intertribal village called Prophetstown on the Tippecanoe River, above its confluence with the Wabash. That same year he sent Tenskwatawa to Fort Malden to maintain liaison with the British (Tucker 1956: 121–23). It was the Potawatomi on the Tippecanoe River who had invited Tecumsah to join them there, much to the consternation of the Miami and Delaware who occupied and hunted the area. From Prophetstown, Tecumsah worked outward, beginning a pattern of personal visitations and journeying that would take him from Wisconsin to New York and the Gulf Coast, and eventually away from Prophetstown at the most critical moment in the development of his confederacy. By force of personal example, oratory, and personality, Tecumsah was working carefully to build up the range and power of the anti-American alliance.

In 1807 Main Poche had temporarily succumbed to the influence of the prophet and Tecumsah. That year he traveled west to the tribes in western Wisconsin and Illinois, carrying news of Tenskwatawa's revelations, conducting his own business along the way. The same fall he accepted an invitation to visit the Shawnee brothers at their village near Greenville.[22] Governor Harrison's intelligence service was well aware of Main Poche's power and of his dalliance with the Shawnee brothers. When the Potawatomi leader left the Shawnee to travel homeward, he was intercepted near Fort Wayne by William Wells, United States Indian agent at that post. Wells—who had been a young captive adopted by the Miami, and who was Little Turtle's brother-in-law, a man fully conversant with Algonquian languages and customs—spared no expense in an effort to convert Main Poche to the American cause, wining and dining him and plying him with presents and promises.[23] The astute warrior-leader and his fellows accepted and enjoyed Wells's hospitality: it was a warm and inexpensive way to spend a cold winter. Before leaving Fort Wayne in the spring of 1808 Main Poche told Wells, "My friend you have caught me. Like a wild Horse is caught with a Lick of Salt you have Hobled me—that I can no longer range the woods as I please. You must now get a Bell and put on my neck when I shall always be in your Hearing. . . .you must also put Bells on the necks of my two war chiefs. This will in able you to know at all times where the warriors of the west are and what they are about" (TP-US 7: 556). Main Poche demanded that the United States provide him and his young chiefs with medals, carrying through with the oratorical metaphor of belling the wild horse. But he also reminded the Indian agent that the Master of Life had made him a warrior, and he would soon go to war against the Dakota.

In April 1808 Wells reported to the secretary of war that Main Poche was an extremely dangerous fellow, that he was "the pivot on which the minds of all western Indians turned." But Wells was reasonably certain that he had swayed him to the American cause. Main Poche was further encouraged to align himself with the Americans when Wells accompanied him and a group of other tribal leaders to Washington City in the fall of 1808 for a meeting with President Jefferson. This delegation was followed east by another party of Potawatomi and other tribesmen from eastern Michigan and Ohio. The result of such American pressures was a temporary lull in Indian hostilities in the Old Northwest, a calm that was shattered when Governor Harrison was instructed to secure another major cession of land in 1809. By this time the lands obtained at the Greenville and subsequent treaties were nearly all settled, and the Americans were preparing to carve away yet another slice of Indian territory. Given the fragile peace and the raw state of tempers on the Northwest frontier, the Fort Wayne treaty in the fall of 1809 rubbed coarse salt into already festering wounds.

At Fort Wayne that fall the animosities and resentments lay just beneath the surface of public negotiations. The sides were clearly drawn, and they came close to blows. Tenskwatawa had been using the tactic of witchcraft accusations to counter the influence of pro-American village leaders (and others who were indifferent or antagonistic to his views) and had wanted to kill all the unconverted okamek; but Tecumsah had kept him in check, preferring to play for the loyalties of the warriors in all the tribes and to employ them to undercut the influence of village leaders (Tucker 1956: 121–23). The result was a confrontation between younger men and elder, of warriors against those more peacefully inclined. This tactic had paid off, so much so that okamek who had previously accommodated themselves to American designs and interests were fearful of participating in the Fort Wayne treaty. Of the major Potawatomi leaders, Topnebi, Gizes, and Five Medals did not appear, although Topnebi's brother Shisamko was present, signing for himself and his elder brother, as did Five Medals' son and brother who also inserted his name on the treaty. The most prominent Potawatomi at the treaty was the faithful Winamek, who joined with Little Turtle and the Delaware (also intrusive in the area) to pressure the unwilling Miami into the surrender of some 4,700 square miles of valuable southern Indiana real estate.[24]

The 1809 treaty involved a complex play of interests between competing parties. A group of immigrant Stockbridge, Delaware, Mohican, and Muncies were involved because they claimed the Potawatomi had granted them lands along the White River, although these were clearly recognized as Miami lands by the Greenville treaty in 1795. Little Turtle, the pro-American Miami leader, certified this claim and worked with Winamek and the Eastern Algonquians to bring about the treaty, against the interests and wishes of the Mississinewa Miami, who were pro-Tecumsah, anti–Little Turtle, opposed to further American expansion, and more than a little annoyed with the Potawatomi. But they were outmaneuvered by Winamek, Little Turtle, and William Henry Harrison. Governor Harrison, in turn, accepted the cooperation of the Potawatomi, although he knew the 1805 Treaty of Grouseland had prohibited them from participating in further cessions of Miami lands (Kappler 1904: 81). Harrison approached and rode away from the 1809 treaty with studied, and greatly misplaced, optimism. He seemed convinced that there was little danger of Indian hostilities, ignored the growing influence of Tecumsah, and believed the treaty would bind the Potawatomi and Delaware to the American cause. "If any ill blood yet remains," he informed the secretary of war that November, "a little attention to the influential chiefs will soon remove it."[25] But this was to be the last treaty completed and ratified by the Senate before the War of 1812. In the tense atmosphere of the Old Northwest in 1809, it was one treaty too many.

The two years between the Fort Wayne treaty and November 1811 were busy with alarms along the frontier, additional raids against the Osage and American settlements, American efforts to neutralize the growing influence of Tecumsah and the Shawnee prophet, and Tecumsah's attempts to consolidate his strength in the Northwest by adding the support of the southern tribes. By mid-summer, 1810, the warriors gathered at Prophetstown—a group composed mainly of Potawatomi, Shawnee, and Kickapoo, but including some Ojibwa, Odawa, Sauk, and Winnebago—swelled to a considerable force, one which apparently fluctuated in size from less than a thousand to nearly three times that number.[26] The opposing groups were increasingly polarized, with anti-American tribesmen gravitating towards an affiliation with Tecumsah, but at least as many sitting by, taking no position, waiting for tensions to ease. This was particularly true of most Potawatomi village okamek, who found themselves trapped by the perennial problem of dissension among their young men, appeals for their support by American agents, and threats coming from the prophet's camp. Few took a position of such open support of the Americans as did Winamek, who regularly served Harrison as messenger, spy, and advocate. More adopted a stance of uncomfortable neutrality like that of Gomo in his village near Peoria on the Illinois River. Gomo was made increasingly miserable by the fact that the warriors of the aggressive Main Poche passed by his village on the way south to raid the Osage and American settlements, while American officials from southern Illinois repeatedly called upon him as a dependent "medal chief" to do the impossible, to take hold of and surrender the warriors responsible, to return prisoners and booty, to keep the peace generally, and to declare himself openly for the American cause.[27]

While Governor Edwards of Illinois Territory and Governor Hull at Detroit sought to cajole the support of nearby Potawatomi and other tribal leaders, Governor Harrison calculated that time was in his favor, being convinced that Tecumsah would have grave difficulty in maintaining a sizable, effective force at Prophetstown for any significant period. He was correct in assuming that the hostile warriors and their leaders would periodically move away from Tecumsah's camp; but when they did so it was often to launch another assault towards Missouri or southern Illinois.[28] In the spring of 1810 some Potawatomi and Shawnee warriors rode south of the Wabash River to harass new American settlers there. Early in July the hostile Winamek raided the Osages and an American settlement in Missouri. On 20 July 1810 Main Poche's brother-in-law Mad Sturgeon defeated an American party on the Wabash. And in September of that year Main Poche himself led the attack on the Osage during which he was wounded. The raids were resumed the following spring and continued with no respite through the fall, causing disorder and panic among the American settlements south of the treaty boundaries and moving American leaders towards more determinative action.

The opportunity came in late fall, 1811, after Tecumsah had departed for the south to solicit the support of additional tribes there. By this time the American leaders were firmly convinced that Tecumsah—after the fashion of Pontiac—was plotting a well-coordinated, decisive blow, to be launched simultaneously against all major American positions in the Northwest.[29] While such plans were most certainly discussed by many of the enthusiasts gathered at Prophetstown, the overtly hostile actions of leaders such as Main Poche were not good evidence for such a conclusion by Americans. Main Poche and other Potawatomi village and warrior leaders were not working out any prearranged plans or conforming themselves to the views and discipline required by Tecumsah. They were in fact in open competition with the Shawnee's leadership, themselves pursuing a traditional tribal pattern of raiding while he was working to forge a larger solution, a massive coalition of forces operating under tight, centralized coordination. Indeed, before leaving for the south (with solid promises of British support), Tecumsah had advised the Potawatomi to keep the peace with the Americans; but during his absence their impulsive hostility combined with provocative moves by Governor Harrison to precipitate open warfare on the Northwest frontier.

Governor Harrison saw Tecumsah's absence as an opportunity to break up the concentration of anti-American forces at Prophetstown. In late summer he gathered a thousand troops—including the Fourth United States Regiment, an additional company of riflemen, and militia units—and marched up the Wabash River valley. Following a deliberate strategy like that of Anthony Wayne, whom he had served as aide seventeen years earlier, he paused twice to construct two small forts along his path. His move was a demonstration-in-force, aimed at impressing the assembled tribesmen with American prowess and firmness of intent.[30] But for the warriors gathered at Prophetstown it was a defiant challenge, one which they accepted. The movements of Harrison's forces were no secret to their opponents, who scouted his trail carefully. Harrison was accompanied by the faithful Winamek, who acted as his messenger and advisor while his forces were being observed and harassed by other, hostile Potawatomi. On one early October morning, for example, a young Potawatomi warrior from the Fox River in northern Illinois, the younger brother of Mkedēpoke—Black Partridge, seized an opportunity to ambush a supply party moving up the Wabash River, killing one of the boatmen single-handed. From this exploit the young Potawatomi took a new war-name, Wabansi—Break of Day, which he carried proudly until his death in 1845.[31]

Harrison and his troops reached Prophetstown on the Tippecanoe River

Plate 2. Wabansi, okama of the villages along the Kankakee River, helped lead the Potawatomi of the Prairie to the Iowa Reservation in 1837. He died before the Prairie People again moved to Kansas in 1847. (Copy of a painting by C. B. King; courtesy of the Bureau of American Ethnology, Smithsonian Institution.)

November 6 and cautiously made camp scarcely one mile from the forces of Tenskwatawa. The number of fighting men available to the Shawnee prophet had been depleted, as many slipped away upon the approach of the American troops. Tenskwatawa had dispatched messengers to the west calling for reinforcements, and the Winnebago and Potawatomi from Michigan and Illinois responded just in time to greet Harrison's arrival. Meanwhile, the prophet met with Harrison's messenger, Winamek, and sent him back with a call for an armistice; but Winamek, perhaps deliberately, missed Harrison on his final advance. The governor kept his men on guard the night of November 6, taking no chances, although anticipating a council with Tenskwatawa the following day. But the meeting that occurred was not peaceful. Those warriors who remained in Prophetstown represented the hard-core supporters of the Shawnee brothers, while the newly arrived reinforcements came prepared for and anticipating battle. That night the Potawatomi and Winnebago successfully pressed for support of an attack, which they prepared and launched just before dawn the next morning. The warriors believed they were protected by the prophet's great spirit-powers and anticipated that the American soldiers would break and run before their sudden assault. But Harrison's troopers were well-experienced fighters. His sentries detected the approach of the warriors, who did not achieve the vital ingredient of surprise. Their initial attack and a subsequent one were broken, and Harrison followed up with a counterattack, including a cavalry charge. The outnumbered warriors were driven off, ending the prophet's chance once and for all to demonstrate the superiority of his power over the Americans, and seriously diminishing his reputation.[32]

Harrison achieved his goal of breaking up the concentration of hostile Indians supporting the Shawnee prophet, but he did not follow-up his limited tactical success. He destroyed Prophetstown, then shortly returned to Indiana's territorial capital where his little army was disbanded. The Potawatomi and other Indians scattered, going back to their home villages, much less impressed with Tenskwatawa than they had been, but yet strongly anti-American. When he arrived back at Prophetstown from the south in late February 1812, Tecumsah found the village wrecked, his main supporters much dispersed. His vision of a well-controlled confederacy that could be used to counter American power had been struck a disastrous blow. Tecumsah directed his ire against the inept prophet, who had allowed the battle to develop, and especially against the Potawatomi, on whom he laid the major blame for bringing about the disaster. The Potawatomi had been led into the fight by the hostile Winamek, who continued his fight against the Americans until he was killed in 1812, and by Shabeni—He Has Pawed Through, an Odawa who married into the Potawatomi tribe in Illinois, and who served Tecumsah throughout the War of 1812 until the Shawnee leader's death, whereupon he became a strongly pro-American "medal chief" in Illinois.[33]

During the late winter of 1811–1812, Tecumsah had to pick up the pieces of his confederacy and to placate the British and those tribes who had been angered by the premature attack on Harrison's troops. Speaking on behalf of the Shawnee, Kickapoo, and Winnebago to the Huron at a council in the village of Machikethic, Tecumsah let go a blast at the ill-disciplined Potawatomi:

> Our younger brothers the Patawatamies (pointing to them) in spite of our separate council to them to remain quiet and live in peace with the Big Knives would not listen to us—When I left home last year to go to the Creek Nation I passed at Post Vincennes and was stopped by the Big Knives and did not immediately know the reason, but I was soon informed that the Patawatamies had killed some of their people. I told the Big Knives to remain quiet until my return when I should make peace and quietness prevail. On my return I found my village reduced to ashes by the Big Knives—You [the Hurons] cannot blame your younger brothers the Shawnees for what has happened: the Patawatamies occasioned the misfortune . . . Fathers and Brothers, the Patawatamies hearing that our father and you were on the way here for peaceable purposes grew very angry all at once and killed twenty-seven of the Big Knives.

William Claus (superintendent of Indian Affairs in Upper Canada), who on 8 June 1812 reported Tecumsah's speech to Isaac Brock (the military commander), added the comment that Tecumsah's forces were not yet well enough organized or armed to go into battle, that Tecumsah was still "avoiding precipitous action," and that he had "called on the nations who had murdered Americans to deliver the culprits to him." The Potawatomi were singled out as the most culpable of those responsible. Claus reported their speakers—in reply to Tecumsah's exhortation—as saying that they could give no immediate answer to his demands, that "they must consult their nation so that at the next full moon they might give him" a reply. Claus noted Tecumsah's further warning to the Potawatomi: "if he did not hear from them by that time he would march against them and cut them off."[34]

There was to be no time for such niceties as imposing intertribal discipline on the unruly Potawatomi. Americans in the west, too, were fully as warlike and impulsive as these tribesmen. By June 18—ten days after Claus sent his report along to Isaac Brock–the aggressive western congressmen had elbowed President Madison into declaring war against Great Britain. Meanwhile, the Potawatomi—paying little heed to Tecumsah's injunctions or his warning—made their own preparations for further battles, laying the foundation for additional surprise attacks against the most exposed of those American positions north and west of the line of frontier settlements.

THE POTAWATOMI
IN THE WAR
OF 1812

The result of Harrison's minor victory at Prophetstown was to scatter the most bloody-minded Indian zealots across the frontier, eliminating for a while what little discipline Tecumsah could exercise within his confederacy.[35] Throughout the winter and into the spring of 1812 the Potawatomi, seconded only by the Winnebago, increased their pattern of raiding and harassment of frontier settlements, while making preparations for more serious efforts as the season for proper war approached. In the same months Tecumsah labored to restore some semblance of unity—by early June he had reestablished himself at Prophetstown and had gathered around himself three hundred men in that place and another six hundred at a nearby village (likely Machikethic). But his men had no powder or lead and were busily occupied making bows and arrows and relearning the skills of their use. Main Poche—who had developed a considerable taste for the creature comforts—in contrast placed himself next to the source of British largess. He spent the winter alternating his residence between a village on the Raisin River and Amherstburg. From there he sent his messengers, including Wapmimi—White Pigeon, westward to Indiana, Illinois, and Wisconsin, prompting the villagers there towards war. In April, Matthew Elliott, who was acting as British control for Main Poche and other warrior-leaders, reported that he had persuaded this "greatest of all the war chiefs of the Putawatamies" to remain at Malden to wait out the results of British-American negotiations.[36]

Potawatomi raiding during the winter and early spring was limited only by the weather, the disposition of the warriors, and the shortage of arms and ammunition.[37] The few hundred soldiers of the tiny regular army who were stationed beyond the frontier in isolated forts could have no effect. Scratch militia units dispatched to patrol the gaping expanses between settlements did not often even detect raiding parties. And American efforts at diplomacy were similarly useless. Councils such as those held by territorial governors and Indian agents at places like Cahokia, Fort Wayne, or Vincennes attracted only already American-leaning leaders such as Five Medals, Winamek, and Gomo, or Tecumsah's agents, such as Wapewi—White Head (of hair). The tendency of frightened and angered frontier settlers to attack any Indians, including those invited to councils, did not ease tensions or make new converts to the American side. By the spring of 1812 events were beyond the control of diplomatic talks. The village okamek sometimes came to councils when invited, but when they did it was to tell American officials what they thought they wanted to hear, to consume the rations provided, collect their presents, and depart. Leaders such as Gomo then had little to gain from the Americans and a great deal more to fear at the tender hands of hostile elements in their own tribe.

By late June the western Indians were assembled in force at several strategic locations: on St. Joseph's Island at the head of Lake Huron, controlling access to Lake Superior and serving as a jumping-off place for an assault on

Mackinac Island, which in turn governed the water route to Lake Michigan and the Fox–Wisconsin River waterway; at Fort Malden, screening a major invasion route into Upper Canada, and threatening Ohio, Indiana, and Michigan; and in northern Illinois, convenient for attacks on American posts and settlements south of Lake Michigan. Anti-American Potawatomi—the great majority of the tribe—were concentrated at Malden and near Lake Michigan. News of the declaration of war reached the British in these places before it did the adjacent Americans, giving them two fresh advantages—the first move and surprise—in addition to several they already enjoyed, superior leadership and more adequate naval and logistic preparations.

As war approached, Governor William Hull was marching towards Detroit with an army of two thousand men; but the British—learning of the declaration of war three days earlier than he did—captured a ship in the Detroit River that Hull had dispatched. Among Governor Hull's personal effects on the vessel were his official papers, including his plans for the campaign. The first word of war received by the American garrison on Mackinac Island was on July 17, in the form of a demand for their surrender by Captain Charles Roberts, of the British army, and Robert Dickson, the principal British Indian agent in Wisconsin. The night before, these two had led a force of seven hundred Indians, fur trappers, and soldiers from St. Joseph's Island to a silent invasion of Mackinac, during which they took control of a hill overlooking the American fort. The loss—without a shot being fired—of Mackinac Island was disastrous for other American garrisons in the upper lakes area, particularly so for the soldiers and settlers at Fort Dearborn, for the supply route to these posts was now severed and their position made untenable. There was as well a symbolic loss at Mackinac: not only were all the cannons pointing in the wrong direction, but they were inscribed with the words "Taken at Saratoga" and "Taken from Lord Cornwallis."[38]

The loss of Mackinac Island brought great pressure on Governor Hull to capture Fort Malden. He had moved his army across the Detroit River on July 12 and occupied Sandwich (now Windsor); but hesitancy and ineptness, combined with skillful management of the defense by British officers and Tecumsah, had blocked Hull's advance. The American supply line led from the east or south, along the south shore of Lake Erie or from the Ohio River, then through the morass of the Black Swamp at the mouth of the Maumee River and up the west side of the Detroit River. It was a long, slow, and highly vulnerable path, which the British and Indians promptly moved to cut. Some Potawatomi were involved in both the defense of Fort Malden on the Canadian shore and the attempt to isolate Governor Hull's army from his base of supply.

On July 19 and 24 a few Potawatomi, led by Main Poche and his brother-in-law, were involved in minor encounters with Governor Hull's advance parties and patrols at the Canard River and at the Petit Côte on the Canadian shore north of Fort Malden. Then, early in August, the British began seriously to threaten Hull's exposed supply line on the American shore. Some Potawatomi, led by Tecumsah and Alexander Elliott (Matthew Elliott's son by a Shawnee woman), on August 5 joined an odd-lot party of two dozen warriors in a successful ambuscade that terrorized and defeated a far larger party of Ohio militia near Brownstown, south of Detroit. This was their first full-scale battle, and it was of precisely the kind the Potawatomi most enjoyed. On August 9 a more serious attack on Hull's supply line occurred at Monguagon. Again the Potawatomi were involved in the mixed ambush party, this time led by Main Poche and Billy Caldwell (William Caldwell's son by a Mohawk woman). On this occasion the British and Indian forces were driven off, but only after a hot fight in which the larger American units received much the heaviest casualties. The younger Elliott and Caldwell were junior officers of the British Indian Service, acting as liaison to the Indian parties, with the mission of imposing some discipline and restraint on the Indians, particularly their after-battle conduct. In this the young liaison officers were not entirely successful, for after the Brownstown fight there was a minor massacre of prisoners, while during the Monguagon battle Main Poche himself killed one American captive.

With the loss of Mackinac to further worry him, attacks on his supply line proved too much for Governor Hull—a hapless, harried soldier. By the morning of August 9 he had hurried his troops back across the Detroit River into the shelter of the fort and town. Thus the tactical initiative was handed to a bold, imaginative professional, Major General Sir Isaac Brock. Brock arrived at Fort Malden with 340 reinforcements on August 13. Within two days he had demanded the surrender of Hull's garrison, alluded to the strong possibility of a massacre should an open battle develop, sent his Indian auxiliaries across the river to harass the Americans, and followed with his British regulars and militia. Tecumsah heightened Governor Hull's dread by passing and repassing the same body of warriors across a clearing in full view of the Detroit garrison, convincing Hull that large numbers of Indian reinforcements had arrived from Mackinac. It was all too much for the governor's shattered nerve: he surrendered his garrison on the sixteenth. Thereby, at the cost of a little British bluff and bluster and some skillfully executed Indian ambushes, the threat of an invasion of Canada in 1812 ended, and the Americans were handed a crushing defeat. So far the Potawatomi had taken only slight casualties—Main Poche had received a minor wound at the Canard River fight. But they had participated in a major victory and had taken much plunder, particularly horses, from the homes and pastures around Detroit.[39]

The day before Detroit surrendered, a bloodier if less strategically significant loss occurred three hundred miles to the west at Fort Dearborn. News of the declaration of war had come to the many Potawatomi concentrated around the foot of Lake Michigan in mid-July, but they delayed undertaking any major action against the garrison, the traders, and the few settlers near Chicago. There the Potawatomi were seriously divided over the issue of what policy to adopt. Some of those nearest to the small settlement counseled neutrality or peace. The pro-American leaders included Black Partridge and Alexander Robinson, also known as Shishibinkwa—(Docile) Rattlesnake. Robinson, the son of a Scots trader and an Odawa woman, had served as a middleman in the fur trade for some years.[40] Those Potawatomi and others friendly to the United States had some success in countering the influence of Main Poche's messengers, until Mad Sturgeon and Blackbird arrived to sway the assembled warriors towards a war policy.

Commanding the small garrison at Fort Dearborn was Captain Nathan Heald. On August 9 he received Governor Hull's order to evacuate Chicago and carry off all Americans to Fort Wayne. The message was carried by the still-faithful Winamek, who strongly advised John Kinzie—then Chicago's most prominent citizen—that their only hope of salvation lay in immediate, swift retreat. Heald would not accept the advice and delayed six fateful days. While Captain Heald organized his evacuation, the Potawatomi swarmed about the fort, increasingly under the sway of their war leaders, Mad Sturgeon and Blackbird. By August 13 William Wells had arrived with thirty-odd Miami from Fort Wayne to provide additional escort for the retreating party. Then on August 14 the Potawatomi welcomed a messenger from the east, who encouraged them with news of Tecumsah's successes and Hull's retreat. That night Captain Heald made final preparations for departure the next morning. His party of evacuees numbered no more than ninety-six soldiers and civilians, men and women, adults and children. Outside the fort upwards of six hundred warriors—largely Potawatomi, supported by a few allies from other tribes—fasted, incensed their war-bundles with tobacco smoke, and worked-up their courage for an engagement the next day.[41]

Heald's party departed Fort Dearborn early on the morning of the fifteenth. The slow, vulnerable column moved hardly more than a mile south on the beach-shore before Wells—riding at the point—spied the Potawatomi waiting behind the cover of the inshore dunes. The Miami covering force rode off, taking no part in the sharp fighting that quickly commenced and as quickly ended. First attempting a charge to break the Indian line, then putting up their best defense, Captain Heald's men (and the women who also fought) were soon enveloped and swiftly overwhelmed. Agreeing to Blackbird's demand that ransom be paid for the survivors, but demanding in turn a guarantee of safety for the remnants of his command, Captain Heald surrendered. The guarantee was not honored. Ninety-six marched out of the gates of Fort Dearborn that morning. When Heald surrendered, fifty-one of them were already dead. Another thirteen prisoners were tortured and killed in the next several days. Of the fifty-five regular army troopers, but nineteen survived. The Chicago militiamen fared far worse: all eleven were killed. William Wells—his face blackened in preparation for the battle he knew was coming—was killed, his price for not following Main Poche's earlier sarcastic advice to hobble and bell that fearsome warrior-leader and his assistants. Three of the nine women and twelve of the eighteen small children were killed. Rather—ten children huddled in a wagon for protection were butchered by one warrior who demonstrated his artistry with a tomahawk in a kind of homicidal frenzy that moved some Potawatomi in the excitement of a battle such as this.

Most of the survivors were saved only by the actions of friendly Potawatomi and by others whose tempers had cooled after the fighting ended. Kawbenaw—The Carrier captured and saved the badly wounded Mrs. Heald, for example. His exploit won him a new war-name—Captain Heald—that he affixed to several treaties after 1814. Potawatomi casualties, in turn, were few: several killed, a dozen or so wounded, including Mad Sturgeon and his brother Wasachēk—The Clear Day. Within twenty-fours hours of the battle some Potawatomi began having second thoughts about the future consequences of their great victory. Meeting with John Kinzie and Captain Heald, they "acknowledged having deceived us and asked Captain H. if he thought the prest. of the U.S. would forgive them," and they "asked Capt. H. his opinion of the probable continuance and result of our war to which he gave a suitable reply." But Heald remained in serious danger of his life, for some of the warriors continued to debate when and how to kill him, until Kinzie managed to spirit him and his wife away to safety (Williams 1953: 351).

With the capture of Detroit, Mackinac, and Fort Dearborn, on August 17 the British and their Indian allies controlled the Upper Great Lakes. Acting independently, the Potawatomi then began organizing for an attack on the American garrison at Fort Wayne, which controlled the headwaters of the Maumee River and access to northern Indiana and Illinois from the east. They were led by Pierre (or Perish) Moran, the hostile Winamek—Blackbird, and Awbenabi—He Looks Back.[42] Most of the warriors involved came from villages along the Tippecanoe and the St. Joseph (of the Maumee) rivers. By late August they had surrounded and invested the fort; but without the support of the British their only hope of success lay in outwitting the garrison or reducing the palisades by fire. Inside Fort Wayne the commanding officer, Captain John Rhea, was frightened into insensibility; but the Indian agent, Benjamin Stickney, kept his wits and took control of the defense.

On September 4 the guileful Winamek led a large party of warriors into the fort under a flag of truce, ostensibly to parley but actually to survey the garrison's weaknesses. Again the next morning he attempted to take a large armed party inside, planning a surprise assault on his prearranged signal, but he was outbluffed by Stickney and the traders. His subterfuge discovered, Winamek was forced to withdraw. He then settled into a siege, hoping to burn the fort or to reduce its garrison by sniping. While the Potawatomi were waiting for British reinforcements and artillery, Awbenabi fashioned two home-made cannons out of hewn oaken logs, loaded them with powder and iron weights, and fired them off. Both cannons burst on the first shot. Meanwhile, William Henry Harrison had left his Ohio base to force-march two thousand reinforcements to the relief of Fort Wayne, stealing a week's lead-time on the British coming from Detroit. At the approach of Harrison's army the siege was lifted, and by September 12 the Potawatomi had dispersed.[43] The tribesmen had thus a foretaste of what was to come the following year. If they had British logistic and artillery support, or faced incompetent, irresolute American leadership, or fought outnumbered American parties in the open, they could win battles. Lacking one or more of these ingredients, they would lose their engagements and the war.

In late fall and early winter of 1812 Governor Harrison of Indiana and Governor Edwards of Illinois attempted an offensive against the hostile Potawatomi, Miami, and Kickapoo in their territories. Theirs was an uncoordinated and inconclusive effort. On September 14 Harrison launched an attack on the villages along the upper Wabash and the Elkhart rivers, which succeeded in destroying two abandoned towns, those of the friendly leaders Five Medals and Little Turtle. A month later another attack, by Ohio mounted rangers, against Wapmimi's village (near present Coldwater, Michigan) was aborted when most of the militiamen deserted. Learning of Harrison's successful defense of Fort Wayne and his moves into Indiana, in mid-October Governor Edwards attempted to strike against the base of operations for the tribes in central and northern Illinois. His plan included a two-pronged move, with one large party of Kentucky rangers to hit against the Kickapoo villages southeast of the Illinois River, while his own smaller party rode north from (present) Edwardsville towards a meeting with the Kentucky volunteers on the Sangamon River.

The meeting never happened, for the Kentucky militia, also plagued by desertions and harassed by the Kickapoo, got lost on the prairielands and returned to their home state. Governor Edwards, proceeding alone with his smaller force, succeeded only in burning two Kickapoo villages and attacking two Potawatomi villages near Peoria, those of Wapewi and the friendly Black Partridge. A third party of Americans coming from southern Illinois reached

Peoria on November 5, weeks after Governor Edwards's militiamen had retreated south. This group, led by Captain Thomas Craig, found no Indians and worked off its wrath by burning the Métis village and capturing Thomas Forsyth, the United States' main source of intelligence and influence among the Indians of the area.[44] American tactical maneuvers in this late fall campaign were too complicated for the limited military skills of the troops then available. Faulty communications, an absence of overall command control, and the inadequacies of the untrained, ill-disciplined, short-term militia units, all blunted the impact of the strokes planned. But the American effort did further press the already off-balance tribesmen, who once again were learning they could not simultaneously conduct a serious war and hunt. American maneuvers in southern Illinois, for example, blocked Potawatomi access to their prime winter hunting grounds and forced them to move their villages farther north out of range of American assaults. Their raids against American settlements in southern Illinois were thereby slowed and diminished, but not halted entirely.

American maneuvers in Indiana and Illinois were little more than holding and spoiling operations: the critical theater of war lay on the western shores of Lake Erie. To gain access to the upper lakes and to secure a base for the major strategic move planned—an invasion of the Ontario Peninsula—the United States had to obtain control of Lake Erie and to retake Detroit. Such an operation would also nip off the British salient established the previous October—a supply depot for the Indian allies on the lower Maumee River. American operations were aided by a change in British leadership, for, soon after capturing Detroit, General Brock left for the Niagara frontier (where he was killed in an attack on October 13), and command in the west had fallen on the weaker shoulders of Colonel Henry Proctor. By December 1812 the Americans were moving in substantial force towards Detroit.

The first engagement occurred on 18 January 1813, when General James Winchester's troops defeated a smaller party of British regulars and Indians on the Raisin River. Winchester followed up by moving his main force forward, but on January 22 he met total defeat at the hands of Colonel Proctor, who had counterattacked with fourteen hundred soldiers and warriors. Winchester himself was captured in the heat of the battle and soon surrendered his ammunition-short regiments to Proctor, who promised him they would be treated as prisoners of war. This was not to be. A few Potawatomi had fought on the eighteenth and many on the twenty-second. When Proctor marched his regulars and their prisoners away that evening, he left eighty wounded Americans guarded by some fifty Indians (mainly Potawatomi) and five interpreters. That night and the next morning the Potawatomi led a massacre of the wounded, killing many of them and herding the survivors away to their villages.[45]

By April 1813 Governor Harrison had completed a major new base of operations, Fort Meigs, near the rapids of the Maumee River, close to the old battleground at Fallen Timbers. For the British this was a critical position, since it interdicted their supply depot at the rapids and cut off access to the Maumee valley. Their attempt to reduce Harrison's position commenced May 1. Led by the newly promoted Brigadier General Proctor and by Tecumsah, twenty-two hundred British soldiers and an intertribal force invested the American fort. To relieve the pressure on his position, Harrison launched eight hundred newly arrived Kentuckians against the British opposite Fort Meigs. This relief force was successful in its assault but failed to withdraw swiftly enough. Some seven hundred of the Kentuckians were killed or captured in the ensuing melee. Once more, Proctor failed to take proper precautions, and the Potawatomi moved among the prisoners and wounded, killing thirty of them before Tecumsah arrived and irately halted the slaughter. Proctor was soon forced to withdraw, however, for most of the Indians dispersed after the battle, taking their prisoners and booty with them.[46] The remainder of the summer, until September 10, was a see-saw of minor engagements and skirmishes, with Harrison sending raiding parties to punish Potawatomi villages in Michigan and Indiana, and the Potawatomi joining the British in ineffective attacks on Fort Meigs and Fort Stephenson (on Sandusky Bay). But on September 10 the balance of the campaign tipped decisively in favor of the Americans.

On that day Lieutenant Oliver H. Perry defeated the British fleet at the battle of Put-In-Bay, swinging control of Lake Erie to the American side, providing Harrison's army easy access to Detroit and Fort Malden, severing the British supply line to their Indian allies in the Old Northwest, and assuring the Americans the capability of landing at any point on the north side of the lake. Proctor's forces in the Detroit-Amherstburg area were now in an untenable position, and he prepared a hasty retreat towards British positions on Lake Ontario. Tecumsah and other Indian leaders were vastly disturbed by the preparations for this move, not understanding the implications of the American naval victory, but recognizing the consequences of the loss of British support in the west. Tecumsah expressed his contempt for Proctor but gathered together his remaining warriors to cover the British retreat. A few hundred Potawatomi warriors—those faithful to Tecumsah's cause—led by Shabeni and Mad Sturgeon, and accompanied by their families, joined in the withdrawal eastward along the valley of the Thames River. But most Potawatomi and other Indians who had earlier fought with the British remained in Michigan or Indiana. The American pursuit followed closely at the heels of the retreating

British until, on October 5, Tecumsah shamed Proctor into making a stand at Moraviantown. There, as the British line broke before the American attack, and while the flanking Indians were driven off, Tecumsah was killed. With his passing died also the guiding spirit of the Western Confederacy.[47]

The day following Proctor's defeat, the Indian agents, including Matthew Elliott, William Elliott, Billy Caldwell, and Billy's half-brother William Caldwell, gathered approximately two thousand Indians and moved them east to a refuge at Burlington Bay, near the head of Lake Ontario. Most of the remaining Potawatomi had escaped after the battle and returned to Michigan, but some accompanied Elliott and the Caldwells east. How many remained in Upper Canada is uncertain, for the British Indian Service thereafter did not separately enumerate the several western tribes who provided occasional aid in the defense of the Niagara frontier. On 7 June 1814 Captain Billy Caldwell reported 428 Odawa, Ojibwa, and Potawatomi men available at Burlington, while on November 1 of the same year his father, Colonel William Caldwell, Sr., gave 324 men as present from these three tribes. But most of these men were old or infirm, incapable of further service in war. The few available warriors had with them their elders and their women and children. They remained in the east, subsisting off army rations until the war ended, when the British encouraged them to return to the United States so as to reduce the costs of Indian Service administration.[48]

Potawatomi casualties in the 1812–1813 fighting along the Detroit-Amherstburg frontier and during Proctor's retreat had not been heavy. Early in 1816, as part of his official duties with the British Indian Service, Captain Billy Caldwell finished compiling a record of those Potawatomi who had been killed or wounded in this period. There were just eleven names on his list. They included Meteya—He Sulks, the hostile Winamek, Windigo—Cannibal, Oshkēsh, Pinase—Little Turkey, Kiseyanēm—Black Dog (Wolf Clan), Wa-wasēk—Distant Flash of Lightning, Mēshkigwa—Sunfish, Kitchigami—Great Sea, and two others whose names cannot be translated.[49] Caldwell apparently did not count such minor wounds as Main Poche received early in the war, but otherwise he made as full and accurate a record of casualties as possible, for the widows and orphans of those killed in battle were entitled to pensions, while the wounded veterans received special consideration in postwar years in the form of larger quantities of better-quality presents at the annual distributions by the British Indian Service.

After Proctor's retreat and his defeat at Moraviantown, the war in the west began winding down for the Potawatomi. Before this major loss fourteen thousand individual rations a day were being issued by the British to Indians in their service, including both warriors and their families (WHC 12: 148). With their supplies cut off and the Americans obviously in the ascendancy, the Potawatomi and other tribesmen were forced towards an accommodation. On 14 October 1813 Governor Harrison grudgingly extended a general armistice to the Potawatomi, which Topnebi and Five Medals more-or-less willingly accepted, and to which Main Poche and other warrior leaders gave only lip-service. Harrison had little confidence in the trustworthiness of all the Potawatomi, a judgment justified by the later actions of Main Poche and his fellows, and one—curiously enough—shared by Robert Dickson, the principal British Indian agent in Wisconsin. At the same time this armistice was ratified, General Benjamin Howard's troops completed the construction of Fort Clark at Peoria. The garrison at Fort Clark was in a position to block Potawatomi raids against settlements in southern Illinois and to cut off access to the major winter hunting range as well. Meanwhile, the British at Mackinac Island and in Wisconsin were increasingly without the wherewithal to command (or to purchase) Potawatomi loyalties.[50]

The winter of 1813–1814 was a hard one for this tribe. Whatever the long-range political interests and designs of its leaders may have been, and despite the short-term goals of perennially hostile warrior-leaders such as Main Poche, Mad Sturgeon, and Pierre Moran, the critical issue that season was one of subsistence and survival. Thus hunger forced old divisions of opinion to open up once more. Some okamek moved directly and immediately towards making peace with the Americans. Others tried to sustain some measure of a warlike posture. Most played a calculated double game, pressuring both the British and the Americans to the best of their ability, and for their best advantage. Throughout 1814 support of the war effort in the west declined, and progressively more hostile attitudes were expressed towards the British remaining in the upper lakes area.

The Potawatomi in the area did not oppose an American raid on the English traders on the St. Joseph River in January 1814, and later they would not support the British against an American party come to announce an inter-tribal peace council planned for later that year. That same month Black Partridge and some of his people visited Governor William Clark in St. Louis to express their adherence to the American cause, leaving behind them nine warriors as hostages to their promises of peace (and nine fewer men to feed).[51] In June a large number of Potawatomi began assembling at Greenville for the peace treaty that was concluded on July 22. At this treaty William Henry Harrison and Lewis Cass, on behalf of the United States and its Indian allies, the Wyandots, Delawares, Shawnee, and Seneca, gave peace to the Miami, and they extended "this indulgence also to the bands of the Putawatamies, which adhere to the Grand Sachem Topinipee, and to the Chief Onoxa" (Kappler 1904: 105). This treaty was signed by Topnebi, Five Medals (who put down his clan name, Onaksa—He Flies Away), Meteya, Bear's Foot, He Sees All

Over, The Mad Odawa, He Walks At Night, The Crane, Deaf And Dumb, The Crow, Flat Belly (who was of Miami origin), and six other Potawatomi okamek. They again promised to keep the peace and to aid the Americans in war against the British.

However, two months later, when they learned of a planned attack on their villages by General Duncan MacArthur, the more hostile Potawatomi leaders were able to assemble over eight hundred Odawa and Potawatomi warriors along the St. Joseph River to meet the anticipated invasion of their territory. Similarly, the same anti-American okamek had—since the winter of 1813–1814—regularly been visiting the beleaguered British at Mackinac Island as well as sending messengers to Burlington, far to the east. In January 1814 Topnebi's younger half-brother, Chebanse—The Duckling, together with other hostile leaders, visited Mackinac to pledge his loyalty and to make a desperate plea for rations, ammunition, and a cannon. The Duckling boasted that the Potawatomi were preparing an assault on Fort Wayne in the spring, which would have been a most ambitious undertaking at that time. Chebanse was back at Mackinac in August, when he and some of his warriors helped the British garrison hold off an American attack on the island. Another party of anti-American Potawatomi, this time led by Shawnese—Southern Fog, arrived later in the year to plea for support and complain that communications were cut off with the British to the east. And, in spite of great difficulties, some Potawatomi managed to get through to the British lines at Burlington. On 25 March 1814 Matthew Elliott reported that two of Main Poche's warriors had arrived there carrying messages and intelligence; the Potawatomi in the west were "sitting on their war clubs waiting to take it up when an opportunity may offer," he wrote.[52]

As Main Poche, Chebanse, Shawnese, Moran, and Mad Sturgeon worked to keep the Potawatomi warlike, many other okamek moved towards closer and friendlier relationships with Americans. Black Partridge, Gomo, his younger brother Senajiwan—Swift Current, and others had moved their villages back to the vicinity of Peoria following the completion of Fort Clark. In part, this migration was encouraged by the failure of the British supply effort in northern Illinois and Wisconsin, by the growing antipathy of some Potawatomi in Wisconsin and Illinois towards the British, and by the worsening suspicions of Robert Dickson, who eventually refused the Potawatomi what small aid he might have provided.[53]

Rendered near paranoid by his isolation and the many pressures on him, Dickson had fair reason for his growing skepticism, for Gomo and others by early spring were regularly reporting British moves and plans to American agents, and they had restored trading relations with the garrison at Fort Clark, bartering venison for ammunition, whiskey, and other necessaries. In one of the more emotion-laden moments of the war, the Potawatomi managed to drive Dickson over the edge of sanity. On 4 February 1814 Dickson wrote his compatriot John Lawe, "The Poutewatamies have always been villains to both parties and will continue to do so until the end of the Chapter. I will work with them a [plot] they are little aware of" (WHC 11: 289–90).[54] A month later Dickson's self-control deserted him. By then he had failed in an effort to marshal the Indians around Green Bay to make war against the Potawatomi near Milwaukee, while some Potawatomi (particularly Onangizes and The Big Winnebago) insisted on visiting him to inquire about the state of his health and how long he thought he might live. His response was that of a rational man harried past the point of reason by great stress, isolation, and too many Potawatomi displaying too much barbed concern for his welfare: driven near psychotic by fear and hate, he wrote up a long bill of particulars, all justifying his obsessive suspicion of these Indians. This episode represented a classic and successful example of Potawatomi psychological warfare, of strong men sure of their own spirit-powers meddling maliciously with the anxieties and doubts of others.

By midwinter 1814–1815 many Potawatomi villages were in a starving condition, and American officials began issuing rations to lure them over to a peaceful course. A few more abortive efforts at generating renewed enthusiasm for warfare were made by such hard-core fanatics as Main Poche and The Duckling, but for most the war was over. On January 10 the elusive White Pigeon went to Fort Wayne to surrender and to obtain rations for his village; in May, Mad Sturgeon—deserting his still aggressively hostile brother-in-law Main Poche—also went to Fort Wayne to make his peace. Although the Treaty of Ghent was signed by Great Britain and the United States on 24 December 1814, it was three months before the first news of peace reached the Upper Great Lakes. At first Main Poche, Blackbird, and Chebanse refused to believe messengers bearing word of the treaty. Even after a visit to Mackinac Island in April, when Lieutenant Colonel Robert McDouall told them the war had ended and they must lay down their weapons, Main Poche, Chebanse, and Moran could not accept the change in their circumstances and continued efforts to stir up interest in further warfare.[55]

There were now few Potawatomi willing to listen to those who counseled yet more hostilities. In mid-July seven okamek of the Illinois River villages gathered at the small village of Portage des Sioux on the Mississippi River to sign a treaty of peace with Governors William Clark and Ninian Edwards. They included Senajiwan (replacing his elder brother Gomo, who had died the previous April), Black Partridge, Odawa, and Wapewi. On the eighteenth of the month the parties agreed to reestablish peace, to forgive prior acts of hostilities, to deliver over any prisoners, and to reaffirm older treaties.[56] Seven weeks later a much larger party of Potawatomi, Odawa, and Ojibwa—together with the formerly hostile elements of the Wyandot, Delaware, Shawnee, and Seneca—gathered at Spring Wells, near Detroit, to write the treaty which finally ended the War of 1812 for the Potawatomi and their allies (Kappler 1904: 117–18). Twenty-five "Sachems, Chiefs, Headmen, and Warriors" of Potawatomi villages in Michigan, Indiana, and Wisconsin signed this treaty. They included Topnebi, Five Medals (who at this treaty signed himself with yet another name, Onangizes), Ashkibi—New River, Winamekos—The Little Catfish, The Crane, Mad Sturgeon, Meteya, Wzawskibi—The Yellow River, someone who signed himself modestly as Honkemani (Okama—The Leader), Louison (i.e., Louis Chevalier, Jr.), and Wamigo—The Thunderbird, who was also named William Henry Harrison. Wamigo was a Potawatomi obviously cognizant of where the power now lay. The listing of Louison Chevalier as a Potawatomi marks the beginning of a process of ethnic-group switching that would increase through the years, for he was the Métis son of old Louis Chevalier and a Potawatomi woman. Moreover, the appearance of so many names on this treaty, particularly those of warriors, was a residue of Tecumsah's teaching. Ever afterward, Potawatomi okamek would not be allowed to sign treaties with the United States by themselves.

At the council preceding the Spring Wells treaty in 1815, one young (unidentified) okama expressed concern with having to accept the provisions of the Treaty of Greenville (1795), which he spoke of as if it were an agreement shrouded in the legendary mists of Potawatomi antiquity. Since his ancestors had accepted it, he said, he would raise no questions that might injure memory of them. He would rather think of their acts as having been wise. But, if "it were to do over again, he would pause and he would reflect. He would look at his children in the cradle, and ask what right he had to injure those innocents? what authority he had to deprive them of their rights? . . . It had pleased the Master of the Universe to place these Indians upon this land, but the scene was now changed. Their ancestors had parted with it" (ASP-IA 2: 25–26).

But there were still those who held out some faint hope of aid from a remote power. Mad Sturgeon had sent for Tenskwatawa, the Shawnee prophet who had inspired so many and lost so much, inviting him to attend the treaty council. Tenskwatawa crossed over the Detroit River and met with the assembly, privately as well as in public. In private he apparently convinced Mad Sturgeon that the fate of America was connected with that of Napoleon Bonaparte, holding out hope that, should the British defeat Napoleon soon, the Western Confederacy might thereupon expect a renewed infusion of British aid. Tenskwatawa was somewhat late in his reckoning, since Wellington had defeated Bonaparte at Waterloo three months earlier, and Bonaparte was already confined to his final exile on St. Helena, with the British showing absolutely no interest in renewing the war (ASP-IA 2: 17–18). William Henry Harrison had to disabuse Mad Sturgeon of this lingering hope, pointing out that the central issue at this council was the proper relations between the United States and the tribes of the Old Northwest. He explained, with little patience, that Great Britain had abandoned the Indians at the Treaty of Ghent, giving up all claims south of the Canadian border.

Spain, France, Great Britain—the influence and support of all these imperial powers were now gone. There remained the issue of working out in detail the proper relations between the United States and the tribes of the Northwest Territory. So ended an era, for the scene indeed was now changed.

THE NEW SCENE:
ON TREATIES
AND TRIBULATIONS

From the viewpoint of the Potawatomi and related tribes in the Old Northwest, the War of 1812 brought only defeat, impoverishment, increased dependency on things American, and a brief four-year pause in the advance of the frontier. As their population increased, and with the threat of British intervention greatly weakened, Americans no longer found it necessary to placate these tribes so as to neutralize their threat to exposed and isolated settlements. The United States was now determined to gain possession of the rich lands of central and northern Illinois and Indiana, according to the preemption clause of the Treaty of Greenville and following the established procedure of treaty council and purchase. But first there had to be a demonstration of sovereign might, genuine provision for the security of Americans settled on or beyond the frontier.

In the eight years between 1814 and 1822 more than a dozen rebuilt or newly constructed forts were garrisoned in the west. Forts Wayne and Harrison in Indiana were reconstructed; Fort Shelby at Detroit was built to replace the old French-British post; Forts Gratiot and Mackinac were improved and garrisoned on the Lake Huron shore; Fort Howard was constructed on Green Bay; Fort Dearborn at Chicago and Fort Clark at Peoria were reestablished; and Fort Edward in western Illinois, Fort Armstrong at Rock Island, and Fort Crawford at Prairie du Chien, all were built in 1816 to cover the Mississippi River. Between 1819 and 1822 were constructed Fort Snelling on the Upper Mississippi, Fort Brady at Sault Ste. Marie, and Fort Saginaw on Saginaw Bay (Billington 1960: 291). At that point, the Potawatomi tribal estate was both completely surrounded and effectively penetrated by a chain of substantial American military positions.

Thereafter, from time to time some of the okamek would speak threateningly of possible hostilities, but only to gain temporary concessions. On several occasions there would be a brief scuffle, and even a very few classic ambuscades and raids; but these were small actions precipitated by local conditions. Concerted military action was no longer a feasible tribal policy. On the few occasions when hostilities between the United States and some other tribes seemed imminent—principally during the Winnebago outbreak of 1827 and the so-called Black Hawk War of 1832—Americans were able quickly to muster and move regular army and militia forces far out of proportion to the actual threat. But by then the Potawatomi had ceased to make war against the United States and its citizens forever.

After the peace treaty at Spring Wells the stark fact of Potawatomi life involved questions of economics and subsistence, not political-military action. The tribesmen faced severe shortages of food and lacked the wherewithal for trade and barter. Such matters are, of course, relative. What was scarcity in one decade was plenty in the next. But certain gross dimensions are clear: the large herds of buffalo and elk that once populated the prairies of Illinois and Indiana were long gone. The Potawatomi's principal large-game animal after the eighteenth century was deer, and the large populations were in the prairie lands, oak-openings, and bottoms of central and southern Illinois and Indiana, not in the forest to the north. Indeed, as much as for any other motive, it was the search for this prime source of animal protein that had moved the Potawatomi southward long before the War of 1812. Their move down the Wabash River valley, the Potawatomi explained to William Henry Harrison, was because of the shortage of deer in the north: "they were tired of eating fish, and wanted meat" (Esarey 1922 2: 636–41). Even after the War of 1812, the Potawatomi continued their drift southward down the Illinois River valley. Following the peace treaty at Portage des Sioux, on 1 September 1815, Black Partridge wrote to President Madison explaining that before the war only the "neutral" Potawatomi had lived south of Lake Peoria, but now that peace had come he anticipated a great increase in the number of Potawatomi hunting and living in the area, to as many as five or seven hundred families (about thirty-six hundred individuals) (TP-US 17: 226–28). Mkedēpoke was certainly exaggerating as well as staking out a claim, but he had a point.

In 1820 John Tanner—by now trying to give up his life as an Ojibwa hunter in the far north—traveled below Peoria on the Illinois River with his children. As his canoe drifted south he found "great numbers of Potawattomies, their lodges standing many together in almost every bend of the river." Tanner was much impressed with the ample supply of game in the area, as well as with the generosity of the Potawatomi who provided him and his children with large quantities of honey and venison (James 1830: 256). Tanner was probably exaggerating the quantities of deer in the area; his base of comparison was the boreal forest of the north, where life was harsher and large game scarcer than in central Illinois. Besides, by 1820 the Potawatomi there were experiencing sharp competition for the available game. The American population to their south was increasing rapidly, migrating northward, and hunting over much of the same territory as the Potawatomi. Some of the tribesmen had already taken to killing American cattle for meat (Edmunds 1972b: 241); and they regularly had to eat fish, as did their kinsmen to the north more often than they (Forsyth 1812b; and Gerend 1920: 126). The shortage of large game animals in southern Michigan exacerbated the problem, for it regularly brought the Potawatomi and other tribesmen from the area south to the prairie country for a winter hunt.[57] There was apparently more large game available in southeastern Wisconsin in the years immediately following the war; while along the Milwaukee River, as on the Des Plaines, the Chicago, and the Calumet rivers, and in the Kankakee marsh, muskrats were especially plentiful (WHC 11: 240).

But the availability of game mammals, large and small, diminished rapidly as the size of the Potawatomi estate declined with each new treaty and as a greatly concentrated and expanding population hunted over a smaller and smaller territory. With the cession of their lands to the east and south, the general movement of the Potawatomi was west and north, and it was in a restricted area near Lake Michigan that the game supply finally dropped to the point of causing actual starvation. In March of 1825, for example, there was a significant if minor scuffle between a small group of Potawatomi and Odawa and a party of American surveyors of similar size south of the Grand River in Michigan. The Indians, near starving after a hard winter, were busy making maple sugar. When the well-fed and amply supplied survey party approached, the Indians protested their blazing trees (which both wasted the precious maple sap and symbolized their loss of the land). They then demanded food from the Americans and threatened them with their firearms. The surveyors easily subdued the angry but weakened Indians and bound them up until morning, when they fed and released them (TP-US 11: 667–69).

The next year, in the winter of 1826–1827, the subagent at St. Joseph, Ramsay Potts, reported that the Potawatomi along the Kankakee and Iroquois rivers were literally starving. An investigator was sent, and he found the shortage of game was being worsened by the presence of a pack of whiskey dealers: "The Indians at most camps are drinking their children starving and the trader selling flour to the Indians at one pint or pint and half for a muskrat skin" (Robertson & Riker 1942 1: 647–48). A few years later, when the tribal range had been contracted to almost nothing by further treaties, the situation worsened. In the late fall of 1835 some five hundred Potawatomi and other Indians were trapped by an early blizzard near Kenosha, Wisconsin, while on their way north after an annuity distribution in Chicago. The small American settlement had to feed these Indians to keep them from starvation (WHC 3: 403–5). That same year, as far north as present Sheboygan, Wisconsin, game animals were so rare and the peltry so scarce that the only trader closed up shop and moved off (Buchen 1944; WHC 15: 158–60). The Potawatomi who remained near Sheboygan turned back to fishing for their subsistence and a source of cash income—they became processors of fish oil for the American market.

The Potawatomi's own techniques of hunting contributed to the decline in the game populations. Popular American stereotypes have the noble Algonquian savage gliding through the forests practicing conservation techniques worthy of members of the Sierra Club. But the hard truth was far from this pleasant fiction. The Potawatomi, as did other tribes of the woodlands, believed that so long as they paid proper respect to the spirits of the hunted animal there would always be an ample supply of game. Actually, they lived from day to day, killing and eating whatever animals they could find (Ray 1974: 199–203). They used, for example, a reed call in the spring to imitate the bleating of a fawn so as to decoy the doe, which allowed the fawns to die of starvation. And by the late 1820s they were repeatedly hunting over the same limited territory in all seasons, further diminishing the game populations (Copley 1890: 263).

The decline of the animal populations is recorded in the condition of the fur trade in the years after the war. In 1806 the United States had started the federally controlled factory system with the aim of regulating and controlling the trade and underselling British and Spanish-French traders. The factory system was not very successful and actually consisted of a disguised system of presents, since the income from furs never met the costs of the program (Tyler 1974: 38–39). Factories were opened at Chicago and Green Bay in 1815, specifically to cut the Potawatomi and other tribes off from contacts with the British traders, but the furs and hides delivered by the Potawatomi were few. The factory at Chicago was a particularly small operation. In 1819, for example, the Potawatomi brought in only 362 deerskins and 1,914 muskrat pelts, compared with 64,332 deerskins and no muskrat traded at the Choctaw factory the same year. The Chicago factory's peak year was 1817, when furs valued at $4,598 were brought in; but this figure declined to $521 in 1819, the year the establishment was closed (ASP-IA 2: 208). However, such figures do not represent the whole of Potawatomi participation in the fur trade; they did much business with private traders close to their villages.

Some Potawatomi also continued regularly to do business with the British in Upper Canada in the years following the Treaty of Ghent. In early summer of 1814 those Potawatomi who had been lodged and rationed near Burlington were ordered to move west to the Amherstburg area, which they did. By July of 1814 there were 1,331 Potawatomi, Odawa, and Ojibwa near that British post, on the Canadian shore, dependent on army rations. In February of 1816 there remained 1,130 Indians from these three tribes near Amherstburg, still unable to support themselves. William Claus estimated that he would need 130,000 daily rations to feed the Indians dependent on Amherstburg in 1816, a ration at that time consisting of six ounces of salt pork or eight of beef, and ten ounces of flour. But by spring of that year, there were no Potawatomi subsisting at that post. The British had strongly encouraged them to move west into American territory and to return to hunting, gardening, and trapping. This they did by the spring of 1816, when no Potawatomi were reported residing on the Canadian shore. They had moved west, passing by Detroit into central Michigan and Indiana. When some of these tribesmen next returned to Amherstburg it was from 230 miles to the west, and they were few in number, arriving only in small parties of two or three dozen.[58]

When the British surrendered Fort Michilimackinac in 1815, they set up shop temporarily on St. Joseph Island, but the next year a new military–Indian Service post was established on Drummond Island, a mile west of the eastern tip of the Upper Peninsula of Michigan. Until 1828 (when it too was determined to be American territory) Drummond Island served as the main point of contact between the tribesmen of Wisconsin, Iowa, and Minnesota and the British. A persistent tradition has it that Drummond Island lodged a community of Potawatomi, but this report stems from a typographical error in one Canadian document, which substituted "Potawatomi" for "Potaganase" (Many Inlets), the name of a small Ojibwa village there (Clifton 1975b: 105–9). In fact, regardless of American suspicions, Potawatomi visits to Drummond Island were extremely rare. The 1817 report of Major Henry Puthuff, United States Indian agent at Mackinac, that a group of Illinois River Potawatomi were visiting the island is not confirmed by British records (Buck 1967: 14).

However, in 1822 forty-five Potawatomi did arrive unexpectedly to see the British at this far northern post. They were a war party from Wisconsin, who arrived "as grim as red and black paint, red-moose hair, spears, clubs, and guns could make them." These unexpected visitors received a cool welcome from the British commander, one that turned frosty when he discovered they had brought him three American scalps, anticipating a generous reception and reward. This officer gave them a basic food ration but no presents or weapons; and much to the surprise of the Potawatomi he told them they would have to accept, without British help, the wrath of the Americans. No specifics of the incident were noted. Indeed, because the garrison commander took no official notice of it, the events would have gone completely unrecorded, except that a curious English topographer was visiting the island at the time (Bigsby 1850 2: 142–43).

Those Potawatomi interested in maintaining their British connections traveled eastward to Amherstburg, and they did so regularly until 1837. After 1817 a fairly steady stream arrived there seeking counsel, supplies, weapons, approval for blows struck, promises of support, and assorted pleasures that were available near the town and military post. In August of 1817, after a large intertribal council in which they enumerated their complaints, they were told (probably by Agent John Askin), "Tell your brothers who have sold lands to the Big Knives that they have done themselves a great injury. . . .but there is no remedy for this now. Remain peaceful and quiet for the present— when your Great Father requires you, he will raise his voice."[59] The British Indian agents were walking the same diplomatic tight-rope they had in 1805, working to keep the western Indians on good terms as a force-in-readiness to aid the British in the event of hostilities with the United States, regularly spilling vinegar into the wounds infecting Indian-American relationships, but not exactly advocating immediate violence.

The Americans, knowing how restive were the Potawatomi as treaty after treaty pressed new demands on them for the cession of additional blocks of real estate, were understandably upset with the continuing contact between the tribesmen and their old British allies. There were repeated reports that the Potawatomi were planning to join in fresh hostilities, and such rumors were amplified by the knowledge that Tenskwatawa—the Shawnee prophet—remained in Upper Canada (until 1826), still hoping to realize his old dreams of power (TP-US 10: 873 and 885–86). In late fall, 1819, Governor Lewis Cass of Michigan Territory resolved once and for all to cut the Potawatomi and other tribes off from contact with the British at Amherstburg (Fort Malden). His efforts at control consisted of speeches only, and these had little effect (ASP-IA 2: 219). The Potawatomi continued to visit the British as before. There was little to stop them, and they had much to gain in the form of goods, praise, acknowledgment of their worth, and the pleasures of ritual renewal of an old alliance. As events developed, the British never again had need of Potawatomi military support against the United States, although from time to time there was some suggestion of the need to mobilize them for defense. Indeed, it would be a full century before any Potawatomi warrior would again fight alongside the Union Jack, and then it would be against a different enemy far to the east, in Flanders Field. However, in addition to the annual generosity of British Indian agents, Potawatomi visits to Upper Canada gained many of them an escape route, one which—when pressed too hard by the United States to do other than they wished—several thousand used to evade American Indian policies and to find a place of refuge.

Following the peace treaty at Spring Wells, there was only a dozen month's respite for the Potawatomi from American pressures for land cessions. In the fall of 1815 the Potawatomi learned that American officials believed the United States had acquired much of their estate northwest of the Illinois River in an 1804 treaty with the Sauk and Fox, a spurious transaction which the Potawatomi okamek quickly repudiated (as did the Sauk and Fox themselves). On September 1 Black Partridge, in a letter to President Madison, protested that it was at the Portage des Sioux peace council the Potawatomi had first heard of this questionable surrender of their lands by another tribe (TPUS 17: 226–80). The following March, Thomas Forsyth met with The Big Seagull and Main Poche—who now was seriously ill, nearly deaf, and drinking very heavily. Forsyth reported the Potawatomi were greatly alarmed about the surveying of their hunting grounds and that they forecast trouble if the Odawa and Ojibwa were not included in any new treaty for Illinois lands. Thereupon, American agents went about arranging the first postwar cession of territory, with the aim of resolving questions concerning the 1804 Sauk and Fox cession and acquiring full title to Potawatomi lands in Illinois, including a tract providing access to Lake Michigan from the south (see Figure 11).[60]

No full record or journal is available of the 1816 treaty; however, both Chambler (Shabeni—He Has Pawed Through) and The Odawa spoke to the effect that the Potawatomi, Ojibwa, and Odawa were united as one and opposed to dividing the lands.[61] Both men had a pronounced vested interest in this contention, as they were of Odawa origin and represented the few members of that tribe and the fewer Ojibwa who had earlier assimilated into Potawatomi villages. Legally, the treaty that was signed on 24 August 1816 at St. Louis was a wash transaction, cleaning up questions of title to part of the territory in a manner acceptable to the participants; it involved, as well, the exchange of some lands in central and southern Illinois for new land in the northern part of the territory (ICC 1974 3: 347). The treaty itself was made with the Odawa, Ojibwa, and Potawatomi of the "Illinois and Melwakee rivers and their waters, and on the southwestern parts of Lake Michigan" (Kappler 1904: 132).

There were twenty-eight Potawatomi and assimilated Odawa who signed the 1816 documents, including Black Partridge, Swift Current (by his brother Ignatius), The Little Blackbird, Pemasaw—The Walker, The Odawa, Onangizes, Shabeni, Kakak—The Duck Hawk, Shawano—Back Rain, Wabansi—Break of Day, The Great Sea, The Little Spaniard, The Little Odawa, The Trader, Alexander Robinson (who signed as Chichibinway), and Mwas—Little Wolf.[62] Jointly they represented villages of the Illinois River, northern Illinois, and southern Wisconsin; and the Eagle, Ocean, Thunderbird, Man, Bear, and Wolf clans, as well as the growing number of individuals of partial

Spanish, French, Scots-Irish, Anglo-Saxon, Odawa, and Ojibwa ancestry who were in process of assimilating into the Potawatomi tribe.

At this treaty the Potawatomi received, in exchange for the lands ceded, "a considerable quantity of goods" delivered immediately following the signing of the documents, a thousand dollars in goods to be delivered annually for twelve years on the Illinois River at or above Peoria, and a strip of northern Illinois above a line drawn due west from the southern tip of Lake Michigan. The lands surrendered were those they had conquered in the second half of the eighteenth century; they included much of their most valuable hunting ground. This was also the first treaty where the United States knowingly and deliberately negotiated with a part rather than the whole of the tribe. It was, thereby, a step in the direction of producing American-fostered and American-recognized "bands," a process that would accelerate a process of political fragmentation in the coming twenty years. Moreover, as the lands ceded at this treaty were surveyed and settled, the Illinois Potawatomi were forced to migrate northwards and to concentrate near Lake Michigan.

In the next two years the eastern Potawatomi were involved in additional treaties. The first of these was made on 28 September 1817 at Fort Meigs, near the foot of the rapids of the Maumee River; and the second was drawn up on 2 October 1818 at St. Mary's, Ohio. Thirty-one Potawatomi signed the 1817 treaty, mostly from west of Detroit, and from villages along the St. Joseph and the Wabash. They were led by Winamek—once more back in a position of accepted leadership—and by Meteya, whose disposition was turning sour. The other signers included The Little Catfish, Yellow River, Flat Belly, Pierre Moran, The Corn, The Mosquito, The Full Moon, New River, The Black, White Elk, The Crane, and Gabinay—Gabriel. Representatives of the Ocean and Fish clans predominated at this council, where the Potawatomi gave their assent to the cession by other tribes of the remaining Indian-held lands in Ohio, together with a small tract in eastern Michigan. Sigenak—The Blackbird was present and signed the treaty, but his name was listed in the Ojibwa column, as were those of Okamanse—Young Leader and Manitogabowit—Standing Spirit, two Potawatomi okamek from the Upper Wabash who twenty years later led a major migration of Potawatomi into Upper Canada.

From the 1817 proceeding, these Potawatomi received (for their cooperation, the lands were not theirs to sell) a fifteen-year term annuity of $1,300 per annum payable in hard cash at Detroit. Of special interest is the fact that they also accepted or arranged a number of special exemptions and awards, unlike any that had appeared on earlier treaties. One of these involved an award of 1,280 acres of land on the Raisin River to St. Ann's Church and College in Detroit, a kind of tithing on the part of some of the okamek, who were strong Catholics. They also approved a number of special payments or indemnities proposed by the commissioners, Lewis Cass and Duncan Mac-Arthur, payments made to Indians who had served the United States during the late war, as well as to former prisoners and to children made orphans by Potawatomi raids. Of particular interest is a new phrase first appearing in this treaty, involving special grants made to individuals related to the Potawatomi "by blood or adoption." One such grant of 640 acres was made to Alexander D. and Richard Godfroy, sons of the Indian agent G. Godfroy, who were labeled "adopted children" of the Potawatomi. These new special provisions created a mechanism for distributing part of the proceeds of a treaty to Americans of dubious ancestry and to others, like the Godfroys, who had close business dealings with these tribesmen. Within a few years there would be a loud clamor from many more such individuals, once Americans came to recognize there was land and silver to be obtained at Indian treaties if they could get themselves accepted as "Indians by blood [descent]" or "adoption." Such a process would contribute to a large, if curious, increase in the Potawatomi population during the late 1820s, particularly involving the many French-Canadian Métis who then changed their status to "Indian by blood."[63]

In the fall of 1818 seven treaties were negotiated at St. Mary's, and these attracted a great many Indians from the Upper Great Lakes and the Ohio valley, including Potawatomi from all parts of the tribal estate. On October 2 these tribesmen had their turn and signed away a large tract in present Indiana and Illinois, along the upper Wabash and the Tippecanoe and Vermilion rivers.[64] Among the thirty-four Potawatomi signatures were those of Topnebi, The Duckling, Little Corn, The Little Catfish, The Crane, Mad Sturgeon, The Prairie Man, Back Rain, The Menomini, Bear, Meteya, Gizes, Bear's Foot, Five Medals (as Onaksa), Shapagizhek—Sound Going Through The Sky, Swift Current, Pierre Moran, and Black Wolf. Representing the Bear, Fish, Ocean, Thunderbird, Man, Wolf, and other clans, these okamek and warriors came in from as far away as the Milwaukee, Des Plaines, St. Joseph, and Wabash rivers. This treaty was drawn with the tribe as a whole, now called the "Potawatamie nation of Indians." From this cession the Potawatomi present received a large share of the ample supply of presents that were distributed, and a perpetual annuity of $2,500 in silver coin, half payable at Detroit, half at Chicago. Six of the Burnett children, the sons and daughters of Topnebi's daughter by a Scots trader, were awarded one or two sections of land each, the first of a number of expensive special privileges given these young "Potawatomi by descent."

Nearly three years later, on 21 August 1821, the process of eliminating Potawatomi control and occupation of land in the Old Northwest began in earnest. On that day the "Ottawa, Chippewa, and Pottawatamie Nations of Indians" ceded the southwestern quarter of Michigan and an eleven-mile-deep strip of land across the northeastern edge of Indiana.[65] The country above the St. Joseph River, particularly directly along the Grand, was principally Odawa territory, although some Potawatomi occasionally occupied or used it, while the United States listed the Ojibwa as participants in the treaty mainly to quiet whatever claims more distant members of this tribe might later make to the lands ceded in 1821. Only one Ojibwa and ten Odawa, as compared with fifty-five Potawatomi, signed the treaty. The latter included Topnebi, Meteya, The Duckling, Louis Chevalier, Shomin—Dried Berry, Bear's Foot, Awbenabi —He Looks Back, The Bear, Swift Current, Winamek, Shawota—Southern (Summer) Spirit, Mzhikteno—Thunder Coming Down, Southern Fog, The Little Megis (i.e., Mide shell), Back Rain, and New River.

The council before the signing of the treaty documents did not proceed easily, well, or quickly. It was by far the largest such meeting the Potawatomi had ever participated in. Some three thousand of these tribesmen arrived, their leaders fully aware that an ominous new step was being taken. Meteya was particularly angry. He spoke strongly against selling such a large tract. Acting out the traditional role of speaker for the whole tribe, Meteya argued that before arriving the Potawatomi had reached a consensus position not to cede so much land. They may well have done, but little consensus was displayed once on the treaty grounds. Lewis Cass, the main treaty commissioner, and Alexander Wolcott, United States Indian agent at Chicago, argued back that the Potawatomi were divided into separate "political communities" and each had separate rights and interests. No one man, nor any few leaders, could speak for the whole, they contended. Meteya could not win the day by oratory alone, and his opposition to the treaty was undercut by the disaffection of many, who had pressing immediate needs. Topnebi, now a wasted old man, instead of backing Meteya with the dignity of his years of experience, spent his time pleading for whiskey, which Cass refused to provide until the treaty was signed. When the opposition to the treaty was dissolved, the Potawatomi sold their title to most of the lands they had taken from the Miami starting in 1699, including a large part of the ancient territory they had occupied when Samuel de Champlain first arrived on Lake Huron in 1616. They received in payment a twenty-year term annuity of $5,000 per annum in silver coin, plus a $1,000 per year award for the payment of a blacksmith and a teacher to service the tribe's needs.

At this treaty a new category of people, "Indians by Descent," emerged full-blown. Dozens of parcels of prime land in 640 and 1,280 tracts were awarded to the wives and children of American men, mainly of French (Métis) or Scots-Irish descent. These men were using their relationships with Potawatomi women, or through their children by same, to gain access to valuable personal estates. These included the Burnett children once again, the La

Limes, the Daze family, the Chandonaises, the La Clercs, the Chandlers, the Beaubiens, the Rolands, the Bertrands, the Rileys, and the La Framboises. They also included the children of G. Godfroy and William Knaggs, both United States Indian agents who helped to arrange the treaty and bring the Potawatomi around to accepting its provisions. Apparently, the United States statutes held no conflict-of-interest titles at the time, or, if they did, they were not applied to Indian affairs. Meanwhile, the old Potawatomi veterans of the War of 1812 were growing older; and the men who had acted as okamek for the villages and clans in the days when the tribe was an autonomous political unit wielding the balance of power in the Northwest Territory were passing one by one. Topnebi drank himself to death in 1826, followed by Meteya in 1827.

By 1825 there was greatly increased tension in the Upper Great Lakes region. The loss by many tribes of much of their territories through treaties, the prospects of further cessions to come, the consolidation of the Indian populations in restricted areas, and continuing invasions of the existing lands by American settlers, hunters, trappers, and miners, all contributed to intertribal friction. In 1825 an intertribal delegation in Washington called for a grand peace council, and the Congress approved this, with a special view towards fixing tribal boundaries so as to both prevent war and to facilitate later cession of the lands. The United States badly needed to know which tribes were the legitimate owners of what lands. No territory actually changed hands at the subsequent treaty which was held at Prairie du Chien on the upper Mississippi on 19 August 1825, and very few Potawatomi participated, although more had been expected to arrive. The four Potawatomi who signed the documents were unknowns: Ignace, Keyokek, Little Crane, and The Trading Man. What was at stake were Potawatomi claims to territory on the Lake Michigan shoreline north of Milwaukee—their old refuge occupied by them since 1650, and the valuable but much contested lead-mining region in southwestern Wisconsin and northwestern Illinois. There were few if any Potawatomi summer villages in this latter area, and its ownership was in dispute, being claimed by the Sauk, Fox, Ojibwa, Odawa, and Winnebago as well. The Potawatomi were awarded a share of the lead-mine district by this treaty,[66] but their claims to the Lake Michigan shoreline were left uncertified. In consequence, six years later the Menomini were able to go off to Washington and to lay claim to all the lands north of Milwaukee, a territory long occupied and heavily used by the Potawatomi (Kappler 1904: 319).

By this time the pressure on land in Indiana had become extreme, and state and federal officials there were being pushed to extinguish title to all remaining Indian lands and to remove the Potawatomi and Miami from that state. On 16 October 1826 Lewis Cass and John Tipton were finally successful in securing Potawatomi agreement to the cession of two large tracts in northern Indiana, plus a one-hundred foot wide right-of-way for a road from Indianapolis to Lake Michigan.[67] The Potawatomi were led by Meteya and Awbenabi, both aging men in the last years of their lives. Meteya again acted as speaker for the whole, but six days later Awbenabi—a particularly arrogant man who was eventually executed by his own family—rose to talk on behalf of the young men, the warriors, and the peace chiefs. These two were unsuccessful in blocking the surrender of additional lands, but they did manage to resist pressure to remove westward. Sixty-one Potawatomi signed this treaty, a larger number than ever before. A few of the names are familiar from previous events and proceedings, such as Topnebi, Swift Current (who signed under his other name, Peche'o), Pierre Moran, Wabansi, and Thunder Coming Down; but most of them were of men signing their first treaty, such as Wapsi —White Skin (Swift Current's son), Kiwani, and Sawkina.

At the 1826 treaty council the Potawatomi immediately received more than $30,000 in presents, much to their relief, for as Lewis Cass observed they had arrived hungry and destitute. The treaty also provided a twenty-two-year term annuity of $2,000 per annum, the expenses of a blacksmith and a miller, the cost of a mill on the Tippecanoe River, and 160 bushels of salt annually, all payable at the Fort Wayne Indian Agency. Like crows drawn to carrion, a flock of traders, Métis, and other predators were present, helping the commissioners persuade the Potawatomi leaders to capitulate and sharing substantially in the proceeds. Members of the numerous Burnett family were again awarded from one to three sections of land each. Fifty-eight "Indians by birth," all past or present students at the Carey Baptist Mission School, were awarded a quarter section of land each; and dozens of other Bourassas, Joneses, Ashes, Dicks, Plummers, St. Combes, and Conners were each deeded one or more sections of Indiana real estate. Some of this land was never actually used but was instead sold or deeded back to the United States at later treaties. However, the cultural process is clear: American treaty commissioners and other agents were using the resources at hand differentially, to reward most those who cooperated in securing the treaty or who were providing the best examples of progress towards "civilization." However, the commissioners were being none too particular in whom they selected to denominate as Potawatomi.

In the following year, on September 19, there was a small transaction at St. Joseph, conducted by Lewis Cass, aimed at consolidating in one place a number of small scattered "bands" of Potawatomi from eastern Michigan. Those few Potawatomi involved ceded their small, personal reserves on the Rouge, Raisin, and headwaters of the Kalamazoo rivers, tracts that had been awarded in earlier treaties. They received in exchange and soon moved to a new 63,000-acre reservation adjacent to the Nottawaseppe Prairie in western

Michigan. This treaty has to be seen as the first move in the drama of removal, for Governor Cass's intention was to move these Potawatomi away from the heavily traveled Detroit-to-Chicago road and from American settlements. Some Potawatomi were now collected and resettled on a proper reservation, away from disturbing contacts with civilization (Kappler 1904: 283–84). Except for a very few names such as Wakaya—The Bay, and Pierre Moran, none of the signatures on this document are familiar from earlier events, including Shekomek—Marsh Fish, Abtegizhek—Half Day, and Mjipenash—Bad Bird.

Meanwhile, during the summer of 1827 in Wisconsin and Illinois, an eruption among the Winnebago once more threatened to draw some Potawatomi into hostilities against the United States. A Winnebago war leader named Red Bird, reacting to a wrong done several of his people, took revenge against nearby Americans and then organized a small war-party. As soon as American troops arrived and prepared to attack his village, Red Bird surrendered. But in the process, Winnebago messengers had gone out calling for the support of nearby tribes. One Potawatomi okama, Makesit—Big Foot, who was from a village on Lake Geneva in southern Wisconsin, agreed to cooperate. He tried but could get no additional support from other Potawatomi. Big Foot succeeded only in making the Americans suspicious and in demonstrating that there were now more Potawatomi willing to fight for rather than against the Americans. Indeed, a group of old warriors left Chicago to scout Big Foot's village and to determine his plans. It was a curious party, including Alexander Robinson, who had tried to keep the peace at Fort Dearborn in 1812; Captain Billy Caldwell, late of the British Indian Service but now back in the Chicago area working as an intercultural broker; and Tecumsah's old supporter, Shabeni. Not one of them was born or raised a Potawatomi. They were, respectively, a Scot-Odawa, an Anglo-Irish-Mohawk, and an Odawa turned Potawatomi.[68] There was no real evidence that any Potawatomi actually cooperated with the Winnebago in hostilities against Americans. Indeed, it was obvious at the time that the tribesmen generally rejected the appeals of Red Bird's messengers and that some Potawatomi and their agents sought to intercede to help keep the peace. Nonetheless, the incident was used to bring additional pressure against the Potawatomi to accept new land cessions and to move themselves out of Illinois.

There followed quickly a series of six treaties through 1832, punctuated that year by the tragic outbreak of hostilities known as the Black Hawk War, followed by the massive cession of remaining Potawatomi lands in the fall of 1833 at Chicago. In 1828 at Green Bay, Wisconsin, Lewis Cass and Pierre Menard met with a small group of Wisconsin and Illinois Potawatomi to draw up a preliminary agreement for the cession of the lead-mine district along the Mississippi River. The American agents again employed the 1816 treaty appellation for the Potawatomi west of Lake Michigan, once more calling them the "United Tribes of Potawatomie, Chippewa and Ottawa Indians." But they were not very united at this meeting. Although Swift Current was present representing the Illinois Potawatomi, the Wisconsin Potawatomi dominated the meeting. Among the other ten signers were Wzawakiwaw—He That Leaves a Yellow Track, Wzawginawnibe—The Yellow River, Nēnkewebe— Thunder Resting, Obwagen—Thunder Turn Back, Tēskegēn—Last Feather, Makesit—Big Foot, Wawmeksigo—White Wampum, and Pamawbeme— He That Gazes Over.[69] They fixed boundaries between the United States, the Winnebago, and the "United Tribes" and agreed to a full-scale treaty council the next year at Rock Island.

A month later Governor Cass and Menard traveled to the Carey Mission on the St. Joseph to negotiate a treaty with the "Potawatomi tribe of Indians," specifically representatives of those along the St. Joseph and Elkhart River valleys. At this more convenient central location a great many more Potawatomi participated than had attended the Green Bay meeting a month earlier. Seventy-one "chiefs and warriors" signed the document, ceding much of the Potawatomi land remaining in Michigan and Indiana. By now the six Potawatomi villages along the St. Joseph River were surrounded by American settlements, while the citizens of Indiana wanted to gain access to the remaining Potawatomi lands in their state, particularly so as to connect American communities near Fort Wayne with those along the upper St. Joseph.[70] The Potawatomi representatives signing the document included the younger Topnebi, Awbenabi, The Bay, Wiske (the Potawatomi culture hero's name), Abtegizhek—Half Day, who managed to sign the treaty twice, and Louison Chevalier, who also signed twice. Wabansi, Senajiwan (who signed as Peche'o), and other Illinois River Potawatomi were present to obtain their share of the enormous quantity of goods and the large amount of silver coin the Potawatomi received at the treaty grounds. But the most prominent figure present was Pogagēn—The Rib, generally known as Leopold Pokagun.

Leopold Pokagun was a strong Catholic and an upstart "chief," one promoted actively by his patron, the Métis trader Joseph Bertrand. Married to the niece of the now deceased Topnebi, he had taken the old leader's son of the same name into his care, manipulated his way into a position of considerable influence, and founded a modest dynasty.[71] At the Treaty of Carey Mission, Pokagun acted as speaker and *éminence rouge*. With the cooperation of the traders and other interested parties, Pokagun and his fellows managed to secure from the United States a long list of considerations for the lands transferred: a permanent annuity of $2,000; a twenty-year term annuity of $1,000; $30,000 in goods delivered on the treaty grounds; an additional $10,000 in goods and $5,000 in specie to be paid over the next year; $7,500 to be spent by the United

States in clearing and fencing land, erecting houses, purchasing domestic animals and farm tools, and for paying laborers to work the farms; 2,000 pounds of tobacco, 1,500 pounds of iron, and 350 pounds of steel, all to be delivered annually; an education fund of $1,000 annually; a personal life annuity of $100 for the young Topnebi; and the wages of three laborers four months each year to work for the Potawatomi villages on the St. Joseph.

The Potawatomi leaders at this treaty certainly intended to set themselves up in style, but those who witnessed the treaty proceedings noted that the Potawatomi did not hold on to this wealth for very long. Indeed, the Baptist missionary Johnston Lykins commented that the treaty was made by and for the benefit of the traders, while Robert Simmerwell—Lykins's fellow Baptist missionary—saw one Potawatomi trade fifty shirts for two quarts of whiskey. The treaty also provided that $10,895 be directly applied to the claims of certain traders against the Potawatomi. These included long-familiar names, such as the heirs of John Kinzie, who were paid $3,500, supposedly for the elder Kinzie's losses at Fort Dearborn. But new names were added of men who had begun earning their living, and who were striving to make their fortunes, out of transactions between the Potawatomi and the United States, men such as Alexis Coquillard and George W. Ewing. Pokagun's patron and teacher, Joseph Bertrand, was paid $2,000 and his wife was awarded one section of prime land. Seventeen other tracts were deeded to individuals, eleven of them to the Potawatomi wives of Métis and other Americans, seven of them small personal reserves for older Potawatomi okamek such as Awbenabi. At this treaty there was a little something for everyone, a lot for others, and wealth for a few. However, the United States Senate balked at one of the more obviously shady provisions, refusing to approve the award of two sections of land "To Joseph Barron, a white man, who has long lived with the Indians, and to whom they are much attached" (Kappler 1904: 296). There was a line beyond which even the Senate would not go.

With this model business transaction fresh in their memories, Swift Current and Wabansi traveled home to Illinois, where the former was soon complaining about arrangements for the 1829 treaty covering the lead-mine districts he had earlier agreed to. The United States gave the old man his opportunity by changing the location of the treaty negotiations from Rock Island (which would have been convenient to Senajiwan's home ground) to the more inaccessible Prairie du Chien (which was the Winnebago and Wisconsin Potawatomi's bailiwick). The change was made at the insistence of the Winnebago, whom the United States—remembering the hostilities of 1827—did not wish further to antagonize. Senajiwan and his associates from the Peoria area were preparing to leave for Rock Island when they first learned of the change in place. Angered, he and some others of the Illinois River Potawatomi boycotted the treaty council, although Wabansi and others from northern Illinois and Wisconsin were conspicuous by their cooperative presence. Thirty-five of the eighty Potawatomi from Illinois and Wisconsin in attendance signed this treaty, including Wabansi, Shawnese, Big Foot, Dried Berry, Padekoshĕk— Pile of Lead, Alexander Robinson, Manebozho (the name of the culture hero's twin), Shawanipine—Southern River, and Skabewis—The Herald. They were all represented and led by a triumvirate, Captain Billy Caldwell, Alexander Robinson, and Shabeni. These men had now emerged as full-blown, highly successful intercultural brokers, servicing the needs of the Potawatomi, Americans, and themselves. Indeed, it was in preparation for this treaty that Alexander Wolcott, Indian agent at Chicago, supposedly maneuvered to have Robinson and Caldwell appointed or recognized as "chiefs" of the Potawatomi, so as to secure further influence over the transaction.[72]

This treaty was drawn by the United States with the "United Nations of Chippewa, Ottawa, and Potawatomie Indians, of the waters of the Illinois, Milwaukee, and Manitoouck Rivers," whose representatives agreed to cede two tracts west of the Rock River and south of Prairie du Chien in Wisconsin and Illinois, plus a large triangular tract north of the Fox River and due west of Chicago (see Figure 11). From this cession the Potawatomi obtained a perpetual annuity of $16,000 in silver payable in Chicago, $12,000 in goods to be delivered at the next forthcoming annuity payment, fifty barrels of salt annually, and a permanent blacksmith's shop at Chicago. As was now customary, a number of special exemptions and payments were made. Caldwell's payment for his services was two and a half sections of land on the Chicago River, Robinson's two sections on the Des Plaines River, Shabeni's two sections at Paw Paw Grove, and Wabansi's five sections on the Fox River. The treaty proper identifies both of the latter as chiefs of bands (villages), but not so Robinson or Caldwell. Alexander Robinson occasionally signed treaties under his Odawa name along with other Potawatomi leaders, but Caldwell did so only at Chicago in 1833.

The Prairie du Chien treaty in 1829 also provided for the interests of a small assortment of Métis and other American traders and settlers. Antoine Ouilamette—probably a Métis descendant of the Ouilamette who had served Robert La Salle so capably in the 1680s—was paid $800 for losses suffered in 1812, while his wife was deeded two sections of land. Similarly, John Kinzie's heirs were compensated once more for his losses in 1812, to the amount of another $3,500. However, the Peoria area Potawatomi apparently got no consideration from this treaty, the price Senajiwan paid for absenting himself in a pique; but later complaints resulted in a distribution of a share of the annuities to those Potawatomi farther down the Illinois River.[73] This treaty is further distinguished as the first ever signed by Potawatomi women, five of whose names are listed last in the columns of signatures. Who they were and what exactly was involved in this innovation is not made clear in any contemporary documents, but in later treaties women signers were clearly widows or heirs of various deceased village okamek.

Following the Prairie du Chien council, the Potawatomi experienced three years' relief from the pressures of treaty making. Remarkably enough, relationships between the tribesmen and settlers in the new states and territories of the Old Northwest during the postwar treaty period had been marked by relative peace and calm. There were, certainly, occasional minor incidents. In May of 1828, for example, one Potawatomi was killed during a squabble with a whiskey dealer in central Illinois, while in July of the next year a half-dozen men of this tribe attacked and injured a settler in his house near Beardsly Prairie, Michigan.[74] But these were modest affairs compared with the disturbance that erupted in 1832. Early that spring Black Hawk—the great warrior-leader of the Sauk and Fox—led some two thousand of his tribesmen east across the Mississippi, determined to abandon the reservation assigned his people in Iowa and to reoccupy the old Sauk town on the Rock River. Much opposed to the accommodationist leaders of his tribe, Black Hawk had been making war against his enemies for fifty years. During the War of 1812 he was one of the strongest supporters of the British cause; and since the Treaty of Ghent he had regularly visited their posts at Drummond Island and Fort Malden to renew the old alliance and obtain advice and supplies.[75]

Black Hawk had long harbored an exalted and unquenchable ambition. He thought of himself as "rising and becoming a great man—exceeding all my brethren in Magnitude like a pine tree in the forest higher and stronger than all around me."[76] His move back into northern Illinois in 1832 bought him the reputation he wanted, at the expense of disaster for the Sauk and Fox who accompanied him. He came with an unrealistic expectation of support from several sources. Among his old allies, Wabansi of the Potawatomi had seemed to promise that tribe's active cooperation; but it was not to be forthcoming. A new prophet, the Sauk-Winnebago Wabokieshiek—The Light, had arisen to foretell that the Master of the Universe and a great army would join him if Black Hawk would make his move. And the Sauk leader's own aide Neopope, on returning from Fort Malden that winter, had falsely reported the British were standing ready to support their old ally in his opposition to American removal policy. But these were not made available either. And the American military reaction was quick and overwhelming.[77]

The unwanted arrival of two thousand Sauk and Fox led by a feared leader was bad enough, but American officials with a vested interest in Indian removal distorted and exaggerated reports of the threat, and soon settlers and newspapers were spreading frightening rumors throughout the states around

Lake Michigan. Large militia forces were quickly mustered into service and regular army regiments dispatched by steamboat from the east. On his first confrontation with an American unit on May 14, in what became known as Stillman's Run from the speed the militia used in leaving the scene, Black Hawk discovered the Potawatomi would not support him with warriors in a fight, and he soon learned they would not even supply his people with desperately needed corn. What was billed as an attacking force was actually a retreat, as Black Hawk's dwindling "British band" made its way across northern Illinois, thence north into Wisconsin, and back again to the Mississippi, where the remnants were finally trapped.

In the same months that Black Hawk's harried people sought to evade contact with militia and regular army troops, some Potawatomi engaged in the last recorded acts of violence against American citizens and settlements. A few warriors were probably involved in the ambush murder of one lone itinerant preacher on the Fox River west of Chicago, while on May 1 a proper Potawatomi war-party was certainly accountable for a major attack on one homestead. Neither incident was directly related to or caused by Black Hawk's incursion. Rather, both grew out of local circumstances and antagonisms that were released by the tense, fearful atmosphere in northern Illinois that spring. The larger incident, known as the Indian Creek massacre, occurred twelve miles south of Ottawa, Illinois. Earlier, a vicious, violent, Indian-hating settler, William Davis, had built a mill-dam across the stream, blocking the spring spawning run of fish upstream to the nearby Potawatomi village. In April, when a Potawatomi man attempted to wreck the obstruction, Davis beat him badly and sent him away. On the morning of May 21 Shabeni—who with his sons was then riding around the countryside warning the settlers of potential trouble—arrived at the Davis mill site and advised the family to seek refuge. But Davis refused to accept the warning. That afternoon over sixty Potawatomi warriors, accompanied by perhaps three Sauk, arrived to take their revenge. Sixteen adults and children were killed, and two young girls captured. The girls, Sylvia and Rachel Hall, were taken into Wisconsin and later safely ransomed (Scanlon, 1915). The two war-party leaders, Toquamee (Dgwagek —Autumn) and Comee (possibly Okama—Leader), were subsequently arrested and tried for murder, but both were acquitted when the Hall girls failed to make a positive courtroom identification.

Instead of actively aiding Black Hawk, most Potawatomi sought to avoid contact with both the fleeing Sauk and overly eager American militia units, who were scouring the prairies and woods searching for hostile Indians. Many moved closer to Chicago into temporary camps for their safety. In Chicago, not as well defended as it had been in 1812, Indian agent Colonel Thomas Owen took charge of the defensive arrangements. A company of ninety-five

Potawatomi was raised and served until July 22 with a scout battalion before being mustered out of service. It was this company of Potawatomi which finally located the main Sauk camp in Wisconsin's Koshkonong swamp during the final days of Black Hawk's retreat. The names of those who undertook this duty are most familiar (Whitney 1970: 560–62). Billy Caldwell, now serving the United States, was back in his old position working with a force of Indians. His second-in-command was Alexander Robinson. Among the sixteen chiefs listed on the muster role were Shawnese, Wabansi, White Pigeon, Mzhikteno, Pile of Lead, and Big Foot. David Laughton, Mawbis—Marble, Mitchel Ouilamette, White Spirit, Joseph La Frombois, and seventy-two others also served. Rather than making war against the United States and its citizens, the Potawatomi—whatever their ethnic origins—now had a vested interest in demonstrating both their loyalty and usefulness if they, too, were to avoid removal west of the Mississippi River.

However, loyal service in times of hostilities did not for long stave off further treaties and land cessions. Less than ninety days after being mustered out, the "Potawatomi Scouts"—together with their kinsmen from Michigan and Indiana—traveled to Camp Tippecanoe in Indiana, there to negotiate three new treaties. The Miami, too, were invited, but they refused to attend these councils, as they did again in 1833 (Anson 1970: 194–96). Knowing full well that they had to face and deal with the prospect of removal west of the Mississippi, as had all the eastern tribes since the passage of President Jackson's Indian Removal bill in 1830, the Potawatomi were split into warring camps, each looking to advance its own parochial interests. The treaty commissioners, Jonathan Jennings, John W. Davis, and Marks Crume, finally resolved to settle the differences by drawing up three separate treaties, the first on October 20 with leaders and men from the "Potawatamie Tribe of Indians of the Prairie and Kankakee."[78] This first treaty was signed mainly by northern Illinois Potawatomi, although a few from southern Wisconsin managed to intrude themselves, including Ashkewi—Mud All Over His Body, from Milwaukee, and Shomin—Dried Berry, from Sheboygan. The second treaty, signed October 26, was agreed to by leaders representing the "Pottawatimie Indians," mainly from villages along the Wabash and Elkhart rivers. On October 27 the last was signed with representatives of the "Potawatomies of the State of Indiana and Michigan Territory," including leaders from southern Michigan and northern Indiana. Altogether, a total of 162 Potawatomi put their marks on these three treaties.

All parties arrived at the council grounds determined to make the most of the situation, and a great deal of wealth changed hands, much of it several times. Potawatomi from more than forty villages arrived in force, as did an assemblage of assorted officials, agents, missionaries, traders, tinkers, bootleggers, gamblers, short-change artists, and ordinary spectators. Included were numerous persons claiming affiliation with the Potawatomi tribe by blood, marriage, descent, adoption, debt, or plain propinquity. Potawatomi leaders —of various kinds and ancestries—came prepared to drive a hard bargain, and they did so.

In comparison with the proceeds of earlier treaties, the dollar amounts and quantities of goods involved were staggering. Term annuities running from twelve to twenty years were awarded, with a total value of $880,000. Billy Caldwell received a personal life annuity of $600, and Alexander Robinson one of $200. Goods to the value of $177,000 were delivered on the treaty grounds and another $70,000 worth arranged for the coming year. Individual Potawatomi were paid a total of $1,400 for one hundred horses stolen, presumably by militiamen, during the Black Hawk affair. It was clear that many Potawatomi were now living with some fair degree of comfort on credit, for they approved payment of their debts to traders amounting to $111,879. Ninety-one parcels of land averaging more than one section each—a total of some sixty thousand acres—were deeded over to a number of individuals of "Indian blood or descent." At a fair market value of three dollars per acre, this represented a transfer of land worth some $120,000 from the tribal estate into the hands of the pernicious fringe population that had grown around the edges of the neshnabek. A grand total of some $1,374,279 was transferred in these three transactions. Not that the Potawatomi always got a dollar's worth of goods for a dollar receipt signed by Commissioners Jennings, Davis, and Crume. The traders and contractors who provided the goods were notorious for jacking up their prices, and the commissioners as well for adding their percentage to the traders' bills. As Billy Caldwell complained to his old patron Thomas Forsyth some months before the treaties were arranged, the Potawatomi feared that "some underhanded work may be put into practice, you know in all negociations, there is more or less of fraud going on."[79]

Subsequent events made it clear what the treaty commissioners had in mind by their discrimination between "Indian by blood" and plain, ordinary Potawatomi. The former had their tracts handed over to them in fee simple, as private, individual property, to use and hold, or to sell and dispose of as they saw fit. Not so the thirty-five "band" reservations that were set aside for the heads of some thirty-nine extended family villages (several of the reservations contained two villages). These ranged from two to thirty-six sections in extent; they consisted of the home village or villages plus a modest amount of surrounding acreage. There was no need for the Potawatomi residing on them to be greatly concerned about exhausting the soils in these reservations, however, for they remained under federal control and all of them were reacquired by the United States within five years. By 1837 all had passed out of

Potawatomi ownership in preparation for moving the last Potawatomi out of Michigan, Illinois, and Indiana.

Shabeni's experience with his personal reservation—two sections of prime prairie near Geneva, Illinois—was a case in point. These lands were the doughty old warrior's reward for turning his coat after the Battle of Moravian-town, and for twenty years of faithful service to Americans in northern Illinois. During an absence beginning in 1836—he once again was aiding Americans, this time to move a group of Potawatomi beyond the Mississippi—local citizens and officials arranged to have his lands repossessed. On his return from the west years later Shabeni thus found himself homeless, having to live out the remainder of his years dependent upon the charity of his sodbuster neighbors.[80] Deprived of his personal reservation, Shabeni was also held in low esteem by traditional Potawatomi. Many years later the Kansas Potawatomi had no pleasant memories of him. They remembered him as a traitor, who did not dare join them in the west, as "they threatened to hang him up by his ears" (Skinner 1924/27: 392).

The list of "bands" contained in these three treaties provides a useful inventory of the number and distribution of Potawatomi communities in 1832. The treaties make entirely clear what was intended by the word "band." Each consisted of a village under a named and specified "chief or headman." Thirty-nine such villages were identified within the bounds of the three tracts ceded in these treaties. Since there were at least a dozen more in northern Illinois and Wisconsin outside the areas ceded, we can thereby identify in excess of fifty Potawatomi villages as of 1832.

There was no relief from the double burden of new treaty making and removal after the cessions of 1832. What had for some years been a gentle-manly request to migrate voluntarily at their convenience soon became a strident demand backed by treaty stipulations, various efforts to encourage and persuade, and finally—in a very few instances—the application of armed force. Pressure had been building since 1818, and in 1819 the Illinois River Potawatomi witnessed and tried to cope with the example of the Kickapoo, who were the sole remaining tribe serving as a buffer between their villages and the Americans in southern Illinois and Kentucky. That year, when the Kickapoo agreed to go and make arrangements for their removal, the Pota-watomi threatened to "waylay, attack, plunder and murder them."[81] Unsuc-cessful in this tactic, some Potawatomi thereupon joined the more traditional and hostile Kickapoo, emigrating west with them, eventually settling in the Nacogdoches country of East Texas, where they served first the Spanish regime and later the Republic of Texas in defense of the border against marauding Southern Plains tribes, such as the Comanche and Kiowa. These Potawatomi were led by one Nozhakēm—Downward Bolt of Lightning, whose descendants in Kansas today are still known as the Mexican Nozhakums.[82]

Soon the pressure was stepped up, but American tactics still emphasized Quaker-like persuasion and voluntary removal. In 1825 Indian agent Richard Graham, for example, reported the Potawatomi unmoved by his words. They remained "friendly with the whites," he noted, "but are unwilling to remove from their present location which is on military bounty lands."[83] Thereafter, American policies and the presence of more and more settlers began taking their toll. The key processes and procedures have been fully described. The major one was reduction of the land base occupied by the tribesmen and their concentration in many small "band" reservations isolated from one another and scattered through Michigan, Indiana, and Illinois. By the winter of 1832–1833 the Potawatomi owned in common only one large tract, in northeastern Illinois and southeastern Wisconsin. The balance of the tribesmen were segregated on some forty-two small reservations, which ranged in size from two to forty-nine sections of land. Another half-dozen Potawatomi villages were located outside the lands recognized by the United States as belonging to that tribe, on the Wisconsin shoreline north of Milwaukee. Their leaders were now being heard from, protesting the fraudulent transfer of their lands to the Menominee in the 1831 treaty. American agents, presumably so as to cover their tracks, had taken to calling these Wisconsin Potawatomi Chippewa, and so they would be designated in the coming Treaty of Chicago. But the depletion of the game supply; upsets and dislocations caused by the Black Hawk War, which prevented the Potawatomi from planting and harvesting their corn in 1832; increased dependency on trade goods and purchased rations; and the growing hostility of state and local officials, all pointed to one inescapable fact: the Potawatomi would have to migrate soon. The only questions and options open to them were: When? Under what conditions? At whose expense? In what direction and toward what destination? In working out answers to these issues during the next eight years, the Potawatomi began developing the reputation they have since enjoyed, as being among the most skillful negotiators and the most stubborn and recalcitrant Indians American officialdom ever had to contend with.

The Potawatomi who joined the hostile fraction of the Kickapoo in their move to Texas were not the only elements of the tribe voluntarily to remove themselves from the stresses of life in Illinois, Indiana, and Michigan. On 21 May 1833 some 119 Potawatomi arrived at the Kickapoo Reservation in northwest Kansas, along with 375 other converts to the new religion of the Kickapoo prophet Kenakuk. By that year, also, another small group of "heathen" Potawatomi had settled in with a community of Catholic Odawa on the Lake Huron shore at Wikwemikong on Manitoulin Island, where they busied themselves planting corn and fishing. And in Illinois another group of Pota-watomi, led by Kikito—Sun Goes One Place, finding themselves starving and harried by state officials in the confused and fearful months after Black Hawk's escapade, elected to migrate to a refuge near the Logansport, Indiana, Indian Agency, where they agreed to undertake an (aborted) removal west of the Mississippi in 1833 (see pp. 000-00).[84]

All the pressures for new treaties, new cessions, and full-scale removal of the Potawatomi came to a head in the summer of 1833. They were only in-creased by the hordes of new settlers pouring into Michigan and Illinois, now made easily and cheaply accessible from the east by the opening of the Erie Canal. Such new arrivals promptly unpacked their belongings on the most accessible lands—those ceded by the Potawatomi in 1832—even before they had been surveyed and placed on the market, and then started clamoring for access to more. Local political officials, responsive to the needs of their new constituents and with an eye towards the large profits that were the fall-out of any major Indian treaty, soon had Washington convinced of the need for immediate action. That spring Lewis Cass, now secretary of war, appointed three commissioners to secure the remaining Potawatomi lands. These were the governor of Michigan Territory, George B. Porter, the Indian agent Thomas Owen, and a minor political luminary from Illinois, William Weath-erford. By mid-September arrangements were complete. Some six thousand Potawatomi, plus many from other tribes, arrived—bag and baggage, whole families and villages—and set up camp on the north shore of the Chicago River, just outside the limits of the recently incorporated city of Chicago, then a village of 140 shanties. They were quickly surrounded and besieged by an army of counterfeiters, whiskey peddlers, land sharpers, restaurateurs, sutlers, Indian agents, greenhorns, horse thieves, journalists, portrait painters, confi-dence men, and assorted officials of high repute if questionable ethics.[85]

For outside spectators, the Chicago treaty took on the character of an absurdly theatrical happening; but for those involved, its conduct expressed dead-serious business, since anything from a grubstake to a fortune could be extracted by those quick and nimble enough to find the right advantage. In Potawatomi historical perspective, this 1833 spectacular had special meaning. Before the end of the month they would sell the last remaining fragment of land they had occupied a century or more before the first Europeans arrived in the upper lakes, their three small tracts in southeast Michigan. And the Wisconsin-Illinois Potawatomi would cede the largest remaining Indian-owned block of land remaining in the Old Northwest, the valuable lands north of Chicago and south of the Milwaukee River. After this cession, there remained in the whole area acquired by Anthony Wayne at Greenville only a few dozen tiny band reserves in Ohio, Michigan, and Indiana, and the major—but then valueless to American farmers—blocks of Menomini and Ojibwa forestland in northern Wisconsin. Therefore, those who attended anticipating to fill their strong-boxes had their wits specially sharpened—this was to be the last of the great Indian treaties in the upper lake country.

The Potawatomi came in droves but gave no appearance of being in a hurry to open the affair. When all parties were finally assembled on September 14, Aptegizhek—Half Day (who had recently moved his village from Indiana to Illinois) fired the first bolt on behalf of the Potawatomi. It was a stroke worthy of a modern contract negotiator for the teamsters' union. Apparently wearing Meteya's moccasins, Aptegizhek stood and informed Commissioners Porter and Owen that the Potawatomi had no wish to consider moving west of the Mississippi until they had been given the opportunity to inspect the country there. Meanwhile, he insisted, there could be no discussion of selling additional lands. The Potawatomi had assembled merely to enjoy their Great Father's beneficence and liberality. Could the annuities due the Potawatomi be distributed quickly so that they might go back to their villages to tend their gardens?

Properly impressed, the commissioners then settled down to the serious business of striking a bargain. After stalling for another four days, the Potawatomi rolled in their largest guns, announcing that Billy Caldwell and Alexander Robinson would serve as chief negotiators in their behalf. These two soon went to work hammering out the details of an agreement. In process, the Potawatomi of northeastern Wisconsin at last gained their innings. White Wampum, okama of their village on the Manitowoc River, again raised the question of the Menomini treaty of 1831; and Commissioner Porter was quick to agree that an injustice had been done, that the lands were properly the Potawatomi's, who would have to be amply compensated for them.[86] Two days later, confusion was generated by many of the assembled okamek, who declared they were ignorant of just exactly which lands the government wanted. The good Democrat Porter, President Jackson's personal appointee, then had sternly to remind the assembled Potawatomi that what Old Hickory wanted badly enough he was prone to take by force. Thereafter there was a suspect five-day gap in the journal of what transpired, of the sort that encourages attorneys to raise the issue of collusion and conspiracy. When the official record again begins on September 26, the treaty was already written and ready to be marked and certified. During the interim, Commissioners Porter and Owens (Weatherford had little to do with any of the negotiations) apparently had introduced their own secret weapons, Subagent Ardent Spirits, Colonel John Silver, and the Reverend Utmost Chicanery. One example of the last variety of special commissioners' helpers was named John F. Schermerhorn, a minister of the Protestant Dutch Reformed Church with an unexcelled if noxious reputation for persuasiveness (Gerend 1964: 129–30). Exactly what new steps were taken to encourage the Potawatomi to agree to the details of the document are unknown, but on the twenty-sixth Porter indicated that in a general council they had done so. Commissioner Porter thereupon read the treaty into the oral records of the Potawatomi, and seventy-seven leaders promptly placed their marks on the document.

The names on this treaty read like a Who's Who of Potawatomi village okamek in 1832, plus some that rose above the crowd. The first name was that of the younger Topnebi, a person about half the stature of his distinguished father, who was regularly used as a front man for one clique of Michigan traders. When Aptegizhek called upon Governor Porter to present Billy Caldwell with a presidential medal so that he might "smile upon them as the Sun Shines upon the Earth," no one seconded the idea with the suggestion that the young Topnebi too receive such recognition. But Billy Caldwell, old hand at Indian diplomacy that he was, and master of Anglo-Irish *noblesse oblige* as well, on accepting the medal insisted all remember that Topnebi held the rank of "hereditary chief" of the whole tribe. Good Irish Catholic that he was, Caldwell likely crossed his fingers on uttering this tactful fib (ICC 1974 2: 231). The second name on the treaty is spelled "Sau-ko-nock," probably a corruption of the one the Potawatomi used in referring to Caldwell, Sakonosh. (Caldwell placed his Indian appellation in two other places on the treaty, certifying the receipt of the treaty goods delivered to the Potawatomi and approving the supplementary articles. See Kappler 1904: 410 and 413.) Next came Alexander Robinson's Odawa name, Shishibinway, followed—apparently in order of influence and rank—by those of White Wampum, Break of Day, Big Foot, Half Day, Pile of Lead, Little Odawa, Swift Current (the younger), Southern Fog, He Has Pawed Through, Big Odawa, Black Sky, Little Miami, Pelican, Young Chief, Lellow Lightning, Mide Man, Little Fire Eater, Dried Berry I (of Two Rivers, Wisconsin), Dried Berry II (of Sheboygan, Wisconsin), Man Goes Through, Sun Goes One Place, The Sauk, Played Out, and The Buffalo. Except for Topnebi, all these signatories were from Wisconsin and northern Illinois. The Michigan Potawatomi were to have their chance the next day.

Acceptance by the Michigan Potawatomi of the terms of the Chicago treaty had been slowed by sharp and potentially deadly dissension in their ranks. Pokagun's people had appointed a committee to kill anyone—including Topnebi—who signed a treaty selling their reservation, but the influential Métis trader Joseph Bertrand, Jr., persuaded them not to. These dissidents were brought around with the promise that they would not be required to emigrate westward. Instead, they were allowed to settle with the Catholic Odawa at their reserve near L'Arbre Croche on Lake Michigan. With this concession, the Michigan Potawatomi ceded their remaining three tracts in that territory, the sixteen sections at Notawasepe Prairie, the nineteen sections adjacent thereto, and Topnebi and Pokagun's villages and forty-nine–section reservation south of present Cassopolis near the Indiana state line. This supplementary treaty was then signed by forty-seven Michigan Potawatomi, led by young Topnebi, and countersigned by eight Wisconsin-Illinois leaders, led off by Caldwell (as Sakonosh) and Robinson (as Shishibinkwa), certifying their acceptance of the additional provisions. Thereafter, until October 4, the commissioners worked at paying off the Potawatomi's debts, certainly including some of their own. It was hard work trying to determine just which of the many claimants would receive how many dollars each from the Potawatomi's now liquid wealth.[87]

The compensation paid the Potawatomi for these cessions was substantial and varied. They were to receive—on an acre-for-acre basis—five million acres of land west of the Mississippi, located by the commissioners undiplomatically just east of the Missouri River in an area the state of Missouri was then busy trying to acquire for its own citizens (see my Figure 12; also, Edmunds 1974). This was in compensation for the some 3,668,000 acres ceded in Wisconsin and Illinois south of the Milwaukee River, and the estimated 1,332,000 in Wisconsin north of that stream.[88] ·The Michigan Potawatomi were to have a fair share of these western lands, but in addition were awarded an additional $100,000, including $10,000 in lieu of personal reservations, which dollars were parceled out to Pokagun (who got the largest award, $2,000) and a long list of Métis offspring, including the Burnetts once more, as well as the numerous Bertrands, Du Charmes, Chandonaises, and Navarres; $25,000 for debts to traders; $25,000 for goods, provisions, and horses; and $40,000 in an annuity payable for twenty years in $2,000 installments. The Michigan Potawatomi again expressed a desire to provide for the Godfroy offspring, in the form of a section of land on the Notawasepe Prairie, a petition whose worth was certified by R. A. Forsyth, Robert A. Kinzie, G. Godfroy, and Richard Godfroy. These four were being economical with their time, simultaneously acting as agents for the government and in their own private business interests. They constituted part of a primitive version of what would later be called an "Indian Ring."

The Potawatomi further agreed in this treaty to emigrate to the west as quickly as possible, at the expense of the United States. They wanted first to send an exploring party to look over the ground, and the government agreed to pay the expenses of same and the subsistence costs of the whole tribe for one year once they were moved. Their emigration was encouraged by the stipulation that a pro rata share of treaty proceeds would be paid west of the Mississippi to those Potawatomi who did move, and that after 1836 all the benefits of the 1836 treaty would be paid out in their new location. For the first time in the Potawatomi's experience a deadline for removal was now fixed. They had to abandon all of the lands in Illinois as soon as the treaty was ratified (which did not occur until 21 February 1835, for the Senate put first some minor questions of a political, legal, and ethical nature); and they agreed to depart all of the lands north of the Illinois line no later than September 1836. As we will see in later chapters, the Potawatomi never did entirely desert Wisconsin, but they soon vacated Illinois.

The treaty also provided for the payment of $100,000 to "sundry individuals, in behalf of whom reservations were asked" (which request for land was refused by the commissioners), also to "indemnify the Chippewa tribe [i.e., Wisconsin Potawatomi north of Milwaukee]." Instead of paying the indemnity to the "Chippewa," however, the commissioners drew up a long list of claimants against the tribe and paid the dollars over to them. These included $600 for each of the Hall girls, Rachel and Sylvia, who had been captured at Indian Creek the previous year, as well as a long list of wives of Métis and Scots-Irish men and their children. These included $200 to each of Billy Caldwell's three then living children and a similar amount for Robinson's two offspring. Caldwell was also awarded another life-annuity of $400 per annum, Robinson one of $400, and Shabeni $200 a year in annuity income. The treaty stipulated that both Caldwell and Robinson would, in addition, receive cash grants of $10,000 each; but this was one of the provisions that made the Senate hesitate, and they were reduced to $5,000 apiece.

There was more. The Potawatomi were to receive $100,000 in goods, part to be delivered in 1833 and the remainder the following year. The sum of $175,000 was set aside to be paid over to traders in satisfaction of their claims against the tribesmen; plus $280,000 to be placed in an annuity fund, to be paid out at $14,000 each year for twenty years; plus $150,000 to be applied to the costs of building mills, houses, blacksmith shops, and for the purchase of agricultural tools and supplies to set the Potawatomi up as farmers in the west; plus another $70,000 to be placed in an education fund, the income from which would be used to support schools. Finally, the small "band reservations" of Break of Day and Awnkote in Illinois were purchased outright for $3,500.

It was the proposed distribution of the $175,000 in traders' claims which made the United States Senate stumble and hesitate in the process of ratifying this impressive treaty document. Not only the method of distribution made the Senate hesitate; news had reached Washington to the effect that Chicago area merchants had been so hard-pressed to supply from their limited stocks the large amounts of treaty goods required, they had drastically increased prices in compensation therefor, and some were in fact breaking into the warehouses filled with Indian goods to replenish their own supplies. The 1833 treaty indeed placed a very considerable strain on the free enterprise system in the Chicago area that autumn (Gerend 1964: 134–35). Hence a major part of the Senate's opposition to the Chicago treaty derived from the restricted and questionable distribution of the proceeds therefrom.

The social organization of American communities in the Lake Michigan area then consisted of a small set of business and political elites, partly old-line Métis families, such as the Grignons in northeastern Wisconsin and the Vieaus in Milwaukee, partly the Anglo-Saxon and Scots-Irish *nouveau riche,* such as the Kinzies and Forsyths, who dominated trade around Chicago. These latter constituted an interlocked web of affinal kinsmen and business partners. Billy Caldwell, for example, was married to Thomas Forsyth's daughter by an Ojibwa woman, while Benjamin Kercheval—Kinzie's partner in trade—was also married to one of Forsyth's daughters, Maria. The Forsyth-Kinzie-Kercheval-Caldwell kindred, between themselves, collected at least $105,152 cash in hand, as payment in lieu of reservations (i.e., part of the money that was supposed to be paid the Sheboygan–Two Rivers Potawatomi), and as compensation for debts the Potawatomi supposedly owed them. However, the total sums paid them are hard to determine exactly, for the schedules of receipts are skillfully drawn in such a fashion as to confound any auditor not intimately acquainted with kinship and employer-employee relations in Chicago.[89] In any regard, not every claimant received enough specie to prevent complaints being sent to the Senate.

However, the more serious question involved the reservation awarded the Potawatomi between the Missouri River and the then western boundary of that state. Missouri's senators both strongly opposed ratification until different lands were substituted for the Platte region west of their state. When this was accomplished, exchanging the Platte country for lands to the north in present Iowa (see Figure 12), the treaty was provisionally ratified on 22 May 1834. Final ratification had to wait approval of these substitutions by the Potawatomi. Seven leaders signed their approval only after much further negotiation and additional concessions by the United States, on 1 October 1834. These seven included an R. Caldwell (likely a misprint for Billy Caldwell), Break of Day, Alexander Robinson, a Joseph, a White Sky, and an unknown—Kaykotemo. Together they were acting as an incipient business committee, a new form of tribal management group that would emerge full-blown once the Potawatomi were established in the west. Within a year after the signing of the Chicago treaty, most of the Potawatomi in northern Illinois and southern Wisconsin were on their way west, moving away from their old Great Lakes habitat forever.[90]

When the Chicago treaty was signed on 27 September 1833, there remained, out of all the thousands of square miles they had acquired by conquest in the previous two centuries, only thirteen small tracts still owned by the Potawatomi. These were the small "band reservations" awarded by the Tippecanoe treaties in October 1832. By 1834 these reservations were occupied by twenty-six "chiefs and headmen," the leaders of as many small villages. All were in northern Indiana, west of Fort Wayne, on the upper Tippecanoe, Yellow, and Wabash rivers. Altogether they totaled no more than 149 sections, or 95,360 acres of land, including a 1,280-acre mill site owned in common on the Tippecanoe. It was recognition of the problems caused by these small reservations that had made Secretary of War Cass insist that no personal or "band" reservations be allowed at the Chicago negotiations in 1833. The American divide-and-dispossess policy of the 1820s had been successful in separating the Potawatomi tribe from the largest blocks of land it controlled, but American officials had not reckoned with the economic viability and social strength of the fundamental building block of that tribal society, the lineage-based extended-family village.[91]

After being awarded these small reserves in 1832, the small groups of villagers in Indiana literally dug themselves into their newly reduced environment in the hope of avoiding removal out of the area. Their economic adaptation was mixed, a combination of dependency on their modest annuities, subsistence gardening, and small-scale hunting and trapping, sufficient to provide the minimum necessities of an existence on the fringes of booming American farm settlements. They were by then a highly acculturated, ethnically mixed group in process of working out new varieties of adjustments to their changed circumstances of living. However, in American thinking and under United States law, they were "Indians," and in the 1830s President Jackson's Indian policy allowed for no exceptions in their removal to a new territory far to the west. This was accomplished only after much expense, prolonged negotiations, and—in the instance of one leader, Menomini—the threat of armed force. The United States had acquired five million acres of land in Wisconsin, Michigan, and Illinois in a few weeks during one treaty negotiation in 1833. Acquiring the small tracts in Indiana consumed three and a half years and required thirteen additional, separate treaties, before being wrapped up with the 11 February 1837 treaty in Washington, D.C., described earlier (see pp. 183–85).

The thirteen agreements, drawn up and signed between 4 December 1834 and 23 September 1836, were all of a piece. In each of them, one or several okamek and a few or a dozen adult men agreed to the cession proposed by the commissioners. Each group of villagers received, in exchange, a small amount of cash and goods, plus a modest short-term annuity for one or two years. The payments averaged about one dollar per acre for the land they ceded, and in most of the treaties the commissioners specified that they would pay off the "just debts" of the village concerned, deducting the amounts paid to traders from those allowed in compensation for the lands ceded. Several of these treaties, like that of 1829, had women as well as men signatories. These included the treaties of 29 March, 11 April, 20 September, and 22 September 1836. Eleven different women signed these four treaties, none of them more than one treaty each. It is clear from the marginal notes on the treaties that these women were either widows of deceased okamek or elders, or representatives of those otherwise indisposed. By itself, this represents a movement away from the strict patrilineal descent system long practiced by the Potawatomi, a movement toward the American bilateral inheritance pattern. It represents, as well, the beginnings of the emergence of Potawatomi women to positions of social and political power such as they had not enjoyed earlier, a process nudged along by the growing failure of their men to provide for their families and villages and by their increasing demoralization.

All thirteen treaties also provided for removal of all Potawatomi from the state of Indiana. In each instance, they were given a sharp, no-nonsense deadline. Within two or at most three years they would be required to vacate Indiana and emigrate west to a new reservation along the Osage River west of the state of Missouri. Most did so readily enough. Some had to be evicted and marched along by military escort. A great many decided they did not care for a country lacking Sugar Maple trees and filled with Salt Mountains and Horned Toads. These invoked their old alliance with Great Britain, packed their numerous ponies with their belongings, and fled into Upper Canada. When they were all gone—except for some hundreds hiding out in the northern forests of Michigan and Wisconsin—the Potawatomi became only a memory in the states created out of the Old Northwest Territory.

9
Persistence and Change in the Treaty Era

Serving the British as valued allies, confronting Americans as dangerous antagonists, living amidst other tribal societies as fearsome equals, the Potawatomi reached the peak of their historical development in the first two decades of the treaty era. But with their defeat in the War of 1812 came an end to this power and prestige. The lease on their freedom to expand the tribal estate lapsed when they came up against a people who overcame them in the struggle for territory, while after 1815 the United States foreclosed the mortgage on Potawatomi lands written at Greenville in 1795. American respect for this tribe was limited to their political and military prowess. It did not extend to admiration of their basic institutions, their language and culture, or their persons. In consequence the Potawatomi experienced a sudden historical and cultural shift, from a position of preeminence or parity to one of political subordination, social inferiority, and linguistic and cultural discrimination.[1]

The decline had set in before 1812. Those Frenchmen, Englishmen, and Americans settled within the borders of the tribal estate were not important sources of lasting strength to the Potawatomi. On the contrary, they had pecked away at the surface of the tribe's cultural and ecological integrity, ultimately reaching and eroding the foundations of confident belief on which these tribesmen had constructed their distinctive cultural adaptations. Well before 1812 the Potawatomi had started serving the instrumental purposes of the French, British, and Americans, less often and less so the reverse. Relationships between the Potawatomi and the new settlers had become fundamentally unbalanced. It was Euro-Americans who defined and determined ends: the Potawatomi produced the furs, provided the corn and game, became henchmen in wars, were sources of profit in trade and land sales, acted as clients for French and American patrons.

In relationships between the sexes, this inequality in the distribution of valued goods and the asymmetry of interactions reached their extreme. Potawatomi fathers and brothers regularly delivered their daughters and sisters

over to the newcomers, a traditional courtesy that was rarely if ever reciprocated. To borrow Joseph Jablow's apt phrase, before 1812 the Potawatomi
were becoming a "frontier proletariat."[2] They were being moved towards a
position of subordination and dependency on the dominant American society.
It was this critical issue the Potawatomi debated and lost between 1807 and
1814. Their defeat further contributed to and intensified another process already begun, a developing sense of cultural confusion, an inability to account
for their decline in ways that were psychologically tolerable or comprehensible
in traditional terms. There followed a partial loss of faith in old traditions and
styles, accompanied by a period of experimentation with new values, novel
institutional forms, and innovative ways of coping with a radically altered
social environment.

RESPONSES TO
AMERICAN INDIAN
POLICIES

Political and economic subordination meant that the Potawatomi were
progressively subjected to policies and programs designed and dictated by
Americans. These policies did not develop easily, quickly, or coherently. On
the other side of the cultural frontier, Americans too had to face their special
problems, those created by the presence of many defeated and enclaved tribal
societies within the sovereign boundaries of the United States. The formidable
task of managing affairs with these tribal peoples was approached with much
ambivalence and anxiety. Many years later, John Quincy Adams phrased the
matter squarely. From the beginnings of the American republic onward, he
wrote in 1841, Indians were a "perpetual harrow" on the feelings and con-
sciences of Americans (Parsons 1973: 339). The development of Indian policies spoiled the treasured American sense of justice and righteousness, forcing
many to confront the dissonance between much valued ideals and the realities
of American social life.

Efforts to design policies for dealing with Indians created, in American
thinking, a confused morass of ethnocentric conceits wrapped in ethical dilemmas, and of high political ideals subverted by economic self-interests.[3]
Although defeated in battle and humbled at treaty council, the Potawatomi
and kindred tribes continued sorely testing the fabric of American institutions.
How best to deal with Indians raised many weighty, painful issues, none of
them easily or readily resolved. Questions about the separation of powers came
forth. President versus Congress versus Judiciary—which unit of the federal
government had how much of what kind of legitimate authority in dealing

with Indians? Did the federal government have any legal authority whatever, if a tribe were located within the boundaries of an established state? Here was raised the issue of states' rights, and the lurking threat of nullification and disunion. Was a standing federal army required? Of what dimensions; and, what was the proper use of armed force? How best to treat culturally distinctive minorities? How would world opinion judge American treatment of Indians? What was the proper geographic size and shape of the new republic? These were some of the specific issues raised by efforts to generate a body of policy guidelines.

The handling of Indian problems even generated regional conflicts. Easterners, who had earlier solved their Indian problems, remained sharply critical and moralistic about westerners, who in turn became convinced that the only good Indian was a distant one. Southerners, once removal of the Indians from the eastern half of the continent became a probability, were adamant in insisting any new western reservations could not block formation of a tier of sympathetic states from Louisiana to California. Hence such reservations had to be located north of Arkansas.[4] So much controversy of so many disturbing kinds could only be resolved by the distinctive American political tactic, a compromise acceptable to all interest groups. In the wake of the frontier, Indian policies were floated as a series of temporary and leaky expedients, built on the basis of pragmatic but flawed designs, each with limited buoyancy in the turbulent waters of American national development.

The problem confronted by Americans was the same faced by all societies expanding their land base into areas occupied by other peoples, whether the growing society was an intertribal confederacy, such as the New York Iroquois, or a new industrializing nation, such as the United States: how best to cope with alien peoples who remained within the new territorial limits? The kinds of strategies available to any society for dealing with such problems are limited and few in number (Clifton 1976e). From time to time Americans have tried most but not all of them. Sometimes these policies were adopted several at the same time, in confused and contradictory combinations.

First of all, alien peoples can be expelled or driven away. In the early colonial period this was a possible approach for Americans; but once the continental limits of the nation were approached, not so, except as a temporary measure which in effect placed an alien group on the shelf, in an undesirable out-of-the-way place until other policies were developed. However, in the Potawatomi instance, some few of the tribesmen after 1815 voluntarily elected to migrate out of the United States into the Republic of Texas and then into Mexico, while after 1837, similarly, a great many more moved into Canada. A second possible strategy is that of genocide, the systematic, deliberate effort to exterminate a whole population. Some few American leaders from time to time have raised this possibility, but it was one never seriously considered or carried into effect.

A third tactic presumes both a measure of tolerance for cultural differences and a respect for minority rights that were never in ample supply in the United States. The policy would have been one of allowing the tribes to live in peace, segregated in different parts of the continent. This needed, in addition to the acceptance of cultural pluralism, well-defined boundary lines and territories acceptable to all parties, with borders that could be respected and enforced. Experience with efforts at establishing such a policy was never encouraging. Beginning with the proclamation line of 1763, hardly had such a border been defined before it was extensively penetrated by Americans. No such line drawn by well-meaning diplomats and government officials was ever able to contain the rapidly expanding American population, particularly the frontier folk seeking opportunity and wealth in free or cheap land. In sequence, the proclamation line dissolved, as did the Ohio River boundary, the Muskingum River line, the Greenville treaty line, and then the surveyed boundaries of most of the enclaved reservation tracts east of the Mississippi. Nonetheless, the idea of some kind of border separating Indians from Americans and of segregated reserves persisted well after 1837, always as a temporary expedient, one usually joined to some other policy that encouraged cultural change and isolated Indians from disturbing contacts with Americans. The Potawatomi, as we have noted in detail, were by 1837 thoroughly familiar with the lasting benefits of having boundaries drawn separating their lands from those of the United States.

Another kind of strategy, perhaps the one most heavily favored by Americans from the earliest days of the republic, involved organized efforts to resocialize an entire alien population. Technically, such an approach is called forced acculturation, and it stresses a kind of heavy-handed, extensive reeducation. In the history of American-Indian relations, this was generally called the "civilization policy." For Americans this reflected an overwhelming faith in progress and the perfectibility of mankind, a literal acceptance of the teachings of John Locke, and an unswerving ethnocentric conviction that American institutions and culture represented the high point of human evolution. Beginning in 1803, some Potawatomi had their first experiences with this civilization policy, which intensified with the establishment of Isaac McCoy's Carey Mission School in 1822, while others were being exposed to American culture in Catholic schools in the same period (Schultz 1972: 64–65).

The results of such efforts at reeducation were not entirely satisfying to the missionaries concerned, and a number of unanticipated consequences were encountered. Most of the students enrolled in such schools were the children of French-origin Métis, who thus obtained an education for their offspring at the expense of the federal government and tribal education funds. Hence the mission schools, intended to make civilized "white men" out of uncivilized tribesmen, actually helped convert a large number of French-speaking Métis into legal "Indians" (James 1830: xxvii–viii). But of greater weight from the perspective of changing American policy needs, officials found that the more Indians or Métis learned to speak, believe, and act like Americans, the harder it was to separate them from their remaining lands and to move them west beyond the frontier. Furthermore, the more pious Americans soon discovered that Indians on reservations adjacent to American frontier communities were selecting their own models and teachers from among the less desirable elements in nearby settlements—bootleggers, gamblers, the ungodly, and the sexually promiscuous (Sheehan 1973: 261–75). In consequence, there was increasingly less faith in the miracles that might be wrought by missionary education.

This conclusion grew alongside the rise to influence of an American racist doctrine, specifically one applied to Indians. In 1825, for instance, Henry Clay voiced his conviction that Indians were "essentially inferior to the Anglo-Saxon race" and his doubts that they were "an improvable breed."[5] The growth in popularity of such racial beliefs helps partially to explain the increasing importance and prestige of the so-called half-breeds during this period. Some Americans had started thinking about Indians as if they were a breed of cattle: the path towards improvement of the herd lay in selective cross-breeding with superior stock, preferably Anglo-Saxon or Scots-Irish, but French Métis, if that was all there was available. Assuming that such cross-breeds were a step towards improvement of the "Potawatomi race," officials then began selectively rewarding such individuals. However, from the perspective of a Métis or a Scots trader living with his Indian wife and his children among or near the Potawatomi, no such exercise in homespun biological thinking was needed. They had immediate social and economic concerns to deal with. In their efforts at self- and family-improvement they had themselves or their children identified as Potawatomi by "blood or adoption." In so doing, they perceived and seized the numerous advantages and perquisites available to them upon a switch in ethnic status: additional and reliable income, free lands, free educational facilities for their children, added influence, expense-paid travel, jobs in the Indian business, and a more securely established ethnic identity.

Doubts about the educability of Potawatomi and other Indians were basically rationalizations for matters of more genuine concern to American officials and settlers. Underneath the ideological verbiage was a pressing political-economic fact, the continuing need for more cheap land on which new settlers might carve out their homesteads. By the 1820s both ideology and economics combined to block further serious consideration of another possible kind of policy, assimilation. Racist convictions erected barriers around the general American population, blocking the entry of those deemed inferior or inadequate; and the need to acquire Indian land required their expulsion and resettlement elsewhere. With assimilation eliminated as a possibility, another kind of policy, amalgamation, emerged, tentatively, as a kind of implicit undercurrent to official thinking.

Closely associated with the idea of resocialization—or of civilizing the Indian—was the notion of assimilating Indians into the mainstream as fully accepted Americans. American policy makers and officials generally spoke of their civilization programs (i.e., forced acculturation) and assimilation as one and the same kind of social process. But they are in fact significantly different (Clifton 1976e). A great deal of acculturative change is a necessary precondition to assimilation but is not sufficient to bring it about. Indeed, as we have seen, the Potawatomi before 1837 were subjected to two centuries of acculturative experiences without becoming Frenchmen, Englishmen, or Americans. Two additional ingredients were required before full assimilation could occur. First, the host population had to want the potential assimilees to join them as full-fledged, accepted members of the dominant society; but this was never the case for Americans with respect to the Potawatomi, at least not so long as they looked, talked, or acted like Indians. Second, those invited by the host society had to want and accept a wholesale change in their social and personal identities; but this was never the case for most Potawatomi. Because they resisted such a radical alteration of their identity, and since most Americans were never serious about the invitation in the first place, full assimilation for the many was never a feasible policy.

Resistance to assimilation by those persons identified by Americans as Potawatomi was of two kinds. After 1837 those Potawatomi who still knew, lived, and valued the traditional culture engaged in a series of complicated migrations and maneuvers aimed at avoiding or reducing further damaging contact with American change agents. One substantial group, those who migrated to Canada, did so with just this end in mind. They departed the United States with the conviction they would find a more culturally tolerant reception on the other side of the border. Similarly, another cluster of culturally conservative Potawatomi, largely from northern Illinois and southern Wisconsin, but with some smaller groups drawn from Michigan and Indiana as well, eventually settled in western Iowa and there built a social barrier around themselves, again with the objective of avoiding further acculturative change and assimilation.

But there was a second kind of resistance to assimilation that involved elements marginally Potawatomi, mostly from Michigan and Indiana, who, from 1837 on, resettled in (present) Kansas, where they were under the guidance of Baptist and Jesuit missionaries. These culturally diminished Potawatomi were dominated by the children of people who were not, to begin with, practitioners of the old culture or native speakers of the language. They were the descendants of Métis, Scots, and Anglo-Saxon traders and settlers, and of long-missionized, highly acculturated Potawatomi. This cluster of people, first called the Mission and later the Citizen Band, avoided assimilation for obvious reasons. Most had earlier opted for identification as Indians because of the numerous rewards attached thereto. Having worked out a novel cultural adaptation, one that allowed them to draw upon such benefits as were available for persons legally defined as Potawatomi, and because they were already well enough equipped with appropriate language, values, and skills to cope with the institutions of the larger society, they were not about to voluntarily abandon their privileged status for the risks of American citizenship.

Another possible way for dealing with Indian problems is resocialization and social assimilation, plus a kind of biological amalgamation that is facilitated by systematic interbreeding. This was the preferred means of dealing with aliens employed by such societies as the Eastern Iroquois, but it was never adopted as a full-scale policy by Americans. To be certain, a great deal of interbreeding has occurred, but a curious refinement of American racial thinking blocked full social assimilation of the descendants of such unions. American beliefs about descent hold that any degree of "Indian blood," however remote or fictional, allows an individual to claim the status of "Indian." For this reason, today there are a considerable number of self-identified Potawatomi in the United States whose claim to this identity is based upon one sixty-fourth or one one-hundred-and-twenty-eighth degree of "Potawatomi blood." What this means is that a contemporary child may claim the status of Potawatomi on the basis of having one such ancestor out of a possible one hundred and twenty-eight, seven generations past. The strength of such racial thinking, added to the increasing glamorization of the Indian and his past, guaranteed that effective amalgamation, and this potential solution of the Indian problem, could never occur.

The idea of removing tribal peoples far outside the range of contact with American communities dates to 1803 when, soon after the acquisition of the Louisiana Territory, it was first proposed by Thomas Jefferson. Even then it was clearly a transient measure, designed to free eastern lands for immediate development by Americans. Thus removal as policy had to have some other ingredient added to it if any lasting solution to Indian problems was to be anticipated. Jefferson himself envisioned a different fate for the new territory. In one breath he proposed Indian removal, and in the next added the thought, "When we shall be full on this side [of the Mississippi] we may lay off a range of States on the western bank from the head to the mouth, and so, range after range, advancing compactly as we multiply" (Randolph 1829 4: 512). The problem was that Jefferson and his peers were vague about the geography and climate of the newly acquired regions, and early reports on conditions there soon spread discouraging rumors that it was a barren wasteland ill-suited for American agriculturists (Billington 1960: 470). This story began with Zebulon Pike's report of his findings in 1806, but it gained greater currency fourteen years later through the exaggerations of Dr. Edwin James, the surgeon-scientist who wrote the report of the Stephen Long expedition of 1819–1820. With Americans believing that west of the Mississippi and Missouri lay a Great American Desert unsuitable for their crops or habitations, the next step was to draw the conclusion that it might be appropriate for Indians.

By the early 1820s American leaders were beginning to learn that their philanthropic programs encouraging Indians to accept the benefits of civilization were not paying the dividends anticipated. One unexpected consequence of the policy of forced acculturation, characteristic of a few local Potawatomi groups in Indiana, but more so of the larger tribes such as the Cherokee and Chocktaw in the Southeast, was a rejection of assimilation, rapid economic and social development, and an increase in community consciousness (Sheehan 1973: 243–75). Another disturbing outgrowth of extensive contact with Americans was a surprising amount of demoralization, apathy, alcoholism, and economic dependency, also true of various Potawatomi communities in Michigan and Indiana. In the former instance, Americans discovered that some Indians were indeed making substantial progress, but not towards becoming Americans. Instead, they were building surprisingly viable new kinds of composite cultures, some of which threatened to become alien states within the American states where they were located. In the latter case, Americans were equally disturbed that many Indians seemed to be turning themselves into dependent wards, living off the limited amounts of charity available in new western states. However, in both instances the Indians occupied lands wanted by American settlers.

By 1825 there came together the notion that the Far West was a sterile land and that it was necessary to remove from the East the remaining Indian communities—whether fast developing or degenerating. The superintendent of Indian Affairs, Thomas L. McKenney, long an advocate of the civilization (or acculturation) policy, then became an advocate of a policy of removal. On 27 January 1825, President Monroe, in a special message to the Congress, recommended that Indians be encouraged voluntarily to migrate westward. He and his advisors believed that nothing more was needed than this offer, that "the prospect of a home beyond white interference would be inducement enough to leave the East" (Viola 1974: 202).[6] The idea of improving the condition of the Indians through an education program was not abandoned, while separating the Indians from the disturbing influence of lower-class frontier Americans was a major aim. President Monroe, Superintendent McKenny, the Reverend Isaac McCoy, and other advocates of Indian removal wanted to "send the Indians forth to the wilderness in order to train them in good civilization" (Berkhofer 1965: 100). In 1823 McCoy had conceived one fresh idea he wanted added to the new policy of removal and separation from contacts with traders and bootleggers. Believing that all Indians had one national (i.e., racial) identity, regardless of language or culture, he hoped to congregate all the tribes in one segregated territory west of the Missouri River, there to form a colony where the Indians could be safeguarded, detribalized, advanced in civilization, and eventually admitted into the federal union as a new Indian Territory and then a state.[7]

President Monroe's doctrine of the American frontier was designed to find a new western homeland for all the eastern Indians and to bring a halt to the advance of the frontier. With the line of American settlements stopped at the Missouri and upper Mississippi rivers, the next two decades were to be years of internal improvement in a compact American republic east of these great watercourses. In June 1828, Isaac McCoy—who had grown disillusioned with the prospects of civilizing Indians in the east, adjacent to American settlements —accepted a commission to lead an exploring party into the western country, there to select sites for Indian colonies. Before departing, he tried to persuade Indian agents in the Lakes country of the worth of his plan for colonization; but they—good bureaucrats concerned with the security of their own positions —opposed the removal policy. He departed Carey Mission 1 July 1828, for the West, taking with him two Potawatomi, Shawanetēk—Southern Noise (of Thunder) and Naganwatek—Leading Noise (of Thunder); a Métis attached to the Potawatomi community, Jean Chandonnai; and three Odawa. That summer and fall he explored the country 150 miles west of the Missouri, up the valley of the Kaw River, and including the lands along the Marias des Cygnes (Osage), where a few years later a Potawatomi Reservation would be established. McCoy thought the country excellent for Indians, with good soils, ample water and wood, and plenty of game. But the Indians accompanying him displayed little interest in the landscape—where they kept getting lost, displayed no concern for hunting, deplored the lack of sugar maple trees, and at every opportunity sought refreshment in the nearest wayside tavern. They were a thoroughly acculturated lot of missionized Métis and Indians.[8]

That same year Secretary of War Peter B. Porter called for an end of federal support of civilization programs in the East. He had seen that this policy was inconsistent with plans for dislodging the Indians from their lands. Still, many officials and missionaries strongly opposed removal, although some, like McCoy, were increasingly drawn to this new policy. But a major migration west was not a prospect that appealed to many Potawatomi. Except for the few hundred who joined the Kickapoo prophet on the eastern Kansas reserve and some sixty-seven Illinois Potawatomi who allowed themselves to be moved to Kansas in the summer of 1833 (Edmunds 1972b), it was not until after the 1833 Treaty of Chicago that any large fractions of this tribe moved out of the Great Lakes habitat.

Added to those who opposed the removal policy in favor of continued missionization and assimilation in reservations in the East were a few voices who expressed an alternative, more pessimistic view. One such was Edwin James, who after 1823 served as an army surgeon at Prairie du Chien and Mackinac (DAB 9: 576). James, looking back on two centuries of European-Indian contacts, was convinced that the "feeble and misdirected efforts" for the "civilization and instructions" of Indians did not express any sincere regard for their rights and welfare. "The utter failure of all these attempts," he wrote, "ought to convince us, not that Indians are irreclaimable, but that we ourselves, while we have built up with one hand, have pulled down with the other" (1830: xxvii-xxviii). He was appalled when he heard of "the project of congregating the Indians . . . in those burning deserts that skirt the eastern base of the Rocky Mountains" in an area already crowded with other tribes, where "nothing but inevitable destruction could there await a congregation of fierce, subtle, and mutually hostile savages."

"Mr. McKoy" and others who advocated removal and colonization, James thought, believed "the region west of the Mississippi . . . a kind of fairy land where man can feed on moonbeams" (1830: xxxiii). He had a lower opinion of this country, which was, at least as he had reported in his account of Stephen Long's explorations, a "land of salt mountains and horned frogs." His own policy for Indians was brief and simple: "Of all plans hitherto devised to benefit the Indians, by far the best, though doubtless attended with great difficulty in the execution is, *to let them alone* . . . necessity might again make them industrious." Edwin James's opinions on noninterference as an Indian policy never achieved any recognition by the Congress, but they warrant attention in order to appreciate the development and adaptation of the Prairie Band of Potawatomi on the United Bands Reservation in Iowa (see Figure 12). There—in 1837—James became an active adversary of the Reverend Isaac McCoy's colonization program. That year he accepted an appointment as the first subagent for those Illinois and Wisconsin Potawatomi who had avoided congregation on McCoy's Osage River reserve in Kansas. Under the guidance of James, a fanatic Vermont individualist and abolitionist, these Potawatomi for a time enjoyed less intervention in their affairs as they went about, once again in their fashion, becoming industrious.

With the election of Andrew Jackson to the presidency came a radical shift in the Indian policy of the United States. Jackson's thinking on key issues was ingenuous and uncomplicated. The tribal peoples within the sovereign boundaries of the United States were dependent societies, conquered peoples with no sovereignty of their own, subject to the laws and regulations imposed on them by the Congress.[9] They could not, Jackson was convinced, continue to exist as independent societies inside the boundaries of established states. The government was now firmly on the side of American settlers on the frontier. In 1830 Jackson's thinking was expressed in the Indian Removal Act, which passed the Congress by a very narrow margin of votes. This legislation created an Indian Territory west of the Mississippi and Missouri rivers and made provision for the exchange of Indian land holdings in the East for reservations in the new territory. Removal was obligatory, not an option as it had been in earlier years. Once in the West the tribes were to be protected from interference from American settlers, subjected to an intensified reeducation program aimed at their development and assimilation, and encouraged to develop themselves into a self-governing territory.

The development of an all-Indian state within the federal system was the particular wish and concern of Isaac McCoy, one of the minority of churchmen who actively supported Indian removal. It was the subject of new legislation in 1834, but the bill establishing an Indian state foundered and sank in the House of Representatives, and with it any prospect for developing a quasi-independent Indian Territory. With the success of Jackson's efforts to stamp new ideas into effective policy, the United States now stepped away from the older colonial model for the management of tribal affairs. For more than a century the Potawatomi had been accustomed to dealing with Euro-American governments through their own leaders, a system of indirect rule by foreign powers. After 1834 the United States, without using the phrase or recognizing the change by legislative act, initiated a system of direct rule through appointed agents. Thereafter, American policy was one of straightforward assimilation. Indian agents became responsible not only for management of tribal affairs, they were also agents of directed change, supposedly accountable for their efforts to nudge the Potawatomi and other tribes along the path of Americanization. But congressional policy was one thing, the actual management of Indian affairs something else. The Office of Indian Affairs was a simple and at best ineffective bureaucracy. Its local agents and subagents were all products of the patronage system, and few of them had any substantial, lasting interests in Indian affairs.[10] Operating at long distances from Washington under the loosest conceivable supervision, their character and personal bent strongly affected how each relocated tribe was managed. The Potawatomi, in particular, were to experience a great range of differences in how their affairs were managed and what influences were brought to bear upon them. This variation would, in the next three decades, further contribute to intratribal divisions and increased cultural heterogeneity.

IDEOLOGY III:
AMERICAN AND POTAWATOMI
VIEWS ON HUMAN NATURE

When Potawatomi and Americans came into intensive firsthand contact, two dissimilar ways of thinking about the causes of human behavior, individual temperament, and group membership helped to structure the development of new relationships and roles. One of these sets of folk beliefs was appropriate to a highly egalitarian tribal society, the other to a rapidly developing and expanding nation-state characterized by increasing social stratification. Both were well loaded with ethnocentric vanities. But they differed in their fundamental assumptions and implications. As Americans achieved a position of dominance, their theory of the nature of human nature began to submerge the beliefs held by the Potawatomi. Few Americans ever came to understand Potawatomi convictions. Most tribesmen, on the other hand, had to accommodate themselves to American thinking. Indeed, many individuals of varied biological and cultural ancestries acquired the social identity of Potawatomi by virtue of the application of American, not Potawatomi, principles of descent and group affiliation.

American thinking about human nature operated on two levels, the one traditional, deep-rooted, and persistently influential in molding the beliefs of government official and frontier settler about Indians, the other restricted to an intellectual minority and dignified by philosophic or pseudoscientific thinking about different groups of humans. The former—an American version of a widespread belief that there is a causal relationship between biological and cultural traits—has persisted as a kind of substratum of thinking about human behavior and group differences. In the first decades of the American republic this traditional-level set of racial beliefs was partially checked by an alternative philosophic position, one based on an enthusiastic faith in the perfectibility of mankind, buttressed by the conviction that societies practicing more rudimentary cultures could readily—through education—acquire the knowledge, beliefs, and skills of a more advanced "civilization."

Although this great American faith in reason, education, and progress generated Indian policies stressing encouraged acculturation and assimilation, it had inadequate popular support. It was an ideology out of phase with the imperatives facing the expanding nation, which could only accommodate population growth and economic development through acquisition of the lands occupied by such tribal peoples as the Potawatomi. Thus the conviction that Indians were an "improvable breed" fell into decline. What had been an undercurrent of belief held by a minority of American thinkers in the 1800s, by the 1840s became a strongly voiced, dominant view. By then America had "bred its own scientific prophets who provided an intellectual rationale for the realities of power" (Horsman 1975: 153). By the 1830s many in positions of power were convinced that Indians, as a "race," suffered fixed, biologically determined inferiorities.

In this fashion the ideology of racial differences came into concert with both widespread popular beliefs and the imperatives of national development. However, the older traditional American beliefs about human nature persisted, little affected by debates between political leaders, philosophers, or academics as to whether Indians were an inferior race, a perfectible breed, or simply a distinct genetic strain or type of human differing from Americans in insignificant, biologically determined ways. American cultural beliefs about group membership derived from a folk theory of conception: both wife and husband make equal contributions to the creation of a child, in this view, and the offspring of any union obtains from each parent half of its "blood"—a vital fluid which determines the child's character, social status, and future behavior. Since there are different kinds of "blood," some superior, others inferior, the children of any breeding pair will vary accordingly. Because "blood" was believed to "mix" in the process of procreation, the offspring of parents of different "races" were believed to be and were characterized as half-breeds, quarter-bloods, and the like. The question in American popular thinking, then, was whether "Indian blood" was superior or inferior to that of "whites." The general answer to this, whether spoken or left implicit, was that Indian blood was inferior to white; but Indian blood was also assumed to have the peculiar characteristic of a kind of dominance over that of whites. Thus a child with only fractional inheritance of "Indian blood in its veins" was classified automatically as Indian.[11]

Viewed objectively, from the perspective of social organization, American beliefs about race and human nature are part of the culturally fixed semantics of this society. With blood, or, more properly, socially specified rules of descent determining group membership, the yield was a social order characterized by a number of major "races": white, black, Indian, each of which contained a variety of subraces—Mohawk, Potawatomi, half-breed, Jewish, Anglo-Saxon, English-speaking, and the like. Objectively, American thinking about race confused a wide variety of human groupings, gratuitously confounding linguistic, religious, cultural, political, and social phenomena together in one simplified semantic scheme for fixing the social identities of individuals and groups. In terms of scientific biology, such socially defined races embraced groups of people who might be genetically similar or dissimilar, phenotypically alike or widely variable.

The most obvious example of this kind of thinking is the racial name "Indian," which automatically brings together peoples of widely different cultural and linguistic characteristics, many of whose ancestors by the 1830s were —as we have seen—not even North American in origin. It was the application of this racial doctrine, and the associated semantics of group membership, which promoted increased biological, cultural, and linguistic diversity within the Potawatomi tribe. In the emerging American social order, the Potawatomi thereby became a kind of subbreed, one variety of the larger Indian race. In the view of Americans the principle of admission or assignment to membership in the Potawatomi variety of Indian was simple. It was fixed at birth for an individual's lifetime by possession of some fraction of Potawatomi "blood." The power of this descent rule is best seen in the treatment of the offspring of so-called mixed marriages. Regardless of their physical appearance, language, cultural characteristics, or individual preference of personal identity, such children were automatically affiliated with and assigned the status of the lower-ranking parent. As such, they were subject to whatever disabilities were associated with this social status, as well as being eligible for such privileges as were available to members of the Potawatomi variety of the Indian social race.

The traditional beliefs of the Potawatomi concerning procreation and their principles of assigning group membership in the early historic period of contact with Euro-Americans cannot be determined with absolute certainty. By the time any outsider began systematically to inquire about such matters, they had already been subjected to many years of acculturative experience, while the population had grown increasingly heterogeneous in its biological and cultural composition. By and large, those persons assigned the status of Potawatomi by application of American principles of descent and racial affiliation, and who were least like the traditional Potawatomi in language and culture, had the largest vested interest in defending the American-derived definition of racial grouping. What is certain is that ancient Potawatomi tradition contained no conviction that "blood" determined social status. Like their closest cultural kinsmen the Ojibwa, Odawa, and Sauk, they held other kinds of beliefs about procreation, descent, group affiliation, and ways of acquiring social identities, beliefs very different from those dear to Americans.[12]

Traditional Potawatomi beliefs about these matters, still expressed today by a very few culturally conservative elders, combined a set of social organizational allegories with a cosmological metaphor. Matchimadzhēn—The Great Chain of Being was like the Milky Way, which was a huge bucket handle fastening the earth firmly in place. Were the Milky Way broken, the earth would fall into nothingness. Similarly, Matchimadzhēn must be maintained, for it is a vital chain binding departed ancestors to their living descendants and to future generations. Matchimadzhēn has two sides to it, a male and a female, which must be regularly joined together. Thus women must bear children for men, or else the lineages and clans will die out. Procreation required the regular sexual collaboration of man and woman. A single sexual act was insufficient to cause conception: it must be practiced regularly over several months for a new link in the chain to be forged. However, sexual intercourse by itself was insufficient to generate living progeny. A man and wife had to live proper, upright lives, observing all appropriate clan rules and prohibitions, or else the child (who carried the identity and powers of an ancestor) might refuse to live.

All new-born children brought with them the potential for assuming the identity of an ancestor; but often some particular ancestor would intervene directly. Sometimes the ancestor's chipo'o—Soul would return from wojitchok —the spirit-land beyond the western rim of the earth to invade the womb of the mother. If an ancestor had done so, then the child's wiyo—corporeal body would have some distinguishing, unusual mark. A child with a streak of white hair, for example, was a reincarnation of some Kakiyat—Old Person, or one with a deformity or birthmark resembling a healed wound was a reborn warrior who had been wounded in battle. This was how Main Poche obtained part of his great spirit-power. At his birth, with his deformed hand, he was recognized as some ancient wounded warrior reincarnate.

Potawatomi beliefs concerning conception, group membership, and human nature cannot be squared with those of Americans. They were based upon cosmological, not biological, analogies, and they were appropriate to an egalitarian, segmented, patrilineal society, not to a social-class structured one stressing human inequality. Moreover, the Potawatomi theory of inheritance was highly individualistic: it emphasized connections between particular ancestors and their individual descendants. Main Poche's inheritance of the characteristics of an ancestor was not conferred by him on his own children. There was no sense of inherited group attributes contained in this Potawatomi belief system. Indeed, the accident of birth made a child a member of a particular clan, not—in Potawatomi thinking—an Indian, or a white man, or even a Potawatomi. The children of Potawatomi women sired by members of other tribes were members of clans belonging to those tribes; conversely, the children of women from other societies born of Potawatomi men were assigned membership in the clan of their father and acquired their Potawatomi status indirectly in this fashion. The fundamental, solidary unit of Potawatomi social life was the clan and village, each of which was, structurally, equivalent to others.

This principle of the equivalence of clans was recognized by the systematic rotation of the position of leadership in the conduct of important, interclan rituals. In this fashion, the Potawatomi believed, each would regularly have a chance to demonstrate the strength of its special manitowek, and the people would themselves judge which clans were more powerful or effective than others. Thus the obvious fact of potentially real differences in hunting skills or war-making capacities between clans was taken care of in such a fashion as to prevent the development of built-in inequality, while allowing each clan's abilities to be tested pragmatically from time to time.

The fact of birth into a household belonging to a particular clan was not in itself sufficient to fix the social identity of a child. Nor was it the only means of entry into a family and clan. Each child had to undergo a special naming ceremony which ritually fixed his or her identity, with the choice of a name by an elder itself determining which of the possible ancestors the child would be affiliated with through the Matchimadzhēn. This was the normal experience of each child with living parents and kinfolk. However, there was an alternative means of entry into clan membership, one that required a special adoption and naming ceremony. Such rituals, in Potawatomi belief, effectively transformed the identities of an orphan or an adult alien, replacing his or her former social affiliation and personal identity with new ones.

It was through such rituals that Americans—that is, persons with American fathers if not American mothers also—might have been incorporated into Potawatomi clan and society. In the treaty period this may have been the mechanism through which numerous French-affiliated Métis and Americans acquired, as noted in the treaty records, the status of "Potawatomi by adoption." However, the adoption ritual is an elaborate, expensive, public affair which requires considerable time and manpower. It is doubtful that all or even most such ethnic emigrants were formally and voluntarily adopted into Potawatomi clans. The fact that few such individuals gave indication of any clan affiliation at all supports the conclusion that most Americans who shifted their identities to Potawatomi did so on a sham basis, via an invalid claim or an imperfect understanding of Potawatomi principles and practices, either or both reinforced by a strong sense of opportunism. There is no doubt that many such Americans who became Potawatomi thought of their new status in terms of citizenship or nationality, which in the treaty period could readily and easily be altered according to personal ambitions and economic opportunities. Many Americans in these decades became, more or less wholeheartedly and permanently, British or Spanish citizens, while others were trying on an Indian identity, all for about the same reasons.

Potawatomi attitudes about what Americans thought of as "racial differences" are well expressed in the thoughts of Meteya, while he was being interviewed by William H. Keating in 1823. Meteya explained his people believed that the Master of Life had created the neshnabēk, and when they first became acquainted with "the different races of men, they supposed a couple of white, and another of black, had likewise been created." But Meteya had not "troubled himself much with thinking on the subject." Racial differences, of much importance to Americans, simply did not greatly excite the attention of Potawatomi (1824: 109). Meteya's replies to Keating's questioning about religious issues also illustrate an important point. The discussion above of Potawatomi beliefs about ancestors, a life after death, and conception are cultural-level descriptions, not equally shared or accepted by all individual Potawatomi. In these matters Meteya was a profound skeptic. He did not share a belief in the immortality of the soul, believing that "after death both body and spirit decayed and disappeared." He observed, "as a dog dies, so man dies—the dog rots after death, so does man decay after he has ceased to live" (Keating 1924: 110).

RELIGION II:
CHANGING PATTERNS OF
MYTH, RITUAL, AND CULT

At the time the Potawatomi signed the Treaty of Greenville their religious institutions were essentially the same conglomerate of cults and beliefs that had served them since 1680. Each of these cult institutions had its own special kinds of rituals, aims, myths, and beliefs. They varied in the number of personnel involved and the degree of complexity of their organization. But each drew its personnel from the same roster of available individuals, who would each assume a ritual role appropriate to whatever cult was mobilized for the conduct of a particular ritual at any one time. These cults also shared the same kinds of ritual ingredients (fire, tobacco, water); and they used similar sorts of ritual prescriptions and paraphernalia (a preference for clockwise movement, a circle-entrapment symbolism, the ritual number four). A straightforward inventory of these several different cults will indicate some of the ritual choices open to the Potawatomi in this period and will as well lay the foundation for understanding latter changes and adaptations.[13]

On the individual level coexisted the vision-dreaming complex and the spirit-helper complex, together with a variety of personal hunting, gardening, love, and similar rites. Strictly speaking, these were not precisely individual cults except in the sense that a ritual performance was aimed at bringing some benefit to one person, the practitioner or worshiper. All such ritual performances involved some individual in a social relationship with at least one other, no more than one of the pair or trio being imaginary. A single Potawatomi worshiper would address himself, for example, to a spirit-helper, or the soul of an ancestor might invade the body of a woman to impregnate her. Similiar to the individual-level rituals were those of the several shamanistic cults—those of the physician, the diviner, and the fire-handler—except that these ritualists each had a special calling and skills and powers that went beyond those available to the ordinary person. Such shamans, moreover, regularly practiced on behalf of the welfare and interests of others: they were part-time religious specialists. The Potawatomi may have also separately identified witches and sorcerers—shamans who used their powers regularly to bring harm to others—but there are insufficient facts to draw such a conclusion. At minimum, each physician or diviner had the potential to use his powers for evil purposes, and some did so on some occasions.

Past the individual level were a set of communal cults, which consisted of a temporarily mobilized group of religious practitioners acting out the mythic prescriptions of some ritual on behalf of a specific group of Potawatomi. These communal-level cults included both regularly scheduled calendric rites and rituals conducted for special purposes at appropriate times. They included the clan-village and bundle complexes; the war ritual complex; the naming, adoption, and burial complexes; communal hunting, fishing, gathering, and gardening rites; and the intertribal calumet ceremony. These communal cults served a variety of aims, from the incorporation of new members into the community to the ritual disposal of the deceased and sustaining relationships with the ancestors. They provided means for handling problems of friendship and enmity in intertribal relations, organized the settlement of intravillage disputes, and regularly served to intensify sentiments of clan, coalition, alliance, and tribal solidarity.

After 1667 the Potawatomi were also involved in at least one pantribal ecclesiastical cult, the Midewiwin. This widespread religious institution consisted of a powerful, semiprofessional ritual elite organized as a hierarchical, loosely bureaucraticized, semisecret sodality. The Mednanenwek, Mide priests, served several important tribal and pantribal aims. They conducted rituals dealing with problems of illness that had reached epidemic proportions; they concerned themselves with problems of social control within the tribe, managing deviant warriors and chastizing overly ambitious okamek; and they served to bind together the scattered clan-villages into a larger solidary unit, the tribal society. The Midewiwin differed from counterpart ecclesiastical cults of European origin, such as Christianity, mainly in that its priests were less disposed to missionization of alien groups, while they expressed no sense of exclusive identification with one religious cult only, and they remained part-time practitioners. No Potawatomi regularly expected to contribute to the support of a full-time religious specialist, until the rise of such prophets as

Tenskwatawa after 1807, and the Kickapoo visionary Kenakuk and their own prophet Menomini in the 1820s.

Two persistent common misconceptions concerning Potawatomi and other Algonquian religious beliefs must be mentioned and disposed of. One consists of the popular stereotype that Indians were not strongly motivated by economic matters, and the other involves the conviction that the Potawatomi and related tribes worshiped a high god.[14] As regards the economic issue, for the Potawatomi, whole rituals, ritual paraphernalia, spells, medicines, and the like were highly valued personal and communal properties that were not transferred to or used on behalf of others without substantial payment. One reason why the Potawatomi remained suspicious of Christianity, for example, was that in the origin myth of this cult the founding prophet Christ was said to have used and given his medicines away freely, rejecting compensation. Such behavior was incredible to Potawatomi ritualists, unless the rites and medicines were valueless.

As to the alleged belief in and worship of a high god, this represented both an effort on the part of some Potawatomi informants to explain their belief system in terms that were comprehensible to untutored Euro-Americans, and the tendency of Euro-Americans to simplify and misconstrue Potawatomi ideas into forms better fitting their own religious beliefs. Kitchimanito, for example, translates very roughly as Very Great Supernormal Power, not Great Spirit. To phrase traditional Potawatomi thinking into a few English words, Chipumama—The Master of Life was a vital principle of cosmological being, not a person or thing. If pressed, the Potawatomi might identify Chipumama as Gizes—the Sun, or perhaps Wiske, one of the twin culture heroes. But in Potawatomi mythology Wiske did indeed attempt to achieve supreme power, seeking to have all neshnabĕk and the other manitowek and supernormal beings that populated the Potawatomi pantheon to worship him and him alone. For this he was deposed and banished to the far north (Skinner 1924/27: 46–48). There was no place in the thinking of this individualistic, egalitarian people for any concept of a single, all-powerful high god, just as there was no place in their tribal social organization for a single, all-powerful okama. Indeed, their pantheon included a variety of different kinds of supernormal beings, including the ancient spirits of the Sun, Moon, Fire, Great Lake, and Water, of the four cardinal directions, of Tobacco, Corn, Beans, and Squash, of Bear and other important animals, of the Merman and the Underwater Panther, of the Thunderbirds, and the culture heroes, Wiske and his fractious twin Chipiyapos. The Potawatomi inventory of supernormal beings in 1794 was fully as complicated, varied, and sometimes contradictory as their numerous cult institutions.

Adaptive changes in Potawatomi religious life after 1794 were largely a creative product of alterations in the tribe's external relations. Broadly speaking, these developments consisted of the participation of some Potawatomi in at least three identifiable cultural revitalization movements, together with the incorporation into the conglomerate of traditional religious practices of numerous individuals who had, at least on the surface, converted to Christianity. Because they represented indigenous responses to the stresses of life in the Old Northwest, the three revitalization movements—those led by Tenskwatawa and Tecumsah, Kenakuk, and Menomini—are the more interesting. Each of these movements involved a conscious, organized attempt on the part of some of the tribesmen in the area to create a more satisfying group identity, adaptation, and culture.[15] But each differed in its type of organization, attitude towards other cultures, ideology, aims, and methods.[16]

Of the three revitalization movements some Potawatomi found attractive, the one founded and guided by Tecumsah and Tenskwatawa had the largest following, the highest expectations, and the shortest life-span. As mentioned in earlier pages, the elements of the new religious ideology worked out by the two Shawnee brothers represent a partial inventory of the most pressing social problems facing the tribes of the Old Northwest in the middle years of the treaty era. In Thomas Jefferson's phrase, the brothers' "budget of reform" prohibited the use of alcohol, preached monogamy, forbade adultery, and stressed peaceful relations between husband and wife.[17] Such teaching aimed at returning internal order to Indian communities marked by increasing dissipation, intrafamily conflict, and disorder. But these were lesser problems compared to others identified by Tenskwatawa and Tecumsah.

The major objectives of the Shawnee brothers included an effort to restore a greater degree of cultural integrity to Indian communities, and particularly to decrease, if not eliminate, the growing dependency of the tribesmen on Euro-Americans, their products, and their practices. The former aim was pursued by requiring all Indian women living with American men to abandon their husbands and children and return to their home villages. In this fashion the prophet recognized that such children had been socialized in ways that would make them a threat to Indian communities. In addition, converts were required to abandon a long list of things and practices borrowed from American culture: European varieties of dogs, cats, and other domesticated animals, American grown or cooked foods, the use of money in economic exchanges (replaced by a traditional barter system), American-style manufactured clothing and American weapons, tools, and medicines. This Shawnee-led revitalization movement also provided for internal discipline and orthodoxy. Miscreants were required to make public confession of misdeeds and beg forgiveness. Those who did not accept sanctions imposed and whose misbehavior continued were threatened with death.

The Shawnee prophet and his brother also introduced new ritual ingredients into their doctrine and preached against the traditional pantheons, ritual practices, and culture heroes of the tribes. They substituted the new concept of a high god, the Great Spirit, who was to be addressed through prayer morning and evening, and of whom Tenskwatawa was the sole prophet. The ancient, powerful medicine bundles were to be destroyed, and the Midewiwin Cult abandoned. There was to be no competition allowed with the preachings of the new prophet, who with his brother sought spiritual and temporal powers that were to be centralized in their hands. On the social and political side of this effort to revitalize Indian cultures were Tecumsah's efforts to generate support for and to organize a massive intertribal confederacy which could act as a third force, relatively autonomous of the British and other European colonial powers, but strong enough to halt and block the expansion of American agricultural settlements into the Ohio valley and the Upper Great Lakes.

The Shawnee-arranged revitalization movement, in one radical, sweeping reorganization of traditional Indian cultures, sought to cope with the major dilemmas facing the tribes in this period. It tried to eliminate some traditional religious and cultural elements, attempted to refurbish and rekindle faith in others, introduced new elements appropriate to the realities of the time, aimed at eliminating disorganization and confusion, and tried to bring about a simplified and improved organization of the whole religious, social, and cultural field. On the political side, Tecumsah's efforts were striking—visionary in a sense different from that true of his brother. He accepted the prospects of an alliance with Great Britain, which posed the least threat to the tribes in the area; but it was to be one in which the Indians would be wary equals, not dependent, short-term mercenaries. He allowed for the more remote possibility of friendship and alliances with Spain and France, who similarly did not threaten to convert hunting lands into farmsteads. But he strongly opposed the expansion of the United States. The instrument to this end was the great intertribal confederacy he advocated up to the point of his death. Between the tribes themselves he insisted on peace and discipline. Little of these great plans were achieved; given the cultures and situations of the tribes at the time, perhaps they were simply not achievable.

The problem in implementing Tenskwatawa and Tecumsah's design was that, whatever the soundness of their political thinking, not many of the tribes saw their problems in precisely the same way as did the Shawnee leaders. Some were not as disorganized as the Indian communities in the Ohio valley. Others were not so threatened by American encroachment. Still others were working out different kinds of adaptations to the presence of the new American nation, making their peace with frontier agricultural settlements, rapidly adopting American technologies and converting their economies, or creating their own alliances. More were unwilling to abandon their traditional enmities with neighboring tribes. There was, on the whole, a belated, differential, and inadequate response to what the Shawnee brothers proposed. Thomas Forsyth noted, for example, that "the Pottawatimie Indians in the course of one season got tired of this strict way of living, and declared off, and joined the main poque" (1812a: 278).

One problem in gaining acceptance of this new doctrine was that there was very little that was claimed, said, or done by Tenskwatawa or Tecumsah that could not be attempted by many other ambitious men with political ambitions or supernormal pretensions. The Shawnee prophet, essentially, was cast in the mold of a traditional Algonquian shaman, slightly larger and more ambitious than usual. Thus he inspired imitators and competitors as often as converts. Soon after the visit of Tenskwatawa's disciples to Manitoba in 1807, for instance, John Tanner noted that there was a small rash of new prophets springing up, each drawing sustenance through his own revelations from the Great Spirit. Tanner's own adoptive father, Manitogezhik—Spirit Sky, was one such, and a second notable Ojibwa prophet in the same years was Ayskabewis—the Messenger (James 1830: 183–86). Tanner, likely expressing the skepticism of successful Ojibwa hunters and warriors, concluded that if a man were inept as a hunter, inadequate in war, and incapable of feeding himself and his family, then the claim to special supernormal powers was one means of gaining recognition and subsistence. Such a pragmatic attitude could not have made many tribesmen susceptible for long to Tenskwatawa's appeal.

The revitalization movement conceived, planned, and advocated by the Shawnee brothers was similar to other such movements in earlier and later years. But it was marked by important differences as well. Although basically a loosely structured affair, it was characterized by a unified, central leadership hoping to obtain control over the loyalties and sentiments of many tribes. Its appeal was addressed to all tribes threatened by cultural disintegration but was heeded only by some members in a minority of the tribes affected, mainly young men. It created a plan for a culture by selective elimination of old elements (mainly those competing with Tenskwatawa and Tecumsah's power) and the addition of new ones. It rejected completely an identification with and the acceptance of American cultural elements; and it sought a position of equality for an Indian Confederacy in relations with European powers and Americans. Tecumsah and Tenskwatawa, in brief, hoped to reform and to restore lost power and integrity by creating appropriate conditions for a separate Indian state, one fashioned upon adequately powerful political and military force, and made possible by a restoration of pride, harmony, and solidarity in the separate tribal communities. But it foundered on the shoals of tribal ethnocentrism, pride in local autonomy, and variant, divisive cultural interests.

Although many individuals and groups from different tribes found the new vision powerfully appealing, too many others were simultaneously indifferent or even threatened and antagonistic.

The lasting impact of Tenskwatawa and Tecumsah's visions and teachings on Potawatomi religion and culture are few. In the political area, there were later repeated attempts of warriors to counter the growing vulnerability of their village and clan leaders. When Meteya agreed to his interview with William Keating in 1823, for example, the aging okama told the latter that "he would very willingly reply to all their questions, but that according to usage he was bound to repeat to his nation all the questions that would be asked, and the replies which he would make; that there were certain points, however, on which he could give no information, without having first obtained the formal consent of his community" (Keating 1824: 91). The warriors of Meteya's village allowed their leader little leeway and freedom of action. Undoubtedly, such constraints represented, in part, the teaching and example of Tecumsah, who had set warrior against village chief; but adult Potawatomi males had ample experience of their own with the weakness of some of their leaders to draw this conclusion on their own.

As regards Potawatomi responses to other specifics of Tecumsah and Tenskwatawa's "budget of reform," Thomas Forsyth was quite right. He may have exaggerated the speed with which Potawatomi abandoned their enthusiasm for this strict way of living, but these tribesmen never lost their cultivated tastes for American whiskey, firearms, and milled flour, while the Midewiwin and their medicine bundles were in active service well into the twentieth century. The one lasting ritual, a minor cult institution at best, that might possibly be traced to the influence of Tenskwatawa is the Shawanoga, a spring rite sponsored by relatives of persons who died the previous winter. This ritual, still practiced in the 1960s, was essentially duplicative of other mourning, adoption, and naming ceremonies, except that the position of warriors was particularly prominent among the ritual roles. In this instance, the Potawatomi seem simply to have taken over one of the cult institutions learned from the Shawnee, while bending it to fit their own beliefs and purposes.[18] Overall, the lasting effects of the Shawnee-prompted revitalization movement were slight. Intended to simplify and to solidify Indian cultures in the face of American threats, the consequences were a modest, lasting increase in the complexity of Potawatomi religious beliefs and rituals. Although some Potawatomi came to doubt the powers of Wiske and their medicine bundles, the alternative beliefs they espoused were fashioned by Potawatomi, not alien patterns.

The teachings of Kenakuk, the Kickapoo prophet, were in pronounced contrast to those of the Shawnee brothers. Like Tenskwatawa, Kenakuk had led a dissipated life until about 1818, when he too underwent a major conversion experience.[19] Expelled from his own village for having murdered his uncle in a drunken rage, he resettled near American settlements in Illinois, where he often frequented frontier revival and Methodist church meetings. Drawing on what he learned from such experiences, he synthesized a blend of Kickapoo ritual elements and some drawn from Christianity. He preached abandonment of the forms of clan bundle rituals, for example, but retained much of the content in his own tribe's other cult practices. With respect to relations with Americans, he taught humility and the avoidance of warfare. The values he stressed centered on increased responsibility to family and community—sobriety and hard work. His followers were to take up American-style agriculture, live in monogamous families, observe the Sabbath faithfully, and attend ritual services in the home each morning and evening (Howard 1965: 22). Isaac McCoy, who was visited by Kenakuk in 1833, and who knew and degraded an active competitor when he saw one, commented that Kenakuk's new faith was "a step from savage blindness to blind absurdity" (McCoy 1840: 456). By that year Kenakuk had some four hundred followers, about half of whom were Potawatomi.

Jointly, this mixed population was organized as a village ritual congregation. In essence, its membership had embraced a compromise with American society and the acceptance of a selection of elements from American culture. Kenakuk thus became the leader of the accommodationist faction of the Kickapoo, but his appeal was also strong among the Potawatomi, who began joining him in 1819. His aim was to make a cultural adjustment within the limits set by the Indian policy of the United States, while preserving a distinctive Indian community identity. More modest in aims and limited in appeal than the doctrines offered by the Shawnee brothers, Kenakuk's efforts —objectively—were also more realistic. After leading his people west of the Missouri to a new reservation in present Kansas, his followers were able to fend off further efforts to missionize them by Methodist and Catholics. This new religion persists today, still observed in the basic forms created by Kenakuk, as an important cult institution for the Kickapoo and some of their Kansas Potawatomi neighbors.

In the years following the War of 1812 a third prophet emerged to influence the lives of the Potawatomi of northern Indiana. Known as the Potawatomi Preacher among the Americans in the area, his clan name was Menomini.[20] With this Man Clan appellation, the Potawatomi Preacher was probably either himself an emigrant from the Algonquian tribe of the same name or a descendant of one. Much less is recorded of his doctrines and aims than is true of either the Shawnee brothers or Kenakuk; but the information available indicates that he was a less independent thinker, an obsessively imitative personality more dependent on the models afforded by aliens.

When Isaac McCoy first settled in Fort Wayne in 1821, Menomini had an already well-established reputation as a deviant Potawatomi ritualist. He had acquired, through contacts with Catholic traders in the area, some of the surface elements of this foreign ecclesiastical cult. He and his followers, for example, came to meet McCoy with their faces painted black, the traditional symbol of approaching death or catastrophe. But they had the Christian cross marked on their cheeks and made a great show of genuflecting. By this time Menomini had worked out a new origin myth for the several varieties of humankind the Potawatomi now recognized. The myth combined elements of Christian doctrine recast into Potawatomi forms and styles. The Virgin Mary was made the hero of the myth. She first rejected the idea of virgin birth outright, and next refused a single statue which was to become the homonucleus of a single variety of man. When the third party of the Holy Trinity made for her two statues, one the original Indian, the other the first European—both boys—she accepted them. The Bible appears in this myth as a power-laden, mysterious book, a charm whose spirit-power gave vitality to the two prototype-statues. This new myth combined a few pieces of Christian rite and observance with a traditional style Potawatomi origin myth, but not enough detail was recorded to allow a full, genuine understanding of Menomini's thinking.

What Menomini had in mind on visiting McCoy was to have the latter act as his patron and advocate, particularly with respect to explaining to both Americans and Indians alike that he and his followers intended no harm. Substantial numbers of his followers traveling around wearing black paint indeed would have been worrisome to sensitive frontiersmen at that time. Menomini also wanted McCoy to establish the new Baptist establishment in his village. McCoy had other plans, however, although his attitude towards Menomini remained tolerant and cooperative, unlike the negative stance he took towards Kenakuk. Menomini's behavior McCoy found somewhat nettlesome. The Potawatomi Preacher followed the Baptist Preacher around, watching his every move, inspecting him closely as he wrote in his journal, observing his manner and behavior. Clearly he was an obsessive imitator, a man who mimicked the external forms of a Christian practitioner without penetrating the surface of Christian doctrine. McCoy—the self-taught, self-made frontier evangelist—had met his match, another able man with a passionate call for improving himself and the lot of his people.

The quality of Menomini's religious innovations is revealed in several incidents. Learning that as a prospective Christian he was supposed to be monogamous, he was placed in a quandary, for he was—as a good village okama—married to two sisters who did not want to be separated. He reverted to a traditional Potawatomi form of decision making and fasted, seeking a vision and supernatural guidance to show him which sister to send away. But no vision came to him, and he kept his two wives. On another occasion he revealed to Isaac McCoy that he was keeping count on a coupstick of the number of sermons he preached, as an earlier okama might have recorded the number of enemies killed or beaver pelts traded. Such instances do not suggest that Menomini was as successfully creative as either Kenakuk or Tenskwatawa. As a kind of compulsive mimic, adding bits and pieces of American ritual and culture to his repertoire in an effort to maintain and enhance his leadership position, he did not fashion a whole new cult institution as did other prophets in this period.

When the Baptist missions in northern Indiana declined in influence, Catholic missionaries began drifting back into the area. By 1835 Menomini and many of his people were practicing Roman Catholics, attempting to work out an agricultural adaptation within the boundaries of the state of Indiana. With the feeble patronage of Fathers Louis Deseille and Benjamin Petit, who supported his efforts to avoid removal to the western territory, Menomini attempted through passive resistance to nullify the impact of the United States policy. His efforts came to naught. In one of the very few examples of the application of military force to bring about Potawatomi removal, in 1838 the Indiana militia rounded up Menomini's villagers, put the old man in hand-cuffs, and forcibly moved the population west.

LEADERSHIP AND GOVERNANCE IV: MIDDLEMEN, BROKERS, AND CHIEFS

In the 1820s and 1830s the Potawatomi underwent a crisis in their style of leadership and governance. The old tribal society, faced by the onrush of American agricultural settlements, divided into small local populations by American policy, and increasingly incapable of managing critical events, was breaking down into multiple political-subsistence units. The smallest of these were in Michigan and Indiana, where by the late 1820s every senior adult—most often male, sometimes female—was being identified as chief, headman, or simply the principal person of an extended or nuclear-family subsistence group. Concerning the 1,325 Potawatomi identified as living along the St. Joseph, Wabash, and Elkhart rivers in 1828, for example, thirty-nine such family groups were identified. They ranged from just two up to 210 members, and had a mean size of thirty-four persons. The following year the local Indian agents identified seventy-four such units of similar size in the same area, totaling some 1,781 Potawatomi. Many of these were married to or children of Métis or other Americans in the area.[21]

In northern Illinois and southern Wisconsin there was far less fractionation in this period. There larger political units endured, substantially like the clan-village units of traditional Potawatomi society, but supported by new kinds of leaders. In most instances traditional okamek continued in positions of power within their clans and villages, men such as Big Foot and White Wampum in Wisconsin, or Wabansi in Illinois. But new varieties of leadership roles were emerging. The prototypes for these roles did not lay in the responsibilities assigned or the skills expected of traditional okamek. Instead, the role models were set by those Frenchmen, Métis, Scots-Irish, and Anglo-Saxon men who for nearly two centuries had been influential in building effective relationships between Indian tribes and Euro-American nations. The earliest full-scale practitioners of these roles were British Indian agents such as Alexander McKee, Matthew Elliott, and William Caldwell, or French traders such as the Bertrands and Bourassas, or American tradesmen-agents such as John Kinzie and Thomas Forsyth. The first incumbents of comparable new leadership roles among the Potawatomi of Illinois and Wisconsin, more often than not, were the sons of such men by Indian women. Indeed, beginning in the last half of the eighteenth century, there was an informal Anglo-Irish policy of deliberately fostering offspring by Indian women. Such sons would then be raised to serve as clients for their entrepreneur fathers, advancing the latter's interests in the fur trade and Indian business.

Two such men, Billy Caldwell and Alexander Robinson, rose to positions of considerable power and influence among the Illinois Potawatomi in the 1820s. Robinson was the son of a Scots trader and an Odawa woman, Caldwell the child of William Caldwell, Sr., who—alongside Walter and John Butler—was a famed leader of Tory Rangers and Iroquois auxiliaries during the Revolutionary War. Billy's mother was a Mohawk woman, the daughter of Rising Sun; but he was raised by his father near Amherstburg until, about 1799, he entered the fur trade as an independent.[22] Both Robinson and Caldwell, acting as clients for powerful traders and political figures in the Chicago area such as John Kinzie and Thomas Forsyth, worked to bring about the series of treaties which in 1833 ended Potawatomi ownership of lands in Wisconsin and Illinois. Well before that time, for purposes convenient to Forsyth, Kinzie, and other entrepreneurs and Indian agents, Caldwell and Robinson had achieved recognition as Potawatomi "chiefs." From the point of view of men like Thomas Forsyth, such a denomination was valuable insofar as it served to create the illusion of legitimacy in the shadier aspects of treaty transactions. Serving as their clients' "chiefs," Caldwell and Robinson would facilitate, approve, and validate transactions desired by their American patrons.

Plate 3. Shabeni, of Odawa origin and a village okama in Northern Illinois, actively promoted the removal of the Potawatomi west of the Mississippi River, but himself returned to live out his later years in DeKalb County, Illinois. (Ambrotype by H. B. Field, 1857; courtesy of the Chicago Historical Society.)

However, both men had personal interests of their own, while the Potawatomi also had a clear interest in gaining control of their skills, influence, and loyalties. In the purest sense of the term they became middlemen or, more accurately, intercultural brokers. Eventually, Caldwell severed his ties to the newly rich entrepreneurs of Chicago and cast his lot with the United Bands of Potawatomi from northern Illinois. As we will see, with his expert advice and guidance, the traditional village and clan leaders of this area were able to escape much of the destructive influence thrust on their kinsmen in Indiana

and Illinois. With Caldwell's aid, and because of other factors, these Potawatomi from west of Lake Michigan were able to reinstitute a substantial
measure of political autonomy and to refurbish the basic patterns of Potawatomi culture in a new ecological setting in Iowa. There occurred the genesis of
a new tribal structure, out of some of the parts of the old one.

Intercultural brokers were not the only new kinds of leadership roles that
emerged in this period. Brokers such as Caldwell and Robinson are distinguished from other kinds of intercultural middlemen insofar as they are responsible both to outside patrons and to local communities. In this same period
the Potawatomi were becoming increasingly familiar with other kinds of
middlemen and agents, especially technical specialists of various kinds. Interpreters, blacksmiths, gunsmiths, physicians, traders, farmers—these were some
of the kinds of men whose services the Potawatomi were using more and
more. They would shortly find the skills of attorneys of considerable value in
prosecuting their claims against the United States and Great Britain, and in
1845 the Iowa Potawatomi would obtain for themselves the novelty of the first
press agent ever known to hire out his talents for the purpose of advancing
the cause and polishing the public image of an Indian tribe. Meanwhile, traditional Potawatomi okamek continued to serve the needs of their kinsmen
within those parts of their society that managed to retain an important measure
of cultural integrity. Aided by such men as Caldwell and Robinson, they had
begun mastering some of the skills needed to fashion a satisfactory adaptation
in their new relationships with the United States.

The rise to power of men of Scots-Irish and Anglo-Saxon antecedents in
the Old Northwest between 1816 and 1835 was, thus, paralleled by a rise to
influence of their sons and daughters by Indian women among the tribes of the
area. Accompanying the development of these new elites was a decline in the
prestige, power, and influence of the long-resident, French-origin Métis. In
earlier years these had been a French-speaking folk, regardless of their hybrid
biological backgrounds culturally identified with their congeners in Lower
Canada and Louisiana. As the social system of the states formed out of the
Old Northwest became increasingly class-stratified, with Anglo-Saxons and
Scots-Irish occupying the peaks of power, these old guard Métis were faced
with a hard choice. They might stay on in this rapidly developing area to
compete with the new elite for the leavings of wealth, which some did. Or
they might continue their traditional adaptation as trappers and middlemen
in the fur trade by moving west to where the pickings were still adequate,
which many did. Or they might, following American practice of assigning
ethnic status on the basis of "blood," become Indians, which a goodly number
did. The alteration of the status of the Métis in this area by 1822 is well illustrated by their fall and exclusion from power in the United States Indian

Service. In that year, of the ten agents in the area, only one—Nicholas Boilvin at Prairie du Chien—was Métis, while of the fourteen subagents again only one—Pierre Menard of Kaskaskias—was of French origin. The rest were the Forsyths, Wolcotts, Princes, Johnstons, Boyds, O'Fallons, and Kinzies who had achieved control of the major positions giving access to power and wealth in these new states and territories (ASP-IA 2: 365). Those Métis who aligned themselves with the Potawatomi obtained positions of some influence, but as Indians. They also often served in lesser positions in the Indian Service, as interpreters and clerks for the Scots or Anglo-Saxon agents and superintendents placed in control of Indian reservations.

SOCIAL ORGANIZATION II: DEMISE OF THE TRIBE

By the mid-1830s the single, unitary tribal structure of Potawatomi society was no more. This fracturing was the result of numerous internal strains and external pressures. The basic segmentary structure of the society contributed. Combined with the extreme territorial expansion and the distances between Potawatomi clans and villages located at opposite ends of the tribal estate, it meant that the fundamental, traditional processes of intratribal decision making and policy formation were no longer efficient. In 1819 John Kinzie commented on this structure in a way that revealed a hidden strength. Like the Ojibwa and Odawa of Wisconsin, Kinzie noted, the Potawatomi were "scattered over a large tract of country, divided into small villages, at the head of each . . . a Chief who holds himself independent, on this account it is impossible to get the general consent of their nations without calling a meeting of every individual composing them who are perfectly republican & will not acknowledge anything *well done*, which is not done by the whole or a majority of them."[23] The requirement that a consensus of the whole be obtained before reaching any significant, tribal-wide agreement on policy, while cumbersome and time-consuming, also slowed down and delayed American efforts to dispossess and remove the tribe. It was this strength of the tribal structure that American agents worked to counteract with the deliberate policy of promoting divisiveness.[24]

During the 1950s it became fashionable to speak of the Potawatomi as a "loosely organized" society, with a "weak and progressively divisive" political structure."[25] Such evaluations, generally made in support of the Justice Department's efforts to defend the United States in land claims cases, are both ethnocentric in their bias and incorrect as to their basic assumptions. American agents on the scene in the 1820s, men such as Lewis Cass, John Tipton, William Henry Harrison, Thomas Forsyth, and John Kinzie, would have been amused at such evaluations. With all the growing power of the United States behind them, they had to work, wheedle, and maneuver for two decades to facilitate and accelerate the breakdown of the single "loosely structured" tribal system.

Captain Samuel Levering, Governor Ninian Edwards' agent among the Potawatomi in 1813–1814, provided a sharp insight into the strengths and the weaknesses of this society in the decade prior to its first major division. The Potawatomi were then, Levering reported, "so far one Nation, that those of another name and nation aggrieved by any of them revenge themselves on the first Putowatomie they meet, no difference what tribe [clan], or whether situated north of the lakes in Michigan, Indiana, or Illinois Territories—yet there are different interests, and opposing ambitions and jealousies among the tribes [clans]."[26] Levering's suggestion for counteracting this strength was to consolidate the Potawatomi in one location under one or a few appointed chiefs who could be readily influenced by American agents. It was a policy followed in part, especially in the Chicago area, but only as companion to the basic divide-and-rule program that played on the "opposing ambitions and jealousies" to disrupt Potawatomi political organization in Indiana and Illinois.

As Levering noted, however scattered the Potawatomi clan villages might be, others thought of and treated them as a single society. Similarly, throughout the treaty era the basic internal peace of the tribe also prevailed. Although efforts were made by Americans to provoke internal conflict during the War of 1812, the Potawatomi villagers refused to respond by making war on one another on behalf of outsiders.[27]

Nonetheless, irrespective of deliberate policy moves on the part of American agents, the basic structure of Potawatomi society would certainly have fractured sooner or later. The social environment which is prerequisite to the adaptation of any tribal society was fast disappearing. Those other tribal societies which had balanced and countered or supported and opposed the Potawatomi during the course of their history were themselves rapidly changing or disappearing. The ecological and economic conditions on which tribal adaptations are dependent, as Tecumsah and Tenskwatawa fully appreciated, were also passing: tribal societies do not persist unchanging as technological and economic dependencies of complex industrial states. Moreover, the internal harmony of the tribe was, in critical ways, a function of shared similarities of value and viewpoint, language and attitude. And these elements of Potawatomi culture were rapidly changing as the tribesmen gained new experience with alien ways, and as—progressively—new members were admitted from other societies, emigrants with radically different views of family life, economic goals, and religious observance. In cultural, political, and religious ways, Potawatomi tribal society by the early 1830s was becoming too complicated and heterogeneous to hang together. The only solution to this was schism and separation, a process quickly facilitated by the American policy of removing all Potawatomi from the Great Lakes area.

10

Migration and Resettlement: 1835-1847

The Potawatomi were very busy Indians in the fourteen years after the Treaty of Chicago. Pushed out of their old estate by land cessions and American policy, they had no choice but to migrate somewhere. Simultaneously pulled in several directions by a variety of attractions, neither had then any option but to seek out fresh ways of coping with critical problems of cultural and societal survival. This historic era was known as the period of Indian Removal. In these years American policy aimed at clearing all Indians out of the territory east of the Mississippi River. Standard historical portrayals of the relocation of Indian tribes during the Jackson administration and subsequent years have been made to read like horror stories.[1] In such characterizations the Indians—Potawatomi and other tribes—are drawn as helpless, pitiable creatures who waited about passively until they were herded together in chains by ruthless dragoons and militiamen, to be driven westward at bayonet point on their "Last Trek" along the "Trail of Tears."

The cultural and historical facts of the Potawatomi migrations in this period, if read in their entirety, present a very different and more complicated picture. In the first place, the experience of migration into new habitats was nothing new to these tribesmen. From the year they first entered the historical scene, down to 1833, there was no time in which some portion of the tribe, large or small, was not on the move somewhere else. Indeed, for nearly two centuries migration had been a favored adaptive strategy, one used to cope with internal strains within the tribe as well as with external stresses.

The great diaspora of the 1640s was, for example, a strategic move that placed the Potawatomi out of reach of marauding Neutral war parties. This earlier great removal, like that of the 1830s, involved the relocation of the entire tribe, but it differed from the latter in two important respects. First, contemporary popular accounts notwithstanding, in the 1830s Americans were not bent on a "war of extermination." Second, in the 1640s the Potawatomi soon congregated again in northeastern Wisconsin and reconstituted the tribal society as a solidary unit. In the 1830s and 1840s, in spite of American encouragement and pressure to bring about a reunion of the whole tribe west of the Mississippi, the Potawatomi never again reassembled as a whole in one place. At the point of departure from the old Great Lakes estate, the tribe was rent with internal divisiveness. To a large degree the great dispersion of the parts of the tribe during the 1830s reflected these existing internal conflicts and divisions. And, once completed, the dispersion of the Potawatomi population into widely separated habitats reinforced the divisiveness that had preexisted the great migration. In this respect, the diaspora of the 1830s more resembled the kinds of adaptive migrations some Potawatomi group was always making after 1680. The dual processes of fission and dispersal once again relieved strains within the tribe. Although pressed by American policy to move else-where, the Potawatomi after 1833 began sorting themselves out into new kinds of separate groupings. Americans provided the push; but the Potawatomi themselves—to a considerable extent—elected the directions and the desti-nations of their movements.

The facts of Potawatomi migrations after 1833, in broad outline, tell their own tale. Some twelve hundred Wisconsin and Michigan Potawatomi never left the Upper Great Lakes habitat at all. They simply drifted northward away from the press of American settlement and held out until the pressure for removal diminished. Another twenty-five hundred packed their belongings into canoes or onto their ponies and moved, not westward as specified by treaty, but east into Upper Canada. Of the some 7,232 Potawatomi who were counted trekking west beyond the Mississippi, just 1,195 were actually forced to relocate under military escort. Even in this instance the military guard for one group of 439 Potawatomi consisted of a single imperious, loud-mouthed officer, Major Robert Forsyth. The other 756 that were in fact herded together and marched west under substantial military guard consisted of Menomini's group of Indiana Potawatomi, and as was suggested earlier they were a very special case. The Potawatomi Preacher's followers, belatedly, had been seeking to accommodate themselves to the earlier American "civilization" policy. They wanted to become Christian farmers in Indiana. But by 1837 this was made impossible for them by intense settlement pressure and President Jackson's stringent and unyielding removal policy.

In contrast to the 1,195 Potawatomi who moved west under military escort a larger number, 1,287, voluntarily transported themselves into present Kansas or Iowa. These included the 179 Potawatomi who in 1833 joined the Kickapoo prophet Kenakuk in Kansas, another 266 led west from northern Illinois in 1836 by Padekoshek, and the major migration of Big Foot and his 842 Pota-watomi from southern Wisconsin. After several seasons of dallying along the headwaters of the Skunk and Des Moines rivers, this last group eventually settled in 1837 on the United Bands Reservation in western Iowa (see Figure

12). Finally, approximately forty-five hundred Potawatomi were enumerated as on the way west by civilian "conductors." These individuals, generally men who had been active in the Indian trade in the upper lakes area, contracted with the federal government to provide transportation and rations for the westward movement of the bulk of the Potawatomi population between 1833 and 1852, when the last substantial group from this tribe was counted moving toward Kansas.

These figures total close to eleven thousand persons; but this number is certainly excessive as an estimate of the total number of Potawatomi in this period. It includes, for example, at least six hundred Métis, who joined the

Figure 12. Potawatomi reservations in the west, 1833–1867.

western migration like a school of pilot fish following a wounded shark. Not only were these marginal people counted as Potawatomi by most Indian agents, missionaries, and traders, they were generally considered by them to be exemplary Indians, because of their cooperativeness and their degree of "civilization." However, most Potawatomi found them suspect, disputed their claims to tribal membership, and protested their sharing in annuity payments and other tribal resources. The Potawatomi on the United Bands Reservation in Iowa, for example, after 1838 purged themselves of the "half-breed" elements and sent them packing. These displaced Métis then resettled on the Osage River reserve in Kansas, where they were welcomed by the missionaries and tolerated by the more disorganized, missionized Potawatomi in that locale.

In addition to these marginal Métis, the count of Potawatomi migrating west was further inflated by several other factors. One such consists of duplicate migrations by the same individuals and groups. A fair number of individuals made several moves after 1833—west to Iowa and then back to Wisconsin and Canada, or west to Iowa and then back to Indiana and again west to Kansas, for example. In consequence, some Potawatomi were counted as migrating two and even three times. Moreover, the removal era spans a full decade, so that children who were born in that period were counted as migrants, while those adult migrants who died in the same years were not deleted from the total of those moved. However, other Potawatomi, as individuals or in tiny groups, fled north into Michigan and Wisconsin where they quickly assimilated into Ojibwa and Odawa communities and hence were never officially enumerated after 1833 as Potawatomi at all. Overall, in order to reach a reasonable estimate of the total Potawatomi population about 1835, we may delete some two thousand from the total estimate of those who migrated in the period. These, roughly, consist of duplicate enumerations and the excess of births over deaths. Including the Métis, because they were counted as Potawatomi by the federal government, and because they soon emerged as a favored elite stratum in the reservation population in Kansas, we can estimate that in 1835 there were approximately nine thousand Potawatomi in the old tribal estate, of which body, by 1833, some had already begun seeking their futures elsewhere.[2]

Once Michigan, Indiana, Illinois, and Wisconsin were cleared of their Potawatomi residents, the attention of the federal government focused narrowly on those Potawatomi who were officially recognized, namely, those residents on and under the supervision of Indian agents at reservations in Iowa and Kansas. Local officials and citizens in Michigan and Wisconsin were well aware that there were a fair number of Potawatomi in the north woods, but except for the Christian Pokagon group in southern Michigan these received almost no formal recognition until the early twentieth century. Similarly, until 1907 the several thousand Potawatomi who had voluntarily moved into Canada were near totally ignored by the United States.

In the west, federal concern was focused on the management and disposition of the Potawatomi who had resettled there. The Iowa reserve was a particularly serious problem because the several thousand Potawatomi there were at constant odds with the plains tribes, while the lands they occupied were—once again—directly west of the most rapidly expanding agricultural frontier. These "Council Bluffs" Potawatomi, from 1837 onward, were under constant pressure to cede their new reservation and to migrate again, this time into Kansas. Such pressure the Council Bluffs bands successfully resisted until, after some extremely adroit maneuvering on their part in 1845, they agreed to the treaty of 1846. By 1847 the Potawatomi in the west were once again inhabiting a single contiguous if much diminished estate on the Kansas River, but they were no longer a single solidary society, and the plans of missionaries and Indian agents to reconstitute a "Potawatomi nation" were doomed before they began.

FIRST MOVES: TOWARDS LEAVENWORTH, UPPER CANADA, AND THE PLATTE

The most important of the early western migrations was the one which, between 1835 and 1837, brought the bulk of the Potawatomi from southern Wisconsin and northern Illinois into the Platte country of western Missouri. But this was not the first of their migrations, west, north, or east. The first Potawatomi to move west were the 119 from Illinois and Indiana who had aligned themselves with Kenakuk. Conducted by James Kennerly, in company with 375 Kickapoo they arrived near present Leavenworth, Kansas, on 21 May 1833, where they settled. A second, smaller group of Potawatomi arrived on the Kansas Kickapoo Reservation later in the year, on August 26. Led by Kikito—Sun Goes One Place and Mishikaba—Snapping Turtle, these few Potawatomi were the remnants of a larger group who had assembled near Logansport, Indiana, earlier in the year. They had constituted a community led by Kikito, mainly affiliated with the Kenakuk religion, who had been so harassed by Illinois settlers after the Black Hawk War that they had fled that state for refuge near the Indian Agency at Logansport. There Kikito requested that his people be moved west of the Mississippi; but delays in getting the removal started, fears of a cholera epidemic in St. Louis, and the excitement and promise of cash and goods at the coming Treaty of Chicago lured away the great majority of those who elected to make this move. Of the some four hundred finally assembled by conductors Abel C. Pepper and Lewis Sands, only sixty-seven completed the move to Kansas that year.[3] In 1833 also began the first tentative migrations of Potawatomi into Upper Canada. That year several "cabins of heathen Potawatomi" settled at Wikwemikong on Manitoulin Island adjacent to a small settlement of Catholic Odawa. These Potawatomi had to have come to this remote island by bark canoe, and they were probably from northeastern Wisconsin.[4] They likely numbered no more than about twenty persons.

In the summer of 1834 another 199 Illinois and Indiana Potawatomi moved west to join those already settled on the Kickapoo Reservation near Leavenworth. Led by Wabanēm—White Dog (i.e., male wolf) and Mishikaba, who had returned to Indiana to encourage more Potawatomi to move west, they were conducted on their journey by William Gordon. These Potawatomi were largely from the Iroquois River valley in northeastern Illinois and adjacent Indiana, and they included many of those who had abandoned Kikito's group in the abortive 1833 migration. Like the earlier emigrants, they were affiliated with the Kenakuk religion. Leaving Illinois on July 11, they arrived at Leavenworth in early September 1834. At that point there were nearly four hundred Potawatomi west of the Mississippi. Their recognized wokamek were Kikito, Mishikaba, Wabanem, and Nozhakēm—Downward Bolt of Lightning. Voluntary emigrants who had espoused Kenakuk's new ideology, they were seeking to avoid further demoralizing contacts with American settlers while they worked out an agricultural adaptation beyond the frontier.[5]

These early migrations were minor affairs compared with the larger movements that started in 1835. In that year began the major population shifts that would, within seven years, remove some 90 percent of all Potawatomi from the old tribal estate. Of special interest is the fact that the first stream of emigrants in 1835 aimed, not for the reservation in western Missouri that had been specified by the Treaty of Chicago, but at Upper Canada. On July 16 Thomas G. Anderson, superintendent of Indian Affairs at Penetanguishene (on the south end of Georgian Bay), reported to his superiors that on returning from a trip to Sault Ste. Marie he had discovered 215 Potawatomi and Ojibwa from Milwaukee camping near his post. Anderson, who had thirty years of experience with the Potawatomi and other tribes of the upper lakes, the previous year had reported the Indians on the American shore to be in a very disturbed state. The Potawatomi, he wrote, were either to be forced north into Odawa territory "or to fly beyond the Rocky Mountains." He then predicted that as many as half of the Potawatomi would seek refuge in Upper Canada.[6]

Events in 1835 seemed to partially bear out Anderson's forecast. On finding the Milwaukee Potawatomi at Penetanguishene, he asked for instructions. His superior, Colonel James Givens, replied granting permission for these emigrants to remain in Upper Canada under British protection and for them to have lands assigned for their use. The Potawatomi were to be given asylum; but no funds were available to aid their resettlement. That same summer 233 more Potawatomi arrived at Amherstburg, and early in September another thirteen Potawatomi men and their families (approximately eighty in all) arrived in Toronto seeking permission to settle on the British shore. These requests were also approved, and the emigrants were directed to Superintendent Anderson, who was then responsible for resettling the Indians of Upper Canada on Manitoulin Island. The claim these Potawatomi made on the Canadian officials was that of loyalists who had served the British well during the War of 1812. In 1834, supposedly threatened by Americans with confiscation of their British medals and flags, some had left these valued symbols on deposit with Anderson at Penetanguishene. Thus by the winter of 1835–1836 some 528 Potawatomi had avoided President Jackson's removal policy by seeking asylum in Upper Canada. They represented two streams of migrants who pioneered the major routes into British territory, one by canoe via the upper lakes, and the other overland on horseback into the Ontario Peninsula (see Figure 13).[7]

Recognizing that many Potawatomi were migrating into Canada at the same time that others were relocating westward provides vital historical context and balance. The Potawatomi of that period were aware and took advantage of options open to them that later historians have largely ignored. The fact that these migrations were voluntary and that they were made with these tribesmen's own resources and under their own leadership provides an opportunity for appreciating the strength and viability of tribal institutions in this period, positive aspects of Potawatomi life that are obscured by too narrow a focus on forced relocation toward the western reservations.[8] As we will soon note, a fair number of Potawatomi were shopping around in these years, inspecting, testing, and comparing the alternative possibilities of Iowa, Kansas, northern Wisconsin, or Canada before finally settling in somewhere. Their freedom of movement in this period was far greater than has generally been appreciated, while—in an age of total dependence on the automobile and jet aircraft—their willingness to travel very long distances by canoe or on foot and horseback nearly defies comprehension. But unless these fluid back-and-forth migrations are understood, the Potawatomi's own perceptions of their options will be missed, as would be the full range of their adaptive maneuvers after 1835 and the complexities and causes of the sorting process that finally saw these tribesmen scattered from Manitoulin Island to Oklahoma.

For example, to assume that the Potawatomi who voluntarily moved into

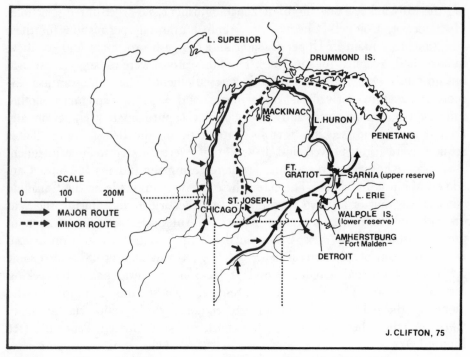

Figure 13. Migration routes into Upper Canada, 1833–1845.

Upper Canada were those who had been most strongly attached to the British cause during the War of 1812 is an easy interpretation quickly placed in doubt. To be certain, the leaders of the clans and lineages that moved into British territory generally proclaimed their long devotion to the Union Jack, and they claimed asylum as their just reward for military services delivered in past years. But although the vast majority of all Potawatomi had, more or less, sided with the British in that earlier conflict, by no means all of them elected to move into Canada. Indeed, some of the most prominent British supporters of earlier years led the migration of Potawatomi from northern Illinois and southern Wisconsin to the Platte country in 1835. Of these, only Alexander Robinson had avoided an identification with the British during the War of 1812. On the other hand, Billy Caldwell, Wabansi, Big Foot, Shabeni, and Young Miami had not exactly been notable for their friendly support of American interests before 1817. Caldwell is of particular interest in this respect, for, although American traders and Indian agents regularly spoke of him as a Potawatomi chief, the title he personally preferred and the one he used to sign his own correspondence until his death in 1841 was that of captain—of the British Indian Service. And his former associations and loyalties were often raised in an effort to discredit him, when he refused to go along with what a particular trader or agent proclaimed was in the best interest of the Potawatomi.[9]

The migration of a part of the Potawatomi from northern Illinois and southern Wisconsin into the Platte country was beset by numerous confusions and problems. This area, comprising some two million rich, fertile acres, coinciding with the six northwestern counties of present Missouri, had been excluded from the territory of that state when statehood was granted in 1820. These two million acres were part of the five million granted to the Potawatomi for their western reservation, in exchange for their remaining lands around Lake Michigan, at the Treaty of Chicago in 1833. The additional three million acres lay immediately to the north, east of the Missouri River and north of the present Missouri state line. Problem was that the state of Missouri wanted the Platte country for its own citizens, and that state's senators were unwilling to accept ratification of the Chicago treaty until the Platte country was deleted from the lands granted the Potawatomi. At the same time, the Reverend Isaac McCoy, supported by the Indian agent at Fort Leavenworth, Anthony Davis, both being in collaboration with officials and trading firms from Indiana, notably John Tipton and the Ewing family, wanted to substitute a reservation along the Osage River in eastern Kansas. These were the lands McCoy had surveyed for Potawatomi use in 1828, and he hoped to assemble all the migrating Potawatomi there where they could be brought under the influence of Baptist missionaries and his political and trader associates from Indiana.[10]

From the Potawatomi perspective, the developing conflict over the Platte country and the alternatives of accepting substitute lands in Iowa or Kansas reflected a schism within the tribe that predated the Treaty of Chicago. This split was exacerbated by negotiations for that treaty, which led to the dominance of Potawatomi leaders from the Chicago area and southern Wisconsin, notably Caldwell, Robinson, Wabansi, and Shabani. This division roughly followed a line of conflict between the two Indian agencies at Chicago and Logansport and the several coalitions of traders, political figures, and entrepreneurs associated with each. In this respect, the northern Illinois and southern Wisconsin Potawatomi were allied with and served as clients for the agents and traders at Chicago, while the Michigan, Indiana, and some of the central Illinois villages were similarly linked to agents and entrepreneurs in Indiana. In passing judgment based on the outcome of the controversy over the Platte country and subsequent developments, it will be evident that the leadership of the Chicago-based division was more capable, disciplined, and effective in promoting Potawatomi interests than were their counterparts in Michigan and Indiana, who were a far more fragmented, demoralized, and dependent lot, generally subordinated to the demands and interests of missionaries, traders,

Indian agents, and American political figures. This schism did not reflect any neat division between "Prairie" and "Forest" Potawatomi, as some have thought. The first movements west to Kansas in 1833 and 1834, we must recall, were of Potawatomi from the Kankakee and Iroquois River valleys of the Illinois and Indiana prairie country. These emigrants chose a course which at first took them outside the controversy between the Chicago and Logansport factions, but they were eventually affiliated with the heavily missionized Indiana and Michigan Potawatomi who subsequently settled on the Osage River in Kansas.

An understanding of the development of the Platte controversy requires mention of a key tactic of the United Bands and of one of their important objectives. The tactic, first expressed during negotiations for the Chicago treaty, more fully developed in process of settling up for the exchange of the Platte lands, and polished to a fine art a decade later in Iowa when the time came for exchanging the United Bands Reservation there for new lands in Kansas, consisted basically of stalling for time as the value of lands occupied by the tribe increased with growing settlement pressure. Leaders such as Caldwell and Robinson were men long experienced in trade. They were fully aware of the supply-and-demand dynamics of a market economy. They appreciated that the greater the demand for the lands occupied by Potawatomi the higher the price would be. They understood the importance of coalition and combination, of negotiating from a position of relative strength. And they were sound judges of the kinds of pressures frontier settlers and political officials would bring on Washington to secure the cession of lands badly wanted for new homesteads. They were also aware of the risks involved in protracted stalling and delay, namely, preemption by squatters, vigilante raids, and, ultimately, the threat of federal force.

The major objective of the United Bands from northern Illinois and Wisconsin in this period was to achieve a greater measure of control over their own affairs. This was an aim difficult to disentangle from the consequences of the tactics they used, an end scarcely separable from the means employed. Success in negotiations, the capacity to manipulate events for the benefit of the Potawatomi involved, and the ability to turn American agents to their own purposes, all involved a satisfactory exercise of power. And the power to manage their own lives, to make their own choices in their fashion, was an end clearly desired by the United Bands and their leaders. To be certain, those Potawatomi who slipped north into the forests of Wisconsin, as well as the many others who crossed into Canada, similarly sought greater control over events affecting them; but they went about securing this goal in a different way. Theirs was a strategy of escape and evasion. They simply avoided further contacts with Americans. The United Bands, in contrast, developed an adaptation which involved maintaining relationships with Americans, but these were relationships in which they had more than a little say and from which, on more than one occasion, they would derive a very high order of satisfaction. The strategy of the United Bands, in brief, was one of manipulation of their opponents' weaknesses.

A point of clarification concerning the internal organization of the United Bands is in order. In the 1830s and early 1840s they were known and identified as the United Bands, the United Nations, or the United Tribes of Potawatomi, Odawa, and Ojibwa. The fact that the Odawa and Ojibwa were minor elements, long assimilated into the Potawatomi villages involved, was discussed at length earlier. The point at issue here is the importance and significance of the pluralization—bands, tribes, or nations. Too often, in recent years, the plural has been misplaced, yielding the denomination of United Band or United Nation, generally with the associated conclusion that the "band" was under the leadership of one or a few individuals, usually Caldwell and Robinson.[11] The fact is that the constituent social elements of the United Bands consisted of a number of villages or clusters of villages in northern Illinois and Wisconsin. Because they formed a major solidary coalition in this period, and since the phrasing "band" or "tribe" was used by Americans to designate an Indian village or clan, they became known as the United Bands.

The basic leadership for this United Bands coalition came from the traditional wokamek of the constituent villages, men such as Wabansi, Big Foot, and Padekoshēk. To the influence and skills of these men—who functioned as a traditional council—was added a superstructure of leadership specialists, men such as Billy Caldwell and Alexander Robinson, who did not have traditional roles in a village. Caldwell, Robinson, and similar individuals were men who obtained great influence by providing highly specialized services, employing skills not possessed by traditional wokamek. Such men were multilingual, literate, experienced in trade, accustomed to keeping books and accounts, adept at making calculations, skilled in business and political negotiations, and knowledgeable concerning American political institutions and processes. Thus the Potawatomi group known as the United Bands might more accurately be called the United Villages, and this solidary unit can, with some gain in insight, be seen as an incipient tribal society in process of reconstituting itself out of some portions of the old one, albeit on a slightly altered pattern.

It is also clear that the leaders of the United Bands held themselves in very high esteem. At the Treaty of Chicago, and later, they sought a position of ascendancy and dominance with respect to other elements, an effort which led finally to an irrevocable schism in the tribe as a whole. Concerning the specialized, non-Potawatomi leaders such as Caldwell and Robinson, within a few years after the Treaty of Chicago their work was done. After seeing the United Bands moved to the Platte country, Robinson returned to his personal estate and severed his connection with the Potawatomi. Caldwell, on the other hand, stayed active among the United Bands until his much-mourned death at Council Bluffs in 1841. The Potawatomi never saw his like again. Following his death the established, traditional okamek in Iowa secured the specialized skills required to accomplish their aims by simply hiring men with the necessary talents or by subverting Indian agents to their ends.

Missouri Senators Benton and Linn made the first move in the controversy over the Platte country by blocking ratification of the Treaty of Chicago until the lands desired by their constituents were deleted and other territory, in present Iowa, substituted therefor. Caldwell and Robinson, representing the Potawatomi in northern Illinois, took the lead in resisting this alteration of the treaty. They offered to exchange the Platte country for their choice of four hundred sections of land in northern Illinois or for agricultural equipment and teachers to help establish themselves as farmers in the west. Thomas J. V. Owen, Indian agent in Chicago and chief negotiator for the United States, refused this proposal; but on 1 October 1834 Caldwell, Robinson, and their associates made a new offer which was accepted. They acquiesced in the substitution of lands in present Iowa for the Platte country but demanded the payment of an indemnity of $10,000 to themselves and $3,000 to Gholson Kercheval and George E. Walker, two traders who had provided various services to the tribe. The government agreed to this alternative, which was made for the benefit of the United Bands, without the consent of the Michigan and Indiana Potawatomi. Leaders of villages in these states immediately protested that the United Bands representatives did not speak for the whole tribe, but to no avail. The senate approved the revised treaty on 21 February 1835.[12] This revised agreement did not, however, stop Potawatomi settlement of the Platte area. Several hundred of the Potawatomi already on the Kickapoo Reservation near Fort Leavenworth in 1834 crossed the Missouri and began settling there. They found numerous Sauk, Fox, and Iowas still living in the area; and shortly there was an influx of Missouri "pioneers" who established squatter's rights prior to annexation of the Platte by their state.

The confusion over the final destination of the Potawatomi and which parties were the rightful occupants of the Platte country increased in 1835. In late June of that year, following the terms of the 1833 treaty, an exploring party went west to examine the new Potawatomi lands. Led by Billy Caldwell, who took his younger son Charles along, the party included thirty-eight Potawatomi from thirteen villages in Wisconsin, Illinois, Indiana, and Michigan. Among the notables were Swift Current, White Pigeon (the younger), Iowa, Black Wolf, Big Foot, Crane, Break of Day, and Dried Berry. Two Odawa leaders from L'Arbre Croche also joined the expedition, which was accompanied by a retinue managed by Major William Gordon, whose support group included cooks, horse-wranglers, wagoners, and general handymen. The Potawatomi leaders were traveling in some style—their expenses came to $9,453; but they did not at all like what they saw on the proposed reservation in present Iowa. During their trip they inspected both the Platte country and the Iowa lands they had supposedly accepted in exchange therefor. The comparison they made was strongly negative with respect to the terrain north of the Missouri state line—it was barren, treeless, swampy, infested with swarms of voracious mosquitoes, and too close to the Dakota tribes west of the Missouri. The United Bands leaders decided to petition President Jackson, pleading for permission to remain in the Platte country for some years.[13] Caldwell and company were stalling. They understood full well that the federal government and Illinois state officials wanted the Potawatomi out of northern Illinois quickly.

While the exploring party traveled west, John Russell—superintendent of removal in the Chicago area—was busy collecting Potawatomi at a camp on the Des Plaines River, preparing them for their move. He encouraged their leaders to start the migration first, before sending their appeal to the president. And he also gave them permission to live temporarily—five or perhaps twenty years—in the Platte country until the issue was resolved. With this vague understanding 712 Potawatomi—led by Caldwell and Padekoshĕk—left the Chicago area in late September for the west. Conducted by Russell and traveling overland, on October 21 they reached and soon crossed the Mississippi. On October 28 Padekoshĕk's party of 224 Potawatomi, with some 226 others, broke away from the emigrant train and journeyed north into eastern Iowa, where they spent the next several years hunting along the Skunk River and other tributaries of the Mississippi. The balance, the 252 Potawatomi with Caldwell and escorted by Russell, continued west, arriving in the Platte—near present Liberty, Missouri—on December 2. When they arrived, they found 454 other Potawatomi already living in western Missouri—some of those who had first temporarily settled on the Kickapoo Reservation with Kenakuk.

While this exploration and first migration was occurring, more sand was thrown into the grease oiling the wheels of the Potawatomi trek. John Tipton of Indiana and his confederates Isaac McCoy and Anthony Davis—the Indian agent at Leavenworth—were busy attempting to block Potawatomi migration to either the Platte or the Iowa lands. They wanted all Potawatomi resettled under their control along the Osage River in Kansas.[14] But the delegation the United Bands sent to Washington in January 1836 brought back a commitment from Commissioner of Indian Affairs Elbert Herring, confirming that offered by Russell earlier. They were to be allowed temporary residence in the Platte until they moved, finally, into Iowa.

The composition of the party led west by Caldwell is of considerable interest, for only on occasions such as this did the government prepare a careful census, allowing us a glimpse into the internal organization of Potawatomi villages of this era. The official roll of this emigrating party provides the names of household heads, the ages and sexes of persons in each family group, and fragments of information concerning the group's experiences en route. Aside from Padekoshēk's party of 224, for which census information was not provided, the remaining 488 Potawatomi consisted of fifty-six households, with an average size of nearly nine persons each. Caldwell, who was getting along in years, had his latest wife with him and three of his children. There were practically no Métis in the group. Other than Caldwell's, the only other Euro-American name appearing in the roll is that of Francis Valdier. Moreover, of the 712 persons who started this long, hard two-months' journey in early winter, only one died en route. It was a particularly hardy group, or one well cared for.[15]

The Potawatomi population in the Platte country and tensions with Missourians increased during 1836. On June 20 Padekoshēk arrived with 266 followers, leaving 352 behind on the Des Moines River in Iowa where they had spent the winter. In mid-July there were another two hundred Potawatomi temporarily camped on the Grand River, seventy miles west of Leavenworth, near present Gallatin, on their way to join Caldwell. And that autumn Gholson Kercheval conducted 634 additional Potawatomi from northern Illinois to the Platte, arriving there November 15. By that time nearly eighteen hundred Potawatomi had left northern Illinois and arrived in the Platte country, but responsible army officers could estimate only sixteen hundred as actually present in the winter of 1836–1837. The Potawatomi were hard to count, for many did not stay long in one place and their camps were scattered over a large territory.[16]

The arrival of so many Potawatomi, the growing influx of squatters from Missouri, and ambiguities over the status of the Platte country aggravated existing tensions in the area. Technically, this was still Indian country, subject to federal law and control. Indian agents warned the trespassers from Missouri away, and in February dragoons from Fort Leavenworth burned the cabins of several who refused to move. Missouri's senators then began lobbying to have the status of the area altered, so that it could be annexed to their state. Their efforts were successful; on 28 March 1837 the Platte country was proclaimed part of Missouri. Meanwhile, the Potawatomi gave little indication of any willingness to move elsewhere, and relations between the tribesmen and Missourians worsened. The federal government then decided to move all Potawatomi out of the newly annexed northwest corner of the state. The problem was deciding where they would go. The United Bands people under Caldwell and his associates were scheduled to move north of the Missouri line, but they displayed no eagerness to leave.[17] Those Indiana and Michigan Potawatomi near Leavenworth refused to move north to join their Chicago area cousins, as did others not yet removed from their villages along the Wabash and St. Joseph rivers. With the prompting of the Reverend Isaac McCoy, still nourishing his vision of an Indian Canaan, of Agent Davis, and of trading interests from Indiana, on 11 February 1837 seven Potawatomi leaders from Indiana signed the treaty establishing a second reservation in the west, along the Osage (Marias des Cygnes) River in eastern Kansas.[18] Soon Anthony Davis was appointed subagent for this proposed Potawatomi "national homeland." On April 28, Dr. Edwin James was made subagent for the new post across the river from Council Bluffs.[19] A protégé of the new commissioner of Indian Affairs, C. A. Harris, James had, briefly, been a candidate for the Osage River subagent's position, but the Baptist missionary–Indian trader combination had—as he put it—caused him a "*dis*-appointment."

Creating the new Council Bluffs subagency was intended to encourage the United Bands into moving north. Indeed, they were almost ready to migrate, for the pressures in the Platte country were rising markedly. Missourians were threatening armed intervention; new settlers were flocking into the Platte; and the Indian Department at Fort Leavenworth was ordered to cease issuing rations to the Potawatomi in Missouri by June 30. This last step was intended to provoke the United Bands into moving; it succeeded only in vexing them, creating further resistance. Their leaders began quoting their treaties, chapter and verse, arguing that under the provisions of the Chicago concord they had not yet reached their agreed-on reservation, and, being technically yet in transit, they were fully entitled to subsistence provided by the government. That June the secretary of war wrote the commanding general instructing him to take steps to move the United Bands out of the Platte, if necessary by the use of force.[20]

However, instead of acting as an instrument of coercion, the army came to the rescue of the United Bands. Before Brigadier Henry Atkinson, commanding at Jefferson Barracks, Missouri, could receive and implement his orders, Major General Edmund Gaines intervened. Gaines, commanding the Western Department of the Army, had been inspecting the western posts. Learning of the Potawatomi situation from Colonel Stephen Watts Kearney, commanding the 1st Dragoons at Fort Leavenworth, he took control of the situation. Little inclined to accept directions from distant political appointees, protocol-minded, an upholder of the law, and determined to keep the peace on the frontier according to his own lights, General Gaines ordered that the issue of rations be resumed. He quickly met in council with the leaders of the United Bands, agreed with them that under the terms of the 1833 treaty they were due rations while in transit and for a year after settling in Iowa, sniped at the secretary of war for his "breach of faith," placated the angered Missourians, arranged an escort, hired two river steamers to transport the aged and the infirm, and directed his subordinate Atkinson to carry out his detailed plans for the orderly movement of the United Bands to their new homes. Under Atkinson's supervision, by July 22 these Potawatomi were on their way upriver.[21]

General Gaines's actions caused great consternation, both among those who had a vested interest in resettling all Potawatomi on the Osage River reservation as well as among some in Washington, where the secretary of war was angered by this independent action. Even before Atkinson set about implementing Gaines's plans to move the United Bands north, instructions were on their way from Secretary of War Joel Pointsett, directing him to move the United Bands onto the Potawatomi "National Reservation." The ostensible reason for this change in plans was the threat of a Dakota war against the Potawatomi emigrants, and the need for economy of management in Indian affairs; but the powerful hand of the Baptist-Indiana lobby was waving in the background. To be certain, there was a pressing need for economy in government that summer, for a decade of rampant land speculation and inflation had brought on a grave economic depression. In May, New York banks had suspended specie payments, and quickly many banks failed. This economic depression raised the value of the Indian trade and intensified the importance of controlling the Potawatomi migration, for this was an important source of income to entrepreneurs in Indiana and Chicago. Nonetheless, the Dakota threat was real. In late June, Edwin James himself had reported that the Dakota were trying to establish an alliance with the Oto and Omaha against the Potawatomi. Well aware of the "ancient hostilities between the Dakota and the Algonquians," this development had him worried.[22]

But the Reverend Isaac McCoy, Subagent Davis, and John Tipton were less concerned with the Dakota threat than they were with their personal visions of glory, power, and income. In July, McCoy reported to Tipton on developments in the Platte. He and Davis had anticipated the United Bands would move to the Osage; but the arrival of Dr. James and General Gaines, he complained, had changed all that. Both were to blame, but especially Gaines, for with his "dashing movements and fair speeches [he] has got the Indians anxious to go up the river." After twenty years of experience, McCoy was still unable to concede that the Potawatomi might have any interests or plans of their own. He was still shepherding the tame Topnibe around, pretending he was the chief of all the Potawatomi, trying to employ him as a magnet to attract all to the Osage River. Anthony Davis was also outraged. He saw a scheme afoot aimed at capturing Indians that "were properly his." McCoy commented, "if Davis cannot obtain a tolerable share of the Puta-watomies we cannot hope for the improvement of his situation, nor even that his present situation will be permanent." He was convinced that Gholson Kercheval was acting in the interests of the United Bands and that he would direct new parties to Council Bluffs rather than to Kansas. He was quite right. Kercheval, the Chicago entrepreneur, was amply paid by the United Bands leaders to heed their words.[23]

Dr. Edwin James was a peculiar choice for an Indian agent. Highly educated and broadly experienced, he was a practicing physician, geologist, geographer, botanist, and biographer, as well as an accomplished ethnographer and linguist whose writings about Algonquian cultures and languages remain of value today. The sort of man who delights any historical researcher, he wrote a perfectly regular hand that is as legible as if it were professionally typed, and he wrote a very great deal. More importantly, from the perspective of Potawatomi interests, he was a radical humanitarian, utterly devoted to the welfare of his charges, and thoroughly honest. He approached his responsi-bilities with an energy and intellectual ability that, combined with his other failings, soon had him in trouble with the Office of Indian Affairs. Vitally concerned with the successful development of the United Bands, he was com-mitted to what, in the language of the present, would be called sovereignty and economic self-sufficiency for these Potawatomi.

The theory of development James employed was taken, neither from Christian mythology nor the American spirit of Manifest Destiny nor laissez-faire capitalism, but from the writings of John Locke and the Baron de Montesquieu. On arriving at his new post at Council Bluffs, he reflected on the values, skills, and wishes of the Potawatomi; conducted a careful study of the reservation's topography, soils, fauna, and climate; and concluded that, preferable to an agricultural economy, the immediate future of the Potawatomi lay in stock-raising. He assumed (following Locke), that "the habits of the Pastoral life form a convenient and early stage between the hunter state and one of fixed and permanent agricultural industry." And he noted that the Potawatomi were "very fond of cattle and horses," hoping that it would "suit the views of the government to second their desire to become possessed of a goodly number of domestic animals." It did not so suit the views of the gov-ernment. Hardly had the Potawatomi arrived in Council Bluffs when they and their agent were brought under sharp pressure to move once more, back south into Kansas. The line of American agricultural settlements in Iowa Territory was moving rapidly toward the west, and to obtain the support of western voters a cheap western land policy was an imperative for the incumbent president as well as aspirants to that office. But the only cheap land in Iowa was occupied by the United Bands, and so their period of occupation of the reserve along the Missouri was foreshortened from the beginning. Edwin James, who defended Potawatomi interests against distant policy-makers, survived in office scarcely more than a year. He was the first of a half dozen subagents at that remote Council Bluffs post, whose average tenure of office was only eighteen months. Regardless of their own personal interests, which were generally focused on economic gain, all were more or less subverted by the leaders of the United Bands, who had a positive knack for turning the loyalties of isolated Indian agents to their own cause.[24]

DIASPORA— WEST, EAST, NORTH

Irrespective of what McCoy, John Tipton, Secretary of War Poinsett, or other American officials wished, during the years 1837–1842 most Potawatomi continued to move when and where they pleased. This was true even of the migrations to the west that were—nominally—those most highly organized by the federal government. But federal policy and federal planning were one kind of thing, the execution of policy on the local level quite another. In fact, local officials and interested private parties were squabbling bitterly over the control of and disposition and resettlement of the Potawatomi emigrants. In late summer 1837, for example, Lewis Sands was appointed to replace Gholson Kercheval, with the responsibility of moving a large number of Potawatomi west from the St. Joseph River and northern Illinois. Sands intended to move more than a thousand, but was able to assemble only 470 Potawatomi at Shabbona's Grove, west of Chicago, for the move. On September 5 this group started off. When they reached the little Platte in western Missouri, the party split. The 287 northern Illinois Potawatomi, led once again by Caldwell's staunch friend Padekoshēk, headed north for Council Bluffs. With the young Topnebi 164 St. Joseph Potawatomi continued to the Osage River reservation. Sands, who had fallen out with McCoy, was castigated for his failure to deliver all into the latter's hands. Equally detested by the Potawatomi, he went home in disgrace. Sands defended himself by saying that the Illinois Potawatomi had refused to go to the Osage, but McCoy was convinced he had been bought off.

Meanwhile, many of the Potawatomi clustered on the Kickapoo Reservation had moved down to settle at Potawatomi Creek on the Osage Reservation. This was a boon to McCoy and Davis, for most of these were from the Kankakee and Iroquois rivers, and hence entitled to annuities from the 1833 Treaty. At that moment, in mid-November, there were only 62 proper

Chicago-area Potawatomi on the Osage River reserve. The Baptists were certain there was "*a secret spring* some where operating to send the Indians to the Bluffs." Convinced that there were some 2,400 Potawatomi with Caldwell, only by "hard scuffling" had they been able to get "850–900 on the Osage." McCoy, Davis, Tipton, and associates now set to work to find a suitable replacement for the discredited Lewis Sands, one who would employ such means as were necessary to deliver the maximum number of Potawatomi to their establishment in Kansas. By this time their anger had focused on Billy Caldwell, whom they thought "was the greatest curse that could possibly be entailed upon" the Indians.[25] Specifically, the conspirators on the Osage River Reservation were convinced that Caldwell's plan was to get "all the annuities paid where he can manage it." This, of course, is what Tipton, McCoy, and Davis had in mind with their scheming. They countered with an effort to undercut the position of Caldwell and the Council Bluffs Potawatomi. Tipton, following a suggestion from the Métis, J. N. Bourassa, in 1838 arranged to have their puppet Topnebi initiate a petition, to be signed by all the Osage River Potawatomi, requesting that their interests in the Council Bluffs reservation be sold. It was an adroit stratagem—the Osage River Potawatomi had no claim to the Council Bluffs lands.[26]

In October 1837 the Osage River population was augmented somewhat by the arrival of 150 (or perhaps 53, estimates vary) Potawatomi from northern Indiana. Led by Neswaki, Nebosh, Kiwani—The Lost One, and Okamase—Young Leader, they included the first of many Potawatomi from nothern Indiana to move west and some of the first Catholic Potawatomi. Thus they added the beginnings of interdenominational strife to the existing conflicts between trading firms and intertribal rivalries that already existed on the Osage River. However, along with his companions, Young Leader apparently did not like what he saw in the west. Whether it was the Kansas prairies or the growing factionalism on the Osage reserve or whatever that displeased them, most soon returned to Indiana. Less than three years later Young Leader joined forces with Manitogabowit—Standing Spirit to carry 267 Indiana Potawatomi into Upper Canada.[27] But this late 1837 migration to the Osage was a minor affair compared with the move of Big Foot's people out of southern Wisconsin in September. Big Foot's migration was voluntary, unescorted, and accomplished in his own style and at his own pace. Securing permission from the Sauk and Fox to pass through and spend the winter in their country, Big Foot's 842 Potawatomi set up their winter hunting camps on the upper reaches of the Des Moines and bided their time, waiting for spring.[28]

The year 1838 witnessed two additional migrations to the west, the first and smallest of them in September to Council Bluffs, with the second being the sorriest episode in the whole history of the great diaspora, the forcible removal of Menomini and 756 Potawatomi from northern Indiana in September. The first of these migrations stands in stark contrast to the latter. In August, Isaac L. Berry collected 163 southern Wisconsin and northern Illinois Potawatomi at the Des Plaines River assembly point and led them west to join the United Bands at Council Bluffs. It was a peaceable, uneventful trip, with no serious illnesses or deaths.[29] The forced removal of Menomini, on the other hand, was marred by a record of deceit, violence, epidemic illness, numerous deaths, and tragedy. Because the story of Menomini's migration has been the one episode in Potawatomi history most often retold, there is little need to continue the agony here, except to underscore several matters of historical context which may make the actions of John Tipton and his fellow conspirators more intelligible, if not more easily appreciated.

By the summer of 1838 the Tipton-McCoy-Davis combination was becoming desperate. The economic situation in the nation was not improving, while the United Bands at Council Bluffs were obviously having more success in securing immigrants to that reservation. After months of controversy in which Edwin James had failed to "cooperate" in securing the removal of the United Bands to the Osage, he was relieved of his responsibilities, to be replaced with a man supposedly more amenable to orders, John Dougherty, who headed the subagency at Bellevue across the Missouri River. Moving large numbers of Potawatomi that summer out of somewhere, whether Indiana or Iowa, spelled badly needed dollars for those involved: payments to the contractors who supervised the migration, access to the substantial annuities due the United Bands, and income from the sale of lands relieved of their Potawatomi occupants. Recognizing the powerful motivation of John Tipton and his partners does not relieve their memories of any blame, but it does help explain why the blow fell on Menomini and the Indiana Potawatomi rather than some other group. They were giving indications of wanting to stay on in Indiana; Menomini refused to accede to any of Tipton's wishes; the lands they occupied were extremely valuable; and the population was substantial, concentrated in a few places, and easily brought under control.

The tragic events leading to Menomini's removal from Indiana began on 5 August 1836. On that date Abel Pepper rammed through a treaty, boycotted and bitterly protested by Menomini, ceding the twenty-two sections on the Yellow River that had been awarded four wokamek jointly in 1832. The other three leaders, Black Wolf, Rattlesnake, and Pepinawa, were bribed or otherwise persuaded to sign the 1836 cession. Through 1837 and the spring of 1838 Menomini continued to fault this transaction, receiving moral support from his priest, Father Deseille, who eventually was forced by Pepper to leave the area, being replaced by Father Benjamin Petit. The obstinate Menomini's village then became an assembly point for the many Potawatomi reluctant to leave Indiana and Michigan, and thus a special focus of attention for those interests who wished Indiana cleared of all its Indians.

On 24 August 1838 Senator Tipton wrote McCoy complaining, "our potta-watomies are stubborn. I lerned lately by traveler that the michigan Indians have refused to emigrate & have left mr. Lykins camp. Our [Indiana] potta-watomies refused but I will go to their camp in 8 days & they shall not tell me they wont go, *they must go.*" Tipton did not wait eight days. At this point Governor Wallace intervened, authorizing the use of one hundred militiamen to dislodge Menomini and his followers. Using a ruse to lure Menomini and other dissident leaders into their chapel, on August 29 Tipton surrounded and captured them all. Six days later 850 Potawatomi were assembled under mili-tary guard and started on their way west. Of these, 756 finally reached the Sugar Creek camp on the Osage River Reservation, where the Catholic Pota-watomi were congregating. This dismal journey coincided with a major en-teric (typhoid) fever epidemic in Indiana and Illinois, and 5 percent of the total body, forty-two persons, died along the route. More than fifty others escaped from the guards and avoided this removal.[30]

In the summer and fall of 1840 two additional streams of Potawatomi emigrants made their way to Kansas. The first of these parties departed South Bend, Indiana, on August 17 and numbered 526 persons, including fifty of those who had escaped from Menomini's migration the previous year. Mostly from southern Michigan, these Potawatomi had been trying to settle around Nottawaseppe Prairie, living off what little credit they had with traders, who in turn opposed the migration. Their conductor was Alexis Coquillard, who delivered the whole party of 526 to the Sugar Creek settlement on the Osage River Reservation. This was, by and large, another Catholic Potawatomi group, which was accompanied by its priest, Father Stanilaus A. Bernier. This first move west in 1840 was accompanied by some of the Michigan Métis, in-cluding Abram Burnett. By now Potawatomi available for removal were be-coming difficult to locate, as well as increasingly unwilling to move west. A great many had fled north into Wisconsin and Michigan, and already more than two thousand had moved into Upper Canada.

In June, Major J. T. Sprague of the Eighth Infantry Regiment had cautioned against the use of troops to effect further removals, advising that conciliatory measures and judicious and influential agents could do a better, more humane job of it. But his advice went unheeded; that summer Brigadier General Hugh Brady mustered two hundred regulars and one hundred Mich-igan militiamen to round up the stragglers. It was a singularly ineffective military action; in two months of scouring the woods, only sixty-five Pota-watomi were captured.[31]

The second party left Marshall, Michigan, on October 15 and arrived on the Osage November 25. The contractor for this party was Gholson Kercheval, and it was led by the imperious Major Robert Forsyth, whose bold manner provided the only military escort needed. Among the leaders escorted west was the elusive Black Wolf, who had several times been captured and then escaped Brigadier Brady's troopers. Again, most but not all of these Potawatomi were nominal Catholics and settled in the Sugar Creek community, while the balance went to the Protestant Potawatomi Creek settlement.[32]

By the winter of 1840–1841 the great majority of the Potawatomi had left their old habitat surrounding Lake Michigan, whether as voluntary migrants to Iowa, with civilian escort or military guards to Kansas, or voluntarily into the north woods and Canada. With them had gone as well the Kerchevals, the Coquillards, the Bertrands, the Bourassas, the McCoys, the Petits—those whose parasitic attachment to Indians made them dependent on migrating also—to where their hosts resided. During the next five years the attentions of such specialists in the Indian traffic were turned to establishing themselves in secure positions of influence on the reservations in the west. A major item of business was securing the removal of the United Bands from their reservation in western Iowa. Not until 1846, when the United Bands wokamek finally obtained the terms they sought and a new treaty was drawn ceding both the Iowa and the Osage River reservations for the new "Potawatomi National Reservation" on the Kansas River, did additional removals from the Great Lakes to Kansas occur (see Figure 12). In June 1847 the first of these took place. That year Alexis Coquillard spent three months rounding up an odd-lots party of Indians from Indiana, Michigan, and Wisconsin, including some two hundred Potawatomi. These arrived at the St. Mary's settlement on 1 September 1847.[33] In 1847, as well, the United Bands finally condescended to move south to the new Kansas River Reservation, but they did so in their own time, unaided and unprompted by conductors or military escort.

Over the next four years there were fragmentary reports of moves of Potawatomi both to the west and back east again, but not until 1851 did another proper removal party make the trip. Once again the perennial Alexis Coquillard was the contractor, this time in partnership with George W. Ewing. In August he departed Wisconsin with 639 Potawatomi, mainly from villages between Sheboygan and Manitowoc, but including some stragglers from Ohio and Indiana. They almost did not finish the journey. As they approached Fort Leavenworth a cholera epidemic broke out, and the Potawatomi scattered to the four sacred directions, regardless of the efforts of the contractors to hold them together. These Potawatomi were not made entirely welcome by their cousins in Kansas. Most of those who had remained in the east had for years not been sharing in the annual annuity payments, and the arrival of so many who were eligible for a share of the limited funds available diminished the per capita amounts of those in Kansas who had long been dependent on their fixed annual cash payments. This precipitated a conflict between the Kansas and the Wisconsin-Michigan Potawatomi that persists today. In connection with this 1851 migration, one of the mechanisms employed by the Potawatomi to raise cash and by the removal contractors to increase their profits came to light. On January 26 Francis Lea, an agent seemingly so new and untutored at his job that he acted astonished at the covert money-making deals he discovered, reported the contractors were in the habit of issuing ration tickets to the Potawatomi. Normally, they were expected to make a reasonable profit from the delivery of food in exchange for the tickets, which in turn served as their receipts; but instead they would buy them back from the Potawatomi for cash at very substantial discounts. It was this device the Potawatomi used to raise money, especially to pay the expenses of their return journey back east. Lea, who was not so innocent as he pretended to be, expressed concern that if this practice continued a great many of his Potawatomi would move back to the Great Lakes area again.[34]

The last recognized formal relocation of Potawatomi from Wisconsin to Kansas occurred in the spring of 1852. That April a mixed party of some two hundred Potawatomi and Winnebago were noted at St. Joseph, Missouri, on their way toward Kansas. By that date, except for the ebb and flow of small groups of Potawatomi moving back and forth on their own, a cycle of movements that has never ended, the westward tide of emigrants from this tribe was over.[35] More than seven thousand had been counted leaving the Great Lakes area and arriving in Missouri, Iowa, or Kansas. Aided by private arrangements with the contractors, who were paid fifty-five to sixty dollars a person for moving them west and nothing for persuading them to stay there, upwards of two thousand Potawatomi did not remain in the west but returned to Wisconsin, Michigan, and even Canada.

In profound contrast to the western migrations, those Potawatomi who elected to move into Upper Canada amply demonstrated that they would not and could not be bound by American Indian policy and practices. That they had considerable freedom of movement and the personal and cultural resources to take advantage of perceived opportunities is well marked by a single fact: between 1833 and 1845 some twenty-five hundred members of the tribe, about 30 percent of the total population, packed their belongings and moved out from under the impact of President Jackson's removal policy. The factors that pushed these and other Potawatomi out of the old tribal estate are now apparent. What needs understanding and explanation is the basis for selection of those who elected to move east, into an area of British sovereignty, rather than west, where they would remain under American control.[36]

The Potawatomi migration into Upper Canada consisted basically of two major waves and a prolonged trickle. Preceded by the twenty or so who settled on Manitoulin Island in 1833, the first large group of 215 arrived at Penetanguishene in early July 1835. Their arrival was not unanticipated, for the British Indian agents in the area were well aware the tribe was under extreme pressure and on the move; but no official British policy as regarded their reception had yet been formulated. This was soon provided by Colonel James Givens, who instructed his subordinate, Thomas Anderson, to welcome them. Two years later, in July 1837, Henry Schoolcraft, United States Indian agent at Mackinac Island, reported that "three hundred united Ottawas, Pottawatomies, and Chippewas" had stopped briefly at his post on their way to Manitoulin Island and Penetanguishene, where they intended to settle. These, he indicated, were from Wisconsin and Illinois. But Schoolcraft made these emigrants unwelcome, and he was forbidden to issue them rations. Thereafter the Potawatomi on their way to Canada rarely stopped at Mackinac Island. Also in early July another three hundred Potawatomi had crossed over the St. Clair River from Michigan and arrived at Sarnia, where they proved burdensome to the Ojibwa residents of the Upper St. Clair Reserve there. These Potawatomi were also mostly from Wisconsin and Michigan, but they arrived on horseback. A month later, Thomas G. Anderson reported that 432 Potawatomi from "Millwackie" were already settled at Manitowaning on Manitoulin Island, clearing land for spring crops, while another 218 were similarly occupied further south on the Saugeen River (near present Southhampton, Ontario).[37]

Thus by late summer of 1837 some 1,465 Potawatomi are known to have been on their way toward or already settling at various locations in Upper Canada.[38] Moreover, this first large stream of emigrants had pioneered the major routes that would be used by others in subsequent years (see Figure 13). The northern avenue involved a coastwise canoe trip along the shore of Lake Michigan to the Straits of Mackinac, and from there along Georgian Bay to Manitoulin Island or Penetanguishene, or south along the east coast of the state of Michigan to the head of the St. Clair River. The southern route was overland, west to east on horseback, with the migrating Potawatomi assembling in remote spots near the headwaters of the Kalamazoo River before striking east for Sarnia. In general, the Potawatomi emigrants avoided heavily traveled roads and densely settled American areas, particularly the Detroit region.

In 1838 Schoolcraft noted another 137 Potawatomi in their canoes passing by Mackinac Island on their way to the British posts on the eastern shore of Lake Huron. Likely these were from Wisconsin. But for several years thereafter the border region was made unsettled by the Patriot Rebellion in Canada. Many of the rebelling Canadians had fled across the American border, where they attempted to organize an invasion of Canada. In an effort to keep the peace and to restrain its own citizens, the United States had regarrisoned Fort Gratiot and tightened up control of movements across the international boundary. These efforts made the movement of Indians into Canada more difficult but did not stop them. What it did end was the attention British officials had been giving to Indian migrations. They had more pressing problems to occupy their time.[39]

Nonetheless, Potawatomi migrations continued. On 17 September 1840 J. W. Keating, Indian agent at the Lower St. Clair Reserve, reported that a total of more than two thousand Potawatomi and some Ojibwa had by that date moved into Canada via Sarnia. More than eight hundred in Michigan were preparing to move, he wrote, but were being "frustrated by American authorities." These were, according to Keating, being pursued by American troops from Kalamazoo and blocked by others at Fort Gratiot—not very effectively, as we will see. Keating, eager to encourage Potawatomi movement into Canada, then became embroiled in a correspondence with Major Thomas Gardiner, commanding at Fort Gratiot. For two months these dignitaries rattled their pens at one another. Did the United States have any objection to the emigration? inquired Keating. Indeed, replied Gardiner, the United States objected officially and formally. The Potawatomi were under treaty obligations to go west, but they were instead "proceeding in the opposite direction." Keating lied, diplomatically, in reply to Gardiner's inquiries about the number of Potawatomi on the Canadian side of the St. Clair River. This tactic particularly annoyed Gardiner, for he had a good firsthand accounting, obtained from a spy, one John W. Dowell, who was working for General Hugh Brady on the Canadian shore, and whose activities were well known to Agent Keating.[40]

In the midst of these diplomatic exercises occurred the one documented incident of near violence in the whole chronicle of the Canadian migrations. For many months a large group of Potawatomi had been dallying on the American shore, avoiding General Brady's troops, who did not seem to be searching too ardently, for their prey had wigwams and cornfields comfortably established a few miles north of Fort Gratiot. Finished with gathering in their crops, on October 21 these Potawatomi made their move across the border. After them came a detachment of Major Gardiner's troopers, hallooing and firing their carbines into the air. They succeeded in capturing a few laggard Potawatomi pack-ponies, a loss which annoyed the warriors, who went through the motions of planning an assault to recapture them. Rather than developing into an international incident, fortunately, this contest was resolved by a further exchange of letters between Major Gardiner and Agent Keating, who denied that there were more than a few families of Potawatomi on the Canadian shore, a number substantially less than the two thousand plus he had reported to his own superiors on September 17.[41]

This group of Potawatomi were the remains of a larger number who had been with Manitogabowit—Standing Spirit and Okamanse—Young Leader, north of Fort Gratiot. But these two had preceded by some months the party chased by Major Gardiner's troopers. The whole company had been very tentative about selecting where finally to settle. Young Leader, probably with others in the group, had been to Kansas and had returned in 1838 with negative reports of conditions there. Both he and Standing Spirit had visited Sarnia several times in 1839. Finally, Chief Superintendent Jarvis demanded that they make up their minds, and so between January 7 and April 29, some 267 of their party came over to the Canadian shore. By summer they were temporarily settled in the Thames River valley, their pony herds pastured in the fields of the Canadian farmers there, hungrily devouring their host's "pease, potatoes, and apples."[42]

Between 1841 and 1845 more Potawatomi continued to straggle into Upper Canada in small parties and as individuals. They came from several parts of the old tribal estate, and little specific accounting was made of who they were or where they were bound. Looking back, it is clear that the first major wave of migration from Wisconsin and Illinois coincided with the aftermath of the Treaty of Chicago and the major removals of the United Bands west to Iowa Territory, while the second wave was partially in response to the concerted effort to clear Michigan and Indiana of Potawatomi that began in 1837, but which was not over in 1842. Because the administrative structure of the British Indian Service was small and uncoordinated, and inasmuch as the Potawatomi scattered in all directions once in Upper Canada, settling for the most part only temporarily in different administrative districts, no comprehensive, central accounting was ever made of their numbers, movements, or whereabouts. Unlike other tribes moving into Canada in the same period, the Potawatomi were not considered "Treaty Indians." That is, they were not entitled to annual annuities for earlier land cessions, and consequently this possibility of a clear, comprehensive accounting is unavailable.

Adding together the streams of migrants that were carefully counted along the northern route and the total provided by Agent Keating in 1840, the total is about thirty-five hundred emigrants. But this number is probably excessive as an estimate of those who came and actually stayed on, for many returned to the United States after a few seasons. The most reliable estimate of the total Potawatomi emigration into Canada comes, not from British sources, but from a 1907 attempt by the American Bureau of Indian Affairs to carefully enumerate American Potawatomi long resident in Ontario. That year Agent W. M. Wooster traveled up and down the Lake Huron shore with an interpreter from Wisconsin, carefully counting noses. He found, from Wisconsin alone, 1,423 Potawatomi then living in Canada, and he estimated there were at least one thousand more from other states present. Thus a respectable estimate of the total number of Potawatomi migrating into Canada after 1833 and staying there is some twenty-five hundred.[43]

Counting the number of Potawatomi who moved into Canada is one matter, accounting for which special elements of the tribe moved east into British territory and why is another. First, we must recall that the Potawatomi were a society well experienced with migration and that they had employed this strategy as a means of adapting to changed circumstances from the very earliest times. Second, for many who moved into Canada it was not an all-or-none affair which required a grave decision. Instead, it was an extension of a pattern of regular annual visits to Amherstburg and other points to renew an old alliance and to receive their share of the yearly presents. Beyond these background, conditioning factors lie a variety of specific attractions. Of these, an important consideration is the fact that the British believed they were obligated to offer the Potawatomi asylum, and the more pressing consideration is that there just might be some need of the services of this tribe's warriors in a future war with the United States. This was, in the first place, the major motive for the annual presents—to keep the Potawatomi on the string as potential allies. As Sir James Kempt reported in 1829, in justifying why 9,422 Indians had been given presents at Drummond Island and Amherstburg, "There is little doubt, that by a continuance of kindness, they will be disposed again to take up the Tomahawk, when required by King George."[44]

The Potawatomi who were attracted by such prospects, and those who migrated into Upper Canada, understood this relationship and its implications perfectly well. All who arrived immediately declared their loyalty and fidelity and recounted past services and exploits. None was more eloquent than old Standing Spirit in June 1839. Pulling open his clothes to display seventeen wounds (his count; his brother, Young Leader, similarly displayed, or complained of, fifteen), Standing Spirit intoned his loyal commitment to the king: "aged and infirm tho' I seem, it is not the snow of many winters which blanched my head or bent my frame, neither have the fiery waters which have been brought among us impaired my energies—see my scarred head and wounded body and in them trace the cause of my premature decay . . . should you want us again . . . shall we echo back the reply that we are ready and tho' broken down by age and disabled by wounds, my tribe shall not march to war without its Chief."[45] Understandably, the regular expression of such sentiments cleared some modest anxiety in American minds, and protests concerning the movements back-and-forth of the "Western Indians" were regularly dispatched to Toronto and London.

The flow of American complaints coincided with changes in British Indian policy, alterations better fitted to improvements in relationships between the United States and Great Britain and ones more appropriate to the imperative needs of an emergent Canadian nationality. While the prospects of employing Indians in war against the United States declined and the costs of buying their loyalties rose annually, Upper Canada was rapidly developing, its population increasing, and new agricultural settlements springing up monthly. The pace of development was slower and it lagged behind that of American territory south of Lake Erie, but the results were the same. Before 1836 the British Indian Service defined two categories of Indians in Upper Canada, "Resident Indians" and "Visiting Indians." Until that time all Potawatomi had been counted in the latter category—there were no permanent Potawatomi settlements in the province until 1833. After 1836 a third category was defined, "Wandering Indians." For decades nearly all Potawatomi, except those who settled on Walpole Island, were enumerated in this new class, if they could be found and counted at all.

Changes in British Indian policy and practice followed nearly exactly those of the United States, differing only in detail. In 1830 Thomas G. Anderson began an experiment in civilizing Indians at Coldwater, on the narrows of Lake Simcoe. This was followed in 1836 with a decision to start a removal and concentration program: all the Indians in the province were to be resettled in a very few locations, mostly on Manitoulin Island, where they would be converted into Christian, farming citizens. Manitoulin Island was, in British thinking, the "Great American Desert" of Upper Canada, unsuitable for Euro-American agriculturists but fine for Indians.

Thus in 1834, when Thomas G. Anderson anticipated the arrival of many Potawatomi who would be placed in his care, he set down what he had planned for them. If they emigrate, he wrote, "we will send them proper teachers from our Church." In 1835, he planned in more detail what he had in mind for the emigrants:

> If concentrated and civilized the Indian Nations would be useful and loyal subjects during Peace, and in the event of War might become an important support for the Government. Our Indian allies emigrating from the United States and seeking our protection as well as the British Indian whose means of subsistence are exhausted, have claims upon our humanity, which would be most easily satisfied by forming one extensive establishment for the purpose of leading them to the arts of civilized life.

In 1836 Sir Francis Bond Head, lieutenant governor of Upper Canada, established Manitoulin Island as the major reservation to which the Indians would be removed. A year later, at the annual distribution of presents on that island, he issued a proclamation which provided a further stimulus to Potawatomi migration eastward. After three years, he announced, Visiting Indians would no longer be provided presents. They were required to make a choice. Remain in the United States with no further support from Great Britain, or emigrate.[46]

The prospects of settling at Manitoulin Island did not delight many Potawatomi, for they saw it as a cold, bleak, isolated place, and much preferred the warmer climate of the Ontario Peninsula. In 1836 Shayte—The Pelican and Shawon—Rain, two Potawatomi wokamek then living on the Maumee River in Indiana but originally from northern Illinois, had to explain to Sir Francis Bond Head that they were not exactly the kind of Indians he thought they were. "We have long since abandoned the idea," they said, "of ever visiting in our frail wooden canoes beyond the rivers and bays in our neighborhood. Crossing the Great Lake would cause us great hardship and danger." Even to cross the St. Clair River the Potawatomi regularly employed ferrymen to transport themselves and their pony herds.[47]

The Potawatomi migrating from the United States to Upper Canada came as intact extended family and lineage groups, and these traditional social units were the basis for their resettlement in Upper Canada. Those originally from Sheboygan and the Door Peninsula in Wisconsin settled first at Cape Croker, those from Two Rivers and Manitowoc at Sheshewoning on Manitoulin Island, those from Kewaunee at Wikwemikong and Parry Sound, those from Racine, Kenosha, Waukesha, and Waukegan on Christian Island, and others from Chicago and Milwaukee at Stony Point and Walpole Island. The census information taken by British agents on or soon after their arrival indicates that these were well-balanced populations, with a good distribution of children, adults, and the elderly, males and females. Generally, females outnumbered males by 20 to 25 percent, and about that fraction of marriages were polygamous. Those coming from Wisconsin and northern Illinois, who were 60 percent of the whole emigrant population, were largely members of four clans from three phratries, the Thunder and Eagle clans of the Thunderbird Phratry, and the Fish and Great Sea clans of the Water Phratry. Only a minority of males represented a few other clans, such as Rabbit, Bear, Turtle, and Warrior. In brief, the Potawatomi moving into Canada came as functioning, whole village communities organized around traditional lineages. The structural basis for the migration was precisely that which had conditioned patterns of Potawatomi migration after 1680.[48]

French and other European names on lists of Potawatomi migrants are exceedingly rare and are generally given- rather than surnames. When they occur, they are Potawatomized, e.g., "Mani" for the English "Mary." All British observers were fully agreed that there were practically no "half-breeds" among the Potawatomi migrants. They had left their Métis behind them in the United States, as they had their missionaries, traders, and other specialists in the Indian business. The most frequent adjectives used by the British to describe them were "pagan," "heathen," "wandering," "hunting," and "drunken." When the old soldier Major John Richardson witnessed the distribution of annuities at Sarnia and Walpole Island in 1848, he thought the Potawatomi much finer specimens of Indiankind than their "deteriorating countrymen," the long-resident, now heavily missionized Odawa and Ojibwa. The Potawatomi still appeared in their war paint with their weapons, calumets, and other traditional paraphernalia and clothing. They continued to live in bark and mat wigwams, unlike the log and frame cabins used by Canadian Indians nearby.[49]

These Potawatomi also carried with them the Midewiwin, which had been unknown in this part of Canada until their arrival, and other traditional religious practitioners, who disturbed the missionaries and frightened the missionized Canadian Indians. On the whole, the Potawatomi disappointed the expectations of their British hosts. Official reactions to their presence after several years were generally negative. They were, an official report commented, "wild, turbulent, mendicant, and dishonest." Kindly received by the British and resident tribes, they were but skillful hunters, "rovers averse to settling." Indeed, commenting on the whole character of the migration, one agent noted that "they sought refuge as from an enemy not that they came willingly as settlers." Worst of all, "their wandering life . . . is not only prejudicial to themselves but sets a bad example to the rising generation in whose minds it is desirable to inculcate habits of steadiness and industry."[50]

Quite clearly, in contrast to the Potawatomi who remained in southern Michigan and those who settled on the Osage River Reservation in Kansas, but more like the United Bands of Iowa, the Potawatomi who moved into Upper Canada were a culturally conservative segment of the total population bent upon maintenance of their way of life in the new social and physical environment. Regardless of the plans designed for them by British Indian agents, they saw an opportunity for greater autonomy, a chance to resist forced reeducation programs and the influence of missionaries and traders. Relative to the experience of their kinsmen who remained in the United States, particularly the Mission Bands, their forecast was justified by their later experiences.

Those Potawatomi who migrated into Canada suffered from one disability. They were not, under British law, considered "Treaty Indians" and consequently were not entitled to compensation for any land or annuities. The one exception to this generalization, which gave some Potawatomi the legal right to settle on specific parcels of land, involved a reserve established in 1790, part of which was known as the Lower St. Clair Reserve, and a lesser, included portion thereof known as the Huron Tract. It was an area some ten miles square on the St. Clair River just north of the Chenail Écarte. Similarly, the emigrant Potawatomi had a right to settle on the reserve at Walpole Island.

These two reservations had been ceded to the crown in 1790 and were specifically set aside as future homes for Potawatomi, Odawa, Ojibwa, and Huron Indians living on the American side of the border. After Jay's Treaty in 1796, which required that the British abandon their posts on American soil, it was to these reservations that emigrant Indians were directed.

However, as an old settler, Thomas Smith, explained to Sir John Colborne in 1829, the Potawatomi were involved in the 1790 cession as a matter of British Indian policy, not as a consequence of their occupation or ownership of the lands. It was the policy in 1790, as Smith explained, "to unite the interests of the four tribes to consider their lands in common, and a common cause in defending them." It was on the basis of this transaction that the Detroit-area Potawatomi acquired the first recorded attorney ever hired to serve the interests of the tribe and pioneered the use of litigation as an adaptive strategy, a fund-raising device in near constant use ever since. But from the perspective of the officials of the Indian Department giving the Potawatomi permission to enter and reside in Canada, this was an act of grace, not of law, a matter of hospitality, not right. The net result of this was to provide the Potawatomi in Canada an ambiguous status, and to make them poorer than other Indians living in Canada. Not being entitled to lands or annuities by law, they had to seek out other means of adjusting themselves to life in their new habitat. They were, Thomas Smith wrote, being offered only "a place of refuge for Indians for all time."[51]

The situation of those Potawatomi who remained in Wisconsin and Michigan throughout and after the removal period was quite varied. The whole area was characterized by a large number of small-scale migrations, both within the two states and between them, Canada, and the western reservations. There was, for example, a modest back-migration from Canada into both Michigan and Wisconsin which continued well into the early 1900s. Similarly, there were substantial back-migrations of Potawatomi from Iowa and Kansas, but these parties lodged exclusively in western and northern Wisconsin, among the Winnebago, Menomini, and Ojibwa. In the Lower Peninsula of Michigan two distinct communities eventually formed, one known as the Pokagon band, settled in Cass County near the Indiana line on land that was originally Pokagon's private reservation. The other, consisting largely of elements from near Detroit, eventually settled on a parcel of land set aside for them by the state in Calhoun County. These Lower Michigan communities consisted of highly acculturated, Christianized products of early mission schools, most of whom became recognized as United States citizens in the late nineteenth century.[52]

In Wisconsin the picture is more complicated and indistinct. Basically, the Potawatomi presently found in the state represent the descendants of those

Plate 4. Coe-Coosh, The Hog, was one of the many Potawatomi who remained in Wisconsin after the removal period. The Canadian artist Paul Kane, who painted this portrait in 1845, reported that Kokosh was a "regular black-leg," who fleeced the Menomini of their annuity money. (Courtesy of the Royal Ontario Museum.)

who never left the area, plus some who did and returned to their communities along the Lake Michigan shoreline. By 1872 they were, however, widely scattered, from Sauk, Wisconsin, to Duluth, Minnesota, and were said to number some two hundred families.[53] This dispersal was the consequence of the march of American settlements north along the Lake Michigan shoreline and through the center of the state after statehood was granted in 1848. The basic social and residential unit throughout much of the second half of the nineteenth century seems to have been nuclear families or fragments of extended families, which lived widely separated in the north woods. During these years they were known as the "Strolling Potawatomi." Not until 1913 did these tribesmen come together and form distinct, sedentary communities. In that year they were granted homestead lands, jointly constituting a reservation, at Hannahville (north of present Menominee) in the Upper Peninsula of Michigan, and at Wabeno and Stone Lake, Wisconsin; together they were known as the Forest County Potawatomi. The second major group of Potawatomi in this state consisted of an infusion from the west in the 1870s. These settled on lands in the west-central part of Wisconsin, near Wisconsin Rapids, where they became known as the Skunk Hill Band. Out of this composite Wisconsin Potawatomi population in the 1880s developed a new religion, the Dream Dance or Drum Cult, some of whose adherents eventually settled around Zoar, on the Menomini Reservation (see Figure 15). Overall, the picture of those Potawatomi who returned to or else remained in Wisconsin is that of a fragmented group of refugees, trying to hold onto a distinctly Indian style of life under extremely adverse circumstances. In this respect they have been successful, for they remain for the most part as culturally conservative as their kinsmen in Kansas.[54]

GEOGRAPHIC DISPERSION
AND CULTURAL DIVERGENCE

The dislocations and stresses of the removal era left the fragments of the Potawatomi tribal society widely separated from one another, located in several political jurisdictions. The scattered parts of the tribe varied considerably in size, ecological situation, and disposition. In consequence, each began moving in quite different cultural directions, working out variant and disparate kinds of adaptations.

In southern Michigan the small groups known as the Pokagon and Huron Potawatomi experienced the greatest amount of acculturation and assimilation. Whereas the Pokagons were strongly Catholic, the Huron Potawatomi became Methodists, while both groups became completely accommodated to the American wage-work pattern, finding their employment and subsistence in farm-labor or in service and industrial employment. The flavor of their adaptation can best be captured, perhaps, with an account of the career of Simon Pokagon. Born in 1830, he died in 1899, having achieved considerable regional and national notoriety. Indeed, he had become a very considerable celebrity in an age when Indians, believed to be disappearing as a culturally distinctive population, once more started to come back into popular consciousness, but only if they were "good Indians." Simon Pokagon was considered to be an ideal product of American Indian policy, the last of the proper chiefs, a devout Catholic, the "Indian Longfellow," and the "best educated full-blooded Indian of his time," having attended Notre Dame and Oberlin College for several years. Very popular on the Chautauqua circuit, his name was attached to a number of harmless essays on Indian affairs published in national periodicals, including *Harper's Weekly*. But he was best known for what was supposed to be a semifictionalized, partial autobiography, *Ogimakwe Mitigwaki, or Queen of the Woods*.

This work bore no relationship to traditional Potawatomi literary style, form, or content. Instead, it was a cloying, romantic fable in the tradition of James Fenimore Cooper, with a plot and theme designed, not to excite the minds of schoolboys, but to rend the hearts of virgins and spinsters. Actually, Pokagon seems to have been little more than literate, with his creative writings being the result of a collaboration with the imaginative, middle-class wife of a local attorney. It was a curious *ménage à trois*. While the wife ghosted Pokagon's essays, poems, and novels, the husband, working on a contingency basis, prosecuted his claims against the United States government. Proper celebrity that he was, in the matter of claims cases Pokagon had a certain inimitable and successful style about him, which he bequeathed to his son Charles, who succeeded him as the recognized "chief." In 1901 Charles Pokagon, working on the famous, long-standing Sand Bar Claim, booked passage from St. Joseph, Michigan, to Chicago for himself, two hundred adults, one hundred children, forty ponies, and one thousand pounds of baggage per family. He was supposedly taking his people to Chicago to settle in Grant Park on a strip of land which allegedly had not been properly ceded in the 1833 treaty. This Sand Bar Claim had been initiated well before the Civil War, and for a short while it was serviced by a struggling young attorney named Abraham Lincoln.[55] To such heights by 1900 had the descendants of Catfish, Mad Sturgeon, and Puckered Hand risen.

Until 1913 those Potawatomi who remained in northern Wisconsin and the Upper Peninsula of Michigan had the legal status of propertyless squatters. Living scattered in small family groups over a large extent of country, they became an embittered, sullen population, thinking of themselves as refugees deprived of their just portion of the proceeds of the Treaty of Chicago. After 1837 they did not share in annuity payments from this treaty, which were distributed only on the western reservations, while the Bureau of Indian Affairs only rarely provided them any basic services. But in the 1890s two missionaries developed an interest in their condition and devoted the next decade to obtaining recognition, legal aid, and relief for these Potawatomi. One missionary, the Reverend Erik Morstad of the Evangelical Lutheran Church, worked with the Wisconsin group; the second was the Reverend Peter Marksman, of the Methodist Church, who serviced those in the Upper Peninsula. Eventually, the Washington law firm of Kappler and Merillat saw the case through Congress, securing in 1913 for the Wisconsin–Upper Michigan Potawatomi an award of $447,339 in past-due annuities. From these funds were purchased the small reservations in Menominee County, Michigan, and in Forest County, Wisconsin, where the Potawatomi soon resettled. Through the years the Wisconsin–Upper Michigan Potawatomi maintained some contacts with their kinsmen in both Kansas and Ontario. A small number of Canadian Potawatomi after 1900 returned to settle again in Wisconsin and Michigan, but the contacts with Kansas were of a more traditional nature. These often consisted of the exchange of ritual specialists, who regularly visited back and forth, for the Wisconsin Potawatomi remained a less acculturated and more traditional group than those in Canada and Lower Michigan.[56]

If the Potawatomi of Wisconsin and Upper Michigan had been deprived of their rights under earlier treaties, those who emigrated into Upper Canada had none at all, except for the privilege of taking refuge at one of the reserves set aside for the use of emigrating American Indians. In British legal usage, this privilege involved "an Act of Grace, not of law" (Clifton 1975b: 93–98). When plans were first laid in 1834 for their arrival, Thomas Anderson and other officials anticipated that they would soon be converted into useful, loyal citizens of the province. Indeed, the great majority of the migrating Potawatomi did become assimilated, but not according to a Euro-Canadian model. Instead, they settled in with and intermarried among those Odawa and Ojibwa communities that did have treaty rights and reserves of their own. Gradually, beginning in the 1860s, these Canadian Indian communities started to admit the resident Potawatomi as recognized members of their communities, entitled to share fully in whatever resources were available to the reserves' populations. This step was not everywhere taken willingly or easily. At the Sarnia and Kettle Point reserves, for example, there was considerable strain, for the dominant Ojibwa there considered the Potawatomi second-class citizens. Eventually, many Potawatomi at these reserves packed their belongings and returned to the United States. At Walpole Island—where the largest single group of Potawatomi lodged—on the other hand, well into the twentieth century the Ojibwa-Odawa and the Potawatomi lived on separate parts of the island, maintaining their own separate band structure, councils, and meeting places. Eventually, these were merged, as they were at all other locations where the Potawatomi settled.

While the Potawatomi in Upper Canada evaded the impact of American policy, those who were guided toward the Osage River in Kansas experienced its full weight. Located adjacent to American settlements in western Missouri, the reservation was easily accessible to horse-traders, bootleggers, gamblers, and others with a passing or seasonal interest in the Indian business. Such types usually arrived in force at the time of annuity payments, hoping to separate the Potawatomi from their silver coin. On the reservation proper were a number of full-time specialists—the missionaries, Indian agents, traders, teachers, physicians—permanent residents with a professional stake in maintaining control over one or another of the developing factions among the Potawatomi there. Overall—compared with the Potawatomi who remained in Wisconsin, those in Canada, and especially those in western Iowa—the Osage River population experienced the most varied, intensive, and damaging contact with the many agents bent on Americanizing them. They were made the more vulnerable by the presence of a great many Métis whose status as "Indians" was already partly dependent on maintaining the good will of Indian agents and missionaries. Such collaborationists helped to undermine what little political autonomy and cultural integrity remained among the several traditional groups who settled on this reservation.

In the spring of 1837 Anthony L. Davis, then agent on the Kickapoo Reservation, together with the Reverend Isaac McCoy and his associate Robert Simmerwell, inspected the Osage River lands and selected a location for a settlement along Potawatomi Creek. McCoy, however, was in a rush and did not complete his official survey of the reservation until the following year. With his 164 Potawatomi from the St. Joseph River area, Topnebi arrived about November 1 and established a camp at the site selected by Davis and McCoy, near present Lane, Kansas. By that time Robert Simmerwell and family had arrived to develop the Baptist Mission station among these emigrants. So far as McCoy and his associates were concerned, their mission was to have exclusive rights to all Potawatomi; but they consulted neither the Catholics nor the Methodists, and certainly not the Potawatomi, about this ambition, which was quickly thwarted.

In January 1838 the Reverend Christian Hoecken, from the well-established Kickapoo Catholic Mission, came to explore the ground and to service those Potawatomi and Métis from Indiana who had come in after Topnebi's group. Hoecken continued to visit the Osage Reservation until October 1838, when he established a temporary station near the Protestant center of operations. The following March he moved his establishment and the nominally Catholic Potawatomi and Métis away from the Protestant settlement to a new location fifteen miles distant on Big Sugar Creek, near modern Centerville. Meanwhile, in the fall of 1838 a second Protestant denomination entered the picture. At that time, in the face of considerable opposition from both Baptists and Jesuits, the Methodist Episcopal Mission Society opened a station on

Potawatomi Creek, close to present Miami, Kansas. Thereafter, until the Osage River reservation was again ceded in 1847, life was characterized by a near constant interdenominational struggle, with Baptist missionary pitted against Jesuit, Catholic Potawatomi and Métis against Protestant. There was more at stake than simply the spiritual loyalties and souls of the Indians. Since all denominations were dependent on income derived from jobs and categorical funds awarded in earlier Potawatomi treaties, the infighting raged over the hiring of a physician, a blacksmith, or a teacher, the award of contracts for construction of schools and mills, and the disposition of educational funds set aside—supposedly for the benefit of the Potawatomi—in treaties drawn before 1838.[57]

Along with the missionaries came the traders, also representing several different competing firms, but in larger numbers than their spiritual compatriots. By the early 1840s Pierre Chouteau, Jr., had eleven men employed at three locations on the reservation, the Boone and Hamilton firm six men at Sugar Creek, and Cornelius Davey three men at Sugar Creek and Potawatomi Creek, while the old Indiana firm of Ewing and Clymer was in full operation in the Protestant community. Generally, these trading outfits represented a link between the national political scene and the reservation community, as well as with the missionary groups. One early trader, for example, was Robert Polke, Isaac McCoy's brother-in-law. Similarly, Senator John Tipton of Indiana continued to serve as patron for the Ewings, who had transferred much of their operations to the west. These traders habitually conducted business on a credit basis, knowing that the controls they exercised over domesticated "chiefs" guaranteed them payment when annuity funds were delivered annually. However, they also continued to serve the Office of Indian Affairs, bidding on contracts and offering their services, together with those of the missionaries, so as to promote what was allegedly in the national interest as regards Indian problems. It was traders such as Alexis Coquillard and missionaries like Isaac McCoy, for instance, who worked hard at persuading the Council Bluffs Potawatomi to cede their Iowa lands and move to Kansas.[58]

The Potawatomi and Métis population on the Osage River Reserve rose steadily after 1837 but never for long exceeded 2,000 persons. In 1838 about 1,000 were reported, in 1839 some 1,650, and the population peaked in 1840 when, for a time, some 2,439 were counted on the reservation, but this figure included the largely unwilling emigrants under Black Wolf and Pamtipi, most of whom apparently did not long remain. In 1842 Agent Davis reported that there were 1,949 Potawatomi on the Osage Reservation. These included 625 persons identified as from the old Wabash River villages, and some 1,324 from the St. Joseph and the Kankakee and Iroquois rivers. In keeping with McCoy's efforts to claim legitimate control over all elements of the tribe, the several hundred

Potawatomi from the Kankakee and Iroquois rivers were identified as representatives of the Prairie Band. This was, however, a convenient fiction, since the vast majority of the Illinois Potawatomi were at Council Bluffs, together with those from southern Wisconsin. The 1,324 figure Davis reported included some 270 individuals who had moved south from the Council Bluffs Reservation, mainly Métis who had been made extremely unwelcome there.

Although Davis generally reported the Potawatomi to be among the most drunken and dissolute of all the Indians in his jurisdiction, he saw important differences between those in the Protestant community at Potawatomi Creek and those on Sugar Creek. The latter, served by the considerably larger and better disciplined team of Catholic missionaries, were under firmer control, subject to more extensive and more consistent missionary teaching and influence, and—in substantial part—were more compliant. Here were the Potemkin villages of the Osage River Reservation, the evidence, however spurious, of success of both agent and missionary in moving the Potawatomi along the path to civilization. More people there lived in log-cabins, broke and cultivated the prairie, constructed rail fences, and remained sober and industrious. In 1841, 812 Catholic Potawatomi were reported and in 1842, 940. Exactly how many of these were actually Potawatomi in origin and by socialization is impossible to say; clearly, the majority were Métis. Here we have one of those anomalies of Indian-European culture contact, so-called. Situations of forced acculturation are generally thought to involve white, Anglo-Saxon Protestants forcing their ways on unwilling, traditional, native-born Indians. In the instance of the Sugar Creek Catholic mission, in contrast, we find French-speaking Belgian and French Jesuits being most successful among old-resident, French-speaking Métis. One of the rules of thinking about acculturation situations is to understand that like seeks out like. The Jesuits had their earliest and greatest successes among those "Indians" who already most resembled them.[59]

Whatever their national origins—French, Scots-Irish, Anglo-Saxon, or American frontiersmen—the Métis of both the Protestant community at Potawatomi Creek and the Catholic community on Sugar Creek were not only admitted and recognized as Potawatomi, fully entitled to share in whatever resources were available to the tribesmen there, but they quickly emerged as a powerful and relatively affluent elite. By 1839 some of the more influential among them were already signing themselves as "chiefs" on petitions, receipts, and other official documents, and their influence among both Americans and Potawatomi steadily increased. They were, on the whole, more prone to take what opportunities came available to them than were the traditional Potawatomi. While nearly all of the latter, for example, resisting having their children sent east to the Choctaw Indian Academy, the Métis were more willing to use this as an opportunity to obtain a free education for their sons.

But the former nationality of the Métis on the Osage River Reservation was no permanent and reliable index to cultural style, economic adaptation, or religious affiliation. Until 1844, for instance, Abraham Burnett was a staunch Baptist and a virulent anti-Catholic, a power in the Potawatomi Creek community and congregation. But as the influence of the Baptist missionaries declined, he changed his affiliations, becoming a Catholic in 1845, marrying a German emigrant woman, and going on to greater peaks of power. On the other hand, Mackinaw Beauchemie, former Catholic trader, by 1843 had become a Methodist minister. One of the more interesting cases is that of Anthony Navarre. The son of Pierre Navarre, a French trader in South Bend, Indiana, as a boy he was sent to school at the Choctaw Academy, his expenses paid from the Potawatomi education fund. Finishing his education, in 1848 he returned briefly to the Council Bluffs area just in time to have his attention captured by the westward stream of Mormons heading for Utah. Joining one of their parties, he was long absent from Potawatomi affairs, until the mid-1850s when he returned as a full-fledged Mormon missionary. This was a religious endeavor he soon abandoned to return to free-enterprise trade, at which work he flourished, soon emerging as one of the wealthiest and most powerful men on the Potawatomi National Reservation in the 1860s.[60]

Life on the Osage River Reservation continued as a round of denominational, economic, and cultural conflicts until late 1847. Increasingly, the more traditional Potawatomi there were out-maneuvered by coalitions of traders, missionaries, Métis, and Americanized Indians; they were politically weakened, economically deprived, and culturally threatened. Their traditional ways were denigrated and their lives demoralized. Then in the fall of 1847 the occupation of the Osage Reservation came to an end, for the treaty signed that year required them to move north and west to the banks of the Kansas River. On October 1 the last annuity payment was held on the Osage, a day which combined elements of carnival with an atmosphere of county fair and an undercurrent of tragedy. The annuity payment had become a great market day, with $60,000 and more in Potawatomi silver flowing into the hands of an army of tradesmen, pack peddlers, counterfeiters, gamblers, and horse-swappers. It was the last such Potawatomi-financed market day on the Osage.[61]

THE IOWA EXPERIENCE—
EMERGENCE OF
THE PRAIRIE PEOPLE

Between the population known as the United Bands of Odawa, Ojibwa, and Potawatomi who settled in western Iowa after 1837 and the group in

Kansas who came to be known as the Prairie Band after 1861, there was a near straight-line development. But the emergence of the culturally conservative Prairie Band during the 1840s should not be confused with the earlier, geographic nomenclature, whether that used by Americans or Potawatomi. The first known use of the Prairie Potawatomi appellation dates to about 1804 and comes from John Kinzie's establishment of branch trading posts among the Potawatomi of the Kankakee and Illinois river valleys. It was a phrasing loosely employed by Kinzie and others to distinguish Potawatomi in one broad area from those in another. After the War of 1812 this distinction was overlaid by a different one, which separated the Potawatomi of Illinois generally from those in Indiana. This distinction, though, followed administrative lines, not differences in the environments occupied by the many local Potawatomi villages. It expressed bureaucratic ties to the Indian agencies in Chicago or Logansport, not the primary vegetal cover in the habitats occupied by the Potawatomi.

By the 1870s this old distinction of Prairie versus Forest Potawatomi, particularly influenced by the writings of John Dean Caton, had solidified into a nearly unshakabe stereotype. According to Caton, who was a crude environmental determinist, not only was there a firm difference between the Forest and Prairie Potawatomi, but the different environments had "stamped upon their tenants distinct characteristics." The Forest Potawatomi, Caton and others after him believed, were much more susceptible to and influenced by "civilization" (Caton 1976: 10–11). It was this popular contrast that Alanson Skinner picked up and applied in 1912 when he began identifying the Kansas Potawatomi as the Mascoutens, supposedly representing the modern descendants of the old Illinois River or Prairie population. Most recently, Joseph Francis Murphy, in searching for the origins of the Citizen Band of 1867, has also employed the standard Forest versus Prairie dichotomy. He has recognized differences in the degree of acculturation between the several groups and added a variety of racial explanation to the existing confusion by attributing to the Prairie Potawatomi an infusion of "primitive blood" which he believed influenced their resistance to forced acculturation.[62]

In truth, the core of the ancestry of the modern Prairie People in Kansas derives from the United Bands of northern Illinois and southern Wisconsin who first settled in the Platte country, then in Iowa. In Iowa the United Bands consisted of at least six clusters of villages, each cluster identified by American agents with the name of its most prominent leader, Billy Caldwell, and Shabeni, Wabansi, Padegoshĕk, Shayte—Pelican, Big Foot, and Little Miami, and occasionally, also Perish Le Clere. Each of these groups settled along a stream valley in a different part of the huge Iowa reservation. Edwin James, their first agent, generally wrote the accepted appellation for the whole group in quotation marks, "United Bands," for the reason that to his practiced eye they did not seem particularly united. They were in fact organized along traditional lines as a segmentary tribe, each part established in its own part of the tribal range, with the political structure consisting of a council of okamek drawn from the constituent villages.

Seen in this fashion the United Bands group was formed out of the forces which divided the old unitary tribal society in the Great Lakes area. They represented one of the large pieces which broke off in consequence of a major factional schism. The migration of the constituent village groups from Missouri, Wisconsin, and Illinois to Iowa, in spite of severe pressures from American officials on them to join forces with their kinsmen on the Osage River Reservation, clearly represented an effort on their part to dissociate themselves from contacts with the more acculturated, intimidated Potawatomi who were resettled there under missionary and governmental auspices. It represented an attempt to gain a greater share of political and economic autonomy, to avoid damaging acculturative pressures, and to sustain a distinctive Potawatomi cultural and social identity. Their leaders spent the next full decade fending off American efforts to remove and to "civilize" them, in restoring tribal morale, and in developing skills that would serve their descendants well in later generations. They were successful partly because the Iowa Reservation constituted, temporarily at least, a more isolated area, both geographically and culturally. Some two hundred miles from the nearest American settlements, government offices, and missionary establishments, they were cut off from contact with the outside world nearly half the year. Indeed, it was rare even for any of their Indian agents to spend more than six months in Council Bluffs. But they also deliberately isolated themselves in social ways, in effect erecting a barrier around their communities, refusing to have anything to do with missionaries or distant schools, and by expelling dissident elements from their ranks—particularly the Métis. The population on the Iowa reservation was nearly exclusively from northern Illinois and southern Wisconsin. However, some from the villages north of Milwaukee joined them, as did a few from Michigan and Indiana. Similarly, there were always at least a few French-speaking, Scots-Irish, and Anglo-Saxon Métis admitted to their communities. The principle of acceptance in this segment of the tribe was neither geographic nor racial origins, but tribal commitment and cultural style.

Hardly had they arrived in Iowa before these Potawatomi came under pressure to return to the Osage Reservation. One of the first duties assigned Edwin James was to persuade them to do this. This goal James refused to press for. Instead, he spent the balance of his short tenure in office strongly advocating the interests of the United Bands, attempting to obtain for them their full share of annuities, goods, and services due under their treaties, and communicating their wishes to his superiors. In December 1837 he informed William Clark in St. Louis that the leaders in Iowa vehemently refused to move again or to further vary the stipulations of the Treaty of Chicago. "They answer all applications by reference to their treaties," he wrote, and "they cannot understand that a subordinate agent can be clothed with the power to set aside the authority of solemn treaties." The leaders had refused also to accept payment of their annuities in goods, rather than in silver, a substitution that remained a sore point for years.

James made it quite clear he personally recognized the Council Bluffs Potawatomi were faced with ultimate eviction, due to the rapid westward advance of agricultural settlements in Iowa, and that the Potawatomi leaders also fully appreciated this hard fact. While they might consider another reservation separate from the one on the Osage, he noted, they simply refused to move to the latter location. There was a question of identitfy involved, James emphasized: "It will I hope be remembered that they are essentially a distinct people from the Potowattomies of Indiana and by far the larger and more reputable part of them wish to remain so."[63]

The much disputed issue of accepting goods-in-kind rather than hard money as annuity payments illustrates how far these Potawatomi had come from the days when they bartered furs and corn for French trade goods, and how resistant they had become to arbitrary changes in their lives. As the old speaker Half Day expressed the sentiments of the group in 1842, "your red children were never fond of change at any time and now we feel our dislike for it increase." In June of that year, following a lengthy council that debated the latest proposal to substitute goods for hard money, Half Day patiently explained why they would accept neither merchandise nor paper money: "Traders bring us goods," he said, "and if they are a little dear we can get just as suits us, and if any of us wants to buy a cow, or a hog, we can get it much more readily with money than with goods, and we want no change, we are satisfied." For many years these Potawatomi had enjoyed the freedom of choice provided by the flexible purchasing power of money, which they had long used to translate their wants into satisfactions by buying such goods and services as they wished. They were unwilling to return to a clumsy barter system, whatever the depressed state of the American economy.[64]

One of the first tasks Edwin James set himself after reporting for duty as the subagent at Council Bluffs was to obtain an accurate accounting of the number of Potawatomi under his care. On 10 August 1837 he reported the results of a long series of interviews he had completed with the leaders of the several villages then established on the reservation. In this fashion he obtained a record of the Potawatomi's own perceptions of who deserved to be enumerated as a Potawatomi and who not. The results tallied 1,482 persons in some 236 household groups, or about 6.5 persons per family. Aside from Billy Caldwell's family, among these 236 households there was just one headed by a person with a Euro-American surname—François Bourboinne. Perish Le Clere was listed, not as a Potawatomi, but as the official United States interpreter. Unsatisfied with these results, James completed another count that winter, to include Big Foot's and Little Miami's groups who had come in later in the year. Although several hundred had already moved south, he estimated there were then a total of 2,500 Potawatomi on the Iowa reservation. Thereafter the population remained relatively stable. On 6 February 1844 Richard Smith Elliott, then subagent, reported some 2,028 at Council Bluffs, indicating that "this is but an approx. to the real number." In December 1846, six months after they signed the treaty ceding the Iowa Reservation, D. D. Mitchell (superintendent of Indian Affairs at St. Louis) provided an official estimate of 2,243 Potawatomi in Iowa, noting that this number was likely short. He could not obtain the exact number, since the Potawatomi had taken "up the idea that the government wished to tax their property and they utterly refuse to give me information necessary to base a satisfactory report upon."[65]

Superintendent Mitchell had made the Potawatomi suspicious by conducting a census of their livestock and major items of property, preparatory to their migration the following year to the new reservation in Kansas. However, the main reason why the agents had difficulties in enumerating the Iowa Potawatomi is that they were scattered over hundreds of miles of territory. At least six clusters of villages can be identified with some certainty, all of them being inhabited throughout the decade spent in Iowa. Until his death in 1841 Billy Caldwell was established in a village at Point aux Poules, also known as Trader's Point, some ten miles south of the center of present Council Bluffs. This was the administrative center of the reservation, and here the agents generally settled, the short-lived Jesuit school was located, the dragoons camped, and the traders did most of their business. Later this modest settlement was relocated to Indian Creek, in present Council Bluffs. Wabansi's people established their villages thirty miles to the south, near present Tabor. Shayte's village was near Lacey Grove, while Big Foot's people settled on the upper Nishnabotna River, forty miles eastward, close to present Iranistan. South of Big Foot's villages were those of Little Miami, also on the Nishnabotna, near present Lewis. The Potawatomi mill, contracted for and its construction supervised by Caldwell in the last months of his life, was located on Mosquito Creek, three miles east of Council Bluffs. In Iowa the Potawatomi were duplicating the settlement patterns of the Upper Great Lakes, scattering their permanent summer villages widely so as not to deplete the local game supply, to express the individuality of each, and to avoid too frequent and intense contacts between different parts of the population.[66]

Billy Caldwell, a distinctive figure acting out a unique role on successive frontiers, died of cholera 28 September 1841. Although the early historians of Chicago and Illinois romanticized him, making him into a great Potawatomi chief, while a recent generation of historians have castigated him as a traitor to his race, he is best seen as one of the last of a type thrown up by the special conditions of Indian affairs on a rapidly expanding frontier, the end-point in a series of developments that started with Sir William Johnson's estate in colonial New York. Although some continued to refer to him as a chief, and others as Mr. Caldwell, until his death he personally preferred the title of captain he had earned in British service during the War of 1812. In fact, he thought of himself as an Irish-American, especially proud of the fact that he had been born on St. Patrick's Day. The role he played in his own and his family's interest was that of a kind of frontier squire; he served the Potawatomi long and ably as their business advisor and manager, and they respected, trusted, and admired him highly for his work.

During the last years of Caldwell's life, when the Iowa Potawatomi were repeatedly pressed to sign a new treaty ceding their lands, their wokamek refused to go to Washington to do business without him. When an agent arrived attempting to obtain a treaty on their own ground, the wokamek would listen and refer them to Caldwell, as old Half Day did in 1839 when he told Colonel Stephen Watts Kearney that Caldwell "will give you our answer tomorrow and should he sell this country for fifty cents we will be satisfied. I have done!" On the other hand, American agents in the period 1837–1841 rarely missed an opportunity to put him down. The view of American officialdom toward Caldwell was best expressed by an exasperated subagent, John Dougherty, in 1839:

> This man Caldwell is a cunning, designing, dangerous, speculating, unprincipled drunken spoilt character. I have had my eye on him for the past two years and am forced to the opinion that the Pottawatomies will never prosper until he is put down and no longer considered as a chief among them. The officers of government have given him his present influence over the tribe and it should be taken from him without delay, for I feel confident in my own mind that he is exercising said influence against the American government secretly, though as fervently as he did during the last war. He has I think no indian blood in him, but is a red coat savage at heart of the first order, even educated in the school of the notorious Genl. Proctor at the River Raisin.

Such assessments were mildly slanderous. Captain Caldwell had in fact been stabbed through the throat by a wounded Kentuckian at the River Raisin while attempting to save the man's life.[67]

The Métis, generally, also thought ill of Billy Caldwell. Years later, Joseph

Napoleon Bourassa told Lyman Draper that Caldwell had disgraced his last days by drunkenness, to the degree that the Potawatomi lost faith in him. Bourassa had good reason to remember Caldwell with less than fondness, for it was the latter who encouraged the Iowa Potawatomi to send the French Métis packing.[68] He was very jealous and suspicious of them, with good reason, for the agents regularly made motions to use the Métis to bring the Potawatomi around. But when all is said and done, Billy Caldwell spent most of his adult life among and earned his living serving the United Bands: rightfully, these Potawatomi should have a say in evaluating the man's character and contribution. They did their best to leave behind something of a memorial to him. Within months of his death the wokamek in Iowa were petitioning the commissioner of Indian Affairs to approve a new name for their people. Thereafter they wished to be identified as the "Prairie Indians of Caldwell's Band of the Pottawatomies." Four years later, in another and even more intense round of negotiations, Wabansi, Little Miami, Padegoshĕk, and Half Day, with their junior wokamek supporting them, made it a prime condition of any new treaty that they would thereafter be known officially by the name they had selected earlier. Whatever later historians may say, the Potawatomi of his own time calculated that Caldwell's name carried with it highly respected, supernorml power.[69]

With Caldwell's death the Iowa Potawatomi were at a loss for the special, technical kind of leadership he had provided them. That is, they lacked the services of a man who was literate, knowledgeable of the American political system and process, skilled in basic accounting, and loyal and dedicated to their interests. Thereafter they worked at subverting to their own cause the most likely candidates for his replacement, their Indian agents. This was one of the things they needed and used hard money for. Half Day was quite right in his assessment of the importance of silver—it was indeed hard to barter for the services of a bookkeeper and negotiator with blankets and salt pork.

These Potawatomi probably did not need Caldwell's suspicions of the Métis to convince them they were a danger. They may have remembered Tecumsah's old injunction to send half-breed children back to their French and American fathers; and they certainly witnessed the experience of the Indiana, Michigan, and Osage River Potawatomi in this wise. In any respect, there were many fewer Métis on the Iowa reservation. With a few exceptions those who remained were not accepted as Potawatomi, and their status was generally much lower than that of the many living amidst the Osage River communities. Perish Le Clere was one who remained, and he was generally listed as an interpreter. Claude La Fromboise was another, also a sometime interpreter, but engaged in trade and bootlegging on the side. The situation and tactics of the Métis were well and aptly summarized by old Padegoshĕk in 1842 in a memorial to the president. After cataloging other serious concerns, such as the whiskey traffic, gambling, and the presence of idle Americans in the vicinity, he castigated the Métis, saying, "Many of these half-breeds claim exemption from the operations of your laws—professing to be indians—and at other times claim the protection of them—because they are *whites*. These things they do as it suits their convenience. We wish them placed on the same footing as white men, when they violate your laws. We will give them a home among us so long as they behave themselves—but no longer." Padegoshēk's complaint was an exact précis of what later sociologists would call the dilemma, or the advantage, of the marginal man.[70]

These Métis provided a kind of reserve labor force for the small community around the subagency at Council Bluffs, when employment was available for them. Then they served as the splitters-of-rails for fences, field laborers in preparing agricultural lands, timber fallers, and house builders. When the Jesuits arrived—unwelcomed by the Potawatomi—for a brief stay in 1838, it was among the Métis that they had their only successes. Indeed, Stephen Cooper—Edwin James's replacement that year—thought the Jesuits served as the "only check we have to restrain" the Métis. The Potawatomi generally forbade them to speak in council, although, in a debate over sending Potawatomi children to the Choctaw Academy, on one occasion the wokamek allowed the Catholic Métis to rise to protest sending any children to a Protestant establishment. The wokamek, likely influenced by the prejudices of Billy Caldwell, did favor a few Métis of Scots-Irish or Anglo-Saxon parentage, such as William Holiday. But the Métis as a whole led a poor, marginal, hand-to-mouth existence. They were landless squatters, not entitled to share in annuities, generally unemployed, and hence dangerous to the economically more secure Potawatomi. The local Americans thought ill of them, the Potawatomi less. In the end, some hung on long enough to make the trek to the Kansas River in 1848, where in a more benevolent climate they were able to clarify their ethnic status and improve their economic condition by gaining acceptance as Potawatomi.[71]

During their decade in Iowa the United Bands—or as they preferred to call themselves, the Caldwell Band of Prairie Potawatomi—had other more pressing problems besides that of dissident Métis in their midst. Half Day complained of two of the more serious concerns in 1842 when, in council, he said, "We have the enemy of the Sioux above, and the whiskey below, and can hardly tell which is the worst."[72] Both were perennial and probably seasonal problems, of which whiskey can most briefly be dispatched. The availability of whiskey, in violation of United States trade and intercourse laws, but in satisfaction of Potawatomi wants, indicates that Potawatomi isolation on the Iowa reservation was relative. Traders and other enterprising sorts could pack-in modest quantities overland from the centers of production in Missouri on horse or mule back, or by ox-cart; but the largest quantities seem to have arrived with the first steamboat about June 1, when the spring freshets on the Missouri River had subsided. Little if any drinking liquor apparently was produced in the immediate vicinity of Council Bluffs before 1847 (when the first Mormons arrived to settle temporarily), for the reason that too little corn was grown in the area and there were no stills. Thus the Potawatomi were dependent on an outside supply, and with transportation facilities then available the supply hit seasonal peaks. It happened that whiskey was most abundant at the end of the long winter, when the women had already gotten their corn and squash crops in, before the start of the summer hunt. Thus the drinking of the Caldwell band took on the pattern of a massive spring binge.

With the first steamboat in June, of course, also came (usually) their annuity payments, and thus demand and supply were balanced by availability of the wherewithal. It seems clear that the village leaders took a dim view of excessive, prolonged Potawatomi drinking, and they were in a position to exercise some considerable discipline. Overall, occasional exaggerated reports of visiting missionaries and other dignitaries notwithstanding, these Potawatomi hardly seem to have drunk themselves into states of insensibility year round. The one most often cited, highly poetic report of Potawatomi excesses in this respect was that of Father Pierre Jean De Smet in 1838. However, gentle Christian that he may have been, De Smet was new to the frontier and inexperienced with the alcoholic frolics that were customary among both Americans and Indians in those years. Moreover, he had some reason for unconscious bitterness, likely expressed in an exaggeration of what he witnessed after his arrival at Council Bluffs. He had been led to believe that there were five hundred Catholic Potawatomi in Iowa, all unserved by priests for years and praying for his arrival. Thus, when the steamer nudged up to the landing on 31 May 1838, he was overjoyed to find two thousand Potawatomi dressed in their finest clothing, all carefully painted and decorated, waiting for his arrival.

However, the Potawatomi were not piously awaiting the coming of De Smet or his party of missionaries. They were, instead, hungrily and thirstily waiting for the steamboat and its cargo. Apparently not a single Potawatomi was informed of, and not many more were interested in, the arrival of the priests. Billy Caldwell, himself a good Irish Catholic, finally rescued the party and found accommodations for them, but it was two weeks before they located another communicant. This inauspicious arrival of the Jesuits was followed by three bleak and unsuccessful years of labor with the Caldwell Band. In the fall of 1841 the mission station was abandoned, and this ended further Catholic efforts at schooling and conversion to Christianity among these Potawatomi.

Overall, there seems to have been no overwhelming pattern of excessive, year-round drinking in the Iowa villages. Morale was higher, to begin with, cultural stress lower, community discipline better, and the supply of beverages more limited and seasonal, while the men and women who under other circumstances might have been compelled to drink had other things to occupy their time and attention. More than anything else, the patterns of drinking among the Iowa Potawatomi in this period seem to have resembled those characteristic of trappers during the spring rendezvous. It was a period of culturally controlled license after a long winter and before the hard work of summer.[73]

Edwin James's 1830 forecast of troubles between resettled eastern tribes and those already occupying the plains was, by and large, verified by later events. Even before the United Bands had moved from the Platte country to Council Bluffs, word came in of impending trouble with the Dakota, many of whom were already being displaced from their favored hunting grounds in central Iowa. Soon after their arrival at Council Bluffs, James reported that the local supply of game was insufficient to meet their needs and that the Potawatomi were "cooped in by hostile tribes." The intertribal environment consisted of more than the Dakota tribes, however. West of the Missouri River, more than one hundred miles up the Platte River, were the powerful Kitkehahki tribe of the Pawnee confederacy, themselves embroiled in continuing conflict with the Dakota for control of prime buffalo-hunting ground on the High Plains. On both sides of the Platte near its confluence with the Missouri River were the near-defeated remnants of the Oto and Missouri tribes, and to their north on the west side of the Missouri River were more than a thousand Omaha. But the real, long-range danger lay to the north among the numerous Dakota bands, whose territory stretched from Minnesota into the present Dakotas. Among these the principal adversaries were the Santee (or Eastern Dakota) on the upper Mississippi and lower Minnesota rivers, and the Yankton (or Central Dakota) on the upper Missouri River. These Dakota bands were accustomed to hunting over the country east of the Missouri, and they did not take kindly to the intrusion of more competitors from the Great Lakes.[74]

Upon their arrival in eastern Iowa the first problem facing the emigrants was that of dealing with the parties of Ota, Omaha, and Missouri hunters who regularly ranged over the new United Bands Reservation. This required some delicate diplomacy, for in effect the long-resident tribes, however weakened, constituted a barrier between the Potawatomi and marauding Dakota raiders. The United Bands' response reflected two centuries of experience with intertribal war in the east, for they soon set to work establishing alliances and the rudiments of a defensive confederacy. A disaffected band of two hundred Iowa, for example, were invited to live on the United Bands Reservation, but they proved to be unruly neighbors and unregenerate horse and hog thieves and were soon sent across the river to live with their kinsmen the Oto. For some time, as well, the Potawatomi—unfamiliar with the ground and uncertain of their prowess on the plains—hesitated to cross the Missouri to hunt in the best buffalo country up the Platte River. Instead, they continued to hunt locally for the deer and elk that were none too numerous and also sent parties across the Missouri state line into the Platte country.[75]

Staying within the confines of their own reservation provided no assurance of safety, however, while Potawatomi men—themselves skilled hunters and aggressive warriors—could not long be confined. Shortly after getting settled, a pattern of minor back-and-forth raiding between the Dakota and the Potawatomi began, and soon enough their wokamek and Indian agents were petitioning the superintendent of Indian Affairs at St. Louis, the commissioner of Indian Affairs, the secretary of war, and the president to send them regular army troops to defend the reservation against Dakota raiders. It is difficult to assess exactly how well such petitions expressed an actual sense of threat among the Potawatomi themselves. The problem is that a company of dragoons stationed at Council Bluffs served other purposes than that of defense against the Dakota. Clearly, an important secondary motivation was to use the troopers as a constabulary, enforcing the law and protecting the Potawatomi against unwanted American intruders, particularly the proprietors of "vile spirit houses" and the "reckless indian traders." But thirty or forty dragoons at Council Bluffs also provided a very large increase in population and a substantial boost for the local economy. In addition to these economic incentives, the Reverend Isaac McCoy used the alleged threat of full-scale war between the Dakota and Potawatomi for additional leverage in his continuing effort to get the Council Bluffs Potawatomi moved back into Kansas. Hence, from time to time the traders and Indian agents likely exaggerated the extent of the Dakota threat. In 1843 and 1844, for example, Richard Elliott vacillated, unable to make up his mind as to whether troops were needed or not, and finally reported that a messenger scouting for Dakota had come in to report none could be found, for the "Sioux are as much afraid of the Pottawatomis as the Pottawatomis are of them."[76]

Nonetheless there was a real threat involving the Dakota—from their small glory-seeking, strike-and-run parties aimed at stealing Potawatomi horses and collecting a few scalps, and from vengeance-seeking parties of Potawatomi warriors returning the compliment. After 1837 hardly a year went by without at least one minor assault by such a Dakota group on the Potawatomi and a similar blow in return. On several occasions the Dakota parties penetrated into the heart of the reservation, but generally they hit at hunting groups far west of the Missouri River or in northern Iowa. But Potawatomi casualties in this decade did not exceed twenty dead. It was the old established tribes which reeled from the full weight of major Dakota assaults on their villages. By 1847 the Oto, Missouri, and Omaha were desperate and decimated, while the hard-pressed Pawnee had been driven south of their lands on the upper Platte. In contrast, Potawatomi involvement was minor and marginal. On 7 February 1838, for example, the Santee killed two Potawatomi who were scouting the headwaters of the Des Moines River. Similarly, in early September 1840, four Santee raided near Billy Caldwell's village, killing one Potawatomi, whose scalp they displayed to Father De Smet at Fort Vermillion a few weeks later.[77]

Such raids were enough to convince the secretary of war of a need to station troops at Council Bluffs. Over the protests of Colonel Stephen Watts Kearney, commanding the First Regiment of dragoons, and General Winfield Scott, in April 1842 a company of dragoons was ordered to Iowa to protect the Potawatomi. At that time the First dragoons numbered less than six hundred effectives divided into ten widely scattered companies, and they were the only mounted force available to protect the vast spaces of Indian country. The senior officers of the army much preferred to keep their scanty forces consolidated and to send out large, regular patrols. They were especially concerned about stationing a detached company at Council Bluffs, far from supporting units and its base of supply. But politics overrode strategic and logistical considerations, and in early June Captain John H. K. Burgwin arrived on the United Bands Reservation with his small and badly armed company. They were no more than forty men, many raw recruits, armed with antique horse pistols and sawed-off, smooth-bore musketoons.

Captain Burgwin and his men soon constructed a modest fortification, hardly more than a blockhouse, on Trader's Point. At first named Camp Fenwick, in November this less-than-imposing structure was renamed Fort Croghan. Unfortunately, it was located on low ground so that in the spring the floods made it uninhabitable. This small force stayed on among the Potawatomi only until October 1843, whereupon they returned to Fort Leavenworth. During their months on the Iowa Reservation, the dragoons seem to have been more effective in controlling bootleggers than the Dakota, who were not much in evidence during their stay. With nothing much warlike to occupy them, Captain Burgwin spent much time training his troopers. The Potawatomi, seemingly not very impressed, developed something of an attachment to the dragoons. Soon after they arrived, some Potawatomi warriors and wokamek began coaching the army men in the best techniques of scouting and fighting the Dakota. But the Potawatomi also spent a fair amount of time carefully watching the drills, and, if their later tactics against the Pawnee and Dakota were any indication, apparently learned a great deal. For these dragoons were not proper cavalrymen. Instead, they were mounted infantry, trained to use their horses to approach an objective or their enemy, whereupon they would dismount and fight on foot, forming ranks and firing their weapons in volleys.

The Potawatomi, much impressed by the formal theory of dragoon tactics, could not have been envious of dragoon weaponry. The government had sent these soldiers off, not only in numbers insufficient to patrol and protect the frontier, but armed with the worn-out left-overs of the War of 1812. They carried as their main weapon highly inaccurate, short-range, smooth-bore, flint-lock muskets, cut down to two-thirds the original barrel length, making them dangerous only to an enemy who stood stock still less than eighty paces away. The Potawatomi, spending their silver coins wisely, were already themselves better armed, being supplied with superior hunting weapons, muskets, and—increasingly so—long rifles with far greater accuracy and range. Thus equipped, with superior arms and mounted infantry tactics learned from the dragoons, the Potawatomi a few years later would prove themselves a highly disciplined, formidable enemy, severely punishing far larger parties of plains warriors who struck at them unsuspectingly.[78] By sending the dragoons to Council Bluffs the secretary of war had unwittingly provided the United Bands with an advanced course in tactics. Always willing to learn something they could adapt to their own use, the Potawatomi profited greatly from the experience.

THE TREATY
OF 1846

While the young warriors were attentively watching the dragoons at drill that summer of 1843, their elders had other business to conduct. In June, Wabansi and Half Day, among others, attended a great conference of emigrant tribes at Tahlequah, in present Oklahoma. Prompted by American officials and sponsored by the Cherokee, the conference lasted four weeks. This meeting was an outgrowth of Isaac McCoy's old scheme of developing an all-Indian territory, long since foundered in the United States Congress. But the aims were modest, to develop a loose confederation of eighteen emigrant tribes and through agreements and compacts to reduce friction with those long-resident on the plains. Surrounded by nearly four thousand persons attending the conference, the delegates met and deliberated, producing a weighty compact which, in the end, had little effect. For Wabansi and Half Day this was one more of the many broadening experiences that had enlivened their years and expanded their wisdom. Both spoke frequently and at length, enjoyed the respect paid them by their hosts, and then returned to Council Bluffs to turn their attention to more pressing matters.[79]

These old experienced wokamek knew the United Bands were close to the end of their stay in Iowa. Pressures to cede the Iowa Reservation had never ended, and by 1843 they were mounting rapidly. Iowa's American population was steadily increasing and expanding westward toward the Missouri River. Territorial status had been granted in 1838, and the prospect of statehood loomed on the near horizon. For seven years the leaders of the United Bands, with consummate skill, had stalled, neatly side-stepping all proposals to sell their lands, fending off all maneuvers aimed at undercutting or subverting their positions. And the Potawatomi had not yet identified and secured the loyalties of an appropriately skilled man to replace Billy Caldwell. They had worked carefully with several of the agents who had succeeded Edwin James, but each time they developed a private understanding and an effective relationship the party either departed for greener pastures or was fired by the commissioner of Indian Affairs for dereliction of duty.

At one time or another between 1837 and 1843 almost every American associated with the Potawatomi was called into play in an effort to persuade the United Bands to cede their reservation and move to Kansas. Edwin James lost his job in 1838 because, instead of persuading the United Bands to move, he honestly advocated their wish to remain in the north. In 1838 Agent A. L. Davis from the Osage, Agent John Dougherty from Bellevue, and Senator John Tipton worked jointly at securing a treaty. That year the commissioner of Indian Affairs blocked delivery of equipment and goods needed for the development of farming operations in order to persuade these Potawatomi to cede their lands and move. In 1839 the Reverend Isaac McCoy offered his services, which were accepted a year later. Meanwhile, in 1839 Colonel Stephen Kearney and Captain John Gantt visited and counciled with the Council Bluffs wokamek while on a patrol along the upper Missouri. Instructed to sound out Potawatomi sentiments, they reported that they were utterly opposed to the idea of moving. Billy Caldwell summed up the position of the United Bands for Kearney and Gantt by telling them his people were quite familiar with the environment in Kansas and did not care for it. The leaders did not want the government to go to any unnecessary expense, such as funding an exploration party, he told the dragoons. Kansas was an unhealthy place, he said, and the Potawatomi were "from a cold climate therefore you cannot expect to organize an exploring party at this time or at any future time."

Operating on the theory that the United Bands were Catholic, in 1840 Alexis Coquillard first secured acceptance of the idea of removal and reunion from the Sugar Creek Potawatomi, then took the Catholic Métis leaders Luther Rice and Joseph Napoleon Bourassa to Council Bluffs to work out the details. Coquillard was very badly informed, both about the number of Catholics in Iowa and the acceptability to the United Bands of Métis spokesmen. His party was rebuffed. Then in 1841 Wabansi and a small delegation, not to miss out on all the free travel, came south to Westport, Missouri, there to visit McCoy, talk politely, complete their shopping, and return home. That year Alexis Coquillard joined forces with the Protestants and accompanied Isaac McCoy to Council Bluffs. The commissioner of Indian Affairs had promised them five dollars per day in expenses for negotiating a treaty, to be raised to a per diem of eight dollars if they were successful, which they were not. Coquillard and McCoy then fell to accusing one another and entered into a long, complicated correspondence trying to fix the blame for their failure, while also attempting to recover expenses. The next year William Ewing came on the scene, also attempting unsuccessfully to obtain agreement for a cession. There, briefly, matters lay for a year. When news of Caldwell's death reached D. D. Mitchell, superintendent of Indian Affairs in St. Louis, he was enthusiastic. Now, at last, he exulted, the United Bands could easily be brought to heel. By then Caldwell had become the scapegoat of everyone's frustration. Not a single American official recognized that the wokamek of the United Bands employed Caldwell as only their spokesman-advisor, who had little authority. On the next contact in 1842 the wokamek drew a firm line—not another word about a new treaty until each and all of the stipulations of earlier treaties had been observed to the letter.[80]

In late May 1843 the Iowa Potawatomi found their replacement for Billy Caldwell, one Richard Smith Elliott. But it required another full year for them to sample his skills and test his mettle. By all means of reckoning, Elliott was, as the Potawatomi shortly discovered, consummately representative of all the mid-nineteenth century American virtues Daniel J. Boorstin has described so well (1965). One of the great versatiles, Elliott was a sometime scientific farmer, land speculator, railroad promotor, town booster, canal and levee builder, attorney-at-law, newspaper publisher, government servant, and would-be political boss. Within a year of their first meeting, the Potawatomi had accepted him as their new *éminence blanche*. Working together as a team so as to satisfy their mutual needs—the Iowa Potawatomi to bring off a treaty on terms desirable to themselves, and Elliott to increase his income—by the fall of 1845 they had invented a professional role new on the American scene. Just ahead of P. T. Barnum, these Indians helped create the press agent, in which capacity Elliott served them in Washington.

One of the great transients, Elliott migrated from Pennsylvania to Illinois, to St. Louis, to Washington, to Council Bluffs, to New Orleans, and places in between, always in search of the greatest opportunity. Bankrupt as a newspaper publisher, and a none-too-successful criminal lawyer, in 1842 he sailed off to Washington, there to collect on outstanding political debts from President John Tyler. Offered a clerkship in the capital city for $1,500 per year, he declined the post in favor of the job as subagent at Council Bluffs at the salary of $750. Such a position held greater chances for advancement and wealth, he was advised. His own assessment of the opportunities went right to the heart of the matter. "It looked as if an 'Indian sub-agent' was expected to steal enough in some way to make his pay correspond to his responsibilities," he wrote in his memoirs (1883: 160). Also a magnificent upstart booster, as the Potawatomi soon discovered, Elliott was willing and able to advocate almost any cause if the money was right. The Prairie People, long accustomed to purchasing what they needed, had their boxes of silver secreted away: soon they and Elliott had struck an agreement.

Elliott arrived in St. Louis, en route to his new responsibilities, on 13 May 1843. Paying the minimal requisite compliments to his nominal superior, D. D. Mitchell, he gave more attention to the high dignitaries of the American Fur Company, with whom, soon, he was also to make a private business arrangement. Two weeks later he was in Council Bluffs, making friends with and influencing the Potawatomi there. The first season with his charges was successful. By June 1 he was writing the commissioner of Indian Affairs of his certainty that a treaty could be obtained—if the Office of Indian Affairs were capable of cooperating with him. This treaty, he promised, would make available large amounts of the best agricultural lands that would "yield to the treasury thousands in return for the few hundreds which may be expended to obtain it."[81]

Shortly, he was advising the commissioner that, if the dragoons were moved away, an increase in the threat from the Dakota would encourage the Potawatomi to cede their land. Then he went to work advising the wokamek, who were eyeing his maneuvers with growing interest. He advised Wabansi and Half Day not to join the "league-of-nations" that had been proposed at Tahlequah earlier in the year, and then reported to his superiors no treaty could be obtained until their faith in the government was restored. This would require settling "*old* business before entering on any new," he wrote. The old business, from the Potawatomi viewpoint, consisted of those provisions of the Treaty of Chicago that had not been fulfilled—Padegoshēk and Little Miami wanted to be paid their expenses for transporting their people to the west unescorted. In a petition to the president that accompanied Elliott's letter on August 9, the wokamek indicated they recognized Iowa was soon to become a state. They wanted to visit the president in Washington where they could meet "face-to-face and smoke together." Their new mentor advised his superiors the Indians wanted him to accompany them. Actually, he had business of his own in the east and no desire to spend the winter isolated in Council Bluffs. When permission for the joint journey did not come, Elliott persuaded the Potawatomi to send thirteen of their boys to the Choctaw Academy in Louisville, no mean accomplishment in its own right, but one which provided the subagent the excuse and expenses for a trip to his home. He had little personal regard for the quality of education delivered at the academy. The school was built by the government so as to reward its superintendent, Richard Johnson, he commented in his narrative, adding, "Indian boys may have profited by the institution, but I never heard of any that did so."[82]

After concluding his personal business in Pennsylvania, Elliott returned to St. Louis, where he spent the winter in some comfort. It was 17 March 1884 before he made his way back to Council Bluffs with his family, leaving behind him temporarily his part-time duties as free-lance columnist for the *St. Louis Weekly Reveille*. The summer of 1884 was spent fairly quietly, since the people of Iowa Territory were in dispute over the content of their new constitution, thus briefly delaying statehood. Thomas Harvey, the new superintendent at St. Louis, was appointed treaty commissioner and briefly visited the Potawatomi at Council Bluffs, but with no success. Elliott spent his time with his wife and young children, occasionally working at his duties as subagent. His family departed that September and he spent the winter among the Potawatomi, enjoying the limited social life available, reading, writing, and planning for the immediate future. The main business concerns for the coming summer were the provisions that would be made to pay off those outstanding claims against the Potawatomi held by various trading firms, another matter promising profit soon to engage Elliott's attention.[83]

Eighteen forty-five was Elliott's, and the Potawatomi's, busy year. In spring the subagent had to journey to St. Louis to welcome his family again, then return to Council Bluffs to deal with an invasion of Mormons, who that winter had started using the Potawatomi Reservation both as a trail west and a way station—Kanesville, their winter quarters, was then established near Council Bluffs. But of weightier concern was the perennial question of a treaty for the Potawatomi. Iowa's statehood was pending in the Congress, and it was time to move the Prairie People elsewhere. This time bigger guns were freighted in. President Polk in April dispatched Thomas H. Harvey, T. P. Andrews, and G. C. Matlock as treaty commissioners, instructing them in the strongest terms to carry back a land cession. Bringing with them representatives of the Osage River Potawatomi, the three commissioners arrived at Council Bluffs in late June and spent the entire last week of the month trying to persuade, cajole, and pressure the Iowa *wokamek* into selling their land.[84]

The commissioners were limited by their instructions to an offer of $250,000 and a half-million acres between the Kansas and Neosho rivers in exchange for both the Iowa lands and the Osage River Reservation. Moreover, the treaty was to be drawn with and approved by all elements of the tribe, and it had to be done with dispatch. The Council Bluffs Potawatomi—well understanding otherwise—could pretend they had all the time in the world.

These wokamek refused to listen or pay attention to those of their more domesticated cousins present from the Osage River. And their conference strategy was impeccable. The elders would sit up all night rehearsing their speeches, plotting their moves, and assessing their opponents. Daily they alternated their principal speakers, switched and increased their demands, and kept the commissioners confused, off-balance, and exasperated.

On June 24 Wabansi, with elaborately feigned finality, turned down the commissioners' offer, knowing it was the only one they carried. The next day Perish Le Clere—interpreting for Little Miami—put the Potawatomi's position poetically: "You have made an offer for only one leg of our horse. If you buy only one leg—he will be lame. He is a good horse and we love him." But, as the Potawatomi soon acknowledged, even the finest horse has his price. "Our chiefs will consider what we will sell our horse for," interpreted Le Clere, "for we do not refuse—but we want to put our price on him." That night, after adjourning the meeting, the wokamek met in private council, working out the details of their counteroffer. More likely than not, as later events indicated, Elliott met with them, advising them how far they might expect to push the commissioners and making suggestions for their bill of particulars. They continued their council the twenty-sixth of June. On the twenty-seventh the weather was so bad they could not meet. On the twenty-eighth, when they did finally come together, the commissioners were expectant, but Little Miami and Half Day merely said that the Potawatomi had refused to sell. Did the commissioners wish to make a better offer?

When the council finally reassembled on June 30, old Wabansi stood to speak. Now carrying the authority and the aches of more than eighty years, he hinted at a reason for the delay. It seemed that during the interim Little Miami had tried to break party discipline and had needed a few reminders of where his loyalties, and his future, lay. "I had a paper made," said Wabansi, "but the bad birds came and scratched it and spoiled it. I have sent away the bad bird . . . Meamis [Little Miami] now talks like a man. That is what I like." Wabansi next stated the position of "Mr. Caldwell's band." He handed Commissioner Harvey his "paper" and said, "take it to the President. We want to talk over your decision at annuity pay [time] this fall." The wokamek were not willing to strike a final agreement with any mere messengers. The commissioners were sent away, while the Potawatomi had bought another summer's grace and a stronger bargaining position.[85]

Wabansi's "paper" was a long, detailed, exorbitant list of demands. For their lands in Iowa, and in exchange for the lands of their kinsmen on the Osage River, the wokamek would accept, he affirmed, a reasonable recompense, including one million acres on both sides of the Kaw (Kansas) River west of the Shawnee reservation. This million acres was to be deeded over to the wokamek in "fee simple" (here the able hand of attorney Elliott is evident). The United States was to grant them a perpetual annuity of $100,000 per annum, and the interest on their old $150,000 improvement fund was to be paid them in silver annually. A payment of $120,000, in two installments, was required to meet the costs of moving to the Kansas River. All those individuals and groups that had moved to Iowa at their own expense would have to be reimbursed for their out-of-pocket costs, which were considerable. Others, listed by name, were to be well paid for improvements they had made on their lands in Iowa. School funds were to be paid in hard cash on the Kansas Reservation. So, too, all annuities under this and other treaties. An indemnity of $200 per head was required for each of the eighteen Iowa Potawatomi who had been killed by Dakota raiders. The United States would have to pay the chiefs immediately after ratification the sum of $55,000, in silver. The treaty would have to be ratified within six months or it would be "null and void." All Americans would be kept off the Potawatomi's million acres. Wabansi would be awarded ten sections of land for his own use and benefit, and a life annuity of $200, which on his death (which was only six months away) would pass to his son and heir, Wapgizhek—Bright Day. And, the final demand—forever after, the United States would officially recognize and refer to them as "The Prairie Indians of Caldwell's Band of the Pottawatomies." Billy Caldwell, capably assisted by the fresh advice of Richard Smith Elliott, had indeed left a legacy behind him.[86]

The mission a failure, the treaty commissioners departed. Some time thereafter, the wokamek began to reconsider their position. Where had their strong rejection and their long list of demands landed them? There was then, as Elliott recorded in his autobiography, a lot of "mysterious pow-wowing among the chiefs." Something was going on, he observed years later, but he had to wait for it to come out. Such innocence as Elliott expressed in his memoirs was nowhere in evidence during the summer and fall of 1845. It is obvious he was busy conspiring with the leaders of the Prairie People, evaluating their prospects and situation, laying plans for the immediate future. In August, for example, he went to St. Louis to collect the annuity payments due the Potawatomi, and on September 18 he reported that he had paid out $16.50 in silver to each of 2,314 persons, with a fraction of $531 left over that was given to the wokamek. The leaders had need of the cash, for they were about to hire themselves the services of a man whose measure they had taken. Meanwhile, in St. Louis, Elliott learned no instructions had come back from Washington concerning the Potawatomi's demands. He also discovered Superintendent Harvey was to be conveniently absent from his post. Indeed, after Elliott departed from St. Louis for Council Bluffs with the Potawatomi's silver annuity pay, Harvey had received instructions to proceed north and obtain a treaty while Elliott was paying the Indians. Neatly sidestepping the possibility of another failure, Harvey begged off, on the grounds that the payment was over, and took his leave.[87]

About the time of the annuity payment, the sense of the "mysterious pow-wowing" came out, explained Elliott later.

> They had not been averse to a fair treaty, but the stately old Wah-bon-seh, with the snows of eighty winters on his head, had "dreamed" that Major Harvey was but a little Father after all . . . and that the treaty could only properly be made with their Great Father at Washington. It was a wonderful revelation, especially as his dream had indicated the very Chiefs who were to be in the mission to the Capitol—himself among them; and he had "dreamed" again, after the departure of Major Harvey, that "Cosenon" [Our Father, i.e., Elliott] was to go along with the chiefs as their guide, philosopher, and friend. (1883: 198)

Elliott then had a "dream" of his own, and again, like Wabansi, a second one. Curiously enough, the messages in his dreams neatly coincided with the desires and the freshly replenished financial condition of the wokamek.

"It was clearly revealed," wrote Elliott, "that the Chiefs, out of the funds of the tribe, were to bear all expenses and pay me fifteen hundred dollars to take care of them and their interests" (1883: 199). Elliott claimed then to have honorably resigned his job as subagent for the Potawatomi so that, free of his public responsibilities, he could undertake his new duties as a private citizen. In fact, he accompanied the wokamek to Washington very much still a subagent and at public expense; and while in Washington—when not discharging his duties as a civil servant, or earning a box and a half of silver coins from his contract with the wokamek—he carried on a little additional private enterprise on the side. In Washington he continued to earn the ample gratitude of the important fur traders from St. Louis and managed to serve as public relations man for a visionary transcontinental railroad developer. It was only after President Polk and Commissioner of Indian Affairs William Medill saw plainly what he was up to in the capital that Elliott and his position as subagent parted company. But then he was fired.[88]

Elliott, in company with Wabansi, Half Day, Little Miami, Shabeni, White Pigeon, four other wokamek, and two Métis interpreters, passed by St. Louis October 1 on his way to the seat of power and wealth. In his memoirs Elliott claimed to have surprised Superintendent Harvey with a visit while waiting for their steamer, but Harvey was in fact absent and the group proceeded without official permission. The eager delegation reached Washington in late October and put up at Fuller's Hotel. During their journey they passed the time in a variety of amusements. On the steamer *Amaranth* the Potawatomi leaders were exposed to the latest fads, including Mesmerism and phrenology, and they provided entertainments of their own. Regaling the ladies with tales of his exploits as a young warrior, for instance, Wabansi embroidered the truth modestly in narrating how he had obtained his war name. As a young lad, said he, setting out alone to revenge a murdered friend, early one misty morning he had surprised and single-handedly killed a full dozen fierce Osage warriors (see page 199). Once in Washington, there was more of the same. Elliott escorted his clients to all the favored places of entertainment and regularly paraded them up and down the avenues. Wabansi and Shabeni had their daguerreotypes made at John Plumbe's new gallery, they all witnessed a demonstration of the new telegraph, and they got another dose of phrenology. This was all part recreation, part work. Little that Elliott had his clients do in Washington that fall and winter was without a purpose. Nearly every move was staged carefully to achieve a desired effect.[89]

All the visiting, parading, displaying, and touring was a carefully crafted prelude to the first movement, a visit with President Polk. Elliott and his clients were on their way toward creating a mid-nineteenth century media event. The wokamek, in fact, had paid him fifteen hundred in coin to create for them a "Pottawatomie atmosphere" in the east. They had reversed their bargaining posture. In Iowa they were isolated from the seat of power and influence and forced to deal with minor representatives. In Washington, on the other hand, they were in the midst of power itself, and next door to the places where public sentiment could be molded and directed against the executive branch.

"I was using the Press," Elliott explained in his later years. A great many Americans had heard of the Potawatomi, but few had ever seen one, and fewer knew of their situation and wants. The early presentation of the wokamek to the public had been crafted to attract attention; but, explained Elliott,

> only a limited public sentiment could be created by all this marching and counter-marching. Besides, how would the gazing public know what to think of us? But the newspapers carried us everywhere, and told the people what views they ought to take of us; and the public, as if duty bound, was on our side. There was a Pottawatomie atmosphere everywhere. The National Intelligencer . . . gave us an editorial puff. We were in all thoughts and on all tongues. Never before or since has an Indian delegation in Washington been so much talked about or so heartily sympathized with.

As a pioneer in the fine art of press agentry, Elliott can be excused some glamorization of his personal contribution to these events. But the impact was in fact considerable. Representatives of the trading firms, with whom Elliott was on very comfortable terms, were enthralled, for their profits depended on the success of Elliott's and the Potawatomi leaders' efforts. Elliott's personal expenses were picked up by one firm, while the Ewing and Ewing company quickly offered him a retainer as their attorney. And the newspapers were well satisfied, for it was a dull season on the East Coast. The *National Intelligencer*, the *New York Herald*, the *Philadelphia Ledger*, and President Polk's own party organ the *Union*, all joined in the litany. Justice had to be done "our red brethren." "Great wrongs had been committed against the Indian." "The Noble Pottawatomis" were the finest example known of Indiankind, and the most deserving.[90]

After the preliminary fanfare, actual negotiations for the treaty—including several exits and encores—required a full month, from November 3 through December 2. The first scene consisted of a reception with President Polk, Secretary of War Marcy, and Commissioner of Indian Affairs Medill. These high dignitaries referred the Potawatomi delegation to the special commissioners—George Gibson and T. P. Andrews—who were empowered to treat with the tribe. With the advantage solidly on their side, the wokamek meant to keep it, and this required careful strategy and the avoidance of hasty commitments. Thereafter the Potawatomi delegation carefully planned, rehearsed, and staged their presentations. Their costumes and makeup were selected to attract the maximum attention to themselves and to bedazzle the eyes while confounding the reasoning of their opponents. They attired themselves in the brightest colored, most garishly designed face-paint and the most outlandish combinations of clothing they could conceive and assemble. Fancy moccasins and buckskin leggings were topped with loose-hanging calico shirts trimmed with black silk cravats, covered with blue frock coats, and surmounted by blue vermilion-painted faces in a variety of inventive designs. With tomahawk or sword-cane in hand, a few feathers and other oddments tucked into their topknots, the wokamek were ready to negotiate.[91]

The night before their meeting with Commissioners Gibson and Andrews, the wokamek plotted their conference strategy, assigning roles to each according to his skills. Wabansi was to open the meeting and to end his remarks with a comment calculated to bring a twinge of sympathy from his listeners. He hoped they might make a wise treaty, the white-haired elder planned on saying, "as he did not expect ever to take part in making another." Then Perish Le Clere was to enter—harping on treaties the United States had failed to honor and promises that were never kept. Le Clere was also to "expatiate on the charms of the country about Chicago, where the frogs in the marshes sang more sweetly than birds in other parts," the Potawatomi's lost and lamented homeland that they had occupied two centuries before the white man appeared (which was a considerable exaggeration). After Le Clere finished singing the praises of Chicago and the Platte country, it was old Half Day's turn. His task was to praise the Iowa reservation and to "magnify the reluctance of the Pottawatomies to give up so fine a country, with a suggestion that their brethren in Kansas might come up there, if the government wanted them all in one place."

The wokamek were prepared for anything. If Commissioners Gibson and Andrews made an immediate, firm offer, then Little Miami was scheduled quickly to rise and call for an overnight recess so that the delegates could think it over. There was a scenario focused on Elliott's special role, as well. He was to remain silent, keeping his eyes on the commissioners. If they gave any evidence of sharp practices, then he would signal Wabansi, who would immediately adjourn the meeting. "No lawyers in consultation over a difficult case ever arranged its management more carefully," he noted in his later years. But all the initial preparations went for nothing. Gibson and Andrews were still bound to their original offer of $250,000 and a half million acres on the Kansas River. The offer was rejected and the meeting broke up with hard words: the dignity of the wokamek had been insulted; there was evidently no respect in Washington for Indian feelings; with great and grave regrets, the Potawatomi would have to visit the president one more time to take their leave of him before returning home.[92]

Before going to the White House with his clients, Elliott once again turned his attention to the newspapers, who cooperated willingly. He and the Potawatomi leaders were well aware that President Polk was already under sharp pressure to obtain a cession of the Iowa lands, and they fully appreciated how easy it was to bring additional force to bear on that one vulnerable point where maximum responsibility was lodged. But the first meeting, on November 21, broke up in moderate confusion, with the president and his advisors half convinced that the wokamek were serious in their threats to break off negotiations, and the Potawatomi themselves becoming concerned, for they could not return to Council Bluffs empty-handed to face the scorn of their younger men and women who had been promised miracles. President Polk, who seemed to have imagined that Wabansi and his fellows enjoyed the privileges and security of absolute, hereditary monarchs, apologized and promised another, better effort the following Monday.

When the council reopened, Half Day acted as the principal speaker. He was at his much-experienced best in portraying the Potawatomi domain in northern Illinois, which his kinsmen longed for so, where were located the "graves of their fathers for unknown generations—all given to the white man." The president was hugely rich, asserted Half Day, but those "little braves" he assigned to council with the Potawatomi acted as if he were poor. The offer they had received was "like giving a poor fellow the tail of a buffalo to keep him warm. He wanted the whole robe or nothing." The oratory and negotiation continued day after day, until it became worrisome to Elliott. Sensitive to the public pulse, he was aware that the newspapers were getting bored with their thirty-day wonder. "The novelty was wearing off, and the public, I think, was getting a little tired of us," he commented. On December 2 the parties reached a compromise. The Potawatomi would receive $850,000 and a reservation on the Kansas River for their lands in Iowa and along the Osage. That night the Potawatomi leaders and Elliott celebrated their success at Fuller's Hotel. Once more they "dreamed" together. Elliott's "dream was to the effect that the Chiefs were to pay me three 'boxes' [$3,000 in coin] in the spring . . . for going to their country to aid in completing the treaty; and the Chiefs 'dreamed' that the arrangement was good."[93]

But Elliott and the wokamek were not to meet again. On their way homeward the stagecoach carrying the Potawatomi to their steamboat on the Ohio River overturned on a sharp bend in the road. While the other wokamek were only injured, Wabansi was killed instantly. Elliott returned to St. Louis near penniless. He whiled away his time unsuccessfully attempting to recover expenses from the commissioner of Indian Affairs while waiting for spring and the realization of his dream of three thousand silver coins for aiding the Prairie People with the final details of their treaty. But this was not to be, either. Superintendent Harvey concealed from him the timing of the treaty negotiations in Council Bluffs, and, finally, the rapid expansion of the American frontier took Elliott into its grasp. While he had been serving the Potawatomi, John L. O'Sullivan began preaching the doctrine of Manifest Destiny, which brought an offer of statehood to Texas and the Mexican War. Always versatile, Elliott took a commission in the LaClede Rangers and rode off to the west with the regiment of Missouri mounted volunteers. During his period of military service he added one more first to his list of innovative roles, becoming known as one of America's original war correspondents.[94]

When Commissioner Medill fired Elliott from his position as subagent, it was a symptom not so much of the former's distaste of Elliott's special relation with the Prairie People as it was his association with the trading firms who flocked around attempting to lay hands on the funds made available by the coming treaty. These maneuvers delayed the final treaty somewhat but did not block it long.[95] Medill was especially hard on traders' claims, which he regularly reduced sharply, when they were not disallowed. The traders, in keeping with their old practice of granting credit to individuals and collecting payment from tame chiefs or corrupt agents, were claiming that the Potawatomi's debts were "national." But they could not prove this, and Medill's refusal to honor the claims provoked a long legal squabble that involved the Potawatomi well into the 1860s.

With the efforts of the traders blocked, Medill again appointed Andrews,

Harvey, and Matlock treaty commissioners. This trio went west in May 1846, and on June 5, after prolonged negotiations in Council Bluffs, they brought the Prairie People to an agreement. The treaty of 1846 delivered into the hands of the Potawatomi far less than they had demanded in the summer of 1845, and less than they had expected of their successful tour in Washington that same fall. The wokamek and Elliott had departed Washington not with a finished treaty but with an ambiguous, unsigned "protocol." On 5 June 1846 the figure of $850,000 was included, but this was a gross amount paid to both the Prairie People and the Potawatomi of the Osage River Reservation for both parcels of real estate. Even then, from the $850,000 were deducted several sums: $87,000 reimbursed to the United States in payment for the 567,000 acres of Kansa tribal lands granted on the Kansas River; $50,000 advanced the Potawatomi to pay off their debts and to purchase equipment, wagons, and supplies for their move; and $30,000 to be paid for the actual expenses of migrating to the new reservation. The balance was placed in trust at 5 percent interest, which would be paid out annually as an annuity. At this point Commissioner Medill had inserted into the treaty document a perfectly noxious proviso, one which reflected his conviction that tribes like the Potawatomi were rapidly dying out. The full interest would be paid, provided Article 7, only "until the nation shall be reduced below one thousand souls." After thirty years, if the Potawatomi population was found to be lower than that number, then the survivors would receive only a pro rata share of the total "so long as they shall exist as a separate and distinct nation." Medill's forecast for the future of this tribe was not exactly optimistic.[96]

Little Miami, who had emerged as a major power after Wabansi's death, led off the signatories. Whatever happened to Wabansi's son and heir apparent, Bright Day, is unknown; but he did not sign this treaty. Fifty-six other Potawatomi men, including six that were literate Métis, added their names. Joseph Le Frambeau, Perish Le Clere, and M. B. Beaubien acted as official interpreters. All these agreed to the document on the assumption that the Prairie People were signing as the dominant leadership for all Potawatomi in the west. The treaty commissioners thought otherwise. With the names of the Prairie People certified, they immediately traveled south to the Osage River Reservation where, on June 17, they collected the signatures of the Potawatomi and Métis there. In this fashion was created a great fiction. The preamble to the treaty stated it was the wish of all Potawatomi to reunite as one people and community on the new reservation in Kansas, where they would live their lives and receive their annuities in common. Thus the stage for further factional conflict was set.

In their treaty the Prairie People agreed to move from Council Bluffs within two years of its ratification, which occurred on July 23, a few days after the commissioners carried the signed document back to Washington. There was no delay in Congress this time—the people of Iowa approved their new constitution twenty days later, on 3 August 1846, and statehood soon followed. On this occasion the Prairie People had stalled the treaty-making process right down to the wire. After it was signed they gave little indication of great sentimental attachment to the lands they had occupied a short decade in Iowa. Allowed a grace period which ran until August 1848, by the fall of 1847 nearly all had abandoned their villages along Indian Creek and the Nishnabotna River.

REUNION
ON THE KAW

Their last months in Iowa were not entirely pleasant for the Prairie People. The winter had been a hard one, with much illness and a high death rate. Exploring parties sent to the Kaw valley carried back discouraging reports of the environment there. Unsettled and unwilling to put in their corn crops, the Potawatomi awaited their next move to yet another habitat. There was a new, unfamiliar, and inexperienced agent. Spring brought unseasonably hot and humid weather. With the spring rains came a vast increase in the most notorious local predator, the swarms of insatiable mosquitoes that plagued the bottoms and wetlands. In full summer arrived yet another host, an Army of the Lord, one more group of emigrants moving outside the hostile reach of an unwelcoming frontier, the main parties of the Mormons.[97]

By late summer more than eight thousand of the latter day saints had passed through the Potawatomi lands. With permission from eight wokamek to stay temporarily on their reservation—which would of course not be the Potawatomi reservation for many months longer—the Mormon's friend, Colonel T. L. Kane, petitioned President Polk for the privilege of establishing a substantial way-station on the long road west to Utah. The new subagent, R. B. Mitchell, spoke highly of this gathering of Zion—the Mormons had cleared two farms for the benefit of the poor in the area, one of them for the Prairie People. Some of the newly arrived Mormons soon were illegally engaged in the fur trade; others were occupied with the distillation and selling of whiskey—not all of the harvest from five thousand acres of corn they put in went for bread. Commissioner of Indian Affairs Medill was concerned that the arrival of the Mormons might delay the departure of the Prairie People. It did not. The Potawatomi were waiting only for the fall annuity payment. So it was that autumn of 1847—the Prairie People departing and the Camps of Israel staying. The Mormons remained the dominant population in the Council Bluffs area until 1852, when most again moved on. But a faction under Joseph

Smith, Jr., who had abandoned polygyny, remained to form an important element in the development of western Iowa.[98]

In late summer, 1847, the Prairie People expressed their willingness to move, once their fall annuity payment and emigration funds were delivered to them. At the request of the commissioner of Indian Affairs, the secretary of war directed that a company of troops from the volunteer Oregon battalion be dispatched to keep order at the payment, since trouble was expected with the traders. The commissioner, William Medill, determined to break the hold of the major firms, had written into the new trade and intercourse laws the provision for payment of annuities directly to the heads of families rather than through the wokamek, who were too easily bought by the companies. Nonetheless, the traders were present in force, displaying for sale everything from "pins to the heaviest articles," including both standard fare and the latest items in trade—allspice, harness wagons, bed ticks, India rubber, and silk stockings. Thomas Harvey arrived from St. Louis on Sepember 30, and by October 5 he had paid out a total of $90,000 in silver to the heads of families. The Prairie People took full advantage of the great market-day, spending much of their cash-in-hand and putting their marks on notes for an additional $90,000 in debts to the trading companies.[99]

Thomas Harvey commended Joseph La Framboise, Perish Le Clere, and Half Day for the valuable assistance they had rendered at the payment grounds and for encouraging the Prairie People to move expeditiously towards Kansas. Within a week nearly all were on the trail, but not all in the direction of the new reservation. Little Miami instead led about half his people, some two hundred, east and north to the headwaters of the Des Moines River, where they established winter hunting camps. Another one hundred and fifty of his people kept going east, to Wisconsin. Probably no more than fifteen hundred of the Council Bluffs Potawatomi made their way south that fall, although others joined them the next year. Those who made the move settled for the winter on the branches of Soldier Creek, north of the Kaw River. Their distant kinsmen from the Osage River arrived a month later and settled south of the Kaw. On their way south through the Blacksnake Hills to St. Joseph, where they would ferry the Missouri, the Prairie People spent their time along the trail hunting the numerous deer in the brakes and sloughs of the Missouri River valley. It was, on the whole, a pleasant and uneventful journey, for the Potawatomi proceeded in their own time at their own pace, unencumbered by escorts or conductors. Some of the Métis who accompanied them did not tarry on Soldier Creek, however, but moved south of the Kaw to join the more receptive Mission Band.[100]

In early spring, 1848, subagents Cummins and Vaughan picked a site for the new reservation's headquarters, the agency house, traders, and blacksmiths.

Plate 5. Chief Johnny Green and family. Johnny Green, or Chemewse, of the Buffalo Clan, was the recognized okama of those Iowa Potawatomi who did not move to Kansas in 1847–1848. (Photograph by Elliott Brothers; courtesy of the Bureau of American Ethnology, Smithsonian Institution.)

It was south of the Kaw in the midst of a good stand of timber on high ground near the geographic center of the Potawatomi National Reservation. But geographic centrality does not always coincide with social organization and political aims. The Prairie People shortly protested this decision and petitioned for their own traders and blacksmith. As independently conservative as ever, these

Potawatomi were attempting to gain as much isolation and autonomy as they might in a now much more restricted setting. But the central site, soon called Union Town, remained and flourished, serving not only the Potawatomi but the emigrant wagons headed west, for it was on the California–Oregon trails at the location most favored for fording or ferrying the Kaw.[101]

Of those Prairie People who had spent the prior winter hunting on the Des Moines or visiting Wisconsin, some drifted back to the national reservation in the summer and fall, 1848. Their movements past St. Joseph, Missouri, happily corresponded with the presence at that place of the noted Swiss artist and traveler Rudolph Friederich Kurz, who talked and traded with them. Kurz found the Potawatomi, like the Fox, a far more reserved people than the Iowa, who had been open and friendly with him. Commenting on what he knew of their long history of displacement and migration, he rightly questioned "how long they would have the benefit of that retreat [on the Kaw]." Only time would tell, he reflected. He found an easy answer to his query "whether this continual displacing of tribes . . . is a benefit or menace

Plate 6. Prairie Potawatomi family on the trail, 1848. (Sketch by Rudolph Friederich Kurz; courtesy of National Anthropological Archives, Smithsonian Institution.)

to . . . friendly relations with the Americans." It made of them "inveterate foes," he concluded.

Kurz was under the impression that the Prairie People were specialized stockbreeders and farmers, an idea contradicted by his own observations of them living in wigwams covered with hides and white cotton fabric. The Prairie People had obviously been adapting to life on the plains, substituting new housing materials for the sheets of bark and reed mats they had used in the upper lakes. Kurz left one excellent drawing of a young Potawatomi family on the trail—father, mother, and child (see Plate 6). Both parents sit astride their ponies on blanket-covered wooden saddle frames of Great Lakes Algonquian style. A youthful father is armed with bow and arrow, and stares attentively off into the distance. Mother, with her child seated in front of her, rides a horse laden with large woven-reed carrying bags holding the family's possessions. One of the very rare visual images of the Potawatomi of this era, it is a sketch which reflects strength and health. The Prairie People may have lost their Iowa lands; they had not lost their vigorous identity (Kurz 1970: 30, 33, 37).

11

The Reservation
Experience:
1848 ~ 1905

After crossing the Missouri River into the Kaw valley the Prairie People experienced a radical alteration in the conditions of their lives. They soon discovered their most recent relocation was one of the first steps in the development by Americans of a full-scale reservation policy. This emergent program for the solution of the Indian problem had one major aim, the assimilation of tribal peoples into the political and economic fabric of American society. Beneath these publicly proclaimed goals lay also a familiar objective, a further sharp reduction of the land-base occupied and used by the tribesmen. The means to these ends included the breakup of tribally owned tracts in favor of individual agricultural allotments, close supervision and control over the daily lives of the tribesmen, increased educational efforts aimed at preparing them for the responsibilities of agricultural production and citizenship, and the transfer of responsibility for law and order from the federal to state and local governments. In Iowa the Prairie People had flourished in relative isolation; once resettled in Kansas they had to cope with overwhelming interference in their lives of a kind and volume they had never previously experienced. The next half century of their history, thereby, is a record of a loss of political and economic autonomy, a near failure of the integrity of their traditional culture, and the growth of a resistance movement the ideology and tactics of which carried the few remaining traditional Potawatomi forward into the twentieth century.[1]

The migration of the Prairie People into the Kaw River valley was one of the last moves in the faltering removal policy that was supposed to have established a permanent Indian frontier along a natural environmental barrier, one that would serve to contain American expansionism while protecting the relocated tribes from damaging contacts with the frontier. By the mid-1840s this policy had been successful insofar as it had cleared the eastern states of most of their Indian populations. By that time a north-south line of large reservations was established just west of the Missouri River (see Figure 14). But the tribes were not long remote from the hazards of American expansion. They were, instead, directly in the path of an agricultural frontier that hardly paused before spreading into the Great Plains. Indeed, the resettlement of so many tribes in this area, by increasing American experience with the habitat, actually accelerated the growth of American settlements and designs upon the lands that had been certified as belonging to the relocated tribes forever.

As traders, trappers, Indian agents, missionaries, and soldiers became familiar with the territory west of the ninety-fifth meridian, and as explorers, emigrant parties, gold-miners, and adventure seekers added their new knowledge of what the tall-grass prairies were actually like, the myth of the Great American Desert quickly dissolved. One of the most eloquent, if not the earliest, commentator on the attractions of the West was Julia Lovejoy. On her way to the Methodist Mission station in 1858, she wrote glowingly of the vast, rich, level bottomlands of the Kansas River valley, where roamed herds of swine, fat cattle, and horses, all owned by the "lazy Indians." "O how many, many times," she observed, "we wished that poor working men from the East, who need farms, or poor Methodist preachers . . . could have the doors thrown open to them here in this paradise." Miss Lovejoy's deep jealousy of the "Indian nabobs" was typical of others of her era and profession. Cath-

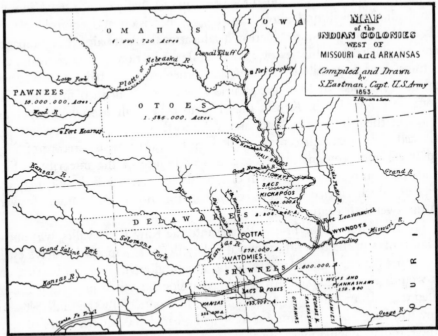

Figure 14. Potawatomi and other tribal reservations in the west, 1853 (section from Captain S. Eastman's map of 1853, in Schoolcraft 1851/57 1: 519).

olic and Protestant alike, the missionaries were supposed to bring to the Potawatomi and other tribes Christian charity and understanding. What they too often expressed was envy, and sometimes outright hatred, for the relative wealth and ease of the lives of the tribesmen they saw. Miss Lovejoy commented that Indians would not work unless forced to do so, yet each could (she believed) freely select two hundred or more acres of prime land, while many had more cattle and horses than any New England farmer.[2]

With such awareness of the riches of the West growing in the minds of Americans, the resettled eastern tribes could not long remain secure in their new domains. In 1848 Superintendent Thomas Harvey at St. Louis and Commissioner William Medill first proposed the rudiments of the new reservation policy. During 1849, seeing that the future held out the prospect of further arbitrary separation from their lands, some of the Mesquakie Fox abandoned their lands in Kansas and returned to Iowa. There, after selling their pony herds, they purchased a small tract on the Des Moines River. The next year they were followed by a fragment of the Prairie Potawatomi, who settled west of the Mesquakie near present Marshalltown. By 1851 the old permanent Indian frontier was fast disappearing; and in 1854 Commissioner George W. Manypenny declared that the removal policy must end. There was no place in the West where Indians could live unmolested, he argued, while the policy of frequent forced relocation interfered with the goal of developing settled agricultural habits. Moreover, it had become apparent to Manypenny and other officials that the policy of doling out large annuities annually was not making Indians into self-sufficient farmers, while the huge communally owned land holdings actively blocked initiative for the development of individually owned farmsteads.[3]

Commissioner Manypenny's views were expressed while awaiting ratification of a series of treaties he had negotiated in 1853–1854. In these transactions he arranged the cession of thirteen million acres in eastern Kansas, which lands were soon thrown open to American settlement. The tribes involved were the Delaware, Shawnee, Iowa, Sauk and Fox, Wyandot, Odawa, Miami, Kickapoo, and other relocated eastern tribes. By the winter of 1854–1855 the only intact tract in the Kansas River valley was that occupied by the Prairie Band and their more acculturated kinsmen south of the river. Although the Manypenny treaties varied in detail, their common features were the more striking. These provisions made up a package that was the direct forerunner of the full-scale assimilation policy which would become dominant in the years after the Civil War, to be expressed finally as a uniform nationwide program in the Dawes Allotment Act of 1887. The Manypenny treaties set aside a fraction of the lands on each of the reserves, which tracts were allotted in severalty to those persons recognized as attached to the Indian community,

Plate 7. Wawasēk in 1865. Namesake of the Wawasēk whose name appeared on the Treaty of Greenville, this Wawasēk was a Prairie Potawatomi subchief in the mid-nineteenth century. (Original photograph published by Blackmore Museum; courtesy of the Bureau of American Ethnology, Smithsonian Institution.)

whether or not they were of Indian ancestry. Those who wished it had citizenship made available to them immediately, while only a limited and ambiguous federal guardianship was provided others who did not then elect political assimilation. The largest share of the lands on these reservations were sold to the United States and quickly placed on the market for purchase by American settlers and land speculators. In such fashion most of the relocated eastern tribes in Kansas were dispossessed, divided, and surrounded by American settlers.

At this time the Prairie People had more to worry them than the experience of neighboring tribes with the Manypenny treaties. By the mid-1850s the future of relocated Indians in Kansas was caught up also in the great sectional controversy dividing North from South. They were confronted now not only by American settlers, but by free-staters and slave-staters, and by a growing conflict that bloodied the prairies east of their reservation. In the same year Commissioner Manypenny called for an end to the removal program and pointed the way for the eventual assimilation of the tribes, the Kansas-Nebraska Act provided territorial status for the area, while Senator Stephen A. Douglas's rider to this legislation, an amendment handing determination of the slavery issue over to local option, guaranteed a decade of strife in eastern Kansas. Only the slavery issue delayed statehood for the territory, which attained a population of over sixty thousand by 1860.[4]

In the midst of a great civil war the population of Kansas continued to rise and statehood was finally granted in 1861. That same fall the Potawatomi were maneuvered into signing a treaty with provisions similar to those which had afflicted the Shawnee, Delaware, and other eastern tribes in 1854. On November 15 the Prairie Band legally separated from their missionized kinsmen, who soon became known as the Citizen Band. Of the 576,000 acres contained in the National Reserve, the Prairie People retained 77,358, while 152,128 of the remaining 498,642 acres were allotted in severalty to the Mission Potawatomi, who were now supposed to move rapidly along the path towards individual entrepreneurship and citizen status. The remainder of the old National Reservation—346,514 acres—was scheduled for sale to the Leavenworth, Pawnee, and Western Railroad Company. In effect the Prairie People boycotted the intent of this treaty-making session, insisting they would hold on to their share of the reservation in common. Five years later, when another treaty was required to provide homes for the now destitute and landless members of the Citizen Band, the Prairie People again stood aside. That year, in 1867, the Potawatomi signed the last of their long series of treaties with the United States. There were only eight signatures on the document providing new lands in Indian Territory (present Oklahoma). Three of them were those of well-tamed, titular "chiefs." The other five were the elite Métis and Anglo-Saxons who had long conducted the business of the Mission Band, B. H. Bertrand, Joseph Napoleon Bourassa, M. B. Beaubien, L. H. Ogee, and George L. Young.[5]

The missionized, and now citizenized, Potawatomi were soon almost but not quite entirely divorced from the affairs of the Prairie People, who settled in for a long siege, resisting all efforts to separate them from their communally owned eleven-mile-square reservation and attempts to assimilate them into American society. A minority of the landless, impoverished Citizen Potawatomi never moved to Oklahoma, but continued to live with or on the edges of the Prairie Band's diminished reservation. Some of them were embittered by their experience and supported the Prairie People in their resistance effort. Others served as a labor force, working the lands the Prairie People did not themselves care to farm. A few emerged as part of another elite stratum, one that served the interests of the Indian agent, local American farmers and businessmen, and anyone else who offered them income and opportunity. Although few in number, they constituted an extremely dangerous element and a threat to the integrity of the Prairie People's resistance.

The influence of a relatively few Métis, the dissident Citizen Potawatomi, and of American settlers who got themselves accepted as legitimate members of the Prairie Band was great because the coalition of political-economic forces known as the Indian Ring needed cooperative local representatives who could give the semblance of legality to the procedures used to separate the Prairie People from their land and wealth. Their influence was the greater, also, because as the years rolled by the Prairie People were increasingly few in number.

From a peak population of 2,500 in Iowa in 1846, by the turn of the century the population had declined to little more than 400. The latter figure represented an actual count of the number of Potawatomi residing on the diminished reserve at the time of annuity payments. But after the 1850s there were more Prairie Potawatomi in being than those who lived on the Kansas Reservation. Some 250, for example, resided in west-central Wisconsin and were carried on the rolls as members of the band, entitled to all benefits, although they rarely even visited Kansas. There were hundreds of others, scattered from Iowa to Mexico, who had effectively severed their relationships with the reservation population. The decline from a peak of 2,500 in 1846 to 436 in 1900 did not, thereby, entirely represent a natural decrease caused by an excess of deaths over births. The Prairie People had responded to the grave stresses of living in Kansas with their tried and tested adaptive tactic of migration: most simply moved away from the reservation. The number used to calculate the Prairie People's share of the National Reservation under the terms of the treaty of 1861 was 680, of whom some 200 were then recognized as living in Wisconsin. In the forty years thereafter, the reservation's population remained relatively stable. Thus the great decline in population occurred in the dozen years after 1848, when there was yet open land to the west and south, as well as in Iowa and Wisconsin, to which disaffected portions of the population could migrate.[6]

After the treaty of 1867, which moved most of the Citizen Potawatomi out of Kansas, the Prairie People could do little more than fight a holding action, striving to fend off the powerful forces arrayed against them. There was never a year when the pressure was reduced. Indeed, the movement for full assimilation gathered force season by season until 1887, when a curious coalition of social gospel Christian humanists—middle-class zealots who believed themselves defenders of Indian rights—allied themselves with the senators, local traders, land speculators, and railroad interests who made up the Indian Ring to bring about the Dawes Allotment Act of 1887. In 1890, under the authority of this legislation, President Benjamin Harrison, grandson of the Potawatomi's old nemesis of Indiana days, ordered the reservation allotted and the balance of their lands (of which it turned out there were none) sold.[7]

By then the few remaining traditional Potawatomi on the reservation had embraced a new religion, the Dream Dance cult, which promised supernatural assistance in their efforts to resist this latest intervention in their affairs, the damaging effects of which their leaders were well aware. But even the most powerful rituals and magical devices added to adroit political maneuver and efforts to keep the local population in line failed those leaders who opposed allotment. By 1904, 812 individual allotments had been made, about one-fourth of them to persons with no claim, or only the most dubious claim, to the status of Prairie Band Potawatomi. By that date, because the Prairie People were now subject to state inheritance law, large parcels of their land were already passing out of the ownership of the Potawatomi as the older people died intestate and their allotments were sold at auction. Thus the Prairie People entered the twentieth century, their traditional leaders defeated but not cowed, their affairs managed directly by the authoritarian edicts of an agency superintendent, the villages broken up and their homesteads scattered across the whole reservation, which was increasingly occupied and owned by American farmers. They carried with them into the modern world a new tradition of bitterness, negativism, secretiveness, and rigid resistance that effectively perpetuated important elements of their traditional culture, if it interfered with further creative adaptation to the changing conditions of their lives.

CULTURAL CHARACTER
AND SOCIOPOLITICAL
ADAPTATIONS

The composition and character of the Potawatomi group that became known as the Prairie Band is of special interest. Although not all of the Council Bluffs Potawatomi ever moved to or settled in the Kansas River valley, the large majority of the Prairie Band were derived from Iowa, and ultimately from northern Illinois and southern Wisconsin. To this core population regularly were added individuals and small groups of persons of two basic kinds. Both groups consisted of emigrants from other cultures and places; but their motivations for taking up residence among the Prairie People and the impact they had upon this society were very different. One group consisted of Americans of varied ethnic backgrounds, at first French-speaking Métis, but in later years Anglo-Saxon and Scots-Irish. These persons, who were invariably males, came seeking opportunity, power, and fortune, at the expense of the traditional Potawatomi. Some of them were Anthony Navarre, Eli G. Nadeau, George L. Young, and George W. James, who moved in on the Prairie People, assumed positions of technical leadership in economic and political affairs, acted as middlemen and brokers with traders, railroad developers, and Indian agents, and eventually usurped much of the powers and responsibilities of the traditional okamek.

On the other hand, because the Prairie People had developed a regional reputation for cultural conservatism, dispossessed representatives of other bands and tribes also sought residence with the Prairie People, but with the aim of identifying themselves with a traditional Indian way of living. Mostly drawn from Central Algonquian tribes that had lost the lands in the West, these new members included both men and women. The most striking example of this class was Wakwaboshkok—Roily Water, a powerfully charismatic man of Sauk origin who achieved prominence in the 1880s, and who led the opposition to the Dawes Allotment Act and its implementation (see Plate 8). In this fashion the Prairie People became a composite group and, as the years passed, one increasingly heterogeneous in language and culture.

However resistant the conservative Prairie Potawatomi were, the same divisive and differentiating pressures of acculturation acted on them after 1848, just as they had on the whole tribe after the 1760s. In particular, the arrival and establishment of aliens as technical leaders expressed the same old weakness in patterns of governance and styles of dealing with Euro-American powers that had plagued the tribe for more than a century. The powerful old leaders of Illinois and Iowa days, such as Little Miami, Padekoshĕk, and Wabansi, left behind them a heritage of pride and a sense of moral and cultural autonomy which became obsessive in their sons and grandsons, but they did not pass on to their descendants the requisite skills for successfully coping with the vastly increased pressures of American society that soon fell upon them. Thereby, the Prairie People were dependent on aliens for technical leadership; but never again were they to find someone as skilled as Billy Caldwell, who would devote his life and energy to their welfare and interests, or even a happy scoundrel such as Richard Smith Elliott, who would at least temporarily lease his talents and know-how to their cause.

For a few years after settling along the Kaw the Prairie People went on their own way, little molested by Indian agents and missionaries, who at first had plenty to occupy their time in organizing the affairs of the Mission Bands. But by the mid-1850s the Prairie People had developed a reputation for stubborn resistance, restive independence, and unruly self-direction that has made them the bane of the Bureau of Indian Affairs ever since. In 1855 Agent George W. Clarke compared them, in less than complimentary terms, with their more docile and cooperative kinsmen south of the Kaw. The Mission

Plate 8. The "Gentil Brave," Wakwaboshkok in 1895. Wakwaboshkok—Roily Water was of Sauk origin, but led the opposition of the Prairie Potawatomi to the Dawes Allottment Act in the last decade of the nineteenth century. His reward was a stay in the Fort Riley stockade. (Photograph by DeLancey Gill; courtesy of the Bureau of American Ethnology, Smithsonian Institution.)

Potawatomi, he reported, faced the "formidable obstacle of the 'Prairie Band' or 'Bluffs Indians' to oppose, thwart, and defeat every measure of improvement among this unhappy people." The Prairie People, Clarke noted, were "hunters, despise farming, and denounce those who cultivate the soil." "This band," he observed, "arrogantly claims ownership of all the land and declares that the other bands have no rights here, nor to the annuities, they being *permitted* to participate in them only as a *courtesy* of their condescending brothers. The Prairie band frequently kill and steal the stock of their brothers, burn fences, turn their ponies into cultivated fields, and threaten lives." Agent Clarke characterized the Prairie People as a "bold and reckless race, and though they form a minority of the tribe, they domineer over it, and rule and misgovern the people in a lawless manner." By this period the Prairie People were claiming to be the "Royal Chiefs" over the whole tribe and the National Reservation.[8]

Over the years the leaders of the Prairie People opposed nearly every program presented to them by their agents. In the fall of 1855, when the government elected to distribute their annuities every six months, one-half at a time, they refused to accept any annuity money until the whole amount was delivered and appointed the warrior sodality to keep discipline and prevent any Potawatomi from accepting partial payment. The following year the Prairie Band leaders got into an acrimonious dispute over purging the rolls. At is turned out, many of the Prairie Band families were inflating their numbers so as to receive larger payments. By 1857 they had taken an adamant position opposing allotment of the reservation. After the treaty of 1861, once settled on their diminished reserve, they successfully opposed any new treaty disposing of these lands. When they felt like it, they would dispatch a delegation to Washington, there to attempt a replay of Wabansi's successful expedition of 1845; but if their agent proposed that they visit Washington on business, they refused.

Throughout the years in which they remained affiliated with the Mission Band on the National Reservation, they consistently insisted on a separation of their annuity funds, and separate schools, blacksmith shops, mission stations, and agency buildings. They regularly resisted attempts to obtain an accurate census, knowing that annuity payments were conditioned on the size of their population. And when pressures mounted for political assimilation and the final allotment of their diminished reserve in the 1880s, their resistance became the stronger and the more vehement. This recalcitrance cannot be judged in terms of some abstract sense of moral outrage, of some great wrong done by the "white man" to the "Indian," with the response proper and proportionate to the evil done them. Instead, the Prairie People were expressing a profound sense of ethnocentric superiority, of moral ascendancy and political domination with respect to other Potawatomi. They aimed not simply at obtaining their

Plate 9. Potawatomi delegation to Washington, 1898. Note the great variety of costume of these Kansas Potawatomi on one of the regular visits to Washington, D.C. (Photograph by DeLancey Gill; courtesy of the Bureau of American Ethnology, Smithsonian Institution.)

fair share of resources available and payments due them, but at controlling the largest possible portion of the good things of life, whatever the cost to their kinsmen and other tribes. They were becoming increasingly preoccupied with their own rights and interests, in an era when common cause and the development of mutual interests might have strengthened the position of all.[9]

By 1865 the Prairie People had concentrated their small villages along the branches of Soldier Creek on their diminished reservation. In that year an official roll drawn under the provisions of the treaty of 1861 fixed the official count of the Prairie Band at 780, including 217 men, 200 women, and 363 children. One hundred seventy-four adults were identified as heads of households, and of these twelve were American men, including a half-dozen Métis. About 300 of the persons on the roll lived elsewhere. This roll indicated something of the indecisiveness of many when faced with the question of whether to elect citizen status or to join with the Prairie Band. Twenty persons on the roll had originally signed up for allotments, only to switch the choice later to the Prairie Band, and of these ten later changed back again to citizen status. By this time there was almost no game on the reservation, while hostilities on the High Plains and the decline of the buffalo prevented the men from engaging in the major annual wide-range hunts that had earlier been their custom.[10]

In the entire second half of the nineteenth century very few observers other than Indian agents and missionaries recorded much in the way of descriptive materials concerning the culture and social life of the Prairie People. In June of 1859 the pioneer social anthropologist Lloyd Henry Morgan spent a very few days among the Potawatomi in Kansas, but he failed to develop any rapport and obtained only a few bits of information. He noted that the Midewiwin was still very strong, with some two hundred active members, and collected a fragmentary and confused list of kinship terms, but otherwise the information he gleaned from his hostile informants tells us little about the conditions and customs of the Prairie People in that year. Then, twenty-one years later, Perry Armstrong visited the Kansas Potawatomi collecting information for his history of the Black Hawk War. Armstrong spent more time with the Prairie People and was in a more advantageous position than had been Morgan, for he had grown up with the Potawatomi in Illinois and was able to renew friendships with men he had hunted and fished with as a boy.[11]

Armstrong found that the reservation contained no large game at all, and only a few prairie chickens, quail, and rabbits. He was particularly struck by the absence of dogs, which the Potawatomi had likely killed and eaten. There were, he discovered, only 2,035 acres under cultivation, which was far fewer than the exaggerated reports of Potawatomi progress in agriculture submitted by the agents. Of these, the largest share was farmed by a small minority of elite Métis and Americans; traditional Potawatomi women continued to cultivate their small kitchen gardens of little more than two or three acres, but they had now added potatoes to their customary crops of corn, pumpkins, beans, squash, and tobacco. All the farms and gardens were well fenced—their construction for years had been an obsession of the Indian agents, who used the number of yards of fences laid annually as a measure of progress towards civilization. But the Prairie People found these fences highly functional; they protected their crops from their pony herds and the droves of razorback hogs which ran half-wild on the reservation.

In 1880 Armstrong noted that the Prairie People lived mainly in log cabins, some in frame homes. But most abandoned these large American-style structures in winter for the traditional wigwam, which was easier to heat. Interestingly, Armstrong observed also that traditional Potawatomi marriage customs were breaking down, with numerous divorces and desertions, and a growing rate of illegitimacy. He commented on, but did not document the details of, a similar breakdown of the extended kinship system. Likely he was referring to a decline in the functions and importance of the clan and patrilineage system. Armstrong's best day was when he renewed his friendship with Mskwas—Little Red, whom he had played with as a boy in Illinois, now speaker of the Prairie Band. Old Mskwas welcomed his boyhood friend in his "state dress." On his head was a "black felt Kossuth [Cossack] hat, ornamented with the tail feathers of a Leghorn Rooster. His feet were encased in Oxford ties . . . his nether limbs were covered with a pair of Kentucky jeans pants ornamented with bands of sea grass rope. He wore a shirt with an immense ruffled bosom, which came down below his knees and [was] starched till it could stand alone." All the Prairie Band women wore American-style clothing, like that of the working class or rural poor, and in a fashion a generation out of style.[12]

In some areas of their lives the Prairie People's okamek found their traditional skills useful, particularly so with respect to the management of intertribal relations, the organization of wide-ranging hunting parties, and in war. During October of 1848, for example, the Potawatomi participated in an attempt to rejuvenate the old Northwest Confederacy. That month, along with representatives from other relocated Great Lakes Algonquians and the Wyandot, they participated in a large intertribal council on the Delaware Reservation near Fort Leavenwortth. There was much ritual hustle and bustle, with a renewal of the old ties of friendship and the confirmation of the Wyandot as traditional keepers of the council fire, but the council had little long-range effect. The members were already too divided, and too easily further subdivided by American agents, for them to sustain a united front in pursuit of their common long-range interests. However, so far as the tribes of the High Plains were concerned, they were one people, and dangerous intruders on the buffalo hunting grounds at that. The Cheyenne, for example, called all the resettled tribes Savane—The Easterners, and could not tell them apart in their fringed buckskin hunting coats and American felt hats, with their accurate long-rifles.[13]

In one respect some of the resettled Algonquians did find a common cause that encouraged them in a limited amount of joint effort. This involved attempts to exploit the buffalo herds in central Kansas and Nebraska, which brought them into immediate conflict with the plains tribes, first the Kitkehahkis band of Pawnee, and then a coalition of Cheyenne, Dakota, Crow, Arapaho, and Kiowa. The old residents of the High Plains sought and eventually succeeded in blocking the hunting parties of the Prairie People and other Algonquians. They did not accomplish this, however, without some sharp and costly encounters.

At first, between 1848 and 1852, the Prairie People were opposed by the Pawnee, for together with the Kickapoo and Sauk and Fox they were hunting into the latter's territory along the Republican River. In July 1848 old Padekoshēk's niktotem got into a fight with an outnumbered party of Pawnee on the upper Kansas River and bested them, bringing home five scalps. By 1850 hostilities were general, with the Pawnees arrayed against the Algonquians, who were sometimes joined by a few Kanza and Osage. Until the summer of 1852 these fights, which were mostly small hit-and-run raids, raged back and forth. The Pawnee regularly raided up and onto the Potawatomi Reservation, especially the area north of the Kansas River. The settlement around St. Mary's was particularly vulnerable. In turn, the Prairie People systematically ambushed Pawnee parties, who were in the habit of harassing emigrant trains traveling west of the Potawatomi Reservation. Shortly, the Pawnee and other marginal tribes on the plains developed a high respect for the Prairie People, their allies, their superior weaponry, and their cool and deliberate battle tactics. The Potawatomi, who had learned much from the dragoons while at Council Bluffs, had trained their horses to stand steady while they fired their rifles. Dismounted, they formed two ranks and—using crossed sticks as rifle rests—alternately fired and reloaded. It was in the spring of 1850 that Kakak—Duck Hawk, of the Bald Eagle Clan, demonstrated his prowess in battle against the Pawnee and earned the reputation for supernormal power which enabled him to found one of the last of the traditional patrilineages ever to be formed among the Prairie People. By 1852 it had become obvious to the Kitkehahkis Pawnee that there was little profit or future in battling against the Algonquians to their east, for the allied plains tribes posed a formidable threat to all. That summer the Pawnee, the Potawatomi, and the other Algonquians made peace and organized an alliance against the warrior tribes to the west.[14]

In the summer of 1853 the Kitkehahkis, the Shawnee, and the Prairie People, now allied, joined forces for a major buffalo hunt on the upper Republican River. Meanwhile, the Cheyenne had organized a large intertribal war-party composed of their own men joined by those of the Dakota, Crow, Arapaho, and Kiowa. While hunting, the Potawatomi separated from their allies. It was then that the Cheyenne and their allies attacked the Pawnee and Shawnee. The latter took shelter in a ravine and held off the Cheyenne-led charges while the Pawnee leader Sky Chief rode off to call in the Potawatomi. Shortly, forty Potawatomi warriors arrived at the gallop like a troop of the Seventh Cavalry. Aiming their accurate rifles, one "platoon rode forward and fired a volley into the mass of prairie Indians, then fell back to reload, the second platoon at once advancing and firing a volley. They came on and on, being driven back a little at times by a hard charge, but always coming on" (Hyde 1974: 234–37). The Potawatomi's dragoon tactics and rifles were too much for the Cheyenne and their allies, who fought as best they could before retreating away from the accurate, disciplined, long-range fire of the Prairie People. The numbers involved in this battle were impressive. There were about one thousand warriors led by the Cheyenne, and they were opposed by some eight hundred Pawnee, which number included many women and children. Thus forty disciplined Potawatomi and their rifles proved decisive against the tactics and the bows, spears, and clubs used by the plains warriors. The latter suffered some fifty killed, with another hundred or more wounded, and they lost 170 horses to the Potawatomi and Pawnee.

In 1854 the Cheyenne, with fifteen hundred of their allies, tried again, this time striking against a small force of less than two hundred Sauk and Fox that included some Potawatomi. This fight occurred on the Santa Fe Trail at Pawnee Fork, near the upper Kansas River. On this occasion the Osage had joined the Cheyenne, so that the Potawatomi found themselves arrayed against an old enemy. The battle was a repeat of the previous year's. The Algonquians would allow the enemy to charge within one hundred yards, and then loose a devastating volley, followed quickly by a second before the broken line could regroup. This time the Cheyenne and their allies lost twenty-six killed and another hundred wounded. Agent Whitefield, who was one of those who reported this fight, commented that the Algonquians had saved the government the trouble of fighting the notorious Osage. The resettled Algonquians, in effect, were serving as a kind of auxiliary constabulary, combating the depredations of the plains tribes at a time when the United States Army units available were still too few to be adequate to the task. By 1854 the Prairie People were offering their services to the army as guides in expeditions against the Dakota.

However, successful though the Algonquians may have been in battle against the warriors of the plains, in the end the Cheyenne and their allies prevailed. They were entirely too numerous and dangerous to make buffalo hunting on the plains adequately safe or economic for the Potawatomi and their friends. The Cheyenne, Dakota, and other tribes were fighting a defensive war in their own territory against a better armed, but badly out-numbered, intruder. The glory earned by the Potawatomi warriors could not compensate for the fact that ammunition expended against the Dakota was an expensive waste. In the 1854 fight the Prairie Band warriors cut out the hearts of the Osage dead and carried them home for a ritual feast—the last recorded instance of ceremonial cannibalism by the Potawatomi. But their bullets and powder would have been better spent against buffalo. By the time of the Civil War the Prairie People were effectively blocked from hunting on the High Plains, for the Cheyenne and their allies, too, were adapting to the new technology of war and developing improved tactics for dealing with intrusive tribesmen.[15]

However skilled they were in war against the plains tribes, and whatever their capabilities for maintaining peace and order within their home villages, the Prairie People discovered soon after arriving on the Kansas River that their traditional leaders lacked the knowledge and skills to cope effectively with Métis and other Americans who infiltrated their ranks, usurping power and mulcting them of their wealth. These upstart, alien leaders, who assumed various titles, quickly moved to where lay the greatest opportunity. Soon enough the traditional okamek found themselves bypassed, outmaneuvered, ignored, suppressed, corrupted, and even discharged and jailed.

The Prairie People's own view of these events is contained in a fragment of legend told to Alanson Skinner as a historical tale in 1912 and repeated in similar versions in the 1960s. The themes remain the same. Only the principal actors change, since the Prairie People are interested mainly in identifying the most recent scoundrels and heroes to complicate or enrich their lives. As the legend goes, a poor American woman gave one of her sons to the Potawatomi interpreter, who was a Métis. Later on the tribesmen adopted him and allowed him to draw annuity money. His name was James Blandin, and the Prairie People spoke of him as the Eye of the Potawatomi. Later another young man was similarly adopted, trusted, and privileged. His name was George W. James, and he was called the Ear of the Potawatomi. Both men became government employees, managed the whole reservation in their own personal interest, and amassed great wealth. Together, so the legend goes, they came to own more than half the lands on the diminished reservation, which they acquired by robbing the Prairie People. Later the immigrant Sauk Wakwa-boshkok, who became okama of the influential Fish Clan, attempted to have the Eye and the Ear of the Potawatomi removed from power. Wakwaboshkok went to Washington, where he got the support of the commissioner of Indian Affairs, but when he returned to Kansas, Blandin and James outmaneuvered him and won. This was how, the legend narrates, the Dawes Allotment Act was implemented on the reservation, and how the Prairie People lost their land and wealth. But in the end both Blandin, who went mad, and James, who was killed in a suspect buggy accident, received their punishment. Lacking political acumen, the Prairie People had turned to their medicine bundles and by magical means inflicted appropriate sanctions on those who abused their trust and defrauded them.[16]

It must be remembered that this is Potawatomi, not American, historiography. It is basically a morality tale based on traditional interpretations of a long series of complex historical events with numerous individual actors. Thus the Métis, Blandin, and James are personified prototypes, as is Wakwaboshkok. All were actual historical figures, but in the tale they represent more, especially so basic trends of human nature as understood by the Prairie People. The bad guys, we can see, much outnumber the good ones. The Potawatomi cannot manage affairs directly with their own leaders but are dependent on aliens, whether Indian or American, and they must travel to a powerful, distant place, Washington, to safeguard their interests. Even the functions of the alien Americans taken in are revealed by the names given them: they were to serve as the special senses of the Prairie People, tuned in on the machinations of outside agents and organizations.

Here again is revealed the old and fundamental dilemma of Potawatomi governance. They did not develop in their own families and communities the kinds of technical leaders they needed to cope effectively with the changing outside world. Hence they were dependent on aliens on whom they placed great trust and who obtained much influence, both of which were abused to deprive rather than to support and protect the Prairie People. On the way to becoming a myth, this legend provided a blueprint for understanding their past as a charter for organizing present behavior. As first recorded by Skinner in 1912, the tale was of special interest, since George W. James had died at the height of his power only ten years earlier, while Blandin was yet living, if afflicted by the supernatural punishment supposedly inflicted on him by Prairie Band shamans. Men who abuse their power do not live to enjoy their ill-gotten gains is the moral of the tale. And it is obvious that the Potawatomi did not wait long before imposing their own mythopoeic imagery on the events of the past.

The actual historic events portrayed in this tale cannot be described with anything like the same brevity, much less the poetic force, of the Prairie People's own oral narrative. Essentially, the substance of the tale is historically accurate, if bent by the Potawatomi's own cultural prescriptions, and if we remember that there were many Métis, Blandins, Jameses, and Wakwaboshkoks who created and acted out the roles depicted. For example, the Potawatomi who narrate these legends did not remember the names and identities of any of the numerous Métis who were the first influential aliens to penetrate their defenses in Kansas, mainly because soon after the treaty of 1867 nearly all of these upstart leaders had followed the Citizen Band to the greener pastures of Oklahoma. By then the Métis, who were adapted to unsettled frontier conditions where the American government needed the services of cooperative middlemen, were once more being displaced by those Americans of Anglo-Saxon and Scots-Irish descent then flooding into Kansas. Similarly, the Potawatomi did not fully understand the actual historical events and the political and economic devices that were employed to reduce their power and render them impoverished. As full-time participants caught up in and oppressed by the swirl of historical events, they had no time for seeking detached comprehension, but experienced only the impacts and the consequences, which they had to interpret in the light of their own traditional belief systems.

Within a few years of the Prairie People's arrival in Kansas the Métis, who had earlier expanded their power and established their position among the Mission Bands, moved to achieve influence on behalf of American authorities and firms among the Prairie People north of the Kansas River. They were

quickly joined by those few of their kinsmen who had remained, barely tolerated and powerless, among the Potawatomi at Council Bluffs. At the same
time, a few men of Anglo-Saxon or Scots-Irish heritage, generally poor, landless, unemployed individuals, began aligning themselves with the Métis leadership, who treated them as protégés. Lucius R. Darling was typical of these
men. From northern Illinois, he had married Antoine Ouilamette's daughter
in the late 1830s, worked as a trader's employee among the Potawatomi at
Council Bluffs for a time, and eventually obtained a government job as ferry-
man at Union Town on the National Reservation.[17]

By the time of the treaty of 1861 the Métis had emerged as a politically
dominant, economic elite among the Potawatomi, including both the Mission
Bands and the Prairie People. Together with their intermarried Anglo-Saxon
and Scots-Irish allies, they monopolized practically every government or private sector job associated with Potawatomi affairs then available, and they
intruded on whatever other opportunities for gain came to their attention.
Using Potawatomi funds, they built and operated the ferries and toll-bridges,
managed inns and hotels, conducted much of the local trade (including the
whiskey traffic), acted as official interpreters, guided Potawatomi delegations
to Washington annually on generous expense accounts (which usually provided them with new wardrobes of clothing yearly at Potawatomi expense),
had most of their personal services (such as blacksmithing) done for them by
government employees supposedly serving the tribesmen, and managed substantial farms, which were equipped with tools and implements delivered for
the benefit of the Potawatomi.

If these sources of income did not add up to sufficient wealth to meet
their needs, the Métis shared payments from trading firms and government
employees, claimed a percentage of all improvements due the Potawatomi as
their just reward for services rendered; and when these did not suffice, they
collected and pocketed the annuity payments of the long deceased and the
absentee Potawatomi. Throughout, they followed the basic principle described
by Padegoshĕk in his 1842 protest to the president: when it served their interest they claimed to be Indians; when not, they were Americans. They
evaded the necessity of licenses for trading operations or of paying territorial
taxes on their hotels, and they obtained considerable federal subvention for
their farming and cattle-raising enterprises, for example, on the grounds that
they were Potawatomi. There was no one like Billy Caldwell to hold them
in check and no powerful traditional leader such as Padegoshĕk to say no to
them. As their numbers decreased in Kansas, the Prairie People were both
overwhelmed as well as outmaneuvered by the more numerous Métis and
Mission Potawatomi. It was for this reason that the "hunter class" of Potawatomi had to resort to occasional threats and force. These were the only

devices available to them to obtain some portion of the tribal resources that were slipping out of their hands.[18]

The Métis were a most adaptable lot who took their religion as they sought their livelihood, wherever the greatest opportunity lay. In 1873, when under President Grant's peace policy a modest effort was made to infuse honesty into Indian administration by handing over the agencies to the control of religious denominations, and when the Potawatomi Agency had been awarded to the Orthodox Quakers, Joseph Napoleon Bourassa—lifelong Catholic and some-time Baptist—converted to the friendly persuasion. In the summer of 1875 he wrote to Enoch Hoag, the Quaker superintendent at Lawrence, appealing that funds be made availabe for the now impoverished Citizen Potawatomi. His letters to Hoag were full of the appropriate "thees" and "thous," and he closed one of them with the wish, "Let us imagine for a short time we are living in the days of William Penn, the best friend the Red Man ever had, then we would all feel like aiding in the good cause." Ten years earlier, when Lyman Draper—Wisconsin's famous frontier historian—wrote Bourassa for informa-tion concerning Billy Caldwell, Bourassa replied briefly and told Draper that he himself had been writing a history of the Potawatomi so as to make money. He wanted Draper to help him edit the manuscript for publication, promised to pay him well for these services, and then asked for advice as to how he might gain entry to the Chautauqua circuit—Joseph Napoleon wished to travel in the East lecturing on the Indian problem, for a reasonable fee.[19]

Serving as technical leaders in economic and political affairs, the Métis and their followers occupied the difficult if profitable battleground between American and Potawatomi institutions. Those who played the more stable, prominent roles were few in number, and this small, elite group changed little in composition over the years. In the early 1850s Joseph La Framboise, Joseph Napoleon Bourassa, and Eli G. Nadeau, together with their protégé George L. Young and the old Illinois trader John D. Lashley, serviced the interests of the Prairie People. However, in these early years their composition and activ-ities were not much differentiated from their counterparts who worked on behalf of the Citizen Bands. This was the period when the government and missionary groups were trying to sustain the fiction of a single, unified, Pota-watomi nation. But within a few years, as the determination of the Prairie People to maintain their separate identity and interests came to the fore, the Métis leadership of this group became clearly divided from that of the Mission —or Citizen—Band. Nonetheless, they continued to work together in an often uneasy alliance, functioning as an incipient executive branch. During these early years they called themselves the "counselors of the Potawatomi."[20]

In late 1857 a new figure appeared, Anthony Navarre, who had finally returned to the fold after a decade spent among the Mormons in Utah. A dozen years later George W. James appeared on the scene, and later in the century James Blandin. After Navarre departed Kansas for Oklahoma in the 1870s, the business affairs of the Prairie People were conducted by James, Blandin, and the nearly indestructible Eli G. Nadeau, who was one of the few wealthy and influential Métis to remain associated with the Prairie People after the 1880s. These men expressed a number of virtues and values; they were literate, better educated, oriented to business enterprise, bilingual and often trilingual, long-term residents who made their careers and spent their lives among the Potawatomi, and were dedicated as well to amassing personal fortunes. They acted out a role that was particularly valuable to the Indian agents, the large trading firms, missionary groups, and various government and private agencies. The Indian agents, particularly, found themselves uncomfortably dependent on the counselors or business committeemen. The agents, all of them political appointees playing the patronage game, rarely spent more than two or three years working with the Prairie People. Hence they needed the services of (more-or-less) trustworthy and dependable local residents who had aspirations compatible with their own.

The common ground of the counselors and agents—and a hotbed of competition and conflict it was—was their shared interests in separating the Potawatomi from their land and wealth. In terms of their actual wealth and their power to manage their own affairs, quite literally beneath the counselors and agents were leaders drawn from the ranks of the Prairie Band itself. The names that were most frequently listed as chiefs on petitions, reports, memorials, and other official documents, roughly in the order of their historical succession, were Wapsi, Shawanese, Mskwas, Mazhi, Half Day (the younger), Wawasēk, Senajiwan (the younger), Matsapto, Miyanko, Shawge, and Kakak. There were many more than these whose names appeared over the years listed as chiefs once or a few times; and there was another category of leaders, also of Potawatomi origin, frequently listed on such documents as well. These were generally called braves, or sometimes headmen. Apparently these were younger men, aspirant chiefs, or leaders of extended families and lineages. Thus, beginning in the 1850s, the affairs of the Prairie People were managed by counselors, agents, chiefs, and braves, with the first two having by far the greatest effective power and the easiest access to wealth and resources.

By 1860 Anthony Navarre was well established alongside Eli G. Nadeau as the major power figure working with the Prairie Band. That year, as the pressures for selling and sectionalizing the National Reservation mounted, Navarre made a major play for even greater influence. Without consulting Agent William E. Murphy he hired an aged attorney, one Lewis F. Thomas of Washington City, to draw up a constitution for the Potawatomi Nation. The instrument Thomas designed was submitted to a poorly attended National

Council which failed to ratify the document. At this point Agent Murphy intervened, for the interests of himself, his patrons in Washington, and the railroad developers were apparently threatened by this move. Murphy called a National Council of his own choosing, then had Attorney Thomas arrested and jailed for interfering in Indian affairs.[21]

After the treaty of 1861 had been signed, but before it was ratified five months later on 15 April 1862, the business affairs of the Potawatomi were unsettled. In March 1862 the Métis, again sparked by Navarre, moved to solidify their control of the whole reservation and its affairs. On March 10 a six-member group set themselves up as the new business committee, with three of the Métis supposedly representing the "Bluffs Band," three the "Catholic Band." Agent W. W. Ross approved this step when he dispatched a report to the commissioner, arguing that "the department will readily see what difficulty attended the transaction of business with a heterogeneous mass of men and boys without any system of organization." However, this business committee immediately fell into conflict, and two weeks later Navarre was forced out of office. Two months later, following a visit with Commissioner Dole, yet another version of the business committee was formulated, and by January of 1863 the causes of Navarre's difficulties came out. He was then identified as the leader of "a small band of wild Indians opposed to the 1861 treaty and against the order system." The "order system" entailed the use of vouchers in place of cash by the Potawatomi in making their purchase of goods and supplies.[22]

Through the 1860s and into the 1870s, there were several attempts on the part of the Prairie People to gain greater control of their affairs, but these met with little success. The new executive institution of the business committee, with its seats occupied by Métis and other Americans, had come to stay. It served as the major administrative mechanism employed by the United States government to manage the affairs of the Prairie People into the twentieth century, by which time the committee had become little more than a rubber-stamp group doing the bidding of the agent, who had emerged as the sole and only authority on the reservation.

As might be expected in a complex, fluid, changing situation such as this, where no sharp or firm line divided Potawatomi from American, chief from counselor, or even business committeemen from Indian agent, the same individuals were often found occupying several such positions and offices, either simultaneously or in succession. The careers of two men, Anthony Navarre and George W. James, are instructive in this regard. Navarre, the son of a French trader in South Bend, Indiana, had gone west with Brigham Young in 1848. He next reappeared on the National Reservation in Kansas in 1857. At first he presented himself as a Mormon missionary, claiming that "he was inspired by the Holy Ghost, that he could foretell events, and that the Mormons would eventually whip the U.S. Govt. and give them all their land back in the various states they had been swindled out of." This was precisely the kind of message, of ultimate justice combined with economic gain mixed with supernatural power, that was greatly appealing to the Potawatomi. Navarre came on like a latter-day Tenskwatawa.[23]

Navarre first took up residence with the Mission Band, where he attempted to organize a group of warriors to go west in support of the Mormon challenge to the authority of the United States, whereupon Agent Murphy had him arrested and jailed until his ardor cooled somewhat. After his release he moved in with the Prairie People north of the Kansas River. By 1859 he had gained considerable influence among them, taken a stand against sectionalizing the reservation, persuaded them to sell part of their pony herds to pay his expenses, and opposed the Indian agent, whose activities he began investigating. At first he signed himself among the Potawatomi chiefs and headmen on memorials and petitions but shortly assumed the title of counselor. His political and business activities were varied. He advocated opposition to the treaty of 1861 in public on behalf of the Prairie People and supported it in private in his own interest and in that of his Métis kinsmen. Regular trips to Washington and other parts were his specialty, always at the expense of the Prairie People's exchequer. He became an expert on Potawatomi treaties, the detailed provisions of which he would cite and interpret for various ends. In 1859, for example, when four Potawatomi men were murdered by horse thieves of eastern Kansas, Navarre called for an indemnity payment from the United States under the 1789 Treaty of Fort Harmar.[24]

Soon after the Treaty of 1861, when Navarre partially and conveniently aligned himself with the Citizen Band, he demanded that he be recognized as a Potawatomi headman, which would give him a half section of prime land, rather than the quarter section made available to the ordinary head of a household. In spite of his acceptance of citizen status (and he was a U.S. citizen to begin with anyway), Navarre continued to work with the Prairie People. In the late 1860s he joined with other Métis leaders in promoting the various devices by which the Citizen Potawatomi allotees rapidly lost their individualized lands and became impoverished. Through most of the 1870s he continued his association with the Prairie People, although early on he had moved his home to Oklahoma where he took up land on the new Citizen Band Reservation. In his later years in Kansas his partner in business was Eli Nadeau, who maintained his own trading and farming operations on the Prairie Band Reserve. This was well after they had both become naturalized U.S. citizens, and hence legally no longer could claim to be Indian. It was Navarre's partner, Nadeau, who was finally tripped up during the Quaker regime on the Prairie Band Reservation. That year charges were pressed against him for collecting large sums of annuity and other payments for deceased Citizen Potawatomi; but Nadeau managed to escape by repaying part of the sum, $6,340, to the superintendent of Indian Affairs in Lawrence.

Somewhere, before 1879, Navarre gradually ended his association with the Prairie People, but Nadeau stayed on, prosperous and influential, until his death many years later. These men missed few opportunities for gainful work. Early in the Civil War, for example, Navarre and Nadeau, using Potawatomi funds, constructed several toll bridges across the tributaries of the Kansas River and collected substantial payments from the supply wagons of the Union Army. Some idea of the wealth these men and other Métis like them had gained is evidenced in an 1878 inventory of cattle and agricultural production on the Prairie Band Reservation. That year the average Potawatomi household owned 3 ponies, 9 hogs, and rarely any cattle, while producing 200 bushels of corn and cutting 6 tons of hay. The ten households identified as those of Potawatomi chiefs or headmen, in comparison, owned an average 23 horses, 1.4 cattle, and 11 hogs, and produced about the same amount of corn and hay as the ordinary neshnabē. In contrast, Eli G. Nadeau was by far the wealthiest man on the reservation. He personally owned 81 horses, 7 mules, 53 sheep, 260 cattle, and 160 hogs, while the crews working his (actually the Prairie People's) lands raised 4,970 bushels of corn and 380 tons of hay. But these figures are only a partial measure of his gross worth and cash-flow, since he was also the largest trader on the reservation, while he and his children had been awarded, as Citizen Potawatomi, allotments south of the Kansas River and in Oklahoma as well. To top this all off, Nadeau managed to have the tuition of his children enrolled at St. Mary's Academy paid from Prairie Band education funds.[25]

Those Anglo-Saxons and Scots-Irish Americans who came into power after the departure of the Métis elite occupied positions similar to their predecessors, who had created the business committee, but circumstances and opportunities had changed. The career of George W. James illustrates the characteristics of this class. James arrived on the National Reservation about 1858 and obtained a position as clerk in the Indian Agency. Although this was a low-paying position, he lived on the reservation at the agency headquarters most of his life and gradually worked his way up to a position of considerable power. In his day, as earlier, the men who every few years were appointed as Indian agents spent only a fraction of their time in the conduct of their official duties. As Richard Smith Elliott had observed in 1843, they were certainly not attracted by the high rate of pay or the possibilities of advancement in government service. They obtained their positions as political favors, came seeking quick fortunes, and departed after a few years. Thus men like George W. James represented continuity and know-how. He was familiar with the people, the language, the records, the accounts, the rules, and the procedures as the agents were not. By the 1870s he had become the *de facto* agent, living and working full-time at the agency. The agents, in contrast, generally made their residences elsewhere, in Westport, Missouri, or Lawrence or Topeka, Kansas, and would occasionally visit the agency when the weather permitted and important business beckoned.

After arriving on the National Reserve, James followed a familiar life pattern. He took his wife from among the Métis—she was a Bourdon by birth. Although for purposes of obtaining access to Potawatomi annuities, resources, and lands she and her family were considered Potawatomi, in 1880 Perry Armstrong found them to be pure "White in ways, company, and status." Thus the "handsome Baltimorian," James, was not adopted into the tribe by the Prairie People as the twentieth-century legend suggested; instead, he worked his way up the ladder of success by the tested route of government service and intermarriage with the established Métis elite. By the 1880s he had become a very restive man, impatient with the succession of Indian agents who were sent out allegedly to manage Potawatomi affairs, certain that he was more capable than any of them (with more than a little justification), entirely too imperious for the comfort of some of his superiors, and, finally, unable to control himself.

In 1894, when an unusually incapable agent arrived, James finally broke loose and managed to secure the man's removal. Then, after nearly forty years of government service, in 1897 he obtained the position of agent for himself, in which capacity he served until 1899. Thereby, in his later years, James occupied a curious multi-ethnic status. Comfortable in his position as government employee and United States citizen by birth, he became a self-adopted Prairie Potawatomi and served as a sometime member of their business committee. While serving as official Indian agent charged with responsibility for protecting his Indian wards, he promoted and supervised the allotment of the Prairie People's lands in severalty, against the violent opposition of the traditional Potawatomi. Among those wards to whom land was deeded, needless to say, were himself, his wife, and his children. Together they were granted five allotments, a full section, 640 acres of prime Kansas real estate. These were among the first fifty allotments made, and among those which helped break the back of the embattled Prairie People's bitter resistance to the Dawes Act.[26]

The counterparts of the Prairie Band's counselors and business committeemen on the American side of the institutional fence were the Indian agents. The latter, serving nominally as the local administrative representatives of the federal government, actually served their own interests, those of their families and political parties, and as well the financial interests of the Indian Ring, that interesting coalition of senators, senior federal administrators, trading firms, railroad developers, and political parties that saw and exploited a mother-lode in the western Indian lands. Whereas the business committeemen had to have his powerbase, if not his cultural roots, in the Potawatomi community, he also necessarily had to maintain a flexible posture as regards the Indian agent and his cohorts. It was necessary that the committeeman have influence among the Prairie Band, and that he be able to provide the semblance of legality to the implementation of national policy. But it was also imperative that committeemen cooperate effectively with the agent, for ultimately it was the agent who accepted, tolerated, and validated the committeeman's position. The committeeman could not have access to Potawatomi funds held in trust in the federal treasury, which were required, for example, to pay the large expenses of the annual junkets to Washington, without the approval of the agent who served as fiduciary for trust funds. The influence of the committeeman without access to such funds would have declined precipitously.[27]

The Indian agent, on the other hand, drew his authority from his official appointment, and his power and influence from the political figures and parties that placed him in office. The agents were expressive of the spoils system, rampant and rapacious in this era of American history. Committeeman and agent together thereby formed an interlocking system of patron-client relationships. Both were intercultural brokers, tying together the institutions of the Prairie Band with those of the United States. On the one hand individual members of the Prairie Band (except those who rejected and opposed the system) were clients benefiting from their relationship with the committeeman, while on the other the committeeman was client to the agent. In turn, the agents had to serve the interests of the trading firms, railroad companies, senators, and presidents who sought and obtained their appointments; but they were usually powerful enough to take ample care of their own needs as well. The committeemen, in addition, did not suffer economically from the exchange.

There were important historical trends, and an interesting interlude, in the evolution of this system during the last half of the nineteenth century. In the first three decades, while the Potawatomi were, yet, relatively powerful and wealthy, the position and influence of the committeeman loomed large, while the whole system was highly personalized and operated on an extralegal, informal basis. During the last decades of the century, in contrast, once the political resistance of the Prairie People had been beaten down, and when the mechanisms for separating them from their lands and wealth had been perfected, the whole arrangement became institutionalized and assumed a rigid, arbitrary, bureaucratic form. It was then, in the first years of the twentieth century, that a few proper members of the Prairie Band began appearing on the business committee. But these were well-domesticated men, appointed by the agent himself to serve his office's needs. Overall, throughout the period, there can be little doubt whose needs were better served—those of the Prairie Band and the commonwealth of the United States, or those of private interests who benefited from most of the wealth and valuables disbursed. The Prairie People began the period a viable, relatively wealthy community. They entered the twentieth century culturally deflated and impoverished, and the United States none the better for the exchange.

Luke Lea, one of the Prairie Band's first agents in Kansas, was a sterling example of the breed. Born in North Carolina, he was of that transmontane frontier stock which settled the Tennessee country, where he became an important political figure and a United States congressman. A good Democrat, he commanded a regiment under Andrew Jackson during the Creek and the Seminole wars. In 1850 he accepted the position of agent to the Potawatomi in Kansas. Like Richard Smith Elliott before him, he had refused an appointment in Washington in favor of the opportunities of the West. Some measure of the relative value he placed on the job as agent to the Potawatomi is given by the fact that the position he rejected in Washington was that of Commissioner of Indian Affairs. This post he declined in favor of his nephew, also named Luke Lea. The elder Lea's tenure in office was not long. Within the year—on 17 June 1851—he died unexpectedly, aged sixty-eight, killed accidentally when thrown from his horse.[28]

The elder Lea's sudden demise precipitated a minor crisis in the office of Indian Affairs and among his kinfolk. At the time of his death the agent had been under investigation for misconduct in office and irregularities in his accounts. Charges against him had been brought by Isaac McCoy and his protégé, Johnston Lykins, the erstwhile physician to the Potawatomi. These charges were prosecuted before an ad hoc administrative tribunal headed by D. D. Mitchell, superintendent of Indian Affairs at St. Louis. The prosecutor was one A. Cumings of Independence, Missouri, who would shortly replace Mitchell as superintendent at St. Louis. Superintendent Mitchell also appointed a J. Brown Harvey of Independence to defend Lea, with the promise of a fee to be paid by the Office of Indian Affairs. Upon Agent Lea's death none of the principals voiced great regret at his passing. Instead, a collective sense of relief was expressed. The charges were not further prosecuted, and the report was forwarded to Washington where it might conveniently disappear and be forgotten. But the elder Lea did leave behind him something of a void—in his accounts: the sum of $154,366 was unreceipted and missing.[29]

On the day following the elder Lea's death, his friend Thomas Moseley, who was agent for the Wyandots, wrote Commissioner Luke Lea. Moseley gave less attention to regrets than he did to recommendations. As a friend, he informed the younger Luke Lea that his uncle "may have left his public business somewhat unsettled." He recommended, keeping the good of the service and family in mind, that one of the agent's surviving sons or sons-in-law "would be better qualified to settle his business" than some stranger. Commissioner Lea then conferred with his kinfolk in Tennessee, and his cousin— the elder Lea's son, Francis W. Lea—was appointed as replacement. Thereafter there was some scurrying about. In August the defending attorney Harvey demanded his fee from Commissioner Lea, hinting that the alternative of suing the deceased Lea's estate might not prove comfortable to those concerned. The following June, an A. B. Earle of Westport wrote the commissioner claiming that Uncle Luke had appointed him physician to the Potawatomi and calling for his salary. Earle, in reinforcing his bill, also suggested strongly that he knew too much for anyone's comfort. He added, in a postscript, "I hope it will meet with your prompt attention . . . I will remain mum . . . there is a screw loose somewhere!"[30]

Francis W. Lea arrived at Fort Leavenworth in November to pick up his father's affairs. He stayed on as agent only long enough to complete this family business, to make a long series of appointments to the numerous positions open on the Potawatomi Reservation, and to find himself charged with irregularities in his own accounts. The younger Lea abandoned his position in June 1853. His brief administration was marked by a remarkable indecisiveness, at least on the public record. Except for the many appointments he made, he remained deferential to all the conflicting interests engaged in the Potawatomi's business, but on no occasion took a clear position for or against any party, and rarely did he specifically advocate or openly reject any policy or practice.[31]

The affair of the Leas was exceptional only in the degree of informality and the importance of nepotism, which prevailed in the earlier years of Potawatomi administration in the West. The younger Lea was replaced by John W. Whitefield (in office from 1853 to 1854), who promptly moved to replace all of the agency employees hired by Lea with his own appointees, including several of his own relatives. In 1854 an R. C. S. Brown was appointed to replace Whitefield, but died of cholera upon taking his post. George W. Clarke (1854–1857) was next in succession. Clarke was a strong proslavery man, notable for his involvement in the guerrilla warfare that raged in eastern Kansas in these years, and for his practice of collecting fifty cents per capita from the Potawatomi annuities. He was replaced by Isaac Winston, who never arrived to take up his duties, and then by William E. Murphy (1857–1861).[32]

During Murphy's administration the confrontation between proslavery and antislavery factions declined, so far as their joint interests in separating the Potawatomi from their reservation merged, overriding sectional prejudices.

Agent Murphy came quickly into conflict with the powerful Ewing and Clymer trading firm, whose local representatives, the Métis leaders of the Mission Potawatomi, worked at having him removed. However, much of Murphy's attention was given to laying the groundwork for the treaty of 1861, an issue on whose value all Americans could agree, and he soon made a workable if uneasy peace with the Métis and the trader patrons. Murphy resigned in the spring of 1861 to run for Congress on a platform advocating the sale of Indian lands in Kansas. He was replaced by W. W. Ross (1861–1865). Ross, inexperienced in Indian affairs, promptly appointed Joseph Napoleon Bourassa as his assistant. It was Ross who legitimized the practice of accepting Americans married to Potawatomi women as Indians, eligible for all rights and privileges in the tribe. By now the population of the National Reservation was irrevocably divided, with the Mission Bands supported by the traders and the agent in the ascendancy, and both they and the Prairie Band regularly sending separate delegations to Washington.[33]

Following the treaty of 1861 one of the first items of business of the now functioning business committee was to pass a resolution indicating the high regard they held for Agent Ross. Their esteem was displayed by awarding him a half-section of land, under the same terms that land was to be allotted in fee simple to other members of the Potawatomi population. Joseph Napoleon Bourassa, Ross's official interpreter and a salaried federal employee, was president of the business committee. By 1864 Murphy came under sharp pressure from Kansas Senator J. H. Lane, who sought and obtained his dismissal on the grounds that he opposed Republican party candidates for Congress and the presidency. The successor to Murphy was a party man nominated by Senator Lane, Luther R. Palmer (1865–1870), who supervised the dissolution of the National Reserve and the treaty of 1867. He was replaced by Agent Joel H. Morris (1870–1873). By then the Quaker leader Enoch A. Hoag had become the superintendent at Lawrence, and in 1874 he secured the appointment of one of his own coreligionists to the Potawatomi agency, M. H. Newlin (1874–1878).[34]

It was Agent Newlin who supervised a brief, four-year interlude in the generally dismal picture of Potawatomi administration. Unlike other agents he gave full attention to his duties and actually lived with his family on the Prairie Band Reservation. Shortly after taking up his post, he proceeded to appoint other good Quakers to the positions available on the reservation. Devoted to his responsibilities and honest, if not entirely tolerant of the wishes of the Prairie People or politic as regards the interests of local businessmen and political figures, he quickly came into conflict with the latter. By the summer of 1875, when Newlin had refused the application of a Topeka merchant, H. C. Linn, as trader to the Prairie People, the Kansas Republican party came down hard on the good Quaker. Linn immediately protested to Senator J. J. Ingalls, requesting as his patronage due Newlin's position as agent.

The embattled Quakers held out for three years, but in the end the spoils system prevailed over President Grant's attempt to bring some modicum of honesty into Indian affairs. It was a specific issue that brought Newlin down. The trader Linn was demanding a monopoly on the trade with the Potawatomi, and he was opposed by the Prairie People, who did not like doing business with him. Newlin, in contrast, was encouraging the Prairie People to take their business where the prices were the lowest and the quality and services the best. He argued that the Potawatomi were quite competent to select their own places of trade, and that this experience contributed to their self-sufficiency. But in the end Republican party politics and federally supported restraints on trade overrode Quaker good sense. In August 1878, over the protests of Superintendent Hoag, Newlin was summarily discharged by President Rutherford B. Hayes himself, and the trader H. C. Linn appointed in his place.[35]

Linn's regime, which lasted until 1885, set the model for Potawatomi management for the next two decades. He worked little at his duties, which were conducted mainly by the *de facto* agent, George W. James, and Eli Nadeau, but he kept his local political fences well mended among the merchants of nearby Holton and Topeka. Thereafter, a sequence of agents carried on in the same fashion into the twentieth century: I. W. Patrick (1884–1887), C. H. Grover (1887), John Blair (1888–1891), J. A. Scott (1891–1894), L. F. Pearson (1894–1897), George W. James (1897–1899), and W. R. Honnell (1899–1903). O. C. Edwards and G. L. Williams were superintendents, respectively, of the Kickapoo and the Potawatomi training schools. By 1903 the management of Potawatomi affairs had become so routinized, and the desire to economize on the costs of Indian administration had achieved such a peak, that the business of reservation administration was handed over to the superintendent of the nearest Indian school. There administrative responsibility lay until 1927, when the superintendents at Haskell Institute in Lawrence were handed the additional responsibility of attending to the management of the Prairie People's affairs.[36]

TRADERS, MISSIONARIES, AND ECONOMIC ADAPTATIONS

Indian agents and their clients the counselors and business committeemen were not the only intercultural brokers to have an impact on the lives and institutions of the Prairie People in the second half of the nineteenth century.

Two other categories of outside agents very important in these years were the traders and missionaries. In addition, as the years went by, a wide variety of other contact agents influenced the Prairie People's lives: promoters of wild west and Indian medicine shows, for example, as well as local farmers and merchants, state and local officials, a substantial number of individuals of ambiguous ancestry claiming rights of access to Potawatomi resources, and interested spectators at the annual Pow Wows the Potawatomi began staging near the end of the century.

Of all these the trader, Indian agent, and missionary certainly had the greatest influence in bringing about significant changes in Potawatomi culture, language, and social institutions. Together they aimed at a total revision of all aspects of the life-style of the Prairie People. Their successes in this respect were highly variable. They had their greatest victories in the areas of technology and political and economic institutions, much less so as regards traditional religion and basic values. Although aimed at producing fundamental revisions in Potawatomi culture—deleting the old and substituting the new—the actual consequences of all this labor was to produce important reactive adaptations. If at the end of the century there were many fewer Potawatomi in Kansas practicing the traditional religious forms, they were doing so more intensively and privately.

At mid-century, when the Potawatomi were wealthy in lands and annuities, many outsiders—either private parties or public figures—were grabbing at the spigots. Within a few decades the Potawatomi cow was giving only skimmed milk. Then fewer could earn their livings in the business of managing the Prairie People's affairs; and there was a decided shift from private entrepreneurship to public administration. While in Iowa, when the Prairie People numbered over two thousand, a part-time subagent, an interpreter, a blacksmith, and occasionally a farmer were the only public employees involved in Potawatomi affairs. By 1897, when the Prairie People living on the Kansas Reservation numbered only 436, ten agency employees and twelve training school employees—all under Civil Service rules—were required to see to their needs. At that point in their history the Prairie People still retained all of their 77,357 acres, although by then most of it had been allotted to them as well as to many outside people. And they still had some $597,037 in treaty funds drawing interest in the federal treasury, yielding approximately $30,000 annually. But this income was not paid over to the Prairie People directly. Instead, the bulk of it went to pay the costs of the very substantial bureaucracy that flourished on the reservation. By that year the trader and the missionary had largely slipped out of the picture, being replaced by the allegedly civil servant. It was not so in the 1850s and 1860s.[37]

In these earlier years a few major firms controlled most of the Potawatomi trade and had the greatest influence in their political affairs. These were Pierre Chouteau, Jr., and Company, the Boone and Hamilton firm (who were successors to the interests of the Forsyths and Kinzies of Chicago), and Ewing and Clymer Company (which conducted the business of the Ewings of Indiana). Generally these companies financed local factors who obtained the necessary licenses to do business with the Potawatomi. The competition between these companies, and with their lesser rivals, was intense. To conduct their business effectively, and to counter the opposition, each worked at obtaining the support of a coterie of "chiefs" on the reservation. More often than not, these chiefs were elevated to their position by a trading company, which in turn attempted to denigrate the client chiefs of opposing companies. Two of George Washington Ewing's favored chiefs, for example, were Andrew Jackson and John Tipton. In March 1850 Ewing wrote Chief Jackson instructing him to spread the word among his followers about all the good things the Ewings were accomplishing on their behalf. Ewing, bolstering his own position, argued that the government was depriving the Potawatomi, paying them ten cents for land worth a dollar an acre. The commissioner of Indian Affairs was the principal cheat, he wrote, and if the Potawatomi cooperated with him he could get them six or seven hundred thousand dollars. A few months later Agent Clarke commented that the efforts of the various firms to secure powers-of-attorney from the Potawatomi were causing grave agitation and conflict on the reservation, generating much gossip, scandal, and slander. The efforts of the Ewings and others were both corrupting and destructive of the influence of the Indian Department, Clarke commented.[38]

At issue in this controversy was the effort of the Ewings and other firms to reinstitute the practice of "national debts." The trading companies had never accepted Commissioner Medill's earlier ban on this method of debt collection. The procedure, first adopted in 1834, allowed the tribal leaders to control the annuity funds and other payments due their people, and to pay their personal debts and those charged against their followers from these "national" funds. As the wealth of the tribe was concentrated in a few hands, the large trading firms had found it easy to corrupt those who had control over these resources. Commissioner Medill's 1846 decision concerning this practice was aimed at reducing the power of the traders and the chiefs, and contributing to the individualization of the tribesmen. In effect, while seeking the most convenient means of increasing their own wealth, traders such as the Ewings opposed the government policy of individualization of responsibility with one of collectivization, with fiscal power lodged in the hands of an easily corrupted few.[39]

In the interim the Potawatomi accumulated very considerable debts among the traders, which Indian agents had been required not to honor. The traders had been cut off from the pipeline of annuity funds, which often had not even passed through Potawatomi hands before being paid directly to the traders by the Indian agents. Thus the income, the personal fortunes, and the future welfare of men like the Ewings was at stake. The divisive consequences of such a controversy were immediate, deep, and lasting. By 1852 factions had emerged among the Potawatomi, one favoring one group of traders, another a second, yet others opposed to the whole practice of delivering tribal annuities to the leaders and indirectly to the traders at all. To a degree this factional split reflected, but it also encouraged, older divisions. The Ewings's main support came from the Mission Bands, while the Prairie People favored mainly their old traders from northern Illinois, the Forsyths, Kinzies, Lashleys, and their associates. Each side provided its favored firms with a power-of-attorney authorizing the direct collection of the trader's debts, each claiming to be the only legitimate representative of the "Nation," and each sending off delegations to Washington to plead their case, at the "national" expense. Agent Francis Lea's comments on this dispute indicated that, so far as he could determine, the several groups of chiefs represented only themselves and their own personal interests, certainly not the tribe as a whole.[40]

The conflict over the nationalization of Potawatomi debts, which was really a fight for control of the tribe's purse-strings, raged for many years. All parties on the reservation were involved, trader, agent, missionary, Métis, and chief. In 1853 Ewing fought to have the tribe's agricultural improvement fund paid in cash, rather than in tools and equipment, acquiring more than $30,000 in this fashion. That same year he praised the Catholic Mission, raged against the "half-breeds" who opposed him, and condemned the Protestant Mission for providing the Potawatomi with "Rogues and prostitutes." In November he tried to obtain the land warrants due certain Potawatomi for their services during the Black Hawk War. The following spring old Padekoshĕk dictated a memorial to Commissioner Manypenny, accusing Ewing of forging his and other chiefs' names to legal documents. By 1855 some elements of the problems Agent Francis Lea had with his accounts in 1853 came out: he had, illegally, authorized payment of $30,860 (the agricultural fund) to the Ewings, and was responsible for still another $18,987 in Potawatomi funds that were missing and unaccounted for. That year also a young traditional okama, Wawasĕk, explained to the commissioner how the Ewings obtained influence, by bribing selected Métis, including the interpreter Joseph Napoleon Bourassa. For the next several years the contest continued as a battle of rival Potawatomi delegations to Washington, each backed by its favored trading company.[41]

Once the treaty of 1861 was signed the furor over the nationalization of individual debts died down, but another issue soon emerged to engage the attentions and emotions of the Potawatomi, their agents, and the traders. This involved the "order system," which was developed as a substitute means of delivering Potawatomi funds into the hands of the businessmen. As Agent L. F. Pearson explained many years later, when the order system itself had fallen into disuse, it consisted of and functioned as a solution to the perennial problem of "promiscuous credits and problematic collections." The "orders" were vouchers, made out and certified by the agent, drawn payable from the account of the individual Potawatomi (usually a head of household), and specifying the dollar value but not the name of the payee. Thus the order system reinforced the role of the agent (and considerably increased his clerical and accounting work), bypassed Potawatomi leaders, delivered a medium of exchange directly into the hands of household heads, and guaranteed payment to the trading firms. Theoretically, when the system was first devised, the orders were supposed to be a "circulating medium redeemable at each payment from the hands of any member of the nation." Agent Ross, who advocated this innovation, also promised the commissioner of Indian Affairs he would prevent their use "outside the reservation." The order system was intended, so Agent Ross explained, to promote competition between traders.[42]

It also bypassed the Trade and Intercourse laws, which restricted trade on the reservation to licensed firms. For this reason, and because the orders—intended to be as good as silver money—were subject to other abuses, the commissioner rejected the plan. Nonetheless, Agent Ross proceeded to issue some vouchers anyway, and these began circulating on the reservation. Shortly, the major source of abuse came to light. This was the same problem that had been discovered years earlier with the "ration tickets" during the removal era. The Potawatomi, accustomed to and preferring cash transactions at the time they wished to make a purchase, were exchanging the vouchers for coin at discount rates. Moreover, it was the Métis leaders—those who had promoted the order system in the first place—who were benefiting from such transactions. These leaders, now established as the business committee, had a comfortable relationship with Agent Ross. In 1862, while Ross was recommending to the commissioner that each of them be paid a salary (from "national" funds) of $200 yearly, they were petitioning the commissioner that he be awarded a half-section of Potawatomi land. But in the fall annuity payment that year there was disorder and confusion. Superintendent Branch, who conducted the payment, refused to honor the outstanding vouchers, and the Potawatomi refused to pay their debts to the traders.[43]

The traders and the Métis thought well enough of the order system to provide Agent Ross with a clerk to aid him in added responsibilities. So powerful were its attractions that, regardless of the periodic protests of the commissioner of Indian Affairs, the order system persisted in use, in attenuated form, subject to short-lived curtailments. From the perspective of the struggling Potawatomi family, the system had the advantage of providing them with a ready source of small cash or goods throughout the year. They would deposit their vouchers with a local merchant and proceed to draw against them over the months until their annuities were again due. The ne'er-do-well, similarly, could trade his voucher in at a discount for ready cash (although they were supposedly exchangeable only for useful goods and food), in preparation for a fast débouché. Finally, the trader and merchant was, as Agent Pearson explained years later, saved the problem of "problematic collections." But in the end the system foundered, as the Prairie People developed other means of obtaining money besides their annuities, and as the growth of American market towns around their reservation offered enticements and competition to the licensed traders. In deference to the local tradespeople it must be acknowledged that the Prairie People were by no means dull in regard to their understanding of the weaknesses of the whole system. Living on credit was a centuries old habit, and more than a few over-extended their indebtedness with numerous traders and merchants. As Indians, federal wards living on a reservation where they were protected from the short-arm of state law, they were safe-guarded against their transgressions in the marketplace.[44]

Both trader and Indian agent found allies among the missionaries, Catholic and Baptist, who worked with the Potawatomi on the National Reservation. St. Mary's mission was established by the Jesuits on the western boundary of the reservation in 1848. A boys' school was started the next year, and one for girls soon thereafter. For the next fifteen years the Catholic establishment flourished, supported by funds drawn from the Potawatomi educational and agricultural development accounts, with some aid from the Society for the Propagation of the Faith. By 1860 the mission and school were largely self-sustaining, dependent on tuition payments from an average sixty-five boys and fifty-five girls in attendance, as well as on the products of the model farm, which had supposedly been established for the benefit of the Potawatomi.

The great majority of the students in attendance at St. Mary's were children of Métis and other Americans. Very few Prairie Band children ever attended this institution. Indeed, a profoundly anti–Prairie People sentiment developed among the Jesuits there, feelings that were reciprocated by the Potawatomi. Father Duerinck, until his death in 1858, was particularly bigoted and remained an avid supporter of assimiliation policies, in general, and the prospect of sectionalizing the reservation, in particular. With growing anti-Catholic convictions, the Prairie People soon began demanding a school of their own, but one managed by a different denomination. After Isaac McCoy's departure from the mission scene the Baptist facility had fallen on hard times. But in 1858 their school was in operation again, with some seventy-seven Prairie Band students nominally enrolled. It is doubtful that anywhere near that number of students regularly attended the school, which was closed down in 1861, for it was run by the Southern Baptist Conference. After the treaty of 1867 St. Mary's, too, fell into a sharp decline, since most of the Catholic Potawatomi and Métis migrated once more, southward to the new reservation in Indian Territory.[45]

The machinations of trader, Indian agent, Métis, and missionary in the 1850s and 1860s associated with dispossessing the Potawatomi of the bulk of the National Reservation, the pressures of thousands of emigrants traversing the trails west, the disorders in the 1850s in eastern Kansas over the slavery issue, and the Civil War, all caused grave stress among the Prairie Band. In large part they responded to these disturbances as they had to the strains of earlier decades, by migrating away from the source of the problems afflicting them. As was discussed in the previous chapter, not all of the Potawatomi in Iowa ever resettled in Kansas. Of those who did, many moved away. More than any other single cause this outward flow was responsible for the dramatic drop in the Prairie Band population after 1848.

About 1850 a group of some fifty Prairie Band members moved back into Iowa and settled in Marshall County near where Johnny Green's people had been living for some years. They lived by hunting and trapping until the game was depleted and then became dependent on local citizens for charity. By 1859 their number had grown to 228 persons, including Green's people. In that year the Iowa legislature, by law, gave them permission to remain in the state. By 1879 they had all become farmers; they sent their children to schools like other Iowans; and the citizens of Marshall County petitioned their congressman to arrange permission for them to remain there in peace.[46]

About 1850 a smaller group of Prairie Potawatomi joined with some Seminole and moved with a Kickapoo band to Coahuila, under the auspices of the Republic of Mexico. There they were given land, and they agreed to provide warriors to aid in the defense of the Mexican frontier against marauding parties of Comanche and Apache. They were joined in Mexico early in the Civil War by more Potawatomi moving away from the problems caused by the treaty of 1861. These Prairie Band members did not abandon their connections to the reservation, nor did they escape the attentions of the sharpers busy separating the Potawatomi from their Kansas lands. Several local businessmen were appointed executors of their estates, had them declared legally dead, and sold their lands. By 1874 only three identifiable Potawatomi families remained in Mexico, and some of these soon returned to the Prairie Band Reservation. Among the businessmen involved in this affair were some familiar names, Eli G. Nadeau, George L. Young, and Lewis Ogee.[47]

Another migration away from the stresses of the Kansas Reservation took the form of a move south into Indian Territory. The Potawatomi involved likely consisted of a patrilineage, led by a man noted for his conservatism, influence, and boldness. This was Shakwas, who for long had maintained his village off the reservation proper, near present Wabaunsee, Kansas. Given to annual visitations to the Osage and Cherokee to begin, in 1856, when he became repelled by affairs on the reservation, he led his people south for a temporary stay, and in the winter of 1864–1865 they finally settled among the Osage.[48] But there were other ways of disappearing from the Potawatomi fold. In June 1862 those Potawatomi long resident with the Kickapoo in eastern Kansas officially amalgamated themselves into that reservation's population, severing their remaining (legal) ties to the Potawatomi tribe.[49]

However, not all migrations were away from the Kansas Reservation. The economic implications and the opportunities of a treaty like that signed in 1861 constituted a powerful attraction for many who had, more or less, a claim to Potawatomi status. When the treaty was done, Anthony Navarre signaled his kinfolk in Indiana, and his brother, Peter, arrived with family to claim eight allotments. Others came in from Iowa and Indiana to take their share of the Potawatomi Reservation. From as far away even as the Ontario Peninsula a dozen Canadian Potawatomi arrived to obtain their due. Few, if any, of those distant Potawatomi became permanent residents. Most soon returned to their homes after arranging for the disposition of the real estate they had claimed.[50]

Of all the scattered groups of "absentee" Potawatomi the most important, from the perspective of later cultural developments, were those in west central Wisconsin. For it was among these Potawatomi, and the adjacent Ojibwa, that a full-scale, organized protest movement emerged in 1876. The protest movement took the form of a new religion, the Dream Dance, that quickly spread among the Algonquian communities of Wisconsin, Upper Michigan, Iowa, and Kansas. The Wisconsin Potawatomi responsible for this development had long ranged through Dodge, Waupaca, Shawano, Portage, Wood, and Adams counties, subsisting as best they could off the land and streams in the area. Early in the Civil War, at the time of the great Sioux outbreak in Minnesota, some of them joined with groups of Winnebago and tried, unsuccessfully, to create a "Western Coalition" opposed to the Union. Relations between them and American settlers in Wisconsin were often strained; and the local Indian agents saw them as a threat to the peace as well as an obstacle to their programs among such reservation communities as the Menomini.[51]

By 1871 the situation of the Potawatomi in central Wisconsin was getting desperate. That year William W. Johnston of Shawano reported to the secretary of the Interior that, because of the depletion of game, the Potawatomi's means of subsistence had failed, which "enraged the Indians more and more every year." Johnston then reported that the Potawatomi were sending messengers to the interior tribes, as far as the Dakotas, urging the other tribes to council with them. "I believe they mean mischief," Johnston added. These Potawatomi, a mounted people, were engaged in a competition with both settlers and loggers in this part of Wisconsin. Their ponies were grazing on the same pastures used for the logging teams, and with intensive clear-cutting of the forests the game supply was severely depleted. In this fashion there broke down the major economic adaptation the Wisconsin Potawatomi had worked out in the years after the removal era—that of occupying and exploiting the lands still unsettled by Americans. Local citizens and Indian agents called for the standard solution, removal to the west or concentration on a reservation in northern Wisconsin. By 1873, encouraged by the Indian agents, some of the Wisconsin Potawatomi were engaged in negotiations with the Prairie Band concerning the possibility of resettling in Kansas.[52]

However, these negotiations and the solutions proposed failed. Then the Potawatomi and the Ojibwa in Wisconsin took matters into their own hands. In 1876 a visionary arose, of very special interest because this new prophet was a woman, supposedly a Santee Dakota, named Wananikwē. She was quickly taken in hand by a coterie of male disciples, all Potawatomi and Ojibwa, who began carrying her message and the tenets of the new faith far and wide. The ideology and the aims of this new religion expressed solutions to both the internal problems of the Algonquian communities and those stemming from contacts with Americans and disloyal Indians. As regards externally caused problems, the disciples were promising the Indians of Wisconsin and other states that "at some future day a great drum will tap in heaven, and at that time all the whites and Catholic Indians will be paralized, when all they have got to do is to walk forth and tap them on the head—and take possession of the land." Political maneuver failing them, military action denied by the overwhelming superiority in men and arms of the Americans, the Wisconsin Potawatomi in their desperation had turned to magic and ritual for a solution to the ills which plagued them.[53]

The first known mention of the Dream Dance (or Drum Cult) among the Potawatomi in Kansas dates to 1884, when Agent Linn reported that during the past year a new system of worship, consisting "principally of dancing and exulting," had been introduced among the Prairie People. This date, 1883, is certainly too late. The Prairie People had been in continuous, yearly contact with the Potawatomi in central Wisconsin and doubtless were well aware of developments there soon after the appearance of the prophetess Wananikwē in 1876. The 1883 date, thus, marks the year this new religion, in a form accepted and practiced by the Prairie People, first came to the attention of the authorities.

Nevertheless, Agent Linn, like his successor, I. W. Patrick, expressed considerable tolerance for the new religion. Linn's opinion was that, aside from

Plate 10. The origin myth of the Dream Dance or Drum Cult tells how Christ put magical power in the first drum of this new religion. Here the late Curtis Pequano holds the staff with which he reenacted this event in quarterly rituals. (Photograph by the author, 1964.)

the "superstition and amount of time spent in these dances, the moral tendency was very good, as the teaching is in accordance with the Ten Commandments." Wananikwē's disciples were preaching against the abuse of alcohol, adultery, violence and murder, gambling, and horseracing. These included some of the internal goals of the new faith, to restore peace and harmony to the sadly disorganized, conflict-ridden Algonquian communities of the region. In 1885 Agent Patrick seconded Linn's tolerance of this new religion. He saw in it a way of making the Potawatomi "chaste, cleanly, and industrious." The Prairie People, Patrick reported, adopted the Dream Dance as a "means of expressing their belief in the justice and mercy of the Great Spirit, and of their devotion to him," and they were "so earnest in their convictions as to its affording them eternal happiness, that I have thought it impolitic . . . to interfere with it any further than to advise as few meetings as possible." Agents Linn and Patrick were perceiving in this new religion only selected elements that met with their approval. The revolutionary aspirations of the founders and faithful were not being exposed in public to American officials. The Dream Dance adherents, in fact, were working to create internal peace and harmony within the separate, isolated Indian communities, and to bind them together into a pantribal movement employing magical devices to oppose American power and encroachment.

Yet it is the nature of magical means that they fail of achieving long-range, concrete, rational ends. Whatever the motivations of the early converts to the Dream Dance religion among the Prairie People (they seem to have been men who were losing faith in the Midewiwin and clan-bundle rites), and however they may have perceived the promises of Wananikē's disciples, the

Plate 11. An early photograph of a Dream Dance drum, ca. 1910, near where the religion was created in the 1870s. Here the piyakskeyonene—drum keeper and his patopet—assistant carry away the sacred drum following a ritual. (Photograph by Frances Densmore; courtesy of the Bureau of American Ethnology, Smithsonian Institution.)

Plate 12. Drum presentation ceremony; one of the two drums presented by the Lac du Flambeau Chippewa to the Menomini in 1910. Such drums eventually worked their way southwest through the ritual pipeline to the Kansas Potawatomi. (Photograph by Frances Densmore; courtesy of the Bureau of American Ethnology, Smithsonian Institution.)

new religion soon began evolving a different kind of promise, while keeping its earlier forms. By the 1950s it had emerged as the major communal cult on the Prairie Band Reservation, but the mythic promise by then was no longer a magical restoration of past power and glory. Instead, myth and ritual promised and helped to achieve cultural stability and the perpetuation of a distinctive Potawatomi identity.[54]

One point emerges from between the lines of Agents Linn's and Patrick's reactions to the Dream Dance religion—they were disturbed mainly by the amount of time the Prairie People were giving to the conduct of rituals. Whatever else American policies and practices had done to the Potawatomi, it had not oppressed them to the point where they had to labor dawn-to-dusk in procuring a bare subsistence, nor had it imbued them with the spirit of the Euro-American work ethic. There is much continuity between such observations in the 1880s and those of an earlier year. The subject of Father Duerinck's hateful, envious remarks at St. Mary's had, for example, focused precisely on this same delict: the Prairie People (especially the men) had large amounts of free time, and they employed it for purposes that outside observers could not recognize as practical or productive.

Somewhere between the funds left over for per capita payments after the Métis, trader, agent, and missionary had collected their large share, and what the Prairie People managed to produce from hunting, fishing, and the small gardens, there was enough to provide for more than bare subsistence. Indeed, more than a half century later the modern Potawatomi looked back with longing at the prosperity of the 1880s and the decades previous to that. The key to what may seem a quandary lies in recognizing the limited wants of the Prairie People in the 1850s and later, and the modest income that was available to them even after the elite elements had provided for their somewhat larger needs, as well as the contemporary tendency to glamorize the past. Beginning in the early 1850s, one agent after another remarked on how dependent the Prairie People were on their annuities for their subsistence as well as for what were, in the perceptions of agent and auditor, their luxuries. An examination of traders' accounts bears out these observations. Beginning in the 1850s—even when the Prairie People were relatively free to hunt buffalo to the west—they were obtaining from the traders in large quantities salt meat, milled flour, and corn meal, as well as a wide variety of manufactured goods, both utilitarian and ornamental. These goods were charged against their individual annuity accounts with the traders and paid for at the annual distribution of funds. Only a very small fraction, less than 5 percent, of such charges were paid off in goods actually produced by the Potawatomi themselves, in peltries, logs, or corn meal, for example. By the early 1850s the Prairie People were dependent on a money economy, and they were living off of income from their capital.[55]

During the 1850s and into the 1860s the annuity payment days created a great attraction on the reservation, taking on the features of a market fair. The presence of large quantities of hard money required armed guards and attracted a variety of sharpers. At this time the traders did their largest business, as most would import goods for this brief period, and then close up shop until the next payment time. The agent generally interpreted the lack of interest shown in work by the Potawatomi as a "want of perseverence and skill." An obvious solution, as Agent Clarke put it in June 1855, was to hire someone who would teach them the necessary attitudes and skills, not to do their work for them. This might be interpreted as the tendency to meet one ill by encouraging another—the expansion of the Indian Service bureaucracy—except that from the point of view of the Potawatomi themselves the blacksmiths, farmers, wagon-makers, and gunsmiths hired were their servants, not their teachers. Thus a considerable portion of the Prairie People's income went into hiring the services of skilled craftsmen, not into the acquisition of skills needed to adapt to a new technology and economy.

In this way the Potawatomi remained technologically backward, capable of functioning effectively only so long as there was income adequate to meet the costs of the services they needed. Several things conspired to render the stability of this adaptation a long-range improbability. Technological change and rapid economic development in the area acted so as to sustain and even increase the gap between the Potawatomi's own skills and those needed to maintain themselves in a modernizing world. Moreover, their own wants increased as new things came to their attention. Beyond these, a constant rate of inflation in the last half of the century gradually eroded the value of their fixed capital and interest income. The Prairie People were trapped in a downward economic spiral that was only accelerated by later developments such as the Dawes Allotment Act, which further diminished their available resources. By the time of the Civil War the United States began engaging in a new practice which sometimes further diminished the income available to the Potawatomi, that of paying out annuities in highly inflated paper money. In 1867, for example, the disbursing clerk of the Department of the Interior made up a $14,725 paper money payment by selling $10,000 in coin at a 47.25 percent premium.[56]

From time to time the Prairie People witnessed the payment of very large sums of money to various groups on the reservation. After the treaty of 1867, once the Atchison, Topeka, and Santa Fe Railroad Company had purchased the surplus (unallotted) portion of the Citizen Band fraction of the National Reservation, several such payments were made. In the fall of 1868, for instance, 600 Potawatomi who had elected to take their land in severalty received "head rights" of $530 each. A total of $317,655.96 was paid out in a few weeks time, starting in October of that year. That same December a half-year annuity payment of $19 was made to each of 1,966 persons, including the minority Prairie People and their departing kinsmen of the Citizen Band. Thus the Prairie People became accustomed to the regular, annual payment of annuities based on their income from their treaty funds, and they developed as well an eager anticipation of the larger windfall amounts that could come to them on very special kinds of occasions. It was this expectation, coupled with their own conviction of past economic injustices and the promises of attorneys and claims agents, that predisposed them to litigation against the United States later in the century.[57]

By the 1870s the fortunes of the Prairie People began to decline, so far as they were dependent on subsisting on their annuity income. In 1872 the total interest due them from their income from prior treaties amounted to only $35 per capita, but most of this was absorbed in the costs of managing the agency, especially its educational functions. Shortly, during a succession of bad crop years, the agents began petitioning the commissioner of Indian Affairs for special relief funds. But they also worked at developing alternate sources of income for the Prairie People. By 1875 the practice of the agent's leasing Prairie Band land to adjacent Kansas farmers for pasturage was established. That year Agent Newlin, the good Quaker businessman, took in $1,200 in fresh, added income for his charges. The amount was small, but the principle sound, and the Prairie People themselves took heed of the practice.[58]

The 1870s were bad years for crops, and they were worsened by the Prairie People's own reluctance to adapt rapidly enough to changing economic circumstances. They still placed great value on their pony herds, which figured importantly in their prestige economy as important goods in ritual exchanges. But there was no longer, as there had been in earlier years, a cash market for these small, wiry animals. Local Kansas farmers had little use for them, since they were too weak and lacked the necessary stamina for arduous farm labor. But they managed to eat up much of the available pasturage on the reservation. By 1876, however, Agent Newlin was able to persuade a few to start cattle-raising and to exchange or to cross-breed their ponies for the larger American stock. Nonetheless, few of the Potawatomi ever kept many cattle for profit or even for their own consumption. The preferred domestic meat animals were hogs, which were allowed to run wild, foraging for themselves (thus providing a minor sport as well as animal protein). These basic patterns continued into the 1880s. The Prairie People then practiced an economy which was based on a small cash income derived from annuity funds and from a collective management and leasing of pasture lands to Kansas farmers. This income was supplementary to the fundamental subsistence gardening and minor stock-raising, still largely woman's work. To this could be added only small amounts of small game, rabbits, duck, quail, and the like, and some fish.

It was at best a highly marginal economy, one threatened by periodic droughts, which necessitated emergency relief in the form of grants of food to prevent late winter starvation. In such a straitened condition, the Prairie People came face-to-face with yet another reduction in the major economic resource owned by them, their 121 square miles of Kansas prairies and bottoms that made up the diminished reservation owned collectively by the community as a whole. In a sense, by Kansas standards of the time, they should have been a relatively wealthy people. In 1883 their net worth, even without counting the value of the land, but including their funds on deposit in the Treasury and the worth of their buildings and improvements, was some $1,411 per capita. However, because of the high costs of management of the reservation, and their reluctance to exploit it in more advantageous fashions, they remained cash-poor.[59]

THE DAWES
ALLOTMENT ACT
AND ITS AFTERMATH

At the negotiations for the treay of 1861, Commissioner Dole came prepared to persuade the Potawatomi either to sectionalize their lands and become citizens of the United States or to sell the reservation and purchase another farther west with the proceeds. The Prairie People's leaders vehemently rejected both alternatives. Shagwe, acting as speaker in the tradition of Half Day and Wabansi before him, and using much the same phrasing these okamek had employed for the treaties of 1833 and 1846, launched bitter, barbed words at the treaty commissioners. When Dole argued that American law would protect those who became citizens, Shagwe replied, saying, "the law protects him who understands it, but to the poor and ignorant like the Indians it is not a shield of protection; on the contrary, it is a cloak to cover the law-giver's malice." Shagwe, when informed that sectionalizing or selling was the president's desire, reflected on how often he seemed to change his mind. He remembered the treaty of 1846, when the president had told him "this land would be my last and permanent home." "What business has he to tell me to change my abode?" he asked. "This place is mine. I can leave it or keep it as I please."[60]

The opposition of the Prairie Band was strong enough to introduce a third option, that of retaining a diminished tract—a large fragment of the whole National Reservation—which they could hold in common. With this alternative successfully negotiated, their leaders placed their names on the 1861 treaty document. Their expectation and hopes were that they would be allowed to hold and enjoy their 121 square miles in perpetuity; but the treaty, the last the Prairie People were ever to sign, was conspicuously silent on this issue. Article 4 simply awarded them a diminished reservation with the understanding that they thereby relinquished all claims to the balance of the lands that had made up the National Reservation. There was none of the fine language found in other treaties of this period, assigning the lands so long as the grass might grow and the waters flow. Clearly, in the perspective of the treaty commissioners—who were representing the railroad development interests—this was an expedient measure only. They had accomplished their aim of obtaining rights-of-way and lands for the railroad companies, and the appropriate mechanisms for separating those who elected citizenship from their allotted lands had already been set in train.[61]

Thereafter, while the Prairie People set about adapting their lives to their new, smaller environment, anticipating that this was once and for all their final homeland, the Indian policy of the United States took a course which would, within twenty years, reduce the reservation to a collection of scattered farmsteads. In 1871 the House of Representatives tagged a rider to the Indian Appropriations Bill which forbade the United States to treat with Indian tribes as if they were sovereign states. In one move Indians were brought under the municipal jurisdiction of the federal government, their leaders were deprived of legitimate authority in dealings with federal officials, and the treaty era was ended. The House, in asserting its powers as regards appropriations and qualifying the Senate's treaty-making authority, had made Indians into subjects of the federal government. Thus Congress acknowledged and brought into the open what had been a fact recognized for decades—treaties were largely unilateral acts on the part of the United States, drawn according to its specifications and at its convenience.

Sixteen years later, in early 1887, the Individual Allotment Act became law. This legislation gave the president authority, without consultation with or the consent of the tribes, to allot lands in severalty to the reservation peoples and to make them citizens of the United States. If an individual Indian refused to select an allotment, the Indian agent was authorized to choose one for him. As Henry E. Fritz has rightly commented, the Dawes Allotment Act "condemned reservation Indian to poverty for many generations." It also deprived them of the power to make important decisions concerning their lives.[62]

While humanitarian reformers supposedly concerned with the welfare of the Indian were gathering enough influence to form a coalition with congressmen interested in benefiting their constituencies and to bring about the Dawes Act, the Prairie People were under constant pressure from local officials and land-jobbers. The sale of surplus Potawatomi lands after the treaty of 1861, and the loss of nearly all individual parcels allotted to the Citizen Potawatomi by 1868, had not satisfied the land-hunger in Kansas. In the winter of 1871–1872 rumors were sweeping the nearby Kansas communities to the effect that the Prairie People were going to sell out, and many Kansans were petitioning the government for homesteads on the diminished reservation. By early 1880 the Prairie Band's okamek learned that the businessmen in Holton had formed an association to bring about legislation forcing the sale of the reservation and the relocation of the Prairie People. The Prairie Band's leaders in this period were Shawnase, Mskwas, Pishedwin, Kakak, Pamoko, Menokwet, and Matsapto, who acted jointly as a tribal council. Their protests against this unilateral action ran on for several years. In February 1881 they asked Agent Linn, while in Washington, to protest this attempt to deprive them of their land. He was to tell Congress and the commissioner of Indian Affairs that the Potawatomi "regard our Reserve in the light of a permanent home and that our improvements thereon will justify such an inference on the part of every reasonable man acquainted with our mode of living." The Prairie People were working hard to maintain a united front. Agent Linn was to inform the Congress that "no party or clique wants to sell."[63]

In January of 1886 the Prairie Band's council issued another protest concerning pending legislation affecting their lands. This appeal to the commissioner was plaintive. "We have relinquished the customs and expectations of our fathers," they wrote. "Our children are advancing in civilization beyond ourselves, and we are determined to transmit them the homes that are dear to us." The Prairie People knew what theme should have been most appealing to officials in Washington, but it fell on inattentive ears. The okamek closed their appeal with a remark indicating their full appreciation of a hard political and economic reality, "We need to be protected in the peaceful possession and enjoyment of our land, without which we would soon become paupers." In this memorial, as in earlier protests, the leaders emphasized they had authorized no one to represent their interests in Washington. They were, rightly, fearful of the old device of dealings between federal officials and self-appointed, self-interested delegations of Potawatomi, or the hangers-on who lived on the fringes of the reservation community.[64]

But there was no one in Washington listening to the Prairie People's appeals, even to protestations about their degree of advancement in "civilization." In 1887 the Dawes Act became the law of the land, and in 1888 Commissioner John H. Oberly pronounced that "the Indian must . . . be taught how to labor; and that labor may be made necessary to his well-being, he must be taken out of the reservation through the door of the general allotment act. And he must be imbued with the exalting egotism of American civilization, so that he will say 'I' instead of 'We,' and 'This is mine,' instead of 'This is ours.'" The following year, in his annual report, the newly appointed commissioner, T. J. Morgan, added that Indians could not escape American civilization. They must "either conform to it or be crushed by it." As President Theodore Roosevelt described it in 1901, this law was a mighty engine, used to crush down the tribal mass. The Dawes Act provided not only the goal but the mechanisms for bringing about allotment, even against the strongest opposition. Land on the Prairie Band's reservation could be allotted to persons who had not lived thereon, to those who had earlier adopted citizen status, to those for whom no reservation was provided, and, in practice, to nearly anyone whom the local agent might recognize as a worthy claimant.[65]

Prairie Band opposition to implementation of the Dawes Act was an extension of their earlier fight against locally initiated legislation designed to deprive them of their land. When the president's message came 1 September 1891, ordering the allotment of their reservation, they were as well prepared for battle as their situation allowed. But the forces arrayed against them were massive and overwhelming, and they were vulnerable within. They had no place to appeal to in Washington, and no powerful allies near the reservation. The agent was not required to consider the wishes of the okamek, and he did not. The only weapon available to the Potawatomi was to stand fast, to maintain a united front against the allotment procedure, and to discipline anyone who indicated his willingness to take lands in severalty.

The forces arrayed against the culturally conservative Prairie People, both within and outside the community, were very similar to those involved in earlier dealings with the federal government. Although a smaller population was associated with the 77,358 acres that made up the reservation, it was fully as heterogeneous as it had been for decades. Except for the missionary, all the familiar actors were present and involved in separating the Prairie People from their lands—agent, trader, Métis, local Kansas settlers and businessmen, dissident and highly acculturated persons who regularly shifted back and forth from Potawatomi to citizen status, absentee Potawatomi, other Indians, and assorted individuals of various backgrounds, all maneuvering to obtain a share of the Prairie People's reservation.

Eli G. Nadeau was the main Métis trader operating on the reservation as the time for allotment drew near. The Prairie People thought ill of him and in 1886 attempted to reduce his influence. That September the okamek petitioned the commissioner for a new trader, "one who will keep a good stock of goods, attend strictly to business, and not interfere in . . . tribal matters." They wanted "someone who had never had any connection to the tribe," and were particularly incensed that Nadeau had recently introduced onto the reservation his protégé and partner, George L. Young. Young frightened the Prairie People, for they know him to be the one person most responsible "for the degradation and poverty of the Citizen's Pottawatomie." Nadeau and Young were by no means the only persons formerly associated with the Citizen Band on the Prairie Band Reservation in this period, although they represented the unscrupulous elite element of this group. After the treaty of 1867 substantial numbers of impoverished Citizen Potawatomi had drifted back to the area, where they managed to gain a marginal living and foothold. The agents generally opposed their presence on the reservation, although some gained official approval for staying. The poorer Citizen Potawatomi worked as servants, housekeepers, stock-keepers, and farmers for the Prairie People. It was from this group that they drew considerable support in their opposition to the Dawes Act.[66]

There were various other Potawatomi from different parts associated with the Prairie People in these years. Nsowakwet, also known as John Young, is an example of those from west-central Wisconsin who joined the Prairie People in fighting against allotment. Nsowakwet was one of the disciples of Wananikwē, and he was instrumental in bringing the Dream Dance to the Kansas Potawatomi. Agent Scott and others were particularly disturbed that this element should oppose the Dawes Act, for the legislation was supposed to reward and encourage hard work, and the Wisconsin Potawatomi had been noted for years as a group who supported themselves without benefit of federal supervision and support. Another representative of the Eastern Potawatomi

Plate 13. Matthew Matchie (now deceased) holds a photograph of himself the day he was initiated into the Native American Church (or Peyote religion) on the Kansas Potawatomi Reservation. (Photograph by the author, 1963.)

active in Kansas at this time was Thomas Topash, from Michigan. Topash was acting as a kind of broker between the Eastern Potawatomi and the Prairie People, and he, too, offended the agent's sensibilities, but for usurping authority that the agents believed theirs. Agent Scott countered the influence of men like Nsowakwet and Topash by demanding that they take up residence on the Kansas Reservation or be dropped from the official rolls. This failing, he attempted to have them arrested and jailed for conduct unbecoming Indian wards.[67]

The organized opposition of the Prairie People to the General Allotment Act took many forms and occupied a great deal of their time and energy for years. They neglected their gardens, hay-making work, and herds. They refused their cooperation to the agent in many of the routine activities of the agency. They threatened violence to the person of the agent, as well as to any Potawatomi who seemed willing to accept an allotment and hence break the unanimity of the opposition. They focused much attention on the Dream Dance, reinforcing their solidarity and spirit of community with ritual, prayer, and magic. Over the opposition of the agent, they sent delegations to Washington seeking aid. They solicited the support of other Indian populations similarly threatened; and they organized the traditional warrior's society as a police force and directed it to keep discipline. None of this was of any avail, except to generate enthusiasm and to raise expectations temporarily, only to find high hopes dashed into bitter frustrations. The agent had a winning hand before he played his first card.

But the Potawatomi meant business. When Agent Scott visited a family in October 1892 to induce them to send their children back to school, the head of the household drew a line on the ground and dared Scott to cross it. Scott, who was alone at the time, retreated instead. He found the Dream Dance meetings particularly disturbing, clearly recognizing this institution as a critical focus of the opposition on the reservation. In early October 1892 he reported that it was becoming "something very nearly like the Ghost Dance," which had recently swept the western plains, generating great fear among many Americans. Scott countered the Dream Dance rituals by enforcing Indian Service regulations prohibiting unsanctioned trips off the reservation, and by threatening the use of military force to break them up.[68]

Much of the organized opposition to allotment was led by Wakwaboshkok —Roily Water and his assistant, Nibakwa—He Walks at Night (also known as James Thompson). It was Wakwaboshkok the Prairie People had appointed okama of the warrior society. A literate man whose prose and spelling was about the same quality as that of George Rogers Clark, Wakwaboshkok habitually signed his letters with the title "Gentil Brave." This appellation he wrote several times at the bottom and on the margins of his letters, each time with the *nom de paix* heavily circled. Obviously, he wanted to emphasize his pacific intentions. But he was not always peaceful on the reservation, when facing dissidents who indicated they might break ranks and take allotments, or countering other Indians and Americans who seized the opportunity to obtain a share of Prairie Band lands. A powerfully charismatic if benign man, Roily Water had been a thorn in the side of the agents for a decade prior to his confrontation with the power of federal law and bureaucracy in the 1890s. Supposedly of Sauk origin, he was a Potawatomi leader of the old school, a master of the several devices the Prairie People had worked out over the years to cope with the government of the United States. However, by 1891 these tactics and techniques were obsolescent. Protest meetings, midnight councils, petitions to the president, delegations to Washington, complaints about the character and ethics of the agent—none of these had significant effect any longer.[69]

Wakwaboshkok's first efforts to stop the allotment procedure were success-ful. When the new agent, J. A. Scott, reported for duty in 1891, charged with the responsibility of sectionalizing the reservation as quickly as possible, mat-ters came quickly to a head. Scott immediately misdiagnosed the problem as being caused by the impoverished Citizen Potawatomi who had joined forces with the Prairie People to oppose the new policy. When persuasion failed him that summer, he called for a detachment of the Seventh Cavalry from Fort Riley to have the Citizen Potawatomi evicted from the reservation. Then Scott and Wakwaboshkok came into an instant, heated confrontation, for part of the okama's support came from the poorer, landless Potawatomi from the

Plate 14. William Wahzowkouck, often called Jack Forty, a major ritualist and leader of the Kansas reservation Peyote religion, sits in front of the sapling framework for a wigwam preceding an evening meeting of the congregation. (Photograph by and courtesy of Dr. Robert L. Bee.)

Citizen Band and the East, and he moved to physically interpose himself between the troopers and the threatened Indians. At this time, in late August, Agent Scott had Wakwaboshkok and Nibakwa arrested and detained by the cavalry. Simultaneously, Scott tried to discredit the dissident Potawatomi leaders, arguing that they had no support on the reservation except among the Oklahoma and Wisconsin elements, and that they had been prompted by a few unscrupulous local businessmen. This was the administrative basis for the agent's efforts to keep the leaders under detention at the Fort Riley stockade; but his aim was swiftly to break the more general Prairie Band resistance to allotment.[70]

Not all Kansans sided with the agent. Wakwaboshkok and the Prairie People did have the support of a few local ranchers and businessmen, who supported them in their opposition to the Dawes Act, as well as that of a scattering of Topekans, who were willing to see the arrest of Wakwaboshkok and Nibakwa as a violation of their civil rights. The economic interest of these ranchers and businessmen was plain. Allotment of the reservation meant that the open range lands would be subdivided and fenced. For some time the Prairie People, picking up on the practice introduced by Agent Newlin twenty years earlier, had been in the business of leasing their open lands themselves. A few leaders, such as Wakwaboshkok, acted as "lease brokers" in making such arrangements, which was one source of their influence. Similarly, again following Agent Newlin's lead, the Prairie People had started being selective about where they took their trade off-reservation. Hence, they were in a position to exert modest economic pressure, and some few Kansans had a vested interest in maintaining the reservation system as it was before the Dawes Act.[71]

With the support of their Kansan friends, in mid-December 1891 Wakwaboshkok and Nibakwa acquired an attorney, who promptly filed habeas corpus proceedings in the Topeka district court. They followed this up the next spring with a civil suit for damages of $11,000 each against Agent Scott and Colonel Forsyth of the Seventh Cavalry. Scott argued strongly against their release. When this failed, he sought to prevent their return to the reservation until both had promised to cease opposition and set an example by accepting allotments. In April 1892, after nearly seven months' imprisonment, the Prairie Band leaders were released from the stockade at Fort Riley and returned to the reservation, where they promptly set about undermining Scott's further efforts to implement the Dawes Act.[72]

Their exertions through the summer of 1892 were largely successful. That August, in his annual report, Agent Scott had to make lengthy explanations of why his attempts to promote sectionalizing had failed. Since 1863, he commented, the leaders of the Prairie Band had "continuously taught that allotment was ruinous to their people." They combated this policy with every

Plate 15. Here a member of the Native American Church plays the small water drum used in rituals. (Photograph by and courtesy of Dr. Robert L. Bee.)

means at their disposal, he explained. Through the date of his report, April 29, only ten heads of Prairie Band families had come forward voluntarily to seek their allotments. Yet Scott reported that as of that date he had made a total of 236 allotments. This he accomplished through two devices, by heeding and honoring the requests of persons who were not accepted by the Prairie Band as legitimate members of their community, and by himself selecting allotments for and assigning them to the very elderly, to small children, and to orphans. Wakwaboshkok and his assistants were maintaining discipline among the Prairie People, but they could not stem the tide of allotments. Control of their lands was slipping away from them.[73]

That October, Scott had to counter a report to the commissioner to the effect that Americans living on the reservation were strongly opposed to the

Dawes Act. On the contrary, he reported, "no class of people—not excepting Officers of the government—are more anxious for the completion of allotments, than they are, for the reason that the ill will of the Indians who are opposing allotments is directed against them with a vindicativeness that subjects them to constant annoyance, if not danger." Scott admitted only to five Americans living on the reservation and enumerated their enthusiastic acceptance of allotments. "On one of the most exciting days I ever saw at the Agency," he noted, one of these was the first publicly to take allotments for himself and his family. This was Charles Sheppard and family of Wisconsin (allotments: 1–5). As soon as was legally possible these allotments—like most of the others obtained by outsiders under similar auspices—were sold. Of the first fifty allotments, forty-two went to nine families, including George W. James, whose claims to Prairie Band status were bitterly contested by Wakwaboshkok and other culturally conservative Potawatomi. The additional six allotments of the first fifty were made to individuals such as Charles E. Maines, Benjamin Preston, and Augustus Pappan. The next fifty allotments went mainly to very elderly Potawatomi, most of whom were deceased in a few years' time so that their lands were placed on sale in the open market, as well as to small children under guardianship, and to a few additional "honorary" Potawatomi.[74]

Agent Scott was not being particularly attentive to the ethnic antecedents of the first four dozen or so individuals he encouraged to take allotments—if encouragement they needed. He may be excused on the grounds that he was carrying out policy directives of a bureau that paid little attention to such ethical issues. The essential thing was to get the process of allotment started and completed, over the concerted opposition of the Prairie People. Scott's future lay in achievements which met with the approval of his superiors in Washington, and the commissioner of Indian Affairs never disapproved of the actions he took. The Prairie People, on the other hand, took a different and dim view of these proceedings. Although Wakwaboshkok did not then accept defeat, the resistance of the Prairie Band to the Dawes Act was effectively broken. Indeed, Wakwaboshkok and other leaders who came after him have never accepted the implementation of the General Allotment Act as anything more than the loss of a single engagement—their war went on. As regards Agent Scott, at the time Wakwaboshkok and other leaders of the period considered him Potawatomi enemy number one. They conducted themselves as if they believed he were personally responsible for the allotment legislation and its execution. They focused their enmity narrowly and concretely on this one individual and followed a course that logically derived from these assumptions, that of attempting to get him removed from office. These *okamek* seemed to believe that, somehow, justice would be waiting for them in Washington.

Scott employed various other stratagems to defeat his opposition. In early 1892 he stopped soliciting leases and tried to prevent the unofficial leasing of Potawatomi lands on the grounds that the income from such a practice made the Prairie People too independent—the funds were largely going to support opponents of allotment. In May 1893 he summarily discharged Kewakok, the elderly leader of the Kansas Kickapoo, on the grounds that he had been supporting Wakwaboshkok. By that summer Scott was viewing the Dream Dance ritual with antipathy and thinking of suppressing it. For many months allotments had been coming through at a very slow rate, intermittently, one or a few at a time. In August 1893 he was able to report only forty-nine more processed since his report the previous year. Meanwhile, he has assigned James Blandin the role of his personal secret service agent. Through 1894 Blandin kept a close eye on Wakwaboshkok, attending meetings and reporting back to Scott the results of his observations.[75]

While Scott was working to break the opposition, Wakwaboshkok labored to bolster it. In 1892 he began a pattern of regular visitations to Washington. Some years he traveled east two or three times. On a few occasions he seems to have flown. That is, he and perhaps Nibakwa would disappear one day, indicating they were on their way to visit the president and sundry officials, and a week later he would surface and report on his great success during a four- or five-day tour of the capital. This was an old shaman's device, used to impress followers with his power. In April 1893 he reported that none other than Anthony Navarre—long absent from both Prairie Band affairs and the planet—was coming to their aid. In early spring, 1894, Wakwaboshkok became convinced he was close to success, for on March 31 Agent Scott announced his resignation (which was not effective until six months later). Roily Water immediately stepped up his attacks, claiming a (premature) victory for Scott's departure, and trying to capitalize on his leaving. Thinking concretely and particularistically, in terms of personalities, Wakwaboshkok and his associates did not appreciate that Scott was an official of a government determined to execute a broad policy on a national scale.[76]

Scott stayed on at his post until that September, when he was replaced by L. F. Pearson. The new agent at first proceeded cautiously, analyzing the situation on the reservation with care before acting. The following February, in reporting to the secretary of the Interior, he outlined what he had discovered. The reservation was divided into two factions, he noted, the "progressive" one dominated by "Half Breeds and Squaw men—who have their eye on the main chance all the time." It was this faction that was pro-allotment, while the "Indians pure" continued to oppose this "progressive policy." Pearson was employing the definitions of his time in construing these alignments as factions, in the sense of major interest groups. At this distance it would be more useful to recognize them as social classes, the Haves being essentially rural Kansas middle-class in value and life-style, politically dominant, carefully attuned to the workings of state and federal law, bureaucracy, and policy, and an economic elite. The Have-Nots, on the other hand—the "Indians pure" —were increasingly powerless, unable to understand, much less cope, with the workings of the larger society, and were economic dependents. It would be entirely misleading to assume that the middle-class "Indians" on the reservation consisted exclusively of persons of Potawatomi cultural and biological heritage. A fair number of them had different antecedents. Some were Kansans to begin with, and many more were the sons and daughters of Métis and American fathers.[77]

Although Pearson was seemingly critical of the "Half Breeds and Squaw men," on whom he blamed much of the Prairie Band's opposition to the Dawes Act, at first he had but little difficulty in working with this group, and few qualms about countering the resistance of Wakwaboshkok and his followers. In January 1895, when the agent learned that Roily Water, James Thompson, and some of their associates were off on their annual trip to Washington, there to conduct the Prairie Band's business without his permission, he reported that upon their return he would "promptly have them locked up in the Agency Calaboose for their having left the reservation without my leave." The powers of the agent had grown rapidly in the past five years. Pearson no longer had need of the Seventh Cavalry to impose sanctions for him; he had his own small Indian Police Force to carry this responsibility.[78]

Among the first special programs initiated by Agent Pearson after he took up his duties was that of leasing out allotted lands to Kansas farmers for cultivation rather than grazing. In this fashion he hoped to more than double the disposable income available to the Prairie People. Similarly, he moved to exercise greater control over a problem that had been bothering the agents for some years, the disposal of the property of deceased Potawatomi. By Prairie Band custom a man's property went to his adult patrikin, not to his wife or children, responsibility for whom was also inherited by the kinsman. When Potawatomi property had consisted of movable tangibles, there was nothing much to raise an agent's interest. But now the estates (by American reckoning) included cash, rents, and real estate. At this time a 160-acre allotment had a market value of well over $3,000, and this very much interested the agent and others with an eye on the resources of the reservation. Although those who wrote the Dawes Act had provided the safeguard of a twenty-five year period in which the allotments of living Indians could not be patented and alienated, this protection did not extend to the lands of those deceased. Since the inheritance law of the state of Kansas operated in these instances, a disastrous loophole had been created. Through this gap poured much of the Prairie

Band's land. Within the twenty-five year period after the first allotment was made, for example, forty-nine of the first one hundred allotments were sold or deeded to others, thus passing out of the control of the Prairie People.[79]

The resistance of the conservative Potawatomi continued through the end of the century, but Wakwaboshkok and his colleagues had worn out their welcome in Washington, while Agent Pearson, and George W. James after him, easily countered their local maneuvers. Wakwaboshkok's main tactic was to persuade some that the allotment system would not last, that the Prairie Band could confidently expect soon to return to holding their land in common. Thus many simply ignored the allotments that had been assigned in their names. The agent, in turn, merely proceeded to lease out the lands to local Kansans, and to deposit the proceeds in their names. When the conservative Potawatomi continued to resist sending their children to school, the agent secured permission to withhold annuity and other payments to those who would not cooperate. The children were held out of school by their parents because Pearson had assigned them allotments. When Wakwaboshkok tried to block the erection of fences around allotments, the agent sent the Indian police to protect those who wanted to thus mark their individual lands. Toward the end of the century the agent was assuming responsibility for the smallest details in the lives of his charges, while the Potawatomi, correspondingly, lost more and more of their freedom of action.[80]

Agent Pearson came into more serious conflict with the "Half Breeds and Squaw men." In earlier years Agent Scott had heavily favored such men as George W. James, James Blandin, and Eli Nadeau, for example, when it was necessary to assign a guardian for an orphan Potawatomi child. Pearson's effort to place this informal system under the Kansas probate courts was a blow to this elite group. Similarly, as Pearson assumed more authority for arranging leases of allotted lands, the old elite was denied another source of income. Much of Pearson's dislike was focused on George W. James, who, under Scott and his predecessors, had enjoyed a very comfortable relationship with the agents. For some years James had been collecting half the pay of the agency's clerk as his share, while acting as *de facto* agent himself. Pearson in early 1895 attempted to break this up, particularly so when the Kansas Democratic party pressured him to hire one of their own as clerk, who expected his full pay. Soon James's family had joined the fray, with his daughter Ellen (who was employed as a teacher at the school) serving as the spearpoint of an attack on Pearson's competence. Eventually, Pearson bowed to the pressure and departed, with James becoming the agent in 1897. Thus the Potawatomi ended the nineteenth century with their affairs directed by a small elite group that was simultaneously their own business committee and in control of the agency.[81]

Irrespective of the continuing opposition of the conservatives and their (declining) refusal to have anything to do with the allotments assigned them by the agent, the process of sectionalizing the reservation continued. Through L. F. Pearson's administration in 1895, 588 allotments had been made. In later years these were generally referred to as the "original" allotments. Between 1896 and 1905 an additional 224 assignments were made to "absentees" and to the children born of original allotees after 1895, making a total of 812 allotments in all. When the last was done, there was no land left surplus. Of the original allotees, a number had received land three times, first following the treaty of 1861, then in Oklahoma on the Citizen Band Reserve, finally in Kansas.[82]

The Dawes Allotment Act, in its publicly stated purposes, was aimed at making self-sustaining, self-reliant individualistic farmers out of the Prairie People. Instead, it left them economically impoverished and, within a few decades, near landless. Their economy and external affairs managed by a small elite, the Potawatomi faced their future politically impotent, with their old values and skills of small effect in coping with the complexities and pressures of the Kansas social environment. By 1900 the tribal council was defunct, the remaining elderly okamek figureheads to be paraded and displayed at public Pow Wows as symbols and relics of the past. By 1903 the Potawatomi Agency disbanded, and such business as remained was conducted by the superintendent of the Potawatomi Training School. So far as the federal government was concerned, the Potawatomi tribal society was no more. In 1914, when Arvel R. Snyder assumed his duties as superintendent at the school, some of the Prairie Band wanted to reconstitute their council of chiefs. He took the position that since no tribe or tribal property existed, no tribal government was necessary, and the federal government would not recognize any such council. Snyder, representing the United States, would deal with the Potawatomi only as individuals. Thus, weakened but not broken, diminished in numbers but not disappeared, subordinated to a larger authority that produced a standing tradition of bitter anger, the Prairie People backed into the twentieth century without leaving the problems of the nineteenth behind.[83]

12

The Prairie People in the Modern World

A peculiar misconception confused the thinking of the legislators who authored the Dawes Act. The social system of the United States, they were convinced, was marked by institutionalized egalitarianism, with a pronounced emphasis on the rights of the individual. In contrast, they believed the institutions of tribal societies such as the Prairie People to be powerfully collectivized, enough to submerge and to deny the natural wants and impulses of their members. Therefore, the General Allotment Act was directed at making the Prairie Band over into a properly individualistic community. What this legislation actually accomplished was very different. A society that had long valued personal freedom highly was forced into the grasp of powerful federal and state bureaucracies, whose rigid, abstract regulations took little account of the distinctive motives and wants of Prairie Band members.

The Dawes Act, and subsequent companion legislation, did bring about the destruction of critical elements of Potawatomi social institutions, those having to do with maintaining an effective sense of community. With the disappearance of their capacity to devise their own polity and to conduct their own external affairs, for instance, came also the demise of the Prairie People's capacity to govern themselves internally. Eventually, the loss of traditional leadership roles and of established procedures for resolving disputes were added to a growing cultural heterogeneity to produce grave disorder. Thus, by the 1930s consensus had been replaced by controversy and confusion, internal order by conflict so pervasive and persistent as to produce near, but characteristically Potawatomi, anarchy.[1]

The Dawes Act did not put the United States out of the Indian business, as some of its authors had hoped. By greatly expanding the legitimate authority of agents and other administrative staff, whole new sets of responsibilities were added. These in turn precipitated a vast increase in specialized legislation, new laws, and new administrative edicts, rules, and regulations, all aimed at rationalizing and regularizing the growing Indian Service bureaucracy. By the 1920s, these rules numbered in the thousands. In this period federal policy was still dominated by the notion of assimilation and characterized by a profound intolerance for things and ways Indian. This approach to the management of Indian Affairs reached its peak influence about 1924, when new legislation awarded automatic citizenship to all Indians who had not achieved that status earlier through the provisions of the Dawes Act or other special statutes. The reaction of the conservative Prairie Band members was characteristic. They had not asked for, did not want, and were affronted by the idea of becoming citizens. Their elders immediately identified this legislation with the provisions of the treaty of 1861 and the Dawes Act, and they opposed it vehemently. In time many were attracted by some of the advantages and rights of citizenship (the protection afforded by the Bill of Rights, for example), while most rejected certain of its responsibilities (particularly taxation). It was many years before the Prairie People came to understand that there were numerous advantages to their dual status as Indians and Americans.[2]

During the late 1920s there was growing sentiment in favor of a major overhaul of federal Indian policy, which found expression soon after the election of Franklin Roosevelt to the presidency. In 1933 Roosevelt appointed

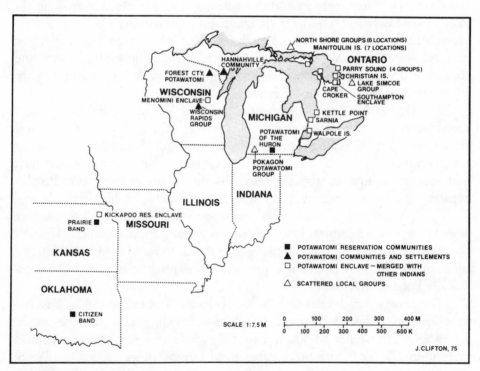

Figure 15. Potawatomi reservations, communities, settlements, enclaves, and other major locations in Ontario and the United States, ca. 1920.

John Collier commissioner of Indian Affairs. Collier, long-time advocate of Indian rights, sometime anthropologist, and perennial romantic philosopher, was dedicated to a position embracing radical tolerance for cultural differences, a near mystic faith in the unique integrity of tribal institutions, and a theory of Indian administration that required heavy use of social science concepts. His views, and those of the advisors who aided him, were shortly translated into the first major revision of American Indian policy since general allotment, the Indian Reorganization Act of 1934. The philosophers, attorneys, and social scientists who drafted this legislation in Washington were convinced their formulations were the wisdom of the age, deeds of pure beneficence designed to work a badly needed uplift in the economic and cultural conditions of Indian communities throughout the United States. The leaders of the Prairie Band at that time thought otherwise. They saw the Indian Reorganization Act in an entirely different light and rejected it outright, both in spirit and detail.

Commissioner Collier's new legislation was designed to bring Indian communities into a therapeutic encounter with responsible, participatory democracy. The specific provisions of the legislation, which could only become operative upon the majority vote of an Indian community in an open election, were aimed at ending the practice of allotment, at severely curtailing patenting and subsequent loss of already allotted land, at expanding existing tribal land resources, at improving economic conditions on the reservations, at reducing the power of the agents and the bureaucracy, and at promoting the development of viable, strong, reservation governments. The legislation strongly opposed the old autocratic style and the assimilation policy, while supporting a position of cultural pluralism and (relative) autonomy for Indian communities. On the whole, the Indian Reorganization Act offered many of the key goals Wakwaboshkok and Nibakwa had fought and been imprisoned for forty years earlier. Yet, beginning in 1934, the culturally conservative leaders of the Prairie Band consistently and successfully opposed its acceptance.[3]

Well aware of their problems, the leaders of the Prairie Band had taken matters into their own hands more than a year before Collier was appointed to office. In early 1932 a small group of vigorous young adults had sought the aid of Superintendent R. D. Baldwin at Haskell Indian Institute in Lawrence, Kansas. These men and women—both culturally and politically conservative —wanted Baldwin's help in drafting a charter regularizing and legitimizing their position as leaders in the community. Their primary interest, and the major authority they wished to secure to themselves, concerned a substantial claims case they were trying to prosecute in the federal courts. The result was a brief, two-page compact, drawn up by Superintendent Baldwin, establishing a seven-member tribal advisory committee to be elected at-large in a general meeting of all adult tribal members. This document, approved by Commissioner of Indian Affairs C. J. Rhoads on 16 June 1932 and thereafter known as the Baldwin Constitution (see Appendix C), the leaders thought of as their enabling legislation.

Although Baldwin, who was of the old Indian Service school, had assigned the committee only advisory powers and the duties of providing leadership in education, farming, and law enforcement, the Prairie Band's new leaders interpreted their authority in a different and more powerful light. It soon became evident that they saw themselves as cast in the mold of the kind of business committee pioneered by Navarre, Nadeau, Young, and James in the 1860s. Indeed, they preferred this title to the advisory committee phrasing used by Baldwin, and they focused their attention on but one of the scant thirty-four lines in the "constitution," that one assigning them the duty of "handling tribal claims." It soon became evident that the new leaders, by judicious use of the substantial funds hopefully to be gained from a successful land claims case, intended to restore the power and wealth of the more traditional Prairie Band members. Therefore, when the Indian Reorganization Act was presented to them they balked, for they had already reorganized themselves in their own fashion and through their own efforts. They had no interest in participating in an experiment in "responsible democracy," particularly one conceived in Washington without their consent and advocated by heavy-handed local Indian agents who actively supported the more acculturated members of their community.[4]

Throughout the 1930s and into the 1940s the Prairie Band's superintendents attempted to persuade them to accept and then to force through the provisions of the Indian Reorganization Act. The culturally conservative Potawatomi, organized under their own business committee, successfully fought back. This controversy added fuel to the already smoldering fires of factional conflict, for the superintendent generally sided with the more acculturated and the absentee Potawatomi, including the descendants of the old Citizen Band elements as well as of the Métis and Americans who had obtained allotments on the diminished reservation after 1891. The conservative leaders of the business committee had no intention of sharing either their power or the eagerly anticipated claims case funds with these elements. However, by relying on the limited and dubious authority of the Baldwin "constitution," in ignoring the economic and political opportunities presented by the Indian Reorganization Act, and by failing to deliver needed services to the community, the business committee severely weakened its leadership position. Their strength was largely negative, the capacity to effectively oppose the Bureau of Indian Affairs and the more acculturated members of the community. There matters lay through the mid-1940s, when the conflict diminished in intensity as many men went off to the armed services during World War II or to take war jobs in other locales.

In 1946 new federal legislation quickly raised the Prairie Band's hopes and increased the value of membership in this community. Until that year Indian tribes were forbidden to bring suit against the United States in the Court of Claims without a special jurisdictional act being passed by Congress. Thus many potentially litigable disputes and complaints had been effectively blocked, for it was unusual for the Congress to allow jurisdiction, and rarer for the Court of Claims to approve a petition for redress. Then, in 1946, the Congress passed the Indian Claims Commission Act. Soon the Potawatomi were expecting quick recovery for damages suffered in the past. The anticipated rewards of successful litigation before the Indian Claims Commission were quickly estimated, reestimated, and overestimated, fanning the factional conflict on the reservation into an open conflagration. As high hopes of soon acquiring several millions of dollars were raised, several unexpected consequences resulted. One was very similar to the effects of the treaty of 1861 and the Dawes Act. As the economic value of being a Prairie Band member rose sharply, there were a great many new claimants to that status. Similarly, because most of these were highly acculturated if not fully assimilated absentees, they were drawn to the more Americanized elements of the reservation community, who had been kept out of power by the maneuvers of the conservative business committee members.[5]

By the early 1960s, when the first of the Prairie Band's several claims cases were settled in its favor, the culturally conservative members of the business committee were themselves being edged out of power. Their narrow and unyielding insistence on the obviously inadequate provisions of the Baldwin document of 1932 was their undoing. This protocol, which did not contain the provisions many of the Prairie People said and believed it did, gave the business committee only advisory functions and no executive powers. In fact, its provisions rested on an earlier tradition, which centered full administrative authority in the hands of the agent or superintendent, and vested sovereign powers of decision making in the general council, a public assembly of all adult members of the band. Therein lay the fatal defect of the business committee's position, for the Baldwin compact contained no specific membership clause. It did not provide a legally acceptable listing of existing members. Neither did it define a procedure for admitting or excluding potential new members. The business committee, in this document, was assigned only the duty of "Making inquiries, recommendations, and suggestions pertaining to Tribal problems and general welfare." Presumably, these recommendations were to be made to the superintendent or to the general council, but no one knew for certain who was a legitimate member and hence entitled to participate and vote in this public assembly. By rejecting the Indian Reorganization Act and failing to adopt a constitution and a set of bylaws under that legislation, the conservative leaders of the Prairie Band had defeated their own aims. They had not drawn a constitutional boundary around themselves by which they might have stemmed the flood of later claimants.

By the mid-1960s the authority for managing Prairie Band affairs had shifted into the hands of the newer, younger, off-reservation members of the band. A great many of these, being rebuffed by the conservatives, had sought guidance and aid from the Bureau of Indian Affairs and the more acculturated residents of the reservation community. These three were natural allies, so that by the weight of numbers, the principles of democratic process, and the skillfully applied legal authority of the bureau, the older conservative leaders were pushed out of power. One by one the elder members of the old business committee passed away, leaving behind them descendants willing to carry on the battle, if ill-equipped to deal with the more numerous and better educated, if less Potawatomi, opposition. Whatever Senator Dawes may have believed of them in 1887, the Prairie People were individualists to a degree and in a fashion inconceivable to him. They saw political power in entirely personal terms, not as the authority of office or role, but as the yield of individual cleverness and ingenuity. Skill and aptitude bought influence during a person's lifetime, and respectful memories after his passing. Their game lay in the trying.

In such fashion the Prairie People passed the first and part of the second half of the twentieth century—preoccupied with the concerns and complaints of an earlier time, committed to the cultural styles and tactics of their grandfathers, unable to take effective hold on the critical problems and issues facing them in the modern world.

ECONOMIC AND
POLITICAL ADAPTATIONS

Through the first three decades of the twentieth century the population on the Prairie Band Reservation remained relatively stable, numbering about 650, with another 150 carried on the roll but living elsewhere, mainly in Wisconsin. With the success of the general allotment program the old villages were broken up. The population now was scattered on homesteads along the section-line roads that crisscrossed the reservation. The Potawatomi preferred living on the southern half of the reservation, in the bottom lands along Big and Little Soldier creeks, although the upland prairies of the northern portion contained the best farm lands. In these years there was little manifest evidence of the

Plate 16. Modern Potawatomi Pow Wow costumes express pantribal styles of dress and Hollywood images of what the Indian should look like. Compare such polyethylene and nylon finery with traditional dress. (Photography by the author, 1963.)

Plate 17. Dakota trophy headdress at the Pow Wow. Curtis Pequano here wears a headdress taken by an ancestor in battle against the Dakota on the High Plains in the 1850s. Note the trade silver ornaments, which were made in Montreal in the early 1800s. (Photograph by the author, 1963.)

Plate 18. The annual Pow Wow provides some Potawatomi the opportunity to make a spectacle of themselves before the wondering eyes of the chimokiman. (Photograph by the author, 1963.)

Plate 19. These Potawatomi dancers stand ready for the annual Pow Wow, an entirely secular, commercial affair whose phototype is the county fair or wild-west show of Midwestern America. (Photograph by the author, 1964.)

persistence of older cultural practices. Public functionaries responsible for managing the Prairie Band's affairs, if not actively suppressing their rituals and the use of the language, were officially blind to the durable features of Potawatomi institutions. The Prairie People were practicing much of their older ways in private, away from the disapproving gaze of agent and teacher.

It was, however, a period of considerable change, involving the erosion and loss of some institutions and the acquisition of others that were new. The elder okamek, those who had won their places in mid–nineteenth-century battles and councils, were dying one by one. Old Mskwas went in 1906, and Kakak—the last of the traditional leaders—followed him the next year. Just

Plate 20. Jess Hale was one of those called "the old bachelors," men who retired to the reservation after a lifetime spent in wage-labor elsewhere. A man of many talents and skills, Jess Hale was shkabewis—herald of the Butler Drum and wigwameyonene—janitor of the Kissus Drum. He was a man with a phenomenally detailed memory of who said what to whom on which occasion. (Photograph by the author, 1964.)

before their deaths, in 1905, Mskwas and Kakak lent their names and prestige to the development of a new secular ritual. Conceived by Agent Williams, sponsored by the Mayetta, Kansas, Businessmen's Association, and managed by the more acculturated Potawatomi, this was the annual Potawatomi Fair. A combination rodeo, agricultural fair, autumn harvest-home, demonstration of present achievement, and celebration of the virtues of the past frontier, the annual fair grew to considerable proportions, generating much interest, income, and conviviality. From the perspective of Agent Williams, the exhibition publicized an important message—the Indian problem had been solved; the Prairie People were making it in terms acceptable to agricultural Kansas. The annual fair prospered until 1929, when it died in the first months of the Great Depression. It was revived in 1956, under Prairie Band auspices, as an annual Potawatomi Pow Wow.[6]

Five years after the Potawatomi Fair was begun a new, missionary-spread religious institution was presented to and accepted by the Prairie Band. Unwelcomed by the agent, who soon called in the county sheriff to help him stamp it out, this was the Peyote religion. This novel doctrine and ritual, centered on the consumption of peyote as a sacrament, was introduced by a Prairie Band member named Shishki, who became the leader of the first ritual congregation on the reservation. It was most appealing to marginal Prairie Band males, those who had drifted away from their faith in older clan rituals and the Dream Dance cult, but who had not found a satisfactory adjustment in American communities. For some years the elder Potawatomi ritualists perceived the Peyote religion as an objectionable rival, although eventually it was assimilated into the accepted ritual inventory of the Prairie Band. Soon enough, the same fundamental patterns that marked much of Potawatomi social life were found also in the Peyote congregation, the pattern of antagonistic opposition and subsequent fission, of gossip and accusations of misbehavior, and of charges of improper use of power. By the 1950s, however, nearly all of the men who participated in Peyote rites were also adherents of the Drum religion and other older religious forms. Acceptance of the Peyote religion by the Prairie People was itself primary evidence of disturbing social change, for this ritual functions as a highly effective kind of group therapy, providing mutually supportive aid and comfort to members confused and disturbed by the pace of cultural change around them.[7]

The Prairie Band reached a peak of prosperity about 1925, after which they fell victim to a double crisis which jointly brought about a failure of the adaptive strategy that had sustained them in the first quarter of the twentieth century. On the grounds that the practice contributed to their demoralization and interfered with their adoption of an agricultural economy, their annuities had been commuted in 1909. Thereafter they were dependent for their living upon the crops they could take from their fields and the income that was obtained by leasing pasture and farmlands. It is in this context that the importance of the annual fair must be appreciated—it was an additional, if minor, source of cash.

In the same period there was, however, a steady decline in the number of acres owned, farmed, and leased out to the Prairie People. The process had

Plate 21. One of the few Potawatomi ever to become a successful practitioner of mechanized agriculture, the late Patrick Matchie developed a fine farm only to see it threatened by the waters of a flood-control dam. He was a leader in both the Native American Church and the Drum religion as well. (Photograph by the author, 1963.)

Plate 22. For years Nora O'Bennick lived away from the reservation; but when illness and unemployment forced her family's return to the reservation, they moved into an unused one-room schoolhouse, where she lived out her remaining years. (Photograph by the author, 1964.)

begun in 1893 as lands assigned to the original allotees were sold on their deaths to outsiders, but it reached a new level starting in 1916, when the twenty-five year grace period specified in the Dawes Act expired for that series of allotments made in 1891. In subsequent years the number of acres on the reservation owned by the Prairie People dwindled rapidly. As individuals obtained their fee patents, many quickly sold their lands for ready cash. There

Plate 23. James "Wild Bill" Wahbnosah and his wife, Suzie, like many conservative Potawatomi, annually grow, dry, and store a crop of maize of the traditional variety. (Photograph by and courtesy of Dr. Robert L. Bee, 1964.)

Plate 24. Mrs. Charles Harrison works at the kind of complex raised embroidery that was once taught as a housewifely skill in early mission schools. Mrs. Harrison became a master of this art and achieved national recognition for her skill. (Photograph by the author, 1964.)

was, for example, a marked surge in land sales between 1918 and 1921, when young men, home from military service during World War I, decided there were brighter prospects elsewhere than in reservation life. By 1925 the Potawatomi owned only 36,540 acres, just 43 percent of the old diminished reservation awarded them in 1861. This loss of land continued into the 1930s, when it was slowed but not entirely halted by the Indian Reorganization Act. Yet by 1962 the Prairie Band's members owned but 17,038 acres, some 22 percent of the original reservation; and much of this was in the hands of absentees, particularly those in Wisconsin, who leased the land out to Kansas farmers and ranchers.

Their economic adaptation through the mid-1920s was effective and satisfactory enough to produce a steady if mild prosperity, although there is no evidence to suggest that many of the Prairie People shared in the great boom of that decade. The reports turned in by agents and visiting commissioners for these years suggested that the Dawes Act had been a great and unquestionable boon. But such reports were based on spurious statistics and carefully selected success stories. It was the atypical achievements of the much acculturated elite

Plate 25. Squaw dice counters. One of the few traditional recreations still practiced, k'sēkēnēk—bowl and dice is a game owned by a woman who has dreamed the right to own the needed counters, but the game is played by men and women she invites. This set includes six round counters and two effigies, Buffalo and Man. Buffalo bone should be used, but now beef bone has to do. (Photograph by the author, 1964.)

minority that were presented as if they were true of all. No one in this decade looked sharply at the foundations on which the Prairie Band's economy were built, and this was unfortunate, for these were literally eroding away.

In 1925 Hugh C. Scott visited the Kansas Reservation on behalf of the Board of Indian Commissioners. He found some 660 Potawatomi living on the reservation and another 150 carried on the roll but residing elsewhere. Of the 36,540 acres owned individually by this population, only 7,041 were under cultivation, while 6,385 were used for pasture. The average Potawatomi farm that year thus consisted of some 50 acres under plow and 45 in pasture. The remainder of the land, some 23,113 acres, was leased out to Kansas farmers and ranchers at very nominal rates, with more than half of the leased lands owned by absentees. Scott's glowing description of Potawatomi industry and success in farming presented an attractive picture, but for the wrong century. He was no agricultural expert: his idealized portrayal of the Indian farmer following his horse-drawn plow down a dusty furrow, while his cheerful wife churned butter with milk obtained from the family cow, was a vision appropriate to 1875, not 1925. Basically, these operations were small, submarginal, nonmechanized, uncapitalized, subsistence operations, in which most Potawatomi had little interest. The steady sale of land by the Prairie People, on the other hand, is unmistakable evidence of a supporting fact—their material wants exceeded their financial grasp. They were living off of their increasingly scarce capital. That process begun at Greenville in 1795 was drawing to a close. Soon the Prairie People would be near landless.[8]

The barely marginal technological and economic status of Prairie Band farmsteads and the steady decline in the number of acres they owned only weakened the community as it came face-to-face with the great disasters of the 1930s. Then two major crises fell upon them. The Prairie People were not the only rural Kansans injured by these events. More vulnerable, they were simply hit harder than most.

The first crisis had to do with the national agricultural economy, supposedly founded on the efficiency of small family farming operations. It was toward this great American myth that the Prairie Band was pushed by the authors of the Dawes Act, who blindly assumed that the one viable path to economic self-sufficiency lay in nuclear-family–based agricultural enterprise. Yet in the same period that the Dawes Act was written began the sharp decline of family farming in the United States and the drift of the bankrupt, landless rural population toward the cities. Thus the Prairie People were caught up in the agribusiness revolution. Never highly motivated by intensive farming to begin with, they were soon worked and priced out of the market. They might better have been left alone in the 1880s to develop a communally based corporate ranching operation.

Plate 26. At over a hundred years of age, Pknokwē had some eighty years of experience in playing k'sēkēnēk, and she made a dangerous adversary. Note her dress, traditional in frontier Kansas communities when she was a young girl in the 1870s. (Photograph by the author, 1964.)

The first crisis was closely connected with the second, which amounted to an environmental disaster. Crowded into a limited range, the Prairie Band could not follow their traditional practice of abandoning fields depleted of their natural nutrients. Encouraged to follow the agricultural practices standard in Kansas in that period, they constantly overcropped and overgrazed the lands they owned. Dependent on the practice of leasing for much of their annual cash income, they handed over the largest share of their most productive and valuable lands yearly to larger, outside operators, who had little concern with long-range protection of the soils, much more in maximizing short-term gains. Therefore, in a decade when most of the Great Plains area was subject to drought, dust storm, and erosion, and when much of the depleted topsoil simply blew away, the Prairie Band soils drifted away with them. Sixty years of misuse had destroyed the natural prairies, rendering them nearly unfit for agriculture. The Potawatomi, like many Kansans, were left dependent on lands that would no longer support them adequately.

The Prairie Band's precarious economic adaptation was ruptured by all these factors in combination—the continuing decline in their land base, the loss in productivity of the remaining soils, the great droughts, the revolution in agricultural technology and management practices that bypassed their farms and gardens, and the national economic depression. In later years adults remembered vividly the grave stresses of these years—there was no game, nor many fish in Soldier Creek; income from leases dropped sharply; crops failed

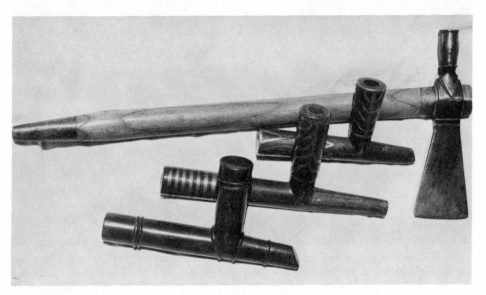

Plate 27. Four heirloom pipes, three of catlinite (two of which are inlaid with pewter) and the fourth a trade item (a brass pipe-tomahawk). (Photograph by the author, 1964.)

Plate 28. The grave house, here used to cover the burial of a deceased Thunder Clan member, became traditional in the late nineteenth century, replacing earlier log and stone cairns. (Photograph by the author, 1962.)

and there was insufficient fodder and water to sustain livestock; there were few paying jobs available, and fewer Indians with the skills and dispositions needed to obtain them. The Prairie People even came close to losing the preciously hoarded seed for their traditional varieties of maize, which was saved only by the skill of a Kansas farmer neighbor who maintained a seed-plot for them until the worst of the drought was over. "There was no meat," adults complained in the 1960s, "only oatmeal and navy beans." And even these were relief commodities grudgingly delivered by charitable organizations and federal agencies. Many of the Prairie People became welfare dependents. Most came close to losing hope, but did not. The Potawatomi still had their devices.

It is in the context of such extreme economic and cultural stress that the search for alternative sources of income must be understood. The Prairie People, like many other Americans in that decade, began wishing for a windfall—this is the sense and meaning of their young leaders' efforts to use litigation in the federal courts so as to secure a financial judgment against the United States. At first their hope was directed at a restoration of the annuity payments that had been ended in 1909. The Prairie Band's new leaders, in seeking solutions to their problems in 1931, looked backward. They aimed at restoring their right to have annuity dollars delivered annually. Only in later years did they add the larger aim of securing judgments for unjust land transactions in the more remote past.

Economic and nutritional stresses added to other social and cultural changes within the reservation community to further exacerbate the problems faced by the Prairie People in the 1930s. With a shift away from the older village settlement organization and the development of small family farmsteads came a decline in the social and economic functions of the traditional extended family and the critically important patrilineal clan and lineage system. By the 1930s the clans had lost their vital functions, such as the regulation of marriage, the organization of political affairs, and the control and management of individual behavior. At that time the clans were no longer corporate organizations structured as patrilineal kin-groups—the sole important function

Plate 29. Wawasēk in 1962. John Wahwassuck (now deceased), beset by a severe coronary disorder, led a life of active opposition to the rule of Bureau of Indian Affairs agents. (Photograph by the author, 1962.)

they retained was that of bestowing names, but even this was increasingly shared by other ritual groups. In this period the whole kinship system had shifted to one very like the American, stressing generational, affinal, and bilateral relationships rather than patrilineal ones. Thus the fundamental building block of Prairie Band social life was no longer the clan or extended-family–based village, but the isolated nuclear-family household. To some extent kin ties continued to be important, but such relationships were created along both paternal and maternal lines of descent, as well as collaterally. Thus, instead of a neatly bounded, coresidential patrilineage, in the late 1930s the larger kin-groups consisted of diffuse bilateral kindreds, whose memberships overlapped one with the other, and whose members were widely scattered. Some of the elders still remembered much of the theory of the traditional kinship system, but this knowledge was not widely shared, and it was no longer the basis for organizing behavior. By the 1950s it was not the fact of a child's birth to a particular father that determined its affiliation with a patriclan—clan membership came with the name given the child by some ritualist. Thus husband and wife might be affiliated with the same totems, while siblings sometimes belonged to different ones, and the names supposedly associated with a clan were coming to be a conceptual hodgepodge.[9]

What was lost was an accepted, systematic means for regulating behavior and for controlling conflict within the community. This loss of organization combined with profound economic stress to produce grave, uncontrolled conflict and disorder. When Ruth Landes studied the Prairie Band in 1936, with her genius for uncovering the covert aspects of a cultural system she revealed a community beset by interpersonal strife. The Prairie People at that moment in their history were consumed with an outburst of witchcraft and sorcery accusations. They had turned all their angers and frustrations inward on themselves. In an earlier day an ambitious male might develop a reputation based on his achievements, found a minimal lineage structured quite like older and well-established clans, and justify his creative efforts before a public tribunal composed of elders who could agree on what was and what was not a worthy accomplishment. If a conflict boiled over that could not be resolved by consensual debate or other devices, the founder of the new lineage could simply gather together his niktotem and move off. By the 1930s there was no traditional council to judge and control; the stresses of living were far greater than they had ever been; consensus on what was proper was lacking; and the escape valve of migration elsewhere was no more.[10]

What Landes discovered and described in 1936 was a situation where the ancient means of laying claim to supernormal power prevailed, but without an organized community to validate such ambitions or to control their misuse. Thus, for some few years, a kind of bully-boy rivalry prevailed. A man would grandiosely assert that he had very special magical powers based on a personal pitchkosan, but instead of founding a lineage, he would try to gather round himself a small group of henchmen. These constituted a ritual brotherhood, putative but not actual kinsmen. Indeed, they often represented different kindreds, and consequently boastful threats, vicious accusations, and (reputed) evil deeds radiated outwards along a complex web of relationships. This uncontrolled outburst of shamanistic sorcery declined with the temporary migration away from the reservation and the modest prosperity occasioned by World War II. Thereafter, it remained an uncomfortable memory, surviving in later decades only as an undercurrent of negative gossip, slurs, and slanders. It represented a period when the evil underside of the Potawatomi ethos had got out of hand.

CONFLICT
AND DISSENSUS

It was in this disorganized social setting and hostile atmosphere that a fresh effort to recreate a legitimate, powerful council of leaders developed. Similarly, it was under these conditions that opposition to the Indian Reorganization Act grew. The two were not unrelated, for spearheading the opposition to the new legislation was one of the principal activities of the new advisory committee. The men and women who first organized this committee, looking back in search of a model for a governing board, clearly fixed on the example set—not by Wabansi, Padekoshēk, and Miyamise in the 1840s—but by Anthony Navarre and his henchmen in the 1860s. In their own lifetimes they had seen traditional clan leaders such as Kakak become toothless relics, symbols to be paraded and manipulated by government agents. It was the prototype of Navarre and his like—with their skillful bent for extracting wealth from the government and their disposition first to take care of their own families—that inspired them. Hence, while they followed the ancient Potawatomi tack of seeking an alliance with a powerful outside benefactor, once his support was obtained and their position validated they twisted the results to their own liking. Whereas Superintendent Baldwin in 1932 designed the new leadership institution on paper as a relatively powerless advisory council, the leaders who had sought his aid soon were speaking of themselves as the business committee, and shortly thereafter as the hereditary, life-tenure, council of chiefs.

The focal concern of the new advisory committee in 1932 was to prosecute a claim against the United States. Indeed, it was this interest which first moved them to seek the aid of Superintendent Baldwin, for they gave little indication of intending to share out the results of their claims case equitably to all persons associated with the reservation community. Self-nominated leaders, they did not represent traditional clan groups or villages. Nor did they represent the community at large. Their power rested on the private support of their own families, kindreds, and henchmen, and these were opposed by many others, representing probably a substantial if incohesive majority of the Prairie People. Hence their maneuvers did not contribute to diminishing the level of factional strife on the reservation, but instead added new fuel to these already disruptive controversies. These new leaders were seeking power via a classic route, that of controlling resources obtained from an outside source. Dealing with a community already divided and pathologically suspicious of leaders, their actions soon confirmed the fears of many and precipitated further dissension.

Such aspirations preconditioned the rejection by the advisory committee of the Indian Reorganization Act, for this legislation required that tribal governing bodies be elected regularly at set intervals, with open nominations in well-supervised plebiscites, and by secret balloting. Those new leaders who had fashioned the advisory (or business) committee were little attracted to the tenets of participatory democracy advocated by Commissioner Collier. Convinced of their own superior right, they much preferred the more manageable, informal, familiar political process by which they had achieved their positions in the first instance. They aspired to becoming an oligarchy, not a representative, parliamentary body.

The advisory committee had an interesting developmental history. That document which later became its charter consisted only of a proposed draft of the organization (see Appendix C). This document Superintendent Baldwin dispatched to the commissioner of Indian Affairs in May 1932 for his perusal, suggestions, and approval. Meanwhile, a general council meeting was held and members of the advisory committee elected, before the charter had been edited and approved. On 16 June 1932 Commissioner Rhoads approved the document, which he termed a constitution, as well as the election. Thereafter, through the 1930s, the committee gave little indication of concern with specified responsibilities outside the area of claims case prosecutions.

Although their several superintendents generally expressed willingness to work with this group, at least so far as soliciting and listening to advice offered, it was an uncomfortable arrangement. For the superintendent believed himself the properly constituted authority on the reservation, with such powers as might be possessed by the tribe lodged in its general council, not in the advisory committee. The latter group, on the other hand, laid claim to and gradually obtained more power than had been granted in its original charter. Reluctant to accept the supervision of the superintendent, and unwilling to deal with public assemblies on the reservation that he had arranged or called, they operated at arms length, unable to cooperate effectively. The superintendent, heavily involved in the day-to-day business of servicing the reservation population's needs, was unable to obtain the aid of the advisory committee in these labors, since they were preoccupied with larger and longer-range aims. For this reason the advisory committee gained little experience with the management of service programs, and less with the fine art of extracting needed resources from the federal bureaucracy.[11]

The controversy between the superintendent and the advisory committee reached a high pitch over the issue of their opposition to the Indian Reorganization Act, with both parties becoming increasingly rigid and imperious. Eventually, when the advisory committee did not follow the specifications of the Baldwin compact for electing new members, and as opposition to its personnel and tactics grew, the superintendent exerted his own authority and removed the remaining incumbents from office. In 1939 and 1940 the superintendent called a number of special general council meetings in his own right and arranged for the election of a new set of committee members. By that time matters had reached an impasse, with the lines of conflict firmly drawn— superintendent and his allies among the Prairie Band in opposition to the surviving members of the advisory committee and theirs.[12]

The advisory committee members and their henchmen were not entirely without their own supporters off reservation. Indeed, the impetus for both the claims case litigation and the development of a new constitution came from a chance encounter with a man who later became their stalwart friend and fervid (if amateur) legal advisor. As the committeemen recalled these events thirty years later, their first meeting with this new ally occurred in the fall of 1932 at the state fair in Topeka (actually, it would have to have been in 1931). Some of the Prairie Band members were at the fair enjoying themselves, and earning some badly needed spending money. While there they were approached by a person whom they at first identified as a Negro; later they came to accept him as a Cherokee. This transition from a despised to an approved ethnic status was eased as it became apparent that the party had an important message for them, a promise of help, and positive recommendations for a desirable course of action.

Seen through the eyes of the Prairie People, this man was a godsend. The superintendent, on the other hand, thought of him as a subversive agent. Viewed in the perspective of Potawatomi history, and with the ideas of the social sciences, he was another in the long series of intercultural brokers who were forever appearing on the Potawatomi scene. Known as Frank Tom-Pee-Saw (or sometimes, Frank Kirk), he represented an organization with an impressive letterhead, the League of Nations of North American Indians. Tom-Pee-Saw (or Kirk) was an immensely if erratically knowledgeable man, something of a technical specialist, a self-taught legal authority on Indian

treaties. In addition to his obvious sympathies for the unorganized and direc-
tionless leaders of the Prairie Band, he offered to throw the weight of his
organization behind their case and soon began acting as their advisor and
advocate.

Thus began the long trail toward successful resolution of the Prairie Band's
claims cases. Tom-Pee-Saw could not guide them very far down that road, for
he lacked the legal credentials, expertise, and funding needed to properly
research, document, and present a complex case on behalf of his clients. Nonetheless, by 1936 he had drawn up a contract (never approved by the commissioner of Indian Affairs) with his Prairie Band clients, and thereafter proved
to be something more than an annoyance to the better-equipped legal firms
which thirty years later saw the Potawatomi cases through to successful conclusion. For more than a decade he acted as aide and advisor to the advisory
committee. In 1946, for example, he was writing the secretary of the Interior
attempting to have Superintendent Bruce removed from office. If the secretary
"did not take *immediate steps* to remove H. E. Bruce," he threatened, "the
League of American Indians will be forced to refer same to other authority
for action, he must go." Tom-Pee-Saw had all the elegance of a depression-era
bill collector. In such ways the Prairie Band's *éminence noire* aided his
clients.[13]

The conduct of Potawatomi business ebbed during World War II, but by
1946 most of the membership returned to the area. That year the Indian
Claims Commission Act was passed, and within weeks many of the Prairie
Band came fervently to believe the pot of gold they had long dreamed of was
nearly within reach. In late autumn a rumor swept the reservation, gathering
force as it was wafted from one farmstead to the next—later in winter, for the
first time in thirty-eight years, there was to be an annuity payment. The wise
counsel of their capable claims attorney, Robert Stone, and the words of their
superintendent could hardly dispel the powerful fantasy expressed in this wish,
which brought only one more bitter frustration (at that moment the Indian
claims commissioners had not even been appointed by the president). But
within a few years the claims cases were going well, if very slowly, much
complicated by the many treaties the Potawatomi had signed and by the dispersal of and divisions within the tribe after 1837.

During the war years the advisory committee had fallen into disrepair.
No elections and few meetings were held, so that by 1946 there was a log-jam
of unfinished business and many serious questions concerning the legitimacy
of the grasp these conservatives had on Prairie Band affairs. The contract with
their claims attorneys expired in June 1947, and the firm was uncertain whether
the old advisory committee could legitimately sign a new one. For years no
action had been taken on up-dating the official roll of the band. Beginning in

1947, and peaking in the mid-1950s, the Prairie Band was under the threat of termination of their federal relationship altogether, and this required concerted, expert attention. Meanwhile, in the prosperity that followed the war, as the surrounding area began booming, many Potawatomi moved back onto the reservation, and a good number of these were not affiliated with and did not become supporters of the aging members of the advisory committee.[14]

As the reservation population swelled, the elders on the advisory committee began losing ground. They were now claiming to be an official business committee, and arguing that they had been elected to office for life. When pressed hard on this issue, they sometimes identified themselves as the tribal claims committee, with similar life-tenure in office. Meanwhile, the younger, better educated, progressive elements of the community were organizing and demanding a hand in Prairie Band affairs. They cooperated gladly with officials of the Bureau of Indian Affairs, who had a long-standing grievance against the elder Potawatomi leaders. The conservatives continued to ignore

Plate 30. Petition signing: The late Mrs. Minnie Evans (shown here on the right) organized a protest petition to be sent the Bureau of Indian Affairs. Under the leadership of Mrs. Evans and others, the Potawatomi avoided termination in the 1950s and successfully prosecuted their cases before the Indian Claims Commission. (Photograph by and courtesy of Dr. Robert L. Bee, 1965.)

these newer elements, arguing that they were not legitimate Prairie Band members and could have no say in the reservation's business. Nevertheless, the progressives struck hard at the glaring weaknesses in the conservative's position —they were a minority; they did not follow even the provisions of the document they claimed gave them their power; and they were inattentive to, and seemingly unconcerned about, many of the issues that preoccupied the younger, progressive elements. Protesting the arbitrary, autocratic, and unrepresentative nature of Prairie Band government, the progressives with the active support of the Bureau in 1961 managed to secure adoption of a new and modernized constitution, one which heavily favored themselves.

The new constitution is of special interest, compared with what the Prairie Band might have enjoyed had they adopted an Indian Reorganization Act constitution in 1935. These early IRA constitutions usually favored the on-reservation, more conservative elements of Indian populations. Voting rights and the rights of office holding were generally reserved to actual residents of the reservation community—the constitution adopted by the Forest County, Wisconsin, Potawatomi in 1937 went so far as to restrict the franchise and office holding to males. More importantly, these early IRA constitutions contained carefully drawn membership clauses, limiting membership strictly to those persons who were of "one-fourth degree of blood."

But in the 1950s and early 1960s the Bureau of Indian Affairs, directed by Congress, was busy trying to move Indian populations off the reservations, to reward those who did relocate, and to reduce or terminate federal supervision of reservation affairs. Thus the provisions of the 1961 Prairie Band constitution granted membership to those persons who had received Dawes Act allotments and to all their descendants, regardless of their "degree of blood." This constitution specifically excluded residence on the reservation as a qualification for membership, voting rights, and office-holding. Thereby the off-reservation, absentee people, who were the more numerous, were heavily favored. In this fashion the 1961 constitution placed power firmly into the hands of the absentee, assimilated, or progressive elements. By giving jural status to a new federal membership corporation, it completely reorganized the basic structure of Prairie Band governance and put the conservative faction temporarily out of power.

The Prairie People were never a group to fade quickly when faced with a fight. Only the lines of battle changed, not the relish felt for combat. In 1934, as one of the first items of business of the newly constituted advisory committee, Minnie Evans, granddaughter of old Wabansi, had sought the aid of Superintendent Henry Roe Cloud at Haskell Institute. The aim then was to find a means of excluding from Prairie Band affairs all the Citizen Band members and the Americans who had obtained allotments after 1891 on their reservation. Roe Cloud then acknowledged, on behalf of the Bureau of Indian Affairs, that a grave injustice had been done. Many persons with little or no claim to Prairie Band status, he admitted, had been awarded allotments. But he knew of no way in which this injustice could be righted, so he advised the advisory committee to swallow their injury and proceed to other business. This they never did. Preoccupied with righting the wrongs of the past, they failed to attend to the pressing business of their own day. Thus they failed to deliver needed services to their people during the hungry years of the 1930s; they gathered power jealously into their own hands; and they failed to adapt successfully to the changing world of Kansas in midcentury. In these ways they neglected to protect themselves against the perils of the present, for many of the absentees who obtained fresh access to Prairie Band resources and influence in its new government from the 1961 constitution were the descendants of those who had helped Agent Scott break Wakwaboshkok's resistance to the Dawes Act in 1891.[15]

THE BELEAGURED COMMUNITY

Although the population associated with the Prairie Band Reservation after 1850 had never much exceeded 800 (including those on the roll but living in Wisconsin), by December 1960 it had risen sharply to 2,101. This considerable increase was the consequence of the generous definition of Prairie Band membership status in the new constitution that was finally approved in 1961. All living "original Prairie Band allotees," together with their "descendants by blood," were embraced in a broad phrasing, which excluded only those descendants who had enrolled with some other reservation group after 1887. The definition of membership did not exclude the numerous allotees who were not Prairie Band members in the 1890s, nor their descendants. In consequence, the 2,101 people on the official roll in 1961 constituted an extremely heterogeneous group. Many had been born and raised elsewhere; only a minority—about one-third—were Prairie Potawatomi culturally, socially, and linguistically.

In 1963 the culturally conservative Prairie Band members, by and large, lived on or near the reservation in Kansas. Only about 22 percent of the lands there were still owned by band members, with many of these tracts greatly fractionated in ownership, due to multiple inheritance. The band itself, corporately, owned but ninety acres, a lapsed allotment that was used for Pow Wows, other social affairs, and public meetings. The reservation proper was heavily checkerboarded by the many substantial farms owned and operated by Kansans. It was also becoming something of an outlying suburb for the state capital, Topeka, some twenty miles to the south, with a growing number of country homes and small estates springing up, especially adjacent to the major north-south highway. Thus the Prairie People lived side-by-side with prosperous Kansans on and near the remnants of their old reservation. They were also surrounded, socially but not geographically, by the many absentees, the descendants of the Dawes Act allotees who had gained membership through the provisions of the 1961 constitution.[16]

At this point in their history the Prairie People were not organized as a spatially bounded community. Their old villages had long disappeared. Their households were scattered here and there along the bottom lands and across the prairies. Many lived in the adjacent towns of Mayetta and Holton, in surrounding rural areas, and in more distant Topeka. The loss of their lands and the failure of their economic adaptation in the early 1930s had forced them to seek economic opportunity elsewhere. Out of the search for jobs and incomes in other places had developed a regular pattern of alternating residence, a pattern with several valences. Some of those who worked in Topeka or Kansas City would return on weekends or holiday periods to visit, to renew their involvement in traditional institutions, and to refresh their identities as Potawatomi. Others, living and working in more distant parts, would remain away most of their adult years and return when they lost their jobs or later in their lives, during their retirement years. Thus the number of Prairie People actually on the reservation fluctuated weekly, seasonally, and with the cycles of the industrial economy. The reservation, thereby, had become something of a state of mind, a magnet attracting many for various and different reasons. For the culturally conservative elders, as well as for their descendants who rejected the larger American culture, the remnants of their reservation remained a powerful symbol of the 1891 defeat they had never accepted, as well as their hope for the future. Some dreamed of the possibility of ultimately excluding not only the assimilated absentee people recently risen to power, but also the Kansans that had purchased acreages out of their lost allotments.

The local reservation-based community in 1963 consisted of a total of 152 households, each containing one or more enrolled members of the Prairie Band. Fifty-three of these households were on the reservation proper, seventy-three in other parts of Jackson County (which embraces the reservation), and twenty-six in adjacent Brown County, on or near the Kickapoo Reservation there. The total population in these households comprised 675 persons, 498 of these being Prairie Band members, the remaining 177 other Indians or Kansans—the Prairie People were heavily intermarried with other groups.

The patterns of intermarriage were very revealing. Some forty-four households—about 29 percent of the total—represented families created by marriages between a Kansan and a Potawatomi. The great majority of these involved a

Prairie Band woman and a Kansan husband, and three-fourths of these lived off the reservation. Some forty-seven, or 31 percent of the total households, were created by marriages where both spouses were Prairie Band members. The remaining 40 percent of the households were formed by marriages between Prairie Band men and women from other Central Algonquian tribes, such as the Kickapoo, Sauk, Fox, and Shawnee. The very few exceptions to this rule consisted of marriages of Prairie Band men and Winnebago and Ojibwa wives, that is, women drawn from other Woodland Culture tribes of the Upper Great Lakes area. Moreover, there was a very pronounced statistical trend emphasizing a patrilocal residence pattern, certainly reflecting an older, traditional cultural imperative. Thus, one of the devices employed by the Prairie People to perpetuate themselves was revealed: they continued to intermarry most heavily with other communities most like themselves, while wives taken from these communities came to live with their husbands on or close to the Kansas reservation.

Similarly, more than one-third of the households on the reservation consisted of composite or generational extended families, with a much lower percentage of this kind of coresidential extended family found off the reservation. Thus the critical carriers of traditional ways—the grandparents—were in daily, intimate contact with the younger generation, insuring transmission of the language, folklore, and values to small children. The age distribution of the total population was of particular interest. In the 1950s the most common impression recorded about the Prairie People was that they were a rapidly aging group, one not reproducing themselves, certain to die out as a culturally distinctive population within a few decades. The actual facts of the population's age distribution entirely refute this antique misconception. Some 52.6 percent of the total population was less than twenty years of age, and on the reservation proper 48.3 percent were young people and children. The most interesting feature of the population was not, however, its relative age or the danger of its expiring, but a discontinuous, bimodal distribution of age groups. One of the age peaks was at about twenty and the other at sixty years. There were, proportionately, many fewer adults in their vigorous middle years actually living on or near the reservation. Their absence was a function of the lack of economic opportunity nearby: they lived and worked at distant places. Which is not to say they were uninvolved or not participants in cultural events on the reservation, to which they regularly returned.

The most interesting feature of the culturally conservative group was that it was about the same size as it always had been since about 1850, some six hundred persons. It was the assimilated, absentee portion of the total population that had greatly expanded in size, not the Prairie People who worked at sustaining the ancient tribal culture. These consisted of a dispersed community with ideological, cultural, and linguistic boundaries, not geographic ones. The location of the community, defined in this sense, did not conform to any governmental or administrative unit. Hence the culturally conservative community of Prairie People was not mutually exclusive with other, surrounding groups, Kansan or other Indian. There was a constant interchange of persons, and a constant round of interactions with different kinds of people in a variety of institutional contexts. This kind of a scattered population with diffuse, permeable boundaries has problems in sustaining its distinctive identity and ways, of course. But such threats to the perpetuation of the culture and language were countered with a constant round of visiting, ritual performances, and political maneuvering, all with the consequence of intensifying and reinforcing group identity, well-being, and cohesiveness.

Clearly, the Prairie People in the early 1960s were reproducing themselves biologically, linguistically, and culturally. They were no fewer than they had been a century earlier and, although a much threatened, beleaguered community, they were adapted to sustaining themselves, employing a variety of well-tested devices to this end. If they were not prospering economically, they were reproducing themselves culturally. Indeed, they resembled a military cadre in peacetime, working hard to maintain the needed values and skills that would be required at some future date, when they might have to train a new and much larger generation in the Potawatomi ethos. In such fashion the Prairie People, one conservative local fragment of a greatly scattered Potawatomi tribal population, survived through the middle of the twentieth century. Stubborn, proud, and imperious, they could not admit defeat, and would not accept assimilation. Thus did the line of Onangizes and his people endure, far from the blue waters of the Mitchigami and the bluestem grasslands of the Ilini, willing to accept a dusty corner of the Kansas prairie as theirs forever.

13

Postscript, 1975

In 1964 I had forecast, with some sense of hope for the Prairie People's own future, that when they gained access to their claims case funds and as they obtained experience with managing their own affairs under the 1961 constitution, they might begin to prosper, to improve the quality of their lives, and to become better integrated as a community. This was no more than wishful thinking. A visit to the reservation in 1975 soon confirmed that these things had never occurred. Indeed, except for some exciting, emotionally rewarding experiences during the previous decade, it was apparent that they had not moved far politically, economically, or as a people. They were, I thought, disturbingly rigid, frozen into a self-defeating posture that had characterized their relations with the larger world for half a century. To be certain, they had learned some new slogans, a few novel tactics, and their words and gestures were more violently hostile; but their basic disposition was the same. They remained very adept at thwarting and disrupting one another's efforts and those of outsiders charged with the responsibility of dealing with them, but they had not again learned how to create and to harmonize, nor to build cooperatively.[1]

The decade starting in 1965, when we finished our research in Kansas, should have been a good one for the Prairie People. Instead it was one in which they replicated the errors and confusions of their recent past. In this they had a very great deal of help, from both Americans and other Indians. Nineteen sixty-five was the year that Indians generally again achieved popularity as America's favorite underdogs, so that a wide variety of charitably—and militantly—disposed people began clustering about, all clamoring for a share of the Prairie People's attention, offering to aid and assist them in their struggle against injustice. As substantial federal and state resources were allocated to Indian development programs, another variety of helper arrived, the grandchildren of the sharpers and confidence men who had helped themselves to a substantial share of the Potawatomi estate and wealth back in the treaty era. This kind of attention did the Prairie People little good, neither from the well-disposed but naïve, self-appointed ombudsman to the oppressed, nor from the enterprising types who sought personal profit in the rapidly expanding Indian business. The latter, of course, often cloaked themselves in the rhetoric of the former. It was an odd decade. Before it was over some younger Prairie Band leaders found themselves working closely with national figures from the Mohawk and Dakota tribes. History, thus, made strange alliances, drawing together as it did the neshnabēk with the nadowe and the nadowesiw.

The major external events impinging on the Prairie People and bringing them and other Indians to national attention constituted an undirected, ill-coordinated conglomerate of public policies and media events. In 1965 the Prairie People, both those on the reservation and the some three hundred then living in Topeka, had their first encounter with the War on Poverty. That year the Indian Division of the Office of Economic Opportunity began operations in Kansas, intending to encourage the Potawatomi into maximum feasible participation in programs using federal grant funds to improve their income, health conditions, educational levels, and housing standards. There resulted the maximum conceivable frustration, as the Potawatomi took this opportunity to vent their hostility on OEO representatives, to thwart program development, and to block the efforts of Indian leaders wanting to become involved in these efforts at self-help. Very clearly and unmistakably, the Prairie People identified the OEO officials as Indian agents and spent their energies on frustrating and driving them away. They anticipated paternalistic treatment, could not bring themselves to become involved productively and creatively, and altogether missed grasping an opportunity that other, better organized Indian groups were exploiting to the utmost.[2]

In 1969 the turncoat Episcopalian, Vine Deloria, Jr., published *Custer Died for Your Sins*, the first of a series of self-pitying satires designed for a mass market. These polemics played heavily on America's favored emotion, guilt-feelings, and were calculated to provide simple, stereotypic answers to the Indian question. The Prairie People took fresh slogans from these works, as they did from Dee Brown's highly popular imitation of history, *Bury My Heart at Wounded Knee*, which many also read avidly. Such materials consisted of skillfully crafted propaganda, effectively aimed at elevating emotional states, but not at setting new directions. In 1968 was created a new organization, the American Indian Movement (AIM), whose skill at staging demonstrations that attracted the maximum press and television coverage soon engaged the loyalties of younger Prairie Band members. Thereafter many of the Prairie People, young and old, participated in a variety of the AIM-staged media events, the 1971 occupation of Mount Rushmore, the Trail of Broken Treaties caravan to Washington, and the takeover of the Bureau of Indian Affairs offices that same year, and the 1973 Wounded Knee incident.

The Prairie People on and around the reservation drew comfort, support, and guidance from such outside models in this decade. Such influence contributed to, but did not entirely determine, their failure to take hold of their own affairs in these years. Since 1961, for example, the Prairie People had had available to them $1,176,788 (less attorneys' fees) drawing interest in the Treasury Department. This was their share of a claims case settlement for the 1846 treaty. That fall their newly elected business committee had resolved to make a per capita payment to each of the 2,101 members then on the official roll. The conservative leaders of the old advisory committee quickly obtained a court injunction blocking this payment. It was not until 1967 that these funds were released and a $490.50 per capita payment paid out, whereupon the business committee attempted to proceed to other development efforts, such as providing for surplus food distribution, the construction of communal housing for the elderly, and the creation of revolving loan funds for students and Potawatomi businesses.[3]

The surviving elders of the old advisory committee, and the young leaders who had joined forces with them, were seeking to restrict the distribution of these benefits to only 204 Prairie Band members, an aim that would have increased the share awarded ten-fold, but to many fewer people. Not successful in this, they began harassing the absentee leaders who had sponsored the broader sharing of resources. Eventually, many of these off-reservation people became discouraged and drifted away from Prairie Band affairs. Simultaneously the conservative leaders began addressing themselves to new goals, many of which they had picked out of the AIM kit-bag of local tactics. In 1971, for example, the conservative leaders—then operating as an unrecognized, *de facto* business committee parallel to the one approved by the Bureau of Indian Affairs —obtained state approval of Potawatomi hunting and fishing rights on the reservation. They now called themselves the tribal action committee, and they conducted a running battle with the elected business committee, charging that the latter did not have tribal support, that the Potawatomi did not come under the provisions of the Indian Reorganization Act, that the superintendent was incompetent, and that only they properly spoke for the Prairie Band.[4]

In the summer of 1971 the tribal action committee was once again in court, this time seeking an injunction to stop the business committee from holding an annual election and attempting to gain approval of the officers at the smaller election they themselves had sponsored. These younger leaders were also engaging in the same kind of irrelevant accusations that their elders had used to oppose the Indian Reorganization Act in 1935. When the business committee sponsored a new housing program, for instance, the tribal action committee spread the rumor that this would cause Prairie Band members to lose their remaining allotted lands. Attempting to undercut the position of the

Plate 31. A new generation of leaders has mastered modern skills of interest-group politics. Here two young Potawatomi leaders hold a press conference, advocating the Kansas Potawatomi case. (Photograph courtesy of *Topeka Capital-Journal*.)

business committee by whatever device was available to them, their own successes were few. The injunction was denied; the official election was conducted; and the same slate of officers was elected to the business committee.[5]

Off-reservation programs and developments were also the targets of the dissident tribal action committee's attention. In June 1972 many of the conservative Prairie People were busily occupied picketing the Boy Scout Jamboree in Topeka. Some, presumably prepared to do battle with the Scouts, carried signs reading "Today Is a Good Day to Die." This kind of sloganeering and confrontation was lifted directly out of the national AIM guidebook, but it provoked a negative response. Whereas the dissident Potawatomi had gotten a good press and a positive response from the state legislature in their hunting rights case, the confrontation with the Boy Scouts produced opposite results. It was seen locally as unnecessary foolishness, and five Potawatomi were arrested for disorderly conduct. The national AIM organization, seeking more headlines and waiting on the sidelines for such a result, immediately moved to the rescue with legal support. AIM could only have been happier had the Scouts actually shed Potawatomi blood on the grass outside the Topeka Municipal Auditorium.[6]

That same summer, believing their opposition on the reservation was weakening, the tribal action committee stepped up the pace of their attacks.

They demanded the firing of Superintendent Carson, concluded negotiations to recover the lands occupied by St. Mary's College (the old mission station), and eventually staged a take-over at the Horton Indian Office. This was followed up by an ad hoc general council meeting at which the ouster of the absentee members of the official business committee was voted. These ousted committee members immediately protested their removal to Washington. That October the commissioner of Indian Affairs withdrew federal approval of the 1961 constitution on the grounds that the Prairie Band's government was no longer able to function, and reverted to the system of direct rule by the superintendent until such time as a new constitution acceptable to the community was drawn up and approved. In autumn many of the militant Prairie Band members were off to Washington, there to accomplish on a larger scale what they had done in Horton, Kansas, earlier in the year. Cooperating with the take-over of the Bureau of Indian Affairs building in the capital city, one young Prairie Band woman phoned the *Topeka Daily Capital* long distance, on the government line, to announce grandly, "This shows Indian people can accomplish something if they stick together." There were, obviously, somewhat different perceptions of the meaning and value of these events.[7]

Some of the dissident Prairie Band members had achieved that great but passing emotional satisfaction which comes from militant demonstrations of this kind, and a kind of transitory celebrity status, if not much else. The following winter national AIM leaders were issuing dire predictions: there was, they claimed, a potential for another Wounded Knee on the Prairie Band Reservation. But this was not to be, for soon the attention of the media were shifting to other excitements. Reporters and television newsmen, reflecting public opinion, were becoming bored with the constant round of impromptu press conferences called by dissident Indian factions, as well as by confrontations and public exhibitions. The Prairie People were forgetting what the elders had well known in Washington in 1845—they had only a limited amount of press appeal to draw upon, and it was wearing thin.[8]

Meanwhile, back on the reservation, there were serious human problems needing attention but not getting it, and there were substantial resources coming available but not being commanded and used. In 1973 the Prairie Band received another installment on the claims cases, their share of 4.1 million dollars awarded for the unjust payment at the treaty of 1829. To obtain this money they had to have an approved roll; but they still lacked even a recognized government. The remaining active leaders were still debating and litigating such issues as whether or not the Prairie Band was an Indian Reorganization Act tribe, whether the Baldwin Constitution was still in effect or not, and how to get their superintendent discharged.

When a general council meeting was called in the fall of 1973 by the

Bureau to discuss the constitutional issue and to select five committeemen, the dissidents vehemently opposed this move, thus delaying it until the following year. The Bureau of Indian Affairs, in desperation, sent in expert arbitrators from the National Center for Dispute Settlements, while the dissidents similarly called in their cohorts, Russell Means and Vernon Bellecourt of AIM. An impasse resulted. The dissident, AIM-supported faction was, it now became clear, seeking only to obtain official recognition and approval from the Bureau of Indian Affairs. They were employing the same strategy their parents had used forty years earlier when they visited Superintendent Baldwin at Haskell Institute. Unable to secure power in their own right through the electoral process, they wanted the Bureau of Indian Affairs to intervene, appointing them the official governing body of the reservation.

So powerfully persistent was their memory of the past century, of the time when the government selected and appointed their "chiefs," that the Prairie People could not conceive of any other route to legitimizing leadership roles. In the 1970s they were still eagerly embracing paternalism, not seeking to avoid its grasp. Dependency, thus, was a root fact of their existence, an imperative with which they remained most uncomfortable. Such extreme dependency could only be balanced by compensatory protests of sovereignty and by rituals of autonomy. In the summer of 1975, for example, they were finally successful in realizing a long-cherished ambition—with one more much-publicized take-over and demonstration they managed finally to have their superintendent removed from office. Thus emboldened, the young leaders began discussions of a further objective, restoration of their control over the lands in the old reservation and eviction of all non-Potawatomi from within its bounds.[9] One question remained to confound their thinking. Who could they get to help them accomplish these ends?

APPENDICES

APPENDIX A
THE POTAWATOMI LANGUAGE

In its phonology and basic structure Potawatomi is much like other Central, Northern, and Eastern Algonquian languages. It is closest to Ojibwa-Odawa, but shares much vocabulary, many phonological features, and basic morphological patterns with the geographic cluster of languages known as Central Algonquian, particularly Sauk and Fox (Michelson 1915; Hockett 1943: 541, & 1966).

A variety of orthographies have been used to write the sounds of Potawatomi since the first contact with the French in Wisconsin, although these have had only limited, regional, and specialized use, with none being adopted as standard. Many of these efforts involved linguistically naïve attempts to render Potawatomi sounds in a French or an English alphabet, with widely varying and often utterly confusing results. The earliest known effort to do anything systematic with the language consisted of a brief word-list set down by Captain William Preston (1796). Some years later an E. Reed published a brief, unsophisticated, and confused outline of the language in the *Detroit Gazette* (1829). As much as anything, this work represented the patronage available to Lewis Cass, then territorial governor, for Reed was one of the governor's protégés.

By 1832 Robert Simmerwell, Isaac McCoy's associate at the Carey Mission in Michigan and the Shawnee Mission in Kansas, had prepared a crude syllabary based on the consonants and vowels of English, that the Western Potawatomi called "babebibobu" spelling, and which some of the Prairie People continued to use in the 1960s, but only to record songs, spells, and recipes for medicines, not the catechisms and hymns the Baptists had hoped for (Simmerwell 1832; Clifton 1962/64). In the same years the famed mission printer of Kansas, Jotham Meeker, developed one of his "articulatory" alphabets for Potawatomi, which was employed to issue a primer and first reader in the language (Schultz 1972: 165; McMurtie and Allen 1930).

A few years later the Kansas Jesuits Fathers Hoecken and Gailland gave longer and more extensive attention to the study of the language, and to the preparation of alphabets, grammars, dictionaries, texts, and religious tracts (Hoecken 1846; Dichls and Gailland n.d.; & Gailland n.d., & 1849). In 1933 the ethnobotanist Huron Smith claimed that a Wisconsin Potawatomi, one Joe Ellick, had invented a Potawatomi syllabary some fifty-five years earlier (ca. 1878), so that "absent members of the tribe could write home to their people" (1933: 12–13). This writing system consisted of some 237 signs, based on four vowels, wherein the phonemes /e/ and /ē/ were compressed as one, and written as "e." This writing system came to be known as the "babebibo" syllabary, and has continued in some limited use in recent years (Nichols et al. 1975). It differed from Simmerwell's "babebibobu" system, which used 145 signs and was based on five vowels and fifteen consonants. More recently, Charles E. Brown, director of the Wisconsin State Historical Society, compiled a substantial Potawatomi-English word-list (1929).

All of these efforts to reach some understanding of the nature of the Potawatomi language, and to devise a writing system for it, were carried on before or aside from the development of modern linguistics. Hence their authors lacked the critically needed ideas and methods that might have speeded and improved their work. In the mid-nineteenth century, for example, all who attempted to study Potawatomi started with glottocentric assumptions; they were convinced that there was a single, natural order to the universe that was expressed in the immutable essence of the one language they most favored, usually Latin or English. Hence, whatever they did with Potawatomi came out looking like an English or a Latin grammar book. Simmerwell, for example, was driven near neurotic by an effort to work out the structure of Potawatomi using the tenses, modes, and inflections of English. This effort, rather like attempting to describe chess with the rules of checkers, yielded millions of permutations and combinations, whose extent the misdirected Simmerwell could conceptualize, without ever coming to grips with the nature of Potawatomi.

Gailland's efforts were similarly biased, although he of course favored Latin as providing the basic forms for describing all the languages of the world. His main informants for studying the language were the inimitable Joseph Napoleon Bourassa and John Tipton (a Métis, not the senator). For years Father Gailland carried around with him a sheaf of penny notebooks into which he had painstakingly copied the entries in standard English and French dictionaries. As opportunities presented themselves he was, thus, able to set down what he thought were the Potawatomi phrasing for such English expressions as "abjuration," "alabaster," "alarm bell," "contumacy," "diocese," "librarian," "unextinguishable," and "vainglory," although he was never able to get anyone to tell him the Potawatomi "words" for such English cultural categories as "fuller" (one who fulls cloth) or "genio." Similarly, his efforts to construct a Potawatomi grammar on Latin principles yielded numerous drafts and revisions full of past, present, future, perfect, and imperfect tenses, and demonstrative, dubiative, indicative, subjunctive, and similar modes. Gailland did come to understand some of the marginal features of the structure of the language, but he missed the basic point, which no one of his era had yet quite grasped, that Potawatomi and other Native American languages were built upon entirely different logical principles than those characteristic of the Indo-European language family.

In the late nineteenth and early twentieth centuries some of the early professional linguists began giving modest attention to Potawatomi. The pioneer linguist Gatschet collected some vocabularies, texts, and translations and made a few notes on the structure of the language (1879, 1889, & 1898). A decade later Truman Michelson similarly worked out a phonology and collected some vocabularies and texts. Michelson soon determined that Potawatomi was quite a separate language, and not a dialect of Ojibwa-Odawa, as had theretofore been assumed, although it was many years before this conclusion was better demonstrated and more broadly accepted (n.d., 1911/1912, 1915, & 1917).

In the late 1930s Potawatomi was studied by one of the most brilliant of modern American linguists, Charles F. Hockett, who reported on his findings in a series of highly sophisticated essays (1939, 1942, 1948, 1950, & 1957). Unfortunately, Hockett's analysis was spun out in a web so innovative that practically no one, not even the most highly trained professional linguist, could quite understand him. Simultaneously, as Hockett himself later willingly explained, his studies and reports on the basic structure of Potawatomi were incomplete. There followed the publication of several essays by other linguists, based upon what they supposed Hockett to have revealed, actually consisting of the kind of linguistic hocus-pocus that preoccupied some scholars in this period (Kelkar 1965; Pike and Erickson 1964; & Erickson 1965). Hockett was then moved to reply with an essay telling, in very basic language, what Potawatomi was really like (1966). This was an improvement over earlier efforts to communicate the nature of Potawatomi morphology and syntax, but not greatly; it still required a reader with at least a year's post-graduate work in technical linguistics to be found intelligible.

In more recent years another quite different kind of attack on the subtleties of this language was launched. This represented the efforts of John Nichols and others at the University of Wisconsin—Milwaukee's Native American Languages Project to prepare basic, comprehensive teaching materials, these to be used in instructing Wisconsin Potawatomi children in the reading, writing, and speaking of their language. With very substantial federal grant funds, this program has steadily turned out high quality teaching materials, beginning at the most elementary levels and working up. Based on a larger and longer investment of professional time and energy, and with extensive assistance from a number of Wisconsin Potawatomi employed by the program, this project should eventually produce basic, comprehensive materials which are both the result of sound analysis and intelligible to the linguistically unsophisticated reader (Nichols, Daniels, et al. 1975).

Meanwhile, in Kansas, a very few of the Prairie Band ritualists continued to use the Potawatomi's own traditional writing system, which consisted of pictographs drawn on birch-bark scrolls, used to prompt their memories in the recall of the sequence and details of lengthy, complex religious ceremonies (Howard 1960). However, already in the early 1960s, the few who attempted to employ these pictograph scrolls were having difficulty recalling the specifics that their ancestors had memorized in association with the signs and symbols drawn on the bark. Thus, unless some systematic effort is made to rejuvenate their use, this skill and practice will likely soon disappear.

The writing of Potawatomi names and expressions in this book employs, so far as is possible, the alphabet recently developed by Nichols and his associates. In many instances, particularly as regards older names and phrasings, their rendition in this alphabet can only be approximate. The reasons for this indefiniteness are several. A fair number of the names recorded in historical documents are both badly corrupted in their spelling and semantically obsolete, to a degree that contemporary Potawatomi speakers, who have never heard the form used, can neither identify the meaning nor reconstruct the older phrasing. In brief, the Potawatomi language, like other aspects of the culture, has changed extensively in the past three centuries. The problems of linguistic acculturation (or interference) and historical development of this language are issues that professional linguists have yet barely turned their attentions to. Consequently, in many instances, only the basic shape of an older expression can be identified with any certainty, with the specific consonants and vowels set down being more or less probable, and little else.

The orthography developed by Nichols and used here consists of twenty-two letters representing fifteen consonants, two semi-vowels, and five vowels, as follows: /a, b, ch, d, e, ē, g, ', i, j, k, m, n, o, p, s, sh, t, w, y, z, and, zh/. The nasals /m/ and /n/ and the semi-vowels /w/ and /y/ are similar enough to English pronunciation that they cause little trouble. However, the balance of the consonants and the vowels are quite different from English and cause much difficulty in perception and transcription. The English speaker, for example, who is accustomed to distinguish the some eleven vowels of English speech and then to transcribe them in the refined torture of the five vowel signs available in the English alphabet, easily becomes confused with the simplier, if different, Potawatomi system, where there are but five vowel phonemes and only one letter for each. Potawatomi vowels are written as follows:

Potawatomi Letter	Similar to English Pronunciation of
a	"a" in "Ma" and "Pa"
i	"ee" in "meet"
e	"u" in "fun"; but also like "i" in "pin"
ē	"e" in "send," or "ie" in "friend"
o	"oo" in "loop," or "ou" in "croup"

The remaining twelve consonant sounds pose a different and more difficult problem for the English speaker. These consonants are of two types, with six sounds in each, as follows:

Type A	Type B
b	p
z	s
zh	sh
d	t
j	ch
g	k

The pairs of Potawatomi sounds in each row are distinguished by a sound feature very different from that which differentiates such pairs as /*b,p*/, /*z,s*/, and /*g,k*/ in English. In English speech these pairs are distinguished by the presence or absence of voicing. Otherwise quite the same sounds, in the instance of each pair the first sound, when spoken, is accompanied by a vibration of the vocal chords that does not accompany the second sound.

It is this feature that makes it very difficult for English speakers to hear and correctly record the Potawatomi sounds represented by these same letters, for the dimension of sound used in Potawatomi to distinguish Type A from Type B consonants is completely different from that found in English. In Potawatomi, Type A consonants, /*b, z, zh, d, j*, and *g*/ are fortis sounds. That is, they are more strongly enunciated and longer in duration; but they are voiceless. On the other hand, Type B sounds, /*p, s, sh, t, ch*, and *k*/, are lenis sounds. That is, they are more softly enunciated and shorter in duration; and they may or may not be voiced. Thus an English speaker on hearing a Type B Potawatomi sound, if it is voiced, will identify it with its voiced counterpart in English, and he may do precisely the same thing with the unvoiced but strongly articulated Type A allophone of the pair. In brief, this part of the Potawatomi language sound system is founded on very different kinds of distinctions from those true of English, French, or other European languages.

What is true of phonology is even more true of Potawatomi morphology and syntax. The structure of this language is based on principles entirely different from those characterisic of European languages. This is where early students of the language went awry, and the complexities of the language are great enough to cause even the best modern linguists substantial differences of expert opinion. Early observers such as Hoecken and Gailland, for example, had a basically simple object in view. They wanted to be able to communicate well enough in something like Potawatomi to teach French and American ideas, and they did quite well at this. However, they were not particularly interested in fully understanding how the Potawatomi were thinking in their own language, much less what they were thinking about. Hence they did not need fully to master the language. It was, and is, easy enough to learn a limited amount of basic Potawatomi, as a tourist masters a phrase book in Spanish. But this does not allow one to think productively in the language, as the Potawatomi do, which is a very different and more difficult problem.

The basic problem with understanding the structure of Potawatomi is that it is a polysynthetic language, one constructed on very different logical principles from those characteristic of English and French. A statement in Potawatomi is expressed only in the form of a complete sentence (except for some commands). Speech thus consists of an arrangement of sentences in each of which disconnected elements do not stand alone as meaningful units, as do many words in English. Each sentence is built up of an arrangement of elements that are stuck together, with prefixes and suffixes tagged on verbal stems to express a complex thought. The elements consist of nouns, pronouns, and personal affixes that stand for some thing or situation, and they are tagged on verbal stems together with other elements expressing several categories, animate or inanimate, for example, or the number of the subjects and objects involved in the expression, and the degree of relevance of each in the statement.

These features of the language are so different from those common to English that they require the analyst or the learner to set aside the principles of his own language before they can be mastered. And it remains true that the language has not yet been well enough studied for its basic arrangements to be fully understood. This remains the task of yet another generation of students.

APPENDIX B
GLOSSARY

Chaskyd	A Potawatomi shaman, specialist in divining.
Chipiyapos	The Potawatomi culture hero; Wiske's twin, who is keeper of the afterworld.
Clan	A unilineal descent group with a corporate identity, organization, and functions. Potawatomi clans (totem) were identified with the eponym of an animal species or natural phenomena, and were patrilineal descent groups. Originally residential groups, later in history they became dispersed.
Clan-segment	A portion of a clan, usually one or more patrilineages, residing separately from the main body of the corporate group.
Kiktowenene	Literally "man who impersonates," this was the title of the speaker.
Kishko	The junior moiety.
Kwē	Woman; female suffix.
Lineage	Essentially a younger, more recently founded clan. The lineage members could actually trace their descent to a known founder. Potawatomi lineages were patrilineal groups.
Manebozho	Alternate, older name for Chipiyapos.
Midewiwin	Literally "spirit-doings," this was the Potawatomi name of the Mide cult or Grand Medicine Society.
Manito	Spirit-Power, or supernormal power. Sometimes mistranslated as spirit or god.
Matchimadzēn	The line of life or great chain of being—a vital principle linking the ancestors with the living.
Nadowe	"Timber Rattlesnake," or "enemy." That is, the New York Iroquois tribes.
Nadowesiw	"Lesser enemy," that is, the Dakota tribes.
Neshnabē	The traditional Potawatomi self-name, i.e., "the People." In contemporary usage it is translated as "Indian" in contrast to "Euro-American."
Niktotem	My clan-mate, i.e., kinsman.
(w)okama	Leader
Oshkēsh	The leading or senior moiety.
Otan	Village
Phoneme	Basic significant unit of sound that differentiates meanings in a language.

Phratry	A grouping of two or more clans with ritual, social, and mythological ties between them.
Pitchkosan	Literally, "Watches over us." One of Wiske's alternate names, and also the name of both the individual and clan medicine bundles.
Wabino	Literally, "Dawn Person." A second kind of Potawatomi shaman who worked as a supernatural advisor and magician.
Wiske	The Potawatomi culture hero. Chipiyapo's twin, Wiske was the great creator and trickster.

APPENDIX C
THE BALDWIN
CONSTITUTION OF 1932

Draft of the Proposed Organization of
The Tribal Advisory Committee of the Prairie
Band of Potawatomies of Kansas

1. Nominations—These will be made in a council of the Tribe, which council will be called by the Superintendent on thirty (30) days notice.
2. Election—Voting will be by ballot and will be limited to the adult members of the Prairie Band of the Potawatomi Band of Kansas.
3. The committee will be composed of seven (7) members, elected for a term of four (4) years except for the first election at which the two nominees receiving the largest number of votes will be declared elected for a term of four (4) years; the two receiving the next largest for three years; the two receiving the next largest for one (1) year. The Chairman & Secretary will be selected from its own membership by vote of the committee, at its first meeting after the annual election.
4. Vacancies—will be filled in the usual way at a general meeting of the Tribe.
5. The annual meeting for the election of committeemen and the transaction or discussion of matters affecting tribal welfare will be held on the third (3rd) Tuesday of September, at two (2) P.M.
6. Duties—(a) Handling of Tribal claims;
    (b) Making inquiries, recommendations, and suggestions pertaining to Tribal problems and general welfare;
    (c) Promoting Tribal Welfare by counseling with the Indians on the Reservation and providing leadership in such things as farming, education, law enforcement, care of helpless, and like matters.
7. The Nominations, elections, and filling of vacancies will be under the general supervision of the Superintendent.

NOTES

CHAPTER 1:
INTRODUCTION

1. Kellogg's 1925 volume on the French regime remains a sound and most readable introduction to this period. Hunt's 1940 study of the fur trade and the Iroquois wars remains of value but has been superseded both in detail and substantive conclusions. The best modern overview of developments in this period is Heidenreich 1971: 220–64. For the best assessment of tribal trading patterns before 1640, see Wright 1967.

2. Brulé was the first example of Champlain's novel policy of sending young Frenchmen to live among the Indians, there to master their languages and to serve as intercultural brokers in the French interest. Jean Nicolet and Nicholas Perrot were later examples of men who acted out the same role, and the discoveries, work, and observations of both are central to the early history of the Potawatomi.

3. "Asistagueroüon" is a Huron, not an Odawa word.

4. For more on tribal identifications, synonymy, and the type of organization of each, see the appropriate tribal entries in Hodge 1910; Vol. 12 of the forthcoming new edition of the *Handbook of North American Indians*; Goddard 1972; Heidenreich 1971; Hickerson 1960, 1962, 1963, & 1970; and Clifton 1976a.

5. Abbreviations used in citations are located alphabetically in the bibliography, cross-referenced to the full source.

6. In his famous "Harangue for the Outaoüa Tribes," Nicolas Perrot, for example, uses "Ottawa" (Odawa) in both the general sense of trading Indians and as a specific tribal name. See Blair 1911 1: 268–74.

7. Hunt 1940, Kinietz 1940, and Deale 1958 are only some of those who have been misled by Le Jeune's remarks, thereby placing the Potawatomi tribe on the shores of Green Bay in 1634.

8. For more on the nature and working of tribal-level societies, see Fried 1969; Sahlins 1965 & 1969; & Service 1962.

9. "Gens" and "sib" are basically synonymous with the technical word "clan," as the latter is defined and used in this book.

10. There are of course exceptions to this rule, the most notable being the tribal societies which flourished in the lush environment on the Northwest Coast of North America, where an ample and reliable supply of food was available for the gathering. There the rich natural environment facilitated the development of tribal social systems.

11. In the Potawatomi instance, an anthropologist who employs such assumptions is Baerreis (1973), and a historian, Edmunds (1969).

CHAPTER 2:
BEFORE HISTORY

1. Estimates of the importance of animal and plant foods are dependent on the remains of bones, pits, and seeds found in archeological sites. Since buffalo were not found in the area of Potawatomi occupation, the tribesmen had to travel long distances via canoe or on foot to hunt them. As in later years— even when the Potawatomi had numerous horses—they did not transport whole buffalo carcasses from the hunting sites. Instead, they boned and dried the meat before carrying it homeward. Hence few buffalo bones would be found in Michigan Potawatomi village sites.

2. See Hodge 1910: 289–90; Skinner 1924/27: 10–12; Schoolcraft 1851/57 1: 308; Copway 1850; & Blackbird 1897. Similar views are expressed today by Potawatomi in Kansas, Wisconsin, and Canada.

3. Indeed, many of Copway's pages are, by today's standards, plagiarized.

4. Blackbird was a very common name in this and earlier eras among the Potawatomi, Odawa, and Ojibwa. As we will see, the Potawatomi had several Blackbirds, Black Birds, Black Partridges, and Black Turkeys of their own.

5. Here Allouez uses "Outaouacs" (Odawek) in the broad sense, including the Odawa proper, the Ojibwa, the Potawatomi, etc.

6. The French generally stated population figures only in terms of the numbers of able-bodied warriors they understood a tribe could muster. This leaves children, adolescents, adult women, the disabled, and the elderly unenumerated. A conservative index of five persons per warrior is used throughout this book, unless more exact historically documented population figures are available.

7. Hunt's 1940 study of these wars remains very readable and useful, although Heidenreich's 1971 book is based on far superior scholarship and a more sophisticated analysis.

8. In his assessment of the Wisconsin wild-rice district, H. Clyde Wilson argues that only the Potawatomi and perhaps the Sauk used canoes, while the Fox, Kickapoo, and Mascoutens did not. He has likely misinterpreted his original French sources. The French carefully distinguished two types of watercraft used by the Great Lakes Indians, the frame and birch-bark type *(canot)*, and the dugout *(pirogue)*. All of the tribes likely knew and could use the simple, cruder *pirogue*, which would give easy access to the wild-rice beds, but which were too dangerous for any off-shore travel.

9. "Méchingan" (from Mitchigami—Great Lake) is of course the origin of "Michigan," state and lake.

10. The successful defense of Méchingan is the more interesting because some of the intruders—perhaps 10 percent—carried firearms obtained from the English and Dutch, while the Indians of the upper lakes were not so armed. The importance of these new weapons and the numbers carried by the Iroquois tribes in this period have sometimes been much exaggerated as the factor responsible for Iroquois military successes (see Hunt 1940). However, in this defense, the lakes tribesmen were operating on interior lines, while the Five Nations warriors were at the end of a very long war road starting in New York, far distant from their base of supply, certainly starving, and possibly out of powder and ball.

11. Raddison's account of these voyages was written many years later from memory.

Untangling and dating his often garbled narrative is difficult. Scull (1967) suggests 1654–1655 as the date of this contact with the Potawatomi, but in a careful textual analysis Adams (1961) places the time as 1658–1659, the dates used in this book. The exact year is much less important than the information about Potawatomi activities, location, and their relations with the Odawa.

12. In 1659 the Potawatomi suffered an epidemic of dysentery which took forty lives (JR 46: 143).

CHAPTER 3:
THE QUEBEC CONNECTION

1. The French were greatly impressed by the Algonquian birch-bark canoe and contrasted it with the heavy, clumsy, crude Iroquoian canoe made from other types of bark. See Margry 1878 1: 156–57.

2. "Tisha" is a Potawatomi pronunciation of the French loan-word *"tissu"*—fabric or textile. Many Potawatomi names, nouns, greetings, and expressions are French in origin. The name Tisha is known nowhere else but in this tale. It is—by Potawatomi literary standards—most appropriate for a man who had not a scrap of hide to cover his nakedness.

3. Sailing ships do not travel over land, of course. Moreover, the French never gave the Potawatomi a sailing vessel. Here the ship, which travels long distances over water, is apparently confabulated with the horse, which travels long distances over land and which was also first acquired from the French. It is remarkable that the Potawatomi have no origin myth for the horse. They apparently could not, from at least the early 1900s onwards, conceive of a time when they lacked horses. See Skinner 1924/27: 366.

4. The writings of Nicholas Perrot and Claude Allouez are among the richest documentations of early Potawatomi culture. One has to come down to the nineteenth century to find anything so detailed and insightful. For Allouez's commentaries, see JR 51: 26–41; 54: 196–237; 58: 36–43. Perrot's long experience with the Potawatomi is documented in his Memoir, in Blair 1911. However, Claude La Potherie also relied heavily on Perrot's unpublished (and lost) journals, as well as personal interviews, for his *History of the Savage Peoples who are Allies of New France*. See Blair 1911 1 & 2.

5. The French habitually identified the several kinds of Potawatomi religious practitioners as *jongleurs*, by which these doctrinaire rationalists meant charlatans, tricksters, or fakers.

6. This is likely the precise point where the Potawatomi and other Algonquian medical practitioners of the upper lakes learned the technique of bleeding, which they continued to practice until late in the nineteenth century, as did their colleagues the Euro-American physicians.

7. When the 1668 trade fleet returned to the bay, in jubilation the young men fired off their newly acquired muskets, frightening the Potawatomi on shore who believed them an Iroquois war-party. The Potawatomi were still extremely skittish about Iroquois raids.

8. The case for this position is argued at some length in an earlier essay; however, in this section, additional facts and clarifications are added. See Clifton 1975a.

9. "Okama" is sometimes also written "wokama."

10. In his glossary of Algonquian words the Baron de La Hontan translated kitchi okima as grand captain (1703 1: 405). At that time, *capitaine* had the connotation of a position achieved by personal effort, valor, or prowess.

11. La Potherie uses "carp," but there were no carp *(Cyprinus carpio)* in North American waters that early. These were more likely lineages of the sucker (Namabin) totem, for there were numerous varieties of suckers *(Catostomidae)* in the Wisconsin habitat and they were important in the Potawatomi diet, especially in the hungry months of early spring.

12. "Onotio" (or Ononthio—Great Mountain) is a French corruption of an Iroquois word. It was a direct translation by the Iroquois of the family name of Champlain's successor as governor, Montmagny; and thereafter it was used by Iroquois and Algonquian alike as a title for all of the French governors.

13. See Ray 1972 for a sophisticated economic analysis of this conflict of the principles of a market with a barter economy in the fur trade.

CHAPTER 4:
CHRONICLES OF THE FRENCH REGIME:
1668–1760

1. In his study of the fur trade Phillips (1961 Vol. 1) overemphasizes the significance of the occasional party of Potawatomi who carried their furs to Oswego and Albany and seems to make them allies of the English prior to 1760.

2. The annexation ceremony is beautifully described by Kellogg (1925: 184–90). The primary sources are Perrot 1911: 220–25; La Potherie 342–48; St. Lusson 1671; JR 55: 105–15; & Margry 1876 1.

3. The only source for these events is Perrot—or La Potherie, who himself relied on interviews with Perrot. Obviously, this able agent had little respect for Durantaye, who seems to have been incapable of dealing effectively with the sophisticated Odawa and Huron politicos.

4. Although the Huron warned the Iroquois, the combined force of Odawa and Potawatomi was very successful, returning to Michilimackinac with thirty Iroquois scalps, thirty-two prisoners, and five hundred pounds of beaver pelts (Charlevoix 1870 4: 278).

5. In this century and most of the next the Indians of the Eastern Woodlands were far superior to either French or British regulars in the military art of pursue and destroy following a successful engagement.

6. The league was a rough time-distance measurement, the distance a loaded canoe could travel an hour. It is variously standardized at from 2.75 to 3.5 statute miles. A three-mile standard is used consistently in this book. See Ray 1974: 6.

7. This was not Potawatomi custom.

8. One must wait until 1795 and 1804 to find further reports of observations of the Potawatomi on the Wisconsin shoreline and when the villages were in basically the same locations as in the late seventeenth century. See Vieau 1888; Anderson 1870; Martin 1888.

9. There is historical significance in the spelling variations of this name. Potawatomi had no "l" sound; other Eastern and Central Algonquian languages did. The Eastern Algonquian "Wilamet" is cognate to the Potawatomi "Winamek," i.e., Catfish. Hence the transition from the French spelling "Ouilamette" (Wilamet) to "Ouilamez" or "Ouilamek,"

and finally to "Ouinamek" (Winamek) marks the assimilation of an Eastern Algonquian form into Potawatomi language patterns. There is more of the same kind of evidence, as we will see shortly.

10. As observed earlier, the Potawatomi remaining on the Wisconsin shore are not mentioned in the very scanty French documentation of that area in the eighteenth century.

11. For examples of historians' stereotyped and ethnocentric treatments of Potawatomi leadership and political organization, see Deale 1958, Edmunds 1969 & 1972a, Wheeler-Voegelin & Jones 1974, Wheeler-Voegelin & Stout 1974, and Conway 1972 & 1975.

12. Kellogg's writings contain the best overview of the Fox wars (1925: 268–340). Edmunds provides a good chronology of events from the narrower perspective of Potawatomi involvement (1972a: 44–76). Some of the principal source documents are Vaudreuil 1716, 1717c, 1719, 1720, & 1723; Beauharnois 1729a, 1729b, 1730a, 1735, & 1736; Beauharnois & Hocquart 1734; Ramezay 1715; Sabrevois 1717; Anon. 1721; Ouashala 1722; DuTisne 1725; Lignery 1722; Deschaillons 1730; Boishébert 1732; Hocquart 1735.

13. This name is so badly corrupted it is difficult to translate. Chichalk—Crane is a good possibility. If correct, then this is another Ocean Clan name.

14. See pp. 107–11 for a discussion of Potawatomi naming customs.

15. "Piremon," often spelled "Pilemon" or "Pilemou" (a typographical error substituting "u" for "n"), was in origin a Sauk name, not Potawatomi.

16. Gibson richly summarizes these activities from the perspective of the Chickasaw (1971: 45–50), and Edmunds from that of the Potawatomi (1972a: 77–85). Some of the primary docu-

ments are Anon. 1743; dan Beauharnois 1733 & 1741.

17. For some of the basic materials for the Huron affair, see Beauharnois 1736b & 1742; Hanna 1911 2: 163–65; Potawatomi Chiefs 1742; WHC 17: 457–86; MPHC 17: 195–206; CHNY 10: 121–24.

18. During the British period, the Huron south of the Great Lakes became known as the Wyandot, an English corruption of their own old self-name, "Wendat."

19. The best summary of these events is the incomparable Kellogg, 1925: 413–22. See also Hanna 1911 2: 282–85; Jacobs 1950: 90–135; and Anson 1970. Some of the primary sources are Céleron 1750; IHC 29: 109–10, 120–23, 205–10, & 147–48; JR 69: 151–99; WMC 18: 58–60, 90–94, & 128–30; and CHNY 10: 247–48.

20. In 1751, the Chicago area Potawatomi called in their kinsmen from the Isle de Poues. (Potawatomi Island) for this raid (IHC 29: 349–51). Edmunds identifies this as Washington (actually Rock) Island at the mouth of Green Bay (1972a: 110). It may have been, but some Potawatomi then occupied a different Isle de Poues. in the Detroit River (Sabrevois 1718). *"Poues."* was a standard French abbreviation for Potawatomi. The translator of the 1718 Sabrevois report mistakenly makes it "louse."

21. The phrasing, not this particular observation, is borrowed from James Thomas Flexner, 1965: 134.

22. Le Jeunesse 1960: 37–39; CHNY 10: 34, 91, 122; WHC 17: 457–58.

23. For the best summary of this disaster, see Flexner 1965: 119–31; also Kellogg 1925: 425–28; Peckham 1964; Billington 1960: 125–28; & Edmunds 1972a: 113–17.

24. Kellogg 1925: 428–32; Peckham 1964: 148–52; & Edmunds 1972a: 119–25 for good summaries of these events. For

documentary details, see WHC 18: 163; CHNY 10: 401–2 & 522; Hamilton 1964: 45–61, 102–21, & 131–33; & Wheeler-Voegelin & Stout 1974: 76–77.

25. Hamilton 1964: 142–44.

26. Kellogg 1925: 431–33; Hamilton 1964: 146–71 & 194–96; CHNY 10: 608, & 629–30; WHC 18: 185 & 203–6; WHC 19: 152–58.

27. Kellogg 1925: 433–35; WHC 18: 205; Peckham 1964: 181–83; CHNY 10: 981–90; Jablow 1974: 227–30; Wheeler-Voegelin & Stout 1974: 80–81 & 140–46; Berthrong 1974: 111–14.

28. NYCD 10: 977–78, & 982–90; & Peckham 1964: 180–85.

29. Stevens 1940–43: 21655: 94–101; WHC 18: 217, 231, & 244–45. Also, Edmunds 1972: 134–44; Tanner & Wheeler-Voegelin 1974: 343–45; Jablow 1974: 228; Wheeler-Voegelin & Stout 1974: 80–81; & Berthrong 1974: 112.

CHAPTER 5:
PERSISTENCE AND CHANGE IN THE FRENCH ERA

1. Key sources for Potawatomi naming customs are: Marston 1820: 167–68; De Smet 1859: 15; Skinner 1924/27: 22–23; Landes 1970: 203–15; McElroy 1968: 20–21; & Clifton 1962/65.

2. Skinner lists 231 translated names belonging to thirteen clans (1924/27: 23–30). Wooster (1907b) consists of a census roll of Wisconsin and Canadian Potawatomi with more than fifteen hundred personal names, nearly 60 percent of which are translated clan names. This author has personally collected approximately sixty-five hundred personal names, about half of which are proper clan names.

3. JR 9: 275–77; JR 10: 181; JR 17: 242–43; JR 20: 310; & JR 55: 137.

4. Father André notes that the original Porceau was giving a "bear feast," and it is quite likely that this personal name was incorporated as a Bear Clan eponym, as this clan included among its names those of most large, hornless, four-legged mammals.

5. Skinner was the only person ever to systematically record in detail the origin myths of a number of Potawatomi clans while there were elders living who knew them as a living part of the tribe's oral literature (1924/27: 56–177).

6. For some of the partial descriptions of the Potawatomi version of the Midewiwin, see De Smet 1859: 15–16; Donohue 1931: 199–204; Armstrong 1887: 611; & Landes 1963: 573–76.

CHAPTER 6:
CONTEST FOR SOVEREIGNTY

1. For an overview of the events leading up to the Treaty of Greenville, see: Tanner & Voegelin 1974 1: 53–127. Horsman (1964) views these events through the involvement of one important British agent, Matthew Elliott. Edmunds 1972: 145–310 & n.d. provides a detailed chronology of Potawatomi involvement in these large events. See also Sosin 1967.

2. For an overview, see Peckham 1961; Parkman 1870; Kellogg 1971: 19–22; & Wallace & Jacobs 1950. Edmunds (1972: 145–93) details many Potawatomi involvements with Pontiac. For some of the primary source materials on

these events, see: Quaife 1958; MPHC 18: 260–61; 19: 47–51, 70–77, 86–94, 114–15, 127–39, 153–54, 186–95, 209–12, 216–17; & 27: 216–19, 259–60, 271–72, 635–54, & 675; Stevens 1940/43: 5-21646: 217–18; 5-21648 2: 74–75, 158, 176–77; 5-21655: 125–26, & 167–75; Flick 1921/62 3: 474–93; & 4: 408–9, 526–33; IHC 10: 293–96, 439–42, 467–71, 491–95, 500, & 534; CHNY 7: 648–50, 711–12, & 854–67; EWT 1: 126–48, 301–2, 323–25, & 164–66; Smith 1973: 47; WHC 18: 255–61 & 244–45. See also Wheeler-Voegelin & Stout 1974: 95–97, 106–11, & 140–46; Berthrong 1974: 113–18 & 323–25; Wheeler-Voegelin & Jones 1974: 86–88; Jablow 1974: 230, 238, & 456; Caton 1876: 5–7; and Phillips 1961: 592–93.

3. For an overview of the period 1763–1775, see ·Kellogg 1971: 23–180; Blasingham 1956; Horsman 1964: 23–59; & Billington 1960: 132–98. Edmunds (1972a: 194–247) provides a detailed chronology of Potawatomi involvement and an excellent record of events. See also Barnhart 1961; DePeyster 1888; Peckham 1939; and Sosin 1961: 190–94. For some of the primary source materials, see CHNY 7: 367–68; EWT 2: 181–83; Downes 1940: 271–74; Flick 1921/62 12: 585–86, 193–94, 226–28, & 585–86; Houck 1901 1: 44; Kinnard 1941 1: 205–7, 391, & 431–32; IHC 1: 220, 232, & 393–94; 8: 33–35, 50–53, 300–1, & 394–95; 10: 484; 11: 157–58, 287–88, 300, 330, 453, 487–95; & 16: 275–77, 331–32, 367, 407, & 579; MPHC 8: 466–67; 9: 347–54, 374–80, 395–97, 442–52, 482–83, 582–83, & 617; 10: 269–77, 348–55, 367, 380–81, 391–99, 435–48, 482–85, 576–78, & 641; 11: 116, 125–29, 178–81, & 210–11; & 19: 310–13, 375, 415–16, 519–20, & 553; WHC 1: 199–200; 11: 120–25, 153, & 178–80; 12: 44–45, 53, 56, & 60; 18: 300, 306, 357–67, 372–76, 384, 394–98, 404, & 413; 22: 7–13; & 24: 297. See also Voegelin &

Jones 1974: 153–54, 333–34, 156–80, & 336–37; Voegelin 1974a: 207–8; Jablow 1974: 253–55, 268–69, 277–90, & 294–97; Caton 1876; Plumb 1904: 10; Phillips 1961: 622–23; Voegelin & Stout 1974: 113–20, 123–24, 405, & 129–39; Fernow 1971: 180–81; & James 1912: 72–73 & 125.

4. A number of historians persist in confusing race with nationality or culture and, lacking a worldwide comparative perspective on the development and evolution of types of cultural adaptations, persist in interpreting this sort of confrontation as a "racial" conflict.

5. For an overview of the period, see Kellogg 1971: 180–210; Horsman 1964: 60–118; & Billington 1960: 199–220. Edmunds (1972a: 248–308) provides many specifics of Potawatomi involvements with the British and Americans. For some of the primary sources, see: Kinnard 1949: 172–75; Downes 1940: 277–98, & 301–4; Reynolds 1887: 153; Cunningham 1967: 14 & 34; MPHC 12: 10–11; & 24: 24–25; Smith 1882 2: 18–19, 108–9, & 130; ASP-IA 1: 5–9; TP-US 2: 31–35, 78–79, 89–90, 119–20, 127–28, & 168; Thornbrough 1957: 122, 159, & 222–25. See also Voegelin & Jones 1974: 111–12; Voegelin & Stout 1974: 129–39; Jablow 1974: 325–26, & 331–32; WHC 11: 238–39; & Buchen 1944; & Plumb 1904: 11.

6. Tanner & Wheeler-Voegelin (1974 2: 377–427) provide an excellent summary of the events of the Greenville treaty. See also Horsman 1964: 109–16; Knopf 1960; & Billington 1960: 224–27 for background and context. The journal of the Greenville treaty and the supplements thereto are in ASP-IA 1: 564–83. The text of the treaty proper is in Kappler 1972: 39–45, although Kappler gives the wrong date of ratification and proclamation, which was properly December 22, not December 2. Some of the primary source materials are in:

ASP-IA 1: 340–44, 359–60, 490, & 527–28; MPHC 20: 380; 34: 73–76, 108–9, 176–77, 620–34, & 674–83; Quaife 1931 1: 550–52, 561–65, & 578–80; & Knopf 1960: 311, 369–70, 386–89, 395–406, 412–13, 422–23, 431–36, 442–46, & 460–63. See also Faben 1958 and Chowen 1941.

7. The individual named Gomo (or, alternatively, Kuomo, Come, Massenogomo, or Nasimagomo) presents an interesting case of translation. His name has also been translated as "Fish Stopping Out of Water" (DRC 21S275, 22S104–6, 9T48; & WHC 11: 336–37); but this is not a translation of "Gomo" or any of the variants. Contemporary Potawatomi speakers hear "Gomo" as an unmistakable corruption of "Okama"—Leader, and they suggest the prefix "Matchi-" (corrupted as Nasimi- or Masse-) was added to make a sarcastic nickname, Big Chief. This interpretation conforms to what is known about this upstart, American-made "chief," who was indeed a fish out of water.

CHAPTER 7:
PERSISTENCE AND CHANGE IN THE INTERREGNUM

1. For specifics on the locations of Potawatomi villages in this and later periods, see: Baerreis, Wheeler-Voegelin, & Moore 1974: 138–67; Berthrong 1974: Jablow 1974: 279–337; Lawson 1920; Tanner & Voeglin 1974 2: 340–75; Temple 1958; Voegel 1962; Wheeler-Voegelin 1974: 155–336; Wheeler-Voegelin & Jones 1974: 89–137; & Wheeler-Voegelin and Tanner 1974: 223–87.

2. For Potawatomi locations in Eastern Wisconsin in 1795 and succeeding years, see: Anderson 1870; Anderson 1912; Buchen 1944; Lawson 1920: 51–57; Martin 1888: 394; Plumb 1904: 11; Vieau 1888; Vieau 1900; & WHC 11: 238–39.

3. The name "Windigo" has its roots in myth, referring to the shared belief of the Odawa, Ojibwa, and Potawatomi in a legendary tribe of cannibals or a cannibal monster who supposedly inhabited the far north woods. In use as a person name, it translates simply as Cannibal.

4. *Bled* in this period was the preferred French spelling for the modern *Blé*—Corn. The North African Arabic loanword *Bled*—Back Country had not entered French as yet. Note that Mitamins was Nicholas Perrot's Potawatomi name, as well.

5. Baptiste Pont du Sable was the Santo Domingo–born French–Afro-American trader on whom some have laid the blame for founding Chicago.

6. The name "Sigenak"—Blackbird and the identity and origins of the man or men who bore it have been a source of particular confusion. It does not translate directly as "blackbird," but means instead a species of bird that was black. It was a very common name among the Ojibwa, Odawa, and the Potawatomi in the period and is found in several variant spellings, depending on the parent language (e.g., "Asiginak" in Odawa). Lyman Draper, for example, confused the name "Sigenak" with "Mkedēpena" —which does translate as "blackbird," as well as with "Mkedēpoke'—Black Turkey (DRC 21S: 274–75; 11YY36–36[1], 37–37[1], & 39[4]–39[5]). Moreover, that particular Sigenak who was detested by DePeyster and respected by Clark in the period 1777–1781 was probably not the younger man of the same name

who, a dozen years later, signed the Treaty of Greenville and then emerged as a bitterly anti-American okama through the War of 1812. George Rogers Clark's Blackbird was also called Le Tourneau by the French. The last known, documented reference to Sigenak (or Le Tourneau) under that name dates to 1789 when Charles Gaultier, British interpreter at Mackinac Island, noted that he was a *"chef de Chicagou"* receiving presents at that post (RG 10 Vol. 26).

7. See MPHC 10: 450–51 & 453–55; & 9: 629; WHC 11: 162; & 18: 413–14; & Kinnard 1: 396–97 & 431–33.

8. The third signatory of the Putnam treaty was Waeachsetch, who likely signed the Greenville documents as Waweegshe, which was probably a corruption of "Wawiyezhi"—Something Round (like a Shield). The fourth signer was Quaquanese, probably Kwakwanese—Little Flying Creature (likely, Grasshopper).

9. Unfortunately, Baerreis cites Gomo as an authority on traditional Potawatomi leadership roles, ignoring the man's own biography and the way he himself rose to a position of influence (1973: 124). See my 1975a essay for an alternative view. For materials on Gomo's early life, see: DRC 9T48, 21S275, & 21S104–106; WHC 11: 336–37; Edwards 1870: 42–48; & IHC 8: 257–58.

10. For an in-depth, psychologically sophisticated, ethnographic assessment of this grandiose, near megalomanic striving for power, see Landes 1963 & 1974.

11. Cited in ICC 1974 2: 228.

12. Cited in Jablow 1974: 333–34; and in Voegelin & Stout 1974: 408.

13. For a good basic statement of what is known in general about tribal-level warfare, see Harris 1975: 259–80. Otterbein (1972) provides a more theoretically sophisticated summary and an excellent bibliography.

14. Keating, who was made very queasy by any mention of Indian cannibalism, and who expended many pages trying to rationalize it away when he found evidence of the practice among the Potawatomi, ended up by confusing the cannibalistic practices of a war-party with the Midewiwin religious cult. Keating was wrong in supposing that Potawatomi cannibalism was limited to "a certain society or fraternity, whose privilege and duty it was on all occasions to eat the enemy's flesh" (1824: 101–3).

15. See Williams (1959) for Boquet's analysis of tribal military tactics. For descriptions of French, British, and American frontier military tactics and arrangements, see Eccles 1966; Stacey 1966; Mahon 1958; Stotz 1958; & Kohn 1975. Sosin provides an excellent, brief summary (1967: 6–9).

16. "Cataboe" is difficult to recognize and to translate with any certainty. It seems to consist of a corruption of "Mkedē"— Black, plus a suffix, making it Black [something]. The "b" may be a typographical error substituting a "b" for a "k." If this is so, then "Cataboe" is rendered phonemically as "Mkedēkwe" —Black Woman, and that possibility certainly offers rich food for speculation.

CHAPTER 8:
THE DIMINISHING ESTATE: 1796–1837

1. Bureau of the Census 1961: 13; & Billington 1960: 246–67.

2. Schultz 1972: 183–81. This is an excellent scholarly biography of McCoy and his involvement with the Potawatomi.

3. Washburn represents another historian confused about Potawatomi political organization. His claim that the "United States helped the Potawatomi ... to achieve a stronger tribal unity" is precisely the opposite of what Lewis Cass and other American officials intended and of what actually occurred (1975: 50).

4. These were the sons of William Burnett of New Jersey, who became a prominent trader in the St. Joseph area, and his wife Kakima, who was one of Topnebi's sisters and old Nanakiba's daughter (Connelley 1915).

5. For the best description of the Kenakuk religion and Potawatomi involvement in same, see Howard 1965. Also Gibson 1963: 109–24; Schultz 1972: 170–76; & McCoy 1840: 456–58.

6. For the texts of these treaties see Kappler 1904: 64–66, 77–78, 80–82, 92–95, & 99–102. Also Smith 1957: 30; ASP-IA 1: 702–3; Wheeler-Voegelin & Tanner 1974: 51–54; ICC 1974 1: 131 & 3: 161–64; Wheeler-Voegelin, Blasingham, & Libby 1974: 337:39, 344–67, & 461–62.

7. In the 1805 Grouseland treaty text, Shissahecon is misprinted as Lishaecon.

8. Wheeler-Voegelin, Blasingham & Libby 1974: 337–39 & 344–67; & Esarey 1922 1: 363–77.

9. For Potawatomi trips to Amherstburg in this period, see Clifton 1975b; MPHC 20: 545 & 23: 39–42; McKee to Claus, 14 Sept. 1801, in RG 10, Vol. 26: 15377–78; & Ironside to Claus, 11 June 1801, in RG 10, Vol. 26: 15368.

10. For the best overview of missionary efforts to "civilize" Indians, see Berkhofer 1965. For Potawatomi involvements with Quakers in the east and in Indiana, Hopkins 1862: 45–90 & 167–73; Woehrman 1971: 115–41; Gibson 1938: 300–2; & Parsons 1960.

11. Quaife 1913: 126–36; NAM M15, R 1:

146–48 & 265–68, & R 2: 243–44; & Esarey 1922 1: 147–51.

12. Wade 1795; Smith 1954: 286; & Hair 1866: 248–52 & 274–77.

13. "Main Poche" is straightforward French, not of Potawatomi origin. It was used as a nickname for this aggressively warlike rogue who had a deformed or clubbed hand. In American and British documents it is variously misspelled as Main Poc, Man Pock, or Mar Pock.

14. For pre-1806 raids against the Osage and against Americans in southern Illinois, Hair 1866: 248–52 & 274–77; Kinnard 1949 3: 110–12; Nasatir 1952 1: 167–68, 173–74, 197–99, & 322, & 2: 528; MPHC 11: 493–96; Houck 1909 2: 94; Matthews 1961: 265–82 & 356; Jackson 1966 1: 253–54; and Jablow 1974: 344.

15. TP-US 13: 243–47; Jackson 1966 2: 33, 115, & 134–45; Esarey 1922 1: 184–87; & WHC 12: 105–6.

16. Good summaries of historical and biographical materials on Tecumsah and Tenskwatawa are in Hodge 1910 2: 714–16 & 729–30; Drake 1858; & Tucker 1956. There is no theoretically sophisticated treatment of either man available.

17. For an introduction to the theory of cultural revitalization movements, see Wallace 1966: 30–39, 157–66, & 209–15; & Wallace 1956; Linton 1943; and Kopytoff 1964. Wallace's study of the Senaca and the Handsome Lake religion is the best available psychohistorical treatment of a comparable revitalization movement (1970a).

18. For Tenskwatawa & Tecumsah's doctrines, see Forsyth 1812a & James 1830: 144–48 & 177–86.

19. Horsman 1964: 157–65 & 1969: 11–16; & Billington 1960: 246–67.

20. MPHC 40: 76–78; Quaife 1913: 192–94; Esarey 1922 1: 110–12; & Tucker 1956: 110–14.

21. For Potawatomi raids against the Osage

and American settlements in this period, Jackson 1966 1: 253–54 & 287, & 2: 33, 115, 131, 134, & 144; Prucha 1969: 91, Matthews 1961: 411; EWT 5: 48–49; TP-US 14: 412–14, & 16: 116–19; & Forsyth 1827: 203–4.

22. MPHC 40: 135–37; TP-US 7: 472–73 & 556–58; & Forsyth 1827: 203.

23. TP-US 7: 555–60; MPHC 19: 42–44; & Esarey 1922 1: 284–85.

24. A small part of the lands ceded west of the Wabash (ca. 75 percent of Royce area 73) was in present Illinois. See Kappler 1904: 101–2; Wheeler-Voegelin, Blasingham, & Libby 1974: 461–62, 337–39, 344–67; ICC 1974 1: 131; & Esarey 1922 1: 363–77.

25. Cited in Wheeler-Voegelin, Blasingham, & Libby 1974: 365.

26. Esarey 1922 1: 417, 420–30, & 433–37. Also Berthrong 1974: 253–55.

27. TP-US 14: 412–14; & Edwards 1870: 46–48.

28. For Potawatomi raids in 1810–1811, Esarey 1922 1: 422–29 & 453–54; WHC 11: 320; Edwards 1870: 37–39; TP-US 16: 116–19; & Forsyth 1827: 202–4.

29. TP-US 10: 317–18, & 16: 162–64. Also Jablow 1974: 360–61.

30. Drake 1858: 146–53; Tucker 1956: 218–31; Billington 1960: 272–78; ASP-IA 1: 776–79; & Esarey 1922 1: 589–92.

31. "Wabansi" translates literally as "a little (east) light" and can be rendered Daybreak, Foggy Morn, etc. He went on to become the principal American-recognized chief of the Council Bluffs or Prairie Potawatomi. See DRC 21S279.

32. Gilpin 1958: 15–20; Whickar 1921; & Esarey 1922 1: 613–15.

33. "Shabeni" in historical sources is generally spelled "Shabbona" or "Shabonee," and mistranslated as "Bear Shoulders" or "Built Like a Bear." It is a Bear Clan name, but does not have these meanings. See Hodge 1910 2: 517–18. Hodge also includes sketches of

the two treaty-era Winameks but confuses biographical facts concerning them (1910 2: 956–57). For the report of the hostile Winamek's death, see Armstrong 1887: 571–86 & Captain Billy Caldwell's official report of Potawatomi casualties during the War of 1812, 5 Feb. 1816, in RG 10, Vol. 32: 18847–49.

34. For the minutes of this council and Claus's covering report to Brock, see RG 10, Vol. 3: 306–13, 8 June 1812. The village of Machikethic (likely, Ill-Looking Sun) was located sixty miles west of Fort Wayne on the Tippecanoe.

35. For the best overview of the War of 1812, see Horsman 1969; the historical-geographic dimensions of the conflict are best treated in Billington 1960: 268–89. Stanley (1964) and Horsman (1963) examine the role of Indians in the war, but not from the perspective of any Indians. Kellogg (1971: 283–312) and Horsman (1962) survey the events of the war in Wisconsin; Edmunds (1969) from the perspective of Illinois Potawatomi involvement; and Horsman (1964: 192–218) as regards events along the Detroit-Sandwich (now Windsor) border. Maj. Richardson's classic treats the war from a Canadian perspective, also that of a personally involved participant (1902). Clifton (1975b: 34–42) examines some aspects of Potawatomi efforts in the Ontario Peninsula. Edmund's forthcoming *Keepers of the Fire* (n.d., Ch. 8) will provide the most detailed treatment of Potawatomi involvement available.

36. For Tecumsah's activities, see Claus to Brock, 16 June 1812, MGC, C676; 144–46. For Main Poche's, see Elliott to Claus, 13 April 1812, RG 10, Vol. 28, File 1813; Esarey 1922 2: 21–22, & TP-US 16: 193–94.

37. For specifics, see Jablow 1974: 363–65; Edwards 1870: 55–60, 291–93, & 300–2; TP-US 16: 193–94, & 531–35; Esarey 1922 2: 41–44.

38. Kellogg 1971: 284–85; Gilpin 1958: 88–91; and Lt. Col. McDouall to Capt. Bulgar, in WHC 13: 136. Col. McDouall was even more mortified in 1815 when he once again had to surrender these same cannon peaceably to the Americans after the Treaty of Ghent.

39. For Potawatomi involvements in the Detroit-Fort Malden campaign, see Richardson 1902: 26–36 & 49–92; Quaife 1931 2: 715–21; Quaife 1940: 80–103; Cruikshank 1912: 139–40 & 180–82; MPHC 15: 129–31; Gilpin 1958: 98–105; Tucker 1956: 256–60; & Horsman 1964: 193–94.

40. Robinson's Indian name was Odawa in origin, and in the historical literature is generally spelled Cheecheebingway, Tsheetsheebeenguay, or something similar. See Hodge 1910 2: 393.

41. For the background to and events of the Fort Dearborn incident, see TP-US 16: 238–65; Quaife 1913: 215–61; Schoolcraft 1851/57 5: 530–31; Tucker 1958: 252–58; & DRC 21S82–84. Williams's publication and analysis of Kinzie's first-hand narrative account is the best single source, one which, as Williams puts it, "blows the froth" off many legends (1953). Also, Kinzie 1856; & Anson 1970: 150–63.

42. Awbenabi was a particularly violent man. Alexander Robinson told Lyman Draper that, when drunk, he was a "very bad Indian." In 1835 Awbenabi murdered his eldest son in a drunken rage; with the approval of the villagers, he was in turn executed by his next oldest son, Pakēshēk (DRC 21S281; Kappler 1904: 457–58).

43. Woehrman 1971: 224–41; Gilpin 1958: 140–42; Tucker 1958: 275–77; & DRC 21S281.

44. Edmunds (1969) provides the best available study of the Illinois River Potawatomi in the war. For some of the specifics of the fall campaign, see Alford 1972: 444–46; Esarey 1958 2: 143–47 & 245–37; Edwards 1870: 69–72; Gilpin 1958: 140–42; Horsman 1964: 200–3; MPHC 15: 151–71; TP-US 16: 261–72 & 279–83; Woehrman 1971: 248–49; & WHC 16: 195–98. Also Jablow 1974: 376–78.

45. Horsman 1969: 81–85 & 1964: 203–5; Gilpin 1958: 163–71; Richardson 1902: 132–47; & Esarey 1922 2: 315–29 & 370–75.

46. Horsman 1969: 85–87 & 99–103; & 1964: 206–9; DRC 12YY62–64; Gilpin 1958: 188–91; Esarey 1922 2: 431–40; & MPHC 15: 293–98.

47. Horsman 1969: 103–16 & 1964: 212–14; Quaife 1940: 140–42; Richardson 1902: 204–40; Tucker 1956: 296–300; Esarey 1922 2: 558–65; Hickling 1877: 4–9; Matson 1880: 25–30.

48. RG 10, Vol. 28: 16995 & Vol. 29: 17461. Also Horsman 1964: 214; & Clifton 1975b: 36–40. William Elliott is sometimes wrongly identified as Matthew's son, but he was in fact no close relation (Horsman 1964: 242, n. 8).

49. See Billy Caldwell Return, 5 Feb. 1816, in RG 10, Vol. 32: 18847–49. This report does not clearly distinguish those killed from those seriously wounded. See also DRC 17S229–40.

50. DRC 26S124–27; Esarey 1922 2: 577–79; MPHC 15: 523–24; Edwards 1870: 287–88.

51. See TP-US 16: 727–28.

52. TP-US 10: 470–71 & 485–86; & WHC 11: 304. For records of visits to Mackinac Island in this period, see Minutes of a Council at Michilimackinac (unsigned, but in John Askin's handwriting), in RG 10, Vol. 29: Sept./Oct. File; WHC 13: 94–97; MPHC 23: 453–55, 469–71, & 558; & TP-US 10: 489–90. The Elliott quotation is from Elliott to D.S.G.I.A., 25 Mar. 1814, in RG 10, Vol. 3: 283.

53. For a summary of Dickson's career, see

WHC 12: 144–50 & Horsman 1962; Materials on the cooperation between Gomo and other okamek with American officials are in Thomas Forsyth's reports to Governor Edwards, May-Aug., 1814, WHC 11: 318–30.

54. DRC 26S194–96; & TP-US 18: 116–17. For some of Dickson's correspondence, which records the decline of his ego-control, see WHC 10: 103–11; & 11: 289–96.

55. WHC 13: 21–22, 82–83, & 144–45; TP-US 16: 446–47; & 17: 145; MPHC 16: 87–88; & 25: 621.

56. WHC 11: 336–41; Kappler 1904: 110–11 & 117–19; & ASP-IA 2: 17–26.

57. John Kinzie to Cass, 15 July 1815, in National Archives, RG 75, Michigan Superintendency, Letters Received, Vol. 1: 90–92.

58. Norton to Holland, 2 July 1814, in RG 10, Vol. 3: 502–10; Claus to Gore, 22 Feb. 1816, in RG 10, Vol. 4: 299–311; B. Caldwell to McDonnell, in RG 10, Vol. 33: 19499; Ironside to Claus, 28 Jan. 1817, in RG 10, Vol. 34. Also, Clifton 1975b: 34–40.

59. Speech of the Saukie . . . , 1 Aug. 1817, RG 10, Vol. 34: 20034. Also Elliott to Claus, 10 June 1816, RG 10, Vol. 27: 16099.

60. TP-US 17: 227–28, & 259–60; WHC 11: 345–47. Main Poche died near present Mainstee, Michigan (DRC8YY57). Wheeler-Voegelin & Jones (1974: 182–89) provide a good discussion of the background of this treaty from the perspective of current Department of Justice needs in claim's case proceedings (1974: 182–89). Also, ICC 1974 3: 347–50. The Sauk and Fox cession of 1804 is identified as Royce area 50, that of the Potawatomi in 1816 as areas 77 & 78 (Royce 1900: 666–67, & 680–81).

61. Cited in Jones, Smith, & Carstensen 1974: 126–27.

62. Kappler 1904: 133. The Potawatomi diminutive suffix/-s/ has the meanings of "little" (in dimensions), "young" (in years), or "immature" (in development).

63. Kappler 1904: 145–55. The lands involved in the 1817 treaty are identified as Royce area 98 (1900: 692–93).

64. Kappler. 1904: 198–201. Designated Royce area 117 (1900: 702–5). For good discussions of the implications of this treaty from the Department of Justice's viewpoint, see Wheeler-Voegelin & Stout 1974: 4–5, & 193–95. Also, ICC 1974 1: 206–26; & 2: 105, 346, & 386–90.

65. The discussion following in the next paragraphs is based partly upon Proceedings of the 1821 Treaty of Chicago, in PF, & Quaife 1913.

66. Identified as parts of Royce areas 144 & 245. See Smith 1973: 122–29; Kappler 1904: 250–55; Hagan 1958: 96–99; & Jones, Smith, & Carstensen 1974: 128–30.

67. Kappler 1904: 273–77. The areas are designated Royce 132 & 133 (1900: 716–17). The following discussion of this treaty is based upon ASP-IA 2: 683–85; NAM T494, R 6: 874–902; Robertson & Riker 1942 1: 595–96. See also, Berthrong 1974: 333–47 & ICC 1974 3: 377–409.

68. Hodge 1910 2: 358; Quaife 1913: 314–15; NAM 234, R 132: 28–35; & R 748: 212–13. See also, Clifton 1976d; & Hickling 1877.

69. Kappler 1904: 292–93; Royce 1900: 722–23; & NAM T494, R 2: 128–47.

70. The lands involved are designated Royce areas 145 & 146 (1900: 772–73). See Kappler 1904: 294–96. The journal for this treaty is in the National Archives, General Records of the United States Government, Treaty Files. Also, Schultz 1972: 118–19; & Berthrong 1974: 348–52.

71. Buchner 1933: 294–98; & Hodge 1910 2: 274–75.

72. This discussion centers on the Potawatomi's involvement in this treaty
council; but the eighty Potawatomi present were far outnumbered by the some
eleven hundred Winnebago who participated. Those Potawatomi areas ceded
are identified as Royce 147, 148, & 149
(1900: 722–23). See Kappler 1904:
297–300; NAM T494, R 2: 185–93;
NAM 234, R 749 : 801–5. Also, ICC
1974 1: 243–334; Smith 1973: 131–32;
Baerreis, Wheeler-Voegelin, & Moore
1974: 57–63 & 155–56; & Jones, Smith,
& Carstensen 1974: 142–43. In ICC
1974 2: n. 71, the Claim's Commissioners wrongly identify the date of the
Prairie du Chien Treaty and Caldwell's
alleged appointment as "chief."

73. ICC 1974 2: 291–95.

74. NAM 234, R 748: 593–94; & Detroit
Gazette, 23 July 1829.

75. American biographers, historians, and
anthropologists almost completely ignore the British documents available on
Black Hawk in the period 1814–1831.
For an example of Black Hawk's breath-
less expectation of British aid, see Minutes of Council No. 3 at Drummond
Island, 7 Aug. 1817, in RG 10, Vol.
32; 19160–82. Much more of the same
will be found in RG 10, Vols. 32–39, 45,
569, & 1836–37.

76. Black Hawk's speech, 7 Aug. 1817, in
RG 10, Vol. 32: 19165.

77. An account of the Black Hawk "war"
should start with his own version in his
autobiography (1834). Perry Armstrong's old history is still very useful,
and expresses precisely the same inter-
pretative bias found in later treatments.
Also, Hagan puts the affair into the
context of Sauk and Fox history, while
Wallace (1970b) stresses cultural factors and confusion that led to this
eruption. See also Hodge 1910 1: 150–
52; & 2: 885–86; Whitney 1970: 560–
62; Walters 1924; & Matson 1876 &
1880. All American treatments are pro-

foundly sympathetic to Black Hawk and
his people, much less so as regards
American officials and settlers. For further details on Potawatomi involvements, see WHC 1: 72; 7: 344; 12:
224–31, 236–46, & 275; & 15: 60–65; &
TP-US 12: 333.

78. The lands are designated, respectively,
for the treaties of Oct. 20, 26, & 27;
Royce areas 177, 180, & 181 (1900: 238–
41). See Kappler 1904: 353–60, 367–
70, & 372–75. For the treaty commissioner's reports and associated correspondence, NAM M1, R 31: 278–80; NAM
T494, R 2: 527–32; & NAM M234, R
354: 874–76; Robertson & Riker 1942 2:
243–44; McDonald 1899: 28–29. Also
Berthrong 1974: 353–58; & Dutch 1941.

79. Caldwell to Forsyth, 8 Apr. 1832. Tes-
son Collection, MHS.

80. Hickling 1877: 38–39; & Hodge 1910
2: 517–18.

81. B. Stephenson & A. Chouteau to J. C.
Calhoun, June 1819, in Pierre Chouteau
Collection; & B. Stephenson to J. C.
Calhoun, June 1819, in Auguste Chou-
teau Papers, MHS. Also, Gibson 1963:
81–82; & Jablow 1974: 420–21.

82. Foreman 1933: 152; Barry 1972: 250–
51; & Clifton 1962/65.

83. Graham to Wm. Clark, 15 Jan. 1825, in
Richard Graham Papers, MHS.

84. For the Kickapoo party, see Barry 1972:
234–35; the Potawatomi at Manitoulin
Island in 1833, Bleasdale 1974: 148–49,
& RAIC 1844; and the Kikito emigration, Edmunds, 1972b.

85. See La Trobe 1835 2: 203–12; Vieau
1900; Caton 1876: 17–20; & NAM T494,
R 3: 60–87. Gerwing (1964) gives the
best recent account of the Potawatomi
treaty, marred only by his confusions
about Potawatomi tribal structure and
the usual racial biases of historians.

86. See Wabmeksigo's speech and Porter's
reply, NAM T494, R 3: 59ff61 (journal
pp. 9–10). Also ICC 1974 3: 473–79;
& Gerwing 1964.

87. For the text of the treaty of 26 Sept. 1833 and its supplement on 27 Sept., see Kappler 1904: 402–16. The Illinois-Wisconsin lands are designated Royce area 187, those in Michigan, Royce areas 188, 189, & 190 (1900: 750–51).

88. ICC 1974 3: 31–45. Also, Wheeler-Voegelin & Jones 1974: 365–81.

89. Kappler 1904: 404–9; Quaife 1918: & Gerwing 1964: 134–37.

90. Kappler 1904: 414–15; NAM M234, R

132: 446–49. Edmunds (1974) contains the best substantive discussion of the Potawatomi move to the Platte area in Missouri.

91. The "band" reservations in Indiana are designated Royce areas 200–201, 204, 208–210, 218, & 223–225. Three of the tracts were never surveyed and are not identified by Royce numbers (1900: 752–67). For the treaties ceding these areas, see Kappler 1904: 428–31, 450, 457–63, 470–72, & 488–89.

CHAPTER 9:
PERSISTENCE AND CHANGE
IN THE TREATY AREA

1. For a good description of a comparable if more extreme example of cultural decline, see Anson's study of the Miami (1970: 186–88).

2. See Jablow's discussion of similar developments among the Illinois tribes early in the previous century (1974: 172–74).

3. The literature on the growth of American Indian policies is very extensive. The following discussion is based partly upon Prucha's excellent overview (1970), Sheehan's study of Jeffersonian policy (1973), Rogin's examination of President Jackson's ideas and adventures (1975), Tyler's official history (1974), Parson's brilliant analysis of President Adams's long experience and conflicts (1973), Berkhofer's general treatment of missionary involvement (1965), Abel's classic history of the removal era (1906), and Harmon's study of policy in the period 1789–1850 (1941). For a good look at British-Canadian policy, see Surtees (1966) and Horsman (1964). Schultz (1972) and Lyons (1945) examine the case of Isaac McCoy, Dutch (1949) that of John Tipton, both local agents who were highly influential with respect to the Pota-

watomi. Viola presents the contributions of Thomas L. McKenney in rich and insightful detail (1974).

4. For discussions of such issues, see Prucha 1970: 224–33; Schultz 1972: 96–97 & 133–38; Berkhofer 1965: 100–2; Dutch 1931: 204–8; & Sheehan 1973: 4–10 & 276–78.

5. Cited in Horsman 1975: 154.

6. See also Sheehan 1973: 261–75; Schultz 1972: 78–87; Berkhofer 1965: 98–101; & Lyons 1945.

7. See Lyons 1945; Schultz 1972: 96–103; & Berkhofer 1965: 100–2.

8. See Barnes 1936. Also Schultz 1974: 97–114.

9. Prucha 1970: 238–77; & Tyler 1974: 35–69. Also Lyons 1945: 39–41; & Schultz 1972: 135–41.

10. See Richard Smith Elliott's humorous account of how he acquired the position as subagent at Council Bluffs (1883: 153–61).

11. For good brief discussions of culturally fixed American beliefs about "blood" and "race," see Harris 1975: 332–33, & 1968.

12. For some of the extensive literature on Algonquian thinking about these matters, see Jenness 1935; Hilgar 1951;

McElroy 1968; Clifton 1962/64; and Landes 1971. Jenness's report on Parry Island mixes information from an immigrant Potawatomi group there (the Eagle Clan) and the resident Ojibwa, as he was mistakenly convinced the Potawatomi were simply one variety of Ojibwa. See Clifton and Isaac (1964) for a discussion of confusion in contemporary Kansas Potawatomi thinking about these matters.

13. The analytic framework for this presentation follows that of Wallace (1966).

14. These misconceptions continue to have great, stereotypic force. For a recent example of the overly idealized, noble, noneconomic savage, see Tax (1972). Both Keating (1824: 24) and Schoolcraft (1851/57 1: 320) record efforts of Algonquian informants to refashion their thoughts into a form compatible with Euro-American notions of a bipolar spirit-world presided over by a good, high spirit (God) and an evil high god (the Devil). Unfortunately, Wilcomb Washburn uncritically accepts such crude efforts at intercultural communication as Indian gospel and perpetuates them in the standard stereotyped form (1975: 56–57).

15. Wallace 1956, & 1966: 30–39, 157–66, & 209–15.

16. The theoretical framework used in the following paragraphs derives from Igor Kopytoff's formulations (1964), and from A. F. C. Wallace's alliance and identity approach to the depiction of conditions stimulating such major cultural changes (1966: 213–14).

17. The Jefferson quotation is taken from Drake 1958: 219–20. For a more detailed inventory of the prophet's perceptions of problems and solutions, see Forsyth 1812a; & James 1830: 144–47, 177–78, & 185–86.

18. Skinner 1924/27: 227–28; & Clifton 1962/64.

19. For more on the Kenakuk religion, see Howard (1965); Gibson 1963: 109–24; McCoy 1840: 456–58; Schultz 1972: 169–72; & Catlin 1850: Plates 185, 186, & 189.

20. There are numerous variant spellings of this name, the most common one being Menominee. For the fragmentary information available on the man and his thoughts, see McDonald 1899: 40–42; Robertson and Riker 1942 3: 312–13 & 682–85; McCoy, Journal entries for 10 Jan., 19 April, & 6 June 1821; Shea 1857: 392–96; McKee 1941: 13–21; & Schultz 1972: 50–52.

21. Robertson and Riker 1942 2: 103–5 & 234–36.

22. Billy Caldwell's maternal antecedents and his supposed status as a "Potawatomi chief" have been the subject of great confusion. Both older and modern American historians uncritically accept the myth of his status spread by John Kinzie and Thomas Forsyth and, following standard American folk beliefs about "blood," think of him as an "Indian." For example, see Conway (1975). For an alternative interpretation and Caldwell's own views of his identity, see Clifton (1976d). The primary documentation on Caldwell's birth and parentage is contained in interviews by Lyman Draper with his younger half-brothers, James and William Caldwell, DRC 175229–240.

23. Kinzie to Lewis Cass, Nov. 1819, TP-US 10: 877.

24. See Lewis Cass's classic statement of 1826 on this policy, quoted in ICC 1974 2: 182–85.

25. For examples of this ethnocentric assessment, see Berthrong 1974: 279; & Wheeler-Voegelin & Stout 1974: 209–11, & 399–402.

26. TP-US 16: 175–79.

27. See Forsyth to Edwards, 12 Sept. 1814, WHC 11: 330–36. Also Jablow 1974: 363.

CHAPTER 10:
MIGRATION AND RESETTLEMENT:
1835–1847

1. The classic of this biased genre is Foreman (1946). Examples of the same kind of exaggeration for the Potawatomi case are McDonald 1899 & McKee 1941. For a more temperate view, and a fine scholarly treatment of two of the many Potawatomi migrations in this period, see Edmunds 1972b & 1974.

2. Another probable cause of over-enumeration of migrants is the fact that the civilian contractors were paid a flat per capita fee. Considering the character and ethics of the men involved, this likely led to generous counts of the numbers of Potawatomi moved.

3. For the Potawatomi with Kenakuk, see Barry 1972: 234–35 & 280–81; IHC 26: 50–51; Schultz 1972: 170–76; & McDonald 1899: 47. McDonald misspells James Kennerly's name as Kennedy and gives the wrong count for the 1833 move, 179 rather than 119. Edmunds's careful study of the Kikito migration is definitive (1972b). See also Barry 1973: 241; Hendricks to Cass, 20 Apr. 1833, NAM 234, R. 361; McCoy 1836; & Dutch 1941: 180–82. Mishikaba was known as the second most important leader in the Kenakuk religion.

4. Bleasdale 1974: 147. Unless otherwise noted, all descriptions of the Canadian migrations are summarized from the author's own monographic study (1975b).

5. Wm. Marshall to E. Herring, 10 May 1834, NAM M21, R 12; McCoy 1835: 5 & 16, & 1836; McDonald 1899: 47. Also Barry 1972: 268; & Wm. Gordon's Muster Roll of Potawatomi near Leavenworth, 30 June 1835, Letters Re-ceived, Commisary General of Subsistence, RG 75, National Archives.

6. Anderson to J. Givens, 5 Aug. 1834 & 16 July 1835, typescript copy in RG 10, Vol. 2789. Also Clifton 1975b: 65–66. For Anderson's background, see WHC 9: 136–206.

7. Givens to Anderson, 28 July 1835; George Ironside's Potawatomi Return for Amherstburg, 31 July 1835; Givens to Anderson, 5 Sept. 1835; all in RG 10, Vol. 2789.

8. The classic historical works on Indian removal give but passing mention to the migration into Canada of large segments of several tribes, an omission which accentuates the basic thesis of such writings (Foreman 1946). Only the movement of the Odawa into Upper Canada has received any systematic attention, but the treatment is uncritical (Bauman 1949 & 1952).

9. For examples, see Caldwell's letter to the *Chicago Tribune* in support of the candidacy of William Henry Harrison, quoted in Wentworth 1881: 60; Wm. Woodridge to Henry Clay, 17 Dec. 1833, Burton Historical Collections, Detroit Public Library; Dougherty to Clark 31 May 1838, NAM 234, R 213; & Dougherty to Clark 29 Jan. 1839, NAM 234, R 215.

10. Edmunds provides a near comprehensive study of the Platte controversy (1974). Also Schultz 1972: 177–78; Robertson & Riker 1942 3: 130, 184–86, 265–68, & 419–22; Babbitt 1916: 24–25; & Conway 1972: 409–11.

11. For examples, see Edmunds 1974: 377–78; & Conway 1974.

12. Edmunds 1974: 377–78; Kappler 1904: 414–16; & Gerwing 1964: 138–42.

13. The title of major used by Indian agents in this era was honorary. The

journal of this exploration is incomplete, starting on July 30 when the party was already near Council Bluffs on their way home, and ending on their return to Chicago, 12 September 1835 (Gordon 1835). For the persons in the party, see Major Gordon's Roll, NAM 234, R 133. Also Rice to Tipton, 23 Apr. 1836, in Robertson & Riker 1942 3: 265–66; Edmunds 1974: 379–81; Barry 1972: 289; & Foreman 1946: 105–6.

14. J. B. Russell to Lewis Cass, 19 Jan. 1836, NAM 234, R 133; Herring to Wm. Clark, 8 April 1836, NAM 234, R 133; J. Tipton & W. Hendricks to Cass, 3 Mar. 1835; A. L. Davis to Tipton, 9 Dec. 1835; & L. Rice to Tipton, 23 Apr. 1836; all in Robertson & Riker 1942 3: 130, 184–86, & 265–68; Petition of United Nations Chiefs, 19 Jan. 1936, NAM 234, R 133; WHC 15: 274–75. Also Foreman 1946: 106; Barry 1972: 297; & Edmunds 1974: 380–81.

15. Muster Roll of Potawatomis, Chippewas, and Ottaways emigrating in September 1835; in MHS.

16. These totals do not include some 444 and more Indiana Potawatomi responsible to agent Davis at Leavenworth. See Davis to J. B. R. Russell, 25 June 1846, NAM 234, R 133; Dougherty to Clark, 26 July 1836, NAM 234, R 215; Barry 1972: 303 & 313; Temple 1958: 153; & G. Kercheval's Journal of Occurrances of Emigrating Indians, Sept. 1836, NAM 234, R 133.

17. Cass to Benton, Linn, & Harrison, 13 Feb. 1836, NAM 234, R 215; & Kercheval to Gibson, 15 Nov. 1836, NAM 234, R 133.

18. Kappler 1904: 488–89. The arrival of many Potawatomi and squatters in the area aggravated existing tensions. Edmunds has the best detailed study of these events (1974: 381–86).

19. E. Harris to E. James, 28 Apr. 1837, TP-US 27: 773–74; James to Harris, 2 June 1837, NAM 234, R 215. Until 1837 "Council Bluffs" designated an area on the west side of the Missouri River near the mouth of the Platte (Van der Zee 1913).

20. Harris to Clark, 3 Nov. 1836, NAM M21, R 20; Davis to Clark, 30 June 1837, NAM 234, R 134; J. Pointsett to Maj. Gen. Macomb, 19 June 1837, NAM M21, R 21; Macomb to Brig. Gen. H. Atkinson, 20 June 1837, NAM 234, R 360. Also Edmunds 1974: 387–88.

21. Col. S. W. Kearney to Brig. Gen. R. Jones, 26 Jan. 1837; Brig. Gen. Atkinson to Maj. Gen. Macomb, 6 Aug. 1837; E. James to Wm. Clark, 28 July 1837 & 27 June, 1837; Gaines to Harris, 26 July 1837; all in NAM 234, R 134. Atkinson to Macomb, 20 June 1837, TP-US 27: 802–3. Also Edmunds 1974: 388–89.

22. Billington 1960: 372–74; James to Wm. Clark, 27 June 1837, NAM 234, R 134; Edmunds 1974: 388–90.

23. Davis to Tipton, 9 Dec. 1835; L. Rice to Tipton, 23 Apr. 1836; McCoy to Tipton, 21 July 1837; all in Robertson & Riker 1942 3: 184–86, 265–68 & 419–21.

24. James to Clark, 11 Aug. & 18 Dec. 1837, NAM 234, R 134. Billington 1960: 372–78; & DAB 9: 576.

25. For the details of Sand's 1837 migration, see Minutes of Council with the Potawatomis, 3–4 Sept. 1837; Sands to Harris, 9 Sept. & 28 Oct. 1837, NAM 234, R 134. Also Barry 1972: 337–38; & Cummins 1933: 6–7. For the details of the McCoy, Davis, and Tipton conspiracy, see Robertson & Riker 1942 3: 362–63, 407, 412, 338–39, 451–52, 458–59, 475–76, 481–82, & 460–62. Also Barry 1972: 330–31.

26. Davis to Tipton, 28 May 1838, in Robertson & Riker 1942 3: 633:34.

27. Pepper to Harris, 20 Aug. 1837; & G. Profitt's Journal of the Emigration, 1837; both in NAM 234, R 361. McDonald 1899: 105; & Barry 1972: 330–31. Also Murphy 1962: 105. The Reverend Mr. Hoecken, at the time, reported 150 Potawatomi in this party, which is the more probable count of those arriving, although George Winter in Indiana noted only 53 departing. See also Clifton 1975b: 71–72.

28. James to Clark, 14 Nov. 1837, NAM 234, R 134. Van der Zee 1913: 22–24; J. M. Street (Indian Agent at Rock Island) to Gov. Dodge, TP-US 27: 755–56. Also A. L. Davis's report, in Wagner to G. Ewing, 18 May 1853, in Special File 69, RG 75.

29. See Berry's Roll of emigrating Ottaway, Chippaway, and Potawatamies, Sept. 1837, NAM 234, R 752.

30. The Tipton quote is from Robertson & Riker 1942 3: 671–72. For the standard versions of Menomini's ordeal, see McKee 1941; Shea 1857: 393–96; McDonald 1899: 42–45; & Foreman 1946: 109–18. Generally, historians have attributed the high death rate in this party to the rigors of the march, if not the cruelty of the escorts. However, the logic is faulty. Typhoid, a disease rapidly spread by infected food and water supplies, took a very high death toll among most populations in this period. The whole issue of mortality rates during the Indian removal period has been subject to moralistic, not adequate scientific, interpretation. It needs systematic study by someone with the proper demographic and epidemiological skills. See also Robertson & Riker 1942 2: 246; Dutch 1941: 192–94; Barry 1972: 358–59; Coulter 1948: 12–14; & McCoy 1840.

31. AR-COIA 1840: 320; Barry 1972: 417–18; Garland Report, 14 Sept. 1840, in Calendar of the American Fur Company Papers, Annual Report of the American Historical Association, 1944 2: Part 1, 927; Sprague to Pointsett, 8 June 1840; & Brady to Crawford, 13 June 1840; both in NAM 234, R 134; MPHC 21: 297–316.

32. Brady to Crawford, 24 Aug. 1840; Ketchum to Crawford, 25 Mar. 1840; both in NAM 234, 361. Buechner 1933; Murphy 1961: 111; & Barry 1972: 420–21.

33. McDonald 1899: 47–48.

34. Lea to COIA, 11 Aug. 1851; Ewing to C. E. Mix, 15 July 1851; Ewing to COIA, 14 Oct. 1851; Ewing's Account for Removal, 5 Aug. 1851; J. Haverty to L. Lea, 21 Aug. 1851; Thos. Mosely's report, 13 Sept. 1851; R. W. Thompson to COIA, 17 June 1851; Lea to D. D. Mitchell, 26 Jan. 1852; all in NAM 234, R 678. Also Barry 1972: 1039–40; & Coulter 1948: 37.

35. Barry 1972: 1081.

36. Only the more critical citations of primary sources will be given for the Canadian migrations, which are summarized from Clifton 1975b.

37. Givens to Anderson, 29 July 1835, RG 10, Vol. 2789; Schoolcraft report, July 1837, NAM 234, R 133; Jones to S.I.A., 7 July 1837, RG 10, Vol. 2789.

38. The three hundred reported by Schoolcraft may possibly have also been reported by Anderson or Jones, the British agents. If so, the total would be reduced to 1165. There is no way of establishing this duplication for certain, as accurate records and details of the origins of the migrants were not systematically recorded on either side of the border.

39. Schoolcraft report, 30 Sept. 1838, NAM 234, R 423. See also Clifton 1975b: 68–70. The single best source of information on Potawatomi migrations from Wisconsin to Canada is in the Potawatomi File of the Charles Brown Papers, State Historical Society of Wisconsin. However, these are difficult

to evaluate, particularly as regards dates and numbers of emigrants.

40. Keating report, 17 Sept. 1840, RG 10, Vol. 2789.

41. Dowell to Brady, 22 Apr. 1840, NAM 234, R 434; & Keating to Jarvis, 17 Sept. 1840, RG 10, Vol. 2789.

42. See the Keating, Higgonson, Jarvis, Jones, and Williams correspondence concerning Manitogabowit and Oka-manse and their travels, 1839–1841, in RG 10, Vol. 2789.

43. Wooster 1907a; & Secretary of the Interior 1908.

44. Kempt to Sir James Colborne, 23 Feb. 1829, RG 10, Vol. 5:22.

45. Manitogabowit's speech, June 1839, in RG 10, Vol. 2791.

46. For an excellent study of British Indian policies in this period, see Surtees 1966. The 1834 Anderson quote is from his report that year in RG 10, Vol. 2789. The 1835 quote is from Anderson to Colborne, 24 Sept. 1835, "Q" Series, Vol. 389, Public Archives of Canada.

47. Memorial to Lt. Gov. Bond Head, RG 10, Vol. 569: 283–85.

48. These generalizations are based on the analysis of names and clan totem marks on census lists, returns of presents to the Potawatomi, memorials, petitions, and similar documentary materials. For a fuller exposition, see Clifton 1975b.

49. Richardson 1924: 81; RAIC 1844; Also Clifton 1975b: 80–84.

50. RAIC 1844; & J. M. Higgonson to Wm. Jones, 1 June 1844, RG 10, Vol. 2789.

51. See Smith's correspondence with Colborne and Mudge concerning this dispute, RG 10, Vol. 5.

52. For some of the primary documentation on the Lower Michigan Potawatomi, see Complaint of Potawatomi Tribe, 19 Feb. 1859, R 406; Fitch to Greenwood, 30 Nov. 1859, R 406; Leach to Dole, 23 Jan. 1863, R. 407;

Micksawbe Tribe, 3 Feb. 1865, R 407; Payment List, 1865, R 407: 675; Harlan to Cooley, 20 Aug. 1866, R 407; Smith to Cooley, 1 Sept. 1866, R 407; Corkhill to COIA, 22 Mar. 1867, R 408; Micksawbe to COIA, 20 May 1869, R 408; Topash to Cox, 19 Aug. 1869, R 408; Micksawby to Sec. Int., 10 June 1875, R 411; Lee to COIA, 21 Mar. 1877, R 412; all in NAM 234. Claspy (1966 & 1970), although uncritical, offers the best available compilation of historical information on the Pokaguns. See also Turner 1911; Van Buren 1908; Winger 1939; Pokagon 1901 & n.d.; Reed 1929; & Quimby 1939.

53. Clark to COIA, 20 Aug. 1872, NAM 234, R 460. The figure of two hundred families, which would make some twelve hundred persons, seems high. But Charles Brown's informants several times speak of epidemic illnesses in the 1880s in Wisconsin, resulting in severe depopulation.

54. Ritzenthaler 1953, Tiedke 1951, & Morstad 1971 are the best summaries on the Wisconsin–Upper Michigan Potawatomi. See also Buchen 1944; Gerend 1920 & n.d.; Martin 1888; Plumb 1904; Bayrd 1948; & Wooster 1907a & 1907b.

55. Quimby 1939; Dickason 1961; Hodge 1910 2: 274–75; & Claspy 1966: 23–27.

56. Morstad 1971; Densmore 1949; Tiedke 1951; & McKeel 1937.

57. See McCoy's Journal, 17 Apr.–3 May 1837; McCormack 1892: 56–59; Connelley 1918: 491–95; Coulter 1948: 18–19; KHC 9: 211–12 & 226–27; AR-COIA 1839: 518, & 1840: 122; Also Barry 1972: 321, 336–37, 342, 348, 355, & 364–65.

58. See Trade Licenses issued in 1841, & D. D. Mitchell's report on licenses issued in 1843, both in NAM 234, R 753; P. Chouteau report of 1839, in Calendar of The American Fur Com-

pany Papers, Annual Report of the American Historical Association, 1944 2: 699. Also see Barry 1972: 341, 431–33, & 490–91.

59. AR-COIA 1838: 320 & 506, & 1840: 320; Davis to Clark, 15 May 1842, in Clark Papers 8: 106; Garraghan 1938 2: 229; & Davis 1839. Also Barry 1972: 449–50 & 453.

60. Ewing & Ewing to R. B. Mitchell, 25 Sept. 1847, NAM 234, R 217; & Patton 1954: 169. Also Barry 1972: 363–64 & 467; Claspy 1966: 14; Murphy 1962: 193.

61. See Jotham Meeker's firsthand account, cited in Barry 1972: 720.

62. Kinzie 1856: 154; Caton 1976: 10–11; J. Tipton to J. R. Pointsett, 8 Feb. 1838, in Robertson & Riker 1942 3: 531–32. Also Michelson 1934: 230–31; & Baerreis, Wheeler-Voegelin, and Moore 1974: 161.

63. James to Clark, 18 Dec. 1837, NAM 234, R 134.

64. Capt. Burgin to COIA Hartley, with Memorial from the Potawatomi Chiefs, 9 Aug. 1843, NAM 234, R 214; D. Miller to D. D. Mitchell, with Report of Potawatomi Council, 24 June 1842, NAM 234, R 215.

65. E. James, Register of Potawatomi, 10 Aug. 1837, 215; James, Roll of Potawatomi, Ottawa, and Chippawas . . . , 15 Dec. 1837, R 134; James to Clark, 14 Dec. 1837, R 134; Census of Chippewas, Ottawas, & Potawatomis at Council Bluffs, 6 Feb. 1844, R 216; D. D. Mitchell, Census & Statistics of Potawatomi at Council Bluffs, Dec. 1846, R 216; all in NAM 234.

66. Cunningham 1961: 39–43; Fulton 1882: 170; Babbitt 1916: 10, & 30–31. Also Stegner 1964: 55, 68; Andreas 1875: 404–5.

67. James to Clark, 26 Dec. 1837, R 215; Capt. John Gantt's Report on Treaty Negotiations to J. Pilcher, Aug.–Sept. 1839, R 215; Dougherty to Clark, 31

May 1838, R 133; Dougherty to G. McGurie, SIA St. Louis, 29 Jan. 1839, R 215; all in NAM 234.

68. J. L. Bourassa statement, DRC 12U 103; J. Gantt's Report to Pilcher, 1839, NAM 234, R 215.

69. T. H. Harvey's Minutes of Council at Council Bluffs, 23 June 1845, NAM 234, R 216.

70. Pah-to-gou-shuk to the Great White Father, 27 July 1842, in NAM 234, R 215.

71. For some specifics on the "half-breed" problem, see: Chittenden & Richardson 1905: 177; Personnel Return, 30 Sept. 1837; E. James to Clark, 28 Sept. 1837; James to Clark, 20 Feb. 1838; Memorial from Potawatomi Chiefs, 17 Mar. 1838; S. Cooper to J. Pilcher, 14 May 1840; D. D. Mitchell to H. Crawford, 10 Dec. 1841; all in NAM 234, R 215. R. S. Elliott in 1845 offered a unique solution to the "half-breed" problem—to use them as breeding stock so as to improve Potawatomi chances to acquire the virtues of civilization—see AR-COIA 1845: 552–53. Also D. Miller to D. D. Mitchell, 1 July 1842; Cooper to Pilcher, 14 May 1840; both in Clark Papers 8.

72. Half Day's words are in D. Miller to D. D. Mitchell, 24 June 1842, NAM 234, R 215.

73. Such a judgment is of course qualitative and relative—in this case as compared to the more demoralized Potawatomi on the Osage, where Missouri whiskey flowed readily and cheaply. Every observer in this period made large judgments concerning Potawatomi drinking; no one collected the statistics that would allow a firm comparative conclusion. For some details, see Chittenden & Richardson 1905: 157–59 & 173. The agents' reports regularly express some sense of a considerable drinking problem, but the commissioner of Indian Affairs would

likely have suspected any agent of deception who did not so report. See NAM 234, Rolls 214 and 215 for examples. Also, Van der Zee 1913: 36.

74. James to W. Clark, 18 Dec. 1837, NAM 234, R 134; Hamilton 1839; Memorial of Prairie Potawatomis, 1 July 1839, NAM 234, R 215; J. Miller to W. L. Marcy, 20 Jan. 1848, NAM 234, R 217. Also Trennert 1975: 133–39.

75. J. Bruce to D. D. Mitchell, 1842, NAM 234, R 215; R. Elliott to Harvey, 18 Mar. 1844, NAM 234, R 216; E. James to W. Clark, 18 Dec. 1837, NAM 234, R 134; & AR-COIA 1841: 257 & 281.

76. Van der Zee 1913: 36; R. S. Elliott to C. O., Ft. Leavenworth, 6 Feb. 1845; & Elliott to Crawford, 18 Mar. 1844; both in NAM 234, R 216.

77. For some of the details of Potawatomi-Dakota raiding, see James to Clark, 26 Feb. & 19 Mar. 1838, R 215; D. D. Mitchell to H. Crawford, 5 Apr. 1842, R 215; Deadrick to Crawford, 5 Apr. 1842, R 215; Elliott to Harvey, 6 Feb. 1842, R 215; Miller to Harvey, 15 Dec. 1846, 12 Sept. 1847, & 15 Sept. 1847, R 217; all in NAM 234. Cooper 1840; Trennert 1975: 133–39; Chittenden & Richardson 1905: 256–57; Flanagan 1970: 179; J. M. Street to Gov. Dodge, 1837, TP-US 27: 706; Van der Zee 1913: 33–34; Cummins to Mitchell, 17 June 1842; & Deadrick to Mitchell, 9 Aug. 1842, both in Clark Papers 8; AR-COIA 1840: 321, 1841: 257 & 281 & 1843: 395. Also Mitchell to Harvey, 28 June 1846, NAM 234, R 216.

78. For information on the dragoons at Council Bluffs, see Deadrick to Mitchell, 23 Feb. 1842; Adj. Gen. R. Jones to Brig. Gen. Atkinson, 19 Apr. 1842, both in NAM 234, R 215; E. Poor, Jr., to Secy. of War, Jan. 1844; R. Elliott to C. O., Ft. Leavenworth,

6 Feb. 1845; Elliott to COIA, 27 Jan. 1845; all in NAM 234, R 216. Also Prucha 1969: 375–83; Barry 1972: 417, & 450–51; Flanagan 1970: 179; Van der Zee 1913: 36; Utley 1967: 22–23 & 25–26; Weightley 1967: 159–60 & 163; & Murphy 1961: 50–52.

79. See report of Ta-Leh-Quah meeting and compact, July 1843, NAM 234, R 215. Also Barry 1972: 485; & Foreman 1946: 206.

80. For some of the details on these prolonged negotiations, see James to Clark, 5 Nov. 1837; Clark to Harris, 29 Nov. 1837; Clark to James, 30 Nov. 1837; James to Clark, 26 Dec. 1837; Disbursing Office to COIA, 20 Mar. 1838; James to COIA Harris, 28 Jan. 1838; Pilcher to COIA, 6 July 1838; Capt. John Gantt, Report Concerning the Potawatomi Mission, Aug.– Sept. 1839; McCoy to COIA, 28 July 1840; McCoy to Gen. Brady, 30 Jan. & 1 Feb. 1841; Coquillard to J. Bell, Secy. of War, 30 Apr. 1841; Deadrick to A. McLea, Actg. Secy. of War, 5 Oct. 1841; McCoy to Crawford 30 Jan. & 2 Apr. 1841; Deadrick to Mitchell, 9 Aug. 1842; W. Ewing to Crawford, 21 Apr. & 19 Nov. 1842; Mitchell to Crawford, 24 Feb. 1842; Deadrick to Crawford, 5 Apr. 1842; all in NAM 234, R 234. Also A. L. Davis to Tipton, 11 Oct. 1838; & McCoy to Tipton, 21 Dec. 1838, in Robertson & Riker 1942 3: 746–47 & 783; & Barry 1972: 440–41.

81. Elliott 1883: 158–73; Elliott to Hartley Crawford, COIA, 1 June 1843, NAM 234, R 215. Also Van der Zee 1913: 39.

82. Elliott to Crawford, 9 Aug. 1843; Petition of Potawatomi Chiefs to President, 9 Aug. 1843; both in NAM 234, R 215; Elliott 1883: 173–76.

83. Elliott, always adept at covering his tracks, used a *nom de plume,* "John Brown," for his articles in Reveille.

See Pelzer 1943; Joost 1970: 219–21; Elliott 1883: 184–87; Hon. S. C. Sample to H. Crawford, 1 July 1844; & Resolution of White Claimants, 10 May 1845, both in NAM 234, R 216.

84. Elliott 1883: 191–99; Harvey to Crawford, 6 May 1845, NAM 234, R 216.

85. Commissioner Harvey's detailed journal of the treaty, and a copy of Wabansi's "paper," are in Minutes of Council, 23–30 June 1845, NAM 234, R 216. Very uncharacteristically, Elliott in his memoirs passes over these proceedings with only the briefest comment. Harvey came, he noted, but "nothing came of the discussion" (1883: 198). Elliott was present and very active—in support of the Potawatomi. He likely wrote, or assisted with the writing of, Wabansi's list of demands.

86. See the copy of Wabansi's "paper" in Harvey's journal, NAM 234, R 216.

87. Elliott 1883: 198; Elliott to Harvey, 18 Sept. 1845; & Harvey to Crawford, 18 Sept. 1845; both in NAM 234, R 216.

88. Elliott 1883: 199–200; Elliott to Wm. Medill, COIA, 27 Oct. 1845.

89. Elliott 1883: 199–203; Clerk, SIA Office St. Louis, to H. Crawford, 2 Oct. 1845, NAM 234, R 216. Medill replaced Crawford as COIA in November 1845.

90. Elliott 1883: 204–7.

91. Combined Journal of Proceedings, 3 Nov.–2 Dec. 1845; Elliott to Crawford, 25 Oct. 1845; Elliott to Medill, 18 Nov. 1845; Potawatomi Power of Attorney to R. S. Elliott, 19 Nov. 1845; Elliott to Secy. of War, 21 Nov. 1845; all in NAM 234, R 216. Also Eliott 1883: 208–11.

92. Elliott 1883: 208–9.

93. Elliott 1883: 209–12; Gibson & Andrews to Medill, 3 Dec. 1845; Elliott to Medill, 13 Jan. 1846; both in NAM 234, R 216.

94. Elliott to Medill, 2 Mar. 1846, NAM 234, R 216. Elliott 1883: 213–20.

95. G. L. Barton to Secy. of War Marcy, 3 Mar. 1846; G. W. Ewing to Marcy, 6 Mar. 1846; both in NAM 234, R. 216. Also Trennert 1975: 36–37; & AR-COIA 1848: 465.

96. Matlock to Medill, 2 May 1846; Combined Journal of Proceedings, 7 May–17 June 1846; both in NAM 234, R 216. Kappler 1904: 557–60. The areas ceded are known as Royce 265 (Iowa) and 266 (Kansas). See Royce 1900: 778–79; & Barry 1972: 592.

97. See Subagent R. B. Mitchell's report, Oct. 1847, NAM 234, R 217. Also Van der Zee 1913: 41–42.

98. For the Mormon occupation of Potawatomi lands, see J. C. Kane to President, 29 Aug. 1846; Mitchell to Harvey, 29 June 1846; Harvey to Medill, 14 Aug., 6 Nov., & Dec. 1846; J. Miller to Harvey, 17 May & 4 Aug. 1847; & Brigham Young to J. Miller, 4 Apr. 1847, in NAM 234, R 217. Also Trennert 1975: 140; Barry 1972: 596–97; Andreas 1875: 404; & Stegner 1964: 74–75, 92, 195, & 223.

99. Harvey to Medill, 9 Aug. & 5 Oct. 1847; Adj. Gen. Jones to Lt. Col. Wharton, 27 Aug. 1847; P. Sarpy to R. B. Mitchell, 25 Sept. 1847; all in NAM 234, R 217. Also McCormack 1892: 68–69; Connelley 1918: 492; Trennert 1975: 27; & Babbitt 1916.

100. Harvey to Medill, 5 Oct., 11 Oct., & 17 Dec. 1847; Medill to Mitchell, 8 Dec. 1847; all in NAM 234, R 217. Also Barry 1872: 725–26; & Richerter 1933.

101. Kelly 1851: 59–60; Vaughan to COIA, 7 Mar. 1848; & Cummins to COIA, 12 Mar. 1848; both in NAM 234, R 302.

CHAPTER 11:
THE RESERVATION EXPERIENCE

1. For an excellent history of the development of the reservation policy between 1846 and 1851, see Trennert (1975). Danziger (1974) traces the development of this policy during the Civil War years, while Mardock (1971) and Fritz (1963) document and interpret the course of Indian policies in the period 1860–1890.

2. Lovejoy 1858: 378–79. Also the Rev. Maurice Gailland's 1854 comments, in Jacobs 1954: 238–47; and Martin 1904: 86–87.

3. Billington 1960: 470–74; Fritz 1963: 18; & Trennert 1975: 40–48. For the Fox migration to Iowa, see Gearing 1955; and for the Prairie Potawatomi move there post–1848, A. M. Cassidy to COIA, 23 Oct. 1859, in R 682, NAM 234.

4. Billington 1960: 595–98; & Clifton 1976c: 44–45.

5. The Potawatomi National Reservation is designated Royce area 434, and the diminished Prairie Band Reservation, area 433. See Royce 1900: 824–25. Also Kappler 1904: 824–28, 916, & 970–74. The best discussion of public land policy in Kansas in this area is Gates 1954: 1–134.

6. Agent G. W. James Annual Report, 1897, in FRC-KC. The author researched the archives of the various Potawatomi agencies at the Kansas City Federal Records Center (FRC-KC) in 1963–1964, before they had been systematically sorted and cataloged. Thus references in this book for materials at that location will not correspond to the more recent, indexed inventory listings, for which see Svanda (1965). Population figures for the Potawatomi are reported in AR-COIA 1848–1905. These are conveniently summarized in Connelley (1918). More detailed reports are found in the special, monthly, quarterly, and annual reports of the agents themselves, which are recorded in NAM 234, Rolls 216–17 & 678–95, and in FRC-KC. The latter archive contains supplementary material for the period before 1880, and the most conveniently accessible, detailed records for subsequent years. See also Barry 1972: 1060–61, 1066, & 1196. Together, these records indicate that significant epidemics of smallpox or cholera erupted in 1852, 1858, & 1859, taking an estimated 170 Potawatomi lives (not all of them Prairie Band).

7. For the best discussion of the Dawes Act and its effects, see Haas 1957, & Fritz 1963: 192–221.

8. AR-COIA 1855–1858; Clarke to COIA, 20 Oct. 1855 & 19 June 1856, R 680; Agent Wm. Murphy to COIA, 21 Apr. 1857, & to SIA, St. Louis, 21 Dec. 1857, R 681; all in NAM 234. Also Connelley 1918: 502–5.

9. For a sampling of reports concerning their resistance, see Clarke's Report on Annuities, 20 Oct. 1855, R 680; Clarke to COIA, 19 June 1856, R 680; Murphy to SIA, St. Louis, 21 Dec. 1857, R 681; COIA Denver to SIA, St. Louis, 13 Dec. 1857, R 681; Ross to COIA, 21 May 1864, R 684; Prairie Band to COIA, Mar. 1869, R 689; Agent & Prairie Potawatomi Agreement on Use of Land, 5 May 1871, R 690; J. H. Morris to COIA, 31 Jan. 1872, R 691; Chiefs & Business Committee to COIA, 29 Jan. 1872, R 691; Agent Newlin to COIA, 6 Aug. 1873, R 691; all in NAM 234.

10. Roll of Potawatomi Holding Land in Common, 18 Apr. 1865, R 685; E. Wolcott to COIA, 4 Feb. 1865, R 685; Agent's Report, 20 Jan. 1870, R 690; all in NAM 234. Also Connelley 1918: 520.

11. The figure of two hundred Midewiwin members seems excessive considering the size of the population at the time. Morgan's informants may have misled him, and he did no checking of what he was told. See Morgan 1858: 57–58; & Armstrong 1887: 597–614.

12. Armstrong 1887: 613.

13. Richard Hewitt's Report, in COIA 1848; KHC 6: 104; Grinnell 1956: 94. Also Barry 1972: 781.

14. AR-COIA 1848–1852: KHC 11: 342; & 17: 457–58; Burke 1951: 507; Hyde 1974: 233–34. Also Barry 1972: 763, 928–29, 944, & 1112; & Connelley 1918: 494.

15. AR-COIA 1853–1855; Grinnell 1956: 88–94; Hyde 1974: 234–36; Matthews 1961: 611–12; Clarke to COIA, 15 Dec. 1854, R 680; Ross to SIA, St. Joseph, 6 Aug. 1862, R 683; all in NAM 234. Also Barry 1972: 1172–73; & Connelley 1918: 499–502.

16. Skinner 1924/27: 392–93; and Clifton 1962/65.

17. See Darling's contract, 10 July 1850, R 303, NAM 234; Also Barry 1972: 952.

18. For some examples of Métis enterprises, see Murphy to SIA, 21 Dec. 1857, R 681; Navarre to COIA, 10 Mar., 12 Mar., & 4 May 1874, R 691; Murphy to SIA, 5 Mar. 1859, R 682; Navarre to COIA, 5 June 1866, R 686; Murphy to SIA, 22 May 1858, R 681; Ross to SIA, 17 Apr. 1862, R 683; Palmer to COIA, 12 Aug. 1865, R 685; Ross to COIA, 5 Mar. 1863, R 684; Memorial to COIA, 1865, R 685; Palmer to COIA, 31 Oct. 1866, R 686; Bourassa to COIA, 1 Jan. 1867, R 687; Agent Murphy, transmitting charges by Prairie Band against Business Committee, 18 July 1867, R 687; Potawatomi Delegation's Expenses, Jan.–Feb. 1867, R 687; Potawatomi Delegation to COIA, 12 Mar. 1868, R 688; Agent Palmer's expense request, 3 Mar. 1869, R 689; Chief Clerk Beede to Actg. COIA, 27 Feb. 1873, R 691;

Agent Newlin's report on Nadeau family, 17 Apr. 1878, R 693; A. Bushman to COIA, 11 Mar. 1870, R 690; all in NAM 234.

19. Bourassa letters to Enoch Hoag, Summer 1873, R 691; Agent Newlin to Hoag, Mar. 1875, R 692; in NAM 234; & Bourassa to Draper, 18 Sept. 1866, DRC 12U103.

20. Ross to COIA, 17 Apr. 1862, R 684; J. W. Bourassa to COIA, 30 Nov. 1857; to SIA, 24 Nov. 1857; to SIA, 24 Nov. 1857; to SIA, 10 Apr. 1858, all in R 681; Bertrand to COIA, 29 July 1858, R 682; Murphy to COIA, 29 Apr. 1862, R 681; Potawatomi Chiefs to COIA, Apr. 1862, R 683; Ross, transmitting resolution of Business Committee, 8 Dec. 1862, R 684; A. Bushman to COIA, 23 Oct. 1868, R 688; Business Committee Memorial to COIA, 1865, R 685; Morris to COIA, 12 Mar. 1869, R 689; Potawatomi Delegates to Agent Newlin, 22 July 1875, R 692; all in NAM 234.

21. L. F. Thomas to President Jas. Buchanan, 28 June 1860, R 682; Murphy to COIA, 7 July 1860, R 682; in NAM 234.

22. Ross to COIA, 10 Mar. 1862, R 683; Potawatomi Board of Commissioners to Agent Ross, 26 Mar. 1862, R 683; COIA Dole to Potawatomi Chiefs, et al., 8 May 1862, R 683; Potawatomi Petition to COIA, 11 Dec. 1862, R 683; Ross to COIA, 19 Jan. 1863, R 674; Murphy to COIA, 18 July 1867, R 687; Palmer Report, Oct. 1867, R 687; J. N. Bourassa to COIA, 1 Jan. 1867, R 687; all in NAM 234.

23. For a summary of Navarre's activities in the early Kansas years, see Agent Murphy to SIA, 21 Dec. 1857, R 681, and to COIA 22 Aug. 1859; all in R 682, NAM 234. Also, Utley 1967: 128, 201.

24. For sample of Navarre's handiwork, see Murphy to COIA, 21 Apr. 1857, R 681; Potawatomi Delegation to President

Buchanan, 13 Feb. 1858, R 681; Murphy to COIA, 5 Mar. 1859, R 682; Murphy to COIA, 17 Dec. 1859, R 682; Navarre to COIA, 8 Mar. 1859, R 682; Ross to COIA, 21 May 1864, R 684; all in NAM 234.

25. For a sampler of Navarre's later activities, and of his associations with Eli G. Nadeau, see, Business Committee to COIA, 12 Mar. 1866, R 685; Palmer to COIA, 29 Mar. 1866, R 686; Navarre to COIA, 5 June 1866, R 686; Report on Toll Bridges, 27 Mar. 1866, R 686; Tolls paid to Peltier & Vieux (Navarre's employees) 1867, R 687; Secy. Int. to COIA, 19 Jan. 1871, R 690; Navarre to Actg. COIA, 27 Mar. 1871, R 690; Agreement between Prairie Potawatomi & Agent Morris, 5 May 1871, R 690; Morris to COIA, 14 May & 18 Oct. 1872, R 691; Navarre to COIA, 14 May & 18 Oct. 1872, & 10 Mar., 4 May, 17 June & 22 June 1874, all in R 691; Report on U.S. Dist. Attorney's action against Nadeau, 1878, R 693; the 1878 inventory of property is in Newlin to COIA, 21 Feb., R 693; all in NAM 234.

26. For a good description of James's situation in 1880, see Armstrong 1887: 599. For more detailed information, see Linn to COIA, 21 Mar. 1881, FRC-KC; Scott to COIA, 5 Nov. 1891, 28 Feb. & 1 Sept. 1893, Box 517, 585, FRC-KC; Pearson to Supt. of Indian Schools, 14 Feb. 1895, and to COIA, 18 Feb. 1895, Box 517, 585, FRC-KC; Agent G. W. James's Annual Report, 23 Aug. 1897, in Box 479, 499, FRC-KC.

27. For partial discussions of the Indian Ring on a national level, see Fritz 1963: 27–29 & 144; Danziger 1974: 7, 163, & 213; and Mardock 1971: 87–88, 106, 119, & 129–32. The best available case study is in Gates 1954; but no full-scale, critical, scholarly study of this important institution has been done.

28. Marquis 1963: 307; Moseley to COIA Lea, 18 June 1851, R 678, NAM 234. Also Barry 1972: 891, 906, & 1012.

29. A. Cumings to COIA Lea, 29 July & 15 Nov. 1853, R 678; COIA to A. Cumings (SIA, St. Louis), 24 Oct. 1853, R 678; G. W. Ewing, Sr., to D. D. Mitchell, 1851, R 678, Frames 93–94; & Auditor Clayton to F. W. Lea, 2 Aug. 1852, R 678; all in NAM 234.

30. Moseley to COIA Lea, 18 June 1851; J. B. Harvey to COIA, 28 Aug. 1851; A. B. Earle to COIA, 10 June 1852; all in R 678, NAM 234.

31. John M. Lea to COIA Lea (Telegram), 27 July 1851, R 678; D. D. Mitchell to COIA Lea (Telegram), 10 Nov. 1851, R 678; F. W. Lea to Auditor Clayton, 15 May 1852, R 678; W. M. Churchwell to COIA Manypenny, 10 Nov. 1853, R 679; all in NAM 234. The appointments made by Agent F. W. Lea and the contracts he drew in his brief tenure are in Rolls 678–79, NAM 234.

32. Barron to Manypenny, 6 July 1855, R 680; Clarke to COIA, 26 Aug. 1854, R 679; Clarke to Manypenny, 8 May 1855, R 680; Potawatomi Chiefs to Clarke, 6 June 1855, R 680; all in NAM 234. Also, Svanda 1965: Appendix E; AR-COIA 1853–1857; & Connelley 1918: 499–508.

33. Murphy to SIA, 24 Nov. 1857 & 10 Apr. 1858, R 681; A. Bertrand to SIA, 29 July 1859, R 682; Murphy to COIA Denver, 29 Nov. 1859, R 681; Ross to COIA, 11 May 1861, R 683; Ross to SIA, 19 July 1861, R 682; Potawatomi Chiefs to COIA Dole, May 1862, R 683; all in NAM 234. Also Gates 1954: 48–113; & Connelley 1918: 507–14.

34. Ross to COIA, 8 Dec. 1962 (transmitting the resolution of the Business Committee concerning the lands awarded him four months earlier), R 684; Senator Lane to COIA, 14 Apr. & 16 Sept. 1874, R 684; A. Bushman to COIA, 23 Oct. 1868, R 688; Hoag to Newlin, 17 Feb. 1872, R 691; all in

NAM 234. Also AR-COIA 1861–1870; & Connelley 1918: 515–21.

35. Newlin to Hoag, 14 Mar. 1873, R 691; Linn to Senator Ingalls, 22 June 1875, R 692; Newlin to COIA, 5 July 1875, R 692, and July 1878, R 693; J. Hammond to COIA, 27 Feb. 1878, R 693; President R. B. Hayes to Newlin, 2 Aug. 1878, R 693; Rhoads & Tatum to President Hayes, 12 Aug. 1878, R 693; all in NAM 234.

36. Linn to SIA, 19 Aug. 1878, R 693. See also the extensive correspondence and reports on the charges brought against Linn during Sept. 1878, in R 693. Linn to SIA, 15 & 16 May 1878, R 693; July 1880 Report of Potawatomi School, R 695; all in NAM 234. Also, AR-COIA 1880–1892; & Connelley 1918: 525–43.

37. George W. James Annual Report, 23 Aug. 1897, FRC–KC.

38. Ewing to Andrew Jackson, 30 Mar. 1850, & 13 Mar. 1855, in R 680; Clarke to COIA, June 1850, R 680; all NAM 234.

39. For a good discussion of the "national debt" issue, see Trennert 1975: 20–23.

40. Chiefs of Potawatomi Nation to COIA, 3 Nov. 1851 (Agent Lea's comments are appended to this memorial), R 678; Ewing & Walker to COIA Lea, 20 Dec. 1852, R 678; Agent Lea to D. D. Mitchell, 28 Apr. 1852, R 678; A. C. Pepper to Rep. J. D. Bright, 27 Nov. 1853, R 679; Deposition of A. Burnett, 20 May 1853, R 679; all NAM 234.

41. Lea to Manypenny, 10 Sept. 1853, R 679; Ewing to Manypenny, 21 Sept. 1853, R 679; F. Lea to Luke Lea, 5 Mar. 1853, R 679; A. Navarre to COIA, 26 Nov. 1853, R 679; Agent Whitefield to COIA, 22 Dec. 1853, R 679, and to SIA, 4 Nov. 1853, R 679; Potawatomi Chiefs to COIA, 22 May 1854, R 679; Ewing to Secy. Int. McClelland, 1854, R 679; Soliciter of Treasury to COIA, 30 Mar. 1855, R 680; Wawasuk to COIA, 18 Jan. 1855, R 680; Jude Bou-

rassa to COIA, 21 Jan. 1856, R. 680; all NAM 234.

42. Resolution of Business Committee, with Agent Ross's endorsement, 17 Apr. 1862; & Business Committee to Ross, 18 Apr. 1862, R 683, NAM 234.

43. COIA to Ross, 21 Apr. 1862; & Ross to COIA, 18 July 1862 & 20 Oct. 1863, R 683, NAM 234.

44. For some examples of the correspondence concerning the order system, see Ross to COIA, 22 Nov. 1862, R 683, & 2 Jan. 1863, R 684; Secy. Int. Usher to COIA, 17 Jan. 1863, R 684; Agent Palmer to COIA, 1866, R 686; & Thos. Ryan to COIA, 5 Nov. 1879, R 694; all NAM 234.

45. Garraghan 1938 2: 510–11, & 635–54; Burke 1951; Carman 1954; 82–85; Wand 1962; Location of Baptist Mission, 1862, in R 684, F. 56, NAM 234; Agent Murphy's Report, 30 June 1858, R 681; & 31 Aug. 1859, R 682; all NAM 234. Also Connelley 1918: 494–96, & 504–14; Barry 1972: 801–3, 889–90, 892, 1103, & 1126; & AR-COIA 1850–1861.

46. For information on Johnny Green's people and other Potawatomi in Iowa, post-1848, see, Report on Iowa Potawatomi, 24 June 1857, R 681; Cassiday to COIA, 23 Oct. 1858, R 682; SIA Branch to COIA Dole, 15 Dec. 1862, R 683; H. C. Henderson to Secy. Int., 1865, R 685; Report of J. Green's visit to President Johnson, 22 June 1868, R 688; & Petition of Citizen's of Marshall County to Congressman Rush Clark, 1879, R 694; all NAM 234.

47. For information on the Potawatomi in Mexico see Pope 1959: 18–19; Armstrong 1887: 606; Secy. of War Grant to Secy. Int., Aug. 1867, R 687; Agent Newlin's Report, 30 Mar. 1874, R 691; Potawatomi Delegation to COIA, 3 Mar. 1879, R 693; & Memorial of Potawatomi to the House and Senate, 27 Apr. 1880, R 695; all NAM 234. Also AR-COIA 1865.

48. For information on Shagwe's people and his migration, see Clarke to SIA, 18 Nov. 1855, R 680; Ross to COIA, 19 Aug. 1864, R 684; in NAM 234; & Matthews 1961: 722. Also AR-COIA 1856 & 1864.

49. See Potawatomi & Kickapoo Compact, 9 June 1862, R 683, NAM 234.

50. See Report on Wilmot (or Wilmette) family of Wisconsin, March 1866, R 686; Palmer to COIA, 11 Dec. 1865 & 17 Jan. 1866, R 686. The supplementary allotment list for the Treaty of 1861 is in R 686, NAM 234. See particularly Allotments numbered 1616–1625 (Iowa Potawatomi), 1626–1629 (Indiana), 1449–1543 (Bourassa family of Illinois), & 1435–1442 (Navarres of Indiana).

51. Special Indian Agent (Plover, Wisc.) to COIA, 30 Sept. 1865, in R 685, NAM 234; Keesing 1939: 165–66; & Skinner 1925: 34.

52. Johnston to Secy. Int., 19 May 1871, R 690; Congressman A. McDill to COIA, 30 Dec. 1873, R 691; Agent Chase to COIA, 20 June 1873, R 691; Citizens of Angelic, Wisc., to COIA, 10 July 1878, A 693; Agent Newlin's monthly report, Mar. 1873, R 691; all NAM 234. Also AR-COIA 1870, & 1872–1874.

53. Keesing 1939: 179–82. The quote is from E. Stephens (Agent at Keshina, Wisc.) to COIA, 23 Aug. 1881 (Stephens 1881). See also Capt. D. W. Benham, 7th Infantry, to Asst. Adj. Gen., Fort Snelling, 20 Oct. 1881, in RG 75. Stephens & Benham's correspondence concerns the "Menomini scare" of 1881, the dates and details of which Keesing, Michelson, and Skinner were unable to pinpoint in their controversy over the origins of the Dream Dance. They could not locate these materials because they had been misfiled in the Bureau of Indian Affairs under the index code "Sioux Dance" for 1881. For further information on the Dream Dance religion (also known as the So-

ciety of Dreamers, the Religion Dance, the Drum Dance, and the Menomini "Pow Wow"), see Barrett 1911; Densmore 1913, 1918, & 1932; MacCauley 1893; Michelson 1923, 1924, & 1926; Skinner 1913, 1915, & 1932; Slotkin 1957; & Sturtevant 1934. For the Dream Dance among the Potawatomi see Clifton 1969; Skinner 1924/27: 222–27; & Landes 1970.

54. The Linn and Patrick quotes are from their annual reports, in AR-COIA 1884 & 1885. See also Clifton 1969; & Connelley 1918: 520, & 529–30.

55. Agent F. W. Lea's report, in AR-COIA 1852. See the Boone & Bernard accounts for 1854, R 679; Clarke to SIA Cumings, Oct. 1854, R 679; & Clarke to COIA, 13 Nov. 1854, R 679, 19 June 1854, R 680.

56. Agent Clarke to COIA, June 1855, R 680; 29 July & 29 Nov. 1856, R 680; Agent Murphy to SIA, 9 Feb. 1859, R 682; Murphy to COIA, 30 Apr. 1860, R 682; Disbr. Clerk, Dept. of Int. to COIA, 9 Jan. 1867, R 687; all NAM 234. Also AR-COIA 1860.

57. Asst. Adj. Gen. McKeever to Lt. Col. English, 21 Oct. 1868, R 698; Agent Murphy to SIA, 10 Nov. 1868, R 688; Lt. Col. English's report on annuity payment, 7 Dec. 1868, R 688; all NAM 234. See also a newspaper report of the 1870 payment, from Kansas State Record, in Kansas Historical Quarterly 10: 207–10.

58. Agent Newlin to COIA, 12 June 1874, R 691; 25 Jan. 1875, 3 July 1875, 29 Mar. 1875, & 28 June 1875, R 692; all NAM 234. Also AR-COIA 1872.

59. Such are their memories of the razorback hog that in the 1960s the Kansas Potawatomi classified it as a native American game animal and could not believe it was an European import reverted to the wild. See Newlin to SIA, 3 Apr. 1876, R 692; 21 Feb. 1878, R 693; in NAM 234; Agent Linn to

COIA, 4 Feb. 1880 & 31 Aug. 1881, FRC-KC. Also AR-COIA 1876–1883. The annual Agent's Report generally glamorized actual economic conditions and exaggerated the amount of progress.

60. Shagwe's speech is quoted at length in Donohue 1911: 149–53.

61. Kappler 1904: 824–25. For the best available study of the cabal that manufactured this treaty, see Gates 1954.

62. Fritz 1963: 84–85 & 211–15.

63. Agent Morris to COIA, Jan. 1872, R 691; Potawatomi Chiefs to Linn, 23 Jan. 1880, R 695 in NAM 234. Linn to COIA, 22 Jan. 1881 & 12 Jan. 1882, FRC-KC. Agent Patrick to COIA, 22 Mar. 1886, RG 75.

64. Potawatomi Chiefs to COIA, 25 Jan. 1886, RG 75.

65. Washburn 1973 1: 422, 425, 465–67.

66. Agent Patrick to COIA, 24 Sept. 1886 (transmitting petition of Potawatomi Chiefs), in RG 75. For details on the status of the poorer Citizen Potawatomi on the Prairie Band Reserve, see Scott to COIA, 12 Sept., 28 Sept., & 29 Sept. 1891; 11 Nov. 1891; & 16 Oct. 1893; all in Box 517, 586, FRC-KC. See also Rodnick 1936.

67. See Scott to Asst. U.S. Attorney, 17 Dec. 1891; Scott to COIA, 7 Apr. 1892, (ca.) 15 Apr. 1892; Scott to John Young, (ca.) 18 July 1892; & W. H. Upham's List of Members of John Young's band of Wisconsin Potawatomi, (ca.) 1 Nov. 1892; Scott to Upham, 4 Dec. 1893; Scott to COIA, 8 Jan. 1894; Agent Pearson to "Whom it May Concern" (a pass for Shawnese), 6 July 1896; all in Box 517, 586, FRC-KC.

68. Scott to COIA, 7, 15, & 31 Oct. 1892; in Box 517, 586, FRC-KC.

69. For an example of Roily Water's correspondence, see Wahquaboshkok to COIA, 29 Apr. 1886, in RG 75.

70. Scott to Lt. Gresham, 7th Cav., 26 & 27 Aug. 1891; to COIA, 29 Aug. 1891; to Capt. Jackson, 7th Cav., (ca.) 30 Aug.

1891; to COIA, 17 Dec. 1891; all in Box 517, 586, FRC-KC.

71. Scott to COIA, 29 Jan. & 12 Feb. 1892. Box 517, 586, FRC-KC.

72. Scott to COIA (Telegram), 17 Dec., (letter) 17 Dec., 21 Dec., & 22 Dec. 1891; & 20 Apr. 1892. In Box 517, 586, FRC-KC.

73. Scott's Annual Report, 29 Aug. 1892, Box 517, 586 FRC-KC.

74. Scott to COIA, 31 Oct. 1892, in Box 517, 586, FRC-KC. The most conveniently accessible list of allotments under Dawes Act of the Prairie Band's lands is in Connelley 1918: 555–69.

75. Scott to COIA, 12 Feb., 17 May, & 27 Aug. 1893; & Jas. Blandin Deposition of 19 Apr. 1893, in Box 517, 586, FRC-KC.

76. For some details of Wakwaboshkok's travels, see Scott to COIA, 1 & 14 Feb. 1893; Blandin Deposition, 19 Apr. 1893; Scott to COIA, 29 Apr. & 25 July 1893; 30 Jan., 31 Mar., 10 Apr., & 3 Aug. 1894; in Box 517, 586, FRC-KC.

77. Pearson to Secy. Int., 23 Feb. 1895, Box 517, 583, FRC-KC.

78. Pearson to COIA, 25 Jan. 1895, in Box 517, 586, FRC-KC.

79. Pearson to Secy. Int., 25 Jan. & 23 Feb. 1895, in Box 517, 586, FRC-KC. Connelley's 1918 list of Potawatomi allotments, which includes Superintendent Snyder's notations as of 1917 as regards deaths, sales, patents, etc., is the basis for the latter statement. Much of Agent Pearson's correspondence with COIA through 1896–1898 is concerned with the setting up of executors for the estates of deceased Potawatomi. See also AR-COIA 1895–1898.

80. Pearson's Annual Report to COIA, 19 Sept. 1896, FRC-KC. Secy. Int. to COIA, 21 Dec. 1894, in RG 75, constitutes the administrative authority to withhold annuities to those Potawatomi who refused to send their children to school.

81. Scott to COIA (re Blandin), 22 Dec.

1891; Pearson to COIA, 6 Dec. 1894; to Hon. W. A. Margrove, 9 Feb. 1895; to COIA, 14 Feb. 1895; & Prairie Band Council to COIA, 18 Sept. 1891; all in Box 517, 586, FRC-KC.

82. See Rodnick 1936; & Henry Roe Cloud to Minnie Evans, 21 July 1934, in FRC-KC.

83. See Snyder letter in Connelley 1918: 552.

CHAPTER 12:
THE PRAIRIE PEOPLE
IN THE MODERN WORLD

1. Except where noted, this chapter is based upon research conducted by the author and his associates among the Kansas Potawatomi between 1962 and 1965.

2. For a good summary discussion of federal legislation in this period, see Haas 1957 and Lurie 1957.

3. An excellent discussion of the IRA is in Dobyns 1965. See also Haas 1957.

4. A copy of the Baldwin "Constitution" is attached to COI Rhoads to Supt. Baldwin, 16 June 1932. For other sources on this document, see Actg. COIA Zimmerman to Supt. J. H. Hyde, 2 Mar. 1949; Rhoads to Supt. C. M. Blair, 11 Mar. 1933; Supt. Bruce to COIA, 25 Sept. 1946; Supt. Hyde to Minnie Evans, 25 June 1948; Area Director R. H. Bitney to Supt. B. Morrison, 9 May 1956; COIA Emmons to Area Director Pitner, 3 Dec. 1956; & Minutes of General Council at Mayetta, 7 May 1932. All in HIO.

5. For a good exposition of the 1946 legislation, see Lurie 1957. An earlier version of the development of the factional conflict on the Kansas Reservation will be found in Clifton 1965.

6. AR-COIA 1906; & *Topeka Capital*, 5 Apr. 1958 & 7 May 1959.

7. For a more detailed and penetrating exposition, see Robert L. Bee's prize-winning essay on Potawatomi Peyotism (1966). Also Bee 1965 and Howard 1962.

8. See Scott 1925.

9. For much more detailed assessments of these developments, see Calender 1962: 92–97; & Landes 1970: 203–39 & 317–54. Also Quimby 1939.

10. See Landes 1963 & 1970. Also Rodnick 1936.

11. Rhoads to Baldwin, 16 June 1932; Rhoads to C. M. Blair, 11 Mar. 1933; & Supt. Bruce to Ernest Seymour, 3 Dec. 1937. All in HIO.

12. Supt. Bruce to Wm. P. Wishkeno, et al., 11 July 1939; Bruce to COIA, 31 July 1939; M. A. Bender to COIA, 30 Mar. 1940; Bruce's Notice & Minutes of Special Meeting, 28 Mar. 1940. All in HIO.

13. Kirk possibly may have been both black and Cherokee, that is, the descendant of one of the black slaves kept by the Cherokee until well into the 1880s. For documentation on some of his activities, see Tom-Pee-Saw to Secy. Int., 20 Oct. 1946, Tom-Pee-Saw to Supt. Hyde, 7 Dec. 1947; Bruce to COIA (Minutes of General Council), 25 Sept. 1946; Minutes of General Council at Mayetta, 26 Feb. 1936. All in HIO.

14. Supt. Bruce to James Kegg, 15 Nov. 1946; Jas. Wahbnosah to Supt. Bruce, 30 Jan. 1946; Bruce to Kegg et al., 3 Sept. 1946; Bruce to Actg. Director D. P. Trent, 10 Sept. 1947; H. M. Critchfield to Supt. Bruce, 11 Sept. 1947; & Minutes of Business Advisory Committee Meeting, 17 Sept. 1946. All in HIO.

15. For an earlier version of these developments, one less adequate for want of a detailed historical perspective, see Clifton 1965. See also Roe Cloud to Minnie Evans, 21 June 1934; Actg. COIA Zimmerman to Supt. Hyde, 2 Mar. 1949; R. H. Bitney to Area Director Pitner, 30 Dec. 1956; & Resolution of General Council, 18 July 1959. A draft of the 1961 constitution is contained in Prairie Band Resolution 3-61. All in HIO.

16. For a more detailed demographic study of the population in the early 1960s, see Clifton and Isaacs 1964; and for a study of the major ritual institution in the period, Clifton 1969.

CHAPTER 13:
POSTSCRIPT, 1975

1. Clifton and Isaacs 1964: 23.
2. The brilliant social psychologist Louis A. Zurcher was on the scene as a participant observer and described these events in several telling essays (1967 and 1968). See also Steele 1972.
3. Clifton 1962/64. Also *Topeka Daily Capital*, 8 June, 9 June, and 8 Aug. 1961; and 8 June 1968.
4. *Topeka Daily Capital*, 8 Mar., 19 Mar., and 4 June 1971.
5. *Topeka Daily Capital*, 3, 6, 11, and 13 June 1971.
6. *Topeka Daily Capital*, 9 June 1972.
7. *Topeka Daily Capital*, 19 Apr., 24 May, 3 Aug., 4 Aug., 31 Aug., 7 Oct., 27 Oct., 3 Nov., 8 Nov., and 15 Nov. 1972.
8. *Topeka Daily Capital*, 31 Dec. 1972, 13 Feb. 1973, and 3 Mar. 1973.
9. *Topeka Daily Capital*, 4 May, 8 June, 6 Sept., and 28 Sept., 1973; 30 Sept. and 6 Dec. 1974; 10 Apr. and 25 Apr. 1975.

BIBLIOGRAPHY

All abbreviations used in citations and notes are
located in this bibliography in alphabetical order,
cross-referenced to the full title of the source.

Abel, Anna Heloise
  1904   Indian Reservations in Kansas
  and the Extinguishment of their Title.
  Transactions of the Kansas State Historical Society 8: 72–108.
  1906   The History of Events Resulting
  in Indian Consolidation West of the
  Mississippi. Annual Report of the
  American Historical Association for
  the year 1906.

Abraham, R. H.
  1924   Pottawattamie Indians of Walpole Island. The Historical Events in
  Connection with the Settlement of
  Walpole Island. Kent Historical Society, Canada. Papers and Addresses
  6: 32–37.

Adams, Arthur T., ed.
  1961   The Explorations of Pierre
  Esprit Radisson. Minneapolis, Ross &
  Haines, Inc.

Adams, Vina S.
  1934   Mandoka. Wisconsin Archaeologist 14: 41–42.

d'Aigremont, Sieur François
  1708   Report to Count Pontchartrain
  on Enrollment of Indians in Canadian
  Militia. WHC 16: 250–51.

Alford, Clarence W.
  1922   The Illinois Country: 1675–
  1818. Chicago, A. C. McClurg.

American State Papers
  1832/1861   American State Papers—
  Military Affairs. 7 Vols. Washington,
  D.C., Gales and Seaton.

Anderson, James S.
  1912   Indians of Manitowoc County.
  Wisconsin Historical Society Proceedings, 59th Annual Meeting: 160–69.

Anderson, Thomas G.
  1870   Narrative of Captain Thomas G.
  Anderson. WHC 9: 136–206.

Andreas, A. T.
  1875   Historical Atlas of the State of
  Iowa. Chicago, Lakeside Press.
  1884   History of Chicago. 3 Vols.
  Chicago, A. T. Andreas, Publishers.

Anonymous
  1697   Summary of Council at Quebec.
  WHC 16: 166–73. (Also in NYCD
  9: 671–75.)

Anonymous
  1721   Proceedings of Council Regarding Governor Vaudreuil's Letter, October 6, & December 2. WHC 16: 395–
  400.

Anonymous
  1743   Memoir on the Upper Country.
  WHC 17: 335–37.

Anonymous
  1869   Memorial of the Chippeway,
  Pottawatomy, and Ottawa Indians of
  Walpole Island, Touching on Their
  Claim to the Huron Reserve, Fighting,
  Bois Blanc, Turkey, and Point au Pelee

Islands, Sarnia, Ontario, Canadian
Book and Job Office.

Anson, Bert
    1970   The Miami Indians. Norman,
    University of Oklahoma Press.

AR-COIA   Commission of Indian Affairs, Annual Reports.

Armstrong, Perry
    1887   The Sauks and the Black Hawk
    War. Springfield, Illinois, H. W. Rok-
    ker.

ASP-IA   American State Papers—Indian
Affairs. See Lowrie and Clark, eds.

ASP-MA   American State Papers—Military Affairs, 1832–61. See American
State Papers.

Babbitt, Charles F.
    1916   Early Days at Council Bluffs.
    Washington, D.C., Byron Adams Press.

BAE   Bureau of American Ethnology
(National Anthropological Collections),
Washington, D.C., Smithsonian Insti-
tution.

Baerreis, David A.
    1973   Chieftainship among the Pota-
    watomi: An Exploration in Ethno-
    historic Methodology. Wisconsin
    Archaeologist 54: 114–34.

Baerreis, David A., Erminie Wheeler-
Voegelin and Remedios Wycoco-Moore
    1974   Indians of Northeastern Illinois.
    New York, Garland Publishing Co.

Barnes, Lela
    1936   Journal of Isaac McCoy for the
    Exploring Expedition of 1828. Kansas
    Historical Quarterly 5: 227–67.

Barnhart, John D.
    1951   Henry Hamilton and George
    Rogers Clark in the American Revolu-
    tion. Crawfordsville, Ind., R. E. Banta.

Barrett, S. A.
    1911   The Dream Dance of the Chip-
    pewa and Menominee Indians of
    Northern Wisconsin. Bulletin of the
    Public Museum of the City of Mil-
    waukee 1: 251–415.

Barry, Louise
    1972   The Beginning of the West:

Annals of the Kansas Gateway to the
American West, 1540–1854. Topeka,
Kansas State Historical Society.

Bauman, Robert F.
    1949   The Migration of the Ottawa
    Indians from the Maumee Valley to
    Walpole Island. Northwest Ohio
    Quarterly 21: 86–112.
    1952   Kansas, Canada, or Starvation.
    Michigan History 36: 287–98.

Beauharnois, Charles de
    1729a   Letter to the French Minister,
    July 21. WHC 17: 62–65.
    1729b   Letter to the French Minister,
    Nov. 1. WHC 17: 67–70.
    1729c   Letter to the French Minister,
    Oct. 12. WHC 17: 80–81.
    1730   Letter to the French Minister,
    Sept. 9. WHC 17: 109–12.
    1735   Letter to the French Minister,
    Oct. 9. WHC 17: 216–22.
    1936a   Letter to the French Minister,
    Oct. 17. WHC 17: 260.
    1736b   Letter to the French Minister,
    Oct. 3. MPHC 34: 151–53.
    1741   Letter to the French Minister,
    Sept. 26. WHC 17: 365–66.
    1742   Reply to the Potawatomi, July
    22. WHC 17: 355–96.

Beauharnois, Charles de, and
Gilles Hocquart
    1734   Extracts from Reports. WHC
    17: 207–8.

Beckwith, H.
    1884   The Illinois and Indiana Indians.
    Fergus' Historical Series 27: 162–83,
    Chicago.

Bee, Robert L.
    1964/1965   Kansas Potawatomi Study
    Field Notes. Ms. Madison, Wisconsin
    State Historical Society.
    1964   Potawatomi Peyotism: The In-
    fluence of Traditional Patterns. South-
    western Journal of Anthropology 22:
    194–205.
    1965   Peyotism in North American
    Indian Groups. Transactions of the
    Kansas Academy of Science 68: 13–61.

Berkhofer, Robert F.
1965   Salvation and the Savage: An Analysis of Protestant Missions and American Indian Response, 1787–1862. Lexington, University of Kentucky Press.

Bernard, Jessie
1928   Political Leadership among North American Indians. American Journal of Sociology 34: 296–315.

Berthrong, Donald J.
1974   Indians of Northern Indiana and Southwestern Michigan. New York, Garland Publishing Co.

Bettarel, R. L., and H. G. Smith
1973   The Moccasin Bluff Site and the Woodland Cultures of Southwestern Michigan. Anthropological Papers, Museum of Anthropology, No. 49. Ann Arbor, University of Michigan.

Bigsby, J. J.
1850   The Shoe and the Canoe, or Pictures of Travel in the Canadas. 2 Vols. London, Chapman & Hall.

Billington, Ray Allen
1960   Westward Expansion: A History of the American Frontier. 2nd edition. New York, Macmillan Company.

Blackbird, Andrew J.
1897   Complete History of the Ottawa and Chippewa Indians of Michigan. Yipsilanti, Babcock and Darling.

Black Hawk
1834   Life of Ma-Ka-Tai-Me-She-Kia-Kiak. Boston.

Blair, Emma H.
1911   The Indian Tribes of the Upper Mississippi Valley and the Region of the Great Lakes. 2 vols. Cleveland. (Reprinted 1969 by the Kraus Reprint Co.)

Blasingham, Emily
1956   The Depopulation of the Illinois Indians. Ethnohistory 3: 193–224; 361–412.

Bleasdale, Ruth
1974   Manitowaning: An Experiment in Indian Settlement. Ontario History 66: 148–57.

Bloishebért, Louis
1732   Letter to Beauharnois, Nov. 7. WHC 17: 172–74.

Bogue, Donald J.
1959   Internal Migration. In, P. M. Hauser & O. D. Duncan, eds., The Study of Population. Chicago, University of Chicago Press.

Boorstin, Daniel J.
1965   The Americans: The National Experience. New York, Random House.

Brophy, William A., and
Sophie D. Aberle, et al., eds.
1966   The Indian: America's Unfinished Business. Norman, University of Oklahoma Press.

Brown, Charles E.
n.d.   Charles E. Brown Papers. Wisconsin Historical Manuscripts HB, Box 3. Madison, Wisconsin Historical Society.
1929   Vocabulary—Wisconsin Prairie Potawatomi Words (Informant, Daniel D. Shepard). Ms., in, Brown, n.d.

Brown, Dorothy M.
1940   Wisconsin Indian Corn Origin Myths. Wisconsin Archaeologist 21: 19–27.
1941   Indian Winter Legends. Wisconsin Archaeologist 22: 49–53.

Brown, G. W., D. M. Hayne, and
F. G. Halpenny, eds.
1966/——   Dictionary of Canadian Biography. 10 Vols. (Series incomplete, 1975.) Toronto, University of Toronto Press.

Brown, Henry
1844   The History of Illinois from Its Discovery to the Present Time. New York, Winchester.

Brown, Ralph H.
1848   Historical Geography of the United States. New York, Harcourt Brace & World.

Brunton, Sam, Compiler
1970   Notes and Sketches on the History of Parry Sound. Canada. Parry Sound Historical Society.

Brymner, Douglas, ed.
1897   Report on the Canadian Archives, 1896. Ottawa.

Buchen, Gustave William
1944   Historic Sheboygan County. Sheboygan, Wisconsin.

Buck, Solon J.
1967   Illinois in 1818. 2nd edition. Urbana, University of Illinois Press.

Buechner, Cecilia Bain
1933   The Pokagons. Indiana Historical Publications 10: 285–340.

Buell, Rowena
1903   The Memoirs of Rufus Putnam. Boston & New York, Houghton Mifflin Co.

Burden, H. N.
1895   Manitoulin: Or Five Years of Church Work Among the Ojibwa. London.

Bureau of the Census
1961   Historical Statistics of the United States. Washington, D.C., U.S. Government Printing Office.

Bureau of Indian Affairs
1804/1904   Records of the Bureau of Indian Affairs. Record Group 75. Washington, D.C., National Archives and Records Service.

Bureau of Indian Affairs
1957   Social and Economic Survey of Potawatomie Jurisdiction. Bureau of Indian Affairs, Department of the Interior, Washington (Mimeo.).

Burke, Rev. James M., S.J.
1953   Early years at St. Mary's Potawatomie Mission, from the diary of Father Maurice Gailland, S.J. Kansas Historical Quarterly 20: 501–29.

Burley, C. A.
1919   Sauganash (Letter to H. G. Zande), 7 pp. Ms. Chicago Historical Society.

Burnet, Jacob
1847   Notes on the Early Settlement of the Northwestern Territory. Cincinnati, Derby, Bradley Co.

Cadillac, Antoine de la Mothe
1704   Memorandum of M. de la Mothe Cadillac concerning the establishment of Detroit, from Quebec. 14 November. MPHC 33: 198–241.

Cadillac, Antoine de la Mothe
1718   Relation of Sieur de la Mothe Cadillac, Captain on full pay commanding a company of marine troops in Canada. WHC 16: 350–63.

Caldwell, William, Sr.
n.d.   The William Caldwell Papers. Ms. Amherstburg, Ontario, Fort Malden National Historical Park.

Callender, Charles
1962   Social Organization of the Central Algonkian Indians. Milwaukee Public Museum Publications in Anthropology 7.

Canada
18991   Indian Treaties and Surrenders. 3 Vols. Toronto, Coles Canadians Collection. (Facsimile edition reprinted 1971.)

Carman, J. Neale
1954   A Bishop East of the Rockies Views His Diocesans, 1851–1853. Kansas Historical Quarterly 21: 81–87.

Carman, J. Neale, and Karl S. Pond
1955   The Replacement of the Indian Languages of Kansas by English. Transactions of the Kansas Academy of Science 58: 131–50.

Carson, Jack
1974   Report on Prairie Band Affairs to Wisconsin Rapids Potawatomi. (Personal communication from Agent, Horton Indian Office.)

Carter, C. E., et al., eds.
1934/——   The Territorial Papers of the United States. 27 Vols. Washington, D.C., U.S. Government Printing Office.

Case, Thomas
   1963   The Battle of Fallen Timbers. Northwest Ohio Quarterly 35: 54–68.

Cass, Lewis
   1822   Letter to John C. Calhoun. National Archives, Records of the Secretary of War, Letters Received, C-113 (161).

Catlin, George
   1850   Letters and Notes on the Manners, Customs, and Condition of the North American Indians. 9th edition.

Caton, John Dean
   1876   The last of the Illinois and a sketch of the Pottawatomies. Fergus' Historical Series 3: 3–30, Chicago.

Céleron, Pierre
   1750   Journal of an Expedition. WHC 18: 26–58.

Chapman, Berlin
   1946   The Pottawatomie and Absentee Shawnee Reservation. The Chronicles of Oklahoma 24: 293–305.

Chapman Brothers
   1890   Portrait and Biographical Album of Jackson, Jefferson, and Pottawatomi Counties, Kansas. Chicago, Chapman Brothers Press.

Charlevois, Rev. Pierre François Xavier de
   1870   History and General Description of New France. Translated by J. G. Shea. 6 Vols. Chicago, Loyola University Press.
   1923   Journal of a Voyage to North America. 2 Vols. Louise Phelps Kellogg, ed. Chicago, Caxton Club.

Chittenden, Hiram M., and
A. T. Richardson
   1905   Life, Letters and Travels of Father Pierre Jean de Smet, S.J. New York, Harpers.

CHNY   Documents Relative to the Colonial History of the State of New York. See O'Callaghan and Fernow, 1853–1887.

Chouteau, Auguste
   1816   Notes on Boundaries of Various Indian Nations. Glimpses of the Past 7: 119–40.

Chowen, Richard
   1941   The History of Treaty Making with the Potawatomi Nation of Indians. Unpub. M.A. Thesis. Evanston, Northwestern University.

Clark, William
   1812   Letter to William Eustis, March 22. National Archives, Records of the Secretary of War, Letters Received. C-244 (6).
   1830/1855   The William Clark Papers, pertaining to the U.S. Superintendency of Indian Affairs at St. Louis. Ms. Topeka, Kansas Historical Society.

Claspy, Everett
   1966   The Potawatomi Indians of Southwestern Michigan. Ann Arbor, Braun-Brumfield, Inc. (Privately published by author.)
   1970   The Dowagaic-Sister Lakes Resort Area and More About its Potawatomi Indians. Dowagaic, Michigan. (Published by the author.)

Cleland, Charles E.
   1966   The Prehistoric Animal Ecology and Ethnozoology of the Upper Great Lakes Region. Anthropological Papers, Museum of Anthropology, No. 29. Ann Arbor, University of Michigan.

Clifton, Faye A.
   1963/1964   Kansas Potawatomi Study Field Notes. Ms. Madison, Wisconsin State Historical Society.

Clifton, James A., and Barry Isaac
   1964   The Kansas Potawatomi: On the Nature of a Contemporary Indian Community. Transactions of the Kansas Academy of Science 67: 1–24.

Clifton, James A.
   1962/1965   Kansas Potawatomi Study Field Notes. Ms. Madison, Wisconsin State Historical Society.
   1964   The Prairie Potawatomi Community in Kansas—1964. University of Kansas, Potawatomi Study Research Report (Mimeo.).

1968   Factionalism and the Indian Community: The Prairie Potawatomi Case. In, N. O. Lurie, ed., The American Indian Today. Deland, Fla., Everett/Edwards Press. (Penguin Books edition, 1970.)

1969   Sociocultural Dynamics of the Prairie Potawatomi Drum Cult. Plains Anthropologist 14: 85–93.

1970   Chicago Was Theirs. Chicago History Magazine, Vol. 1, No. 1.

1974   The Canadian Potawatomi: Ethnohistorical Notes and Documents, Deposited with Ethnology Division, National Museum of Man, Ottawa.

1975a   Potawatomi Leadership Roles: On *Okamuk* and Other Influential Personages. In, Proceedings of the 1974 Algonquian Conference. Mercury Series. Ottawa, National Museum of Man.

1975b   A Place of Refuge for All Time: The Migration of the American Potawatomi into Upper Canada, 1835–1845. Mercury Series. Ottawa, National Museum of Man.

1976a   Potawatomi. In, Handbook of North American Indians, Vol. 12: Northeast, Bruce G. Trigger, ed. Washington, D.C., Smithsonian Institution.

1976b   Applied Anthropology among Wisconsin's Indians. In, D. E. Hunter & P. Whitten, eds., The Study of Anthropology. New York, Harper & Row.

1976c   The Post-Removal Aftermath. In, R. L. Buchman, ed., The Historic Indian in Ohio. Columbus, Ohio Historical Society.

1976d   Captain Billy Caldwell: An Essay into the Reconstruction of an Abused Identity. Paper presented at the 1976 annual meetings of the American Historical Society, Washington, D.C.

1976e   Acculturation, and Assimilation. Entries in, Encyclopedia of Anthropology. New York, Harper & Row.

1976f   The Master of Life Helps Those Who . . . Comments on the Course of Psychosocial Dependency in Potawatomi History and Culture. Paper read at the annual meetings of the American Anthropological Association, Washington, D.C.

n.d.   Dreamers and Drummers: Potawatomi Religion and the Dream Dance Cult. Ms.

Collins, Joseph E.
1793   Deposition, February 16. Wayne Papers. Philadelphia, Historical Society of Pennsylvania.

Commissioner of Indian Affairs
1845/1905   Annual Reports to the Secretary of the Interior. Washington, D.C., U.S. Government Printing Office.

Connelley, William E.
1915   Abram B. Burnett, Pottawatomie Chief. Collections of the Kansas State Historical Society 13: 371–73.

1918   The Prairie Band of Pottawatomie Indians. KHC 14: 488–570.

Conway, Thomas G.
1972   Potawatomi Politics. Journal of the Illinois State Historical Society 65: 395–418.

1975   An Indian Politician and Entrepreneur in the Old Northwest. The Old Northwest I: 51–63.

Cook, Samuel F.
1896   Drummond Island: The Story of the British Occupation, 1815–1828. Author's edition. Lansing, Michigan. (Also, University Microfilms, O-P Series.)

Cooper, Stephen
1840   Report of Stephen Cooper, Sub-Agent at Council Bluffs. 2nd Sess., 26th Congress, Senate Documents #375, Vol. I. Washington, D.C.

Copley, A. B.
1890   The Pottawattomies. MPHC 14: 256–64.

Copway, G.
 1850 The Traditional History and Characteristic Sketches of the Ojibway Nation. London, Charles Gilpin.
Coulter, Joseph E.
 1948 Catholic Missions among the Potawatomi Indians. Unpub. M.A. Thesis. Norman, University of Oklahoma.
Cruikshank, Ernest A.
 1892 Robert Dickson, the Indian Trader. WHC 12: 1–13.
 1912 Documents Relating to the Invasion of Canada and the Surrender of Detroit. Ottawa.
 1923/1931 The Correspondence of Lieutenant Governor John Graves Simcoe. 5 Vols. Toronto, Ontario Historical Society.
Cummins, Damian L. R.
 1934 Catholics in the Early Platte Purchase (to 1845) and in Nodaway County (to 1930). St. Louis, Lawlore Printing Co.
Cunningham, R. E., Compiler
 1961 The History of Manti (Iowa). Shenandoah, Iowa, The World Publishing Co.
Cunningham, W. M., ed.
 1967 The Letter Book of William Burnett. Fort Miami Heritage Society of Michigan.
Currey, J. Seymour
 1912 The Story of Old Fort Dearborn. Chicago, A. C. McClurg Co.
DAB Dictionary of American Biography. See, Dumas Malone, ed.
Danziger, E. J., Jr.
 1974 Indians and Bureaucrats: Administering the Reservation Policy during the Civil War. Urbana, University of Illinois Press.
Davis, A. L.
 1839 Report of A. L. Davis, Sub-Agent at the Osage River. Sub-Agency, October 15, 1839. Public Documents Printed by Order of the Senate of the United States, 1st Sess., 26th Congress.

Senate Documents #354. Washington, D.C.
DCB Dictionary of Canadian Biography. See, Brown, Hayne, and Halpenny, eds.
Deale, Valentine B.
 1958 The History of the Potawatomi before 1722. Ethnohistory 5: 305–60.
Deliette, Sieur (probable author)
 1724 Memoir of DeGannes Concerning Illinois Country. IHS 23: 302–95. (Attributed to DeGannes, this memoir was likely written by Henri Tonty's nephew, Sieur Deliette.)
Denonville, Jacques Brisay
 1686 Letter to Duluth, June 6. WHC 16: 125–6.
Densmore, Frances
 1913 Drum Presentation Ceremony. In, Chippewa Music II, Bureau of American Ethnology Bulletin 53: 142–183.
 1918 The Grass Dance. In, Teton Sioux Music, Bureau of American Ethnology Bulletin 61: 468–77.
 1932 The Drum Religion and its Songs. In, Menominee Music, Bureau of American Ethnology Bulletin 102: 150–83.
 1949 A Study of Some Michigan Indians. Anthropological Papers, Museum of Anthropology. Ann Arbor, University of Michigan 1: 31–33.
de Peyster, Colonel Arent Schulyer
 1888 Miscellanies by an Officer: 1774–1813. New York, A. E. Chasmar & Co.
Deschaillons, Jean
 1730 Letter to Beauharnois. WHC 17: 100–2.
De Smet, Father Pierre-Jean, S.J.
 1847a Legend of the Potawatomie Indians. A Letter to Fr. Barbeau. Copy made by J. N. B. Hewitt. Bureau of American Ethnology Ms. #3829.
 1847b Oregon Missions. New York.
 1859a History of the Western Missions and Missionaries in the United States. New York, P. J. Kennedy.

1859b   Western Missions and Missionaries: A Series of Letters. New York, Catholic Publishing House.

Dichls, Rev. Francis, S.J., and
Rev. Maurice Gailland, S.J.
n.d.   English-Potawatomi Dictionary. BAE Ms. 2528. (Original in Jesuit Provincial Archives, St. Louis, Mo.)

Dickison, David H.
1961   Chief Simon Pokagon, the Indian Longfellow. Indiana Magazine of History 57: 127–40.

Dobyns, Henry F.
1968   Therapeutic experience of responsible democracy. In, Nancy O. Lurie, The American Indian Today. Deland, Fla., Everett/Edwards, Inc. (Also, Penguin Books edition.)

Donohue, Arthur Thomas
1931   A History of the Early Jesuit Missions in Kansas. Unpub. Ph.D. Dissertation. Lawrence, University of Kansas.

Douville, Raymond, and
Jacques-Donat Casanova
1967   Daily Life in Early Canada. New York, Macmillan.

Downes, Randolph
1940   Council Fires on the Upper Ohio. Pittsburgh, University of Pittsburgh Press.

Drake, Benjamin
1858   Life of Tecumseh and of His Brother the Prophet, with a Historical Sketch of the Shawanoe Indians. Cincinnati, Anderson, Gates & Wright. (Reprinted 1969 by the Kraus Reprint Company.)

DRC   The Lyman Draper Manuscript Collections. Madison, Wisconsin State Historical Society.

Dubuisson, Charles
1712   Letter to Governor Vaudreuil reporting on the war at Detroit with the Fox and Mascoutin. WHC 16: 267–87. (A different translation of the original is in MPHC 33: 537–52.)

DuChesneau, M. Jacques
1681   Memoir on the Western Indians, &c. November 13. CHNY 9: 160–66.

Duncan, Charles T.
1964   An Overland Journey from New York to San Francisco in the Summer of 1859 by Horace Greeley. New York, Knopf.

DuQuesne, Ange
1754   Letter to the French Minister. October 13. WHC 18: 141–42.

Dutch, William
1949   John Tipton of Indiana, with Special Reference to his Activities as Indian Agent of the United States. Unpub. M.A. Thesis. Greencastle, Ind., DePauw University.

Du Tisné, Claude Charles
1725   Letter to Gov. Vaudreuil. January 14. WHC 16: 450–51.

Eby, Cecil
1973   "That Disgraceful Affair," the Black Hawk War. New York, W. W. Norton.

Eccles, W. J.
1966   The French forces in North America during the Seven Years War. DCB 3: xv-xxiii.

Edmonds, John Worth
1837   Report of J. W. Edmonds, United States Commissioner, Upon the Disturbances at the Potawatomi Payment September, 1836. New York, Scatcherd and Adams.

Edmunds, R. David
1969   The Illinois River Potawatomi in the War of 1812. JISHS 62: 341–62.

1972a   A History of the Potawatomi Indians, 1615–1795. Unpub. Ph.D. Dissertation. Norman, University of Oklahoma.

1972b   The Prairie Potawatomi Removal of 1833. Indiana Magazine of History 68: 240–56.

1974   Potawatomis in the Platte Country: An Indian Removal Incomplete. Missouri Valley Historical Review 63: 375–92.

n.d. Keepers of the Fire: History of the Potawatomi to 1840. Ms.

Edwards, Ninian W.
1870 History of Illinois, From 1778 to 1833; Life and Times of Ninian Edwards. Springfield.

Elliott, Richard Smith
1883 Notes Taken in Sixty Years. St. Louis, R. P. Studley & Co. (Privately Published.)

Enjalran, Father Jean, S.J.
1683 Letter to Governor Lefevre de la Barre, August 26. WHC 16: 110–13.

Erickson, Barbara
1965 Patterns of person-number reference in Potawatomi. International Journal of American Linguistics 31: 226–36.

Esarey, Logan, ed.
1922 Messages and Letters of William Henry Harrison. 2 Vols. Indianapolis.

EWT Early Western Travels. See, Thwaites, ed., 1904/1907.

Faben, W. W.
1958 Indians of the Tri-State Area—the Potowattamis. Northwest Ohio Quarterly 30: 49–53 & 100–5.

Farnham, Thomas J.
1906 Travels in the Great Western Prairies, the Anahuac and Rocky Mountains, and in the Oregon Territory. In, EWT 1: 132–35.

Fernow, Berthold
1971 The Ohio Valley in Colonial Days. New York, Lennoy Hill Co. (Reprint of 1890 edition.)

Fitting, James E., and Charles E. Cleland
1969 Late Prehistoric Settlement Patterns in the Upper Great Lakes. Ethnohistory 16: 289–302.

Fitting, James E.
1965 Late Woodland Culture of Southeastern Michigan. Anthropological Papers, Museum of Anthropology, No. 24. Ann Arbor, University of Michigan.

Fitzpatrick, John C., ed.
1931/1944 The Writings of George Washington. Washington, D.C., U.S. Government Printing Office.

Flanagan, John T.
1970 Western Sportsmen Travellers in the New York "Spirit of the Times." In, McDermott 1970: 168–86.

Flexner, James Thomas
1965 George Washington—The Forge of Experience (1732–1775). Boston, Little, Brown and Company.
1967 George Washington in the American Revolution (1775–1783). Boston, Little, Brown and Company.
1969a George Washington and the New Nation (1783–1793). Boston, Little, Brown and Company.
1969b George Washington—Anguish and Farewell (1793–1799). Boston, Little, Brown and Company.

Flick, Alexander, et al., eds.
1921/1962 The Papers of Sir William Johnson. 13 Vols. Albany, State University of New York Press.

Foreman, Grant
1946 The Last Trek of the Indians. Chicago, University of Chicago Press.

Forsyth, Thomas
1812a The Shawnee Prophet. In, Blair 1911 2: 273–77.
1812b Report to William Clark on the Illinois Country. St. Louis, 23 December. Typescript copy. St. Louis, Missouri Historical Society.
1827 A Report to General William Clark on the Manners and Customs of the Sauk and Fox Indians Traditions. In, Blair 1911 2: 183–245.
1888 Letter-book of Thomas Forsyth. WHC 11: 316–55.

FRC-KC Federal Records Center, Kansas City, Missouri. See, Svanda 1965.

Fried, Morton H.
1968 On the Concepts of "Tribe" and "Tribal Society." In, June Helm, ed., Essays on the Problem of Tribe. Seattle, American Ethnological Society.

Fritz, Henry E.
1963 The Movement for Indian As-

similation, 1860–1890. Philadelphia, University of Pennsylvania Press.

Fulton, A. R.
1882   The Red Men of Iowa. Des Moines, Mills & Co.

Gailland, Rev. Maurice, S.J.
n.d.   Three drafts of a Potawatomi grammer. BAE Ms. 2530. English-Potawatomi dictionary. BAE Ms. 1761.
n.d.   Hymns in Potawatomi; Evangelica, quae leguntur in diebus festivis per annum; Epitenitakwog Enemat otinosowin;   &   French Potawatomi catechism. BAE Ms. 2529.
1849   Fragments of the Potewatemi Tongue. BAE Ms. 1855. (Originals in Jesuit Provincial Archives, St. Louis, Mo.)

Galinée, Gabriel, Abbe de Queylus
1671   Narrative of the Most Noteworthy Incidents in the Journey of Messieurs Dollier and Galinée. In, Kellogg 1917: 167–209.

Galt, Anthony
1974   Rethinking Patron-Client Relationships: The Real System and the Official System in Southern Italy. Anthropological Quarterly 47: 182–202.

Garraghan, Gilbert J.
1938   The Jesuits of the Middle United States. 3 Vols. New York, America Press.

Gates, Paul W.
1954   Fifty Million Acres: Conflicts Over Kansas Land Policy, 1854–1867. Ithaca, Cornell University Press.

Gatschet, Albert S.
1879   Notebook—vocabularies, texts, notes. BAE Ms. 68.
1889   Notebook. BAE Ms. 27-a.
1898   Vocabulary. BAE Ms. 1212.

Gerend, Alphonse
n.d.   Album of Indian Portraits and Biographies (ca. 1925). In, Charles E. Brown, n.d.
1920   Sheboygan County. Wisconsin Archeologist 19: 121–92.

Gerwing, Anselm J., O.B.
1964   The Chicago Indian Treaty of 1833. JISHS 57: 117–42.

Gibson, A. M.
1963   The Kickapoos: Lords of the Middle Border. Norman, University of Oklahoma Press.
1971   The Chickasaws. Norman, University of Oklahoma Press.

Gibson, Lawrence H., ed.
1938   The Moravian Indian Mission on White River. Indianapolis, Indiana Historical Society.

Gilpin, Alec R.
1958   The War of 1812 in the Old Northwest. East Lansing, Michigan State University Press.

Goddard, Ives
1972   Historical and Philological Evidence Regarding the Identification of the Mascouten. Ethnohistory 19: 123–34.
1976   Central Algonquian Languages. In, Bruce G. Trigger, ed. Handbook of North American Indians, Vol. 12, Northeast. Washington, D.C., Smithsonian Institution.

Goode, Rev. William H.
1864   Outposts of Zion, with Limnings of Mission Life. Cincinnati, Poe & Hitchcock.

Gordon, Major William
1835   Journal of a Pottawatomie Exploration West of the Mississippi. July 30, 1835. Copy in "Indian Envelope." St. Louis, Missouri Historical Society.

Gossen, Gary
1964   A Version of the Potawatomi Coon-Wolf Cycle: ' A Traditional Projective Screen for Acculturative Stress. Search 4: 8–15.

Graham, Richard
1820/1830   The Richard Graham Papers. Ms. Collection. St. Louis, Missouri Historical Society.

Grant, W. L.
1907   Voyages of Samuel de Cham-

plain: 1604–1618. New York, Scribners.

Great Lakes Indian Archives Project
n.d. Glenn A. Black Laboratory of Archaeology, Bloomington, Indiana University.

Grinnell, George Bird
1956 The Fighting Cheyennes. Norman, University of Oklahoma Press.

Griswold, Bert J., ed.
1927 Fort Wayne, Gateway of the West (1802–13). Indiana Historical Collections 25.

Haas, Theodore H.
1957 The legal aspects of Indian affairs from 1887 to 1957. In, Simpson & Yinger 1957: 12–22.

Hagan, William T.
1958 The Sac and Fox Indians. Norman, University of Oklahoma Press.

Hair, J. T.
1866 Gazetteer of Madison County. Alton, Illinois.

Hallowell, A. Irving
1955 Culture and Experience. Philadelphia, University of Pennsylvania Press.

Hamilton, Edward P., ed.
1964 Adventure in the Wilderness: The American Journals of Louis Antoine de Bougainville, 1756–1760. Norman, University of Oklahoma Press.

Hamilton, Joseph V.
1839 Report of Joseph V. Hamilton, Agent at Council Bluffs. Fort Leavenworth, October 18, 1839. 1st Sess., 26th Congress, Senate Document, No. 354, Vol. 1.

Hanna, Charles A.
1911 The Wilderness Trail, or the Ventures and Adventures of the Pennsylvania Traders on the Allegheny Path. 2 Vols. New York, Putnams.

Harmon, George Dewey
1941 Sixty Years of Indian Affairs: Political, Economic, and Diplomatic— 1789–1850. Chapel Hill, University of North Carolina Press.

Harper, J. Russell
1971 Paul Kane's Frontier. Toronto, University of Toronto Press.

Harris, Marvin
1968 Race. In, D. L. Sills, ed., International Encyclopedia of the Social Sciences, Vol. 13: 263–67. New York, Macmillan & Free Press.

1975 Culture, People, Nature. 2nd edition. New York, Crowell.

HCL Historical Collections of Louisiana. New York, Wiley and Putnam, 1846.

Heidenreich, Conrad
1971 Huronia: A History and Geography of the Huron Indians 1600–1650. Toronto, McClelland and Stewart.

Helm, Linai T.
1912 The Fort Dearborn Massacre . . . with Letters and Narratives of Contemporary Interest. Chicago, Rand, McNally.

Hennepin, Louis
1683 Narrative of the Voyage to the Upper Mississippi. IHC 1.

1903 A New Discovery of a Vast Country in America. 2 Vols. Chicago, A. C. McClung.

Hertzberg, Hazel W.
1971 The Search for an American Indian Identity. Syracuse, N.Y., Syracuse University Press.

Hickerson, Harold
1960 The Feast of the Dead Among the Seventeenth Century Algonkians of the Upper Great Lakes. American Anthropologist 62: 81–107.

1962 The Southwestern Chippewa: An Ethnohistorical Study. American Anthropological Association Memoir 64.

1963 The Sociohistorical Significance of Two Chippewa Ceremonials. American Anthropologist 55: 67–85.

1970 The Chippewa and their Neighbors: A Study in Ethnohistory. New York, Rinehart & Winston.

Hickling, William
1877   Caldwell and Shobnee. Fergus' Historical Series 10, Chicago.

Hilger, Sister M. Inez
1951   Chippewa Childlife and its Cultural Background. Bureau of American Ethnology Bulletin 146.

HIO   Archives of the Horton Indian Office, Bureau of Indian Affairs, Horton, Kansas.

Hockett, Charles F.
1939   Potawatomi Syntax. Language 15: 235–48.
1942   The Position of Potawatomi in Central Algonkian. Papers of the Michigan Academy of Science, Arts, and Letters 28: 537–42.
1948   Potawatomi (Parts 1–4). International Journal of American Linguistics 14: 1–10, 63–73, 139–49, 213–25.
1950   The Conjunct Modes in Ojibwa and Potawatomi. Language 26: 279–82.
1957   Central Algonkian Vocabulary: Stems in /r/. International Journal of American Linguistics 23: 247–68.
1966   What Algonquian is Really Like. International Journal of American Linguistics 32: 59–73.

Hocquart, Gilles
1735   Report to the Comptroller General. WHC 17: 230–32.

Hodge, Frederick Webb, ed.
1910   Handbook of American Indians North of Mexico. 2 Vols. Bureau of American Ethnology Bulletin 30. (Reprinted 1971 by Rowman and Littlefield.)

Hoecken, Rev. Christian, S.J.
1846   Pewani Ipi Potewatemi Missinoikan, Eyowat, Nemadjik, Tacholigues Endjik, Baltimoinak. (Photostat in Newberry Library, Chicago.)

Holmer, N. M.
1954   The Ojibwa on Walpole Island —A Linguistic Study. Upsala Canadian Studies IV.

Hopkins, Gerard T.
1862   A Mission to the Indians of Fort Wayne, in 1804. Philadelphia, T. E. Zell.

Horsman, Reginald
1958   British Indian Policy in the Northwest, 1807–1812. Mississippi Valley Historical Review 45: 51–66.
1962   Wisconsin and the War of 1812. Wisconsin Magazine of History 46 (1).
1963   The Role of the Indian in the War. In, Phillip P. Mason, ed., After Tippecanoe: Some Aspects of the War of 1812. East Lansing, Michigan State University Press.
1964   Matthew Elliott: British Indian Agent. Detroit, Wayne State University Press.
1969   The War of 1812. New York, Knopf.
1975   Scientific Racism and the American Indian in the Mid-Nineteenth Century. American Quarterly, May: 153–68.

Houck, Louis, ed.
1909   The Spanish Regime in Missouri. 2 Vols. Chicago, Donnelley.

Howard, James H.
1960   When They Worship the Underwater Panther: A Prairie Potawatomi Bundle Ceremony. Southwestern Journal of Anthropology 16: 217–24.
1962   Potawatomi Mescalism and Its Relationship to the Diffusion of the Peyote Cult. Plains Anthropologist 7: 125–35.
1965   The Kenakuk Religion. An Early 19th Century Revitalization Movement 140 Years Later. Museum News, South Dakota Museum, Vol. 26, No. 11–12.

Hunt, George T.
1940   The Wars of the Iroquois: A Study in Intertribal Trade Relations. Madison, University of Wisconsin Press.

Hurlbut, Henry
  1890   Chicago Antiquities. Chicago, Eastman & Bartlett.

Hyde, George E.
  1962   Indians of the Woodlands, from Prehistoric Times to 1725. Norman, University of Oklahoma Press.
  1974   The Pawnee Indians. New edition. Norman, University of Oklahoma Press.

ICC   See, Indian Claims Commission 1974.

IHC   Collections of the Illinois State Historical Library, Springfield.

Indian Claims Commission
  1974   Indians of Ohio, Indiana, Illinois, Southern Michigan and Southern Wisconsin: Commission Findings. 3 Vols. New York, Garland Publishing Co.

Innis, Harold A.
  1962   The Fur Trade in Canada. Abridged edition. Toronto, University of Toronto Press.

Isaac, Barry
  1963   Kansas Potawatomi Study Field Notes. Ms. Madison, Wisconsin State Historical Society.

Jablow, Joseph
  1974   Indians of Illinois and Indiana: Illinois, Kickapoo and Potawatomi Indians. New York, Garland Publishing Co.

Jackson, Donald, ed.
  1962   Letters of the Lewis and Clark Expedition. Urbana, University of Illinois Press.

Jackson, Donald
  1966   The Journals of Zebulon Montgomery Pike. 2 Vols. University of Oklahoma Press.

Jacobs, Hubert
  1954   Document: The Potawatomi Mission, 1854. Mid-America 35: 220–47.

Jacobs, Wilbur
  1950   Wilderness Politics and Indian Gifts: The Northern Colonial Frontier, 1748–1763. Lincoln, University of Nebraska Press.

James, Edwin, ed.
  1830   A Narrative of the Captivity and Adventures of John Tanner. New York. (Reprinted 1956 by Ross & Haines, Inc., Minneapolis, Minnesota.)

James, James Alton, ed.
  1912   George Rogers Clark Papers 1771–1781. Collections of the Illinois State Historical Library 8, Springfield.

Jameson, Audrin
  1950   Pottawattomies on Walpole Island. The Totem Pole 25: 1–5.

Jenness, Diamond
  1935   The Ojibwa Indians of Parry Island, Their Social and Religious Life. Ottawa, National Museum of Canada.

JISHS   Journal of the Illinois State Historical Society.

Johnson, Frederick
  1929   Notes on the Ojibwa and Potawatomie of the Parry Island Reservation. Indian Notes 6: 193–216. New York, Heye Foundation.

Jones, J. A.
  1953   The Political Organization of the Three Fires. Proceedings of the Indiana Academy of Science 63: 46.

Jones, J. A., Alice E. Smith, and Vernon Carstensen
  1974   Winnebago Indians. New York, Garland Publishing Co.

Jones, Peter
  1861   History of the Ojibway Indians, with a Special Reference to their Conversion to Christianity. London, A. W. Bennett.

Joost, Nicholas
  1970   Reveille in the West: Western Travelers in the St. Louis "Weekly Reveille," 1844–50. In, McDermott 1970.

Joutel, Henri
  1962   A Journal of La Salle's Last Voyage. New York, Corinth Press. (First printed, Paris, 1713.)

JR   The Jesuit Relations. See, Thwaites 1896/1901.

Kappler, Charles J., ed.
1904   Indian Affairs: Laws and Treaties, Vol. 2 (Treaties). Senate Documents, 58th Congress, 2nd Sess., Document No. 319. Washington, D.C., U.S. Government Printing Office. (Reprinted 1972, Interland Publishing Company, New York.)

Keating, William H.
1824   Narrative of an Expedition to the Source of St. Peter's River, Vol. 1. Philadelphia, H. C. Carey.

Keesing, Felix
1939   The Menomeni Indians of Wisconsin. A Study of Three Centuries of Culture Contact and Change. Memoirs of the American Philosophical Society, Vol. X. (Reprinted 1971 by Johnson Reprint Corporation.)

Kelkar, Ashok R.
1965   Participant Placement in Algonquian and Georgian. International Journal of American Linguistics 31: 195–205.

Kellogg, Louise Phelps
1917   Early Narratives of the Northwest, 1634–1699. New York, Barnes and Noble.
1924   A Wisconsin Anabasis. Wisconsin Magazine of History 7: 322–39.
1925   The French Regime in Wisconsin and the Northwest. Madison, State Historical Society of Wisconsin. (Reprinted 1968, Cooper Square Publishers, New York.)
1971   The British Regime in Wisconsin and the Northwest. New York, De Capo Press. (Reprint of 1935 edition, State Historical Society of Wisconsin.)

Kelly, William
1851   An Excursion to California Over the Prairie, Rocky Mountains, and Great Sierra Nevada. 2 Vols. London, Chapman and Hall.

Kenady, Freda M.
1914   The Early Indians of Council Bluffs. Based on interviews with General Greenville Dodge, Mr. Clutterbuck, etc. 8th Grade Report. Typescript. Council Bluffs, Iowa, Council Bluffs Public Library.

Kent, Donald H.
1974   Iroquois Indians—I: History of Pennsylvania Purchases from the Indians. New York, Garland Publishing Co.

KHC   Kansas Historical Collections. Topeka, Kansas State Historical Society.

Kinietz, W. Vernon
1940   The Indians of the Western Great Lakes, 1615–1760. Occasional Contributions from the Museum of Anthropology of the University of Michigan, No. 10. (Reprinted 1965 by the University of Michigan Press.)

Kinnard, Lawrence, ed.
1949   Spain in the Mississippi Valley, 1765–94. 3 Vols. Washington, D.C., American Historical Society.

Kinzie, Mrs. John H.
1856   Wau-Bun, the "Early Days" in the North West. New York, Derby and Jackson. (Reprinted 1930, Menasha, Wisconsin, Banta Publishing Company.)

Knopf, Richard, ed.
1960   Anthony Wayne: A Name in Arms. Pittsburgh, University of Pittsburgh Press.

Kohn, Richard H.
1975   Eagle and Sword: The Beginnings of the Military Establishment in America. New York, The Free Press.

Kopytoff, Igor
1964   Classifications of Religious Movements: Analytic and Synthetic. In, Proceedings of the Annual Meeting of the American Ethnological Society: 77–90. Seattle, University of Washington Press.

Kurz, Rudolph Friederich
1970   Journal of Rudolph Friederich Kurz. An Account of His Experiences

among Fur Traders and American Indians on the Mississippi and the Upper Missouri Rivers during the Years 1846 to 1852. Lincoln, University of Nebraska Press.

La Barre, Le Febure de
1683   Letter to M. de Seignelay. 4 November. CHNY 9: 201–10.

La Forest, Captain de
1714   Memoir on Detroit. WHC 16: 307–10.

La Galissonière, Michel
1748   Letter to the French Minister. WHC 17: 506–7.

La Hontan, Baron de
1703   New Voyages to North America. R. G. Thwaites, ed. (Reprint edition, New York, Burt Franklin Co.)

Lajeunesse, Ernest J.
1960   The Windsor Border Region. Toronto, University of Toronto Press.

La Jonquiere, Pierre Jacques
1750   Letter to the French Minister, September 20. WHC· 18: 68.
1751a   Letter to the French Minister, September 17. WHC 18: 81–82.
1751b   Letter to the French Minister, September 25. WHC 18: 88–89.

Landes, Ruth
1963   Potawatomi Medicine. Transactions of the Kansas Academy of Science 66: 553–99.
1970   The Prairie Potawatomi: Tradition and Ritual in the Twentieth Century. Madison, University of Wisconsin Press.
1971   The Ojibwa Woman. New York, Norton.

La Potherie, Claude Charles le Roy
1911   History of the Savage Peoples Who Are Allies of New France. In, Blair 1911. I: 275–372; II. 13–138.

Latrobe, Charles Joseph
1835   The Rambler in North America. 2 Vols. London, R. B. Seeby and W. Burnside.

Law, Judge
1958   The Colonial History of Vincennes. Vincennes, Ind., Vincennes Historical and Antiquarian Society.

Lawson, Publius V.
1920   The Potawatomi. Wisconsin Archaeologist 19: 41–116.

Le Sueur, Pierre Charles
1700   Journal Extract. WHC 16: 181–82.

Lignery, Constant Marchand de
1728   Letter to Beauharnois. WHC 17: 32–33.

Linton, Ralph
1943   Nativistic Movements. American Anthropologist 45: 230–40.

Lipscomb, A. A., & A. E. Bergh, eds.
1904   The Writings of Thomas Jefferson. 20 Vols. Washington, D.C., Thomas Jefferson Memorial Association of the United States.

Lohman, Arthur H.
1907   Early Days in Two Rivers, Wisconsin. Milwaukee.

Long, John
1791   Voyages and Travels of an Indian Interpreter and Trader Describing the Manners and Customs of the North American Indians. In EWT 2.

Longuevil, Charles le Moyne
1752   Report to the French Minister. WHC 19: 111–16.

Lovejoy, Julia
1947   Letters of Julia Lovejoy. Kansas Historical Quarterly, Nov., 378–79.

Lower, A. R. M.
1961   The Growth of Population in Canada. In, V. W. Blader, ed. Canadian Population and Northern Colonization. Toronto, University of Toronto Press.

Lowrie, Walter, and
Matthew St. Clair Clarke
1832/1834   American State Papers, Indian Affairs. 2 Vols. Washington, D.C., U.S. Government Printing Office.

Lurie, Nancy O.
1957   The Indian Claims Commission Act. In, Simpson & Yinger 1957: 56–70.

Lyons, Emory J.
1945   Isaac McCoy: His Plan of and Work for Indian Colonization. Fort Hays Kansas State College Studies, General Series. No. 9. Topeka.

MacCauley, Clay
1893   The Dreamers among the North American Indians, as Illustrative of the Origin of Forms of Religion. The Japan Weekly Mail, March 18: 338–40.

McCormick, Calvin
1892   The Memoir of Miss Eliza McCoy. Dallas, Texas. (Privately printed. Copy in University of Kansas Research Library.)

McCoy, Isaac
1821/1846   Journals and Correspondence. Isaac McCoy Collection. Topeka, Kansas State Historical Society.
1835/1838   The Annual Register of Indian Affairs within the Indian (or Western) Territory. (Printed privately in several locations.)
1840   History of Baptist Indian Missions: Embracing Remarks on the Former and Present Condition of the Aboriginal Tribes: Their Former Settlement within the Indian Territory, and Their Future Prospects. Washington, D.C.

McDermott, John Francis, ed.
1970   Travelers on the Western Frontier. Urbana, University of Illinois Press.

McDonald, Daniel
1899   Removal of the Pottawattomie Indians from Northern Indiana. Plymouth, D. McDonald & Company

McElroy, Ann
1964   Kansas Potawatomi Study Field Notes. Madison, Wisconsin State Historical Society.
1965   The Value of Ethnohistorical Reconstructions of American Indian Typical Personality: The Case of the Potawatomi. Transactions of the Kansas Academy of Science 68, No. 2.
1968   Contemporary and Traditional Prairie Potawatomi Child Life. O-P Series. Ann Arbor, University Microfilms.

McInnis, Edgar
1969   Canada: A Political and Social History. 3rd edition. Toronto, Holt, Rinehart and Winston.

McKee, Irving
1941   The Trail of Death: Letters of Benjamin Marie Petit. Indianapolis, Indiana Historical Society.

McKeel, H. Scudder
1937   Report on the Michigan Indians. Applied Anthropology Unit, U.S. Office of Indian Affairs. (Mimeo. Potawatomi Files, Washington, D.C., Bureau of Indian Affairs.)

McKenney, Thomas J., and James Hall
1838   History of the Indian Tribes of North America, with Biographical Sketches and Anecdotes of the Principal Chiefs. Vol. 1. Philadelphia. (Reprinted 1967 by the U.S. Government Printing Office.)

MacLeod, William Christie
1928   The American Indian Frontier. New York, Knopf.

McMurtrie, D. C., and Albert H. Allen
1930   Jotham Meeker, Pioneer Printer of Kansas. Chicago, Eyncourt Press.

Mahon, John K.
1958   Anglo-American Methods of Indian Warfare, 1676–1794. Mississippi Valley Historical Review 45: 258–75.

Malone, Dumas, ed.
1932   Dictionary of American Biography. 20 Vols. New York, Scribners.

Mann, Francis Walker, Jr.
1935   Father Pierre-Jean de Smet, S.J.: His Influence on the History of the Trans-Mississippi West. M.A. Thesis. Los Angeles, University of Southern California.

Mardock, Robert W.
1971   The Reformers and the American Indian. Columbia, University of Missouri Press.

Marest, Father Joseph
1706 Letter to Governor Vaudreuil. WHC 16: 232–39.
1708 Letter to M. de Vaudreuil, June 4. MPHC 33: 383–87.
1712a Letter to Governor Vaudreuil, June 21. WHC 16: 288–92.
1712b Letter to Rev. B. Cermon, Cascaskias, November 9. JR 66: 219–95.

Margary, Pierre
1876 Decouvertes et Establissements des Francais dans l'Amerique Septenrionale. Paris. (English translation on microfilm, 4 Rolls, Burton Historical Collections. Detroit Public Library. Citations in this book refer to the microfilmed translation, by roll and frame number.)

Marin, Pierre de
1730 Letter to Governor Beauharnois, May 11. WHC 17: 88–100.

Marquis—Who's Who
1963 Who Was Who in America, Historical Volume, 1607–1896. Chicago, Marquis—Who's Who.

Martin, Deborah B.
1913 History of Brown County, Wisconsin. Chicago, Clarke Company.

Martin, George W.
1904 Extinction of Reservation Titles in Kansas. Transactions of the Kansas State Historical Society 8: 86–103.

Marston, Major Morrell, U.S.A.
1820 Letter to Rev. Dr. Jedidiah Morse. In, Blair 1911, Vol. 2: 139–82.

Martin, Morgan L.
1888 Narrative of Morgan L. Martin. WHC 11: 385–415.

Mason, Carol, and Ronald J. Mason
1975 Personal Communication Concerning Potawatomi Occupancy of Rock Island.

Mason, Edward G.
1890 Early Chicago and Illinois. Fergus' Historical Series, Chicago.

Mason, Ronald J.
1974 Huron Island and the Island of the Poutouatamis. In, E. Johnson, Aspects of Upper Great Lakes Anthropology, pp. 149–56. St. Paul, Minnesota Historical Society.

Matson, Nehemiah
1876 Sketch of Shaubena, Pottawatamie Chief. WHC 7: 415–21.
1880 Memories of Shaubena. Chicago, Donnely, Gassette & Lloyd.

Matthews, John J.
1961 The Osages: Children of the Middle Waters. Norman, University of Oklahoma Press.

Meyer, Alfred H.
1954 Circulation and Settlement Patterns of the Calumet Region of Northwest Indiana and Northeast Illinois: The First State of Occupance—the Pottawatomie and the Fur Trader—1830. Annals of the Association of American Geographers 44: 245–74.

MGC Military Series C. See, Public Archives of Canada.

MHS Archives and Collections of the Missouri Historical Society, St. Louis.

Michigan Pioneer and Historical Society
1877/1929 Historical Collections. 40 Vols. Lansing.

Michelson, Truman
n.d. Buck Green and Johnnie Green's Pack: Prairie Potawatomi Test. (English translation only.) BAE Ms. 2948.
n.d. Notebook on Linguistics, Ethnology, and Physical Anthropology. BAE Ms. 1854.
1911/1912 Potawatomi Linguistic Notes from Grover Allen. BAE Ms. 2703.
1915 The Linguistic Classification of Potawatomi. Proceedings of the National Academy of Science 1: 450–52.
1917 Linguistics; Ethnology, Notes. BAE Ms. 2743.
1923 On the Origin of the So-Called Dream Dance of the Central Algonkians. American Anthropologist 25: 277–78.
1924 Further Remarks on the Origin of the So-Called Dream Dance of the

Central Algonkians. American Anthropologist 26: 293–94.

1925   Notes on the Fox Society Known as Those Who Worship the Little Spotted Buffalo. Bureau of American Ethnology Annual Report 40: 504.

1926   Final Notes on the Central Algonkian Dream Dance. American Anthropologist 28: 573–76.

1934   The Identification of the Mascoutens. American Anthropologist 36: 226–33.

Mooney, James
1892   The Ghost Dance Religion. 14th Annual Report of the Bureau of American Ethnology, Part 2. Washington, D.C., U.S. Government Printing Office.

Mooney, James, and J. N. B. Hewitt
1910   Potawatomi. In, Hodge 1910 2: 289–93.

Moore, Bessie Ellen
1939   Life and Work of Robert Simmerwell. Unpub. M.A. Thesis. Lawrence, University of Kansas.

Moorehead, Warren K.
1899   The Indian Tribes of Ohio. Ohio Archaeological and Historical Society Publications 7.

Morgan, Loyd Henry
1959   The Indian Journals. Leslie A. White, ed. Ann Arbor, University of Michigan Press.

Morse, Jedediah
1822   A Report to the Secretary of War of the United States on Indian Affairs. New York, Augustus M. Kelly.

Morstad, Alexander E.
1971   The Reverend Erik Olsen Morstad—His Missionary Work Among the Wisconsin Pottawatomie Indians. Clearwater, Fla., The Eldnar Press.

MPHC   Historical Collections of the Michigan Pioneer and Historical Society.

Murdock, George Peter
1965   Algonkian Social Organization. In, M. E. Spiro, ed., Context and Meaning in Social Anthropology, pp. 24–38. New York, The Free Press.

Murphy, Joseph Francis
1961   Potawatomi Indians of the West: Origins of the Citizen Band. Unpub. Ph.D. dissertation. Norman, University of Oklahoma.

Murray, Florence B.
1963   Muskoka and Haliburton: 1615–1875. A Collection of Documents. Toronto, The Champlain Society.

NAM   National Archives Microcopy. See, National Archives and Records Service, and appropriate Microcopy number.

Nasatir, A. P., ed.
1952   Before Lewis and Clark: Documents Illustrating the History of the Missouri, 1785–1804. 2 Vols. St. Louis Historical Documents Foundation.

NASP-IA   The New American State Papers—Indian Affairs. See, Loring B. Priest, ed.

National Archives and Records Service
1800/1824   National Archives Microcopy M 15. Letters Sent by the Secretary of War. Washington, D.C.

n.d.   Finding Aid—History of Agencies and Superintendencies Responsible for Potawatomi. Washington, D.C., National Archives.

1801/1869   National Archives Microcopy T–494. Documents Relating to the Negotiation of Ratified and Unratified Treaties with Various Indian Tribes. 10 Rolls. Washington, D.C.

1814/1851   National Archives Microcopy M 1. Records of the Bureau of Indian Affairs; Michigan Superintendency. Washington, D.C.

1824/1880   National Archives Microcopy 234. Letters Received by the Office of Indian Affairs. 962 Microfilm Rolls. Washington, D.C.

Nichols, John, Billy Daniels, et al.
1974/1976   Potawatomi Language Lessons and Materials. Wisconsin Native

American Languages Project, University of Wisconsin-Milwaukee.

Nicholson, W.
1934   A Tour of Indian Agencies in Kansas and the Indian Territory in 1870. Kansas Historical Quarterly 3: 289–326.

NMC   National Map Collections. See, Public Archives of Canada.

O'Callaghan, E. B., and B. Fernow, eds.
1853/1887   Documents Relative to the Colonial History of the State of New York. 15 Vols. Albany.

O'Connor, Mary Helen
1942   Potawatomi Land Cessions in the "Old Northwest." Unpub. M.A. Thesis. Ithaca, Cornell University.

O'Kane, Harry Ward
1934   The Work of the Methodist Church among the Potawatomi Indians. Unpub. M.A. Thesis. Evanston, Northwestern University.

Otterbein, Keith
1972   The Anthropology of War. In, J. Honigman, ed., The Handbook of Social and Cultural Anthropology, pp. 932–58. Chicago, Rand-McNally.

Ouashala
1722   Speech of Ouashala (a Fox Chief) at a Council in M. de Montigny's house, September 6. WHC 16: 418–22.

Paine, Robert, ed.
1971   Patrons and Brokers in the East Arctic. Newfoundland Social and Economic Papers No. 2. Toronto, University of Toronto Press.

Park, Robert E.
1936   Succession, An Ecological Concept. American Sociological Review 1: 171–79.

Parkman, Francis
1870   History of the Conspiracy of Pontiac. 6th edition. Boston.
1879   LaSalle and the Discovery of the Great West. Boston, Little, Brown and Company. (Reprinted by New American Library, 1963, New York.)

Parsons, Joseph H.
1960   Civilizing the Indians of the Old Northwest: 1800–1810. Indiana Magazine of History 56: 212–16.

Parsons, Lynn Hudson
1973   "A Perpetual Harrow Upon My Feelings": John Quincy Adams and the American Indian. The New England Quarterly, September: 339–79.

Patton, William
1954   Journal of a Visit to the Indian Missions, Missouri Conference. Bulletin of the Missouri Historical Society 10: 167–80.

Peckham, Howard, ed.
1939   George Croghan's Journal of His Trip to Detroit. Ann Arbor, University of Michigan Press.

Peckham, Howard H.
1961   Pontiac and the Indian Uprising. Chicago, University of Chicago Press.
1964   The Colonial Wars: 1689–1762. Chicago, University of Chicago Press.

Pelzer, Louis
1943   The Prairie Log Books. Chicago, Caxton Club.

Perrot, Nicolas, Sieur Cadillac, et al.
1695   Reports to Governor Frontenac. WHC 16: 160–65. (Also in CHNY 9: 619–21.)

Perrot, Nicolas
1911   Memoir on the Manners, Customs, and Religion of the Savages of North America. In, Blair 1911 1: 25–275.

Petit, Benjamin Marie
1941   The Trail of Death: Letters of Benjamin Marie Petit. Irving McKee, ed. Indiana State Historical Publications 14 (1).

PF   Potawatomi File. See, Great Lakes Indian Archives Project.

Phillips, Paul C.
1961   The Fur Trade. 2 Vols. Norman, University of Oklahoma Press.

Pike, Kenneth, and Barbara Erickson
1964   Conflated field structures in Potawatomi and Arabic. International

Journal of American Linguistics 30: 201–12.

Plain, Nicholas
  n.d.   The History of the Chippewas of Sarnia and the History of the Sarnia Reserve. Mimeo. (In, Department of Indian Affairs Library, Ottawa, Canada.)

Plumb, Ralph G.
  1904   A History of Manitowoc County. Manitowoc, Brandt Publishing Co.

Pokagon, Simon
  n.d.   The Lord's Prayer. (Translated by the late Chief Simon Pokagon into the Pottawattomie Language and printed on birch-bark. Copy in Newberry Library, Chicago.)
  1901   Pottawatamie book of Genesis. Legend of the Creation of Man (printed on birch-bark). Hartford, Michigan, C. H. Engle. (Copy in Newberry Library, Chicago.)

Potawatomi Chiefs
  1742   Speech to Beauharnois, July 16. WHC 17: 393–94.
  1796   Speech of the Putawatimies Chiefs of Chikago, July 17. Wayne Papers, Historical Society of Pennsylvania.

Preston, Captain William
  1796   Vocabulary, 7 pp. (Copy in Department of Interior Schedule from originals in possession of author's grandson.) BAE Ms. 6.

Priest, Loring B., ed.
  1972   The New American State Papers: Indian Affairs. 13 Vols. Wilmington, Del., Scholarly Research, Inc.

Prucha, Francis Paul
  1969   The Sword of the Republic: The United States Army on the Frontier—1783–1846. New York, Macmillan.
  1970   American Indian Policy in the Formative Years: The Indian Trade and Intercourse Acts, 1790–1834. Lincoln, University of Nebraska Press.

Public Archives of Canada
  n.d.   Military Series C. Mss. Collections.
  n.d.   National Map Collections.
  n.d.   Record Group 10—Indian Affairs (Red Series, Eastern Canada). Ottawa, Ontario.

Quaife, Milo M.
  1913   Chicago and the Old Northwest, 1673–1834. Chicago, University of Chicago Press.
  1918   Documents: The Chicago Treaty of 1833. Wisconsin Magazine of History I: 287–303.
  1931   The John Askins Papers. 2 Vols. Burton Historical Collections, Detroit Public Library.
  1940   War on the Detroit: The Chronicles of Thomas Vervheres De Boucherville and the Capitulation by an Ohio Volunteer. Chicago, Lakeside Press.
  1958   The Seige of Detroit in 1763: The Journal of Pontiac's Conspiracy and John Rutherford's Narrative of a Captivity. Chicago, Lakeside Press.

Quimby, George I., Jr.
  1939   Some notes on kinship and kinship terminology among the Potawatomi of the Huron. Papers of the Michigan Academy of Science, Arts and Letters 25: 553–63.
  1966   Indian Culture and European Trade Goods. Madison, University of Wisconsin Press.

RAIC   Report on the Affairs of the Indians of Canada. See, Special Commissioners, 1844 & 1858.

Ramezay, Sieur de (and Bégon)
  1715   Letters to the French Minister, September 13 & 15. WHC 16: 311–22.

Randolph, Thomas Jefferson, ed.
  1829   Memoir, Correspondence, and Miscellanies, from the Papers of Thomas Jefferson. 4 Vols. Charlottesville, Virginia.

Raudot, Antoine Denis
  1709   Memoir Concerning the Differ-

ent Indian Nations of North America. In, Kinietz 1940: 339–410.

Ray, Arthur J.
1974   Indians in the Fur Trade: Their Role as Hunters, Trappers, and Middlemen in the Lands Southwest of Hudson Bay, 1660–1870. Toronto, University of Toronto Press.

Reed, Charles S.
1929   Chief Simon Pokagon was last leader of Pottawattomies. The American Indian 3: 8–9.

Reed, E.
1829   A Study of the Pottawatomie Language. Detroit Gazette, August 6, Vol. 13, No. 629: 1–2.

Reynolds, John
1887   Pioneer History of Illinois. Chicago, Fergus' Historical Series.

RG 10   Record Group 10. See, Public Archives of Canada.

RG 75   Record Group 75. See, Bureau of Indian Affairs, 1804/1904.

Richerter, Emma Cones .
1933 A History of Silver Lake, Kansas. (Privately published. Copy in Kansas Collection, University of Kansas, Spencer Research Library.)

Richardson, Major John
1902   Richardson's War of 1812. Edited and with Notes and a Life of the Author, by A. C. Casselman. Toronto, Historical Publishing Co.
1924   Tecumsah and Richardson. The Story of a Trip to Walpole Island and Port Sarnia. Toronto, Ontario Book Company.

Ritzenthaler, Robert E.
1953   The Potawatomi Indians of Wisconsin. Bulletins of the Public Museum of the City of Milwaukee, Vol. 19, No. 3.

Robertson, N. A., & D. Riker
1942   The John Tipton Papers. 3 Vols. Indiana Historical Collections, Vols. 24–26.

Rodnick, David
1936   Report on the Indians of Kansas. Applied Anthropology. Washington, D.C., U.S. Office of Indian Affairs (mimeo.).

Rogers, E. S., and Flora Tobobondung
1973   Parry Island Farmers: A Period of Change in the Way of Life of the Algonkians of Southern Ontario. Mss. Draft. Toronto, Royal Ontario Museum.

Rogin, Michael Paul
1975   Fathers and Children: Andrew Jackson and the Subjugation of the American Indian. New York, Knopf.

Royce, Charles C.
1900   Indian Land Cessions in the United States. 18th Annual Report of the Bureau of American Ethnology, Part 2. Washington, D.C. (Reprinted 1971, New York, Arno Press.)

Sabrevois, Jacques de
1717   Letter to Marquis de Vaudreuil, 8 April. MPHC 33: 582–84.
1718   Memoir on the Savages of Canada as far as the Mississippi River, Describing their Customs and Trade. WHC 16: 363–76.

Sahlins, Marshall D.
1961   The Segmentary Lineage: An Organization of Predatory Expansion. American Anthropologist 63: 322–36.
1968   Tribesmen. Englewood Cliffs, N.J., Prentice-Hall.

Saint Cosme, Jean Francois Busson de
1969   A Letter to the Bishop of Quebec. In, Kellogg 1917: 342–61.

St. Lusson, Simon Francois Daumont
1671   Report on exploration and annexation of lands near Lake Superior. CHNY 9: 803–4.

Salzer, Robert J.
1972   Bear-Walking: A Shamanistic Phenomena Among the Potawatomi Indians of Wisconsin. Wisconsin Archaeologist 53: 110–46.

Scanlan, Charles M.
1915   Indian Massacre and Captivity of Hall Girls. Milwaukee, Reis Publishing Company.

Schoolcraft, Henry R.
1853/1857   Information Respecting the History, Condition and Prospects of the Indian Tribes of the United States. 6 Vols. Philadelphia, Lippincott, Grambo & Co.

Schultz, George A.
1972   An Indian Canaan: Isaac McCoy and the Vision of an Indian State. Norman, University of Oklahoma Press.

Schusky, Ernest L.
1965   A Manual for Kinship Analysis. New York, Holt, Rinehart and Winston.

Scull, G. D., ed. & trans.
1967   Voyages of Pierre Esprit Radisson. Boston, Prince Society.

Secretary of the Interior
1908   A Report on an Investigation of the Claims of the Pottawatomie Indians of Wisconsin. House of Representatives Document #830, 1st. Sess., 60th Congress.

Service, E. R.
1962   Primitive Social Organization. New York, Random House.

Sharp, W. A.
1934   The Pioneer Pottawatamies. Hamburg, Iowa (Reprinted by the Hamburg Reporter).

Shea, John Gilmary
1853   Discovery and Exploration of the Mississippi Valley; with the Original Narratives of Marquette, Allouez, Membré, Hennepin, and Anastase Douay. New York, Redfield.

1857   History of the Catholic Missions among the Indian Tribes of the United States, 1529–1854. New York, E. Dunigan.

Sheehan, Bernard W.
1969   Indian-White Relations in Early America: A Review Essay. William and Mary Quarterly 26: 267–86.

1973   Seeds of Extinction: Jeffersonian Philanthropy and the American Indian. Chapel Hill, University of North Carolina Press.

Silverberg, James
1957   The Kickapoo Indians: First One Hundred Years of White Contact in Wisconsin. Wisconsin Archaeologist 38: 61–182.

Simmerwell, Robert
1832   Catechism and hymns translated into the Potawatomi Language; preceded by an alphabet and notes on phonetics. Potawatomi Ms. No. 6, Ayer Collection Ms. No. 1668, Chicago, Newberry Library.

Simpson, George E., and J. M. Yinger
1957   American Indians and American Life. The Annals of the American Academy of Political and Social Sciences, Vol. 311.

Skinner, Alanson
1913   How I Became a Dreamer. Southern Workman 42: 110–14.

1915   The Society of Dreamers. In, Associations and Ceremonies of the Menominee Indians. American Museum of Natural History Anthropological Papers 13: 173–82.

1923   A Further Note on the Origin of the Dream Dance of the Central Algonkian and Southern Siouan Indians. American Anthropologist 25: 427–28.

1924/1927   The Mascoutens or Prairie Potawatomi Indians. Bulletins of the Public Museum of the City of Milwaukee 6.

1925   Final Observations on the Central Algonkian Dream Dance. American Anthropologist 27: 340–43.

Slotkin, J. S.
1957   The Menomini Pow-Wow: A Study in Cultural Decay. Milwaukee Public Museum Publications in Anthropology, No. 4.

Smith, Alice E.
1973   The History of Wisconsin, Vol. 1: From Exploration to Statehood. Madison, Wisconsin State Historical Society.

Smith, Dwight, ed.
1952   From Greenville to Fallen Timbers: A Journal of the Wayne Campaign. Indianapolis, Indiana Historical Society.

Smith, Dwight
1954   Notes on the Wabash River in 1795. Indiana Magazine of History 50: 285–91.
1957   Indian Land Cessions in Northern Ohio and Southeastern Michigan. Northwest Ohio Quarterly 29: 27–45.

Smith, Huron H.
1933   Ethnobotany of the Forest Potawatomi Indian. Bulletin of the Public Museum of the City of Milwaukee 7: 1–230.

Smith, William E.
1928   The Oregon Trail through Pottawatomie County. Collections of the Kansas State Historical Society 17: 435–64.

Smith, William Henry, ed.
1882   The St. Clair Papers. 2 Vols. Cincinnati, Clarke & Co.

Sosin, Jack M.
1961   Whitehall and the Wilderness: The Middle West in British Colonial Policy, 1760–1775.
1967   The Revolutionary Frontier: 1763–1783. New York, Holt, Rinehart and Winston.

Special Commissioners
1844   Report on the Affairs of the Indians in Canada. Appendix EEE, 1845, Vol. 4, Appendix No. 2, Journals of the Legislative Assembly of the Province of Canada (Acronym 87 LEAS, Call, Can. Doc. 516).
1858   Report of the Special Commissioners to Investigate Indian Affairs in Canada. Appendix No. 21, Vol. 16, No. 6. Appendix to the Journals of the Legislative Assembly, Province of Canada (Acronym 87, LEAS, Call, Can. Doc. 516).

Stacey, C. P.
1966/——   The British forces in North America during the Seven Years War. DCB 3: xxiv–xxx.

Stanley, George F. G.
1964   The Indians in the War of 1812. In, Morris Zaslow, ed., The Defended Border. Toronto, Macmillan Co.

Steele, C. Hoy
1972   American Indians and Urban Life: A Community Study. Unpub. Ph.D. Dissertation. Lawrence, University of Kansas.

Stegner, Wallace
1964   The Gathering of Zion: The Story of the Mormon Trail. New York, McGraw-Hill.

Stephens, E.
1881   Letters to the Commissioner of Indian Affairs concerning the Sioux Dance on the Menominee Reservation, June 18 & 30, August 23, September 2 & 6, & October 2. Record Group 75, National Archives.

Stevens, Sylvester K., ed.
1940/1943   Papers of Colonel Henry Boquet. 18 Vols. Mimeo. Harrisburg, Pennsylvania.

Stiles, Henry R.
1906   Joutel's Journal of LaSalle's Last Voyage, 1684–87. Albany, J. McDonough.

Still, Bayrd
1948   Milwaukee—The History of a City. Madison, Wisconsin State Historical Society.

Stotz, Charles M.
1958.   Defense in the Wilderness. Western Pennsylvania Historical Magazine. 41: 99–101.

Stout, David B., E. Wheeler-Voegelin, and E. J. Blasingham
1974   Sac, Fox and Iowa Indians 2. New York, Garland Publishing Co.

Strong, William D.
1926   The Indian Tribes of the Chicago Region with Special Reference to the Illinois and the Potawatomie. Field Museum Leaflet 24: 17–34.

Stuart, Benjamin F.
1922   Deportation of Menominee and His Tribe of Pottawattomie Indians. Indiana Magazine of History 18: 257–58.

Sturtevant, Gene
1934   The Dream Dance Drum. Wisconsin Archaeologist 13: 86–90.

Surtees, R. J.
1966   Indian Reserve Policy in Upper Canada, 1830–1845. Unpub. M.A. Thesis. Ottawa, Ontario, Carleton University.

Svanda, Harry
1965   Preliminary Inventory of the Records of the Potawatomi Indian Agency. Bureau of Indian Affairs, Record Group 75 (Materials at Federal Records Center, Kansas City, Missouri).

Swanton, John R.
1946   The Indians of the Southeastern United States. Bureau of American Ethnology, Bulletin No. 137. Washington, D.C., Smithsonian Institution.

Tanner, Helen Hornbeck, and Erminie Wheeler-Voegelin
1974   Indians of Ohio and Indiana Prior to 1795. New York, Garland Publishing Co.

Tax, Sol
1972   Let the Indian Speak. In, Clash of Cultures: The American Indian in Higher Education. Canton, N.Y., St. Lawrence University

Temple, Wayne C.
1958   Indian Villages of the Illinois Country. Scientific Papers, Vol. 2, Part 2. Springfield, Illinois State Museum.

Thornbrough, Gayle, ed.
1957   Outpost on the Wabash, 1787–1791. Indiana Historical Society Publications 19.

Thwaites, Reuben Gold, ed.
1896/1901   The Jesuit Relations and Allied Documents. 73 Vols. Cleveland, The Burrows Brothers Company.
1904/1907   Early Western Travels, 1748–1846. 32 Vols. Cleveland, Arthur H. Clark Co.

Tiedke, Kenneth E.
1951   A Study of the Hannahville Indian Community. Michigan State Agricultural Experimental Station, Special Bulletin 369.

Tonty, Henri de
1693   Memoir Sent in 1693, on the Discovery of the Mississippi and the Neighboring Nations by M. de la Salle from the Year 1678 to the Time of His Death, and by the Sieur de Tonty to the Year 1691. IHC 1: 128–64 (Also in HCL 1).

TP-US   The Territorial Papers of the United States. See, C. E. Carter.

Trennert, Robert A., Jr.
1975   Alternative to Extinction. Philadelphia, Temple University Press.

Tucker, Glenn
1956   Tecumseh: Vision of Glory. New York, Bobbs-Merrill Company.

Turner, Jesse
1911   Reminisences of Kalamazoo. MPHC 18.

Tyler, S. Lyman
1974   A History of Indian Policy. Washington, D.C., U.S. Government Printing Office.

United States Congress
1954   Joint hearing before the subcommittees of the committees on Interior and Insular affairs. 83rd Congress, 2nd Sess., on S. 2743 and H.R. 7318, Part 2, February 28. Washington, D.C., U.S. Government Printing Office.

Utley, Robert M.
1967   Frontiersmen in Blue: The United States Army and the Indian, 1848–1865. New York, Macmillan.

Van Buren, A. D. P.
1908   Indian Reminiscences of Calhoun and Kalamazoo Counties. MPHC 10.

Van der Zee, Jacob
1913   Episodes in the Early History of

Western Iowa Country. Iowa Journal of History and Politics, July: 3–43.

Vansina, Jan
1961   Oral Tradition: A Study in Historical Methodology. Chicago, University of Chicago Press.

Vaudreuil, Philippe, Marquis de Rigault
1710   Letter to M. de Pontchartrain. WHC 16: 263–65.
1711a   Words to the Savages who came down from the Upper Country. MPHC 33: 503–6.
1711b   Memorandum to serve as instructions to the Officers and Voyageurs dispatched to bring down to Montreal the Savages of the Upper Country. MPHC 33: 497–502.
1711c   Letter to Pontchartrain, October 25. CHNY 9: 858–59.
1712   Letter to M. de Pontchartrain, November 6. CHNY 9: 862–65.
1716   Letter to the Council of Marine, October 14. WHC 16: 341–44.
1717a   Talk of the Poutouatamis and the Reply of M. de Vaudreuil. MPHC 33: 586–87.
1717b   A Talk with the Ottawas and their Reply, June 24. MPHC 33: 584–85.
1717c   Letter to the Duke of Orleans, October 12. MPHC 33: 589–91.
1719   Letter to Council of Marine. WHC 16: 380–82.
1720   Letter to Council, October 22. WHC 16: 392–95.
1723   A Letter to the French Minister, October 11. WHC 16: 433–39.

Vieau, Andrew J., Sr.
1888   The Narrative of Andrew J. Vieau, Sr. WHC 11: 218–33.

Vieau, Peter J.
1900   The Narrative of Peter J. Vieau. WHC 15: 458–69.

Vincent, John
1965   Midwest Indians and Frontier Photography. The Annals of Iowa 38: 26–35.

Viola, Herman J.
1974   Thomas L. McKenney, Architect of America's Early Indian Policy: 1816: 1830. Chicago, Swallow Press.

Vogel, Virgil
1962   Indian Place Names in Illinois. JISHS 55: 5–30, 157–89, 271–308, 385–458 (Reprinted as one volume).

Wheeler-Voegelin, Erminie
1974a   Indians of Northwest Ohio. New York, Garland Publishing Co.

Wheeler-Voegelin, Erminie, E. J. Blasingham, and D. R. Libby
1974   Miami, Wea, and Eel-River Indians of Southern Indiana. New York, Garland Publishing Co.

Wheeler-Voegelin, Erminie, and J. A. Jones
1974   Indians of Western Illinois and Southern Wisconsin. New York, Garland Publishing Company.

Wheeler-Voegelin, Erminie, and David B. Stout
1974   Indians of Illinois and Northwestern Indiana. New York, Garland Publishing Company.

Wheeler-Voegelin, Erminie, and Helen Hornbeck Turner
1974   Indians of Northern Ohio and Southeastern Michigan. New York, Garland Publishing Co.

Wade, Lt. John
1795   Extracts from a Journal. Mss. Wayne Papers, Pennsylvania Historical Society.

Wallace, Anthony F. C.
1956   Revitalization Movements. American Anthropologist 58: 264–81.
1966   Religion: An Anthropological View. New York, Random House.
1970a   The Death and Rebirth of the Seneca. New York, Knopf.
1970b   Prelude to Disaster: The Course of Indian-White Relations Which Led to the Black Hawk War of 1831. In, E. M. Whitney, ed., The Black Hawk War: 1831–1832. Col-

lections of the Illinois State Historical Library 35: 1–51.

Walters, Mrs. Alta P.
1924   Shabonee. JISHS 18: 381–97.

Wand, Augustin, C., S.J.
1962   The Jesuits in Territorial Kansas: 1827–1861. St. Mary's, Kansas, The St. Mary's Star Co.

Washburn, Wilcomb E.
1973   The American Indian and the United States: A Documentary History. 2 Vols. New York, Random House.
1975   The Indian in America. New York, Harper & Row.

Wax, Murray L.
1968   Religion and Magic. In, James A. Clifton, ed., Introduction to Cultural Anthropology, pp. 224–43. Boston, Houghton-Mifflin.
1971   Indian Americans: Unity and Diversity. Englewood Cliffs, N.J., Prentice-Hall.

Weighley, Russell F.
1967   History of the United States Army. New York, Macmillan.

Wentworth, John
1881   Fort Dearborn. An Address, May 21st. Chicago, Fergus' Historical Series 16.

WHC   Wisconsin Historical Collections. See, Wisconsin State Historical Society.

Whickhar, J. W.
1921   Shabonee's Account of Tippecanoe. Indiana Magazine of History 17: 353–63.

Whitney, Ellen M., ed.
1970   The Black Hawk War: 1831–1832. Collections of the Illinois State Historical Library 35.

Williams, Edward G., ed.
1959   The Orderly Book of Colonel Henry Boquet's Expedition against the Ohio Indians, 1764. Western Pennsylvania Historical Magazine 42: 9–34, 179–200, 283–302.

Williams, Mentor L.
1953   John Kinzie's Narrative of the Fort Dearborn Massacre. JISHS 46: 343–62.

Wilson, H. Clyde
1956   A New Interpretation of the Wild Rice District of Wisconsin. American Anthropologist 58: 1059–64.

Wing, George W.
n.d.   Collection of Newspaper Articles on History of Kewaunee County. Microform Room, Madison, Wisconsin State Historical Society.

Winger, Otho
1939   The Potawatomi Indians. Elgin, Elgin Press.

Winter, George
1948   The Journal and Indian Paintings of George Winter, 1837–1839 (A special publication of the Indiana Historical Society). Chicago, Lakeside Press.

Wisconsin State Historical Society
1855/1931   Collections of the Wisconsin State Historical Society. 31 Vols. Madison.

Woehrmann, Paul
1971   At the Headwaters of the Maumee: A History of Forts at Fort Wayne. Indianapolis, Indiana Historical Society.

Wooster, W. M.
1907a   Report to the Commissioner of Indian Affairs on the Enrollment of Wisconsin Potawatomi in that state and in Canada. In, Secretary of the Interior, 1908.
1907b   Census Roll of Wisconsin Potawatomi in Canada and the United States; and, Selected Documents Relating to the "Wooster Roll." Records of the Bureau of Indian Affairs, RG 75. Wooster Roll (Special Series A, Box 2), and 98659-1907-053-Carter, Part 1. National Archives, Washington, D.C.

Wright, Gary A.
1967   Some Aspects of Early and Mid-Seventeenth Century Exchange Net-

works in the Western Great Lakes. Michigan Archaeologist 13: 181–97.

York, Samuel

1700   Information respecting the Western Indians. 2 September. CHNY 4: 748–50.

Zurcher, Louis A.

1967   The Leader and the Lost: A Case Study of Indigenous Leadership in a Poverty Program Community Action Committee. Genetic Psychology Monographs 76: 23–93.

1968   Selection of Indigenous Leadership. In, Hans B. C. Spiegel, ed., Citizen Participation in Urban Development, Vol. 1. Washington, D.C., NTL Institution for Applied Behavioral Science.

INDEX

Abtegizhek—the elder (Half Day), P. leader, 229, 239, 320, 322, 324, 329, 332, 343

Abtegizhek—the younger, P. leader, 336

A'chawi. *See* Winnebago

Achirwachronnon. *See* French River Algonquian bands

Adams, President John Quincy, 248

Advisory committee. *See* P. tribe, history of: business committee of

Alcoholic beverages: 80–81, 91, 94, 191, 218, 253, 316, 324, 437 n. 73; Wayne blocks use of at Greenville treaty, 147

Algonkin bands, 29

Alliances: English-tribal, 71, 95–96, 162–63; French-tribal, 70–71, 78, 102–4; intertribal, 70–71, 82–83, 87–89, 198–202, 294–95, 326–27, 360–61, 440; United States–tribal, 160

Allouez, Reverend Claude, 34–35, 49–51, 65, 74–75

Amalgamation, policy of, 336–37

Amaranth (river steamer), 336–37

American Bottoms, 189, 194–95

American Fur Company, 332

American Indian Movement, 440–42

Amherstburg, Ontario, 155, 285, 305. *See also* Fort Malden

Amikwa (Bear), Ojibwa clan community, 11

Andaste tribe, 136

Anderson, Thomas G., British Indian agent, 284–85, 302, 306

André, Reverend Louis, 111, 123–24

Annexation: of Illinois country by Louisiana in 1718, 89; of upper lake country by France in 1671, 46, 63–64, 73–74

Annuities: commuted, 416, 431; provisions for distribution of, 172. *See also* Payments

Apache bands, 381

Armstrong, Perry, 358–59

Ashkewi (Mud All Over His Body), P. leader, 235

Ashkibi (Eskibee, The New River), P. leader, 163, 176

Asistagueroüon. *See* Fire People

Askin, John, Jr., 148, 221

Assikinak (Ossigunac, Blackbird), Odawa leader, 31–32

Assimilation, policy of, 250–52, 257, 313, 353, 380, 437

Assiniboine tribe, 13

Atchison, Topeka, and Santa Fe Railroad Company, 388

Atkinson, Brigadier General Henry, 293–94

Atsimethe (Etsimethe), P. leader, 151

Attorneys, 309, 397, 431–32

Awbenabi (He Looks Back), P. leader, 225, 227, 229; at Fort Wayne siege, 207; executed by kin, 464 n. 42; fashions wooden cannon, 208

Awe,atsiwaen'ronnons. *See* Winnebago tribe

Awechisae'ronnons. *See* Mississaugi bands

Babebibobu spelling system, 445–46

Bad River. *See* Matchizibe

Baldwin, R. D., superintendent, Haskell Indian Institute: 407–8; constitution prepared by, 407–8, 428–29, 451

Band level societies, 21–24

Baptist missions, 380–81. *See also* Carey Baptist Mission, Isaac McCoy, Osage River Reservation